The International
Energy Relations of China

The International Energy Relations of China

Kim Woodard

Resource Systems Institute
East-West Center

Stanford University Press
Stanford, California 1980

Stanford University Press, Stanford, California
© 1980 by the Board of Trustees of the
Leland Stanford Junior University
Printed in the United States of America
ISBN 0-8047-1008-2
LC 77-92949

This book is dedicated to Judith Banister,
who is beyond compare

Contents

Part II
Statistical Profile

Tables

Foreword

The global problem of energy supply and demand is of serious concern to the nations of the Asia-Pacific region. Many of these nations, including the United States and Japan, are substantial energy importers, and others desperately need access to new sources of energy if they are to continue along the path of economic and social development. No discussion of present and future energy flows within the region can be undertaken meaningfully without taking into account the energy resources of the People's Republic of China, her prospective demands as modernization takes place, and her energy export policies.

The Resource Systems Institute of the East-West Center is deeply interested in the energy policies of all nations in the Asia-Pacific region and in the ways in which those policies interact. In this respect, the international energy relations of China have been all-too-poorly known and understood. We were delighted, therefore, upon learning of Kim Woodard's pioneering doctoral study, to be able to invite him to become a staff member of this institute and to provide him with the necessary resources to enable him to carry his study to completion.

It is my hope that Dr. Woodard's analysis of the energy situation in China marks the beginning of a process which will provide a continuing overview of Chinese energy policies.

HARRISON BROWN, DIRECTOR
Resource Systems Institute
East-West Center

Preface

Perhaps no task is more difficult for any author than to describe his or her own work, its origins, strengths, weaknesses, and debts. For in doing so, one inadvertently makes reference to oneself. This is not a small book, nor was it written for easy reading. Rather, it is a reference work, the result of roughly seven years of research and writing, starting in 1972. The manuscript for the book is the fourth or fifth version of the study. Each version gets larger and more complex as the sheer quantity of information on the subject mushrooms. Yet it is ironic that now, in 1979, as I summarize the findings of the book, I discover myself returning to the simple generalizations that I started with in 1972—the duality of the Chinese energy system, the constraining effect of the population and rapid industrial growth on energy export potential, the great size of the Chinese energy system when measured in aggregate terms, and the importance of the political factor in determining the pattern of China's energy relations with other countries.

At a root level, the subject of this book is *China's international energy relations.* All four words are an important part of the description. *China,* a rapidly industrializing, centrally planned economy country with enormous energy potential, is the principal actor. The study focuses upward, toward *international* energy relations, rather than downward into individual energy industries, national energy development, or rural energy consumption patterns, although satisfactory analysis requires a solid foundation in China's domestic energy balance. General statistics are provided on energy resources, production, consumption, and trade. Some attention is paid to the level of energy technology and to organization of the energy system, since these domestic factors exert critical constraints on the formulation of Peking's international energy policies. The subject of the study is *energy,* rather than any individual energy industry, such as the oil industry, or offshore exploration. It is a basic premise of the analysis that energy policy cannot be fully understood by reference to a single energy industry or to trade in a single energy commodity. Finally, the heart of the study is its concern with energy *relations* between China and all of the other countries and regions of the world, rather than Peking's energy policy toward a single country or a narrowly defined region. Energy relations with Asian countries do receive special attention because of the high salience of regional proximity in the perceptions of the Chinese government.

The discerning reader will notice that the book owes a heavy debt to the work of previous authors writing on China's energy development, in particular to the books published by Yuan-li Wu (Hoover Institution, 1963), Vaclav Smil (Praeger, 1976), and Selig S. Harrison (Columbia University Press, 1977), and to the articles by A. A. Meyerhoff and Jan-Olaf Willums. I believe that these works represent a collection of the finest materials available on the subject, and in general I concur with the methods used and the conclusions reached. I also make frequent reference to numerous English-language articles and books that are listed in the Bibliography. But the underlying methodology and subject matter in this book differ substantially from earlier analyses and are my own responsibility.

As for methodology, the book rests on the twin pillars of extensive documentary analysis and adequate energy-accounting techniques. When I began the research in 1972, I was a purist and gathered my documentary sources exclusively from the Chinese press, both in the original and in translation. My purity, needless to say, was rapidly sullied as the realization dawned that the unmentioned areas of Chinese energy policy are far greater in extent than would permit total reliance on the Chinese press. I began to divert a good part of my effort into amassing data and press reports from a wide array of foreign sources. This introduces, unfortunately, a higher level of inaccuracy as reports are compounded through secondary and tertiary repetitions. The only method of eliminating the laminations of subjectivity and rumor was to conduct painstaking comparisons among the various sources available on each individual point or statistic. The footnotes and tables frequently, therefore, use multiple sources to document a single assertion. Among periodicals that I used as secondary sources, I am particularly indebted to reports in the *U.S.–China Business Review* (National Council for U.S.–China Trade), the *Far Eastern Economic Review* (Hong Kong), *Petroleum News: Southeast Asia* (Hong Kong), the *Asia Research Bulletin*, the *Asian Wall Street Journal*, the *China Trade Report*, and of course the *New York Times*. I have not used interviews as an empirical tool in conducting the research, a method effectively employed by Selig S. Harrison in his work on China's offshore oil development.

On the statistical side, our picture of the Chinese energy balance is rapidly becoming less subjective as Peking publishes an increasing volume of local, provincial, and national statistics. The validity of these statistics themselves is open to question, but the questions of accuracy to be raised regarding official estimates are of a different order of error than the problems that plague foreign estimates. As for the computer, it does little to relieve the subjectivity of the original data estimates. The computer does, however, greatly extend the power and convenience of energy-accounting methodology. If anything, the utility of computerized data processing increases as the inverse of the reliability of the data. It changes energy balance analysis from a static end point to a fluid process. Within hours of the announcement of a new piece of data, such as the recently published coal production statistics for 1976–78, I can introduce a new set of interlocking estimates for the entire energy balance. The same task on a hand calculator takes a month. On paper it would take a year. The projection analysis would be entirely impossible without the computer, unless one were willing to return to a simple set of exponential curves. But in the end the entire exercise rests on the validity of those fragmentary bits of data that manage to wander out through the corridors of the Chinese press.

As the author, I am naturally sensitive to the remaining deficiencies of the study. As broad as the project seems, it still passes over some questions lightly, defers on certain statistical problems, and avoids outright one or two areas of analysis. Perhaps the greatest weakness of the book is the problem of noncommercial energy fuels. A large proportion of China's rural energy consumption, perhaps as much as half in many areas, comes from the burning of traditional agricultural fuels—firewood, dung, and straw—and from the use of draft animals. Vaclav Smil has made some initial efforts to measure these noncommercial energy flows for China. But there are no reliable data available over the years since 1949. My simple assumption, therefore, is that the contribution of noncommercial energy fuels to China's pattern of energy consumption is basically stable, and does not seriously affect the statistical analysis of commercial energy fuels or the projections of future trends in the energy balance. This assumption may not be entirely tenable in the light of new research on energy flows in other developing countries. In any case, it is quite clear to me that much more research should be done to fully understand both commercial and noncommercial energy consumption in the People's Republic of China (PRC). We have only the vaguest and most aggregative estimates of energy consumption patterns, a critical set of variables for accurate energy balance projections.

A second major weakness of the book is that it avoids more than minimal contact with the economics of the energy sector. There is no consideration, for example, of the effects of the energy commodity price structure, of the allocation of labor in the energy industries, or of the availability, control, and use of capital in the Chinese energy economy. It might be argued that in the past most of China's energy planning was conducted on the basis of largely political objectives, innocent of the intricacies of econometrics. Even if this was the case, however, it is evident from the recent modernization program that energy planning in the future will involve far more sophisticated economic analysis. Further foreign research on China's energy development and trade will depend on an economic as well as political framework of analysis.

A third area of weakness that will bother some readers is the lack of even the most subjective appraisal of the environmental and social impacts of China's rapid industrialization and the growth of the energy system. I am simply not equipped to grapple with this problem, although I believe that some information on environmental impacts might be winnowed from the Chinese press or gathered from foreign visitors to the PRC. This is another area that must be left to future research, although I am fully aware of its importance for China and other rapidly industrializing countries.

There is at least one part of the analysis that will draw critical fire. Some scholars may challenge the strength of my statements in support of China's self-reliant energy development strategy. Self-reliance is passé in the modernization program of the new government, or so it is believed by the media and some researchers. The principal Chinese leaders, after all, scarcely mention it as a leading concept in their new approaches to modernization. Every day new contracts are announced for millions of dollars of foreign plant and equipment imports. China is even experimenting with export-processing zones and joint ventures with foreign firms. Just how far can the technology import program proceed without stretching the concept of self-reliance to the breaking point? The question is of more than academic interest.

I would make just two simple arguments on the issue of self-reliance. The first is a historical point. Chinese society has been struggling to regain its technological and scientific independence and preeminence for at least a century. That struggle was an important dimension of the history of national humiliation, unification, and revolution that took place in China following its encounter with the West. The Chinese communists absorbed the turbulent quest for scientific and cultural renaissance and converted it into the principle of self-reliance. The basic concept of independent scientific, technological, and industrial development may change labels once again, but no one in China is urging a new era of dependence.

The second point is cautionary in nature. There is, perhaps, a temptation even today to seize the credit for China's modernization without paying the bill. The West did little or nothing for China's development between 1949 and 1970, and still the Chinese economy grew at an impressive pace. One may argue that certain factions made a fetish of self-reliant purity at the cost of needed foreign technology, particularly in the period between 1965 and 1975. Indeed, that is precisely the political line of the current leadership in Peking. But the control and management of China's basic industries have not, and probably will not, slip out of domestic hands in the foreseeable future. A substantial proportion of the new industrial infrastructure over the next 20 years will be built at home, using domestic capital, technology, and labor. Priority in the use of natural resources, especially energy resources, will continue to be channeled to domestic requirements rather than to exports. The term "self-reliance" may disappear from the Chinese political lexicon, but the reality will remain, perhaps to reemerge under a different label, as has already occurred several times during the last century. The independent thrust of China's development strategy should surprise no one in the industrial world. Some form of "self-reliance" has been a characteristic of virtually every society that has experienced rapid industrialization. Dependence, on the other hand, is more often than not associated with economic stagnation.

As this book goes to press, it is clear to me that the future pattern of research on China's energy policy cannot imitate the past. The sheer volume of empirical material is rapidly getting out of control. Future studies should be collaborative efforts rather than single-author research. Collaboration should extend not only to the very small circle of foreign experts on various aspects of China's energy development. Rather, it should include the wider community of scholars and government officials who are conducting policy research on international energy problems and alternative energy technologies. Within the last several years, it has been possible for quite a number of scientists, engineers, economists, and other experts concerned with energy to travel to China in their professional capacities. China has reciprocated with teams of its own specialists, which travel extensively throughout the industrial countries in the search for new technologies and wider trade. This broader exchange is needed if significant sharing is to occur between China and other countries. It is no longer necessary to speak or read Chinese in order to share information, particularly in the technical fields associated with energy. Finally, China's energy development should come to be viewed in the context of regional energy development in Asia, rather than standing alone as a special feature of a single country.

Perhaps several specific areas of research could be mentioned that require further work. The Chinese electric power industry is still poorly understood and will be a rapid growth industry over the next two decades. China's electric power system will be particularly important if oil and gas resources prove to be limited, forcing the country toward coal, hydropower, and nuclear power for primary energy production. The coal industry could use a book-length study, in view of its importance in current technology acquisition plans and its heavy contribution to the Chinese energy balance. The natural gas industry is still the least understood energy industry, and further research could be conducted, although documentary sources on natural gas are rare. Aside from these technical studies on the production side of the energy balance, a broad array of analyses would be useful to increase our understanding of rural energy flows in China and to further define the connection between the energy system and the rest of the economy.

The foundation for this book was laid at Stanford University during my graduate years. Once again, I thank my thesis advisers and the rest of the Stanford community for their valuable guidance. During 1976–77 I was a Compton Fellow at Princeton's Center for International Studies, and I extend my gratitude to Cyril E. Black and the staff of the Center for their generous support of my research during that year. The last year and a half of research and preparation of the manuscript were conducted at the Resource Systems Institute of the East-West Center in Honolulu. Without the magnificent support rendered by the Institute and the time it released for me to complete the manuscript, the book would have been but a shadow of itself. Harrison Brown, John Bardach, and Allen S. Whiting (currently on leave at the Center) provided guidance from the perspective of noted scholars steeped in the traditional lore of research and publication. A number of colleagues read and criticized portions of the manuscript, including Richard Sheldon, Selig S. Harrison, Jason C. Hu, Corazon Siddayao, Vincent E. McKelvey, and Martha Caldwell. A number of staff members at the Resource Systems Institute helped me with the preparation of various parts of the manuscript or with the administrative tangles of funding, including Louis J. Goodman, Fred Burian, Harriet Kusuhara, Linda Hamada, Beverly Takata, Rosemary Hilbery, Monica Yoshino, Rita Hong, and Gladys Wong. Jean Morris, a graduate student in the Department of Geography at the University of Hawaii, single-handedly produced the maps and most of the charts for this book. The aesthetic quality of the book owes Jean a special thanks. Arsallah Shairzay, a creative graduate student from Afghanistan, helped me extensively with the hand tabulations for the trade tables. I thank him for his accuracy and his meticulous attention to detail. Ronald K. Lohrding, Andrew Ford, and other staff members of the Los Alamos Scientific Laboratory revised and standardized the projection model. Finally, I would like to thank Jess Bell, the chief editor at the Stanford University Press, for his guidance in bringing the manuscript through a lengthy process of revision. Betty Spurr, Peter J. Kahn, Joy Dickinson Barnes, and Eva N. Nyqvist have edited the manuscript and crafted the tables into type. A first book is always a learning experience. I was fortunate to have been taught and helped by the best.

I would like to append a special note of recognition and gratitude to the many authors and organizations whose data and analyses have been included in this book. I have made an effort to identify the source of information somewhere in the notes or in the statistical tables. Unfortunately, because of the sheer mass of the information gathered and reported in the book and because of the synthesis required in the analysis, it was impossible to repeat the reference for each piece of information at each point where it appears. Without the careful groundwork of other authors and publications, most of which are listed in the Bibliography, a book of this scope would have been impossible. Once again, therefore, I thank all of you who are working on problems related to China's energy development and note the high standard of reporting and analysis that has characterized this area of inquiry.

I use a simplified Wade-Giles romanization system for Chinese language terms and names. Hyphens are deleted from place names (e.g. Taching) and apostrophes are deleted from aspirated syllables (e.g. Teng Hsiao-ping). This convention may irritate Chinese language speakers but makes the name problem more approachable for energy analysts and experts from other fields as well as for the general readership.

K.W.

Part One

Energy Policy

Chapter 1

Rapid Change and Constraints in China's Energy Policy

The world of 1980 is a world of rapid change. Indeed, rapid change has been a characteristic of human communities for the past several centuries. But in the second half of the twentieth century, change itself has taken on some new characteristics. First, the area of rapid change has expanded from a few isolated pockets to humanity as a whole. One is hard pressed these days to find a quiet spot that remains untouched by social, economic, technical, and political upheavals. The spread of rapid change reflects an underlying trend toward a new global community. Just as city-states and feudal baronies once coalesced to form countries, so the world now gropes toward stabilized patterns of communication, exchange, and travel that weave a net across entire regions and around the globe. Second, we are now at a point of intersecting transitions. Changes that began hundreds of years ago in isolated sectors of life are now converging and interlocking. The intersections of technical changes alone—high-speed mechanized communication, reduced travel times, the availability of vast energy supplements to human labor, and so on— are breathtaking. But as we learn repeatedly, technical change occurs successfully only in the framework of societal change and greater organizational articulation. Third, the changes now underway penetrate to individual lives. Literacy, personal philosophy, moral judgment, and alternative states of consciousness were once the realm of a narrowly identified cluster of individuals living at the pinnacle of society, but now are matters of choice for millions. With the pace at which ideas are flowing across international boundaries, one expects that the number of people who consciously order their lives may soon be measured in billions. Fourth, we are conscious of change itself. Like the dragon eating its own tail, we not only change, but change our direction and pace of change. Long-range planning has become a fact of life for governments and most industries and will soon be commonplace. We not only observe ourselves, we model our futures and choose among them, thereby determining in the present the selves that we will retrospectively observe in the future.

Stasis and change are two sides of the same coin in energy studies. This study, while not overtly theoretical in nature, constantly deals with constraints and trends, the forces holding back the development of China's energy system and the forces propelling it forward. Change moves at distinctly different tempos. One need only compare the development experiences of India and China to understand this. In aggregate, both societies are moving, but the concatenation and balance of the process vary enormously between the two. We still lack even the dimmest concept of social change or the variation in modes and tempos of change possible across the spectrum of humanity. Rapid change attracts our attention. But we fail to understand it, caught as we are in the prism of our own perceptions.

If the twentieth century is the century of change, our decades are clearly associated with energy. The shortage of any commodity makes one aware of its existence. The irony of energy problems is that they spring simultaneously from plenitude and paucity. Never in the history of the world has so much physical energy been at the fingertips of some people and some societies. Energy commodities are rapidly becoming a new standard of wealth. And yet the process of "energizing" the world has hardly begun and already we feel the pressure of consumption on production. If the energy crisis were simply a matter of some temporary technological dislocations in the industrial countries, it would be of little consequence. On a world scale, however, what lends the crisis its urgency is that half of humanity has yet to raise itself beyond the most meager access to energy commodities. This is partly a matter of distribution and partly a matter of the balance between production and consumption. Even if we met in the middle somewhere, at a Japanese or European standard of energy consumption, the upward pressure on production would be enormous—far beyond the carrying capacity of conventional fossil-fuel resources. We are, therefore, in the midst of a massive energy transition.

In 1980, the energy development of the People's Republic of China reflects that of the world as a whole. That is, China is midway in its energy transition. Historically, China was viewed in the West as a negligible factor in global energy development. But the Western energy crisis has drawn attention to the rapid pace of Chinese energy development (particularly in petroleum), to China's comparatively large aggregate energy consumption, and to the future potential of China's fossil-fuel resources. With or without large-scale petroleum exports, the People's Republic of China (PRC) will be a substantial component of the global energy system by the year 2000. Accordingly, the central purpose of this project is to examine, both empirically and theoretically, the international energy relations of China. I have attempted to answer four basic questions in this study: (1) What is China's international energy policy? (2) How does it differ from energy policies typical of Western market-economy countries? (3) Why does it differ from typical Western international energy policies? (4) What will be the future direction of China's international energy relations?

Ten years ago, a case study of this sort would have been considered exotic. The few studies of China's energy development then extant were read primarily by China scholars and government specialists concerned with the overall direction of Chinese economic and industrial growth.* Very little attention was paid to the international implications of China's growing domestic energy production system. Precise figures on energy commodity trade went uncollected. Specialists paid little attention to the possibility that China, once considered "oil poor," would soon become an "energy giant" to be reckoned with by the great industrial powers of the mid-twentieth century.

By 1975, the situation had changed. The Western world had suddenly become aware that the People's Republic had in 25 years achieved the energy production and consumption levels of a modern industrial nation. Although still poor in terms of per capita energy consumption, the PRC had developed the third-largest coal industry in the world, was increasing oil and natural gas production at leaps of 20 percent per annum, had discovered major oil and gas reserves, and had become a regional petroleum exporter. This awareness struck precisely at the moment of greatest agony in the Western "energy crisis"—late 1973. The result was instant notoriety for a previously technical and narrow subject. Rumors flew: China's offshore oil reserves would make the country a second Saudi Arabia; crude oil production would reach 400 million metric tons (8 million barrels per day) by 1980, with at least 100 million available for export to Japan; Peking would require enormous purchases of foreign equipment to explore for offshore oil; China would soon overtake the Soviet Union and then the United States in total energy production.

By 1976, the dust had settled somewhat. A spate of articles helped sort fact from fiction. Crude oil exports to Japan, which increased rapidly from 1973 through 1975, faltered in 1976. Chinese negotiators made a few limited purchases of Western equipment, but window-shopped for much more than they bought. Foreign geologists began discussing the physical and economic limits on offshore oil potential. Perhaps the ardor

*See Bibliography for a complete list of studies dealing with China's energy development and policies.

of Chinese energy planners had also cooled under the sobering awareness that many technical problems remained, that capital requirements would be staggering, and that even a rich endowment of fossil-fuel reserves would require conservation and careful allocation to meet the energy requirements of industrialization. Foreign observers settled into more conservative estimates and more realistic projections.

Despite this retrenchment, however, China's energy policies, both domestic and international, will remain a topic of more than technical interest for some time. The importance of the subject is that it lies at the intersection of a number of international problems. Its difficulty is that it spans traditionally separate disciplines.

The Structure of the Study

Because of its scope, this book was written in two parts. Part I is policy-oriented and is entitled "Energy Policy." It covers a comparison of Chinese and Western views of the "energy crisis," China's substantive international energy policies, and the domestic organizational roots of those policies. Although it frequently reaches back into the 1960's and even the 1950's in the development of particular themes, documentation for this part was drawn primarily from very recent articles in the Chinese press—i.e. from the period since 1970.

Part II, the "Statistical Profile," was designed to establish a comprehensive set of energy accounts for China from 1949 through the present, and a set of alternative projections to the year 2000. The "Profile" provides statistics on China's energy resources, production, consumption, and trade. The statistics in each category are presented in a standard coordinated format that provides easy access to particular data. The alternative energy-balance projections are based on explicit growth assumptions. The division into two parts has served to clear the text of the policy section of extraneous statistical material. Where appropriate, statistical material was drawn from the "Profile" to illustrate points in the policy volume.

Taken as a whole, the study is addressed to the *international* aspects of China's energy development and energy policies. It seeks to integrate the disparate fields of China studies, international relations, and energy development. The analytical structure of the study should be thought of as a set of nesting layers of energy-policy constraints—much like the spatial structure of an onion. In the Chinese case, despite enormous data and information-access problems, this concept of layered energy-policy constraints works well in determining the nature and direction of China's international energy policies. Seven distinct layers of such constraints were identified: (1) dominant attitudes toward rapid change; (2) international policy constraints; (3) domestic policy constraints; (4) energy reserves and production capacity; (5) energy consumption patterns; (6) energy trade habits; (7) future energy development options.

In general terms, the book is arranged according to this analytical structure. It begins with the heart of the "onion" and moves out toward successively more sharply defined constraints. Chapter 2 examines distinctive Chinese attitudes toward change in the international energy system. Put in the simplest terms, Chinese planners perceive international energy problems from a different perspective than the dominant Western conception of such problems. They have a different set of expectations regarding the dynamics of global energy growth and distribution patterns. Their view, for example, of the Western "energy crisis" is that it results not from a physical energy shortage but from fundamental disequilibria in the control of energy resources. Such distinctive attitudes toward rapid change in the international energy system affect the choice of energy-policy vocabulary, explanatory factors, and projected options. And at some level, the distinctive attitudes and categories spill over into the day-to-day process of energy-policy formulation.

A number of international policy constraints operate on the formulation of Peking's distinctive international energy policies. Patterns of trade in energy commodities are affected by regional relations with Asian neighbors. There are still very real constraints on China's ability to function as a world power, and Peking views its own capabilities in terms of regional, rather than global, influence. Thus, China will be more comfortable as a regional oil exporter than as a participant in the world petroleum market for some time to come.

International security considerations have also had a direct bearing on China's energy policy. The border confrontation with the Soviet Union, which began in the late 1960's, causes Peking to be very defensive in its regional energy relations with East Asian neighbors. China vigorously opposes Soviet-Japanese cooperation on energy construction projects in Siberia. Chinese exports of crude oil to Japan were partially motivated by the specter of a deal whereby Japan would have received substantial quantities of Siberian oil and gas in return for pipeline construction and extraction equipment. The proposed trans-Siberian pipelines (or railroad) would have cut close to the Chinese border along contested reaches of the Amur River. The projects would have improved Soviet access to the border and supplied Russian divisions stationed there. China's own principal energy-producing areas are close to the Soviet border and therefore vulnerable to conventional military attack. The Soviet army could virtually shut down China's petroleum industry with a few short thrusts across the border into Heilungkiang and Sinkiang provinces.

Peking's territorial claims to the continental shelf have also been influenced by security considerations. The vigor with which China has pressed its claim to the Tiaoyutai (Senkaku) Islands is a reflection of continued uneasiness about Taiwan's de facto independence and ability to defend itself.* The Tiaoyutai lie a short distance north of Taiwan and are said to be highly promising as a subsea oil-production area. Peking's claim to the Tiaoyutai is linked to its long-standing crusade to recover Taiwan itself. For its part, Taipei has sold exploration concessions along the Chinese shelf to several foreign multinationals in areas north of the Tiaoyutai that are part of China's coastal defense system. And Japan has complicated the issue both by making claims to the Tiaoyutai and extensive areas of the continental shelf, and by concluding a cooperative oil-exploration agreement with South Korea.

Even China's diplomacy acts as a constraint on the formulation of international energy policy. Peking very much views itself as a Third World country, still in the relatively early throes of industrialization. Thus China vociferously supports the Organization of Petroleum Exporting Countries (OPEC) and the other raw-materials-producing organizations. And the Chinese press still makes long-winded attacks on the multinationals and on the Western energy economy generally. Nearly every aspect of public energy policy must be rationalized against the background of political ties to the Third World. In general, therefore, China's international energy policy is constrained by a broad framework of foreign-policy considerations—commercial, military, and diplomatic. Chapters 3–8 deal with such constraints in the PRC's relations with the Third World, the industrial countries, and China's Asian neighbors. Chapter 9 discusses China's energy policies in the context of international organization.

International energy options are further limited by domestic policy constraints, whether economic or organizational. In economic terms, the basic constraint is the fact that China began the postwar period as a poor agricultural country, torn by a century of foreign penetration, natural disasters of unprecedented severity, a full-scale foreign invasion, and two decades of civil war. First with extensive Soviet technical and mate-

*To avoid confusion, the Republic of China will be consistently referred to as "Taiwan" and its government as "Taipei." Other authors also make use of "Formosa" to refer to the island and the dominant political party (Kuomintang or KMT) to designate the government. (Publications in both China and Taiwan use strong pejorative labels for the other side.) "China" and the "PRC" in all cases refer to the People's Republic of China excluding Taiwan, and "Peking" designates the government of China.

rial assistance and then completely on its own, China struggled to achieve adequate levels of food, clothing, housing, medical care, and education for its population. The early stages of industrialization required rapidly increasing inputs of commercial energy for agriculture, transportation, the military, household use, and industry itself. In 1975 the domestic energy consumption requirement was already the fourth-largest for any country in the world. By the year 2000, the domestic energy system will approach truly modern proportions. Chapter 10 adopts a comparative perspective on China's energy system. Reserves, production, and consumption (aggregate and per capita) are examined in the light of the experience of other countries and regions. Comparative growth rates illustrate the magnitude of domestic energy requirements and the imperative for further development.

Domestic energy-policy constraints also include important organizational factors. China's domestic energy economy is organized according to distinctive principles, at once highly collective and highly cellular (decentralized). Center-periphery relations dominate energy planning and constrain the overall pattern of development. One energy-production unit (Taching oilfield) was described in some detail to illustrate the domestic organizational constraints operating on the making of Chinese energy policy (Chapter 11).

The final chapter of the first part provides an overview of future energy-policy options facing the Chinese leadership. Here again, the basic theme is the impact of domestic consumption requirements on future export potential. Domestic and international energy-policy constraints interlock directly in determining China's energy future. Under a variety of projected scenarios, the PRC will remain a Third World country in per capita energy consumption for some time to come. And foreign-policy constraints on the use of foreign technology (e.g. in developing offshore oil or nuclear power) may restrict the range of domestic development alternatives.

Part II, the "Statistical Profile," is more technical, more quantitative, and more sharply defined than the discussion of policy constraints that precedes it. The "Profile" begins with a detailed exposition of statistical methods and data sources in its own Introduction, Chapter 13. Energy reserves and production capacity, perhaps the fundamental constraints on the development of any integrated energy system, are discussed in Chapters 14–17; they were determined by examining alternative data series from both Chinese and foreign sources. In Chapters 18 and 19, energy consumption patterns, a particularly important set of constraints in the Chinese case, were estimated by derivative methods from production statistics. Inefficiencies, non-energy use of hydrocarbons, and net trade in energy commodities were estimated and subtracted from figures for aggregate and per capita energy consumption. China has a much longer history in energy-commodity trade than is commonly supposed, and energy trade habits, which developed during the first two decades of the PRC, continue to play an important constraining role in energy policy. Chapters 20, 21, and 22 provide a nearly comprehensive set of energy-trade data by commodity, partner country, and year, and then aggregate the data into an accurate set of trade statistics in common energy units.

Finally, Chapters 23 and 24 define an explicit range of future energy-development options. A simulation based on various aspects of energy-development theory, such as the relationship between reserves and production growth rates and energy/GNP elasticities, provides an array of alternative projections through the year 2000. These projections show a range of likely Chinese energy futures in quantitative terms. Future policy options facing the Chinese leadership in Peking will most probably occur within the framework of this range of alternative futures. And particular policy choices will determine the exact outcome for each of the projected variables. In brief, the simulation projects the quantitative development constraints on future international energy policies.

One caveat should be appended to this introduction to the analytical structure of the study. Every effort has been made to treat China's international energy-policy constraints dynamically. At the PRC's stage of energy development, everything appears to be in motion at once and each parameter is inextricably wound together with all the others. The result feels a bit like riding an N-dimensional roller coaster. Within the space of a few years, not only has the Chinese energy system itself changed rapidly, but the information available outside China concerning the energy system has expanded rapidly as well. And the same explosion could easily happen again over the next five years. The only plausible analytical approach to these changes was to plunge as deeply as possible into detail in each energy sector and then to reemerge, not with a hard set of findings, but with a general set of conclusions. And the entire process will have to be repeated several more times before adequate foreign understanding of China's energy policies will be achieved.

Broader Implications of the Study

Aside from the main task of describing, explaining, and predicting the international energy policies of the People's Republic of China within the limits of current knowledge, this study has produced a number of intellectual by-products. It proved impossible to move too far down any side path without detracting from the focus of the book, but in the long run the broader implications of this study may be more important than the study itself.

First, China's energy policies provide a unique window on broader domestic- and foreign-policy-formulation processes that go on behind a veil of bureaucratic secrecy. The Chinese government and press are proud of the accomplishments of centrally planned energy development and frequently disclose considerable detail on the history of internal organization of particular energy-production units. The problem is not to find articles on energy development in the Chinese press, but to sift through the mountains of information provided looking for important threads of policy or key statistics. The same generalization holds for documentary material on international energy policy. Although frequently propagandistic, the published articles do reveal bits and pieces of the foreign-policy puzzle—sometimes inadvertently.

Second, the book raises, but does not solve, some important theoretical problems in the study of international energy politics. In particular, I discovered in the course of examining Chinese attitudes toward the "energy crisis" that Chinese analysts view international energy problems against an entirely different conceptual backdrop than the usual Western energy analysis. The difference is so great as to be difficult to explain either in terms of Marxist categories or in terms of Chinese tradition. For the evaluative orientation toward energy problems appears to be influenced by an even deeper perceptual current. The perceptual difference between Chinese and Western perspectives on the energy crisis may provide a tip to the discovery of a theoretical dimension with more general implications for international relations theory. If it can be established that attitudes toward rapid change are an important perceptual factor and that such attitudes vary widely, the discovery could lead toward an explanation of cognitive dissonance between governments and across cultures. This type of cognitive dissonance might be particularly important in analyzing international policy problems introduced by technological shift. Such critical areas of international development as energy and nuclear technology may be sensitive to varying process orientations. If different governments perceive change in different ways, they will have difficulty communicating about solutions to policy problems associated with new technologies.

Third, examination of the domestic constraints on energy policy provides a new empirical access to the peculiarly Chinese and Marxist pattern of production organization. China is engaged in a vast experiment with the fundamental principles of industrial organization. The experiment differs from both Western market-economy and Soviet planned-economy models. As an approach to economic development, it appears to have provided a more equitable distribution of the benefits of industrialization than occurred in the West and a more flexible adaptation to local needs than occurred in the Soviet Union. Here again, the Chinese press allows us to get down into the roots of the industrial-planning and management policies.

Finally, the most immediate spin-off value of this book will be to fill an enormous gap in international energy-data collections. China will soon be the world's third-largest energy producer and consumer. Any collection of global energy data or analysis of trends in world energy development is hopelessly inadequate without the China component. The data presented here are still tentative and subject to further revision. But at least a first step has been taken toward setting out energy statistics in a format compatible with international standards. It is to be hoped that energy analysts will be patient with the volatility of statistics on China, and that China specialists for their part will attempt to be technically precise and statistically rigorous in providing each new edition of the truth about the Chinese energy system.

Let us begin, in Chapter 2, with a comparison of Chinese and Western reactions to the "energy crisis" of the early 1970's. This comparison is clearly reflected in comments in the Chinese press. Against the background of common Western analytical approaches, distinctive Chinese attitudes toward rapid change in the global energy system will be seen to stand out in bold relief.

Chapter 2

China and the Energy Crisis

At the height of the Arab oil embargo in late 1973, the energy crisis got almost as much coverage in the *People's Daily* as it did in the *New York Times*. But the nature of that coverage would have startled most American readers. To begin with, Chinese journalists dismissed the entire energy crisis as contrived—a political device of monopoly capital to justify further price gouging, artificial withholding of supplies from the consumer market, special-interest tax breaks, and collusive business practices.[1] According to this view, the energy crisis never existed, except as an artificial creation of the ruling classes of the industrial market-economy countries to further exploit the labor of their own populations and the raw materials of Third World countries.

Certain articles in the Chinese press went so far as to claim that world energy reserves were theoretically and practically boundless and inexhaustible.[2] China's own experience with energy-resource development showed that Western capitalists sometimes have had an economic stake in underestimating the presence of fossil-fuel reserves in areas served by their own oil-marketing structure.[3] The physical law of the conservation of energy demonstrates that resource problems are at root political rather than material in nature.

Views of "energy exhaustion" in human history have been varied. Such views are wrong theoretically, either because they take a metaphysical approach to the problem of energy and deny the infinity of the material world and the indestructibility of the motion of matter, or because they take an isolated and absolute approach to the definite conditions for the transformation of the motion of matter. Politically, such views meet the needs of the declining reactionary classes and are used by them as tools against progress.[4]

The author of this quotation, which defies most of what Western scientists believe about the very real problems of fossil-fuel depletion, went on to argue that all available empirical evidence showed energy resources to be expanding rather than contracting. He claimed that known energy deposits were increasing owing to new fossil-fuel discoveries (with no mention of the declining rate of new discoveries, that new energy resources could be tapped through alternative energy-production technologies (with no mention of the rising costs of such technologies), and that the efficiency of energy use by humans was improving (with no mention of thermodynamic limits on efficiency curves).[5]

The view that the energy crisis really does not exist has its proponents in the West, too. Some of them are prominent experts with considerable knowledge of energy-production systems.[6] However, though these experts might agree with the Chinese press that the energy crisis is unreal, they would not agree about the source of the evident fiction. Whereas Chinese experts have dismissed the energy crisis as deliberately contrived, Western skeptics have believed that it was simply a muddle, arising out of blatantly mistaken and readily corrected policies by either government or business.

But the fact that the Chinese press officially dismisses the reality of the energy crisis has not stopped it from commenting at length on the fiction. Once having established a set of quotation marks around the term "energy crisis," the Chinese commentator is off and running; and what he has to say is often revealing of the general dimensions of Peking's international energy policies.

In broadest outline, Peking sees the underlying forces of production, including energy production, as objective. That is, the role of energy development in history has a certain definable characteristic and an inevitable direction. Energy resources themselves are theoretically boundless; the only limit to energy production is the arrangement of social forces and class relations within the production system itself. Hence the references to the first law of thermodynamics—that energy itself is indestructible. But this mechanical view is tempered by Mao Tse-tung's thesis that "the people and only the people are the motive force in world history." In other words, although the energy resource itself could be considered boundless, the productive forces of humanity move in a historical pattern defined by Marxism-Leninism out of a past and present bound by class relationships toward a future of boundless (and classless) production.

Projected onto the international level, this Marxist design translates into the view that the energy crisis is symptomatic of the deeper crisis of monopoly capital and social imperialism in their struggle for hegemony over the Third World.

Energy exhaustion and "hunger for energy" uttered by the two superpowers actually mean the crisis of their policy of plunder and hegemonism, showing that they can no longer ravage the third world as they please. . . . The frantic cries of the two hegemonic powers about "energy exhaustion" is but a smokescreen to cover up and create public opinion to facilitate their aggression and plunder. . . . All this illustrates that the so-called energy crisis is a crisis of the imperialist system itself. With the victorious advance of the third world countries and the people of the whole world in their struggle against imperialism, there will soon emerge a new and unprecedentedly bright era in the history of development of energy sources.[7]

On an even broader level, this thesis regarding the energy crisis reinforces the general division of the world into two groups of countries, locked in a global revolutionary struggle. The intensification of contradictions between the haves and the have-nots, the enfranchised and the disenfranchised, the raw-material-producing Third World and the manufactured-goods-producing industrial world is cresting on the revolutionary tide of history. These contradictions are being felt in the very centers of the world class system. "The wind in the tower heralds the rising storm in the mountains."[8] And the energy crisis itself should be seen in the same way as the international monetary crisis or the hegemonic struggle between the superpowers for raw materials—as fault lines under the structures of imperialism. The fictional "energy crisis" is but another sign of a deeper crisis in the overextended lines of control over world production by monopoly capital. But the "rising storm" is real enough, generated by turbulence in the Third World as the resource-exporting countries struggle to free themselves from international exploitation.

This general Chinese Marxist perspective on international energy problems will be examined in the context of the specifics of China's international energy policy. But the broad view of the "energy crisis" as a symptom of deeper global rifts, inequities in world energy-distribution patterns, and disequilibrium in international political development will remain central to the rest of the analysis.

Specific Causes of the Energy Crisis

Chinese commentators have analyzed in some detail both the domestic development patterns and the international distribution patterns that precipitated the oil shortage of 1973–74. The key to the entire problem, as they see it, is the profit structure of the Western energy system. This key is thought to unlock a number of different doors in explaining just how the oil shortage occurred in the face of the theoretically boundless global endowment of energy resources.

The search for high profits by large multinational corporations has led to "lopsided growth" in the market-economy countries. This has occurred because petroleum has been favored over coal by corporations seeking cheap energy supplies to market at relatively high prices and wide profit margins. Within the oil industry itself, recovery methods are inefficient because of competitive drilling practices and a high proportion of waste. And the corporations themselves have failed to develop the necessary technology to extract oil from tar sands and oil shale. The electric-power industries in capitalist countries have encouraged wasteful consumption patterns.[9] All of these factors have been exaggerated by the uneven nature of Western economic growth: "Rapid increases in the demand for oil are accentuated by the lopsided and bloated economic build-up in the capitalist countries and an anarchic expansion of the economy."[10]

Japan is the primary example used in the Chinese press to underline the effects of the lack of balance in Western economic growth patterns. The lack of domestic energy resources has made Japan 99 percent dependent on foreign oil supplies. Each price rise in the international oil market is reflected in production cost rises in Japanese industry. Oil produces over 70 percent of Japan's energy, owing to the decline in the domestic coal industry during the 1950's, and oil imports have jumped from 10 million tons per year in the mid-1950's to 250 million tons in the mid-1970's. Since 80 percent of Japanese oil imports came from the Middle East at the time of the Arab oil embargo (November 1973–February 1974), the embargo hit the Japanese economy hard, reducing industrial production by 10–30 percent and shipping by 40 percent, and affecting a number of other sectors of the Japanese production system. The overall effect was to reduce the 1974 GNP growth rate to 2.5 percent, the lowest in 20 years.[11]

These lessons of development are doubtless contrasted in the minds of Chinese planners with the fact that China has maintained 97 percent self-sufficiency in total energy supplies for 25 years (see Chapter 18). The self-reliant development policies strictly enforced by China's revolutionary regime meant that every increment in energy consumption had to be paid for by real growth in energy-production industries. China used oil imports to supplement a seriously lagging domestic petroleum industry in the late 1950's and early 1960's, but the large coal industry, which expanded at a rapid rate during the 1950's, provided the great bulk of China's energy. Not that China has always experienced easy development in the energy sector. The PRC had its own energy crisis in the early 1960's, when petroleum imports from the Soviet Union declined and the coal industry stagnated after the excesses of the Great Leap Forward. And the provision of adequate electric-power supplies for industrial growth has always been a problem for Peking. However, in China production shortages are compensated for by curtailing consumption. Thus it comes as small surprise to Chinese planners that Japan, with its totally unbalanced energy-production and energy-consumption sectors, has experienced severe energy-related distortions in its economic growth pattern. And Peking views increased American dependence on imported oil in much the same light.[12]

The search for "fabulous profits" by multinational oil corporations also led to distortion of international energy-distribution patterns. The cost of extracting a barrel of Middle Eastern crude oil was less than one-tenth the cost of extracting the same barrel of oil from an American well. This drove the American multinationals abroad for crude oil supplies and gave them (the Chinese believe) a profit rate much higher than profit rates for non-energy multinational corporations.[13]

However, the drive for maximum profits based on cheap foreign oil supplies had a number of unanticipated side effects on the market-economy countries. First, they entered into sharp competition with one another for access to Middle Eastern oil during the period immediately following the energy crisis. The United States has entered the Middle Eastern petroleum market on a large scale only since 1970; it now competes directly for oil supplies with Japan and the West European countries, which developed dependency on the Middle East in the 1960's. Following the severe shortages caused by the Arab oil embargo in 1973, each country sought to assure its own supplies at the expense of the others. Japan established "independent exploitation" agreements with several of the oil-producing countries. Western Europe responded by strengthening ties with the Middle East and developing the North Sea oilfields. These events isolated Washington, which attempted a number of political moves to ensure future oil supplies, including efforts to organize the oil-consuming countries under the umbrella of the Organization of Economic Cooperation and Development and its new International Energy Agency. China saw all of these maneuvers as signs of increasing competition among the industrial market-economy countries. By 1976, the oil shortage had shifted at least temporarily to an oil glut. But this fact, in the Chinese view, did not ease the competition among the capitalist countries. By 1977, the United States had incurred a trade deficit in excess of $40 billion, largely because of expanded oil imports. This, according to Peking, precipitated "intensifying trade and monetary wars between the United States and other capitalist countries."[14]

The growing dependence on Middle Eastern oil also caused an unexpected shift in political power toward the governments of the oil-producing countries. The reduction of oil supplies to the market-economy countries during the 1973–74 Arab-Israeli confrontation proved this, as the governments of the oil-producing countries demanded a higher return for exported oil and increased participation in production in their own countries. The sensitivity of the industrial oil importers to the Arab oil embargo demonstrated, to Chinese eyes, that the curtain of history had begun to fall on the resource exploitation of the Third World by the industrial countries. Third World governments were ready, it seemed, to take over control of their own resource bases and to eliminate, or at least contain, the overpowering influence of the multinational corporations. The distortion of world energy-distribution patterns toward the industrial market-economy countries at the expense of the Third World countries was finally ending with the mounting victories of the oil-producing countries.

Finally, the international oil shortage marked a new stage in the competition between the United States and the Soviet Union for world hegemony. Despite large domestic petroleum resources, the Soviet Union, according to Chinese sources, saw both economic and political advantages to entering the scramble for "oil hegemony." Moscow began increasing oil and natural-gas imports from the Persian Gulf at the height of the energy crisis, treating Middle Eastern oil reserves as "international property."[15] The Russians saw an economic advantage in the reexport of Middle Eastern oil and natural gas to the Eastern European countries at world market prices. And Moscow detected an opening for the further expansion of political influence in the Middle East during its period of intense confrontation with the Western governments over the Arab-Israeli conflict. Once ensconced in a position of political preeminence in the Middle East, the Soviet Union would have its hand on the energy lifeline of its Western competitors, a situation that would be viewed with the utmost gravity in Washington. The USSR, however, soon began to run into the same resistances from the Middle Eastern governments that the Western multinational corporations had encountered, making political penetration of the oil-producing countries a difficult task.

These specific elements of the Chinese analysis of the energy crisis are much less surprising to a Western analyst than China's rejection of the reality of the energy crisis itself. There is something familiar about many aspects of China's view, from its reasons for the premature decline of Western coal industries to its analysis of Soviet political motives in the Middle East. Chinese commentators have certainly not been oblivious to events and factors that went into the development of the energy crisis. But a glance at what the Chinese press did *not* say is more revealing of the actual differences between the Chinese and Western positions on the energy crisis than what they did say. Peking has specifically not attributed the energy crisis to the pressure of rising petroleum production on available reserves—the most common Western analysis. China has only begun to enter an era of rapid increases in petroleum production and has consequently felt little if any effect from the depletion of domestic crude oil reserves. But the PRC will face resource limits on crude oil production by the mid-1980's unless China manages in the meantime to settle jurisdictional disputes over offshore oilfields on the continental shelf and musters the necessary extraction technology to produce there (Chapters 7 and 8).

The reasons that Peking has not attributed the energy crisis to economic growth go beyond the domestic stage of development of the petroleum industry. As will be repeatedly demonstrated in the chapters that follow, Peking is committed to rapid economic development, whatever the resource costs. For ideological and historical reasons, China's revolutionary leaders believe that the energy crisis is one manifestation of severe distributional inequities in the global energy system. According to this view, what drives the energy crisis is not the fact of rapid industrial growth but the unevenness in the distribution of its benefits. Distribution disequilibria of global resources have been increasing in intensity to the point that the effects of regional or even national energy shortages reverberate through the entire international economic order. From the Chinese perspective, the energy crisis may have highly salutary effects in releasing the Third World countries from resource bondage to the multinational corporations and the endless cycle of technological dependency.

In order to establish that China's government has viewed the energy crisis from a distinctive perspective, let us digress briefly and discuss prevailing Western energy policies and theoretical perspectives on the energy crisis. The section that follows will provide a basis for comparison of Chinese and Western energy policy throughout the remainder of the study. The comparison has been undertaken in some detail, but it is not intended to convey the impression that there is but a single set of energy policies or analyses in the West. Far from it; different Western governments, and certainly different Western scholars, hold very divergent views of the energy crisis and its most likely cures. The dominant view of change in global energy patterns that prevails in the West should be thought of as a distribution or continuum, not as a fixed "average" point. The point of central tendency in the Western energy policy continuum is quite different from the focus of Chinese energy policy. But there is also a much wider range of variation on key aspects of Western energy policy than is the case in China—at least to judge from the views expressed in the Chinese press.

Western Energy Policy: A Comparison

Western energy policy may be summed up in terms of three basic concepts—growth, crisis, and price. This section will treat each of the three
concepts in turn and will offer illustrations of the implications of each
for the formation of substantive energy policies.

The concept of growth, and particularly exponential growth, has received increasing attention in Western academic circles during the last
decade or so. It has been discovered that the industrial market-economy
countries have been experiencing "exponential growth rates" since at
least 1950 and that these growth rates, particularly in energy production
and consumption, have markedly changed the life-style and expectations of populations living in countries that have undergone industrial
"takeoff."[16] But at the same time, exponential increases of production
for key commodities such as crude petroleum have increased the fundamental demand for raw materials and natural resources. This has created a problem of supply—a problem that has accelerated exponentially
along with the changes in life-style that have accompanied takeoff into
the industrial age.

The entire crisis can be summed up in three words, exponential growth rates.
The population has been growing exponentially; of all people who ever lived,
approximately one-third are alive today. Because energy consumption per person has also grown exponentially, total energy consumption now outpaces the
nation's capacity to produce sufficient energy from domestic resources.[17]

Such exponentially growing economies have carried with them exponentially
growing energy consumption, and this in turn has produced demands for energy
that exceed easily accessible indigenous supplies; thus the industrialized nations
are increasingly dependent upon foreign fuels supplied primarily from the natural resource bases of the developing countries. The technology to produce energy economically from more inaccessible fuels is still lacking, with the result that
for many developed countries domestic energy sources are more costly to exploit
than foreign sources. The domestic costs appear to be setting the base price for
foreign fuels, and the future seems to hold the high probability of very large transfer payments from industrialized nations to the fuel-rich developing nations. . . .

Meanwhile, an awakened population in the developing nations is tracing the
path of western industrialized societies. . . . This raises the possibility of sustained
growth in worldwide energy consumption at a rate even higher than any single
industrialized nation has yet experienced. As energy use increases, the volume of
wastes from energy production and consumption begins to exceed the ability of
natural environmental processes to absorb it without severe degradation.[18]

The image presented by these two extracts is that growth is somehow
self-perpetuating. Once started in one part of the world, the argument

goes, population increases and rising per capita consumption of energy rebound around the globe, causing a sustained and "inelastic" growth in the demand for commercial energy.[19]

The view that exponential growth in energy consumption is self-perpetuating has been reinforced by empirical observation of the close correlation between per capita energy consumption and per capita income.[20] The correlation, which holds for individual countries over time, or cross-sectionally for all countries in a given year, is very strong statistically.* This has led to debate over the relationship between industrial production and energy consumption. There has been some speculation that the GNP and industrial product could be "untied" from energy consumption by rigorous conservation measures. But the outcome of efforts to untie economic growth from energy consumption is still unclear.[21]

The second concept basic to Western energy policy is the belief that the global energy system has entered a "crisis." Exponential growth rates have produced a "supply emergency," an "energy gap," or a "shortage" of primary and secondary energy fuels.[22] The basic argument is simple. World fossil-fuel deposits in the earth's crust are limited to a finite pool. Coal, crude petroleum, and natural gas are nonrenewable energy resources of limited quantity. These fossil-fuel resources can and will be depleted within the foreseeable future. The depletion of crude oil and natural gas has already brought North American production increases for these fuels to a halt. Production levels are slowly declining as the remaining reserves are exhausted and as new reserves become more difficult to locate and extract.

Western experts have predicted that an ongoing energy crisis may be caused by the depletion of vital fossil-fuel resources and the failure of energy production to keep pace with world demand.

Energy is probably the pivotal requirement for continuing growth. For more than a century technology, made effective by investment and the necessary organizations, has been contriving a shifting, rapidly expanding array of energy supplies that has kept a step ahead of our escalating demand. Just now, for the first time, much of the world is encountering an energy gap.[23]

First, let us assume that the default will not be abrupt. It will be slow at first, gathering momentum as oil becomes increasingly inaccessible and we will expend greater amounts of energy to obtain, refine, and transport it.

---

*Some experts have questioned the statistical strength of the energy/GNP correlation for certain countries at the lower end of the development ladder. Others caution against the use of arithmetic energy/GNP elasticities as an effective means of projecting energy consumption requirements. But the consensus continues to support a general statistical relationship between economic growth and commercial energy consumption.

At the beginning, the cost of gasoline and oil products will increase. This increase will represent a minor inconvenience to many and a financial hardship for some. . . . As the shortage grows more severe, there will be restrictions placed upon the use of luxuries. . . . As the oil shortage deepens and begins to approach crisis levels, concern for loss of luxuries or creature comforts will give way to an enormous preoccupation with obtaining life's essentials. Rationing of oil and gasoline will be mandated. . . . The shortage of oil will continue to worsen. Congress will enact legislation restricting the use of gasoline to essential uses, priorities will be established with abuses subject to severe penalties. . . . Decisions will be required that will shortcut our economic and social freedom. Survival will supersede due process.[24]

As frightening and overstated as some of these conclusions may seem to nonspecialists, Western energy technologists insist that the first signs of the long-term effects of the energy crisis have already appeared in the broader economic and political systems of the industrial countries, and that the growth of the developing nonindustrial countries has already been slowed or stopped by the petroleum shortage.

Early in 1973, the growth prospects of most developing countries for the decade ahead appeared good. Twelve months later, these prospects are in grave jeopardy because of the jolt of sudden massive price increases of their essential imports—primarily oil, food, and fertilizers. They also will be hurt by the deepening of the global economic slowdown already in prospect for 1974 and even before the announcement of the Arab oil embargo and the OPEC price increase for oil. The result of these massive changes is that some developing countries will suffer severe, but manageable shocks; others now face catastrophe and their development prospects are endangered for the rest of the decade.[25]

The common element of all of these statements is their sense of urgency. It is not just that a petroleum shortage has occurred, but a distinct crisis atmosphere has been introduced by the element of surprise that such an event could have taken place in the most technologically advanced countries. Some attributed the surprise to a lack of public awareness, others attributed it to insufficient government planning.[26] But nearly all Western analysts agreed that energy shortages constituted a crisis.

What measures could then be introduced to contain the energy crisis within manageable bounds, to avert the sudden destruction of an important pillar of the industrial market economies, and to gain time for the introduction of alternative energy-production technologies? The basic Western countermeasures to the energy crisis have centered on the concept of price, a third major element of Western energy policy. Governments of the industrial countries in particular have believed that manipulation of the price structure both domestically and internationally would dampen the effects of the energy crisis long enough to permit technological solutions to take hold and to avert major repercussions throughout the industrial infrastructures of the developed countries.

The price structure is so important, in the Western view, that some economists have gone so far as to blame the entire energy crisis on OPEC manipulation of the price structure rather than viewing the shifts in the price structure as a result of resource limits on fossil-fuel production.

Some powerful force has overridden demand and supply. This force did not enter before the middle of 1970, at the earliest. Up to that time the trend of prices had been downward, and long-term contracts had been at lower prices than short-term, indicating that the industry expected still lower prices in the future, even as far as 10 years ahead.[27]

It is quite uninteresting to know how many millions of tons of one mineral resource or another there are in the earth's crust. We will only become confused if we ask, "Will a given supply of energy be available at such and such a time in the future?" Such questions are not well posed and cannot be answered in a "yes or no" fashion. Instead the question is: Given certain actions in the interim, what supply will be available at what cost? . . .

The use of energy, like supply, also depends on price. We have to stop thinking of "needs" and start thinking of "demand"—that is, how much of various kinds of energy households and industry will want to purchase at various prices. . . . But on a worldwide basis, oil is not a shortage commodity. Current prices are high, due in large part to the successful cartel agreement among the nations of the Organization of Petroleum Exporting Countries (OPEC). If anyone wants to argue for inevitable long-term shortages, their impact remains hard to detect in current oil markets.[28]

These are obviously extreme statements of the price theory of the origins of the energy crisis. An extension of the argument would be that the oil corporations crumbled in the face of OPEC demands, garnering enormous profits in the process of accepting sharp price increases, and easily adjusting to their new role as "tax collectors" for the OPEC governments.[29] At one edge of the Western energy-policy continuum, the energy crisis was seen as nothing but a price conspiracy between the corporations and the OPEC governments—a conspiracy that could be effectively controlled by government intervention in the bargaining process to control the price of crude petroleum. Although this view may appear at first glance to have something in common with the Chinese perspective that the energy crisis was contrived to maximize profits, the price theorists and Peking could not be further apart in their suggestions for resolution of the international energy problem.

Price increases have had a devastating effect on the balance-of-payments position of many oil-importing countries, severely challenging the adjustment capabilities of the international monetary system and undermining the value of the dollar.[30] Western governments have responded with tariff-induced price increases and price controls that hold domestic oil above or close to the price of imported oil. These measures constrict domestic demand for imported oil, thereby putting long-term downward pressure on the international market price of crude petroleum while assuring domestic "independence" from foreign oil sources. In addition, there have been some rather ineffective efforts by the petroleum-importing countries to cartelize, to share available petroleum supplies in the event of another embargo, to cooperate in restricting the total demand of the industrial oil-importing countries, and through all of these measures to "break" OPEC control over the price of crude oil.[31] What is important to this analysis about all of these measures is not their effectiveness, but the fact that all of them focus to one degree or another on manipulation of the price of crude petroleum as the principal means of containing the energy crisis.

There was some empirical evidence that price control and conservation efforts in the industrial oil-importing countries had begun to have an impact on the international petroleum market. The total volume of 1975 crude petroleum imports from the Middle East dropped somewhat from 1974 levels, and a one-third cut (10^7 barrels per day) in oil imports was projected for 1980, despite projections of long-term demand increase.[32] This would have left the world market in 1980 with a surplus of 15–20 million barrels per day of crude petroleum production, if the projections had been correct. The effect of consumption constraint was temporarily to push the real price of crude petroleum below the "posted price" through the granting of "hidden discounts" by some of the producing countries.[33] OPEC also cut back production somewhat to keep the market tight. Import and production cutbacks caused a depression in oil tanker rates owing to surplus tanker capacity.[34] Crude shipping prices on the "spot market" fell to about one-tenth 1973 levels, and about 9 percent of the world tanker fleet was laid up in early 1975 as more supertankers, ordered under conditions of very high shipping rates a few years before, were delivered by shipbuilders during a period of tanker surplus. But these short-term fluctuations did not reflect the long-term trend, which was toward ever higher current production pressure on world crude oil reserves.

Some governments and economists began to fear a sudden drop in the international price of crude petroleum as much as they initially feared price increases. They therefore sought to establish some means of maintaining a "floor price" under domestic crude petroleum production should OPEC governments suddenly decide to undermine energy development programs and new energy industries by flooding the market with cheap crude.[35]

The Western view that price is the appropriate means of dealing with the energy crisis contrasts sharply with the Chinese view that organization of the international energy market and energy distribution are the critical issues. The government of the PRC believes that a shift in political control over energy distribution away from the multinational corporations and the governments of the industrial market-economy countries toward Third World governments of the oil-producing countries has been the decisive factor in the outcome of the energy crisis. Peking welcomes this event as a shift in political authority over energy resources that will ease the disequilibrium in the global energy-distribution system. The political organization of energy distribution may therefore be seen as the Chinese counterpart of Western efforts at price control. China views shifts in the price structure of the international petroleum market as a result of, not a cause of, changing patterns of political authority. This brings us back to some final comments on the general characteristics of China's international energy policies.

China's International Energy Policies

The energy crisis hit the industrial market-economy countries at a time that coincided exactly with the development of extensive political relations between these countries and the People's Republic of China. The combined effect of the energy crisis and China's "reemergence" into a diplomatic arena dominated by the West was to reveal the general outlines of China's international energy policies. As if to mock the distress of the Western world, Peking denied the very reality of the energy crisis itself, attributing it to the Madison Avenue concoctions of the giant oil corporations. At the same time, China has encouraged its friends in OPEC and the rest of the Third World to seize the energy crisis as a vehicle for establishing domestic governmental control over the petroleum industry within their borders and over their own petroleum resources. Self-reliance, resource sovereignty, and energy distribution became the central political issues raised by the Chinese press in its attack on the energy policies of the industrial market-economy countries. (See Chapter 5.) Real or imaginary, the energy crisis served as an effective political device for the PRC at a critical juncture in the development of its relations with the Third World.

During the 25 years of its own energy development, China sought to maximize domestic energy production and minimize import dependence. Through a long and often bitter struggle, the PRC established its energy independence from the Western corporate energy giants and from penetration by Soviet technology and management techniques (Chapter 4). The political break with the Soviet Union pushed China into a rather steep domestic energy crisis of its own in the early 1960's, a crisis that was ultimately overcome by the timely development of Taching oilfield (Chapter 11).

While seeking energy independence from the "superpowers," the PRC was careful to establish effective trade relations in energy commodities and equipment with the smaller industrial market-economy countries (Chapter 5). Peking obviously felt more comfortable dealing with the aggregate energy capabilities of Japan and Western Europe as energy trading partners than with the very large industrial countries. The trade in energy commodities, initially marginal in China's overall foreign trade and miniscule in terms of domestic energy consumption, expanded rapidly after 1973. Chinese crude petroleum exports to Japan herald a new age for both the Chinese energy-production system and China's international trade. Extensive offshore petroleum reserves may enable China to develop this energy-trade relationship with Japan even further, although a ceiling on petroleum exports will be set by the energy end-use requirement of the domestic Chinese economy and by the political preferences of the revolutionary Chinese leadership. These preferences will be reinforced by the regional scope of China's energy-trade potential (Chapter 8).

All of these substantive energy-policy themes have been developed within the context of Peking's particular approach to the international organization of global energy distribution (Chapter 9). The Chinese leadership ranks organizations dealing in energy distribution according to highly political criteria. Peking advocates concentration of authority over global energy distribution in the hands of governments—especially Third World governments. China is an active participant in most international organizations, and supports an energy-related political role for these organizations as long as they maximize government control over energy resources and energy-distribution patterns. The PRC openly attacks the role of the multinational corporations in global energy distribution, but has been willing to deal with them for the purchase of high-technology energy equipment, as long as such purchases are kept free of long-term commitments and other commercial "strings."

China tends to view the role of commodity cartels such as the Organization of Petroleum Exporting Countries as catalytic, precipitating rapid change in the international energy-distribution system. According to the Chinese perspective, the background field conditions for such rapid change were established some time ago through the historic process of imperialism. Disequilibrium in global energy distribution was the result of centuries of imperial domination of the countries and areas of the Third World by the industrial market-economy countries and their corporate agents. Thus, the current "energy crisis" was the result of fundamental disequilibria in historic global energy-distribution patterns, not a mere breakdown of energy technology as a consequence of overextended energy-production growth rates.

The disequilibrium model for China's international energy policies may help to explain some of the apparent contradictions between the conservative and radical aspects of those policies. Peking views the disequilibria in global energy-distribution patterns as a long-term development. According to the Chinese Marxist perspective, such disequilibria might be maintained over a long period by countervailing pressures for maintenance of the status quo from the centers of international imperialism. China's humiliation at the hands of Western colonialism, for example, lasted at least one hundred years, and much longer if one counts back beyond the opening of the first treaty ports. This relatively long-range Chinese historical perspective is matched by an equally long-range perspective on the future. Peking readily accepts the proposition that it may take China decades, if not centuries, to catch up with and surpass the industrial market-economy countries. And China's revolutionary leaders expect global energy-distribution problems to persist for some time.

The long-term nature of energy-distribution disequilibria helps explain why Peking is willing to deal directly with the multinational energy corporations that it excoriates in the press, why China is willing to sell large amounts of crude oil to Japan, and why the PRC supports the relatively conservative political orientation of OPEC. There is no inconsistency, in China's view, between its own socialist ideology and these aspects of its international energy policies. Energy-distribution disequilibria have been around for some time and will not disappear overnight. Why not then deal with the situation as it is, as long as the domestic Chinese energy system can be effectively insulated from global energy problems by the policy of self-reliance? Dealing with the centers of energy imperialism may facilitate the transfer of energy technology into the domestic Chinese energy-production system. One Western scholar summed up China's attitude toward technology transfer this way:

China shares with the developing countries of the third world the broad objective of economic growth, starting from a condition the Chinese themselves describe as "poor and blank" relative to the material resources of the developed countries. Yet "self-reliance" has been the keynote of Chinese policies for ten years, and the Chinese now urge the rest of the third world countries to adopt the same principle for their own development. In broad terms, "development" refers to the improvement of a society's material welfare, resulting from economic growth and from appropriate measures of income distribution. In Chinese, and increasingly, in general usage, such economic growth is identified with the use of production processes and the production of goods new to the developing economy. "Self-reliance" does not necessarily preclude transfer of foreign technologies into the developing country, but specifies technological change which occurs in response to demands arising within the economy itself, rather than imposed on it from outside. In any country, demand for technological change and distribution of the fruits of technological advance are dependent on its political and social structure, as well as on economic factors, and on the country's international economic and political bargaining power. China, whose leaders have a particular perception of these relationships for their development objectives, is an especially significant "case study" of the use of science and technology for national development.[36]

But there is a far more radical side to China's international energy policies. The radical side corresponds to the revolutionary aspects of Peking's attitudes toward change. The enormous pressures in international relations generated by disequilibria in energy and other resource distribution patterns will eventually precipitate sudden, wrenching, and even revolutionary changes. Such changes will be initiated by the have-nots and will therefore occur along the fault lines between the industrial countries and the Third World. The radical side of the international energy policies of the PRC seeks to identify and reinforce the catalytic events that may precipitate sudden shifts in global energy distribution. Chinese leaders believe that the damage to humanity from inequities in resource distribution will be less the sooner the catalytic events occur. Therefore, China supports OPEC and other organizations that Peking has identified as being catalytic for the resolution of long-term resource disequilibria. The entire energy crisis is viewed in Peking as a catalytic event, or a series of catalytic events, in the global energy-distribution system.

The basic elements of Chinese and Western reactions to the energy crisis might be summarized as follows:

	Field condition	Process	Solution
PRC	disequilibria	catalysis	political organization
West	growth	crisis	price control

The central point in this analysis is simply that China's attitude toward change differs fundamentally from that expressed in statements by Western governments and observers regarding the energy crisis. The differences in their respective attitudes toward change may be what makes the energy policies of each look absurd to the other. The Chinese disequilibrium model is based on the theory of underlying pressures (or "contradictions" in Mao's usage) generated by enormous differentials in energy and other resource consumption. The Western growth model, on the other hand, identifies the source of pressures on the global energy system in the aggregate characteristics of that system, specifically the depletion of fossil-fuel reserves by rising production and consumption. The background field conditions for the Chinese scenario are differentials in energy distribution. The field conditions for the Western scenario are energy-production-to-reserves ratios.

Distinctive official Chinese attitudes toward the energy crisis and toward rapid change in the international energy system act as basic perceptual constraints on the formulation of Chinese energy policy. These perceptual constraints operate with greater or lesser degrees of severity, depending on the policy issue in question. On the one hand, the PRC views its own energy-development lag as the result of earlier injustices. Peking must, therefore, minimize the likelihood that China will ever again fall victim to control of its domestic energy resources or production by foreign corporations or governments.

On the other hand, China has not applied its disequilibrium analysis with complete consistency. As will be seen in Chapter 3, Peking supports the pricing policies of the OPEC governments, even at the cost of further inequities in energy-consumption patterns in other Third World countries. Chinese commentators have proved surprisingly insensitive to the additional burden that the energy crisis has imposed on the poorest oil-importing countries. In many ways, China identifies itself with the rapid growth prospects of the oil-exporting countries. But in doing so, China's development planners have paradoxically accepted some elements of the exponential growth fixation that characterizes Western energy policy. The Chinese government has officially committed itself to the construction of a "modern industrial socialist country" by the turn of the century.[37] Meeting that objective will require an enormous energy input. It is difficult to assess what impact such exponential growth in the energy industries will have on the prevailing process orientation in Peking.

Chapter 3

China's Energy Policies in the Third World

> The awakening and growth of the Third World is a major event in contemporary international relations. The Third World has strengthened its unity in the struggle against hegemonism and the power politics of the superpowers and is playing an ever more conspicuous role in international affairs.
> —Chou En-lai, August 1973[1]

Since the successful emergence of the People's Republic of China into the international arena in the early 1970's, China has repeatedly identified itself as a Third World country.[2] In expressing its solidarity with the Third World, the PRC goes further than simply admitting that it too is "still a poor and developing country."[3] China's Third World identity extends to vicarious support for the policy positions of the poorer countries in their struggles for political independence and rapid industrial growth.

China's Third World identity also implies a categorization of the world's countries and areas according to the relative level of industrialization of each area. This categorization hinges on fundamental distinctions among the Third World, the "second world" (smaller industrial countries), and the "superpowers." China's sense of identification with the Third World has grown steadily since the Sino-Soviet split, when the PRC realized that it was no more a European communist country than it was a Western market-economy country. This trend reached an extreme during the Cultural Revolution, when radicals attempted to translate China's revolutionary experience directly into prescriptions for Third World development.[4] The theme that the Third World is a vast countryside ripe for a Chinese-style revolution did not go down well in Third World capitals, and has since been disavowed. But the underlying concept of the Third World as a distinct political category has remained, and has been particularly pronounced in Peking's statements on international energy and other resource problems.[5]

The distinction between the resource haves and have-nots should not surprise Western analysts, since there has long been a recognition that the newly independent countries and the poor countries of Asia, Africa, and Latin America constitute a group with certain shared characteristics.

In terms of per capita energy consumption, these Third World areas (or "less developed countries," "developing countries," etc.) tend to cluster at well under 1,000 kilograms coal equivalent (kgce) per capita per annum.[6] Even counting noncommerical agricultural fuels, average Third World per capita energy consumption has been under 5 percent of American per capita energy consumption for more than a decade. These simple statistics indicate that a Third World grouping could be justified on the basis of per capita energy consumption, whatever the hazards of doing so on general economic or political grounds.

Despite considerable progress in all of its domestic energy industries and rapid growth in the petroleum and natural gas industries, the PRC is still very much a Third World country in terms of per capita energy consumption. (See Chapter 19.) In the mid-1970's, China ranked ahead of Third World Asia and Africa, but behind Latin America and the Middle East, in per capita energy consumption. China has a respectable but not comfortable per capita energy life-style, even by Third World standards. Low per capita energy consumption creates a set of severe political and economic constraints within which China must choose its energy development policies. For at least the next several decades, China's energy export potential will be sharply limited by the enormous domestic energy end-use requirement. And that end-use requirement in turn will be generated by the high priority placed on rising per capita energy consumption levels. (See Chapter 24.)

The Self-Reliance Policy

One important organizational device that Peking has used to overcome, or at least minimize, the effects of the low per capita energy consumption constraints on domestic development is the "self-reliance" policy. The self-reliance slogan sums up what Peking considers a successful model for both agricultural and industrial development. It has been important in the development of energy production. The concept has intensely political connotations and concerns the locus of political authority and control over the process of development. The slogan "*dulizizhu, ziligengsheng,*" literally translated, means "Independence, self-mastery, relying on oneself, producing more." "Self-reliance" will do as a more compact, if not literal, abbreviation.

Over the last decade, Peking has increasingly applied the self-reliance guideline to the development problems of other Third World countries.[7] Exactly the same Chinese phrase that appears on commune buildings and factories all over China also shows up in discussions of Third World energy-development problems. There are a number of reasons for the use of a domestic development slogan as an element of international energy policy.

Historically, China's own energy development was affected for more than a century by the intrusion of foreign companies and the governments of foreign countries into the domestic energy sector, as well as into all aspects of the Chinese economy. China was open to "semicolonial" Western economic penetration from 1842 until 1949. That penetration brought with it the new energy technologies being developed in the West, but on a very limited scale and in a manner that subordinated Chinese development to Western financial interest.[8] Chinese guides still enjoy reminding Western visitors to any of the large oilfields or refineries that China was once considered "oil poor" by Western geologists and petroleum engineers. The Chinese explanation for this egregious error is usually that the Western oil companies had an interest in suppressing the development of a domestic oil industry in China, in order to preserve the Chinese market for Western petroleum products, particularly kerosene.[9] (Western geologists prefer to believe that the mistake was the result of an underestimation of the oil-bearing potential of China's predominantly lacustrine sedimentary basins.)

Chinese energy development was further disrupted by Japanese imperialism and particularly by Japanese exploitation of Manchurian coal deposits. Although many of the present-day coal mines in northeast China date to the period of Japanese occupation and were actually developed by Japanese industry, little if any of the coal from these mines reached the domestic Chinese energy market. The struggle with Japan raged back and forth across China for a decade, closing many coal mines and disrupting the production activities of others.[10]

But the current historical bête noire of the various Chinese energy industries is neither Western nor Japanese imperialism, but Soviet "social imperialism." The massive influx of Soviet technicians during the 1950's had an enormous impact on the direction of energy development within the PRC, which took a turn toward large-scale, centrally funded projects drawn to the specifications of Soviet blueprints. These projects were interrupted and in some cases severely damaged by the withdrawal of Soviet technical assistance in 1960. When combined with the failures of China's own Great Leap Forward, the result was a domestic energy crisis that deepened the economic depression of the early 1960's. The energy crisis involved a decline in coal production, insufficient petroleum-product supplies, and interruption of large-scale hydropower construction.[11] Blaming the entire fiasco on the Soviet withdrawal, China experienced a serious decline in its total energy-production growth curve. (See Chapter 16.)

The policy of self-reliance was formulated in part as a response to the historical succession of foreign countries that have attempted in one manner or another to penetrate and control the domestic Chinese production system. This historical context helps make clear exactly what the Chinese mean by self-reliance in energy development. Self-reliance means any measure or series of measures that ensures the independent operation of a country's domestic energy system. It connotes a sort of political-economic nationalism that can take effect in a variety of ways, depending on local circumstances and on the exact nature of foreign penetration. It implies ultimate control over the domestic energy system of any country by the government of that country and thus has a definite socialist cast. Self-reliance precludes both domination of the domestic energy-production infrastructure by multinational corporations and penetration of the domestic energy-planning apparatus through foreign technical-assistance programs. It rules out foreign ownership of primary and secondary energy-production facilities (coal mines, oil refineries, power plants, etc.) as well as the domestic energy-marketing structure.

In short, the self-reliance development model is a broad concept and may be applied to different situations in a variety of ways, depending on political circumstances. For one country it may imply reduction of energy imports, for another an increase in energy exports. Self-reliance is often invoked to encourage nationalization of an energy-production industry or the petroleum-marketing structure. Completion of a hydropower project may be praised as a step toward self-reliance, even if it was constructed using generating equipment of foreign manufacture.[12] The self-reliance guideline is more important in ruling out certain types of dependency than in charting a precise course for energy development.

The Resource Sovereignty Policy

A second basic element of China's international energy policies toward the Third World is the concept of "resource sovereignty."[13] Resource sovereignty is related to but distinct from self-reliance. It implies a certain concatenation of fundamental ownership rights over mineral resources, a concept that borders on a new international legal formulation. Roughly stated, resource sovereignty implies that the resources within the territorial boundaries, territorial seas, and contiguous offshore areas should be under the exclusive and ultimate control of the government of the country in question. The principle of resource sovereignty excludes "concessions" of mineral rights within territorial boundaries to a multinational or foreign corporation or to a foreign government. If implemented, it would completely eradicate all forms of control by the major

oil corporations over oilfields in the producing countries. And it would
directly affect control of other mineral resources, such as copper or
aluminum.

The Chinese position is that such controls developed as part of the historical process of imperial expansion:

> National independence and economic development are issues of vital interest
> to the people of all countries and in particular to the people of the developing
> countries. . . . The economic backwardness of Asian, African, and Latin Ameri-
> can countries is the result of oppression by imperialism and colonialism. These
> regions abound in resources and are inhabited by the majority of the people of
> the world, who have created splendid ancient civilizations and made tremendous
> contributions to mankind. But the majority of the Asian, African, and Latin
> American countries suffered in varying degrees from oppression and plunder
> by imperialism and colonialism. As a result, their state sovereignty was trampled
> upon, their national resources were damaged, and their people greatly impover-
> ished. Especially the economy of the colonies and dependent countries was
> turned into a "single-product economy" as a result of lopsided development
> under man-made "division of labor" in the colonial interests of imperialism.
> These countries were reduced to sources of raw materials and markets of manu-
> factures monopolized by colonial and metropolitan countries, and were sub-
> jected to ever more cruel exploitation.[14]

> The Chinese people firmly support the people of the other developing countries
> in Asia and the Far East in their struggles to develop the national economy, to
> protect their sovereign rights over national resources, and to establish interna-
> tional economic relationships that are equitable and rational, and to combat im-
> perialist, and particularly superpower control, plunder, and exploitation.[15]

These quotations illustrate the strength of the Chinese government's
position regarding the principle of resource sovereignty. Peking insists
that domestic control over a country's raw materials and mineral resources is a critical condition for rapid development. Conversely, foreign
control of domestic resources such as petroleum reserves leads, in the
Chinese view, inevitably toward exploitation of those resources in the interest of the foreign company or government involved, thereby diverting income and the resources themselves from domestic development.
Regardless of the short-term advantage (which accrues mainly to the domestic ruling class) of an influx of foreign capital to mineral resource
ventures such as petroleum extraction, the long-term consequences are a
disastrous development. According to this position, the influx of foreign
capital and technology is matched or exceeded by an outflow of profits
and political control over the direction of development. The ultimate result is that the development of the raw-materials-producing countries is

chained to the development requirements of the industrial countries. The principle of resource sovereignty would reverse this process by moving the center of political control over mineral and other resources back to the capitals of the Third World countries.

It would be a serious mistake to underestimate the intensity of Chinese feelings on the issues of resource sovereignty and self-reliance. These principles lie at an important intersection between intense nationalism and equally intense economic development imperatives. Both doctrines will be involved in the willingness of the People's Republic of China to become involved in joint offshore exploration or production ventures with foreign companies or foreign governments. At the end of 1978, it appeared that Peking might indeed, after several years of hesitation and refusal to even consider such an option, offer joint offshore development contracts to foreign oil companies (Chapter 8). This represents a radical departure from previous policy, but not necessarily an abandonment of either resource sovereignty or self-reliance. The critical issue is the matter of control. It remains highly unlikely that China will alienate control over its offshore oil resources (if such resources exist) through direct concession contracts that mark off tracts along the Chinese continental shelf and place the operation of exploration and production completely under the control of foreign companies. It is much more likely that Peking will buy foreign exploration and offshore production through service contracts. A certain proportion of the resulting production will then be guaranteed for "buy-back" and export to pay for the services. This sort of arrangement will leave the ultimate control of each project in the hands of Chinese energy planners. In addition, Chinese teams and offshore rigs will probably work in close coordination with the foreign companies that receive offshore service contracts. This is roughly what Peking means by "joint ventures" or "joint offshore development." The exact form that the contracts will take has not yet been determined. But they will most likely fall within the boundaries defined by the concepts of resource sovereignty and self-reliance. The concept of self-reliance has deeply imbedded historical roots in China's development. One could trace its origins at least as far as the mid-nineteenth century to the "self-strengthening movement."[16] The Chinese press has recently reasserted and redefined this important concept:

Thus, the principle of self-reliance has been very clearly defined; China must maintain its political and economic independence; the destiny of China must be in the hands of the Chinese people; and the tasks of both revolution and construction must be accomplished by the Chinese people themselves. This is the basis on which our policy rests. But on no account does this mean self-sufficient isolationism and refusing to learn from the positive experiences of other countries.[17]

Energy Trade with the Third World

Although China's energy policies toward the Third World have been largely vicarious and have seldom involved direct interaction, the PRC has maintained trade in some energy commodities with a growing number of Third World countries (now about forty).* These trade relations began to develop in the early 1960's, following the Sino-Soviet break, as China moved to establish a wider diplomatic presence in nonsocialist countries. The energy value of such trade has been marginal in terms of the scale of domestic Chinese energy production and consumption. China's balance of trade has benefited from the sale of various petroleum by-products, and the PRC has occasionally made spot imports of critical energy fuels from Third World trading partners. But the principal benefit of China's trade in energy commodities has been political, providing an opening wedge for trade relations, which have often been followed by diplomatic recognition and political ties. Certain Chinese energy commodities have been offered at concessionary prices in the early stages of a trade relationship with a given country. Chinese mineral jelly and wax, petroleum by-products, and low-grade lubricants often appear in export statistics very early in the trade relationship with a new Third World trading partner. Such products are usually of use to the trading partner and can be bought on a small scale at first. China has already developed a wide network of markets for these specialized energy commodities. Should China decide to export energy fuels (crude petroleum, petroleum products, and liquefied natural gas) on a world scale, the marketing infrastructure will be in place and functioning. Chinese trade officials have also gained experience in dealing with transport and financing arrangements peculiar to energy commodities.

China's spot imports of liquid fuels (mostly diesel fuel) have periodically been used to cover domestic shortages. Eastern European or Third World trading partners have been the preferred source of such spot imports, owing to the political hazards of dealing in critical commodities with the industrial countries that applied until the early 1970's. Some of the spot imports may have been bound on Chinese ships for Korea or Vietnam, a politically sensitive matter during the 1960's. The United States was still enforcing an embargo on exports to China during the 1960's. And the Soviet Union had just recently cut back the export of petroleum products to the PRC. Third World sources were the obvious way to avoid political entanglement with the superpowers. For various reasons, including both the embargo problem and the likely destination of the spot im-

---

*The empirical foundation and documentation for this section were derived from the detailed energy trade statistics in Part II, Chapter 20.

ports in Vietnam, the spot import of petroleum products was always wrapped in secrecy and has been difficult to unwrap statistically. It would be safe to say, however, that such imports never exceeded one million metric tons in a single year. Some authors have consequently mistaken spot imports for ongoing trade relations in critical energy commodities.[18]

China has also exported some intermediate-technology energy-production machinery to Third World countries. The most common energy-equipment exports have been diesel engines and electric power-generating and transmission equipment. Such items as ceramic insulators are favorite Chinese exports. The PRC tends to export low- or intermediate-technology energy equipment to the Third World and to import high-technology energy-production equipment from the industrial countries. Chinese exports of intermediate-technology energy-production equipment are an area of great potential in trade relations with the Third World. Chinese equipment, which is cheaper than the equivalent purchased from the industrial countries, is simpler and more closely suited to the energy-development needs of Third World countries than highly sophisticated, expensive units. Chinese electric-power generators, for example, are predominantly low-capacity units, more flexible and less capital-intensive than the usual generating equipment produced in North America or Western Europe. The main constraint on Chinese exports of intermediate-technology energy equipment will more likely be China's own production capacity and domestic requirements than marketing considerations.

Coal and Coke

China's coal and coke exports have been oriented almost entirely toward Asian countries (excluding the Soviet Union). Aside from Japan, the main Third World importers of Chinese coal were Hong Kong, Pakistan, and Cambodia. Coke was exported to a variety of Third World Asian countries in small quantities during the 1960's. Pakistan and Hong Kong have been the most consistent Third World importers of Chinese coke-oven coke. The regularity of Pakistan's coke imports since 1970 indicates some sort of supply agreement between a Pakistani steel mill and the PRC.

Crude Petroleum

China was an importer of crude petroleum until the mid-1960's. Since 1970, crude oil exports have gone to Korea, Vietnam, Thailand, and the Philippines. Chinese crude has run into serious problems in Third World refineries, because of its high wax content, high pour point, and low flash point, characteristics that make it hard to handle without special refinery equipment. Both Thailand and the Philippines found Chinese crude difficult to deal with and have backed away from initial crude oil import agreements with the PRC. This raises serious doubts about the suitability of Chinese crude oil for trade in Third World energy markets. The large domestic Chinese energy end-use requirement compounds the issue by setting a rather low ceiling on potential crude petroleum exports (Chapter 24). Crude oil available for export will probably, therefore, go primarily to Japanese refineries until at least 1985, unless China offers unusually low prices to Third World importers to compensate for the waxiness of Chinese crude.

Refined Petroleum Fuels

China has not been, and probably will not be, a significant exporter of the higher petroleum fractions—gasoline and kerosene. Domestic refinery capacity has never kept pace with the demand for these light distillates. China has exported small amounts of kerosene to Hong Kong since 1971, but has usually been a net kerosene importer.

Diesel fuel, however, is a different matter. After importing large quantities of diesel during the 1950's and 1960's, China began exporting significant amounts in the early 1970's. Initial diesel exports went to Hong Kong and Thailand, although such exports may have been discussed with several other countries at the time. China may also have been exporting some diesel fuel to both Korea and Vietnam during the late 1960's and early 1970's. This would help explain spot imports of diesel from Iran, Egypt, and Kuwait, although some of the fuel may also have been used to cover domestic Chinese shortages.

Diesel fuel would seem to be an ideal potential energy commodity for export to Third World countries during the 1980's. It is the heaviest distillate fraction, produced in relatively large quantities by Chinese refineries. It would not require further refining in Third World countries, and would be suitable for diesel-burning vehicles and small engines. It is cheaper than gasoline. But China has been moving toward greater use of diesel fuel in the domestic transport sector (particularly in railroad engines) and may have only limited quantities available for export. Allowing for domestic Chinese requirements, diesel remains the fuel of greatest potential for trade with Third World partners.

Chinese production of residual fuel oil has almost always matched domestic consumption requirements. No residual oil was imported from the Soviet Union or Eastern Europe during the 1950's. In fact, the only significant recorded imports of residual oil were purchased from Kuwait in 1971–72. Unspecified petroleum-product imports from Singapore since 1972 may also have been heavy fuel oil, as may similar spot purchases from Egypt (1968–69), Albania (1962–64), Romania (since 1965), and Iran (1967). Assuming that these unspecified imports all consisted of heavy fuel oil, the total has been running between 100,000 and 500,000 metric tons per year since 1965. Furthermore, there has been an increase in these purchases since 1970. Taken together, this evidence would indicate that the unspecified petroleum-product imports listed for various countries are predominantly fuel oil for Chinese ships. The locations of the supplying countries and the increase in such purchases after 1970 would also point to fuel oil. Chinese freighters in trade with Europe, Africa, and South Asia apparently make fuel stops in these supply ports on a fairly regular basis. However, the supply of residual oil from Chinese refineries has always been ample for domestic power plants and industrial process heat.

Lubricants

China's trade with the Third World in lubricants illustrates again the proposition that the PRC is a high-technology importer and an intermediate-technology exporter. The PRC has long imported high-grade, specialized, and expensive lubricants and greases from the industrial countries, including both Eastern and Western Europe (predominantly Eastern Europe and the Soviet Union by volume). At the same time, China exported low-grade lubricants (at low prices) to Third World countries—particularly in Asia.

Mineral Jelly and Wax

China has exported mineral jelly and wax (paraffin) to at least 25 Third World countries since 1960. Owing to the extreme waxiness of Taching crude (and the other crudes from China's lacustrine sedimentary basins), paraffin has been available in massive, even unwanted quantities. The obvious answer was to export it at low prices. Wax must have done much better than the PRC expected in the early export years, and it became a leading export commodity in China's foreign trade with the Third World, as well as with several industrial countries. It has almost always been the first petroleum by-product to appear in China's export to a new trade partner. The flag followed the wax to an extent that might lead some academic wag to suggest that wax was largely responsible for China's entry into the United Nations.

Petroleum By-Products

Most of China's export of petroleum by-products (petroleum coke, non-lubricating oils, bituminous mixtures, spent oil shale, etc.) have gone to Japan and the other small industrial countries. Marginal amounts have been exported for more than ten years to various Third World countries in Asia and Africa.

Regional Energy Policies

China's energy relations with the Third World may conveniently be analyzed on the basis of the major regions—the Middle East, Africa, Latin America, and South Asia. East and Southeast Asia will be treated separately (Chapters 6–8), owing to the importance of the regional element in China's energy-trade policies. This section will also be limited to consideration of bilateral relations with various Third World countries, leaving multilateral relations to Chapter 9, on China's energy policies in international organizations.

The Middle East

China's energy relations with the Middle Eastern countries illustrate nearly every aspect of Peking's energy policies toward the Third World. This is true, of course, because of the importance of petroleum trade to Middle Eastern economic development and regional politics.

The Middle East fits the Chinese paradigm perfectly in that the region suffered a long period of penetration by foreign oil corporations and domination by Western governments. The Middle Eastern oil-producing countries have supplied massive quantities of energy resources for Western Europe, Japan, and, more recently, North America. Until 1970, oil prices were dictated by the multinationals, which held iron-clad concession agreements for the region's vast crude petroleum reserves. The Middle Eastern countries were also classic cases of the maintenance of repressive and wealthy ruling elites through external subsidies from oil-tax revenues, which scarcely trickled down to the wider population. At least one Middle Eastern government (Iran in 1953–54) was overthrown at the behest of the oil companies.[19] The Middle Eastern governments paid for their external base of support by massive and cheap crude petroleum exports, and insured it with the maintenance of absolute "order" at home. The result was not particularly advantageous to the standard of living of the wider citizenry, let alone to the political and social development of Middle Eastern countries. Meanwhile, the benefits of an enormous direct energy supplement went to Europe and Japan, as energy production soared by 10 percent annually, but with more than 90 percent of production leaving the region.[20]

During the early 1970's, OPEC and the Western oil-supply gap combined to produce a realignment of political control over Middle Eastern oil resources. The first step was the sharp rise in tax rates and the climbing posted price of crude oil exports.[21] But almost immediately, the governments of Middle Eastern countries began to assert more direct forms of control over domestic petroleum resources. This assertion of political control took the form of participation agreements that transformed the foreign consortia into joint ventures with the governments of the producing countries. The governing boards of the consortia suddenly found themselves with government participants. Most of them are now slated for 100 percent control by the host government. And real political control over petroleum resources has shifted to the governments of the producing countries.

In addition, some of the Middle Eastern countries have directly abrogated or renegotiated the concession agreements. They have thereby asserted direct legal control over petroleum resources and have fulfilled the basic condition for what the Chinese would call resource sovereignty. Peking has, of course, been delighted at these developments.[22] They confirm a key element of China's energy policies toward the Third World.

China has strong political ties to certain Middle Eastern countries—notably Iran and Kuwait. The Peking press has been vocal in its support of Iran's program of nationalization of the domestic oil industry.[23] Iran has also been a champion of higher oil prices, sometimes embroiling the country in struggles with more conservative members of OPEC, such as Saudi Arabia, who wish to hold the line on prices. Iran's oil reserves are limited on the scale of projected world-market demand, and the Iranian government has been taking steps to conserve remaining reserves for long-range exports. At the same time, Iranian development is moving at a fairly brisk clip, and the country requires large amounts of foreign exchange to pay for imports of industrial technology. China has praised Iranian development projects, despite the foreign origin of much of the required technology.[24]

Relations with Kuwait are also quite warm, although less important than with Iran. Peking has been attentive to Kuwait's retrieval of oil concessions and to Kuwait's high level of resistance to Soviet penetration of the Middle East.[25] Good political relations with Kuwait have spilled over into some energy commodity trade between the two countries, in the form of Chinese purchases of fuel oil and Kuwaiti purchases of Chinese wax.

On the negative side, China's hostility toward Israel has reinforced its close relations with the Arab governments. The Chinese press has nothing good to say about Israel, and considers the country a vestige of imperialism in the Middle East. Peking has been a constant political antagonist to Israel in the United Nations and uses every opportunity to demonstrate its loyalty to the Arabs.[26] China also gained political mileage out of the success of the Arab oil embargo during the conflict between Israel and Egypt in October 1973.[27] China was delighted to see the embargo turned against the Western countries, which had long isolated the PRC from full participation in international economic relations with the West. But, on the whole, Israel is an insignificant factor in China's foreign policy, except as a political foil.

Peking has much larger fish to fry than Israel in the Middle East—the largest being the Soviet Union. The USSR borders on Iran, one of China's closest friends in the Middle East. Since China itself has serious border problems with the Soviet Union, the PRC has attacked Soviet border relations with the Eastern European countries, Mongolia, and Iran. Any easing of relations between the Soviet Union and these countries permits Moscow to apply even greater pressure to the Chinese border. China has accused the USSR of selling out the Arabs in a variety of ways, including a soft-on-Israel policy. According to Peking, Moscow has displayed a two-faced attitude toward the Arab-Israeli confrontation, supporting the oil embargo verbally in 1973–74 while selling oil and natural gas to the embargoed Western European countries at high prices, thereby relieving the political pressure of the embargo for the sake of high profits.[28]

The whole matter of Soviet energy trade with the Middle East has become a favorite political scourge, applied with great vigor by the Chinese press.[29] The Soviet Union imports some natural gas from Iran through a pipeline constructed with Soviet aid. The gas, originally purchased under the terms of a barter agreement, was going to the USSR at about one-fourth the price that Moscow was receiving for natural-gas exports to East and West Europe. In 1973, China explicitly accused the Soviet Union of purchasing 289 billion cubic feet of natural gas from Iran for 51.6 million rubles (0.18 rubles per thousand cubic feet) and then selling the gas to Poland, Czechoslovakia, and Austria for twice the price (179 billion cubic feet for 68.3 million rubles, or 0.38 rubles per thousand cubic feet). Embarrassed by the Chinese revelation and under pressure from the government of Iran, Moscow raised the purchase price 35 percent (to 0.24 rubles per thousand cubic feet), retroactive to January 1, 1973.[30] Eastern European governments subsequently began signing direct oil import agreements with the Middle Eastern governments to counter steep rises in the price of Soviet crude oil and to gain some political independence from Moscow.[31]

But the most telling criticism of Soviet energy policies toward the Middle East, from the Chinese perspective, has been over the issue of resource sovereignty:

The Soviet revisionists have concocted various fallacies to justify their imperialist plunder:

One, the theory of "international division of labor": The Soviet revisionists babbled that "the Soviet Union supplies sets of equipment, machinery, spare parts, and materials of all kinds, while the developing countries provide the Soviet Union with commodities it is interested in," and that "the Soviet Union and many countries are willing to take advantage of the 'international division of labor' on the basis of mutual benefit." This "international division of labor" is in fact a neocolonialist policy of plunder—"Soviet industry and Asian, African, and Latin American agriculture" or "Soviet industry with Asia, Africa, and Latin America as accessory factories." Such a policy aims at bringing the developing countries of Asia, Africa, and Latin America into the orbit of the Soviet revisionist sphere of influence after the pattern of East European countries and Mongolia, reducing them into bases of raw materials and markets.

Two, the theory of "limited sovereignty over resources": The Soviet revisionists declared that "the sovereignty over natural resources depends to a great extent upon the capability of utilizing these resources by the industry of the developing countries." In other words, countries with greater industrial capability of utilizing resources enjoy greater sovereignty over their natural resources and those with smaller capability have less sovereignty. According to this imperialist logic, the Third World countries still industrially backward cannot exercise sovereignty over their natural resources, whereas the industrially developed Soviet revisionist social-imperialists could plunder the resources of others and encroach upon their sovereignty at will. This is entirely an extension and amplification of the theory of "limited sovereignty" which the Soviet revisionists apply to some East European countries.

Three, the theory of "international property": The Soviet revisionists babbled that "although Arab oil—in form—is the property of the Arabs, actually it is international property. It is a substance connected with the life of the modern world and its industries." This is an out-and-out imperialist argument, an absurd pretext concocted by the Soviet revisionists to plunder Middle-East oil. It wholly denies the sovereignty of the Arab countries over their natural resources.[32]

This Chinese rendition of the Soviet position on Middle Eastern oil resource sovereignty was stated in the most extreme fashion, and the enclosed quotations were not referenced. However, it does demonstrate that the PRC fears Soviet penetration of the Middle East and has serious reservations regarding Soviet designs on Middle Eastern oil and other Third World natural resources. The Soviet factor is obviously important to China's Middle Eastern energy policy. It also illustrates once again the central position of the issue of resource sovereignty in China's international energy policies.

China itself has traded only modestly in energy commodities with the Middle Eastern countries. In general, the Middle Eastern governments were still influenced by American and European policy toward China during the 1960's and were not eager to break the Western embargo on strategic exports to China. There are occasional reports that Iran or Iraq exported significant quantities of crude oil to China in certain years.[33] I have not been able to confirm these reports through a search of official trade returns or United Nations data. China did import several hundred thousand tons of refined petroleum products (diesel and residual fuel oil) from Kuwait in 1971 and 1972 (Table 20.73). It is possible that some other energy commodity trade with Middle Eastern countries has eluded my net.

Africa

China likes to think of Africa as a proving ground for its self-reliance energy-development model for the Third World. As an extremely energy-poor area (in terms of per capita consumption) and an area with a recent colonial history, Africa fits the Chinese paradigm of the causes of Third World poverty. Furthermore, the United States and the Soviet Union have been competing actively for influence in Africa, strengthening the Chinese thesis that the Third World is now falling victim to a struggle for hegemony by the two superpowers.

The PRC has had a particularly close relationship with Algeria since the early 1960's. There were rumors in 1964 that China was seeking to import Algerian crude oil. A delegation of Chinese oil experts visited the oilfield facilities of French companies in the Algerian Sahara in January 1964.[34] The Algerians apparently introduced the Chinese to the French, and discussions began over the possible purchase of French natural-gas-processing equipment and oil-refinery components. China was also reportedly considering giving technical aid to the national Algerian oil company. Nothing but goodwill, apparently, came of these contacts. More recently, China has supported Algerian President Boumedienne's vigorous efforts to protect Third World natural resources through multilateral discussion of raw-materials and international-trade issues.[35]

China has also been interested in Nigerian and Tunisian efforts to nationalize domestic crude petroleum reserves.[36] The Chinese press has commented favorably on African efforts to develop self-reliant energy industries.[37] But beyond this moral encouragement, the PRC has conducted a number of aid projects related to energy production in African countries. From 1973 until 1975, China assisted in the construction of the Bouenza hydropower station (74 megawatts) and power transmission lines in the Congo.[38] Aside from its big railroad project, Peking has helped Tanzania with geological exploration and the development of a coal mine at Tukuyu.[39] An agreement was signed with Equatorial Guinea in May 1976 that provides for Chinese construction of a hydro-

power station and transmission lines.[40] In February 1978, Chinese aid
personnel signed over a small diesel-fired power station built in Bongo,
Ethiopia, under the terms of a 1973 technical cooperation agreement.[41]
On the darker side of energy cooperation, Libya has requested Chinese
aid in the construction of weapons-sensitive nuclear facilities (Chapter
12).

China has exported minor amounts of petroleum by-products, including lubricants and wax, to a number of African countries (Tables 20.4–
20.6). Spot fuel purchases were reported from Ghana in 1965 (residual)
and Egypt in 1968 and 1969 (diesel).

Latin America

Peking has been remarkably aware of Latin American energy development patterns, considering the primitive state of its political relations
with that region. China is particularly attentive to the process of nationalization of the Venezuelan oil industry and crude oil reserves, something of a model for the rest of Latin America in Chinese eyes.[42] The
Venezuelan experience appeals to the PRC because of the direct confrontation between the President of Venezuela and several American oil
corporations. Political relations with Venezuela have been warm and the
two countries established diplomatic relations in June 1974.[43] China established diplomatic relations with Trinidad and Tobago in the same
month, following a visit by a Trinidadian oil delegation to the PRC.[44]
China's energy policies had political side effects in at least these two
cases. China has shown similar interest in the development of Ecuador's
new crude petroleum production industry. Ecuador joined OPEC in November 1973 and has been attempting to control its domestic oil industry
through the State Petroleum Company.[45] The PRC also verbally supports the nationalized petroleum industries of Mexico and Peru.[46] During 1976, China and Mexico exchanged petroleum delegations.[47] There
have recently been large crude petroleum discoveries in Mexico, a situation parallel to that in China. This may result in some technical cooperation in the petroleum field between the two countries.

In the mid-1970's, Peking was establishing foreign trade networks
throughout Latin America. Mineral wax and other petroleum by-products have played their usual role in this trade. By 1978, energy commodity trade had been initiated with Brazil, Chile, Colombia, Ecuador, and
perhaps some other Latin American countries. China's potential trade
relationship with Brazil is interesting in an energy context. There were
rumors as early as 1974 that Brazil might be interested in Chinese crude
oil.[48] In 1975, the two countries signed their first small trade agreement.[49] In January 1978, they signed a much larger trade agreement,

amid unusual hullabaloo.[50] China and Brazil are at roughly equivalent levels of economic development, although their economic systems could hardly be more disparate. Brazil, like China, is interested in rapid development of its primary energy industries, and has very large hydropower resources. Peking openly supports Brazil's efforts to acquire plutonium-reprocessing facilities and other nuclear technology.[51] There is still no significant trade in energy commodities or energy production equipment, but the prospect would not be surprising.

South Asia

China's energy relations with South Asian countries turn around its close political and military relationship with Pakistan. Continuing friction over the border issue has impeded the development of any energy commodity trade between China and India. There are occasional rumors that India may someday import Chinese oil, but this will not happen without a substantial improvement in political relations between the two countries.[52] India has somewhat better relations with Vietnam, and has offered Hanoi assistance in oil exploration.[53]

The relationship with Pakistan is a mirror image of that with India. China and Pakistan first developed close relations during the Sino-Indian border conflict of 1962, as each country found itself confronted by the common Indian enemy. China supported Pakistan in the 1971 conflict over the independence of Bangladesh and vetoed the entry of Bangladesh into the United Nations. Peking extends considerable aid to Pakistan and in 1972 wrote off $140 million in earlier soft loans.[54] China has also been giving and selling Pakistan military equipment since about 1965. In 1978, after years of construction, the Karakorum highway was opened between the two countries, providing a direct link to China's Sinkiang province. The highway strengthens the security link in a region where both have continuing territorial conflicts with India.

Close political relations with Pakistan brought a measure of cooperation and trade in energy. China has been particularly interested in Pakistan's natural gas industry and sent natural gas study delegations to gas installations in Lahore, Lyallpur, and Multan in 1976 and 1977.[55] The central purpose of these visits was to examine Pakistan's Western natural gas compression and pipeline technology. China helped in the construction of a 150-mile high-voltage transmission line between Tarbela hydropower station and the Northwest Frontier province.[56] In energy commodity trade, Pakistan has imported Chinese coal since the late 1950's. (Table 20.11). This trade, which had averaged 200,000–300,000 metric tons of coal per year, was primarily with markets in East Pakistan. Coal trade therefore dropped precipitously in 1971 as Bangladesh gained independence. Recently, however, Peking's relations with Bangladesh have improved. In 1978, China offered Bangladesh a $57 million loan, technical assistance, and a trade agreement that will restore at least part of the coal trade.[57]

In sum, it could be said that China's energy relations with Third World countries outside of East and Southeast Asia are still dominated by the verbal component. China will remain a vocal supporter of Third World causes, and will support Third World positions on energy issues in various international forums. The PRC has, within its limited capabilities, offered technical assistance in energy to a variety of Third World countries and maintains a broad network of marginal trade contacts with these countries in petroleum by-products, coal, and other energy commodities. Certain countries, such as Iran, Pakistan, and perhaps Brazil or Mexico, will strengthen their energy relationship with China through trade and technical exchange. But on the whole, the priority given to domestic energy development in the PRC will preclude widespread energy aid or trade with the Third World beyond China's immediate perimeter for the next several decades. If my projections are even vaguely correct, China itself will remain a Third World country in terms of per capita energy consumption until the turn of the century. Peking will continue to associate closely, therefore, with the life-style and international economic positions of the Third World countries. The PRC may for some time continue to identify itself as a Third World country, despite its massive industrial and economic growth.

Chapter 4

Energy Policies Toward the Industrial Countries: The Soviet Union and Eastern Europe

Just as China's low per capita energy-consumption level gives the PRC the life-style identity of a Third World country, so the country's large aggregate energy-production capabilities and energy-consumption requirements make China an industrial country by world standards. Foreign observers are often surprised to learn that China already ranks among the world's largest commercial energy producers. By 1975, China ranked fourth among all countries in total energy production, trailing the United States and the Soviet Union by wide margins and Saudi Arabia by a very narrow margin.[1] In the same year, China outproduced Iran, Venezuela (by double), and the whole of Africa combined. China's commercial energy production in 1975 was roughly four times that of India.

On the consumption side of the energy balance, the PRC also does surprisingly well. By 1975, China ranked third or fourth in aggregate energy consumption, with almost exactly the same aggregate energy consumption as Japan, but far behind the United States and the USSR. China's aggregate energy-consumption level passed all of the Western European countries several years ago, although taken as a whole the European Economic Community still has more than twice China's annual aggregate consumption of energy.

This type of comparison should be made with some caution. China is a much larger country, in terms of both population and land area, than France, West Germany, or Saudi Arabia. Size alone would tend to give the PRC a high rank in terms of aggregate energy statistics. But size is not the whole explanation for China's standing as an industrial country in total energy production and consumption. The People's Republic itself started its industrial growth in 1949 with aggregate energy-production and consumption levels well under 50 mmtce (million metric tons coal equivalent). Rapid development of the commercial energy system since 1949 has raised total energy production and consumption to ten times the 1949 level in just 25 years. (The 50-mmtce level was reached in 1951–52.) In terms of the size of China's energy system in the early

1950's, the PRC began with roughly the same commercial energy capabilities as India, and then surged ahead of India and other Third
World countries. Thus, in aggregate terms, China achieved the status of
an industrial country in the early 1970's.

None of this has significantly changed China's ranking in terms of *per
capita* commercial energy consumption. In 1975, the PRC still ranked in
the middle of the Third World in average annual per capita energy consumption, behind many countries in the Middle East and Latin America.
In 1975, Japan, with roughly the same aggregate energy consumption as
the PRC, had about nine times the average per capita energy consumption of China. Again, these comparisons are very crude, obscuring the
effects of different distribution systems and energy-consumption allocation patterns. But even such crude comparisons illustrate an important
feature of the Chinese energy system. *The PRC has the per capita energy
life-style of a Third World country and the aggregate energy capabilities of an
industrial country.*

This "dual energy personality" places a double set of policy constraints
on Chinese political leaders. Peking's planners must constantly be aware
of the energy end-use requirement generated by rising per capita
energy-consumption levels. And, at the same time, Peking must provide
central direction to an enormous array of diverse energy-producing industries, transportation facilities, and distribution networks. In its domestic development programs, China must produce energy equipment
as small as the tiny hydropower generators installed in rural villages to
provide minimal electric-power supplies for home use and to alleviate
the drudgery of simple tasks like water pumping for irrigation, or mechanized grain threshing. But the PRC also must invest large amounts of
scarce capital and foreign exchange in the production or import of offshore drilling rigs. To a certain extent, these dual development requirements can be met by diversified and self-reliant energy-production enterprises working in tandem with the central ministries. But to a large
extent, Peking must simply face the duality of its energy development
position.

China's dual energy personality also has important, and sometimes
constraining, effects on the international energy policies of the People's
Republic. As discussed at length in the last chapter, Peking's verbal position on most international energy issues reflects what it regards as the
interests of the developing countries, particularly the oil-producing
countries. Largely because of its own experience as a poor country, an
experience that is still reflected in its low per capita energy-consumption
figures, China officially seeks to identify itself and its energy policies
with the Third World. The identification with Third World positions on

energy issues is much more than a matter of ideology. Formal Marxist ideology provides little or no guidance on such matters as oil-price policy or intergovernmental cartels. Peking's verbal attacks on the multinationals are consistent with its Marxist outlook, and in general ideology cannot be considered to be irrelevant to the formulation of China's international energy policies. But the strong emotional identification with Third World demands must be considered the result of continuing constraints on living standards in the PRC. And the continuation of low living standards is directly related to the availability of commercial energy supplements on a per capita basis inside China.

However, the other side of China's dual energy personality, high and rapidly increasing aggregate levels of energy production and consumption, also has direct consequences for Peking's international energy policies. The PRC is able to act and react in the international energy system as a full member of the community of industrialized countries. The next two chapters will examine in detail China's energy policies toward the industrial countries (with the exception of Japan, which will be dealt with in Chapter 6). China's large aggregate energy capabilities should be kept in mind throughout this discussion. The PRC seeks, and to a certain extent has already achieved, energy parity with the industrial world. For example, in the purchase of high-technology energy-production equipment on the international market, Peking can command the most favorable credit and delivery terms. In the export of crude oil, China has successfully used equipment and steel purchases to gain leverage for higher prices and larger sales. In territorial and security issues, China obviously has achieved levels of power and status that demand respect from the industrial countries. In short, China's large aggregate energy capabilities permit the PRC to play an active role in the international energy system, rather than the role of a passive bystander or victim. The strength of China's position on international energy issues should be expected to increase further over the next few decades. But the industrial countries already have a new participant among them in the international energy system.

Energy Relations with the Soviet Union

The intensity of China's energy relations with the Soviet Union reflects the general intensity of political relations between the two countries. The Soviet Union gave and sold China the technological base for all of its energy industries during the 1950's. China also became more than 50 percent dependent on the USSR for critical refined-petroleum products. The Sino-Soviet break in 1960 precipitated a Chinese energy crisis and

caused a thorough reevaluation of Peking's energy-development policies. By the mid-1960's the Chinese petroleum industry was off the
ground and Peking had regained its domestic energy balance. In the late
1960's and early 1970's, owing in large part to an aggravated border conflict with the Soviet Union, the energy relations between the two countries were entirely negative, with each trying to play Japan off against the
other and China bitterly criticizing Soviet energy policies in Eastern Europe and the Middle East. Throughout the entire transition from energy
dependent to energy antagonist, China has placed the "Soviet factor"
high on its list of policy priorities. Thus, the relationship has retained its
intense character, despite a complete reversal in its quality from highly
positive to highly negative.

The reversal of China's energy relations with the Soviet Union was
most dramatic in the petroleum industry. Mao Tse-tung visited Moscow
immediately after the establishment of the new government in Peking in
October 1949.[2] He signed the Sino-Soviet Treaty of Friendship, Alliance, and Mutual Assistance in February 1950 and established a $300
million line of credit for the purchase of Soviet industrial equipment.
The Soviet Union moved immediately to the formation of joint-stock
companies in Sinkiang for the development of the promising Karamai
oilfield.[3] This and other joint-stock companies were subsequently abol-
ished in 1954 in the initial stage of the First Five-Year Plan (1953–57).

Soviet assistance to the Chinese petroleum industry during the First
Plan was predominantly oriented toward geological exploration for new
oilfields. A Soviet-assisted aerial magnetometer survey of the whole of
China in 1953 revealed more than one hundred sedimentary basins.[4] By
1956, joint Russian-Chinese teams were carrying out extensive surface
gravimetric and magnetic surveys.[5] It is rumored that one of these teams
discovered what later became the Taching oilfield in 1956, although
Peking has never confirmed that Soviet technicians were responsible for
the discovery.[6]

Meanwhile, Soviet petroleum engineers were busy training Chinese
colleagues, consolidating the development of Yumen oilfield, opening up
Karamai for initial production, and laying the groundwork for new refineries and oil pipelines at Karamai and Lanchow.[7] During the 1950's, petroleum extraction and refinery equipment was imported almost exclusively from the Soviet Union. Since the Chinese petroleum-equipment
manufacturing industry in Shanghai was not organized until 1954, and
grew out of numerous small machine shops and boiler plants, the petroleum infrastructure was developed entirely from Soviet blueprints.

The abrupt departure of Soviet technicians (with their blueprints)
wreaked absolute havoc in the Chinese petroleum industry in 1960.

China's new geologists and petroleum engineers were suddenly required to take up the entire technical burden of designing and developing a modern petroleum industry. One of the large oilfields (Karamai) was flooded in 1960, owing to improper management of water injection.[8] Peking responded well under the circumstances. Faced with the imminent loss of Soviet petroleum-products imports, the central government decided to develop promising formations in the Sungliao Basin. Thousands of oil workers were mobilized from Karamai and Yumen oilfields and dispatched with little equipment and no shelter to build the Taching oilfield (Chapter 11). The first wells came in at Taching in 1960, and within three years Peking claimed that "basic self-reliance" in petroleum production had been achieved.[9]

The rapid development of Taching relieved, but did not entirely avoid, a severe petroleum shortage from 1961 through 1965. China had imported around 50 percent of domestic petroleum requirements from the Soviet Union since 1950. These petroleum imports, which peaked at nearly three million metric tons in 1961, were predominantly of refined petroleum products that could not easily be replaced at China's stage of refinery development. China was particularly dependent on the Soviet Union for the light petroleum fractions—gasoline and kerosene—that were required for ground transport and China's fleet of Soviet-built jet aircraft. The result in the trucking industry was a gasoline shortage that lasted several years.[10] Truck drivers were asked to coast downhill, adjust their carburetors to the leanest possible mixture, and tow trailers. In some areas trucks were converted to natural gas or city gas (methane) carried in large inflatable bags.[11]

One can imagine the vocabulary these truck drivers developed to express their feelings on the subject of Sino-Soviet relations. But to give credit where credit is due, Moscow did not immediately cut off exports of petroleum products to China. The exports declined to 1.5 million tons in 1963 and to nearly zero in 1965. Some of the shortage may have been caused by the confusion resulting from Great Leap policies in the petroleum industry. But the Chinese press has always blamed it on the Soviet withdrawal:

In the early 1960's, the Chinese working class, relying on its own efforts, developed China's first big oilfield—Taching. This ended her dependence on imported oil.

Imperialism and social imperialism had hoped to strangle the young People's Republic by depriving her of oil. One blockaded and put an embargo on our country, the other perfidiously scrapped trade agreements. They both confidently asserted that China lacked oil resources.

Guided by Chairman Mao's revolutionary line, the Chinese workers completely shook off the shackles of idealist theories of geology and found rich oil deposits at Taching. In the following year they determined their areas and volume. In another three years, Taching satisfied the basic needs of the country.[12]

During the 1960's, China carefully dismantled the Russian technological base for the petroleum industry and substituted domestic equipment and imported European and Japanese equipment in both oilfields and refineries. Many articles on the petroleum industry spoke of "breaking the deadly foreign frame" in technological development—meaning the Soviet design of plants remaining from the 1950's.[13] Peking has remained bitter about the disruptive Soviet role in the development of the petroleum industry.

The same pattern of early dependency and later recriminations occurred in the development of other Chinese energy industries. In the coal industry, China imported Soviet and Eastern European mining equipment and was given technical assistance by the USSR and Poland in developing a large-scale coal industry.[14] In return, China exported coal to Russia (about 200,000 tons per year) until 1965. Imports of Soviet mining equipment fell off rapidly in the early 1960's, and here again China turned to the intermediate industrial countries for technology imports, as well as for help in developing a domestic mine-equipment industry.[15]

There was complete disaster in Sino-Soviet energy relations in the electric power industry. The Russians got off to an early start by removing Japanese power-generating equipment left in Manchuria in 1945, including three of the five American and German generating sets in the Feng Man hydropower station on the Sungari River.[16] Moscow then offered to help China replace this equipment during the 1950's and in addition sold or gave the PRC quite a bit of thermal and hydropower equipment for the construction of large stations throughout the country. Not all of the hydropower projects worked out well, and one, the giant San Men Gorge project on the Yellow River near Sian, silted up so rapidly that it became a threat to the city and was unable to produce any electric power.[17] The dam was completely reconstructed with low water-head generators and adequate runoff channels to prevent silting, no doubt an expensive project that did not convince Chinese engineers of the merits of Soviet dam designs. Other hydropower projects, including the giant Liuchiahsia power dam, were delayed by some ten years because of the Soviet withdrawal, damaging the entire base of the Chinese electric power industry. As with the petroleum industry, Peking has not forgotten the lesson:

During the first years of socialist construction, China had aid from the Soviet Union. However, in a vain attempt to undermine this construction, the Soviet revisionist social imperialists withdrew their experts and tore up all contracts with China during the three years of the country's temporary economic difficulties. They claimed that without their help China could never build any high-capacity generating units. Nevertheless, China refused to be cowed. She developed her power industry at high speed, by implementing Chairman Mao's principle on maintaining independence with the initiative in our own hands and relying on our own efforts.[18]

China also received aid from the Soviet Union in the initial stages of its uranium extraction and experimental nuclear power program. The USSR helped in the construction of the Lanchow gaseous diffusion plant, which processes the bulk of Chinese ore into enriched U-235. The most widely publicized nuclear power facility supplied by Moscow was an experimental reactor provided under the terms of a 1955 agreement. The reactor was completed and commissioned in 1958. Its small size (7–10 megawatts) would indicate that it was designed strictly for experimental and educational purposes.[19] In any case, China has not yet developed any significant nuclear power capacity, with or without Soviet assistance.

In the period since the Cultural Revolution (1966–69), Sino-Soviet energy relations have deteriorated to the point of open hostility and rivalry. Chinese imports of Soviet petroleum products stopped completely in 1970 and have not been resumed. There has been very little energy or resource-related trade of any sort since 1969. Mineral commodity prices, oddly enough, are still frozen at 1958 levels in trade between the two countries. This is an advantage to the Soviet Union, which imports tungsten from the PRC at less than $20/mt (metric ton), less than half the world market price for tungsten.[20] Peking probably allows such gross concessions in order to obtain a continuing supply of spare parts for Soviet-built machinery imported during the 1950's. There was a small increase in Sino-Soviet trade in 1976. Total value of the 1976 trade agreement was up 40 percent to 280 million rubles, still a small part of China's total foreign trade.[21] The 1976 agreement included Chinese import of several 200 MW (megawatt) steam turbines with boilers. But otherwise there has been little or no trade recently in energy-production equipment.

Since 1960, the importance of China's security relations with the Soviet Union has increased as trade has declined. The security aspect of the Sino-Soviet confrontation gradually moved to the center of China's Soviet policy, and has affected various aspects of Peking's international energy policies. Peking has been concerned about the security implications of (1) the location of its principal energy industries in regions vulnerable to Soviet attack; (2) proposed Soviet-Japanese cooperation in energy development and transportation projects in Siberia; and (3) increasing Soviet naval capabilities and presence in the Yellow Sea, the East China Sea, and the

South China Sea, where the PRC has laid claim to continental-shelf and island areas.

Vulnerability of Principal Energy Industries

Tension between the Soviet Union and the People's Republic of China over the precise definition of the Sino-Soviet border began as early as 1954, when Mao Tse-tung first raised the issue of the border between Mongolia and Inner Mongolia in a meeting with Khrushchev.[22] The same question was raised again by Chou En-lai in another meeting with Khrushchev in January 1957. In both cases, the Soviet Union declined to respond in detail to the Chinese initiative. The deterioration of Sino-Soviet relations during the Great Leap Forward (1958–60) apparently resulted in border incidents, beginning in 1959. These incidents were probably symbolic, involving the moving of marker posts, the tilling of disputed soil, and so on. The areas of dispute were located in two main sectors—the northern border of Sinkiang province and the border of Heilungkiang, especially along shared stretches of the Amur and Ussuri rivers. (The Mongolian border was settled to the satisfaction of both sides, although the issue could be reopened.) By 1962 traditional cooperation in navigation along the Ussuri River had been replaced by mutual interference and growing hostility.

The implications of the initial border dispute widened during the mid-1960's. Peking began to raise the question of the "unequal" treaties that had established the traditional border in a series of public statements in 1963. Vague Chinese claims were extended to include vast areas of Siberia east of Lake Baikal. Secret consultations on the border issue began on February 25, 1964, but were discontinued before active negotiations had begun.

Border relations worsened seriously during the Cultural Revolution as part of the general deterioration of political relations between the two countries. Border incidents increased in frequency in 1967–68 and may have included some armed confrontations. On March 2, 1969, the first armed hostilities with a significant number of casualties occurred on Chenpao Island (Damansky Island) in the Amur River. They were followed on March 14–15 by a violent clash at the same location, which resulted in several hundred casualties and a complete breakdown of political relations. The Ninth Congress of the Chinese Communist Party met the following month and may have taken important steps to determine the direction of China's border policies. Efforts were made to revive discussions of the border issue, culminating in talks in Peking beginning in October 1969. At this point each side formally stated its position, but little progress was made and the talks again failed to proceed to direct negotiations.

By 1967, the two sides had also begun to increase their military capabilities along the border, particularly in the Mongolian and northeast border regions. In that year, Moscow signed a defense agreement with Mongolia and began to rotate increasing numbers of troops and armored divisions into the forces stationed along the Chinese border.[23] The Chinese responded by increasing the number of their divisions by four or five and tightening border security. The buildup continued to accelerate on both sides until the open hostilities in 1969. By the end of 1972, Soviet forces on the Chinese border had increased to 34 divisions, or approximately one-third of the Soviet army.[24] Soviet forces are highly mechanized and equipped with tactical nuclear weapons.[25] The PRC has increased its force levels in the northeast to nearly one million troops and an undetermined number of militia. Chinese forces are thought to be armed with IRBMs (intermediate-range ballistic missiles) with nuclear warheads.[26] The PRC has also engaged since 1970 in a program of shelter and tunnel construction in its major cities. In short, both sides are equipped to conduct warfare far beyond the scale of limited border attacks. In this atmosphere, little or no progress has been made toward settlement of the original, limited territorial questions at issue. Talks have been held periodically, but with no visible effect other than to avoid further armed clashes. Most recently, the two sides resumed discussion of Amur and Ussuri River navigation in August 1977.[27]

A new border incident in May 1978 indicates that tension remains very high along the northeast boundary. Both sides agree that on May 9 a small contingent of Soviet troops penetrated a short distance into Chinese territory at a point just south of Chenpao Island at Yueh Ya in Hulin county, Heilungkiang province. The Chinese claim that this invasion was accompanied by a helicopter and a number of patrol boats and was obviously intentional. Moscow apologized formally for the incident but claimed that the troops were pursuing a "dangerous criminal." The incident followed Soviet President Leonid Brezhnev's saber-rattling trip through Siberia at the end of March and preceded the Peking visit of American National Security Adviser Zbigniew Brzezinski by just 11 days. This timing indicates that the incident was intended as a warning to China of the continuing vulnerability of its northern border to probes by even small Soviet contingents.

The relevance of these political and military developments along the Sino-Soviet border to China's energy policies stems from the concentration of Chinese energy industries in the northeast. If one includes an area as far south as Peking and Tientsin, more than half of China's total energy-production capabilities are located in the northeast. Since this is the border region of greatest tension between China and the Soviet

Union, the concentration of energy industries happens to coincide with the region of greatest strategic vulnerability. Whatever the outcome of open warfare between the two countries, one likely initial result would be a heavily mechanized Soviet attack on Chinese energy industries in the northeast. It is likely that the PRC would lose half its energy-production capacity—including important oilfields, coal mines, refineries, electric power plants, and transmission networks—within a few weeks (if not days) of the onset of full-scale warfare.

This situation confronts Peking with a serious dilemma in its energy-development policy. Particularly in the petroleum industry, but also in the coal, natural gas, and electric power industries (not to mention such secondary energy-production industries as coke and petrochemicals), the incentive to locate additional industry in the northeast is very high. This region is China's Ruhr. Every necessary resource for heavy industry is available at a convenient distance. Transportation networks within and outside the region are well developed. The region's population is more urbanized and industrially better trained than in the rest of China outside of a few major cities, such as Shanghai, Nanking, Wuhan, and Canton. But the strategic vulnerability of the region to Soviet attack makes further development there hazardous to China's security, increasing the fragility of the Chinese industrial infrastructure in the face of any concerted Soviet effort to close it down. The Chinese have taken steps to minimize the vulnerability of their energy industries—pushing coal development south of the Yangtze, storing crude oil in underground reservoirs, dispersing new refinery and petrochemical-plant construction to the point of consumption, and so on. But the effect of such deployment is marginal when measured against the initial problem.

It is certain, therefore, that the vulnerability of the energy infrastructure in the northeast is an important consideration in the formulation of China's security policies. The loss of Taching oilfield alone would close down half of China's crude oil production capacity. The result of any Soviet attack on the energy industries of the northeast would be a disaster for the country's industry and transport. With the exception of a few industrial centers like Shanghai and Wuhan, Chinese industry would probably come to a complete halt within a month of any such attack. The country would be thrown back on its agricultural base and whatever industry could be supported on the basis of local energy supplies, such as local coal mines and hydropower stations. The People's Liberation Army itself has probably taken precautions to ensure its supply of fuel. But the rail and road transportation network would also be suddenly constricted by fuel shortages. The effects of disturbances such as the Tangshan earthquake (July 28, 1976), or political crises in Peking, which have seriously disrupted the pattern of energy development in the past, illustrate the vulnerability of key energy industries in the northeast. A Soviet attack would have similar effects, except that the result would be far more severely felt in energy production.

There is very little that Peking could do to protect itself against a blitzkrieg in the northeast. The Soviet army could attack from the east, north, or west. Its highly mechanized divisions and air force could carry out a series of coordinated thrusts designed to destroy the energy and industrial centers and could then withdraw without having to maintain an extended occupation of Chinese soil. The weight of the Chinese army could cushion such a blow but could not stop it. In-depth militia defense would be useless against Soviet mobility in the protection of energy-production centers. The only defense available to the PRC is retaliatory nuclear strikes on Soviet industry in Siberia, a strategy of nuclear deterrence. Nuclear deterrence and avoidance of warfare are the only avenues available to Chinese security planners, in view of the strategic vulnerability of the northeast and of the energy infrastructure centered there. An intermediate level of conventional warfare would be one-sided and would inflict unacceptable damage on the PRC.

Soviet-Japanese Cooperation in Siberia

The importance of energy industries in the northeast to Peking's security policy explains the strength of China's negative reaction to proposed cooperation between the USSR and Japan in the development of Siberian energy resources. The PRC has thrown every available obstacle in the way of large-scale Japanese participation in development of oilfields, natural gas, coal mines, pipelines, and rail transport in eastern Siberia. The motive for Peking's position regarding such projects is simple. They would all strengthen Soviet logistics and military power east of Baikal in the region of greatest Chinese strategic vulnerability.

Japan has imported marginal amounts of crude petroleum from the Soviet Union for a number of years. These imports were treated by the Japanese government as a means of diversifying its energy sources and a natural development in trade with the Soviet Union. Tokyo was aware of the immense energy and mineral wealth of Siberia, and a dialogue developed in the late 1960's and early 1970's between Japanese commercial organizations and the Soviet government regarding the possibilities for development of cooperative energy extraction and transportation projects in the region. These discussions were predicated on the assumption that Japan would supply a certain proportion of the needed capital and technical inputs in exchange for an assured long-term supply of coal, oil, and natural gas. The discussions were greatly stimulated by parallel arrangements between the Soviet Union and U.S. corporations for the development and export of Soviet liquefied natural gas (LNG).

By 1971–72, these commercial discussions had begun to crystallize into some specific projects.[28] The main primary-energy production projects were to be located at three major centers—Tjumen (Tyumen) in western Siberia, Yakutsk on the Lena River in eastern Siberia, and the continental shelf of Sakhalin Island to the north of Japan. (See Map 4.1.) Discussions also included proposals for the construction of an oil pipeline of at least 4,000 kilometers (Irkutsk-Nakhodka) for the transport of Tjumen crude oil to an eastern port for shipment to Japan. It was this latter project that stimulated the greatest Chinese resistance. The proposed pipeline would have paralleled the sensitive border of northeast China. It would have included access roads and could have been used to supply Soviet divisions just north of the border with a ready source of fuel. The pipeline also would have strengthened Soviet naval capabilities in the Pacific, again by supplying fuel oil for Soviet ships.

There was also resistance from the start from Japanese industry. Japanese commercial interests were definitely interested in all aspects of the proposed projects, including the pipeline. But the estimated cost of the projects, which totaled some $6 billion, and the requirement that Japan supply the steel for the pipeline appeared prohibitive in view of the estimated return to Japan of some 25–50 million metric tons per year of crude petroleum over a 20-year period. The capital was to be raised in the form of long-term Japanese credits, which would run at a low rate of interest (6–7 percent) and which would be paid off from revenues generated by crude oil sales to Japan.[29] Natural gas and coking-coal projects were to be included in the $6 billion total bill, on much the same financial terms. Some consideration was also given to participation by American oil companies.

By early 1973, the discussions had reached the level of intergovernmental negotiation between Tokyo and Moscow and were formally sanctioned by an exchange of letters between Prime Minister Kakuei Tanaka and Party Secretary Leonid Brezhnev.[30] Capital resources were to be raised by the Export-Import Bank of Japan and a consortium of 20 private Japanese banks. In return, Japan would be guaranteed the sale of 25–40 mmt/year of crude oil for 20 years, as well as long-term LNG and coking-coal supplies.

The Tanaka-Brezhnev letters and formal approval by the Japanese foreign and trade ministries (March 12, 1973) stimulated a direct response from the PRC. China had itself begun discussions with Japan of possible crude oil exports in January 1973 and had initially agreed to supply 0.2 mmt of Taching crude in 1973. In April or May, Chinese dip-

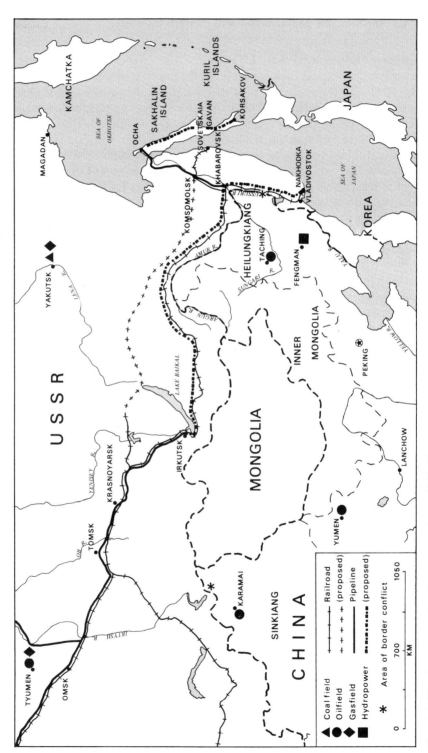

Map 4.1 Siberian energy development projects, 1971–76.

lomats at the new embassy in Tokyo began to raise direct objections to joint Soviet-Japanese energy-development projects in Siberia.[31] Peking was attempting to use both carrot and stick to prevent these projects, particularly the pipeline, from coming to fruition. The Japanese government itself was uneasy about the Siberian projects and expected political resistance because of an unsettled territorial dispute with Moscow over the status of four northern islands (Habomai, Shikotan, Kunashiri, and Etorofu) which the Soviet Union had continued to hold in the face of Japanese claims since the Second World War.[32] In May 1973, a 55-member Chinese "friendship team" under Liao Cheng-chi (China's leading Japan expert) went to Tokyo to try to discuss the Tjumen oil deal and Japanese participation on the proposed pipeline.[33] China simultaneously raised its crude-oil-export offer to 1.0 mmt for delivery in 1973.

These Chinese efforts were not without direct effect. Tokyo began to back down from the Tjumen project and the pipeline, complaining of rising projected costs and a Soviet reduction of the initial offer to the lower limit of 25 mmt/year of assured crude oil supplies. Japanese experts and industry were projecting continued high growth in China's petroleum production and export potential. Peking was willing to sell crude oil to Japan without any capital inputs, and Chinese officials were projecting optimistic levels of potential oil exports to Japan by 1980, perhaps reaching or even exceeding the Soviet offer. By the time of Tanaka's visit to Moscow in October 1973, differences between the Japanese and Soviet positions had begun to harden.[34]

The pipeline project was the most seriously damaged aspect of the Siberian cooperation proposals, and also the most sensitive from Peking's perspective. Final designs for the pipeline had envisioned a buried line with a surface access road on top, running the entire length of the line. This blueprint conformed to Peking's worst fears, and doubtless led to some reevaluation in Japan's own defense ministries. The Soviet government continued to pursue the pipeline project, but shifted emphasis toward the joint development of Yakut coal and natural gas, and the Sakhalin offshore oil exploration program. Brezhnev and Premier Alexei Kosygin sent another letter to Tanaka in February 1974, urging renewal of cooperation talks that had lapsed at the end of 1973.[35] U.S. corporations (Occidental Petroleum and El Paso Natural Gas) were invited to participate in the Yakut natural gas project, perhaps in the hope of stimulating further Japanese involvement.[36] An alternative to the pipeline was proposed in the form of a second railroad across Siberia, parallel to and north of the trans-Siberian railroad.[37] Peking was apoplectic about the railroad proposal, and Japan simply let the matter rest with the death of the pipeline and turned to other parts of the proposed cooperation agreements. In April and May 1974, a series of Soviet-Japanese memoranda were signed that provided $100 million in Japanese credits for Yakut natural gas exploration (matched by $100 million in U.S. credits), $450 million for development of southern Yakut coal deposits, and another $100 million for exploration for oil and gas on the continental shelf of Sakhalin Island.[38] These loans were to be financed at concessionary rates (about 6 percent). In return, the Soviet Union would export natural gas to Japan and the United States via the eastern coast of Siberia, and would guarantee Japan the sale of 3.2 mmt of coal in 1983, 4 mmt in 1984, and 5.5 mmt/year thereafter until 1998. The total value of these memoranda was about $1.15 billion.

The distance between the Soviet and Japanese positions on Tjumen oilfield development and the trans-Siberian pipeline had widened by the end of 1974 to the point where the Japanese government terminated official negotiations on these aspects of the Siberian cooperation projects on November 1, 1974.[39] But the other projects, especially the Sakhalin exploration project, continued to receive Japanese support. A protocol signed in Moscow on December 10, 1974, provided $100 million in Japanese credits for exploratory drilling along the northeast coast of Sakhalin Island.[40] Sakhalin's crude oil production had reached 2.5 mmt/year by the end of 1974. An additional $100 million loan was scheduled contingent on successful wildcat discoveries on the continental shelf. Moscow also expressed interest in joint construction of a nuclear power plant on Sakhalin.

Meanwhile, the three-way cooperation arrangement (including U.S. corporations) for coal and natural gas development in Yakutsk also began to run into some snags. In January 1975 the U.S. Congress placed a ceiling of $75 million per year on Export-Import Bank credits to the USSR, with a sublimit of $40 million per year on U.S. loans for development of Soviet fossil-fuel resources.[41] U.S. participation in Soviet energy projects was also made contingent on item-by-item authorization by the President and Congress. This immediately placed U.S. participation in Tjumen and Yakut natural gas development in jeopardy. The restrictions were a result of mounting anxiety in Congress over increasing Soviet military power in the Pacific region. As we shall see below, this assessment corresponded exactly to the Chinese position. And the Japanese government itself was becoming increasingly concerned over Soviet refusal to negotiate the status of the northern islands, a confrontation in the area north of Japan over fishing rights, and Soviet naval activities in the vicinity of Japan.[42] It was felt that any contribution to Siberian energy and transport development would simply exacerbate the problem. Japan continued participation in coal development at Yakutsk, but has been moving much more slowly on the natural gas exploration project there.

Meanwhile, the Soviet Union had made the proposed Baikal-Amur (BAM) railroad a completely domestic project.[43] Once it became clear that Japan would not participate in a trans-Siberian pipeline, let alone a massive railway project, Moscow moved ahead quickly in the design of the new railroad, which was needed for a variety of development purposes in Siberia, including the strengthening of military mobility and logistic support along the northeast China border. Construction was begun in April 1975 on a rail line 3,145 kilometers long, running from a point near the northern tip of Lake Baikal to the Siberian coast.[44] The railroad is scheduled for completion by 1985, with coal from the huge new open-cast coal mine at Neriungri (Yakutsk) to be transported to the coast for export to Japan starting in 1978.[45] Thus the railroad helped to clinch Japanese participation in the Yakut coal-mining venture. The Chinese press has condemned construction of the railroad in the strongest language, accusing the Soviet Union of building it for the purpose of military expansion in East Asia: "When the Soviet Union steps up construction of BAM, its aim is, first, to contend with the other superpower for hegemony in Northeast Asia, Asia and the Pacific region as a whole, and next, to threaten Japan, with, of course, an eye to other Asian countries as well.[46] This passage leaves little doubt of which "other Asian country" Peking has principally in mind.

Despite the slow pace of Soviet-Japanese cooperation in energy-development projects in Siberia, the potential for such cooperation will remain for some time. Vast Siberian energy and mineral resources have an obvious counterpart in great Japanese demand for these commodities. The transportation advantage of Siberian resources for Japan tends to counterbalance the security dilemma posed by development of those resources. And Moscow, for its part, continues to advance new energy- and resource-development proposals as fast as the Japanese government turns down the old ones. By late 1976, for example, negotiations were rumored for Japanese participation in the construction of nuclear power plants in Sakhalin and maritime Siberia.[47]

The Siberian energy projects also tend to be highly vulnerable to domestic politics in both Japan and the United States. Japan and the Soviet Union have long attempted to achieve a peace treaty that would formally move relations out of the post–World War II era. The PRC was also negotiating a similar pact with Tokyo. The value of these agreements is entirely symbolic, but the state of negotiations reflected the current balance in the Japan-USSR-China triangle. Peking insisted that its treaty include an antihegemony clause directed against Soviet military expansion in

Asia. The USSR resisted any such wording in a Sino-Japanese treaty and went so far as to send high-level officials to Japan to spike negotiations at a critical juncture.[48] Peking on its part discouraged a Soviet-Japanese treaty that might stimulate cooperation on the sensitive Siberian development projects. Japanese public opinion and the Diet were caught up in the swirl of these contending positions. The issue tended to be emotional and to reflect wider Japanese sentiment toward China and the Soviet Union. On August 12, 1978, China won the treaty competition by inducing Japan to sign a Treaty of Peace and Friendship that included the antihegemony clause.

A similar sort of political struggle takes place in the United States over participation in Soviet energy-development projects. In the past, the President tended to take a favorable attitude toward such cooperation, whereas Congress resisted it. President Ford, for example, signed a communiqué with Brezhnev in Vladivostok (November 24, 1974) giving U.S. approval for joint development projects in Siberia just before Congress passed legislation strictly limiting the funding of such projects through the U.S. Export-Import Bank.[49] The U.S. business community favors such projects and has tried to raise private financing for Tjumen and Yakut natural gas development.[50]

Peking has consistently sought to take advantage of such political rifts in Japan and the United States. China has taken a position on the northern islands issue so strongly favorable to the Japanese claim that it has embarrassed the Japanese government.[51] Peking has also emphasized the anti-Soviet theme very heavily in its exchange of delegations with the United States, hoping to strengthen a sense of U.S.-Chinese solidarity in the face of the Soviet threat. As will be seen in Chapter 6, China has used its own oil and energy-equipment trade with Japan to discourage Soviet-Japanese cooperation in Siberia. Peking views such cooperation as an important element of its security problem along the northern border and has therefore given disruption of Siberian energy-development projects a high ranking in its scale of policy priorities.

Soviet Naval Expansion

A final aspect of China's security relations with the USSR that has implications for Peking's energy policy is recent Soviet naval expansion in the Pacific. This expansion was part of the general Soviet program of naval construction and deployment that has been under way since the late 1960's. Reinforcement of the Pacific fleet was probably also related to the long Soviet supply line to Vietnam during the war there. China has been building up its own naval force during the 1970's, concentrating on the construction of fast-attack surface ships and conventional submarines.[52] Most of China's energy facilities are located inland and are more vulnerable to mechanized land attack than naval attack. Nonetheless, China has become increasingly concerned about the Soviet naval presence along its coastline.

The Soviet navy occasionally makes symbolic forays along the Chinese coast. On May 12, 1973, three Soviet warships passed through the Taiwan Strait at the same time that an important Chinese mission arrived in Tokyo to dissuade Japan from participation in the Tjumen oil-pipeline project.[53] Large-scale Soviet naval exercises were held in the East China Sea in the summer of 1975.[54] China has been able to do little about such forays, except to protest vigorously in the press. But in the event of an armed confrontation, the PRC might be able to concentrate a sufficient naval force along its own coast to challenge part of the Soviet navy.

The question of Soviet naval expansion has also become entangled in China's claims to clusters of islands in the South China Sea and with Sino-Vietnamese relations. In January 1974 the PRC seized the Hsisha (Paracel) Islands by force from South Vietnamese contingents stationed there. The islands and surrounding seabed are potentially petrolific. The seizure caused considerable friction in Chinese relations with North Vietnam, which also has an outstanding claim to the area and would have controlled the islands after the defeat of Saigon. Moscow has attacked Peking on the issue, accusing the Chinese of "aggression against the Vietnamese people."[55] In the summer of 1976, China began complaining about Soviet naval activity in the South China Sea and reported a Soviet submarine in the vicinity of the Hsisha Islands.[56]

Soviet naval expansion in the Western Pacific continued through 1977 and 1978. By 1978 there were some 125 submarines in the Soviet Pacific fleet, including 50 nuclear subs. Japan is increasingly concerned about the threat that the Soviet navy poses to its sea lanes. Japan's 60-day crude oil stockpile would be useful, not only in the event of another Middle East embargo, but also as a guarantee against a Soviet blockade. In June 1978, Moscow exacerbated Japanese and Chinese worries by holding naval and marine military exercises at Etorofu, one of the islands under dispute with Japan. In addition, Peking is concerned that Vietnam may turn over Cam Ranh Bay for use as a Soviet naval base, thereby flanking China and exposing its southern coastline and trade routes to Soviet attack.

The naval security problem is not a matter of such intense concern to the PRC as the question of the border dispute in the northeast. However, Peking, like Washington and Tokyo, is concerned about increasing Soviet naval power in East Asia. The Soviet navy would also be a threat to Chinese offshore oil development in the event of active hostilities.

Thus the intensity of China's concern about the Soviet Pacific fleet may increase as the PRC moves further into offshore exploration and extraction projects during the 1980's. And the Chinese naval defense capability will have increased commensurately, particularly within the near-shore areas where offshore oil development will occur.

Energy Relations with Eastern Europe

China's energy relations with Eastern Europe have been shrouded in successive layers of obscurity since the 1950's. During the 1950's, the Chinese press did report regularly on technical cooperation projects in various energy industries that included some East European participation. But even at that time, exact data on such cooperation projects, on the level of energy-commodity trade with East European countries, and on the value of energy-equipment purchases from Eastern Europe were virtually impossible to come by. Both China and its "fraternal" socialist trading partners refused to publish detailed trade statistics on any regular basis. This made the usual back-door access to Chinese energy trade statistics unavailable.

During the 1960's, China's political rupture with the Soviet Union covered Sino–East European trade relations with another layer of obfuscation. East European governments were loath to discuss their continuing technical cooperation and trade with the PRC, and preferred quiet relations that avoided rousing the Russian bear. Peking for its part was not eager to advertise its continuing oil and equipment imports from Eastern Europe, since they shed doubt on the efficacy of the new "self-reliance" policies adopted to compensate for the loss of Soviet trade and technology.

Finally, despite a revival of interest on the part of Peking and the East European capitals in technical cooperation and trade ties since the early 1970's, these new relations have tended to be buried by an avalanche of new information on Chinese contacts with the West. The Western media and specialized Western energy journals have provided very little current information on Sino–East European energy relations. Only the occasional scrap of information filters through the combined screens of poor data-reporting by the East Europeans (and the Chinese), intentional political obfuscation, and the lack of attention by the Western press.

Eastern Europe led Western Europe by about a decade in the development of its energy relations with the PRC. All of the East European countries participated in Soviet technical assistance programs, which laid the industrial backbone of China's energy sector in the 1950's. Poland helped with the Chinese coal industry.[57] Romanian equipment was used extensively in China's new oilfields and refineries.[58] Czechoslovakia, East Germany, and Hungary assisted with the construction of electric power plants.[59] After the Sino-Soviet break, Peking strengthened these ties with East European energy technology to the extent it could within the limits imposed by the Soviet Union on its East European satellites. Poland continued to export coal-enrichment machinery and power generators to the PRC.[60] Romania in particular became a steady exporter of drilling rigs, refinery equipment, oil pipeline, and electric power equipment to China.[61] Romania also continued technical assistance to the PRC, and was reported to have participated in the design of the Peking General Petrochemical Works in 1969.[62] Czechoslovakia was rumored to have refined a certain quantity of Chinese uranium in 1965.[63]

Not all the energy-equipment trade was in one direction. China provided materials, machinery, and technical assistance to Albania for the construction of the Fieri oil refinery in 1969, an oil-processing plant in the early 1970's, the Fierza hydropower station in 1971, the Ballsh thermal-power plant in 1975, and the Mao Tse-tung hydropower station at Van i Dejes in 1965.[64] Peking was also reported to have sold a refinery to Romania, although the report has never been confirmed by a second source and may have been a confusion with the Fieri refinery in Albania.[65]

China turned directly to Eastern Europe for desperately needed petroleum products in the early 1960's, in an attempt to relieve the shortages caused by the loss of imports of Soviet refined petroleum products. Throughout the 1960's Peking imported crude petroleum from Albania; gasoline, kerosene, diesel fuel, and lubricants from Romania; and unspecified petroleum products from Poland. The pattern of this trade, which increased as Soviet exports of the same commodities declined, and the commodity mix, which was heavily weighted toward the high petroleum fractions and refined products, confirm that China was seeking to replace the lost Soviet petroleum supplies. However, imports from Eastern Europe never reached even 10 percent of what imports from the Soviet Union had been at their height (3 million tons in 1961). Some sources have placed Chinese imports of Romanian crude oil at over 1.5 million tons per year in the mid-1960's.[66] But no such transactions have been reported in official Romanian trade returns, and it is unlikely that China would have imported large quantities of crude during a period of short refinery capacity.

After a long break in trade relations with Yugoslavia, China began importing very minor quantities of refined petroleum products from that country in 1969. This trade has increased since, but remains at token levels.

Political factors weigh heavily in China's energy relations with Eastern

Europe. Peking is critical of the economic role of the Council of Mutual Economic Assistance (CMEA) in the region. The Chinese press has accused Moscow of buying Middle Eastern oil and natural gas cheap and selling it dear in Eastern Europe. Above all, Peking wishes to encourage every sign of political independence from Moscow in East European capitals, both because it makes China's relations with the region easier and because Peking would like to see the USSR deeply embroiled on its western border. Among other things, political independence implies less energy dependence on the Soviet Union:

Five Eastern European countries—Poland, Hungary, Czechoslovakia, East Germany, and Bulgaria used to depend on the USSR for 90 percent of petroleum consumption. But the Soviet Union has been reducing exports to Eastern Europe to sell to Western Europe, in order to contend with American influence there. Furthermore, this year Soviet oil prices jumped 130–140 percent to Eastern European markets, damaging their economies. Now Moscow will review oil export prices annually.

As a consequence, Eastern European countries have begun measures to reduce reliance on imported energy sources. Domestic coal production has been stepped up and oil and coal extraction equipment imported from Western Europe.

Bulgaria and Czechoslovakia have assisted in construction of an oil port in Yugoslavia capable of handling seven million metric tons per year, or two-thirds of the import requirement of these countries. East Germany has been constructing an oil refinery for processing Middle Eastern oil. East European countries have been signing oil import agreements with Middle Eastern governments.

Bulgaria and Poland have been seeking Western assistance with offshore oil exploration. Poland has also signed an agreement for American assistance with coal liquefaction and gasification.[67]

The scattered information available indicates an upturn in Sino-Romanian energy relations since the Cultural Revolution. This would conform to the general trend in political relations between the two countries since 1969. Romania has been steadily loosening its political ties to Moscow, a direction of policy that Peking vocally supports. The PRC had been looking for a broader avenue of approach to Eastern Europe than that provided by its singular political relationship with Albania. Technical cooperation in the energy field provided a commercial stimulus for Sino-Romanian political relations.

Romanian technicians were reported to have participated in the construction of the Peking General Petrochemical Works under the terms of a 1969 technical assistance agreement.[68] The Romanian technicians were in China from 1968 through 1973 working on the project. A Chinese Vice-Minister of Petroleum and Chemical Industries attended a meeting of the Joint Commission of Scientific and Technical Cooperation in Bucharest in June 1973.[69] This visit may have concerned potential Chinese crude oil exports to Romania. In May 1975 the two countries signed a trade agreement that provided for the export of 150,000 metric tons of Chinese crude oil to Romania in 1975, and higher exports were planned for 1976.* During 1976, the PRC chartered a 95,000-deadweight-ton tanker for crude oil exports to Romania and signed a new trade agreement for an unknown quantity of oil trade.[70] In the same year, the PRC contracted for renewed purchases of Romanian oil-drilling rigs, again of unknown quantity and value.[71]

Recent energy relations with the other East European countries have been relatively modest' and very sensitive to the political factor. Political and energy-trade relations with Yugoslavia have improved. Yugoslavia reportedly received a contract for the construction of two 45,000-deadweight-ton tankers for China in 1976.[72] President Tito got an ironic hero's welcome in Peking in August 1977. As the tide of political relations with Yugoslavia has risen, so that with Albania has ebbed. The Valias Coal Dressing Plant, completed with Chinese aid in November 1976, was the last major cooperative energy project reported between the two countries.[73] During 1977 the press on each side began engaging in political attacks on the other for the first time.

In 1978, Peking launched a new diplomatic drive in its relations with Eastern Europe, winning two and losing one. Political and trade relations with Yugoslavia were greatly strengthened. In February Yugoslav Vice-Premier Berislav Sefer visited Peking and concluded a trade agreement that called for up to $300 million per year in imports of Chinese commodities, including crude petroleum and coal.[74] Chinese Chairman Hua Kuo-feng took an extensive political tour through Romania, Yugoslavia, and Iran in August 1978, receiving a particularly warm welcome in both Romania and Yugoslavia. In Romania he visited the Ploesti Oil Equipment Plant, which builds 30 drilling rigs for export to China each year.[75] Relations with Albania, on the other hand, turned increasingly sour. In an ironic repetition of the history of Sino-Soviet relations, China terminated aid and technical assistance to Albania in July 1978.[76] The PRC claimed that since 1954 it had supplied Albania with aid that included 91 completed projects and a number of others under construction or in design. Trouble in Sino-Albanian relations was laid to deci-

---

*Estimates of crude oil exports to Romania vary, and some run as high as 500,000 metric tons in 1975 and 6 million metric tons in 1976. But the more conservative figures of 150,000 mt in 1975 and perhaps 500,000 mt in 1976 would be safer estimates, judging from Chinese crude oil production and tanker capabilities. See *USCBR* 3, no. 5 (Sept.–Oct. 1976):55.

sions of the Seventh Congress of the Albanian Party of Labor in November 1976. At the time when aid was terminated, the Ballsh Integrated Refinery and Valias Coal Mine, two of the largest Chinese projects, had just been completed.

This ends our review of China's energy relations with Eastern Europe and the Soviet Union. Hostile relations between the PRC and the Soviet Union are at the heart of most recent developments in energy relations with China's former communist allies. Peking seeks to flank the Soviet Union on the east by blocking cooperation between Japan and Moscow in the development of Siberian energy resources, and on the west by driving wedges into the Soviet grip on Eastern Europe. Most recently, the PRC has signed a long-awaited peace treaty with Japan, a treaty that includes a clause condemning hegemonism (Soviet expansion) in East Asia. The forging of this powerful link between Japan and China infuriates Moscow and has deepened the chasm in Sino-Soviet relations. In November 1978 the Soviet Union responded to the new Sino-Japanese alignment by announcing a 25-year treaty of friendship and cooperation with Vietnam. Regional politics within East Asia appear to be polarizing around the two agreements. This basic regional realignment extends and hardens the contours of the Sino-Soviet conflict. The security problems that underlie these agreements will affect China's pattern of international energy relations for another decade or two.

Chapter 5

Energy Policies Toward the Industrial Countries: The West

Organization and Policy Formulation

The People's Republic of China has developed energy relations with a group of industrial countries that may roughly be termed "the West." The group includes North America (Canada and the United States), Western Europe, and Oceania (Australia and New Zealand). It can be conveniently distinguished from those countries with centrally planned economies on the basis of both political and economic organization. Japan, the other major industrial country, stands in a category by itself in China's international energy policies and will be dealt with as an Asian country in the next chapter. Peking's own formal political lexicon groups East and West European countries, Japan, Canada, and Oceania into a cluster called the "Second World," presumably lying somewhere between the "superpowers" and the nonindustrial countries of the Third World. The Second World, particularly Western Europe, is supposed to be the main arena of contention between the superpowers for world hegemony. This theory is convenient from the point of view both of China's Marxist ideology and of the PRC's security policy. If the United States and the Soviet Union were indeed locked in mortal struggle over the smaller countries of Eastern and Western Europe, Peking would have less to be concerned about along the sensitive Sino-Soviet border.

In reality, however, Peking tends to deal with the West as a coherent grouping, particularly in energy policy. Equipment-purchase policies, for example, are equally applicable regardless of the precise political characteristics of the supplying country. The multinationals all use similar trading practices, regardless of their base country. And all rhetoric to the contrary, size alone is not a determining political or economic distinction among the countries of the West. Taken together, the industrial capabilities of the European Economic Community (EEC) countries are comparable to those of the United States or the Soviet Union. Per capita living standards in many of the small Western countries are comparable to average per capita standards in the Soviet Union. Therefore it is reasonable to treat the West as a coherent grouping in the framework of China's international energy relations.

Energy Commodity Trade Policy

"Trade" is the key word in China's energy relations with the West, just as "security" is the touchstone of Sino-Soviet energy relations. Two types of energy-related foreign trade have emerged between China and the Western countries: commodity trade (in coal, crude petroleum, and petroleum products), and equipment trade (in refineries, offshore drilling rigs, seismic-exploration equipment, etc.). There is a distinct lack of balance in China's energy trade with the West, for by the 1970's, China had become an energy-commodity exporter and an energy-equipment importer. Energy-commodity exports, however, were still limited to Japan and other Asian countries on China's perimeter by China's own domestic consumption requirements. In particular, the PRC lacks the crude petroleum surplus necessary to compete with the OPEC countries in the markets of the industrial countries. Most projections of the energy balance for the PRC indicate that this situation will prevail for the next several decades.

The PRC has been a marginal net energy exporter to Western Europe and Oceania since the mid-1960's, trading only in small quantities of specialized petroleum products, particularly mineral wax and lubricants. Total petroleum exports to the West have never exceeded 100,000 metric tons in a single year, the equivalent of a single moderate-sized tanker load of crude oil. Energy exports to each of China's main Asian trading partners have exceeded this minimal level. These marginal energy-commodity exports have brought China a few million dollars in foreign exchange, a web of energy-trade contacts in the West, and perhaps some goodwill when trade relations were otherwise at low ebb. And the specialized imported lubricants may have relieved some bottlenecks in certain Chinese industries. But on the whole, China's energy-commodity trade with the West cannot be considered commercially significant.

This situation could change by 1980. Chinese negotiators have explored possible crude oil exports to the United States, Australia, and Italy. However, several constraints will continue to maintain a low ceiling on such exports, unless China's offshore oil resources prove to be in the range of the most optimistic estimates. First, domestic energy consumption within the PRC will continue to rise sharply for at least 10–15 years, particularly in the petroleum sector. Second, petroleum exports to Japan and other Asian countries will take priority for whatever export surplus the PRC can muster, for both political and commercial reasons. Third, transport and refining costs for Chinese crude will continue to make it an expensive alternative in Western markets unless Peking is willing to take substantial price cuts in relation to Middle Eastern crudes. Fourth, there is strong supply competition from the North Slope of Alaska and from Indonesia for the U.S. West Coast and for Australia—the two most likely markets in the West for Chinese crude. Taken together, these factors make it unlikely that Peking will be able to substantially raise petroleum exports to the West in the next few decades. The energy-trade imbalance with the West will therefore persist, and China will find it necessary to pay for energy-equipment purchases from Western countries with foreign exchange earned in other trade or in energy trade with Japan and Asia.

Energy-Equipment Trade Policy

The exact level of Chinese energy-equipment purchases in any given year is extremely difficult to determine with accuracy. China seldom publishes information of any sort on foreign equipment purchases and the PRC's trading partners in the West are reluctant to provide detailed information owing to the proprietary information policies of many of the large equipment manufacturers. Government trade returns are of little use, since they break complete plant purchases into components such as valves, boilers, and turbines and provide no information on the capacities or characteristics of these components. Fortunately, the National Council on U.S.-China Trade has collected and published information on major PRC equipment purchases since about 1973. This information was supplemented by a similar collection of data by the U.S. government through a contract with the Rand Corporation. (See Chapter 22.) The summary trade data for energy equipment from these sources should be used with caution. Often the information is incomplete, particularly concerning the precise value and capacities of the unit in question. The Chinese government actively discourages the release of such data. The company may have its own reasons for not reporting the information publicly. The organizations collecting the information may miss some transactions, or may simply consider some transactions too insignificant to report. There tends to be a reporting bias toward contracts completed by U.S. corporations that exaggerates the statistical significance of Sino-American energy-equipment trade. For all these reasons, none of the statistics should be treated as final, and all should be considered underestimates. Nonetheless, certain general conclusions may be drawn from the available data.

First, it may be stated with some certainty that China's total energy-equipment purchases from the West and Japan since 1960 have exceeded U.S. $4 billion. Annual purchases of energy-production and transport equipment (including chemical-fertilizer and petrochemical plants) have run at various levels since 1972, between 5 percent and 20 percent of total imports by value. The peak year for energy-equipment imports was 1973, both in absolute and relative terms, with more than $1.5 billion of contracts signed in a single year (perhaps 20 percent of total Chinese imports during that year, counting the contract year as the year of import). Thereafter, energy-equipment imports declined steadily in both absolute and relative terms through 1977. Total figures are not yet available for 1978, but preliminary reports indicate a big jump in energy-equipment and technology contracts, including several large construction contracts.

Second, identifiable patterns have emerged in the type of equipment the PRC has been purchasing. Nearly two-thirds of all the energy-equipment purchases since 1960 have consisted of refinery, petrochemical, and chemical-fertilizer plants and equipment. Petrochemical plants and equipment alone have exceeded $1.5 billion, or about 40 percent by value of total energy-equipment purchases. The next largest category was offshore-oil-exploration equipment at nearly $600 million, or 16 percent of total energy-equipment imports. Electric power equipment totaled more than $500 million, or about 13 percent of total purchases. Coal-extraction equipment ran about 8 percent of the total. Tanker purchases, which ballooned in 1975, still reached less than 3 percent of total energy-equipment purchases.

The great emphasis on petrochemical and chemical-fertilizer plants and equipment has been consistent since the early 1960's. This confirms suggestions by foreign observers that China's refinery- and petrochemical-equipment industries lagged seriously behind the expansion in crude petroleum production. However, this conclusion should be treated with some caution, since most of the equipment purchases were for "downstream" petrochemical and fiber facilities rather than basic refinery components. Basic petroleum refinery capacity has been only marginally expanded by equipment purchases abroad. The reasons for the large purchases of chemical-fertilizer plants are obvious, given China's expanding population and agricultural production. In contrast to the petrochemical plants, most of the fertilizer equipment was basic ammonia and urea production capacity.

Energy-equipment purchases have proved very sensitive to China's balance-of-payments position. The PRC has traditionally maintained a small favorable balance of payments, but complete plant purchases caused an annual trade deficit beginning in 1973 that grew to about $1 billion in 1974.[1] Corrective action was taken in 1975–76, which reduced the annual trade deficit to well under $500 million, primarily through the drastic reduction of new plant orders. Energy-plant purchases suffered sharp reductions in 1975 and 1976, largely in response to the balance-of-payments situation. This further illustrates the likely long-term impact of the crude oil export ceiling on energy-equipment purchases. China's political preference for self-reliance in energy equipment will continue to be strongly reinforced by the simple but compelling argument that the PRC cannot afford to rely on the West or Japan for the greater part of its energy-equipment requirements.

Currency shortages and balance-of-payments problems may also have pushed Peking toward adoption of Western deferred-payment practices. An increasing proportion of Chinese energy-equipment purchases have been on a deferred basis. The terms vary, but usually include a down payment or series of down payments of from 10 to 30 percent of the total contract price. The PRC then pays over a five-year period after delivery, at an annual interest rate of 6–7 percent. The low interest rate makes these terms concessionary and would be favorable to the PRC even without the balance-of-payments factor. There is also some evidence that Peking was counting on rising crude oil exports to Japan to cover the cost of imported energy-production equipment. In the case of rapidly rising payments from petroleum exports, deferred payments would have greatly eased the burden of equipment imports. But as we shall see in the next chapter, the Japanese crude oil trade fell short of Chinese expectations. The result was that deferred payments on 1973 energy-equipment purchases spread the balance-of-payments problem to later years.*

Technological Exchange Policy

China's attitude toward the acquisition of foreign energy technology should be carefully distinguished from energy-equipment purchase policies. There is a sharp distinction between technology acquisition and equipment purchases in the minds of Chinese energy planners. It is part of the self-reliance ethic to attempt to maximize the former while minimizing the latter.

It is imperative to uphold the principle of maintaining independence, keeping the initiative in our own hands and relying on our own efforts. This is the base from which we advance. We must rely on our own strength and take our own road in industrial development. We must always keep this in mind. However, in order to keep up with and surpass advanced world levels and accelerate the development of the national economy, it is necessary to introduce some essential new techniques and new equipment from abroad and make foreign things serve China.[2]

*See Chapter 8 for recent Chinese policies accepting long-term loans and credit.

This Chinese attitude sometimes irritates Western traders, who accuse the PRC of window-shopping in the process of equipment-purchase negotiations and of other practices designed to acquire the essential technology without paying for it. The Chinese do frequently request equipment blueprints in advance of the contract and push for the maximum training of Chinese personnel as part of each purchase. But to be fair to the Chinese and their trading practices, they frequently include payment for technology as part of the larger plant contracts and in some cases have purchased designs and technology without an equipment purchase. For example, in 1975 Peking signed a contract for the purchase of technology for the manufacture of 150 MW (megawatt) steam turbines from a West German firm (Siemens A.G.).[3] In any case, a great deal of technology transfer has always accompanied rapid industrialization and has never been prevented or even metered by the system of international patent laws and recognized trading practices. The marginal cost of such technology "leakage" across international boundaries is more than compensated for by the benefits of rapid technology diffusion. Payment is eventually returned manifold to the donor country in the form of increased trade potential as the recipient country industrializes. As Peking began its new modernization drive in 1978, commercial law was being revised to protect foreign patents and to provide a structure of laws governing joint development projects. This should ease some of the concern over the conditions of technology transfer.

Aside from equipment purchases and direct purchases of foreign technology, the PRC also receives a certain amount of foreign energy technology through the many technical groups and energy delegations that travel back and forth between the PRC and the Western countries. Here again, as with statistics on trade in energy-production equipment, data on the delegations traveling back and forth from the PRC are incomplete but do provide some idea of general patterns. During the period 1972–76, more than 80 energy delegations from foreign countries traveled to the PRC and about 50 delegations having some energy-related function traveled from the PRC to other countries. The great majority traveled to or from the West and Japan. (Japan alone accounted for nearly half the energy delegations to the PRC, but only about 20 percent of the delegations traveling from the PRC.) The total of 130 energy delegations moving in both directions represented a large proportion of the total interchange between China and the outside world during this period. Peking places heavy emphasis on energy (particularly petroleum) technical exchange, both because of its utility to Chinese energy development, and because it is a type of interchange that is relatively "safe" from a political perspective. Foreign energy delegations can be shown China's proudest industrial achievements and are un-likely to press sensitive political nerves. Delegations of China specialists, for example, with their deep knowledge of Chinese history and current politics, are much more difficult to handle and raise more difficult questions than groups with a narrow technical interest and little background knowledge of the PRC.

Energy delegations are frequently associated with major energy-equipment purchases, a fact demonstrated by the distribution of delegations among various types of energy technology. The largest number of delegations in both directions have been concerned with energy technologies associated with crude petroleum trade, refining and petrochemical processes, chemical-fertilizer production, and various aspects of the petroleum industry. Relatively few delegations have been exchanged concerned with coal, natural gas, or electric power. This follows the general pattern of equipment purchases. The purchase of a complete energy plant, such as a petrochemical plant or a major set of seismological equipment, is often accompanied by an exchange of experts in the technology that has been purchased. The purchase contract specifies the precise parameters of this technical exchange. Chinese engineers travel to the headquarters of the firm supplying the equipment and undertake special study programs in the use and maintenance of the equipment. Foreign engineers frequently accompany plant construction projects and may spend several months in China at the site of the new energy facility. The larger and more advanced the equipment purchase, the more likely it is that a direct exchange of technical personnel will be written into the contract.

There has been a rapid increase in the number of energy delegations moving in both directions during the early 1970's. Records on energy delegations during the 1960's are poor, but indicate that there was little energy-related technical exchange of this nature from 1961 until about 1971 with the Western countries. There was probably some exchange with Eastern Europe and virtually none with the Soviet Union during this period. But the opening of direct political relations with the United States, China's entry into the United Nations, and the wave of diplomatic recognitions that Peking achieved in 1971–72 set the political conditions for technical exchange with the West in various energy fields. At first only a few energy delegations were exchanged and the exchanges were focused on Japan. But by 1975–78 a wave of energy delegations was moving back and forth between China and the West. The general pattern was to send and receive just one or two energy delegations per country per year, except for important energy-trading partners. By 1976 a total of 13 countries sent energy delegations to the PRC, and

China sent energy delegations to 13 countries, for a total of some 60 delegations moving in both directions in a single year. This was a significant increase over the four countries that sent energy delegations to the PRC and the six countries that received such delegations from China in 1973.

The United States has significantly increased its level of energy delegation exchange with the PRC. There were no U.S. energy delegations to China in 1973 and only one energy delegation to the United States in the same year. But by 1976, the United States managed to send more than ten energy delegations to the PRC in a single year, many of which were directly related to equipment purchases. This shift may herald a new period of Chinese interest in American energy technology and equipment, or it may simply be a result of the sophisticated nature of the equipment China tends to import from the United States. In any case, the United States now rivals Japan in its level of energy technology exchange with the PRC.

Organization of China's Foreign Energy Trade

The organizational structure through which Peking controls China's crude oil exports, energy equipment imports, and technical exchange is highly centralized, compared with the organization of such activities in the market economy countries of the West. (See Figure 5.1.) The organizational authority for virtually all forms of energy relationship with the outside world is vested in various agencies of the State Council, China's cabinet-level government agency. The State Council itself is directly responsible to the Central Committee of the Chinese Communist Party, and in practice to the Political Bureau of the Central Committee. Thus, decisions concerning the level of annual petroleum export and equipment purchase are made under the direct guidance of the Party center and are considered a matter of state policy. No Chinese energy enterprise has the authority to buy and sell on the international market without explicit authorization from the center in Peking.

Despite this relatively centralized character, however, the organization of China's foreign energy relations is fairly complex, involving quite a number of agencies under the State Council. The effect is sometimes bewildering to the novice foreign supply agent representing a single office of a single corporation with no direct responsibility to a home government. A single purchase decision may involve representatives of several ministries, an import-export corporation, specialized research institutes under the Chinese Academy of Sciences, and officials of a Chinese shipping company. Technical exchange delegations may represent a single institute or agency or, more commonly, may include representatives of various government, trade, and academic organizations. Even provincial-level organizations may get into the trade and technology act in certain instances, especially when a piece of equipment is destined for an energy production unit (coal mine or electric power station) under provincial control.

Mindful of the complexity of its own trading organizations, Peking has channeled a substantial amount of its foreign energy and equipment trade through the semiannual Canton Trade Fair. The Canton Trade Fair is situated at a convenient distance from Hong Kong and is held in a predictable manner, allowing foreign selling and purchasing agents to register in advance and to plan their contacts with Chinese agencies. However, a great deal of trade goes on outside of the framework of the fair, including the most important and expensive equipment purchase negotiations. Any large purchase will typically involve an invitation to the selling corporation to send agents to Peking for negotiations. Very important purchases usually involve the dispatch of an advance team of Chinese negotiators to the site of equipment manufacture. These negotiations often do not lead to equipment purchases, frustrating the foreign corporations and leading to charges that the Chinese team was "window-shopping" for proprietary technology which has been developed at great cost by the manufacturer. For example, Peking sent negotiating teams to several European countries and Singapore to discuss the purchase of offshore drilling rigs, before ordering two rigs from Singapore's Robin Loh shipyard in 1975.

Crude oil and refined petroleum exports in the 1970's have been handled through intergovernmental negotiation as well as at the level of the trading corporations on both sides. Before China initiated crude oil exports to Japan in 1973, trade in energy commodities with the West was too insignificant to require special procedures and was handled through the Canton Trade Fair. Regular purchases and sales involved only a few thousand metric tons of petroleum by-products such as mineral wax or specialized lubricants. Refined petroleum products were purchased only occasionally on a spot basis from the Western countries. But the initiation of large-scale crude oil and diesel fuel exports to Japan, Hong Kong, Thailand, and the Philippines required direct negotiations between the Chinese Ministry of Foreign Trade, the Ministry of Petroleum and Chemical Industries, and the Foreign Ministry and their counterparts from the trading partner country. In some cases, such as crude oil exports to the Philippines, discussions reached the level of head of state, and were considered an important political event in relations between the two countries.

The Chinese ministries that may get involved in energy commodity

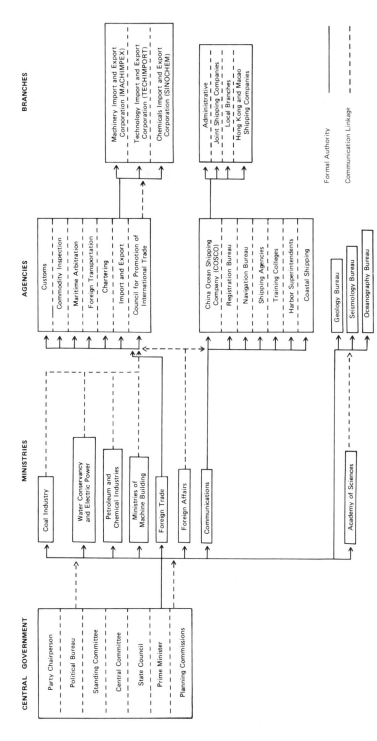

Fig. 5.1 The organization of China's foreign energy trade, 1976. (During 1978, the Ministry of Petroleum and Chemical Industries was divided into the Ministry of Petroleum and the Ministry of Chemical Industries, and during 1979 the Ministry of Water Conservancy and Electric Power was divided into the Ministry of Water Conservancy and the Ministry of Electric Power.)

and equipment trade and in energy technology exchange include those of Coal, Petroleum, Chemical Industries, Water Conservancy, Electric Power, Foreign Trade, Communications, and Ministries of Machine Building. The Ministry of Foreign Affairs may be consulted in important cases. The Chinese Academy of Sciences and its numerous scientific, engineering, and petroleum institutes frequently initiate or respond to direct technical exchanges involving energy delegations to and from China. Specialized agencies of the State Council, such as the bureaus of Seismology, Geology, and Oceanography, are frequently involved in both technical exchange and equipment purchase.

The principal types of organization encountered by the foreign agent interested in energy commodity and equipment trade with China are the numerous "corporations" that the PRC has established for this purpose. The Ministry of Foreign Trade includes three corporations of particular importance in energy trade. China National Chemicals Import and Export Corporation (Sinochem) handles petroleum exports. China National Machinery Import and Export Corporation (Machimpex) is responsible for the purchase of petroleum and other energy machinery at the subplant level. China National Technical Import and Export (Techimport) arranges the importation of complete energy plants, new technology, and technical patents.[4] If shipping is arranged on a Chinese flag carrier, the China Ocean Shipping Company (Cosco) or one of its local branches will make the arrangements.[5] Cosco is an agency of the Ministry of Communications. Cosco also controls a fleet of ships registered under flags of convenience (Somali and Panamanian) and technically owned by a number of shipping companies operating out of Hong Kong. A number of agencies may be involved in clearance procedures at Chinese ports of entry, including the China Commodity Inspection Bureau and Customs (both Ministry of Foreign Trade), Registration and Navigation Bureaus, Shipping Agencies, and Maritime Administrations for various ports and rivers (all under the Ministry of Communications). Coordination of negotiating activities, hospitality, and trade delegations may be handled by the China Council for the Promotion of International Trade and contract disputes by the Maritime Arbitration Commission (both agencies of the Ministry of Foreign Trade). Transportation may also be arranged by the China National Foreign Trade Transportation Corporation and the China National Chartering Corporation (Ministry of Foreign Trade).

Finally, in order to raise the level of confusion still further, or perhaps in an effort to reduce it, China's energy trade organization is constantly in flux. During 1978 the Chinese government split the Ministry of Petroleum and Chemical Industries into a Ministry of Petroleum and a Ministry of Chemical Industries. In addition, Peking has added a new corporate layer to the organizational structure by introducing the Chinese Petroleum Corporation and similar corporations in other energy industries. This last reform may be an effort to centralize and simplify what is otherwise a bewildering array of agencies, commissions, trading companies, and other organizations. The new corporations may also facilitate joint development projects in offshore exploration and other energy ventures. It remains to be seen, however, whether the Chinese energy corporations will simplify or further complicate the lives of foreign trading agents.

Energy Relations with the United States and Canada

There is a general tendency in the United States, in both academic and business circles, to exaggerate the importance of the Sino-American energy relationship relative to China's energy relations with the other Western countries and with Japan. This exaggeration, which is harmless in the overall political and commercial relationship between the two countries, was largely the result of a coincidence in timing between the American energy crisis, the development of political relations between Washington and Peking, and China's first crude oil exports to Japan. For several years in the mid-1970's, it appeared that the PRC might be a potential new source of crude petroleum for the American market and that rapidly expanding Chinese energy industries would provide an open market for U.S.-manufactured energy equipment:

> Only a handful of West European countries, Japan, and the U.S. are in a position to benefit from China's oil industry needs. China, in fact, represents the last frontier in the highly profitable world-wide dispersion of U.S. oil production and petrochemical knowhow.
> That frontier has been breached. Since November 1973 almost $10 million worth of onshore and offshore oil exploration and production equipment has been sold China by various U.S. companies.[6]

This enthusiast missed some Chinese energy transactions with that "handful of West European countries" and Japan. In fact, since 1972, U.S. energy equipment sales to the PRC have amounted to only 10 percent of the total import of such equipment by China. And even this 10 percent figure includes more than $200 million worth of petrochemical plants sold to the PRC by the M. W. Kellogg Company. In addition, American companies were secondary contractors or equipment suppliers in a number of energy plant and equipment deals with China. If one counts subcontracts, the American share of the Chinese energy equipment market was 10–15 percent of the total from 1972 through 1977. (See Chapter 22.)

There are several reasons for the rather poor American showing in energy technology trade with the PRC: (1) trade relations in energy production equipment were established with Western Europe and Japan during the 1950's and 1960's, giving these countries experience in dealing with China's trading habits; (2) Sino-U.S. trade was blocked by the lack of formal diplomatic relations and Peking may have been using the low level of equipment imports from the United States to put pressure on the American business community, Congress, and the executive in the direction of formalizing the relationship; (3) because of its experience with technological dependence on the Soviet Union, Peking is trying to diversify its sources of foreign production equipment rather than depend on a single large trading partner; (4) China feels more comfortable dealing with the smaller industrial countries—the "Second World"—than with the giant U.S. multinationals, because the PRC has achieved aggregate energy parity with these countries while it still lags far behind the United States in energy capabilities.

Among these four reasons for the low level of Sino-American energy relations, the political factor must be rated by far the most important. There were, of course, no Sino-American energy commodity or equipment trade relations at all between 1950 and 1970. The United States refused to recognize the People's Republic as the legitimate regime in China when it came to power in 1949. Rather, Washington waited to see if the Chinese Communist Party would succeed in stabilizing its control of the mainland and would be able to extend that control to the island of Taiwan, where Chiang Kai-shek had fled with the remnants of his Kuomintang government and a large number of wealthy (and pro-American) Chinese refugees. On December 17, 1950, Washington blocked all Chinese assets and dollar accounts in the United States after China had entered active combat in the Korean War.[7] China retaliated two days later by seizing $200 million in U.S. public and private property in China. The United States also imposed a strategic embargo on China, which prevented any American corporation from doing business with the PRC, and encouraged its Western allies to do likewise. This sudden freeze in Sino-American political and commercial relations lasted for more than two decades, until the breakthrough in political relations that was achieved in the spring of 1971.

Sino-American political relations, which were deeply damaged by the recognition issue, the Korean War, and the strategic embargo, continued to worsen during the 1950's. The Taiwan Strait area became the main point of contention after China signed the Korean armistice in 1953. There were two military crises in the Taiwan Strait over the control of Nationalist-held islands lying close to the China mainland (1954 and 1958). Both crises involved air battles and artillery duels between the People's Liberation Army and Nationalist military forces. In both cases, the United States reinforced the Nationalist military position and threatened to intervene directly with military force, should the Nationalists' position deteriorate to a point that threatened their control of Taiwan itself. In December 1954, Washington and Taipei signed a mutual defense agreement guaranteeing the security of Taiwan and the offshore islands. A supplementary agreement was signed on May 7, 1957, providing for the emplacement on Taiwan of U.S. Matador missiles with a potential nuclear capability and a range of 600 miles.[8] The American reaction in 1958 included nuclear threats and the emplacement on Quemoy of eight-inch howitzers with a tactical nuclear capability. The military confrontation over the offshore islands, which continued into the 1960's and flared up to near-crisis proportions in 1962, continued to exacerbate Sino-American political relations and made the Taiwan issue the main point of difference between Washington and Peking. Tension over the jurisdictional status of Taiwan and the military confrontation in the Taiwan Strait became the main block to the establishment of diplomatic relations in the early 1970's. And, as will be seen in the next chapter, the Taiwan Strait issue has direct relevance to China's international energy policy, since the Chinese continental shelf and areas immediately contiguous to Taiwan are potentially petrolific. Wide areas of the continental shelf are claimed by both Taipei and Peking in their continuing political struggle over the Taiwan Strait.

American involvement in Vietnam during the 1960's maintained the level of hostility between Peking and Washington for another decade. Washington sharply increased its military support for the Diem regime (South Vietnam) in 1963 and 1964, and in January and February 1965 began bombing North Vietnam and landing U.S. marines in the south to begin an active combat role.[9] Both actions greatly concerned the Chinese government, which feared that it would become directly involved militarily in the event of a U.S. attack across the demilitarized zone or an extension of the bombing to Chinese border regions. By 1968 (coinciding with the height of the Chinese Cultural Revolution), U.S. troop strength in Vietnam had escalated to more than 300,000, some 25 percent of the population of the south had become refugees, North Vietnamese and National Liberation Front (NLF) troops had launched the "Tet" offensive, and the peace movement in the United States had become a serious political factor. In January 1969, four-party peace talks began in Paris, leading to a gradual withdrawal of U.S. troops. On April 30, 1970, President Richard M. Nixon ordered U.S. and South Vietnamese troops to cross the Cambodian border in force, precipitating a nationwide student uprising in the United States and repeal of the Senate Tonkin Gulf Resolution, which had authorized an escalated U.S. military presence in Vietnam.

"Vietnamization" of the conflict by U.S. troop withdrawals led to secret discussions between the United States and China concerning the possibility of relaxation in political relations between the two countries. Faced with increasing tension along its northern border with the Soviet Union, China invited Secretary of State Henry Kissinger to Peking in July 1971 for secret meetings with top Chinese leaders, and issued a round of public invitations to U.S. groups to visit China for "people's diplomacy." On July 16, 1971, it was publicly announced that Nixon would visit the PRC within a few months for direct political discussions. The visit occurred in February 1972 and culminated in the Shanghai Communiqué, signed by both sides, which established a political framework for cultural and economic exchange and for negotiations leading toward the normalization of diplomatic relations. Warming political relations between China and the United States coincided with gradual de-escalation of the fighting in Vietnam, complete American withdrawal of ground troops, and the ephemeral success of the Paris peace talks. Meanwhile, in November 1971 the PRC was successful in its bid for United Nations membership, replacing the representatives of the Nationalist government in Taipei.

This brief chronology of political events is important to an understanding of the relatively slow pace of Sino-American energy relations since the establishment of direct political relations in 1971. China and the United States had been separated for two decades, not only by ideological, political, and diplomatic differences, but by direct hostilities and military confrontation on the Chinese perimeter. A succession of crises in Korea, the Taiwan Strait, and Indochina maintained a high level of tension between the two countries that not only prevented any sort of energy trade or technological exchange before 1970, but left a deep reservoir of mutual suspicion that has considerably slowed the development of relations since 1971. Neither Japan nor China's other Western trading partners face this burden of recent hostility and mutual suspicion. Their energy relations with the PRC have therefore outstripped those of the United States during the 1970's. Here, as in other areas of China's energy policies, the political factor is predominant, establishing a framework of limiting conditions within which energy relations with other countries take place.

Formal restrictions on U.S.-China energy trade have gradually been relaxed in the period since 1971. In April 1971, the U.S. government relaxed restrictions on oil companies providing fuel to ships and aircraft bound for China, except for traffic between China and Vietnam or Korea.[10] A general list of U.S. goods that could be sold to China was issued in June 1971, followed by a further relaxation on February 14, 1972, that put China in "Country Group Y," essentially on the same footing as the USSR and Eastern Europe.[11] This cleared the way for energy equipment exports to the PRC, except in certain areas of advanced technology that could have military application. President Nixon further lifted the ban on travel to China by U.S. ships and aircraft on November 22, 1972.

February 1973 was another good month for political and commercial relations between the United States and China. A cease-fire agreement was reached at the Paris peace talks on February 23, despite the heavy U.S. bombing of Haiphong harbor which had occurred just two months before, in December 1972. On February 22, a Kissinger visit to Peking resulted in the establishment of liaison offices in Peking and Washington, a step below full ambassadorial relations. Sino-American trade relations began to accelerate in earnest during 1973. In November, coinciding with another Kissinger trip to Peking, Washington announced the withdrawal of 3,000 of the remaining 8,000 U.S. Air Force personnel stationed in Taiwan.[12]

Once liaison offices had been established in the two capital cities, discussions began (March 1973) on the settlement of mutual claims outstanding since 1949. The claims issue is of marginal economic importance, involving only $250 million of private American claims for properties that the Chinese seized in 1950 without compensation and $78 million of blocked Chinese assets in the United States. Both sides have long since adjusted to the financial losses, and the value of Sino-American trade each year exceeds the total value of the claims. The Chinese position is simply to let the matter rest, a solution that would in effect return $0.40 on the dollar for U.S. properties nationalized in 1950. This settlement would be in line with compensation received for nationalized U.S properties in other countries. Washington could simply apply the blocked assets to payment of outstanding claims by private U.S. citizens. However, the issue has retained a certain emotional content in the United States. Settlement of the claims issue would clear the way for U.S. Export-Import Bank credits on transactions with the PRC and would permit the extension of most-favored-nation tariffs for Chinese goods entering the United States. There has been a certain amount of resistance in Congress to the Chinese solution, based on remaining emotional ties to Taipei and a fear of cheap Chinese goods, particularly textiles.[13]

In the closing months of 1976, a change of administration took place in both Peking and Washington. In China, following the deaths of Chou En-lai and Mao Tse-tung, a moderate political faction led by Hua Kuo-feng and (from behind the scenes) Teng Hsiao-ping, rose swiftly to power. They immediately purged the "gang of four," a radical faction based in Shanghai that had been closely associated with the Cultural Revolution. It took the moderates a full year to consolidate their power and launch a new program for industrial modernization of the PRC. Meanwhile, the government in Washington had also changed hands with the election of President Carter and a Democratic administration. While committed to early normalization of Sino-U.S. relations, Carter pushed the China question to the background during 1977 as he dealt with a number of more pressing domestic and international issues and moved past the first halting months of his administration. By the end of 1977, Chinese frustration at the slow pace of normalization rose and a good-will mission by Secretary of State Cyrus Vance yielded little more than a public tongue-lashing by Teng Hsiao-ping.

In early 1978, however, the general climate in U.S.-China relations took a sharp upswing. In January Peking sent a high-level petroleum delegation (nominally from the Chinese Petroleum Corporation) to the United States to tour American oilfields, refineries, and energy equipment plants. The U.S. Department of Energy gave the Chinese visitors the red carpet treatment, stressing the potential for Sino-American technical cooperation in energy. In May U.S. National Security Adviser Zbigniew Brzezinski flew to Peking to discuss the state of Sino-American relations. He stressed common security concerns vis-à-vis the Soviet Union at every opportunity. Brzezinski even gave Chinese officials a detailed briefing on Soviet-American strategic arms limitation talks and explained U.S. security goals at some length. This type of briefing is usually reserved for close American allies in Western Europe. The point was not lost on the Chinese, who responded warmly to Brzezinski, in sharp contrast to the reception accorded Vance just a few months earlier.

During the spring and summer of 1978, Sino-American energy and other trade relations continued to improve. Major U.S. corporations and important corporate executives were invited to Peking, including a number of American oil companies (Chapter 8). These companies were invited to present technical seminars and to discuss the possibility of joint participation in major industrial projects, including offshore oil exploration and development. Washington further eased restrictions on the sale of sensitive technologies to the PRC, licensing advanced geological survey equipment (an "array processor" and infrared scanning devices) that have potential military applications. Meanwhile, in late October, Carter vetoed a proposed sale of Northrop F5G fighter aircraft to Taiwan.

During November, the pace of Sino-American relations quickened even further. Secretary of Energy James R. Schlesinger made an extended visit to the PRC, offering China the latest in American energy technology (Chapter 8). Schlesinger mapped out an "agenda for cooperation" in energy that included coal, electric power, oil and gas, renewable energy resources, and high-energy physics. The Chinese made no explicit trade arrangements, but hinted at a larger role for American corporations in their energy plant and equipment import strategy. The basic payoff for the trip, as Schlesinger himself acknowledged, was political. During November, China also announced plans to increase imports of American agricultural commodities, invited an American company to build a chain of hotels in China, and contracted with the Fluor Corporation for construction of the world's largest copper mine and refinery. The U.S. Treasury Department eased its position on the frozen-assets issue by announcing that henceforward American banks must pay interest on frozen Chinese assets. On November 21, it was announced that an American oil company (Coastal States Gas Corporation) would import half a million tons of Chinese crude oil in 1979 for its California refinery. At about the same time, the National Council for U.S.-China Trade announced that trade would reach $1 billion in 1978 and would be much higher in 1979.

On December 15, 1978, in simultaneous broadcasts from Washington and Peking, it was announced that on January 1, 1979, relations would finally be normalized between China and the United States, and that ambassadors would be exchanged on March 1. This announcement broke a deadlock that had persisted for nearly 30 years. President Carter read a joint communiqué that acknowledged the People's Republic as the sole legitimate government of China, abrogated the security treaty with Taiwan (effective at the end of 1979), and pledged the United States to continue commercial, cultural, and other unofficial ties with Taiwan. In an accompanying speech, Carter reiterated American determination that the settlement of the Taiwan issue be peaceful, pledged continuing sales of military equipment of a defensive nature to Taiwan, invited Vice-Premier Teng Hsiao-ping to visit Washington at the end of January, and denied that the normalization of relations had other than peaceful objectives. With regard to the last point, however, it should be remembered that the joint communiqué commits both countries to resist "hegemonism" in any part of the globe—a clear reference to the Soviet Union.

Sino-American Energy Commodity Trade

There was virtually no significant energy commodity trade between the United States and China in the period from the opening of political relations in 1971 until 1977. The United States imported small amounts of

Chinese wax starting in 1972 and exported specialized lubricants beginning in 1974. The only other energy commodity transaction of interest reported in official American trade returns was the purchase of 150,000 tons of Chinese coal in 1977 (Table 20.12). I have not been able to trace this transaction through the literature, but the size of the purchase indicates that some American industry or utility imported enough Chinese coal to make laboratory tests and a trial run.

Before 1978 there were repeated rumors of impending Chinese crude oil exports to the United States, but nothing materialized.[14] The American oil market is problematical for Peking. The U.S. West Coast, the most likely destination for Chinese oil, is currently taking more crude than it can use from the North Slope fields in Alaska and is resisting becoming a transshipment point for Alaskan crude bound for other parts of the country. The major oil corporations feel that Chinese crude is overpriced relative to Indonesian crude and that insufficient quantities will be offered to justify disrupting normal supply patterns or refinery operations. This could change, of course, in the event of a new tightening in the world crude petroleum market, or if China discovers and exports lighter-grade crude oils at competitive prices.

In November 1978, Coastal States Gas Corporation, one of the larger independent oil companies, contracted with the China National Chemicals Import and Export Corporation for the purchase of about half a million metric tons of Taching crude oil at an estimated price of $50 million. The Chinese crude was to be delivered to a small refinery in Hercules, California, during the first six months of 1979 for the production of low-sulfur residual fuel oil. In its announcement of the transaction, Coastal States indicated that the reason for the purchase was that Chinese crude would meet the stringent environmental standards imposed on utilities and industry in California.[15] The company also said that it would be interested in further crude oil contracts with China. Even if the deal doubled in 1979, or another company followed suit, however, Chinese crude would be supplying less than half of one percent of the American crude oil import market. Peking has opened a tiny crack in the American oil market, sufficient to mop up its surplus export crude, but insignificant in terms of U.S. energy requirements.

Some U.S. multinationals may be supplying Chinese ships with limited quantities of bunker fuel, but these transactions have not yet appeared in official U.S. trade returns as exports to the PRC. Exxon has supplied bunker fuel for Chinese ships since 1975, probably through subsidiaries in Hong Kong and Singapore. Because of peculiarities in the reporting of bunker fuel, it is difficult to trace to the purchasing country.

Sino-American Energy Equipment Trade

As pointed out above, the United States has not done particularly well in energy equipment exports to the PRC, capturing only about 4 percent of the total between 1972 and 1976 (or 10 percent if chemical fertilizer plants are included). The precise character of the transactions that have been consummated, however, reveals an interesting pattern that could have implications for future U.S.-China energy equipment trade. Based on the first few years of experience, it appears that Peking tends to turn to U.S. corporations for purchases of "cutting edge" energy technology (advanced seismological equipment, secondary recovery equipment, specialized monitoring instruments, etc.) while purchasing the bulk of its standard technology· (petrochemical plants, offshore drilling rigs, etc.) from Japan, Singapore, and Western Europe. This is obviously not a hard-and-fast rule. But it may provide a clue regarding Chinese negotiating behavior in transactions with U.S. corporations.

The first energy equipment contracts with U.S. companies were signed in 1973. The bulk of the $36 million in U.S. energy equipment sales to China in that year was made up of coal-mining equipment, including 25 blast-hole drills and five power shovels (Bucyrus-Erie, $20.0 million). But a much more widely publicized deal was made for the purchase of sophisticated computerized seismic-survey equipment in October 1973 (Geospace, $5.5 million). The purchase contact included a Raytheon 704 computer and training for Chinese technicians at the Geospace headquarters in Houston.[16] China also purchased 20 wellhead blowout-preventer stacks for onland use in 1973 (Rucker, $2.0 million), and some unspecified drilling equipment (Hughes Tool, $500,000). One U.S. corporation also sold China technology for a synthetic fiber complex to be constructed near Peking by a consortium of Japanese corporations (Sohio, $8.0 million).

In addition, 1973 was the contract year for the sale of chemical-fertilizer plants to the PRC. The contracts, which surprised even veterans in the China trade in its magnitude, included eight complete ammonia plants from the United States (M. W. Kellogg, $200 million) to be constructed over a five-year period. U.S. technology was also the basis for the sale of an additional eight urea plants by the Netherlands (Kellogg Continental, $90 million). The ammonia-urea complexes are fed by natural gas, and each has a capacity of 1,000 tons per day of ammonia and 1,620 tons per day of urea.[17] The contracts also included the stationing of 140 American technicians and their dependents in eight Chinese provinces to assist in the construction of the plants and the training of about 60 Chinese technicians in Houston and Enid,

Oklahoma. Although not strictly an energy equipment purchase, the chemical-fertilizer plants did increase China's capabilities in an important energy-related technology.

U.S. energy equipment manufacturers did not repeat their major 1973 incursions into the Chinese market in 1974. The main contract signed during the year proved to be highly controversial and took until 1976 to be cleared by the U.S. government. The French Compagnie Générale de Géophysique contracted to sell the PRC an offshore seismic data-collecting and prospecting center that incorporated two Cyber 172 computers of U.S. manufacture (Control Data, $7 million total). Because this computer is relatively large and has strategic-weapons applications in ballistic missile tracking and nuclear weapons tests, it came under the export controls of the U.S. Department of Commerce. The Office of Export Controls reviewed the transaction in consultation with the State Department, the Department of Defense, and the Energy Research and Development Agency.[18] ERDA objected to the sale, which then had to be directly reviewed by the National Security Council in the White House. The National Security Council cleared the Cyber sale on October 12, 1976, and it was referred to NATO's Coordinating Committee for Export Control (Cocom) for final approval.[19] As part of its approval, the NSC required safeguards, including information on use and programming and on-site inspection in China by Control Data officials. The inspections were to continue for three years.

The United States substantially improved its position in the Chinese petroleum equipment market in 1977 and 1978. In 1977, Peking ordered two National 1320 offshore production rigs for installation on platforms of Chinese construction (Armco, $15–20 million). In addition, American petroleum equipment companies sold China at least $15 million of assorted onland oil exploration and production equipment, including workover rigs, a seismic-exploration system, and drilling equipment. By 1978, it appeared that American companies might be moving into a dominant position in China's petroleum equipment trade. Two U.S. subsidiaries in Singapore sold the PRC three jack-up rigs for offshore exploration, loaded with advanced American equipment (Bethlehem Singapore, $20–25 million, and Marathon Le Tourneau, $46 million). Hughes Tool and other companies opened a series of supply contracts for standard drilling equipment (bits, handling tools, and cementing equipment) in the first half of the year. Combined with the 1978 exchange of petroleum delegations, this may indicate a swing toward American petroleum equipment companies. This trend could be accelerated by the successful negotiation of contracts for joint offshore development projects along the Chinese coastline (Chapter 8).

Direct Energy Technology Transfer from the United States

The same pattern (acquisition of U.S. "cutting edge" technology and preference for Japanese and European plant) is evident from the history of direct scientific and technological exchange between the United States and China in the energy field. From 1973 until 1976, the PRC sent one energy technology delegation a year to the United States. These Chinese delegations have been highly specialized and interested in particular areas of U.S. technology, such as liquefied natural gas, oil refining, petroleum prospecting, and pipe laying. Delegations from the United States to China have been more frequent and have typically been associated with the sale of energy equipment to the PRC. One important petroleum technology delegation from the United States in 1975 included representatives of major U.S. oil corporations and was invited to tour a range of petroleum production facilities, including Taching oilfield.[20]

Scientific delegations from the PRC to the United States have occasionally raised the possibility of Sino-American cooperation in nuclear power technology.[21] U.S. nuclear equipment manufacturers are also reported to have sent representatives to China for preliminary discussions.[22] The PRC may be interested in American light-water reactor (LWR) technology for future development of power reactors in China. But so far such discussions have not moved beyond the level of general inquiry and courtesy calls. The November 1978 sale of two French reactors to the PRC indicates a firm choice in favor of West European suppliers for nuclear equipment, although the reactors will be produced under license from Westinghouse. Normalization of diplomatic relations with the United States might open the door for some sales of U.S. nuclear power plants or equipment (Chapter 12).

Energy Relations with Canada

Although the Chinese would never admit it officially, Canada has often been treated as an adjunct to Peking's U.S. policy. Canada has not been involved in direct hostilities with the PRC, and the attitude of the Canadian government toward its relationship with China has been somewhat more flexible than Washington's posture. This makes Canada a good testing ground for political and commercial contacts with the United States. Diplomatic relations between the PRC and Canada were established on October 13, 1970, after months of negotiations in Stockholm. This breakthrough, which preceded the Kissinger visits to Peking, was based on a new Taiwan formula: "The Chinese government reaffirms that Taiwan is an inalienable part of the territory of the P.R.C. The Canadian Government *takes note* of this position of the Chinese Government."[23] A Canadian chargé d'affaires arrived in Peking on November 31, and a full ambassadorial exchange was completed by July 1971. Canadian Pacific Airlines negotiated the first direct air link to China in August 1971. All of these steps had implications for the development of Sino-American relations, and were taken in part to test the official U.S. reaction.

The energy relationship between Canada and China has centered on an exchange of several delegations of petroleum experts. The Chinese initiated this exchange by sending a 17-member delegation under Deputy Fuel Minister Tang Ko in September 1972 for a study of Canadian refineries and gas plants.[24] Canada responded with a 30-member mission of oil equipment suppliers in April 1973, led by Energy Minister Donald McDonald. A second delegation of Canadian petroleum engineers visited China in June 1974 and was among the first Western groups invited to tour the Taching oilfield. Two additional Canadian groups, a delegation of port, harbor, and marine terminal experts and a seismological study group, visited the PRC in October 1975. A rare provincial-level delegation of cartographers from the Hopei Provincial Bureau of Surveying and Cartography visited Canada in June 1976. These various delegations performed a dual function, cementing Sino-Canadian relations and providing the PRC with another route of access to U.S.-based petroleum technology. Some of the refineries and other installations visited by the Chinese groups are managed by American corporations.

Despite this active technological exchange, there has been no recorded energy commodity trade between China and Canada and very little trade in energy equipment. The PRC did import three Canada Westinghouse gas turbines in 1974 as part of a plant purchase from a Belgian corporation (ACEC, $5.0 million). The only other energy equipment transaction with Canada was the purchase of steel casing for oil wells in 1975 ($700,000). There were reports that Canada was negotiating the sale of a synthetic rubber plant to the PRC in 1974 (Polysar, $20 million), but no record has appeared to indicate that this transaction was completed.[25]

Conclusion: The Potential American Role in Chinese Energy Development

The normalization of diplomatic relations between China and the United States in December 1978 achieved the final step in political rapprochement between the two countries. In the final analysis, the Taiwan question proved to be the barrier that had to be removed before normalization could occur. The normalization of relations will accelerate the pace of energy cooperation between the United States and China. However, it remains to be seen whether American companies will be able to displace European and Japanese suppliers of capital equipment. In any case, the political factor will continue to determine the quality and quantity of energy relations. Even without the various formal diplomatic and commercial obstructions that hampered U.S.-China energy trade, geographic and cultural proximity will continue to weigh heavily in the minds of Chinese policy makers. The energy policies of the PRC will continue to be predominantly regional in character, stressing energy commodity exports to Japan and Southeast Asia and energy equipment imports from Japan and Western Europe.

For its part, Washington appears to have accepted this situation as a geopolitical fact of life. For example, the United States has shown little inclination to become entangled directly in the territorial dispute over who owns the potential oil-bearing areas of the Chinese continental shelf. (See Chapter 7 for details of the controversy.) The United States has everything to lose and nothing to gain from involvement in the issue. No matter what position (aside from noninvolvement) Washington chose, it would offend Peking, Taipei, Seoul, or Tokyo, if not all of them at once.

An American oceanographic team (Woods Hole), operating under the auspices of the U.N. Economic Commission for Asia and the Far East, carried out a seismic survey of the floor of the East China Sea, the Yellow Sea, and the Ryukyu island arc in October–November 1968.[26] But since then, Washington has avoided irritating Peking on the issue. The U.S. State Department in 1975 discouraged American companies (Superior and Gulf) from drilling exploratory wells in contested areas of the shelf.[27] Taipei and Seoul had granted paper concessions along wide reaches of the shelf in the East China Sea to various oil companies. But the State Department blocked the more aggressive companies from taking advantage of the concessions in disputed areas and indicated that the United States would not protect isolated drilling rigs from naval enforcement by the PRC of its offshore claims. It is unlikely that Peking would have tolerated an active oil-exploration and extraction program along its coastline.

Control of the Chinese continental shelf is just one of the many areas of China's international energy relations where the United States will remain in a secondary role. American corporations seeking to enter energy commodity or equipment trade with China should be keenly aware of the political and geographic impediments to such trade. Particularly in large-scale energy machinery and plant purchases, Peking will probably continue to display a marked preference for Japanese and Western

European suppliers. China's energy policy planners still feel uneasy about tangling directly with the large U.S. multinationals, backed by the political power of the U.S. government.

Where do these various constraints leave the American role in China's future energy development? As suggested above, there is one very important area within which the United States should expect to develop strong energy relations with the PRC—the area of advanced (and specialized) energy technologies. Much of the energy technology that is incorporated in China's energy plant purchases from Western Europe or Japan originated in processes under U.S. patent. Offshore exploration, petrochemical processing, seismic data processing, secondary and tertiary recovery, natural gas transport, and light-water reactor construction are just a few of the energy technology fields where U.S. research and development have led to technological innovation. China will continue to be interested in such "cutting edge" innovations, with an eye to technological shortcuts that may allow the PRC to bypass some stages in the development of their own energy industries. U.S. corporations seeking a portion of the China trade should concentrate heavily in areas where they have a definable technological lead over Japanese or European counterparts. The energy crisis has further stimulated energy research and development in the United States, providing a stream of innovations, some of which will have relevance and application to China's energy development.

Meanwhile, the level of American interest in Chinese energy development, particularly in the Chinese petroleum industry, remains high. Numerous articles and books have appeared on the subject in the last few years (see Bibliography). A publishing company based in Houston is offering a Chinese-language trade magazine with advertisements from U.S. petroleum equipment manufacturers for circulation in the PRC.[28] Several conferences and workshops have been held in the United States on the subject of China's energy development and energy equipment trade, including a major oil industry conference (Houston, June 1976).[29] American experts were also deeply involved in a February 1978 conference in Singapore on China's offshore oil development.[30] A cautious approach to estimates of Chinese offshore oil and gas resources and to energy plant and equipment sales to the PRC has emerged as a consensus view at these conferences. This more realistic approach is correcting the original overstatement of the potential U.S. role in China's energy development and trade. The media, meanwhile, continue to thrive on speculation and exaggerations fed by the course of political events, rather than basing their reports of Chinese energy development on hard-nosed analysis.

Energy Relations with Western Europe

As with other areas, China's energy relations with Western Europe have been contingent on political relations. Peking views Western Europe (at a convenient distance from Chinese borders) as the principal arena of struggle for hegemony between the superpowers.[31] Given the general state of global energy and economic disequilibrium, the Chinese press talks as if it expects to see a "closing of ranks to oppose hegemonism" between Western Europe and the Third World.[32] Since Peking has encouraged Washington to maintain a strong presence in Europe, China's obvious political goal is to isolate Moscow from the region. The Chinese press views rising Soviet energy exports (oil and natural gas) to Western Europe as an effort to extend its political sphere of influence.[33] And the PRC has been vocal in its support for European unity and the Common Market as an effective method of resisting the Soviet advance.[34]

Despite these various political positions in support of West European countries, China still views the region as incorrigibly capitalist and mired in the economic results of its own obsolete production system. The Chinese press included Western Europe in its disparaging comments about the energy crisis, and encourages the European working class to take its destiny into its own hands.[35]

Once beyond the rhetorical framework of these formal ideological positions, however, one discovers that political relations between Peking and the capitals of West European countries have been cordial since 1970. Badly disrupted by the excesses of the Cultural Revolution, China moved quickly to mend its political fences in Western Europe. Formal diplomatic relations were established between the PRC and several European countries as a prelude to China's entry into the United Nations and to the warming of Sino-American relations. Once formal diplomatic relations had been established throughout the region, Peking began to improve trade relations and commercial contacts as well. By 1975, the PRC had entered into a regular exchange of views with the European Economic Community, leading to the establishment of formal relations with the EEC and the posting of a Chinese ambassador to Brussels in February 1976.[36] Negotiation of a trade agreement between the PRC and the EEC continued for more than two years, and the agreement was concluded on April 3, 1978.[37] Ten years ago any such agreement would have been politically unthinkable. But by the mid-1970's, commercial relations with the EEC were considered just one more element of China's forward political posture in Western Europe.

Energy Commodity Trade with Western Europe

China's energy commodity trade with Western Europe began in 1954 when the PRC imported about 1,000 metric tons of some unspecified petroleum product (probably lubricants) from Britain. Ever since that date, Sino–West European energy commodity trade has consisted entirely of a few refined petroleum products, with the exception of 1959, 1964, and 1965, when the PRC exported minor amounts of coal to some European countries. It is evident from the pattern of the coal exports to Western Europe in 1959 that China was seeking to unload coal originally destined for Japan, and may have been looking for a replacement for the Japanese coal market during the disruption of Sino-Japanese political and trade relations that followed the Nagasaki flag incident (Chapter 6). However, the distances made this alternative less than desirable from a long-term trade perspective, and coal exports to Western Europe were discontinued in 1960.

Throughout the 1950's and 1960's, trade in petroleum products consisted of imports of lubricants from Western Europe (particularly Britain) and exports of mineral wax to a number of European countries. The quantities were quite limited and the total value of this trade never exceeded a few million dollars in a single year in either direction. Exports of wax and petroleum by-products to Western Europe increased in the 1970's, but still barely reached 25,000 metric tons in the peak year (1974). Chinese imports of specialized lubricants from Western Europe have declined to an insignificant level.

As with the United States and Australia, there have been rumors that China would begin to export crude petroleum to some West European countries. China's ambassador to Italy disclosed negotiations for a crude oil–petroleum equipment barter deal in February 1976.[38] But so far, such efforts have yielded little but speculation. The PRC has long imported petrochemical equipment from the Italian state-owned oil company (ENI), and talk of crude oil trade could be designed either as a negotiating tactic in more serious discussions with the Japanese or as a stimulant to better purchase terms for Italian refinery equipment. Unless China were willing to offer a sufficient price incentive to overcome the natural transportation disadvantage it suffers in the European petroleum market, significant petroleum exports to Western Europe are not likely in the near future.

The transportation problem also presents an obstacle to the export of Chinese coal to Europe. In April 1976, Chinese trade officials were reported to be discussing the sale of large quantities of coal to West Germany in exchange for mining equipment.[39] But here again, such talk must be considered highly speculative when found in association with impending equipment purchases. The PRC will have difficulty meeting its crude oil and coal export commitments to Japan and is unlikely to enter into further long-range energy export commitments. But the West Germans were reported to have offered to handle the transportation cost and some expansion of China's coal port facilities in return for such a long-range commitment.

Energy Equipment Trade with Western Europe

China has carried on extensive trade in energy machinery and complete energy production plants with Western Europe since the Sino-Soviet break in 1960. This trade has been almost entirely in one direction. From 1961 until 1976, the PRC imported more than $1.6 billion in energy production equipment from the West European countries, or just over 50 percent of total Chinese energy equipment imports from Japan and the West. China did export some intermediate-technology electric-power-transmission equipment, diesel engines, and other miscellaneous items, but imported a much greater quantity of high-technology energy plant and machinery.

Nearly all of China's energy equipment imports from Western Europe in the 1960's were petrochemical, refinery, and chemical-fertilizer plants. The only recorded exception was about $5 million in oil-drilling equipment imported from France in 1965. Petrochemical and refinery plant purchases alone accounted for two-thirds of the total. Major purchases included oil refineries from Italy in 1963 and 1965 (ENI, $20 million total), and petrochemical plants from France in 1963 (Melle and Speichem, $8.5 million), from West Germany in 1964 (Lurgi-Gesellschaft, $12.5 million), from Britain in 1964 (Simon Carves, $20 million), from Norway in 1965 ($14 million), and from Britain in 1965 (Prinex, $8.4 million). Ammonia and urea plants were imported from Britain in 1963 and 1965 (Humphrey and Glascow, $32 million total), the Netherlands in 1963 (Stork-Werkspoor, $7.0 million), and Italy in 1963 and 1965 (Montecattini, $25 million total).

The Cultural Revolution caused serious political strains between China and a number of European countries, strains that peaked in the sacking of the British embassy in Peking in August 1967. A hiatus in commercial relations with Western Europe accompanied these political disruptions. No new contracts were signed between 1966 and 1970 for the purchase of European energy production plants. Indeed, active Chinese interest in European energy equipment was not evidenced until 1972. In the summer of 1968, Vickers-Zimmer, a company working on refinery construction in Lanchow, was accused of fraud and six of its technicians were expelled from China.[40] One British citizen working on the project (George Watt) was arrested for spying and given a three-year prison sentence. This incident doubtless dampened the enthusiasm of European companies for Chinese plant construction deals.

By 1972 the bad feeling of the Cultural Revolution period had largely been forgotten and apologized for by the Chinese government. Britain received a personal apology from Chou En-lai regarding the embassy matter, Watt was freed, and compensation was arranged for the destruction of the embassy. The euphoria that followed the breakthrough in Sino-American relations helped to overcome residual distrust, and plant purchases began once again from West European companies.

The first such purchases in 1972 were all electric power equipment, including both hydropower and thermal power generators from Italy, Britain, and France with a total value of more than $110 million in 1972 alone. China's imports of European electric power equipment continued in 1973 and 1974 on a fairly large scale, totaling $150 million in each of those years. More electric power equipment contracts were signed in 1975 and 1976, but on a much reduced scale (exact total value unknown), reflecting the general cutback in Chinese energy equipment purchases that followed the balance-of-payments crisis of 1974. The new emphasis on electric power equipment was the result of a rising awareness in China's energy planning agencies of the slow pace of expansion in the electric power industry. Nearly three-quarters by value of the contracts signed by China for electric power equipment (1972–76) were with West European companies. The other 25 percent of the market for Chinese electric power equipment went to Japanese manufacturers. This demonstrates a marked Chinese preference for European generating plants and technology.

By 1973–74 the PRC was purchasing a wide spectrum of West European energy equipment. British companies sold China about $100 million in advanced longwall coal-mining equipment during those two years. A French conglomerate contracted for a complete refinery–petrochemical complex in 1973 (Technip-Speichem, $272 million) slated for construction south of Shenyang by 1978.[41] This plant, which will have a capacity of 2 million metric tons per year and will produce a wide range of petroleum, petrochemical, and fiber products, is the largest single energy plant ever purchased by the PRC. A group of French, British, and German companies sold China a vinyl acetate/menthanol plant using natural gas as the feedstock in the same year (Speichem-Lurgi, Humphrey and Glascow, and BASF, $90 million total). West European petrochemical plant and equipment sales to China continued at a level of about $50 million per year from 1974 through 1976. European companies captured about 40 percent of the Chinese market for petrochemical equipment ($500 million) from 1972 until 1976, with the other 60 percent going to Japanese manufacturers. European companies also shared the Chinese chemical-fertilizer plant purchases with the United States in the same years, capturing about 60 percent of the market ($400 million). European companies have done very well in sales of offshore exploration equipment to the PRC, with about 35–40 percent of the 1972–76 Chinese market ($150 million). Offshore equipment sold to the PRC included supply ships from Denmark in 1973 (Weco, $41.8 million), a seismic survey ship from France in 1974 (Compagnie Générale de Géophysique, no value given), suction dredges from the Netherlands in 1973 (NVIHC, $53 million), and supply helicopters from Germany in 1975 (Messerschmitt, no value given). China also turned to Western Europe, particularly Norway, for tanker purchases in 1974–76. Norwegian shipping companies sold the PRC a 34,000-deadweight-ton (dwt) tanker and a 76,000-dwt tanker in 1974, a 96,000-dwt tanker in 1975, and several tankers in the 85,000–100,000-dwt range in 1976. Most Chinese oil port facilities are geared for 50,000-dwt tankers, but port expansion is still under way, and there is one 100,000-dwt tanker dock in Dairen.

"Diversification" would be the key word that describes best the pattern of China's energy equipment trade with Western Europe. The PRC has bought the entire range of coal, petroleum, and electric power equipment from European companies and shows every sign of continuing to do so. Chinese planners evidently prefer European electric power and coal-mining equipment over equipment of Japanese manufacture, and they split the petroleum equipment purchases between Western Europe, Japan, and the United States. A breakdown of energy equipment purchases by country indicates that the PRC also prefers to spread purchases over a number of trading partners rather than concentrate on one or two European countries for the bulk of imported equipment. Particular countries may be favored for particular types of equipment (Britain for coal-mining machinery, Norway for tankers, etc.), but overall the pattern shows that Peking is unwilling to be dependent on any single trading partner in Europe. This pattern of diversification by type of equipment and trading partner confirms the impression gathered in the analysis of Sino-American energy relations that the Chinese government is still concerned about potential dependency relationships with the West in the development of its energy industries. Japan is the only industrialized trading partner with whom China feels a sufficient parity to permit a disproportionate share of the Chinese energy equipment market. Even in the Japanese case Peking is careful to balance equipment imports with crude oil exports and always maintains the European option for each type of energy equipment purchased from Japanese companies.

Energy Technology Exchange with Western Europe

Despite the fact that more than half of China's purchases of foreign energy production equipment have come from West European companies, the exchange of technical energy delegations with Western Europe has been relatively muted. To a certain extent this impression may reflect reporting deficiencies; but even allowing a considerable margin of error, China's technical exchange with Europe in energy-related fields has not been as vigorous as might be supposed from the trade in energy equipment. From 1972 until 1976, only five major energy delegations from European countries were reported to have visited China. During the same period, fourteen of the approximately 50 Chinese energy delegations visiting foreign countries traveled to Western Europe. Even allowing for substantial underreporting, it appears that only 20–30 of the 130 energy delegations moving in both directions were involved in technical exchange with China's European trading partners. This confirms the impression gathered from analysis of Sino-American and Sino-Japanese technical exchange patterns that Peking purchases standard energy plant and equipment from European companies and prefers Japanese and American sources for advanced or unfamiliar technology.

There are some important exceptions to this generalization. Peking has expressed considerable interest in North Sea offshore oil development and in European nuclear power technology. A group of petroleum experts from China visited Norwegian offshore oil installations in 1975, investigating ferroconcrete drilling platforms, rig supply equipment, geological analysis, and offshore oil storage and transport.[42] In 1976, the PRC exchanged offshore petroleum technology delegations with the Netherlands and sent a team of offshore experts to British North Sea installations. The reasons for Chinese interest in European offshore oil technology are fairly obvious. Exploration and development of oil deposits in the North Sea have encountered more severe conditions and heavier technological demands than similar projects in other parts of the world. The North Sea deposits are located in relatively deep water in seas that are frequently troubled by turbulent weather. These conditions are similar to the depth of the most promising sediments in the East China Sea and the typhoon conditions in the South China Sea. Current Chinese interest in European offshore technology could lead to rig and equipment purchases from Western European companies, although so far Peking has preferred Asian suppliers for offshore rig purchases.*

During 1977 and 1978, China's energy relations with Western Europe

*For a description of China's nuclear energy relations with Western Europe, see Chapter 12.

began to accelerate again, as in 1973 and 1974. The year 1977 was relatively slow for Chinese equipment purchases from Europe. The PRC did buy the "Borgny Dolphin," a large semisubmersible drilling rig capable of deep-water drilling (Fred Olsen, $27–40 million). But Chinese trade officials patiently explained to their European counterparts that big new contracts were on the way, as soon as the new government had settled in and initiated its modernization program. By early 1978, this prophecy was fulfilled. In January, Alsthom-Atlantique began discussions with Peking of a possible contract for a 600-megawatt coal-fired thermal power plant, and one or more nuclear power reactors. In February a Chinese coal industry delegation visited mines and processing plants in West Germany and Romania. By March, rumors were circulating that Britain, China, and Hong Kong might be involved in a triangular deal for the construction of a coal-fired thermal power station in Hong Kong, fed by Chinese coal, and delivering part of its off-peak output to Canton (Chapter 8). In April, a second Chinese energy delegation toured coal mines and electric power facilities in West Germany. These contacts led to contracts for the British National Coal Board and Ruhrkohle, a West German firm, for consulting services for modernization of the Chinese coal industry.[43] By July, Peking was initiating discussions with European banking and finance syndicates regarding long-term loans and other credits for plant and equipment purchases.[44] These discussions continued at the time of writing and appear to hinge around Chinese insistence on credit in dollars without the high interest rates currently prevailing in the Eurodollar market. But even in raising the subject of direct loans, China had departed from its traditional policy eschewing foreign debt (Chapter 8).

In the closing months of 1978, trade agreements and large construction contracts began to roll in like a series of huge waves on the shore. In September a German coal industry delegation went to Peking and met with high officials in the Ministry of Coal for extended contract talks. These talks yielded one of the most spectacular contracts in Chinese trade history. A consortium of German companies agreed to the construction of a large open-pit lignite mine, four underground coal mines, and a coal-equipment-manufacturing plant, for a total of $4 billion.[45] This deal was followed by an even larger one when Schloemann-Seigmag announced a $14 billion tender for construction of a fully integrated steel mill in Hopei province. If this contract goes through to completion, the steel complex will be one of the largest in the world, with an annual capacity of 10 million metric tons. Following this, another West German consortium, Baskalis-Westminster, signed letters of intent for construction of harbor facilities on the Yangtze River. Some of the new harbor facilities will be designed specifically for coal exports. Not all of these Sino-German deals have yet been finalized. China wants dollar credits at 7.25 percent interest, terms that financial institutions in Europe are still unwilling to provide.

Other European countries were not far behind. British companies signed contracts for chemical plants and steel for China's coal industry.[46] On a much larger scale, China expressed increasing interest in British military hardware, especially the Harrier vertical takeoff and landing (VTOL) jet fighters. Peking would like to buy 100 of the jets and position them at remote and scattered spots throughout northeast China as a defense against a lightning Soviet attack. Moscow was not amused over the prospect of this $800 million bargain, and Soviet President Brezhnev sent letters to British Prime Minister James Callaghan and several other governments warning against the hazards of military equipment sales to China.[47] The United States has expressed a deliberately neutral position on the matter, and will not press for NATO clearance of conventional arms sales to China. If completed, the VTOL aircraft sale and similar contracts for French antitank missiles, West German tanks, and American communication satellites could greatly strengthen China's defense of its northeast energy industries (Chapter 4).

Peking has also begun signing long-term trade agreements with West European countries. France and China signed a $13.6 billion trade agreement on December 4, 1978, which includes the sale of two nuclear power plants.[48] The French agreement also specifies two 600-megawatt thermal power stations, steel plants, and petroleum equipment. Sweden followed with a ten-year pact calling for a sharp but unspecified increase in bilateral trade. Britain and other EEC countries can be expected to follow with similar trade agreements. For the most part, these agreements set the general framework for trade, rather than committing the two sides to defined contracts. But the succession of deals and trade agreements between China and Western Europe suggests that Peking is continuing its trade preference for the smaller industrial countries of the "Second World," despite the normalization of diplomatic relations with the United States.

Energy Relations with Oceania

Political relations between the PRC and Australia and New Zealand were contingent on the recognition issue until 1972. Both countries officially recognized Taipei and neither had much contact with Peking before 1970. Australia and China developed some trade contacts in the 1960's and occasional Australian citizens were permitted to travel in China. The first major breakthrough in relations came when China and Australia signed a contract for the Chinese to import more than two million tons of Australian wheat in 1969–70, about one-third of Australia's wheat exports at the time. Australia got caught up in ping-pong diplomacy with China in 1971, and the opposition Labour Party began demanding recognition of the PRC. The Labour Party established diplomatic relations with China on December 21, 1972, immediately after its electoral victory. The Australian formula on the Taiwan issue was far more concessionary than the Canadian and Japanese formulas: "The Australian Government *acknowledges* the position of the Chinese Government that Taiwan is a province of the People's Republic of China and has decided to remove its official representation from Taiwan before 25 January 1973."[49] This position was a simple capitulation to Chinese demands on the issue.

New Zealand also recognized the PRC in December 1972. Both countries sent their trade ministers on visits to China during 1973, and Australian Prime Minister Gough Whitlam visited the PRC from October 31 to November 4, 1974. Trade continued to flourish, based largely on Australian wheat and iron ore exports.

The one political issue that continues to aggravate Sino-Australian relations is the matter of Chinese atmospheric tests of nuclear weapons. The Australian government takes a firm position against such tests and has also been highly critical of French atmospheric testing in the South Pacific. Formal protests were delivered by the Minister of Overseas Trade in June 1973 and by the Prime Minister in November 1974 during their visits to Peking.[50]

The PRC has carried on spot energy commodity trade with Australia and New Zealand since the early 1960's. China imported minor quantities of Australian coal in 1963, 1964, and 1971, possibly destined for Canton or to fill coal export commitments to Hong Kong or Japan. Official trade returns recorded Chinese export of minor amounts of crude petroleum to Australia in 1962 and 1964 for some undetermined reason. The size of the transactions (about 40,000 metric tons in each of the two years) would indicate that the export commodity was actually residual fuel oil sold by China for use as bunker fuel in Australian ships. China has also exported mineral wax to both Australia and New Zealand since 1966.

Rumors began to circulate in 1974 that Australia was considering importing Chinese crude petroleum.[51] A joint trade committee discussed the matter in April 1975, and samples of Chinese crude were tested in Australian refineries.[52] These exploratory efforts, however, did not lead to a purchase contract. Australia's crude oil imports have been declining since 1970, owing to rising domestic oil production. China also faces competition from Indonesian crude in the Australian market.

Australia has not participated significantly in energy equipment exports to China. The only recorded transaction was the sale of two gas turbine helicopter engines (Hawker de Havilland, $318,000) in 1976 for the Messerschmitt offshore supply helicopters ordered from West Germany.[53]

The two countries have, however, carried on technical exchange in petroleum exploration and coal mining. Australian oil company representatives were shown China's offshore drilling operations in July 1974, and a return Chinese delegation visited Australian oilfields in 1975. A delegation from China's Coal Mining Society attended the Seventh International Conference on Coal Dressing in Australia in May 1976, and Australia sent a delegation of coal-mining experts to the PRC in October 1976.[54] Peking is probably interested in Australian open-cast coal-mining technology and in coal preparation methods—both areas in which the Chinese coal industry lags behind world standards. These technical exchanges could lead to Chinese purchases of Australian mining and dressing equipment.

Australia and China are potential competitors in Asian energy commodity markets. Companies involved in Australia's coal industry are particularly concerned about China's rising exports of coal to Japan (Chapter 12). My projections indicate that the Australian worries in this regard are well founded, since the PRC could potentially export 10–15 million tons of coal per year by 1985. Furthermore, certain Australian companies have recently expanded their steaming coal operations in anticipation of new contracts with Japanese thermal power plants that are now under construction. The Japanese market for steaming coal is limited, and it is precisely this market that Chinese coal is expected to enter.

Constraints on Energy Relations with the Industrial Countries

We began Chapter 4 with a brief analysis of China's dual energy personality—high domestic energy production capabilities and low per capita energy consumption life-style. The effect of this unique domestic energy balance is reflected throughout China's energy relations with the industrial countries. On the one hand, China is overtaking the industrial world in aggregate energy capabilities. The Chinese government would like to complete this process of energy modernization within the remaining decades of this century. China should be able to accomplish this goal if current growth rates persist and political disruptions of critical energy industries are minimized. With four times the population of the United

States or the Soviet Union, however, the PRC will continue to feel the per capita energy consumption constraint for some time to come. The most important direct result of this constraint will be that domestic energy consumption requirements will continue to rise rapidly, setting a sharply defined ceiling on potential energy commodity exports. The revenue generated by coal, petroleum, and possibly natural gas exports will in turn be needed to pay for the importation of advanced energy production equipment and technology from the industrial world. As vividly illustrated by the 1974 Chinese balance-of-payments crisis, equipment and plant imports will be closely tied to commodity exports. There is no simple escape from this dilemma. The great energy consumption needs of the Chinese population set a basic constraint within which energy policies toward the industrial world must be formulated.

There are international policy constraints, as well as domestic production and consumption constraints, that set limits on the formulation of the energy policies of the People's Republic of China toward the industrial world. The security constraint ranks at the head of the list for China's policy makers. The basic defense requirements of the PRC set parameters for energy relations with the United States in the 1950's and 1960's and for energy relations with the Soviet Union in the 1960's and 1970's. Energy trade relations with the United States were out of the question as long as there existed a state of hostile armed confrontation ("containment" in Washington's lexicon) between the two countries around China's perimeter. Chinese government leaders were constrained in a number of ways by their growing security problems with the Soviet Union. After 1960, trade in energy commodities declined sharply, forcing China back on its own energy resources and energy equipment industries. Such energy equipment imports as China could afford had to be purchased from the West and Japan. Peking had to take extensive precautions to defend its vulnerable energy industries in the northeast and began to resist any Japanese moves toward cooperation with Moscow in Siberian energy development projects. The prospect of Soviet-Japanese cooperation along China's sensitive northern border led Peking to offer surplus crude for export to Japan. Even China's offshore oil development could potentially be limited by vulnerability to Soviet naval capabilities or by a political liaison between Moscow and Taipei. In all of these ways the security problem with the Soviet Union has set parameters within which China's energy policies must be carefully chosen.

Sino-Soviet security relations also act to constrain the development of energy trade and technology exchange between the PRC and the countries of Eastern Europe. Aside from Romania and possibly Yugoslavia, China's energy relations with Eastern Europe have dwindled steadily since 1960 under the shadow of the Soviet presence in that region. This trend will likely be reversed only by a loosening of the Soviet grip in Eastern Europe.

The geopolitical factor is another international constraint that functions to limit Peking's energy policy options. China's role as an energy-commodity-exporting country has been sharply limited by distance and transportation considerations. Negotiations with Italy, West Germany, Australia, and the United States for the export of Chinese coal and petroleum have failed to produce any major results, largely owing to the comparative cost of transporting Chinese energy commodities in relatively limited quantities to relatively distant points around the globe. The Middle East, Indonesia, the North Sea, and the North Slope of Alaska all enjoy transportation advantages over China as sources of crude oil for the world market outside of Asia. That leaves Japan as the only industrial oil-importing country in China's potential energy commodity market region. This situation will change only in the event that China's offshore fossil fuel reserves prove larger than expected, generating a sufficient surplus to permit bulk transport and lower costs per ton. China could overcome the transportation differential by lowering prices, but would still lack a sufficient export surplus to justify costly shifts in the global oil transportation network. Without huge new additions to reserves, China will remain a commercially weak member of the international energy market, with less to offer than even the smaller OPEC oil exporters.

Security considerations, the geopolitical factor, and traditional political and cultural ties will continue to contain the effective radius of China's international energy exports to the Asian region—particularly East and Southeast Asia. The PRC will reach beyond this radius for additional energy equipment imports, but again only within the constraints imposed by foreign-exchange and balance-of-payments considerations, as well as by Peking's preference for self-reliance as the fundamental political guideline in its energy development. And so we turn next to China's energy relations with Asia. In this instance, because of the importance of the regional factor in China's international energy policies, industrial (Japan) and nonindustrial Asian countries will be considered together within the same analytical context.

Chapter 6

China's Energy Policies in Asia: Japan

Within the framework of China's international energy policies, no region is more important than Asia and no country within the region is more important than Japan. The thrust of China's domestic energy development is part of the process of modernization occurring throughout Asia. Because of its size and enormous aggregate economic and political strength, China increasingly looms as a major power in Asia. The People's Republic is joining the Soviet Union, the United States, and Japan in terms of its ability to influence the future of the region. In the energy field, China has sufficient fossil-fuel and hydraulic resources to supply its domestic energy needs and still export some energy commodities to other Asian countries.

Sino-Japanese energy relations will be at the heart of China's future energy policies in Asia. The development of the hydrocarbon resources thought to exist in the continental shelf will be contingent on the state of this relationship. The political futures of Korea and Taiwan will be influenced by future developments in Sino-Japanese relations. Third World Asian countries will find themselves moving in a political space defined by polar relations with Japan and China. The two Asian giants are potential competitors and potential partners. Both the competitive and the cooperative nature of their relationship will persist for some time. Each will offer the other something critical, but neither will submit to the ideological and structural character of the other. The relationship, in short, will retain its ambivalence.

Energy Relations with Japan

The special energy relationship that has been developing between China and Japan during the 1970's should initially be understood in terms of the crude aggregate statistics that characterize the energy systems of the two countries. It would be difficult to find another example of such disparate energy production capabilities and consumption requirements anywhere in Asia. Japan's commercial energy development began more than half a century ago. Rapid increases in both aggregate and per capita energy consumption in Japan were based on the importation of ever-greater amounts of coal and petroleum from abroad. An oil embargo provided part of the rationale for the Japanese attack on Pearl Harbor in 1941. It would not be an exaggeration to suggest that Japan imported the foundation for its economic miracle of the 1960's in the holds of supertankers carrying crude oil from the Persian Gulf. By 1975, Japan was importing 90 percent of its total domestic energy requirement in the form of crude or refined petroleum products.[1] Thus, all aspects of Japan's economic modernization can be traced to petroleum imports, from the electric power required to light new high-rise cities to the rapid increase in labor productivity. Any serious disruption of supply would constitute a devastating blow to the Japanese economy. The success of OPEC in wresting control of the world petroleum market from the multinationals and the Arab oil embargo hang like a dark cloud over the Japanese hope for continuing prosperity. Oil price increases, an economic boon to producing countries, could largely be blamed for the end of Japan's growth spurt. Even Japan's famed industrial drive has been restrained by the rising cost of fuel and the heavy balance-of-payments pressures generated by oil imports.

The most superficial glance at the Chinese energy balance reveals a production-consumption pattern almost exactly inverse to the Japanese one. The PRC has always produced more than 95 percent of its energy requirements domestically. Even at the height of dependence on the Soviet Union for petroleum supplies, China was importing only about 3 million metric tons per year of Soviet petroleum products—a far cry from the scale of Japanese crude oil imports from the Middle East. On the other hand, China's level of per capita energy consumption is still quite low by world standards, owing to the large and still growing Chinese population. Even with great effort, it will take the PRC at least another quarter-century to approach Japanese energy consumption standards. The potential size of domestic energy consumption requirements in China will constrain every aspect of Chinese energy policy for the indefinite future. Japan has considerable latitude for experiments with alternative energy production systems and for growth through energy conservation. China has no such latitude and must proceed with every form of energy development available (plus conservation) or risk a stagnant economy and frustration of the deep-seated ambition for a "modern socialist" standard of living. All aspects of Chinese energy export policy and equipment import policy must be geared to this objective. Japan's energy vulnerability is its lack of resources. China's energy vulnerability is its abundant population.

These differences between the Japanese and Chinese energy balances have led many observers to emphasize the potential interrelationship between the two energy systems.[2] Given their geographic proximity, Japan's advanced energy technology, and China's vast energy resources, it appears obvious at first glance that a long-range exchange of Chinese hydrocarbons for Japanese plant and equipment would be in the interest of both. Indeed, the prospects for such an exchange of energy resources and technology have often figured prominently in the rhetoric of the current rapprochement between the two countries. It must be recognized, however, that there are a number of constraints operating on energy relations between China and Japan, and that these constraints are durable. Direct trade in energy commodities still represents a minuscule proportion of the energy balance of each. In 1977 China exported about 1–2 percent of its total primary energy production to Japan. Japan imported about 1–2 percent of its aggregate energy consumption from China. Although substantial in absolute terms, the import of Japanese energy production equipment represents only a very small proportion of China's total industrial capital investment and a minor market for Japan's industrial plant and equipment exports. While remaining aware of the future potential of a Sino-Japanese energy partnership, the researcher and policy maker alike must take the constraints operating on that partnership into account.

The energy relationship with Japan is the keystone of China's energy policies in Asia, and Sino-Japanese energy relations in turn are fundamentally constrained by the nature of political relations between the two countries. Just as the domestic energy consumption requirement imposes a ceiling on China's long-range energy export potential, so the political relationship with Japan imposes a framework of policy options within which Sino-Japanese energy relations must develop. Ideologically, Peking groups Japan with the Second World—the smaller industrial countries of Europe. Japan, like Europe, is thought to be an arena of struggle between the superpowers and to lie politically between the United States and Soviet Union and the Third World countries. But practically, Japan is the most important market-economy country in China's energy policies. The Sino-Japanese relationship also lies at the heart of the territorial dispute over the continental shelf.

There are three basic constraints on the development of Sino-Japanese energy commodity trade—limits on Chinese fossil-fuel resources and production, domestic Chinese energy consumption requirements, and the state of political and commercial relations with Japan. This chapter will focus on the third constraint, leaving energy resources and production and the domestic Chinese energy consumption requirement to other sections of the book. Before dealing directly with Sino-Japanese energy commodity trade and other aspects of energy relations between the two countries, we will digress a considerable distance into the history of political and commercial relations between Japan and China since 1945. It will be shown through a historical narrative that powerful centrifugal political forces operate on commercial relations to condition and limit trade. The sensitivity of commercial trade to political issues is critical to understanding the state of energy commodity trade in the mid-1970's. Time and again, political issues have intervened in the development of trade relations. Historical issues that have disrupted trade relations include security relations, the recognition issue, the U.N. issue, the nuclear weapons issue, the peace treaty, territorial issues, the domestic politics of both sides, and the personal politics of various Japanese and Chinese leaders.

On the Japanese side, the handling of these issues was conditioned by the special dependence of Japan on the United States in foreign affairs. In the early 1970's, this dependency was replaced by what may be termed "vulnerability." At present, though not dependent on a single country for direction, Japanese foreign policy is unusually vulnerable to outside influence from a number of directions. Unless this vulnerability is clearly understood in its historical context, the importance and durability of the political constraint on Sino-Japanese energy relations will be underestimated. It will be repeatedly pointed out that the political constraint is less tangible, but just as real, as production and consumption constraints operating on energy commodity trade between the two countries. To a great extent, the two governments have recognized the importance of the political constraint on energy relations and are learning to operate more easily within the boundaries set by the political factor. But Western observers, expecting a sort of mechanical economic "rationality" in trade relations, are prone to miss the political constraint entirely. No projection of future energy commodity trade or energy equipment trade will be even remotely accurate without an allowance for the long-range political constraint on energy relations.

Political Relations with Japan

Observers of the historical development of Sino-Japanese relations have often noted the cultural and geographic affinities and the deep structural divergence between the two societies. The tension between affinity and divergence had persisted into the contemporary era.

Japan was profoundly indebted to the traditional Chinese influences, ranging from its written script and ethical foundations to its educational system and religious practices [so that] even the Anglo-American cultural bonds were hardly closer than those linking Japan and China. However, the general pattern of interaction between these two Asian neighbors in the postwar period up until 1972 was characterized by a mixture of diplomatic, ideological, and strategic conflicts and economic and cultural cooperation.[3]

China's political relations with Japan have always been intense. The Japanese invasion of China in the 1930's was one of the main reasons for the rise to power of the Chinese Communist Party, but it caused 15 million Chinese deaths and set back the modernization of Chinese society by decades. Thus, the initial stages of Sino-Japanese relations after the establishment of the PRC in 1949 were marked by acrimony and recriminations;[4] and the bitterness of the war could still be detected in the Chinese attitude toward Japan until the establishment of diplomatic relations in 1972.

The Japanese surrender in August 1945 placed the administration of foreign affairs directly in the hands of the United States occupation authorities, just as it gave the United States the heavy responsibility for reconstructing Japanese society, dismantling the Japanese empire, and modernizing the Japanese government. It also placed the United States in a preeminent position of military power in the Pacific. Partly as a response to American power, and partly for ideologial reasons, the Chinese and Soviet governments signed the Treaty of Friendship, Alliance, and Mutual Assistance in February 1950. The treaty specifically provided for a Sino-Soviet alignment against revival of Japanese military power in East Asia.[5] The United States and Japan reacted to the Sino-Soviet treaty and to the Korean War by further strengthening the U.S. military presence in Japan and the Ryukyu Islands. Japan, the United States, and 49 other countries signed a peace treaty at the San Francisco Conference in September 1951 over the objections of China, the Soviet Union, and Eastern Europe. Japan renounced all territorial claims to its Pacific empire, including Taiwan, without specifying the future locus of sovereignty for these territories.[6] Prime Minister Yoshida Shigeru simultaneously signed a secret mutual-security treaty with the United States directed against the Sino-Soviet alliance. This security treaty initiated a new period of indirect dependence on the United States for foreign-policy guidance.

One of the first ways in which the United States chose to exercise its indirect control of Japanese foreign relations was to exert great pressure on Tokyo to sign a peace treaty with Taipei rather than Peking.[7] The Tokyo-Taipei treaty, signed on April 28, 1952, helped legitimize U.S. protection of Chiang Kai-shek's refugee government on Taiwan and also drove the final wedge between the Japanese government and the government of the PRC. It also crystallized the Taiwan issue as the central point of contention in China's relations with both the United States and Japan. The treaty not only denied Peking's territorial ambitions toward Taiwan but also placed the weight of the Japanese-American security treaty behind Chiang's claim to legitimacy as president of the "Republic of China." Even the establishment of Sino-Japanese diplomatic relations has not fully disengaged Tokyo from this tangle, which lingers in the form of the territorial dispute over the continental shelf.

Tokyo remained sensitive to pressure from Washington on the Taiwan issue throughout the 1950's and 1960's. Each time there was a move by either Japan or China in the direction of improved political relations, Washington would intervene and the overtures would collapse. This cycle of accommodation, intervention, and collapse occurred in 1955 when Hatoyama Ichiro replaced Yoshida as Prime Minister and China's Bandung diplomacy was in flower. In December 1954 the United States and Taiwan signed a mutual-defense treaty, and in January 1955 the U.S. Congress passed a resolution on the Taiwan Strait question. The Japanese government came under intense pressure from both Washington and Taipei, both of which held a veto over Japan's entry into the United Nations (December 1956). Despite two secret Chinese initiatives in 1955 to get diplomatic talks started, the Japanese position hardened, the Chinese published the secret correspondence, and political accommodation collapsed.[8]

Under the "San Francisco system" commercial relations were less sensitive than political relations to American influence. Four "private" trade agreements were signed between the Chinese government and representatives of Japanese commercial interests between 1952 and 1958. All four received the tacit approval of the Japanese government and the Keidanren (Federation of Economic Organizations). The trade conducted under these agreements was restricted by U.S.-sponsored Cocom regulations, but the U.S. State Department had granted Japan permission to trade with the PRC as early as March 1950.[9] China viewed the private trade agreements as an opening wedge for recognition and the establishment of formal trade and diplomatic relations. Japanese business viewed the agreements as an opening wedge into the potentially lucrative Chinese market for Japanese technology and manufactured goods. Washington grumbled privately and Taipei protested publicly, but the trade continued to develop.

By 1958, however, commercial relations suffered the same fate as the 1955 diplomatic initiatives. Kishi Nobusuke, who became Prime Minister in February 1957, had strong personal commitments to both the United States and Taiwan. The PRC launched a verbal attack on Kishi and began direct support for the Japan Socialist Party (JSP). Tension was increased by the new radical phase in China's domestic politics (Great Leap Forward) and by the accelerating crisis in the Taiwan Strait. Against this background, Japan's continuing diplomatic and political relations with Taiwan precipitated the Nagasaki flag incident. A Japanese youth desecrated a small Chinese flag at a stamp exhibit in a Nagasaki department store. China chose to make this event a major international issue and suspended all economic transactions, exchange programs, and repatriation negotiations in May 1958. Trade was reduced to an insignificant trickle of contracts with pro-Peking companies.

The trade hiatus continued until 1961, when China again began to permit some trade on a "friendship" basis with certain Japanese companies or subsidiaries that were willing to adopt formally pro-China political positions. This friendship trade was conducted on a contract-by-contract basis through the semiannual Canton Trade Fairs. Starting in 1962, it was supplemented by semiofficial "memorandum trade agreements" that were negotiated by members of the Japanese Diet and that included provisions for a minimum total annual trade volume of about $100 million. The practice of memorandum trade continued throughout the 1960's as the formal basis for commercial relations between the two countries. But in fact the friendship trade contracts negotiated at Canton continued to expand to several times the volume of the memorandum trade.[10]

Despite the memorandum trade agreements and the steady increase in friendship trade, political factors continued to plague Sino-Japanese commercial relations in the 1960's. In August 1963 the Kurashiki Rayon Company arranged Japanese Export-Import Bank credits for the deferment of payment on the sale of a vinylon plant to the PRC.[11] The U.S. State Department objected to this arrangement on the grounds that it constituted de facto government-to-government trade relations with Peking. Chiang Kai-shek recalled Taipei's ambassador to Tokyo and suspended government purchases of Japanese products. Kishi succumbed to these pressures and had former Prime Minister Yoshida write a personal letter to Chiang pledging not to extend further credits to the PRC through the Export-Import Bank. The "Yoshida letter" became the keystone in Japanese trade policy toward China for the remainder of the decade. Peking, of course, was outraged by the Yoshida letter when it became public in February 1965 and called for its immediate nullification—without success. The PRC subsequently canceled contracts and negotiations for some 40 industrial processing plants, including large-scale textile and fertilizer plants. The Kurashiki vinylon plant was the last major Japanese industrial plant imported by the PRC until 1972.[12]

Complete plant purchases were shifted to West European companies in the interim. Trade with Japan was limited to raw materials and manufactured products, and excluded potentially important commerce in capital equipment. Once again the centrifugal force of Japan's external dependence in foreign affairs proved greater than the gravitational attraction to China.

Three other international issues complicated the development of Sino-Japanese relations during the 1960's—the China representation problem at the U.N., the development of Chinese nuclear weapons, and the reversion of Okinawa to Japanese control. At the United Nations, Japan showed the same sensitivity to American policy as in the matter of the status of Taiwan. Tokyo joined Washington in support and advocacy of the "important question" resolution, which effectively barred the PRC from U.N. membership for the entire decade. When it became evident in the autumn of 1970 that the Albanian resolution supporting Peking's membership had gained a plurality, Japan joined the United States in seeking a separate U.N. seat for the Republic of China, an outcome that would have in effect further extended exclusion of the PRC. Japanese and American lobbying efforts on behalf of Taipei continued for a year until the PRC was admitted and Taiwan ejected on October 25, 1971.

The nuclear issue is a two-edged sword in Sino-Japanese relations. Japan has objected officially to the atmospheric testing of Chinese nuclear weapons since the first test of an atomic bomb in 1964. Aside from the military threat posed by Chinese atomic weapons, the testing produces fallout over Japan and each new test arouses a public outcry. On the other hand, China fears the potential for Japanese nuclear development. Japan has 19 nuclear power plants in operation, four plants under construction, and plans for another eight. Japan has also successfully launched earth satellites and has the rocket potential for a ballistic missile force. The United States continues to offer Japan its "nuclear umbrella" against attack by either China or the Soviet Union. Japan's nuclear dependence on the United States may be expected to continue as long as Japanese society successfully resists the acquisition of nuclear weapons.

The United States also effectively used the reversion of Okinawa to Japanese control to gain leverage over the conduct of Japanese foreign relations during the late 1960's and early 1970's. Prime Minister Sato Eisaku considered the Okinawa reversion treaty a principal mission of his tenure in office and refused to resign until reversion took place in May 1972.[13] Okinawa was important to Japan both as a territorial matter and as a symbol of the ending of indirect dependence on the United States in foreign affairs that was part of the "San Francisco system."

Japan was completely stripped of its territories in 1945, including the Ryukyus and the four northern islands (Habomai, Shikotan, Kunashiri, and Etorofu). Regaining the Ryukyus from the United States and the four northern islands from the Soviet Union represents to the Japanese public the reestablishment of territorial integrity and national sovereignty. Hence the United States was able to extend the life of the "San Francisco system" by protracting negotiations for Okinawa and the Ryukyus. Sato's personal political inclination was to favor Taipei, and he traveled to Taiwan for state visits and made his antagonism to the PRC clear on many public occasions. The Chinese press returned the feeling and openly attacked every aspect of Sato's foreign policies. Chinese resentment of Sato was so deep that Chou En-lai repeatedly refused to deal with him in the months that followed the "Nixon shock" in late 1971, preferring to await the Japanese elections and a new Japanese prime minister before opening the door to diplomatic relations with Japan. But over and above his personal antipathy toward the PRC, Sato continued to defer to the U.S. position on Asian affairs in order to ensure the smooth reversion of the Ryukyu Islands. He publicly supported the U.S. position in Indochina in a communiqué that followed his November 1967 meeting with President Johnson. And he went further in November 1969 when he signed a joint communiqué with President Nixon that explicitly identified Japanese security with that of South Korea and Taiwan.[14] This gave official Japanese support for Nixon's program of Asianization of the Indochina conflict and containment of communism in Asia. By 1971 Sato was in serious political trouble in Japan over the rigidity and deference he had displayed in his China policy in the name of the Okinawa reversion treaty.[15]

Domestic political considerations on both sides of the Yellow Sea have also exerted a powerful brake on the momentum of Sino-Japanese relations. Chinese foreign policy has repeatedly proved sensitive to domestic political competition and the campaign cycle. Both the Great Leap Forward and the Cultural Revolution, radical phases in the Chinese political cycle, disrupted commercial relations with Japan. The Great Leap Forward was partially responsible for the two-year hiatus in trade relations (1958–60). The Cultural Revolution drastically lowered industrial production in 1967–68, so that China was not able to fulfill its export commitments to Japan. Political events since the Cultural Revolution—the Lin Piao affair, the anti-Teng campaign, and the current purge of the "Gang of Four"—have also been reflected in the general tone of Sino-Japanese relations and in commercial relations. Despite the apparent consolidation of political power in the post-Mao period in the hands of a group favoring strong trade ties to Japan, there is some likelihood that political competition within China will continue to restrain and disrupt external relations from time to time.

On the Japanese side, the effects of domestic politics on relations with China have been equally obvious. The Japanese political structure allows considerable latitude for the foreign policy preferences of the prime minister. Thus the personal attitudes of Kishi and Sato toward the PRC were among the most important factors restraining the development of Sino-Japanese relations during their tenures in office. Conversely, the moderate views of Hatoyama and Tanaka led to diplomatic initiatives toward the PRC. The structure of personal attitudes toward China was, of course, strongly influenced by the intensity of commitment each prime minister felt toward Taiwan.

Peking has also insisted on intruding directly in domestic Japanese politics, a matter of considerable sensitivity to the ruling Liberal Democratic Party (LDP). Faced with Kishi's hostility in the mid-1950's, the PRC actively aligned itself with the LDP's principal adversary, the Japan Socialist Party. Peking has also encouraged pro-China factions within the LDP itself, inviting many delegations of LDP Diet members for visits to the PRC, with selection based on known sympathy for prescribed political positions. Pro-China forces within Japan have mobilized demonstrations on the Taiwan question and such major issues as the United States–Japan security treaty. China developed its "people's diplomacy" in the laboratory of Japanese politics, sponsoring friendship associations, pro-China business organizations, and party factions, and using the prized invitation to visit China as a reward for cooperative groups. Not that Peking has been alone in stimulating this brand of intercultural contact—both South Korea and Taiwan have long engaged in similar practices designed to strengthen their political standing in Tokyo. Commercial relations have been the most active arena of struggle among externally sponsored groups. But the general reaction of the Japanese government has been to attempt to avoid direct pressure from either the PRC or Taiwan, and to avoid antagonizing either. This reaction encouraged an official "nonpolicy" posture, which left the Sato government unaware of, and then embarrassed by, the Sino-American rapprochement.

Richard Nixon announced his impending visit to the PRC on July 15, 1971.[16] The Sato cabinet was in session when it was informed, just hours before the public announcement, of Nixon's plans. The effect on the Sato government was apparently something of a cross between paralysis and panic.[17] Japan, dependent on Washington for more than 20 years for the direction of its policies toward China, had been completely outflanked by the new Sino-American relationship. The event has since been designated the "Nixon shock" in the Japanese political lexicon. The breakthrough was particularly embarrassing to Sato, who had based his China policy on public support for the American position in Asia through the Sato-Johnson and Sato-Nixon communiqués. Sato initiated a series of gestures toward China during what was left of his tenure in office, but Chou En-lai firmly refused to open recognition negotiations with the Sato government or to invite Sato Eisaku to Peking.[18]

In the spring and early summer of 1972, Tanaka Kakuei based an important part of his election campaign on the China recognition issue. He vowed to travel to Peking and normalize Sino-Japanese relations, and repeated his pledge after his election to the LDP presidency on July 5, 1972.[19] Chou En-lai responded positively to this initiative and on August 11 formally invited Tanaka to visit Peking. A series of high-level LDP delegations traveled to China during the following month, before Tanaka's arrival in Peking on September 25. After four days of summit talks, Tanaka and Chou signed a nine-point communiqué providing for Japanese recognition of the People's Republic of China; diplomatic, cultural, and commercial relations between the two governments; mutual noninterference; Japanese "understanding and respect" for the Chinese position on the question of Taiwan; the renunciation of force in relations between the two countries; negotiation of a new Sino-Japanese peace treaty; and termination of the "abnormal state of affairs" between China and Japan.[20] Chou and Tanaka accomplished in two months what the Chinese and Japanese governments had failed to accomplish in two decades.

Did the establishment of diplomatic relations end the "San Francisco system" dependence of Japanese foreign relations on the United States? Did the resolution of the Taiwan issue pave the way for smooth development of commercial relations? Were the constraints imposed by domestic politics in China and Japan written off at the stroke of a pen? Did gravitational affinities finally overcome centrifugal tensions? The answers to these questions are extremely important to a successful analysis of the future prospects for Sino-Japanese energy relations.

Tanaka did advertise diplomatic relations with the PRC under the signboard of foreign policy independence, both before and after his successful campaign to become prime minister. And indeed, the Nixon shock had shattered the Japanese illusion of partnership with the United States in Asia. Perhaps Japan's indirect but explicit dependence under the "San Francisco system" was finally laid to rest by both the Okinawa reversion treaty and the normalization of relations with China. China renounced its indemnity claims and Japan set aside its peace treaty with Taipei. The deep shadow of the war and the Japanese occupation of

China had finally receded to the dim memory of another generation. Japan had reconstructed its international prestige, as had China. Both had risen from the ashes of military destruction. Both had built what amounted to a domestic economic miracle. Both had established conventional military defense capabilities without acquiring a viable offensive capability. Both had entered the United Nations after prolonged absence from the international community (Japan in 1956, China in 1971). Japan had the technology, China the resources. A partnership was the obvious next step.

However, the end of indirect dependence on the United States was not the beginning of foreign policy independence for Japan. The very act of establishing diplomatic relations with China was a reaction to the sudden American initiative. That reaction alone was not enough to end Japan's vulnerability in the international system. Japan continues to be vulnerable to the outside world on three fronts. First, Japan lacks an adequate resource base for industrial production and growth, particularly in energy resources. Second, Japan is vulnerable to the conventional military power of the Soviet Union in the Pacific region. Third, Japan by choice does not possess an arsenal of nuclear weapons. These basic vulnerabilities continue to exert centrifugal pressure on Sino-Japanese relations, particularly energy relations.

Japan's basic foreign policy vulnerabilities have surfaced in a number of ways since 1972. The lack of an adequate resource base, Japan's Achilles' heel since the turn of the century, continues to influence the direction of Japanese foreign relations. After the Arab oil embargo of late 1973, the Japanese government totally capitulated to the political demands of the Middle East oil-producing governments, shunning Israel and voting the Arab line in the U.N. The Japanese effort to develop Asian supplies of fossil-fuel resources has resulted in entanglement in the Sino-Soviet dispute. And the staggering foreign-exchange burden of higher oil prices has exerted tremendous pressure on Japanese trade policies.

Japan's regional security problem with the Soviet Union also reduces Tokyo's flexibility in relations with Asian neighbors. Moscow has proved intransigent on the question of the northern islands and in the fisheries dispute with Japan. Lacking the conventional military means to enforce its position, Japan must continue to try to obtain concessions through the negotiation of the long-awaited peace treaty with the USSR, and through participation in costly cooperative development projects such as exploring for oil off the coast of Sakhalin Island. Any Japanese concession to Moscow is immediately greeted with a hostile reaction from Peking. Even the strength of Japan's territorial claims to the Tiaoyutai and negotiation of the offshore oil development agreement with South Korea are affected by the fear that any concession will lead to a stronger Soviet grip on the northern islands. Tokyo is afraid that any territorial concession might lead to a chain of such concessions.

Japan's continuing lack of nuclear weapons further inhibits the development of a truly independent foreign policy. Japan began an atomic research program during the Second World War, which was suspended under the Occupation and then reinstated for theoretical and civilian applications in 1952.[21] On November 14, 1955, Japan and the United States entered into an agreement to cooperate in promoting nuclear energy research. An Atomic Energy Commission was established in 1956 and initiated an experimental reactor program. The development of nuclear power in Japan was slowed by American caution and by the high capital cost of nuclear power plants. The import of American nuclear power equipment, technology, and fuel has also proved a sensitive issue in public and government debate. By the early 1970's, Japan had constructed a substantial nuclear-power-generating capacity based on imported American enriched uranium. The Japanese government would like to free itself from direct dependence on the United States for enriched uranium and has a spent-fuel reprocessing plant at Tokai Mura, built with French technical assistance, that extracts plutonium 239 from spent fuel rods and thus extends the life of the fuel. Washington objects to the operation of the Tokai Mura plant on the grounds that it violates safeguard provisions of the Sino-American uranium supply agreement. A tentative agreement was reached in June 1977 that permits the use of the plant for "co-processing" or "partial co-processing"—procedures that yield a plutonium-uranium mixture not suitable for weapons applications.[22]

A similar pattern of continuing tension is revealed if one examines closely the development of commercial relations since 1972. Far from improving prospects for Sino-Japanese commercial relations, the establishment of diplomatic relations appears to have led to new difficulties. After 20 years of trade with and investment in Taiwan, Japan was in no position to simply abandon it for the Chinese market. From 1965 until 1973, Japan's trade surplus with Taiwan was three times that with the PRC.[23] Professor Gene T. Hsiao has accurately described the new Sino-Japanese relationship as "ambivalent." Hsiao traces in magnificent detail the development of negotiations over the proposed civil aviation agreement between China and Japan—the first of several such proposed agreements that were supposed to constitute the backbone of the new commercial relationship between the two countries.[24] It took two years to negotiate a simple agreement for direct air flights between Tokyo and major Chinese cities. In the process, all the old demons reappeared—the triangular relationship with Taipei (China and Taiwan would not park airplanes at the same airport), right-wing street demonstrations in Japan, vitriolic articles in the *People's Daily,* flag and emblem confrontations, and the suspension of bilateral civil aviation relations between Taiwan and Japan (a costly matter for Japanese business). Hsiao further documents the continuation of Japanese commercial relations with Taiwan after 1972 and demonstrates that Taiwan continued to outrank the PRC as a Japanese trading and investment partner.[25]

None of this is to suggest that Sino-Japanese commercial relations did not make great strides following the establishment of diplomatic relations. Banking arrangements and currency exchange rates were normalized. The aviation agreement was eventually completed. A fisheries agreement was reached. China's purchase of Japanese plant and equipment was added to the trade roster, as was Japan's import of Chinese crude petroleum. An undersea cable was laid. Negotiations began on long-range government-to-government trade agreements. But throughout one sees the indelible imprint of the political factor. Taiwan did not disappear at the moment of diplomatic recognition. Neither did Japan's special relationship with South Korea. Every commercial accord between Peking and Tokyo is carefully designed to protect both parties against a violation of their own political and economic objectives in East Asia. The familiar ambivalence persists between partnership and competition, self-reliance and development, security and independence, cultural attraction and structural repulsion, gravitational affinity and centrifugal divergence. Japan's vulnerability to outside influence in the making of foreign policy creates tension in the new relationship with the PRC. The ambivalence in Sino-Japanese political relations is less tangible but just as real as the constraint imposed by China's domestic energy consumption requirement.

Sino-Japanese trade relations moved at a desultory pace during 1977, declining even further than in 1976.[26] But high-level trade negotiations in September and November moved the two countries slowly toward conclusion of the long-awaited trade agreement.[27] The agreement was slowed on the Japanese side by a struggle between the petroleum-refining industry and the steel industry over the level of Chinese crude petroleum that should be imported over the five years of the agreement. Refiners, fearing the high cost of specialized facilities to handle Chinese crude, resisted raising future imports beyond current levels. The steel industry, suffering from a long slump because of market limitations, was eager to import more crude oil in order to sell China more steel. The struggle raged back and forth at high levels in Japanese industry and government, and was another round in the traditional Japanese ambivalence toward the PRC. Peking, on the other hand, pressed for a higher level of crude oil export to Japan and firmly resisted any reduction in the market price of Chinese crude to reflect its handling difficulties. The Chinese government was also annoyed about Japanese delays in signing the peace treaty.

By January 1978, however, it became clear that the two sides were close to a final settlement. The China-Japan Long-Term Trade Agreement was signed in Peking on February 16, 1978.[28] The agreement caused a stir in international trading circles, but was far from a radical departure from past practices. It committed each side to exports of about $10 billion between 1978 and 1982. This represented steady growth in the level of Sino-Japanese trade, but not a big jump. In 1978, for example, trade will exceed $5 billion, up from about $3.5 billion in 1977, a low year.[29] Energy commodity trade, an important feature of the agreement, was slated to grow from 1978 through 1981 at just under 15 percent per year (Table 6.1). In 1982, however, the agreement calls for a sudden jump in crude oil trade, bringing a 50 percent increase in energy commodity trade in a single year. It is impossible to tell at this time exactly what will be the impact of the long-term trade agreement. If Japanese refiners found it impossible to construct the necessary hydrocracking equipment by 1982, the projected crude oil imports for that year might be substantially lowered or deferred. On the other hand, it appears that there will be little trouble fulfilling the general targets of bilateral trade stipulated by the agreement, given the brisk pace of trade in 1978. Indeed, much as was the case in the memorandum trade agreements of the early 1960's, the volume of actual trade will probably exceed the terms of the agreement by a considerable margin. The ink had hardly dried on the agreement when Chinese and Japanese negotiators were busy trying to extend it to 1985 or 1990 at even higher annual trade levels.

Energy Commodity Trade with Japan

The importance of political relations to the development of energy commodity trade between China and Japan was evident from the earliest days of the People's Republic. After the U.S. State Department gave Japan permission to trade with the PRC in March 1950, coal was one of the initial commodities China exported to Japan.[30] But the Korean War and the U.S. embargo of December 1950 cut short the first Sino-Japanese effort to establish trade in coal and other commodities.

Sino-Japanese trade in energy commodities resumed in 1953 under the terms of the first private trade agreement. About 140,000 metric tons of coal were shipped to Japan in 1953. Within two years, these coal exports had jumped to half a million tons, twice what the PRC was exporting to the Soviet Union during the same period. However, the political constraint surfaced again in 1958 when this promising coal trade was cut off entirely by the Nagasaki flag incident and disruption of the Chinese coal industry by the Great Leap Forward. As political and commercial relations improved in 1961, coal exports to Japan resumed. At first they were small, but they increased to a peak of more than a million tons in 1967. During the 1960's, high-grade coking and steam coal constituted about 5–10 percent of China's exports to Japan by value.[31] Chinese coal cost Japanese industry about half the price of U.S. coal of comparable quality.[32] The Cultural Revolution reduced the coal export level to 200,000–300,000 metric tons a year, where it remained until 1974.

In 1974, under improving political and commercial conditions, China doubled coal exports to Japan to 400,000–500,000 metric tons. In the same year, both the Japanese steel industry and the electric power industry began to exhibit increased interest in long-range contracts for Chinese raw steam coal and coking coal.[33] Small amounts of boiler coal were imported by Nissho-Iwai for trial burning in the electric power industry. These initial tests were successful, and somewhat larger amounts were purchased at around $20 per metric ton. By 1975, interest in Chinese steam coal had risen sharply in the Japanese electric power industry, and Peking sent a coal mission to Tokyo to discuss a long-range contract with Japan's Power Resources Development Corporation.[34] The Nippon Steel Corporation sent a delegation to the PRC in July 1975 to explore the possibilities for a long-range coking coal contract.[35] By 1976 the prospects for a contract for steam coal exports to Japan from 1980 to 1985 looked favorable. Japan's electric power industry was interested in a stable supply for new coal-fired thermal power plants and was projecting potential coal trade with China at one million tons by 1980 and five million tons by 1985.[36] Yet there were obstacles: the PRC would have to expand its coal-handling port facilities to accommodate Japan's 50,000–100,000-ton carriers, and the price of Chinese steam coal was projected to rise to $30–35 per metric ton. At the height of the contract talks, the Chinese coal industry was hit by the Tangshan earthquake (July 28, 1976), one of the most destructive in Chinese history. The quake destroyed the Kailuan coal complex, the centerpiece of the Chinese mining industry and a key supplier of export coal. The earthquake made it difficult for China to meet its coal export commitments for 1976. Final coal exports in 1976 to Japan were 322,000 metric tons, down from 456,000 tons in 1975 (Table 20.11). Official coal trade data are not yet available for 1977, but I believe that the amount was in the range of 300,000–400,000 metric tons.

TABLE 6.1
Structure of the Sino-Japanese Trade Agreement, 1978–82
(Chinese exports of energy commodities to Japan)

Year	Coal			Crude petroleum (mmt)	Total energy (mmtce)
	Steam (mmt)	Coking (mmt)	Total (mmt)		
1978	0.15–0.20	0.15–0.30	0.3–0.5	7.0	10.8–11.0
1979	0.15–0.20	0.5	0.65–0.70	7.6	12.0–12.1
1980	0.5–0.6	1.0	1.5–1.6	8.0	13.5–13.6
1981	1.0–1.2	1.5	2.5–2.7	9.5	16.7–16.9
1982	1.5–1.7	2.0	3.5–3.7	15.0	26.0–26.2

The long-term trade agreement will substantially affect Chinese coal exports to Japan between 1978 and 1982. Coal trade will be about equally divided between steam coal and coking coal (Table 6.1). This is important, for it indicates that the PRC is entering both the established Japanese market in coking coal and the new market for steam coal. Japan will increase imports of steam coal from negligible current levels to at least 10–15 million tons by 1985 to feed large coal-fired thermal power stations that are currently under construction. My projections indicate that by the mid-1980's, China will be able to fill a substantial proportion of Japan's new steam coal requirements (Chapter 12). Australia, a major coking coal supplier to the Japanese market, is already concerned about Chinese competition for the steam coal market. Japan is also beginning to import some Siberian coal, further crowding the market. Japanese coal requirements will increase rapidly over the next few years, but there will be sharp competition among various regional suppliers for a share of that market.

Aside from the Soviet Union and Eastern Europe, Japan was China's largest trading partner in petroleum products during the 1960's. Starting in 1962, the PRC imported high-grade Japanese industrial lubricants, and Japan imported between 50,000 and 100,000 metric tons of petroleum coke per year, in addition to minor quantities of Chinese mineral wax. This trade was not significant when compared to coal exports or to China's later crude oil exports to Japan. However, it may have helped to establish a valuable trade contact that was later to blossom into large-scale petroleum trade.

Peking began considering long-range crude oil exports to Japan once it discovered that Taching oilfield held substantial reserves that could be economically recovered at the technological level the Chinese oil industry had achieved in the early 1960's. Rumors that China was offering Japanese traders Taching crude filtered through the Canton Trade Fair as early as 1964 and again in 1966.[37] These initial probes came to nothing. The Cultural Revolution intervened in 1967, causing a new low ebb in Sino-Japanese relations and precluding cooperation in any field as sensitive to Peking as petroleum development.

From the very inception of the oil trade in the last months of 1972, the prospects for the export of crude petroleum from China to Japan were fraught with sharp political overtones. During 1972 a succession of major Japanese industrial corporations, including Mitsubishi and Mitsui, had capitulated formally to Chou En-lai's conditions for trade with the PRC.[38] After the establishment of diplomatic relations, memorandum trade was replaced by direct contact between the Ministries of Trade in Tokyo and Peking. The first Chinese initiatives in the direction of crude oil exports are difficult to trace. There were persistent rumors in the autumn of 1972 about the possibility of oil trade. In August, Yoshio Inayama, president of the Nippon Steel Corporation, was reported to have proposed an exchange of Chinese crude for Japanese refined products. An initial agreement was reached for the export of 200,000 metric tons of Taching crude to Japan before Minister for International Trade and Industry Yashuhiro Nakasone visited Peking on January 17–21, 1973.[39] During his meeting with Nakasone, Chou En-lai raised the Chinese offer to a possible one million tons in 1973.[40] The first contract for one million tons was signed the following April with a consortium of Japanese companies formed for the specific purpose of promoting crude oil trade.[41]

The motivation behind the initial Chinese offer of crude petroleum is not difficult to detect. First, Peking was casting about for a commodity that would be of sufficient importance to Japan to properly cement the new commercial relationship between the two countries. Tanaka had made it very clear in his discussions with Chou En-lai that Tokyo intended to continue its commercial ties with Taiwan.[42] The scale of Japanese investment in Taiwan and the flourishing trade with Taiwan precluded a sudden Japanese withdrawal. Tokyo wished simply to reverse the pattern of diplomacy and commerce that had existed before recognition of the PRC. In October 1972, Japan established an "Interchange Association" in Taiwan, staffed by government personnel "on leave." Taipei established its "East Asian Relations Association" with offices in Japan for the same purpose. Against the background of these events, China was looking for a commodity of sufficient value to the Japanese to offset their continuing commercial ties with Taiwan. Oil, long the Achilles' heel of the Japanese economy, was the obvious answer.

Second, Chinese concern over the prospects of long-range Soviet-Japanese cooperation in the development of Siberian energy resources increased sharply in the spring of 1973. An important Chinese mission, headed by Liao Cheng-chih, visited Japan virtually as the first crude oil export agreement was signed (April-May).[43] The task of the Liao mission was to discourage the Japanese government from officially endorsing the use of Japanese capital and technology for the construction of the Ir-kutsk-Nakhodka crude oil pipeline. The Chinese position was simple: Chinese oil could be had for the asking, with no prior investment re-quired. The *quid pro quo* was that Tokyo restrain Japanese industry and finance from pursuing Siberian projects—particularly the pipeline, which had security implications for China related to the Sino-Soviet border confrontation. The combined effects of the crude oil offer, the Liao mission, and growing American concern over the security implica-tions of the pipeline for Soviet naval strength in the Pacific worked mira-cles in Tokyo. Caution replaced optimism in the pipeline negotiations, and the prospects for joint energy development in Siberia began to fade.[44]

The third motivation for China's crude oil offer was commercial. By 1973, Peking was developing a long shopping list for foreign plant and industrial equipment. China's needs were particularly great in the petro-chemical and chemical fertilizer industries. The petrochemical industry was lagging seriously behind the annual increase in crude petroleum and natural gas supplies. By the early 1970's, the PRC had established equipment industries capable of producing basic cracking and refinery components, but Chinese industry still lacked the technology for petro-chemical equipment manufacture. Synthetic fiber plants were particu-larly high on the list of priorities, since synthetic textiles could relieve the pressure on the cotton industry and boost China's textile export capac-ity. Large-scale ammonia and urea plants were also high on the list. Chi-nese agricultural production had steadily expanded since 1949, but per-acre productivity remained relatively low and chemical fertilizer had to be imported at high cost from Japan. Rapid expansion of natural gas production in the early 1970's gave China the potential for high-quality and low-cost chemical fertilizer production. The missing link was large-scale fertilizer plant. By 1973, the world market price of crude petro-leum was rising rapidly under pressure from OPEC, and Peking saw an opportunity to ride the crest of the increases. Crude oil exports to Japan and other Asian countries would provide the foreign exchange China needed for plant and equipment purchases. The crude oil trade also strengthened Peking's bargaining leverage with Japanese corporations eager to sell plants to China: by tying the crude oil trade to plant pur-chase agreements, China managed to pry both higher crude oil prices and better plant purchase terms out of Japanese industry.

It is against this political and commercial background of motivations that China's crude oil export potential should be viewed. In 1973–74, the Chinese government had a direct interest in exaggerating the production and export potential of its petroleum industry. By dangling future crude oil trade before the eyes of oil-hungry Japanese industry, Peking could realize both its political and its commercial objectives—driving a wedge into Japan's remaining ties to Taiwan, destroying the prospects of Soviet-Japanese cooperation agreements in Siberia, and paving the way for favorable plant and equipment purchase terms.

China's crude oil sales campaign took place on a number of different levels. It was conducted at the highest level by Chinese government officials. Premier Chou En-lai himself had discussed the first crude oil contract with Nakasone in January 1973. In January 1974 Chou again raised the matter of China's crude oil potential in a meeting with Japanese Foreign Minister Ohira, "revealing" that China's crude oil production in 1973 had reached 50 million tons.[45] This news startled those foreign observers who had been underestimating the growth rate of Chinese crude petroleum production since the mid-1960's. The sales campaign was even more pronounced in Chinese contacts with Japanese commercial organizations. In September 1973 a Keidanren delegation visited the PRC to press for higher oil exports to Japan. The Chinese hosts solemnly promised that Japan would receive 10 percent of China's crude oil production, or some 40 million tons a year by 1980, if only Tokyo would abstain from collaboration in the Tjumen oil pipeline project in Siberia.[46] On September 17, China's oil tanker "Jinhu" arrived in the Japanese port of Kashima amid great fanfare in the Chinese and Japanese press.[47] By the end of 1973, Peking had managed to convince some Japanese oil experts that as much as 100 million tons of China's crude oil production in 1980 might be available for export to Japan![48]

By 1974, the basic crude oil export pattern had emerged. In that year, Peking contracted with two Japanese groups (International Oil Trading Company and the Japan-China Oil Import Council) for a total of 4.9 million metric tons.[49] Of this quantity, only four million tons were actually delivered in 1974; the remainder was held over for delivery in 1975. The 1974 contracts were negotiated at the height of the Arab oil embargo (November 1973–February 1974), again increasing the dramatic effect of Peking's sales campaign. Moreover, 1974 was the peak year for Chinese plant purchases. The future of a Sino-Japanese exchange of crude petroleum and industrial technology seemed assured.

By early 1975 the first hints began to surface that the crude oil trade might be subject to certain constraints. Vice-Premier Teng Hsiao-ping had once again promised visiting Japanese political leaders, in a meeting on October 20, 1974, that crude oil exports would continue to grow.[50] The combined contracts for 1975 reached 7.8 million tons, including the amount held over from 1974. But the price of Chinese crude had become a point of some concern to Japanese refiners, who reported problems handling the high wax content of Taching-grade crudes. The price of China's crude oil in trade with Japan had been pegged to the price of Indonesia's Minas crude, which was in turn pegged to the price of Arabian light. The price rose from $3.93 per barrel in April 1973 (FOB Dairen) to $4.59/bbl in late 1973.[51] It then skyrocketed to $14.80/bbl in January 1974, under the impact of the Arab oil embargo. This very high price lasted only a few months, and by July 1974 Taching crude had stabilized at $12.85/bbl. Slow price erosion then occurred, with the Chinese offering crude in October 1974 at $12.80/bbl. Then the price simply rose and fell with the international petroleum market. But this situation did not satisfy the Japanese companies receiving Chinese crude. They began to press for substantial price concessions through the two Japanese consortia that had been set up to handle the China petroleum trade.[52] China yielded in February 1975, dropping the price to $12.10/bbl, $0.50 under Minas crude. (The Soviet press thereupon accused Peking of undercutting the Indonesian petroleum industry.[53]) But this minor concession was nowhere near what Japanese refiners were hoping for. During long-term oil trade negotiations initiated in 1975, the Japanese began to press for a baseline price for Chinese crude in the range of $9.10/bbl.[54] The rationale for this demand was simple. Japanese refineries were having problems with the high wax, water, sediment, and residual oil content of the Taching and Shengli crudes shipped from China.[55] This meant that an increasing proportion of the Chinese crude had to be burned without refining in power plants and steel mills. Alternatively, Japanese refiners would be forced to invest in expensive dewaxing and heavy-oil-cracking equipment just after they had finished installing desulfurization equipment to handle Middle East crudes.

The Chinese side, naturally enough, was infuriated by this Japanese position. It both compromised the pride of the fledgling Chinese oil industry and threw a monkey wrench into the future prospects for Sino-Japanese oil trade. The Chinese position on crude oil prices hardened, and Taching crude rose to $12.30/bbl in November. The Japan External Trade Organization (Jetro) meanwhile had begun to reevaluate its early projections of China's crude oil export potential. The 1980 export projection fell from as much as 100 million tons to 50 million tons and then to 35 million tons.[56] There was even some talk of Japanese assistance for construction of a refinery in the PRC for heavy-oil-cracking treatment of Chinese crude before shipment to Japanese refineries. The Japanese side was disillusioned with both the quality of Chinese crude and the long-range prospects for substantial petroleum trade.

However, the promotion bubble in the Sino-Japanese oil trade did not really burst until January-February 1976, when Peking began to negotiate on a year-to-year basis and Masami Ishida, president of the Petroleum Association of Japan, advised Japanese importers to make only spot purchases of Chinese oil.[57] In January, Yoshihiro Inayama, chairman of the Japan-China Friendship Association, was dispatched to Peking with the delicate task of persuading the Chinese to reduce the expected level of crude oil shipments to 10 million metric tons in 1977 and a mere 15 million by 1981.[58] Tokyo was under considerable pressure from Middle East suppliers to maintain its oil imports from OPEC countries despite declining consumption owing to higher prices and government conservation programs. Japanese refiners were set up to process Middle Eastern crudes selling at $0.60/bbl under the Chinese price. Desulfurization capacity was sitting idle, and dewaxing equipment was unavailable. The only countervailing influence on Japan's Ministry of International Trade and Industry was coming from Japanese industrial plant and equipment manufacturers, who feared repercussions in the fading Chinese market, a market under pressure from trade imbalances incurred in 1974–75.

The first response of the Chinese was to press for an oil-steel barter agreement with the Japanese steel industry. Chinese crude would be burned in Japanese steel mills in return for steel exports to the PRC.[59] But by this time (February 1976) the oil export issue had reached the highest circles of the Chinese government and had been translated into an active policy debate between at least two party factions engaged in a struggle to succeed the dying Chou En-lai and Mao Tse-tung at the pinnacle of the Chinese political system.[60] In mid-February the level of monthly crude oil shipments was suddenly slashed to 250,000 metric tons, down from the 600,000–700,000 tons shipped monthly in 1975.[61] The decision to cut oil exports was taken and implemented so suddenly that several Japanese tankers had to be recalled as they prepared to pick up Chinese oil. The constriction of oil exports then lasted into March and April, dooming any remaining hope that 1976 oil trade would even equal the level achieved in 1975. The oil-steel barter agreement talks were abruptly canceled, and in early April Vice-Premier Ku Mu indicated that China's rising domestic demand was placing a ceiling on oil exports.[62]

The abrupt decline in the oil trade in February 1976 aroused considerable debate over the reasons for the Chinese decision. It was variously attributed to negotiating tactics on the Chinese side, to a real domestic oil shortage, to a disastrous fire at Taching oilfield, and to competing crude oil commitments to North Korea and Romania.[63] A year later the Chinese press itself attributed the sudden decline in oil trade to "sabotage" by the

"Gang of Four." The Shanghai radicals were accused of encouraging the burning of crude oil as fuel in electric power plants in Shanghai and Liaoning province, displacing coal and intentionally precipitating an export crisis.[64] Whatever the truth of these accusations and rumors, the political factor was evident in nearly every explanation. Careful review of the events surrounding the Sino-Japanese oil trade denouement would suggest three principal and interlocking factors.

First, it is plausible that China had already begun to reach its petroleum export ceiling in early 1976. The growth rate for crude petroleum production fell from over 20 percent per year in 1970–74 to about 13 percent in 1975 and again in 1976.[65] The trend continued in 1977 with a growth rate of around .11 percent.[66] Even Taching oilfield, the model unit for Chinese industry, appeared to have slackened its pace of development by 1976.[67] Serious questions began to surface among foreign experts regarding the long-range prospects for the Chinese petroleum industry. Meanwhile, energy consumption had continued to shift in the direction of petroleum and natural gas. Petroleum's share in the Chinese energy consumption mix jumped from about 15 percent in 1970 to 21 percent in 1975 (see Table 16.5). Net petroleum exports had jumped from 2 to 11 million metric tons in just two years (see Table 21.2). By 1975, petroleum exports were taking about 15 percent of China's total crude petroleum production, up from 4 percent in 1973. Judging from retrospective Chinese press reports, the combined impact of a slowing growth rate in the petroleum industry, a shift in the energy mix toward petroleum (particularly in electric power generation), and the pressure of rapidly rising export commitments produced a crude oil shortage at Chinese refineries in late 1975 or early 1976. The domestic energy consumption constraint had already placed a ceiling on China's oil export capacity. China's new status as an oil-exporting country was beginning to conflict with the "self-reliance" guideline and the priority attached to domestic energy development.

Second, China's domestic political cycle had once again surfaced to affect the direction of energy development policy and Sino-Japanese relations. The "Shanghai radicals," a group of Politburo members who had come to power during the Cultural Revolution, used the petroleum shortage as part of their attack on the economic development and foreign trade policies of Chou En-lai and his potential successor, Vice-Premier Teng Hsiao-ping. The anti-Teng campaign that followed Chou's death in January 1976 coincided exactly with the drop in crude petroleum exports to Japan. The Shanghai radicals also vigorously attacked the complete plant imports that had led to serious balance-of-payments deficits in 1973–74. Foreign Minister Chiao Kuan-hua reassured the Japanese ambassador in April that the anti-Teng campaign would not affect Sino-Japanese trade.[68] But the damage had already been done in the oil trade. Both Teng and Kang Shih-en, Minister of Petroleum and Chemical Industries, had come under sharp attack for exporting China's petroleum and other mineral commodities to other countries.[69]

Third, the drop in the oil trade reflected long-term political constraints operating on Japan. During the 1960's, the Japanese energy balance had shifted heavily in the direction of Middle Eastern oil. At first, this resource dependence was balanced by political dependence on the United States. The United States and its oil companies tightly controlled Middle Eastern oil until about 1971. Japan's energy lifeline was just about as safe as its security lifeline to Washington. But successful OPEC cartelization of the international petroleum market and the subsequent Arab oil embargo graphically demonstrated the vulnerability of Japan's entire economy where its energy supply was concerned. The Japanese government reacted by shifting politically toward the Arab governments and away from Israel. It also sought to protect its energy lifeline with a series of special long-range petroleum supply arrangements with governments around the Persian Gulf.[70] These agreements were themselves unfortunately double-edged, for by 1976 the situation had reversed itself. Japanese refiners were under increasing pressure from Middle Eastern governments to fulfill long-range oil import agreements, despite declining domestic petroleum requirements. An uncomfortable "oil glut" had seized the international petroleum market. Japan's total crude petroleum imports actually *declined* from 1973 until 1975, the very years when the oil trade was initiated with China.[71] Resource vulnerability, a factor for many decades in Japanese foreign relations, continues to play an important role in determining policy. Ironically, in the case of Chinese petroleum, it resulted in reluctance on the part of the Japanese government to further extend its import commitments. As Tokyo became aware of the domestic consumption ceiling on China's export potential, the entire matter of oil trade with China was pushed to the back burner. Oil imports from the PRC would be encouraged only in the event of further supply shortages on the international market or in the event of major Chinese discoveries along the continental shelf. By late spring 1976, Japan's Ministry of International Trade and Industry (MITI) was actively discouraging the importation of Chinese fuel oil.[72] The limited scale of oil trade with China, the high wax content of Chinese crude, the expense of shipping in "coil tankers" of limited capacity, and the difficulty of negotiating long-term supply contracts had begun to take a toll on trade officials in Tokyo. Further trade would require substantial price concessions or long-term supply commitments, or both.

Among the three constraints that limited China's crude petroleum exports to Japan in early 1976, the domestic consumption requirement should be ranked as the most important. Oil exports to the Philippines were also reduced at the same time, indicating a genuine supply problem that transcended negotiating problems with the Japanese. But domestic Chinese politics and Japan's resource vulnerability were also factors of considerable importance. The political constraints that have long had a centrifugal effect on Sino-Japanese relations persist and should be taken into account in assessing the future prospects of Sino-Japanese energy commodity trade.

Of the three constraints operating on Sino-Japanese oil trade, only the domestic Chinese political factor changed much from the spring of 1976 until 1977. Mao Tse-tung died on September 9, 1976. Hua Kuo-feng and the political "moderates" in Peking seized control, and within weeks the Shanghai radicals had been purged from the Politburo and placed under arrest. Restrictive trade policies characteristic of the anti-Teng campaign were reversed. The Fifth Five-Year Plan was rescheduled to begin in January 1977, with heavy emphasis on large-scale industrial development. Minister of Foreign Trade Li Chiang reassured foreign guests that China would resume trade in industrial equipment in 1978.[73] A series of industrial conferences were convened, culminating in a major "Learn from Taching" conference in the spring of 1977. Once again favorable projections of China's crude petroleum exports began to appear.[74] Peking and Tokyo resumed long-term oil export talks.[75] The Chinese press published a long series of articles attacking the economic policies of the "Gang of Four" in general, and their attitude toward oil exports in particular. The Eleventh Chinese Communist Party Congress, held in August 1977, rehabilitated Teng Hsiao-ping and the economic and trade policies that he represented.[76]

However, despite these shifts in the political climate in Peking, crude oil exports to Japan contracted for in 1977 remained at just 6.5 million metric tons, almost exactly the 1976 figure and below the 1975 level.[77] Previous difficulties remained to hamper new export contract negotiations. The Chinese refused to yield to Japanese pressure for lower prices and greater volume. In February 1977 Peking raised the posted price on Chinese crude to $13.20/bbl, up about 7 percent.[78]

The strength of centrifugal forces in Sino-Japanese political and commercial relations was still very apparent in late 1977. The Chinese government was upset by Prime Minister Fukuda Takeo's campaign in the

Japanese Diet for ratification of the joint offshore development agreement with Seoul. Peking was also displeased with Japan's refusal to include an "anti-hegemony" clause in the peace treaty under negotiation with China. Obviously directed against Soviet influence in East Asia, the clause caused so much difficulty in Soviet-Japanese relations that Tokyo was still unwilling to accept any version of the Chinese formulation, and kept deferring the peace treaty, now some 30 years overdue. Overall Sino-Japanese trade continued to decline in 1977, but a warm welcome for a Keidanren delegation, Chinese interest in a five- to ten-year trade agreement, and a special three-week trip to Japan by Vice Minister to Foreign Trade Liu Hsi-wen in September appeared to augur a resurgence of commercial relations.[79] Crude petroleum exports to Japan in 1977 reached 6.8 million metric tons, up from 6.1 million tons in 1976.

The Sino-Japanese long-term trade agreement calls for a steady increase of annual crude oil exports to Japan to about 9.5 million tons in 1981. In 1982, the figure is supposed to jump to 15 million tons, a 50 percent increase in a single year. In the face of the resistance of Japanese refiners to Chinese crude, MITI is planning a government-sponsored refinery construction project to handle the Chinese crude. Initial plans call for a huge (25 mmt/year) refinery in Hokkaido with hydrocracking units, capable of handling heavy crudes with a capacity of 3 million tons per year. So far, only one private refining company (Idemitsu) is building facilities for Chinese crude. (Prospects for long-range Japanese crude oil imports from China are discussed in detail in Chapter 12.)

The most basic and persistent condition identified in our analysis of short-term trends in energy commodity trade between China and Japan is that the energy trade is subject to the general state of commercial relations, which is in turn subject to the state of political relations. The linkage between commercial and political relations stretches back at least 30 years and should not be expected to disappear in the immediate future. This generalization would of course hold in the commercial and political relationship between any two countries. What makes it especially important in the Sino-Japanese context is that trade appears to be extremely sensitive to even subtle shifts in the political environment. I also believe that the Chinese and Japanese governments are unusually aware of the linkage and have come over time to deal with the political limits on commercial relations as a matter of self-conscious policy. Governments and trade officials in both Peking and Tokyo are sharply aware that they are dealing with one another in a framework determined by limiting political factors. They allow for the political factor in their deliberations and it affects policy directly.

The strength of the political factor in Sino-Japanese relations was illustrated once again on August 12, 1978, when China and Japan signed a Treaty of Peace and Friendship, formally ending the hostilities of the Second World War. The treaty, which followed three years of deadlocked negotiations, accepted Chinese language condemning hegemonism. Article II states: "The Contracting Parties declare that neither of them should seek hegemony in the Asia-Pacific region or in any other region and that each is opposed to efforts by any other country or group of countries to establish such hegemony."[80] The Japanese government was quick to point out that the treaty is not directed at any third party, but the Soviet Union was not convinced. The Soviet ambassador to Japan was immediately recalled for consultations and remained in Moscow for an extended period. Moscow also followed up the Chinese victory by announcing on November 3 that a treaty of friendship and cooperation had been signed between the Soviet Union and Vietnam. Thus, in a period of just a few months, the power alignment in East Asia shifted radically toward a bipolar China-Japan and Soviet-Vietnam face-off. Japan and Vietnam are at pains to soften the impact of their new tacit alliances, but Asia has been split along a new set of fault lines that may persist for some time.

The energy component in the Sino-Japanese peace treaty was not explicit. However, it was no accident that accelerated energy commodity trade was closely associated with improvement in political relations. If the political arrangement stabilizes and is suitable to both sides in that it turns the Soviet flank in the Western Pacific, the Japanese government will be even more eager to push for higher imports of Chinese coal and petroleum. Further concessions from Japan's beleaguered oil refiners are already being called for. At minimum the long-term trade agreement and the peace treaty will stabilize and slowly expand Sino-Japanese energy commodity trade. But it is also possible that China has opened a new door on the Japanese energy market.

Not that this development eliminates the traditional ambivalence in political and commercial relations between China and Japan. The two countries are still structured in completely different ways. Japan is a high-technology, resource-poor, industrialized market-economy country. China is a low-technology, resource-rich, centrally planned economy country. Even if the opposites attract, they simultaneously repel. Each is fully aware that the other is a potential competitor in Asia. Each is chary about its national prerogatives and defensive about its distinctive political, economic, and social systems. During 1978, we did not witness a fusion of China and Japan. Rather, we saw the reemergence of an ancient and rather well-balanced relationship.

Energy Equipment Trade with Japan

Japan inadvertently laid the foundation of the Chinese coal and electric power industries in what was to become the industrial northeast during the occupation of Manchuria prior to 1945. Coal from the area was needed by domestic Japanese industry, and the fledgling Manchurian electric power industry built under the Japanese serviced their other industrial installations and urban settlements in the area.[81] Despite Soviet equipment removals—particularly of electric-power-generating sets—from the northeast between 1945 and 1949, the area prospered under the communists and became China's industrial and energy heartland.

Japan and China engaged in limited trade in coal-mining equipment and electric power machinery during the 1960's.[82] China exported intermediate technology items such as basic electric power transmission equipment (switchgear, insulators, etc.) and imported limited quantities of high-technology Japanese equipment. But this trade was restricted by the Yoshida letter and Chinese policy to various subplant components purchased on an item-by-item basis.

Complete electric power plant purchases began in 1972 when Peking imported a single large generating set (Mitsubishi, Hitachi, and Toshiba, $13 million) and a complete thermal power station that included two generating sets with a total capacity of 250 MW (Hitachi, $30 million). A second coal-fired thermal power plant with two generating sets rated at 250 MW each was purchased in 1973 (Hitachi, $72 million). After 1973, Peking shifted toward European companies for electric-power-generating sets, and the Hitachi deals were not repeated.*

On the basis of the total value of the transactions involved, China's most important energy plant and equipment imports from Japan were petrochemical and refinery components. Peking's first complete plant purchase from Japan was the vinylon plant bought in 1963 (Kurashiki and Dai Nippon, $50 million) that precipitated the Yoshida letter and the end of complete plant purchases from Japan. From 1972 until 1976 China resumed the large-scale import of petrochemical plants from Japanese companies, importing more than $700 million worth in just four years. The plants and components included a wide array of processes and tended to concentrate at the downstream and fiber end of the petrochemical industry. The largest single contract was signed in 1972 for a synthetic fiber plant (Toray, $90 million) destined for Shanghai. Japan exceeded any other country or region in the export of petrochemical equipment to China. Taken as a unit, Western Europe was the

*In late 1978, Hitachi, Toshiba, and Mitsubishi were negotiating a contract for three thermal power plants to be constructed at the site of the new Paoshan integrated steel complex.

closest competitor, with about $500 million in sales of petrochemical components to the PRC during the same four-year period. However, more than half of the West European total was a single complete plant, the petrochemical and synthetic fiber complex sold in 1973 (Technip-Speichem, $282 million). In the petrochemical field, therefore, Japan has dominated the Chinese market.

For a time it appeared that Japanese business might also corner the potential market for offshore exploration equipment. Japan opened that market in September 1972 with the sale of the 400-ton offshore drilling rig "Fuji" (jack-up type) and a supply ship for a total of about $10 million (Nippon Kaiyo Kussaku and Mitsubishi). In December 1973, Peking signed a contract for a Japanese semisubmersible drilling rig, the "Hakuryu" (Mitsubishi, $23 million), but then failed to complete the transaction after an effort to lower the price.[83] During 1975, Peking also signed contracts for five offshore rig supply and service ships (Hitachi, $10 million) and two tugboats ($16.7 million) of Japanese manufacture. Other Japanese ships with possible offshore oil exploration applications were purchased in the same year, including eight self-propelled bucket dredgers (Nippon Kokan, $57 million) and two crane ships used primarily for harbor construction (Mitsui, $7 million). However, as in the case of electric power plants, Chinese trade officials began to look beyond Japan for offshore exploration equipment, and the early purchases did not result in an ongoing important program. By 1974, the focus of Chinese offshore equipment purchases and negotiations had shifted to Western Europe (the North Sea developers, particularly Norway), the United States, and Singapore. Two additional orders were placed in 1975 for jack-up type drilling rigs carrying American equipment and built in Singapore (Robin Loh, $60 million). China did purchase an ocean survey ship from Japan in 1975 (Japan Ocean Industries and Sumitomo Shoji) and a life-saving system for offshore use (Nichimen). Japan received an order for one Robray 300 jack-up in 1977 (Hitachi, $30 million) as a spin-off from China's Singapore rig purchases.

Japan has been involved in trade in a number of other types of energy equipment with the PRC since 1972. Japan participated as a lesser partner in the sales of chemical fertilizer plants to China. Contracts for Japanese ammonia and urea plants were signed in 1972, 1973, and 1976. The largest single transaction in this field was the sale of an ammonia-urea complex in 1973 (Toyo, Mitsui, and Hiroshima Trading, $42 million). But Japan trailed both the United States and the Netherlands as an exporter of fertilizer plants to the PRC from 1972 until 1976. In 1975–76 Japanese shipping companies sold China several crude oil tankers, including the 92,000-dwt "Tatsuta Maru" (Nippon Yusen, $2.6

million). Japan has not been an important supplier for the Chinese coal industry, but did sell 40 mechanical shovels to the PRC in 1974 (Kawasaki, $350,000). Japanese oil pipeline, pipelayers, and filters were sold, beginning in 1973.

The only area of real and sustained strength in Japan's energy equipment exports to the PRC has been in petroleum refining and petrochemical plants. No other type of equipment has come anywhere near the sales volume for petrochemical equipment. Both electric power equipment sales and offshore exploration equipment sales were shifted away from Japanese companies after an initial burst of enthusiasm in 1972–73. This lopsided nature of Sino-Japanese energy equipment trade has several implications. First, it indicates that Chinese refining and petrochemical technology is patterning itself on the Japanese model, particularly in the chemical fiber part of the petrochemical industry. Chinese planners may have discovered a fundamental economic or technical compatibility between their refining and petrochemical needs and Japanese components. This impression is reinforced by the number of Japanese technicians who visited or resided at Chinese petrochemical and refining facilities. Second, it indicates that Japanese heavy industry may have some difficulty competing with American or European technology in the fields of electric power generation and petroleum extraction. This could be particularly important if China moves into an expanded offshore development program or into nuclear power. Third, it is evident that Chinese planners placed overwhelming emphasis on petroleum refining and the petrochemical industry during the mid-1970's. The Chinese government apparently believes that petrochemicals, plastics, and synthetic fibers will revolutionize the national standard of living at a basic level. Abundant petroleum and natural gas feedstocks were available as a result of the great boom in these industries in the late 1960's and 1970's. Refining and petrochemicals represented both critical bottlenecks and industries of rapid secondary growth potential.

Direct Energy Technology Exchange with Japan

It is impossible to gain even a rough idea of the amount of technology transfer in energy-related fields that has taken place between Japan and China since diplomatic relations were established in 1972. At least half of the 80-odd energy delegations visiting the PRC from abroad were Japanese groups. And at least seven major energy delegations were dispatched to Japan by the Chinese government from 1972 until 1976. But the comprehensiveness of these delegation statistics is open to some doubt because of the variety of groups involved. Hundreds of Japanese companies send representatives to the Canton Trade Fair each spring and autumn. Hundreds of Japanese technical personnel have been stationed at or have visited various Chinese energy industry construction projects. Specialized energy trade and technology personnel have doubtless been included in the diplomatic and commercial missions maintained by each country in the other. None of these contacts would be included in the "delegation" total.

The distribution of energy delegations traveling back and forth between Japan and China is roughly what one would expect from the statistics on energy commodity trade and energy equipment trade. About 40 percent of the Japanese energy delegations visiting China were concerned with some aspect of the refining and petrochemical industries. Another 30 percent were involved with establishing and managing China's crude oil exports to Japan. There were a few delegations from Japan concerned with petroleum production technology and chemical fertilizers and coal mining. The remainder were distributed across other aspects of energy technology and development.

Certain symmetrical benefits accrue to each side in the process of the energy delegation exchanges. When Japanese energy delegations visit the PRC, they bring with them advanced energy technologies that may find application in one or another Chinese energy industry. They are likely to take home a purchase contract or at least establish contract negotiations for a particular line of energy equipment. Chinese delegations to Japan have usually been more formal and have occasionally played an important role in crude petroleum negotiations between the two countries.

There are two particularly interesting areas of potential technology transfer between Japan and China: undersea pipelines, and liquefied natural gas (LNG). Peking began to display some interest in Japanese offshore oil pipeline technology in 1973. A delegation of Japanese oil experts visited the Pohai oil fields in October 1973 to advise the Chinese on the technical problems of large-diameter pipelines. The delegation included representatives of Nippon Steel and Mitsui.[84] Undersea oil pipelines were also discussed with Japanese companies at the autumn Canton Trade Fair in 1973.[85] There was even some speculation that China was interested in an undersea pipeline for exports to Japan, an unlikely prospect in view of the conflicting claims to the continental shelf and the inflexibility of such an arrangement with regard to future fluctuations in the crude oil trade. Nothing much has been heard since 1973 on the subject of Japanese undersea pipeline technology, but by 1975 the PRC was importing a substantial proportion of the seamless oil pipeline required for onshore projects from the Japanese steel industry.[86]

Transportation has been a critical bottleneck in the Sino-Japanese oil trade, and at least two of China's major pipelines (Taching-Chinhuang-tao and Taching-Dairen) were built to service that trade. In the event of rapid expansion in offshore oil development, China might again turn to Japan for advice on undersea pipelines, particularly if the lines in question were to serve crude oil exports to Japan.

Chinese acquisition of Japanese LNG technology is also closely related to potential energy commodity exports (and, incidentally, to pipeline technology). For several years, Japan has been gearing up for expansion of its LNG imports. Tokyo has signed a series of long-term contracts for LNG development and import projects, including the Yakut natural gas development project in Siberia (see Chapter 4). Meanwhile, Chinese natural gas production has been increasing rapidly, from both associated and nonassociated gas fields. Much of the development in the natural gas industry has taken place inland in Szechwan province, but some has accompanied the opening of oilfields in the northeast. In 1974 a Japanese natural gas delegation visited China, and a return group of Chinese natural gas experts visited Japan the following year. Concurrently, Tokyo's Bridgestone Natural Gas Company, Ishikawajima-Harima Heavy Industries, and Toko Bussan opened negotiations with China's Techimport for a 300,000 mt/year LNG plant.[87] The plant was to be installed at China's Takang oilfield in exchange for an assured supply of exported LNG. Initial plans called for completion by 1978, a dubious deadline in view of the speculative nature of the project. In fact, the Chinese side was hesitant about the whole affair and slowed the negotiations by complaining that the size of the project should be "scores of times larger."[88] But whatever the outcome of the Bridgestone proposals, the LNG project indicates one possible alternative in China's energy development programs. The hydrocarbon content of the continental shelf could be in the form of extensive natural gas deposits rather than crude petroleum. China may have already discovered more gas and less oil than it expected in the fields around the Pohai Gulf. If so, foreign natural gas and LNG technology will become an important part of Peking's energy development program. But the prospects for LNG exports to Japan were still not very good at the end of 1978. China will face steep competition for the Japanese LNG market from several other Asian suppliers over the next several decades. Australia, Indonesia, Malaysia, and Soviet Siberia all have LNG projects underway or in the planning stage. The LNG export infrastructure (and regasification and distribution systems) are extremely capital-intensive and represent an unlikely alternative for the PRC at this point.

Transport and Handling in the Oil Trade

One final set of constraints should be considered in assessing the prospects for Sino-Japanese energy relations. China's potential fossil-fuel exports are limited on the production side by reserves and by the rising domestic energy consumption requirement. Japan's oil imports from China are limited by the framework of political and commercial relations between the two countries. But even assuming that China could provide substantial oil for export and that political conditions permitted steady expansion in the oil trade with Japan, certain problems would remain. Coal, oil, or liquefied natural gas must be physically moved from the point of production to the point of consumption, in this case Japan. Financial arrangements must be made that facilitate a reciprocal flow of currency. In the case of a new energy commodity trade relationship, such as that between China and Japan, these links do not antedate the initiation of trade. Transportation and handling facilities must therefore be established to accommodate the rising volume of trade, including appropriate financial arrangements. Depending on the pace of development of these facilities, bottlenecks may occur regardless of the availability of the energy commodity for export or the size of the import market. The transportation and handling bottleneck constitutes yet another constraint on Sino-Japanese energy trade.

Pipelines

From the Chinese end, crude oil transportation remains a stumbling block for long-range exports. Nearly all crude oil transport within the PRC was handled by rail tank cars before 1970. This proved difficult in the case of waxy Taching crude, which had to be heated at regular intervals along the rail lines leading south to China's industrial centers. From 1970 to 1973, the PRC constructed its first large-bore (24") long-distance pipeline from Taching to the Pohai Gulf port of Chinhuangtao, a distance of over 1,000 kilometers.[89] The crude oil line was later extended to Peking, where it feeds the Peking General Petrochemical Works and supplies crude for rail shipment south.[90] The total annual capacity of this line is about 12 million metric tons. Following the completion of the Taching-Chinhuangtao line, a parallel line was constructed from Taching to Tiehling and from Tiehling to the port of Dairen.[91] At about the same time, a 200-kilometer line was built from Shengli oilfield to the port of Huangtao.[92] These three pipelines are critical to the development of Sino-Japanese oil trade. They were laid at considerable cost and have both export and internal oil transport functions. China has also constructed pipelines to North Korea and to Vietnam to carry oil exports to those countries (see Chapter 8). Japan exported much of the large-diameter seamless steel pipe used in these pipeline projects.

The political implications of China's new network of oil export pipelines were not lost on Tokyo. Rather than seek Japanese capital, as the Russians had, for oil pipeline construction, China was willing to import Japanese pipe and construct the line themselves, regardless of the cost. Peking made a point of opening the Taching-Dairen pipeline on the eve of Soviet Foreign Minister Andrei Gromyko's visit to Japan in January 1976.[93] Chinese planners were reportedly very angry when Japanese oil importers reduced their projected imports of Chinese crude at about the same time.[94] Chinese investment in oil transport facilities had been very high in 1974–76, and Peking had been banking heavily on the oil trade with Japan to cover the cost of the new pipelines. Chinese pique at falling Japanese interest was one of the factors that led to the sudden drop in crude oil exports to Japan in February 1976.

Ports

Port facilities and oil dock construction have also received considerable attention and capital in Peking's planning priorities in the mid-1970's. The size of the port and dock facilities directly affects the size of tankers that may be used in the Sino-Japanese oil trade and thereby influences the transportation cost per metric ton of crude oil shipped to Japan. The three main oil export ports are situated in the shallow waters of the Po-hai Gulf (Dairen, Chinhuangtao, and Huangtao). The fourth port directly involved in the oil trade, Chankiang in southern Kwangtung province, also has a limited capacity. Even after substantial port construction projects at six Chinese oil ports (Dairen, Chinhuangtao, Huangtao, Shanghai, Whampoa, and Chankiang), most oil dock facilities are only capable of handling tankers up to 50,000 deadweight tons (dwt) and cannot accommodate tankers in a class that would be competitive with international shipping standards. Even the largest tankers in the Chinese fleet exceed this berthing capacity. Just one berth has been constructed with a 100,000-ton-tanker handling capacity, at the new oil port in Dairen.[95] At existing port facilities, foreign shipping companies complain of extraordinarily long turnaround times, again adding to the cost of shipping Chinese crude oil.[96] Incidentally, negotiations for a long-term coal export contract have also encountered a low ceiling on the size of coal carriers that can be accommodated in Chinese ports. Port construction will be a costly development requirement at every step in expansion of China's energy commodity trade.

Tankers and Shipping

Except in the unlikely event of an undersea pipeline between China and Japan, the oil trade between the two countries must be carried on with tankers of either Chinese or foreign registry. Furthermore, Taching crude and other waxy Chinese crudes require "coil" tankers that maintain the oil at handling temperature. The annual volume of Sino-Japanese crude oil trade is substantial enough for small increments in handling and tanker charges to have a differential impact on the cost of Chinese oil relative to Middle Eastern and Indonesian crudes, but too small to justify massive capital expenditures for appropriate additions to the Japanese tanker fleet. The burden of crude oil transport, therefore, has fallen increasingly on the Chinese tanker fleet and shipping industry.

The PRC has responded to this burden with a variety of measures designed to expand its tanker capacity at minimum cost. A tanker construction program has been under way in the Chinese shipbuilding industry. China's shipyards have produced a succession of ever-larger tankers and have now crossed the 50,000 dwt threshold into supertanker construction.[97] Chinese tankers have been reported to have some technical problems, including inadequate heating coils and a narrow temperature control range, limiting the number of petroleum products and crudes they can handle.[98] But past expansion of the PRC's tanker construction program would indicate that China could quickly accelerate the size and capabilities of its domestically produced tankers if the need should arise. Chinese shipyards are confident enough in tanker construction to have offered coastal tankers for sale on the international market.[99]

Peking has also been acquiring tankers from abroad under a variety of arrangements. Numerous tanker purchases have been reported from Norway, Greece, Japan, and other countries (Table 22.4). The China Ocean Shipping Company (Cosco) and its subsidiaries in Hong Kong that own tankers under Somali and Panamanian flags of convenience were thought to have purchased some 40–50 tankers for international oil trade by late 1976.[100] In addition, China has been chartering tankers for specific runs in its oil export agreements with countries other than Japan. Special tanker charters have been arranged for crude oil shipments to the Philippines and Romania.[101] Peking has also ordered several new tankers from shipyards in Yugoslavia, Malta, and Japan.[102]

The tanker bottleneck has caused higher shipping costs in China's crude oil export program than would normally be expected on the international market. The cost of shipping crude oil from China to the Philippines was reported at $0.65/bbl in early 1977, higher than the average $0.50/bbl charged for the trip from the Middle East.[103] This differential

TABLE 6.2
Taching and Other Crudes

	Taching crude	Minas crude	Arabian light
Crude analysis:			
Specific gravity	0.86	0.85	0.86
Wax (% wt.)	22.4%	13.0%	2.8%
Pour point (°C)	32.5-35.0°	32.5°	-15.0°
Product yields:			
Gasoline	9.1%	12.5%	25.0%
Kerosene	4.7%	8.9%	13.5%
Diesel	13.9%	14.3%	13.5%
Residual	68.0%	64.2%	47.8%
Water and sediment (% vol.)	4.3%	0.1%	0.2%

Sources: WES, 20 (1971–75), pp. xxii–xxiii; U.S. CIA, *China: Energy Production Prospects*, p. 11; Susumu Awano-hara, "Snags Facing China's Oil Exports," *FEER* 90, no. 48 (Nov. 28, 1975): 47.

in shipping costs is significant, for it wipes out the geographic advantage enjoyed by China in the Asian petroleum market. High shipping costs have also been used by Japanese refiners as an argument for lower prices for Chinese crude oil.

Refining

China's export crudes are unusually difficult to refine, especially for refineries set up to handle low-wax, high-sulfur Middle Eastern crudes. Taching crude contains more than 20 percent wax (hexane) by weight and has a pour point of 32–35° C.[104] (See Table 6.2.) The wax must be removed before refining at a cost that some sources have placed as high as $2–3/bbl.[105] Most refineries in Asia do not have the necessary dewaxing equipment or heating equipment to maintain the crude at handling temperature. Furthermore, the flash point for Chinese crude is not much higher than the pour point, which narrows the band of suitable handling temperatures. Refiners in the Philippines and Thailand found these characteristics so difficult to deal with that they refused to accept Chinese crude after a few trial runs.[106] This caused repeated delays in the receipt of crude oil shipments and added to the already high cost of shipping.[107] The solution in Japan has been to burn about 50 percent of the imported Chinese crude oil in power plants and steel mills. The remaining 50 percent has been refined by mixing it with light Middle Eastern crudes or by putting it through a special 8,500 bbl/day hydrogen treatment plant operated by Idemitsu Kosan in Chiba.[108] The hydrogenation process adds another $3/bbl to the refining costs. And as if that were not enough, the product yield of Taching crude is 68 percent residuum and less than 10 percent gasoline, requiring additional cracking cycles and lowering the market value of the end products.[109]

The refining problems will be a permanent feature of China's crude oil export program, unless crudes are discovered and developed that have less wax and greater distillate content. But so far all the major fields in the northeast have yielded Taching-type crudes. Inland crudes would require expensive overland transport, and offshore crudes are still in the speculative category. Japanese refiners have taken steps to modify at least a few units to handle Taching crude.[110] High prices or short supply in the international petroleum market, definitely a long-term possibility, would make further refinery modifications a relatively marginal impediment to Sino-Japanese crude oil trade.

Financial Arrangements

Transport and handling problems, and the high costs of shipping and refining have made Chinese crude oil appear less than competitive with Indonesian crude and Middle Eastern oil. On the other hand, the balance-of-payments deficits of 1973–74 have made Peking less willing than it might otherwise have been to consider price concessions in oil trade with Japan. Given the domestic constraints on export potential that had already begun to surface in early 1976, China could only lose by offering Japan lower prices. But within the framework of the price structure that has emerged in the first four years of crude oil exports to Japan, Peking has proved relatively flexible in adjusting its banking, currency, and financial arrangements to international market conditions. Chinese oil officials apparently were alert to the incentives that could be offered their oil trading partners through alternative financial arrangements facilitating or even motivating that trade.

Peking initially insisted on payments for crude oil in Japanese yen or Chinese jenminpih. The Chinese feared losses that could be incurred in the international money market with floating third-country currencies. But in early 1975, at the insistence of Japanese oil importers, and under pressure from China's own balance-of-payment problems, Peking agreed to a 1975 crude oil contract that called for settlement in dollars.[111] Japanese traders prefer a third currency to settlement in yen and jenminpih because of the arbitrary structure of exchange rates set by the Chinese government.

Japan has repeatedly offered long-term oil contract arrangements to China and at times has attempted to sweeten these offers with technical assistance or joint development proposals. In negotiations toward the end of 1975, the Japanese offered Export-Import Bank low-interest financing for Chinese oilfield development, as well as direct technical assistance in transportation and refining.[112] The Chinese government, however, was reluctant to enter into a formal agreement of this nature, which might be construed as compromising the country's resource sovereignty or prized self-reliance in petroleum development. Particularly in early 1976, during the radical swing in Peking's domestic politics, China was highly unlikely to accept such offers. By 1978, Chinese policy regarding the financing of petroleum development had relaxed somewhat with the signing of the long-term trade agreement, preliminary acceptance of bank loans and other forms of direct credit, and open discussions of the prospects for joint offshore oil development in the Pohai Gulf with Japan.[113]

The Chinese government has also encouraged crude oil barter trade whenever it was felt that a direct commodity import-export linkage would improve the level or conditions of the oil trade. The crude oil export agreement with the Philippines, signed in September 1974, specified two-year barter terms for Philippine sugar, lumber, copper, and coconut products.[114] Japan was offered the ill-fated oil-steel barter in January 1976. And the 1976 crude oil sale to Thailand was tied to Chinese rice imports.[115] In each case, the barter may have simply formalized trade that would have occurred anyhow, but such agreements do reassure Third World trading partners that China is genuinely concerned to balance bilateral trade. And the barter deals may have helped in the competition with Indonesian crude, although concessionary "friendship prices" have been much more important in stimulating Chinese oil exports to Southeast Asian countries.

One other type of arrangement deserves passing comment in the context of China's oil trade policy. The PRC has engaged in some downstream marketing activities to stimulate the sale of Chinese petroleum products in Hong Kong. Hong Kong lacks adequate storage facilities for diesel fuel and other petroleum products. In 1976, Peking agreed to build three large storage tanks in the colony for use as depots for Chinese oil.[116] A retail company controlled by China also opened two gasoline stations and has plans for two more.[117] The Chinese government doubtless believes that such arrangements will eventually be terminated in favor of much more direct control of Hong Kong's fortunes.

Short-term and Long-term Constraints

This chapter has identified a number of constraints on Sino-Japanese energy commodity trade. It has been pointed out that future trade in oil and other energy commodities will probably reflect the limits set by such constraints. Some of the constraints are the "bottleneck" type—pipelines, ports, tankers, refining, and financial arrangements. These constraints are operative in the short term or perhaps the intermediate term. They are in no sense insuperable and would be quickly overcome by appropriate investment and construction programs, should the level of oil trade expand sufficiently to justify such expenditures. Other constraints, however, are more enduring. The ambivalence of the political relationship between China and Japan will persist for the next several decades as China enters the modern industrial world and as Japan adjusts to its new regional and global status. The conditions that created the vulnerability of Japanese foreign relations to outside influence will also persist for the next décade or two. Japan will always be dependent on the outside world for the bulk of its mineral resources and raw materials. The security of Japan in a world of nuclear powers cannot be assured in the absence of dependence on one or another of the possessors of nuclear weapons. Territorial and other political problems with the Soviet Union will not disappear overnight. All of these factors will set limits on the political relationship with the People's Republic of China. Oil and other energy commodity trade in turn will remain sensitive to the ebb and flow of political currents between the two countries.

The energy export potential of China (or any other country, for that matter) is defined by the balance between domestic energy resources and the domestic energy consumption requirement. If domestic energy resources and production exceed a country's energy consumption requirements, the country will have a positive energy commodity export potential. If resources and production are insufficient to meet domestic consumption requirements, then energy commodities must be imported and the country has a net import requirement. In the Chinese case, the resource-consumption balance is not yet known, either to the Chinese government itself or to foreign observers. Perhaps the biggest single question mark is the continental shelf. No one knows exactly the extent of hydrocarbon deposits in the Chinese continental shelf. Nor do we have any idea of the composition (oil, gas, tar sands, etc.) of the hydrocarbon deposits that exist. And even assuming perfect knowledge of the extent and composition of hydrocarbon resources in the shelf, no one knows to whom they will belong. The next chapter will systematically explore our ignorance of the character and future of the continental shelf. That ignorance itself may constitute a critical constraint on China's international energy policies.

Chapter 7

China's Energy Policies in Asia:
The Continental Shelf

The Chinese continental shelf is one of the largest of such areas in the world. It extends some 4,000 kilometers along the arching Chinese coastline from Korea on the north to Vietnam on the southwest. The width of the shelf, measured to approximately the 200-meter contour, ranges from 125 kilometers to 450 kilometers from the coast. The surface area of the shelf, including sections in the Pohai Gulf, Yellow Sea, East China Sea, Taiwan area, South China Sea, and the Gulf of Tonkin, is roughly one million square kilometers. Tectonic folding of the basement rock has formed a series of ridges and basins that have captured nearly three million cubic kilometers of sediment from river runoff along the coast. The rivers contributing sediment include the Yellow River and the Yangtze River, having the first and fourth largest sediment burdens among the world's major rivers. In fact, the sedimentary deposits generated by China's rivers have overflowed basement ridges on the shelf proper and have proceeded to form vast sedimentary basins beyond the margins of the shelf in deep-water areas. The average thickness of the sedimentary deposits, an important parameter determining the flow of hydrocarbons into available trap structures, varies widely in different areas of the shelf, but exceeds 3,000 meters across broad reaches. Preliminary seismic analysis indicated sufficient unconformities, anticlines, and faults to provide ample trap structures, although experience in adjoining onland exploration and the high level of tectonic activity in the region might indicate a probability of highly fractured and difficult-to-locate trap structures.[1] In general, the size and characteristics of the Chinese continental shelf and its sedimentary basins warrant consideration from the perspective of hydrocarbon exploration.

The hydrocarbon potential of the Chinese continental shelf is important within the framework of China's international energy policies for a number of reasons. If significant and commercially viable petroleum and natural gas reserves are located by further exploration of Chinese areas of the shelf, energy production from the offshore areas would add to China's annual energy production capacity and would greatly spur the pace of development in the domestic energy production industries. China's oil and gas reserves could be increased by successful exploration and development of the offshore areas. Depending on the extent of offshore reserves and the cost of extraction, China could also significantly increase its energy commodity export potential through investment in a vigorous offshore development program. Exploration of the continental shelf, therefore, may add a significant energy development option to the choices facing Chinese energy planners over the next several decades.

The continental shelf is also significant in terms of its direct impact on the international energy policies of the People's Republic of China. Japan, Korea, Taiwan, Vietnam, and the Philippines all border directly on areas of the Chinese continental shelf or on subsea areas claimed by the Chinese government. The shelf and adjoining subsea areas have never been delineated by international agreement into defined areas of national seabed control. The areas claimed by the littoral states overlap. The territorial issue is further complicated by a lack of consensus regarding the appropriate principles for demarcation. Historical occupancy, midline, and depth criteria provide a bewildering array of rationalizations for conflicting territorial claims along the entire length of the shelf. In addition, the struggle between Peking and Taipei over the jurisdictional status of the two governments greatly complicates the achievement of any settlement of the territorial issue. China's immediate Asian neighbors loom large in the formulation of Peking's foreign policies, as do unsettled territorial issues. The continental shelf controversy is at the intersection of regional political relations and the settlement of China's territorial boundaries. It will, therefore, be a matter of considerable concern to the Chinese government for some time to come.

It should be understood from the outset, however, that the extent and ownership of hydrocarbon deposits in the continental shelf are not the only determining factors either in China's domestic energy development or in the formulation of China's international energy policies. Chinese energy planners have a number of other options that could be developed in the event that offshore oil and gas reserves prove subeconomic. The PRC has an enormous untapped hydropower potential. China possesses both the basic technology and the uranium resources necessary for rapid development of a nuclear power industry. Coal reserves are extensive and could be developed rapidly, especially in combination with advanced gasification or liquefaction technology. Oil and gas reserves in western areas of the country could be exploited if Peking decided to push the construction of a national pipeline network. Under these conditions, offshore oil and gas might accelerate energy development, but the lack of significant offshore reserves will not prevent it.

Nor will Peking necessarily be myopic in pursuit of Chinese territorial claims along the continental shelf. The general state of political relations with near-Asian neighbors may well induce the PRC to move gradually in its offshore exploration program, drilling first in areas conceded by all of the littoral states to be within China's legitimate area of control. Under certain conditions, Peking might even consider cooperative exploration and development programs in order to avoid confrontation over specific territorial claims. The Taiwan issue and the negative relationship with South Korea and Vietnam still limit the political option of cooperative development, but cooperation should not be ruled out within the longer time-frame of offshore development over the next two decades, particularly if political and commercial ties with Japan stabilize and are gradually strengthened.

Finally, there are enormous constraints operating on the pace of China's offshore exploration and extraction program. Even under ideal geological conditions, offshore oil development is roughly twice as expensive as comparable onland development. Conditions along the Chinese continental shelf are far from ideal. The thickest sediments are located in the deepest and most sharply contested areas of the shelf. Weather conditions are highly variable, with the southern end of the shelf subject to violent typhoons. Onland exploration indicates a likelihood of difficult drilling conditions and relatively small individual reservoirs. There is sharp competition within the Chinese economy for available capital and foreign exchange needed to purchase or construct offshore drilling and extraction equipment. For all of these reasons, as well as for important political considerations, the Chinese government may choose to move offshore in a slow and deliberate fashion.

The History of Foreign Exploration

Until recently, virtually nothing was known about the geological nature of the Chinese continental shelf, and little exploration of even the most rudimentary type had been conducted. Lack of attention to the shelf was due to both political and economic factors. The shelf lies in an area of the world that has been politically unstable for more than a century. Japanese occupation of northern China and the Second World War prevented any type of exploration in the 1930's and 1940's. World War II was followed by the completion of the Chinese revolution in 1949 and the installation of a Chinese government in direct conflict with the United States, the other dominant political force in the area in the postwar period. The Korean War, a succession of crises in the Taiwan Strait area, and the war in Vietnam continued this state of hostilities until

1971, making geological exploration of the shelf area a hazardous enterprise for both China and foreign countries. Even under more peaceful conditions, relatively little attention might have been paid to the continental shelf because of more attractive oil-development prospects both abroad (especially in the Middle East) and within China itself (Taching oilfield).

However, beginning in the early 1960's, under the auspices of the United Nations Economic Commission for Asia and the Far East (ECAFE), a series of conferences were held among Asian countries, focusing on regional energy problems. These conferences, combined with growing interest among multinational oil companies in exploration of the continental shelf areas of Indonesia and Southeast Asia, stimulated a more active interest in the geological characteristics of the Chinese continental shelf. In the late 1960's, with China preoccupied with the Cultural Revolution and its northern (Soviet) and southern (Indochina) security problems, a time window opened for a series of quietly organized and implemented oceanographic surveys of areas along the Chinese continental shelf. This time window for foreign exploration was quite narrow and began to close again as early as December 1970, when Sino-American relations warmed slightly and Washington became increasingly nervous about the political implications of seismic surveys and drilling projects along China's coastline. Meanwhile, however, a number of ECAFE and Japanese survey ships and planes had conducted a quick geological reconnaissance of the continental shelf. The results of this reconnaissance precipitated a wave of claims and counterclaims to contested areas of the shelf, the multiple leasing of disputed zones to competing oil companies, and the planning of several wildcat drilling expeditions. The reconnaissance also provided foreign experts with their only data on the continental shelf with which to assess the probability of significant hydrocarbon potential.

The CCOP Surveys

According to its own account, the Committee for Coordination of Joint Prospecting for Mineral Resources in Asian Offshore Areas (CCOP) was established in 1966 by ECAFE "to aid in the reconnaissance exploration for potential mineral resources from the sea floor off eastern Asia."[2] The initial membership included scientists from Japan, South Korea, Taiwan, and the Philippines. West German, French, British, and American scientists were then invited to participate in a Technical Advisory Group. The CCOP investigations drew initially on a reservoir of research on the marine geology of East Asia that had been sponsored during the 1960's by ECAFE, the Japanese government, and the government of Taiwan. The first *CCOP Technical Bulletin* was published in 1968, with the results of an analysis of sediments dredged from the bottom of the East China Sea. There was from the start, however, an awareness that further progress in exploration for mineral resources in the area would require seismic exploration of the continental shelf. In June 1963 the United States Naval Oceanographic Office conducted an initial airborne geomagnetic survey of the shelf as part of its "Project Magnet," the results of which were contributed to the ECAFE research group.[3] CCOP itself conducted a seaborne survey in October and November of 1968, using the "F. V. Hunt," an 850-ton seismic-survey ship then under contract to the U.S. Navy. The "Hunt" conducted more than 12,000 linear kilometers of seismic explorations on the northeastern part of the Chinese continental shelf, obtaining bathymetric, seismic, temperature, and sea color data.[4] These data provided the base for analysis of the seismic profile of sediments and basement structures as well as the tectonic and evolutionary history of the shelf areas of the Yellow and East China seas. The results were preliminary and general, but they greatly advanced knowledge of the hydrocarbon potential of the shelf areas. In particular, the study provided information on the huge sedimentary basins that cover broad reaches of the shelf, including their likely boundaries and thicknesses. The report of this first CCOP-sponsored voyage of the "Hunt" concluded that "A high probability exists that the continental shelf between Taiwan and Japan may be one of the most prolific oil reservoirs in the world."[5]

Taipei, Seoul, and Tokyo instantly recognized the implications of the CCOP survey for the development of their economies and for the politics of the region.[6] Each government in turn loudly reiterated its jurisdictional claims to overlapping areas of the shelf and began to map out concession areas for lease to the foreign oil corporations. About a dozen oil companies bid successfully on these concessions for "exclusive" drilling rights. Seoul and Taipei not only sold overlapping concessions in 1969 and 1970, but encouraged the companies concerned to drill immediately in their areas. Since most of the companies were based in the United States, encouraging their immediate involvement had security implications. Perhaps the United States could once again be drawn into a direct political alignment with these governments, and encouraged to defend an extravagant line of territorial claims along the length of the Chinese continental shelf. Any sign of caution on the part of the oil companies was interpreted as a national insult. Tokyo behaved somewhat more cautiously, but issued a series of preliminary concessions to domestic Japanese oil companies that stretched virtually to the shore of Taiwan.[7]

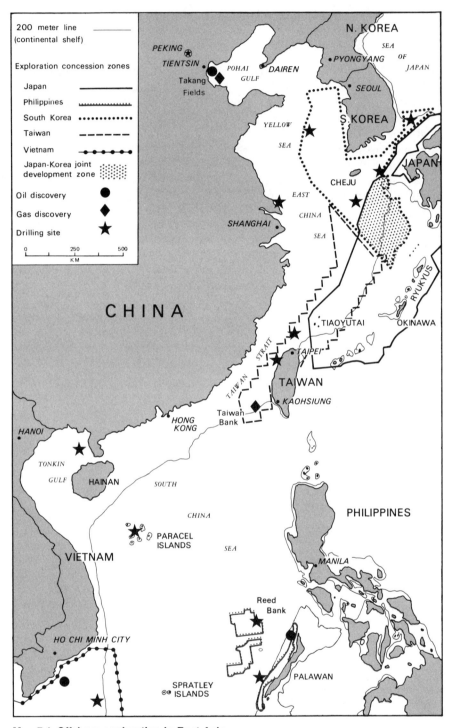

Map 7.1 Offshore exploration in East Asia.

The unexpectedly dramatic effects of the first CCOP reports stimulated another round of oceanographic research by that organization in 1969, covering areas of the South China Sea, the Gulf of Thailand, and the Sunda Shelf (Indonesia).[8] Again the studies were conducted with the assistance of the U.S. Navy and used the seismic survey ship "Hunt," as well as two other survey ships operated on contract to the Navy. Data were obtained from more than 25,000 kilometers of seismic profile traverses by both ships and aircraft.[9] The results were similar to those obtained along northern parts of the Chinese continental shelf. The combined effect of tectonic folding of the basement rock and sedimentation from coastal rivers has produced vast basins with a likely high level of organic content, over areas of the Chinese shelf, the shelves bordering coastal Southeast Asian countries, and on the floor of the deep sections of the China Basin. Any of these sedimentary basins could contain reservoirs of oil or gas. One of the most promising areas for initial exploration was thought to be the basin that stretches from the southern tip of Taiwan west and south along the Chinese coast toward Hainan—an area of certain political contention.[10]

The combination of the CCOP survey results, the overlapping and hastily drawn concession areas, the intense interest of neighboring countries, and rising curiosity among the oil companies led to several initial drilling efforts around the perimeter of the Chinese continental shelf. These efforts by China's neighbors have not been notably successful in finding commercially viable oil and gas reservoirs. But they have added another, more explicit type of data to the growing bank of information regarding the composition and extent of the sediments on the Chinese continental shelf. The drilling tests are still too few and too early to determine with any accuracy the hydrocarbon potential of the shelf.

Japan's Offshore Program

Japan has been drilling offshore petroleum exploration wells since 1880 along the country's immediate coastline (see Map 7.1).[11] Japanese fishing boats collected bottom samples from the East China Sea from 1920 to 1940, and the samples were analyzed by modern techniques in the late 1950's.[12] The Japanese government began serious efforts to explore the continental shelf in 1956 with the formation of the government-controlled Japan Petroleum Exploration Company (JAPEX) and the initiation of seismic and gravimetric surveys in the shelf areas immediately adjacent to Japan. These surveys were followed in 1958 by the construction of the first Japanese offshore "jack-up" drilling rig ("Hakuryu I") and the drilling of test wells along the central western coastline. Surveys and exploratory drilling continued during the 1960's, with new attention to areas south and west of Japan. Some gas was discovered in wells drilled on Okinawa. Shell and Mitsubishi filed an application for a joint exploration concession in the Sea of Japan in 1967.[13] In 1968 and 1969, in the wake of the CCOP seismic survey, Japanese companies filed exploration claims across broad areas of the East China Sea, stretching as far south as the Tiaoyutai (Senkaku) Islands to the north of Taiwan.[14] These companies conducted their own surveys to confirm the CCOP findings, but did not immediately embark on drilling activities because of the political uncertainty generated by conflicting claims in the area. In contrast to Seoul and Taipei, Tokyo had a great deal to lose and little to gain from a precipitate drilling program in contested waters. The Shell/Mitsubishi venture was planning to begin drilling in the area between Japan and Korea in 1971, but was deterred by a decision of the Japanese government to avoid upsetting the delicate process of Okinawa reversion.[15]

Since 1971, Japan has concentrated its drilling efforts in the nearshore areas around the main islands and the Ryukyus. About 40 wells had been drilled by 1975, of which several were listed as oil or gas shows. Just four wells were drilled in 1976, owing in part to opposition from Japanese fishing villages. Japan produced its first commercial offshore oil from the Aga-Oki field in September 1976.[16] But on the whole, the commercial value of offshore oil has not yet been established.

On January 31, 1974, Japan and South Korea initialed an agreement for joint exploration of a zone of some 95,000 square kilometers in the contested area of the shelf between the two countries. The People's Republic of China and North Korea immediately protested the agreement, which was reached without their participation or concurrence. Drilling within the zone was delayed, however, by strong political resistance to the agreement in the Japanese Diet. Final Diet approval was not reached until June 1977, and then only as result of a parliamentary maneuver.[17] South Korea threatened on several occasions to proceed without the Japanese, but was deterred from doing so by the reluctance of its foreign concessionaires to get involved in yet another politically uncertain drilling venture.

Taiwan's Offshore Program

If Japan was the first country to explore the continental shelf for hydrocarbons, Taiwan has been the most vigorous. Taiwan's commercial and political interests in exploration of the continental shelf coincide closely. A major oil or gas discovery under Taipei's auspices would both boost the domestic economy beyond its already rapid pace of development and provide a toehold against Chinese claims to the continental shelf and to Taiwan itself. From Taipei's perspective, significant involvement of American oil companies in Taiwan's concession areas could provide some reinforcement for deteriorating relations with the United States.

Taiwan's domestic petroleum industry arose as a result of a series of natural gas discoveries made on the island during the early 1960's by the state-controlled Chinese Petroleum Company (CPC). In 1967 Taiwan produced about 50 million cubic meters of natural gas and 33,000 metric tons of crude oil from domestic wells.[18] While not significant by international standards, domestic oil and gas production had begun to make a significant contribution to the economy of the island. These onland discoveries and the success of the CCOP survey led the government in Taipei to greatly expand its investment in CPC and to begin offshore seismic surveys of its own. By 1969–70 these surveys had enticed a number of the independent oil companies involved in international ventures to begin competitive bidding, and the Taipei government and CPC together soon signed exploration concession agreements with five U.S.-based companies.[19] Amoco was given some of the safer concessions along the coast of Taiwan as a reward for its early interest and participation in the 1967 seismic survey work. The value of the remaining concessions receded in direct proportion to the distance from Taiwan and the risk of confrontation with China. The concessions reached northward along the shelf to an area opposite Shanghai, China's largest industrial city.

By late 1970, the U.S. government was becoming increasingly concerned about the activities of U.S. oil companies in areas known to be claimed by the PRC. The matter reached high-level circles at the end of December when the State Department, Joint Chiefs of Staff, and National Security Council debated the risk of a seismic survey being conducted at the time by the "Gulfrex," a sophisticated U.S.-owned electronic survey ship operating in waters just off the Chinese coast.[20] Gulf was warned that U.S. forces would not be used in defense of its exploration activities, and the State Department formulated a general policy discouraging the use of U.S.-flag survey ships and drilling rigs off the Chinese coast. This decision was important because of the secret developments in U.S.-China relations and because of the risk that China would seize a survey ship or drilling rig, precipitating an international incident and the possible loss of sensitive electronic equipment.

This U.S. posture did not, however, discourage Taipei from pursuing its offshore exploration program and from encouraging the foreign oil companies to press forward. The CPC continued its own surveys and leased the "Wodeco IV," a drilling barge, for its own offshore program.[21] The foreign companies were just a shade ahead of the CPC, and Amoco drilled the first offshore well in a Taiwan concession in January

1973, using the "Glomar IV."[22] Amoco, Conoco, CPC, and Gulf started a total of seven wildcat wells off the coast of Taiwan in 1973.[23] The seven wells were clustered on a shallow bank 100 miles southwest of Kaohsiung (Conoco), an area very near shore along the central part of the west coast (Amoco and CPC), and midway between the northern tip of Taiwan and the Tiaoyutai Islands (Gulf). Exact data are lacking, but apparently none of these initial wells were productive. Several may have produced significant oil or gas "shows" and other information of geological importance. By 1974, Conoco, Amoco, and CPC had coordinated their drilling programs and were concentrated on the southernmost area of Kaohsiung. Four more wells were started during the year, and one was listed as a gas discovery on July 3, 1974.[24] This well, drilled by "Wodeco IV" on the shallow Taiwan Bank 100 miles off the southwest coast, was the first significant hydrocarbon discovery on the Chinese continental shelf outside of the Pohai Gulf. The well tested at significant but subcommercial levels of natural gas and condensate productivity. The Chinese media immediately attacked Taiwan's exploration program as a sellout of national resources to the foreign oil companies.[25] Meanwhile the Taiwan press claimed that the discovery was ten times the size of the island's largest onland discovery.[26]

The vigorous exploration program continued in 1975. Seven additional offshore wells were started during the year. The CPC reported an oil discovery at 3,600 meters in a well drilled 16 kilometers off the central portion of the west coast.[27] A second Conoco gas discovery was also rumored, but not reported in official drilling statistics.[28] Thus, by year-end 1975, 14 offshore wells had been started with only two or three significant discoveries. Furthermore, the commercial value of these discoveries has not been disclosed, indicating that they were probably all subcommercial. This record is quite mixed and would indicate some caution in assessing the prospects for oil and gas resources in the Taiwan Strait area of the continental shelf. Hydrocarbon deposits are obviously present, but may be limited and difficult to locate. It is likely that the first wells were drilled into the most promising structures indicated by extensive seismic and magnetic profiles of the area. The gas finds off Kaohsiung were the most significant discoveries to date. However, they are some distance from shore and lie in an area that might be contested by the PRC. Even if these discoveries were several times the gas discoveries onland on the island itself, political and commercial considerations might limit the viability of an extraction program. In any case, extraction will have to be heavily subsidized by the government of Taiwan, at least in the initial stages.

By 1976, Taiwan's offshore program suffered serious setbacks. Amoco and Conoco suspended their joint exploration program with CPC, which was forced to proceed on its own. CPC managed to drill just four offshore wells during the year, down from ten in Taiwan's concession areas in 1975. The four main concessionaires—Amoco, Conoco, Gulf, and Oceanic—all reported offshore relinquishments during 1976.[29] The exact mix of political and commercial motivations for this withdrawal is still unclear. But the simultaneous departure of the major concessionaires creates the distinct impression that the offshore discoveries have been subcommercial by international standards. This may not deter Taipei from attempting offshore development on its own. An offshore drill-ship ("Wodeco VIII") was produced for Fluor Drilling Company in one of Taiwan's shipyards in 1975, so the country must be considered to have developed a domestic rig-building capacity.[30] The government was also reported to be considering a $1.8 billion offshore exploration program that would greatly expand the existing drilling program on the basis of domestic investment through the CPC.[31]

However, it must be initially concluded that Taiwan's offshore program has failed to demonstrate the commercial viability of hydrocarbon deposits in the continental shelf areas around the island. Only major new discoveries would reverse this verdict. Development of the offshore gas discoveries, if successfully accomplished, might contribute to Taiwan's energy independence, but will not affect regional energy development patterns in East Asia. The sediments around the Tiaoyutai Islands are thought to be particularly promising and have not yet been explored by the drill. A bonanza discovery in the Tiaoyutai area is still possible, but the title to the islands is under dispute by both Japan and the PRC. The political constraint on exploration of Taiwan's concession areas northward along the thick sediments of the "Taiwan-Sinzi Folded Zone" increases exponentially with the distance from Taiwan.*

South Korea's Offshore Program

To a remarkable extent, South Korea's offshore exploration program has paralleled the Taiwan experience. The U.N. sponsored at least three

*As this book was going to press, I received a recent issue of the *American Association of Petroleum Geologists Bulletin* (Oct. 1978) that reports six CPC wildcats offshore in 1977 (pp. 1994–95). One of these wells was in the gas exploration area southwest of Taiwan. The other five were reported at coordinates in the South China Sea, directly south of Hong Kong, perhaps 200 miles from the Chinese coastline. If true, this report indicates that Taiwan, like the PRC, is planting the flag with the drill-bit. The area is just south of recent Chinese offshore oil discoveries along the coast of Kwangtung province at the mouth of the Pearl River (Chapter 8). All of the six reported wildcats were suspended or plugged and abandoned. See the section below on Taiwan's claims to the South China Sea.

geophysical studies in Korean waters. The first study took place in September–October 1966, before the formation of CCOP.[32] It measured sediment thickness and composition in the Pohang area and recommended initial concentration in other areas of the Yellow Sea, especially around Cheju Island. The second was the CCOP-sponsored geophysical survey conducted by the survey ship "Hunt." The third study was an aeromagnetic survey in February–March 1969 carried out with the assistance of the U.S. Naval Oceanographic Office as part of Project Magnet, also under CCOP sponsorship.[33] As a result of these surveys, the government in Seoul offered five large offshore exploration concessions in 1969 and 1970 to four companies.[34] In contrast to Taiwan, the concessions were made directly, without intervention by a national petroleum company. The majors showed more interest in South Korea's program than in Taiwan's and drilling commenced in December 1972, at about the same time as the first well in the Taiwan concessions. Three wells were started in 1972, and two more in 1973. All five were dry holes and were abandoned.[35] Drilling was suspended in 1974 and then resumed by Shell with two wildcat wells in the Korea Strait in 1975.[36] Shell reported oil and gas shows, but the discoveries tested at subcommercial levels of productivity.[37]

Like the Taiwan program, Seoul's efforts to stimulate offshore oil exploration by foreign oil companies ran into serious political difficulties. The Korean problems were predominantly territorial, with concessions and exploratory drilling contested by both of South Korea's powerful neighbors, China and Japan. The Chinese Foreign Ministry publicly warned Gulf, the most aggressive of the concessionaires, on March 15, 1973, as the "Glomar IV" entered contested waters.[38] Chinese gunboats were reported to have shadowed the Gulf drilling rig at about the same time.[39] The U.S. State Department once again pressured Gulf not to carry its exploration into contested waters. Gulf withdrew from its drilling efforts amid rumors in Seoul that commercial oil or gas had been discovered and relinquished owing to political factors.[40]

The failure of the Japanese Diet to ratify the joint offshore exploration agreement between January 1974 and June 1977 also slowed South Korea's offshore development program. The Wendell-Phillips concession from Seoul formed a large part of what was to become the joint exploration zone, so the company farmed out portions of its concession to three other companies in 1972, retreating to a 10 percent interest.[41] No drilling occurred in the area before the Diet ratified the joint exploration zone, although the Korean government several times threatened to explore on its own.[42] This was an idle threat in view of the country's lack of offshore drilling capability.

As with Taiwan's offshore concessions, by 1976 the oil companies were beginning to back out of their exploration agreements with South Korea. The avenue of departure was simply to allow the concessions to lapse because of failure to fulfill drilling commitments. No offshore drilling took place in 1976, and by early 1977 Gulf, Texaco, and Shell had all relinquished most of their concessions.[43] Like Taipei, Seoul was determined to press ahead without the initial concessionaires, perhaps to discover non-American oil companies interested in the continental shelf. Unlike Taiwan, however, South Korea has not developed a domestic offshore exploration capacity, and the road to a viable drilling program could be long and expensive to travel. Seoul is apparently pinning its hopes on the joint exploration zone and on joint ventures with Japanese companies in the Korea Strait.

Little is known outside of North Korea of Pyongyang's offshore development plans. Offshore oil exploration would be a delicate political matter for the North Korean government in view of its dispute with Peking over the precise demarcation of the continental shelf. China would certainly be hostile to the introduction of a Soviet exploration program, at least along the west coast of North Korea. On the other hand, Peking is unlikely to assist an exploration program that might encourage a firm attitude in the North Korean government regarding its claims to disputed areas of the continental shelf lying between the two countries. For its part, North Korea obtains a substantial portion of its annual petroleum imports from the PRC, a supply that might be sensitive to any aggravation of the offshore boundary issue. Interestingly enough, Pyongyang may follow Hanoi's example in seeking joint exploration agreements with foreign oil companies along its continental shelf: it was reported in December 1977 that North Korea and Asia Exploration Consultants, a Singapore company, signed a preliminary agreement for offshore exploration planning subject only to U.S. and South Korean exclusion from participation.[44]

Philippine Offshore Exploration

Exploration for oil in the Philippines has a long and somewhat checkered history. Onland exploration began in 1896. There are eight major sedimentary basins covering wide areas of the islands and offshore areas. After 1950, exploration programs were sharply increased and about 300 wells were drilled in the next 25 years. None of this exploration activity produced commercial oil or gas discoveries until 1976, although numerous oil and gas shows were recorded. There was a hiatus in the drilling program from 1964 until 1970, although geological and seismic work continued.[45] After 1970, serious attention began to be paid to the offshore areas, particularly in the Sulu Sea and west of Palawan Island.

A combination of domestic factors and the CCOP surveys stimulated a renewed interest in offshore oil possibilities in 1969 and 1970. Geophysical research was stepped up and included shooting seismic lines in the Sulu-Palawan area. At the end of 1971, 65 new concessions for petroleum exploration were granted, including many blocks in the offshore areas.[46] Oriental drilled the country's first two offshore exploration wells in the area northwest of Palawan during May and July 1971. Both were dry holes.[47] On December 21, 1972, President Marcos signed a new petroleum exploration law providing for a "Contract of Service" with foreign oil companies in tandem with local companies for exploration and development of national petroleum resources.[48] The first concessions in the Reed Bank area of the South China Sea were awarded to a joint venture called Fil-Am Resources. The Reed Bank concessions were part of an effort to strengthen Philippine claims in the South China Sea in areas contested by both Vietnam and China (as well as nominally by the government of Taiwan). Offshore drilling in 1972 was limited to one well in the Sulu Sea.

The new petroleum law led to the drilling of four offshore wells in 1973, including a Chevron test well drilled by the "Glomar III" that was the first under a Service Contract Agreement.[49] The Philippines National Oil Company was formed to provide greater government investment and control in both the exploration and downstream marketing phases of the petroleum industry. Japanese oil companies began to express interest in Philippine exploration programs, and a Philippine-Swedish consortium was formed to explore the Reed Bank concessions held by Seafront Petroleum, a Philippine company.[50] China thereupon reiterated its claim to the Reed Bank and the Spratley ("Nansha") Islands.[51]

Offshore activities in 1974 were confined to two dry holes drilled by Superior in the Sulu Sea and extensive seismic surveys of the Reed Bank area by the joint consortium.[52] Not until the following year did the center of gravity in Philippine petroleum exploration shift heavily toward the offshore program. Ten offshore wells were drilled, including five new wells west of Palawan. Ten new Reed Bank concession areas were obtained by White Eagle Overseas Oil Company.[53] During the following year, these offshore efforts began to bear fruit. On March 11, 1976, Marcos announced that the "Nido I" well drilled by Philippine Cities Service had come in as the country's first significant oil discovery in 80 years of exploration. A second Cities Service well in the same area off northwest Palawan produced oil in mid-1977, demonstrating the commercial possibilities of the Palawan shelf.[54] The Philippine-Swedish consortium began drilling two structures on the Reed Bank in the early months of 1976 and struck oil and gas shows.[55] Manila extended the area protected by the Philippine Navy to include the Reed Bank and played up the significance of the discovery. But two confirmation wells drilled in early 1977 came in dry and the oil companies involved were sufficiently unimpressed to suspend drilling operations in the area. Efforts were thereupon concentrated on the Palawan shelf, where a major discovery was reported in the Nido (Cities Service) complex in early 1978.[56]

The Philippine offshore exploration experience provides very little information on the petroleum potential of the South China Sea. The Palawan discoveries were in structures in near-shore areas that may not be entirely analogous with structures in other parts of the South China Sea area. They were certainly located far from the main sections of the Chinese continental shelf. Unless China is able to establish its rather dubious claims to the southern parts of the South China Sea, including the Reed Bank and the Spratleys, the Palawan discoveries will mean very little for the offshore development program of the PRC. The results of initial drilling efforts in the Reed Bank were less than encouraging for the petroleum prospects of the area.

Vietnam's Offshore Program

Vietnam's offshore exploration program is difficult to assess because of the political instability of the region during the period under consideration. The extended conflict in Indochina, the war and change of government in Cambodia, the U.S. withdrawal from South Vietnam and the ultimate reunification of Vietnam into a single political entity have all had a direct impact on offshore oil and gas exploration. The foreign companies engaged by the previous governments of Cambodia and Vietnam in concession agreements were sharply aware of the uncertainties of drilling in waters around an area of active, large-scale, and protracted conflict. They proceeded, therefore, with considerable caution and on a relatively limited scale, despite the reported geological promise of the continental shelf that wraps around the southern Indochina peninsula.

The government of Cambodia issued the first exploration rights in the area on February 21, 1970.[57] The entire Cambodia shelf area was treated as a single concession of 80,000 square kilometers and awarded to Elf du Cambodge, a subsidiary of the French ELF-ERAP group. A seismic survey was conducted in March and April 1970 in an effort to locate promising structures off the Cambodian coast. The company conducting this survey, Compagnie Générale de Géophysique (CGG), was the same French company that has been involved in sales of seismic equipment and services to the People's Republic of China. Elf du Cambodge did not drill offshore until August 19, 1972, and then completed only one well.[58] Elf farmed out part of its concession area to Esso and Marine Associates in 1972 and 1973, and further seismic exploration was conducted by Canadian Reserve in 1974.[59] Elf drilled two more wells in 1974. Operations were completely suspended in April 1975 as a consequence of the capture of Phnom Penh by the Khmer Rouge. No progress has been reported since in resumption of Cambodia's offshore exploration program. No discoveries have been reported in Cambodian waters as a result of the minimal drilling program conducted under the old government.

No exploration activity was reported off South Vietnam until Ray Geophysical conducted a seismic survey in 1969 and 1970 that followed up the CCOP surveys of the South China Sea.[60] The results of the Ray survey were sold to interested oil companies. The government in Saigon passed a petroleum exploration law on December 1, 1970, establishing the procedures for filing offshore exploration bids.[61] The first group of concessions were awarded in 1973, predominantly to U.S.–based oil companies, and these companies began conducting their own geophysical surveys of the concession areas.[62] Final bids were taken on the remaining concessions in 1974, and the first four offshore wells were started in the same year.[63] Several wells had oil and gas shows and one well drilled by the Ocean Prospector for Pecten–Cities Service came in as a significant, but subcommercial oil discovery.[64] Mobil-Kaiyo made a second, slightly larger oil discovery in March 1975, but was forced to suspend operations and remove the rig by the deteriorating military position of the Saigon government.[65]

The political and military cloud hanging over South Vietnam's offshore exploration program was evident from its inception. Seismic exploration and the delineation of concession areas were somewhat slower than in the case of the other offshore programs we have reviewed. Drilling began late, was limited to just eight wells despite encouraging results, and ended abruptly. Saigon's program was also plagued with a boundary dispute with Cambodia on the continental shelf. (Cambodia also has an offshore boundary dispute with Thailand.) A sharp dispute developed between Saigon and Phnom Penh in 1974 over the survey and drilling operations of Elf du Cambodge in contested waters. Saigon issued an injunction against drilling in the area and sent a note to the Cambodian government requesting that it deter the company from further projects in the area until the dispute could be settled. Elf desisted and the matter was laid to rest officially by the two governments on September 16, 1974, in an effort to avoid further strain on their uneasy alliance.[66]

Relatively little is known about the offshore programs or policies of North Vietnam and the government in Hanoi that inherited the oil potential of the southern part of the country in the summer of 1975. The continental shelf is exceptionally broad along the northern coast of Vietnam, extending under virtually the entire area of the Gulf of Tonkin and directly into the Chinese portion of the shelf west of Hainan Island. The exact boundary of North Vietnam's portion of the shelf is uncertain and the subject of dispute between Hanoi and Peking. The CCOP surveys did not extend into the Gulf of Tonkin, but it is thought that Liuchow Basin reaches right to the coast.[67] If so, then the Gulf of Tonkin should contain sediments and structures resembling those of the rest of the region.

North Vietnam may have undertaken some preliminary geophysical research on its continental shelf with Soviet assistance. If so, the scope of such research was probably restricted by the war to insignificant levels. North Vietnamese waters were hazardous during the period of U.S. bombing in the north and any such program would have received very low priority in the war economy. The first reliable foreign reports of Hanoi's interest in offshore exploration appeared in 1973. The Italian national oil company, ENI, was said to have signed a technical agreement with the North Vietnamese government providing for assistance in offshore oil exploration over an eight-year period and the training of Vietnamese engineers in offshore operations.[68] Japanese companies, under the umbrella of the Japan Petroleum Development Corporation, sent offshore oil delegations to North Vietnam in 1973 and 1974 and expressed interest in a joint venture on Vietnam's continental shelf.[69] These contacts established Hanoi's interest in offshore exploration, but did not result in any activities during 1974. The defeat of Saigon in the spring of 1975 brought about a de facto unification of offshore policies and programs in the northern and southern parts of the country.

U.S. oil companies hastily departed South Vietnam in April 1975 as the impending collapse of the government became a certainty. The companies claimed exploration and concession losses as high as $60 million when the Provisional Revolutionary Government canceled all agreements made by the Saigon government, although rumors began to circulate immediately that the oil companies had contacted the Vietcong and were negotiating a new set of agreements.[70] Whatever the truth of these rumors, the new government began public discussions of foreign participation in new offshore programs with remarkable alacrity. Interim arrangements were made with sympathetic Third World countries to fill in the gap left by the departure of the oil companies. Iraq offered free petroleum supplies to tide southern Vietnam over until more permanent arrangements could be made.[71] The Algerian state oil company, Sonatrach, acted as a technical advisory agency and assisted in the establishment of the new South Vietnam Oil Company to deal with all matters relating to petroleum exploration and marketing.[72] In September Foreign Minister Nguyen Thi Binh invited the companies previously engaged in offshore exploration to renew their contacts with the new government and to discuss resumption of the exploration program.[73] This gesture surprised the oil companies, which were unable to respond because of a U.S. law forbidding contact with the "enemy." Bills were introduced in Congress to bypass the law, and several Japanese companies took initiatives in response to the invitation. The Foreign Minister repeated her offer in an interview on May 3, 1976, and the U.S. companies were reported to have held confidential discussions with Vietnamese officials.[74] A French company (Comex) negotiated for a preliminary contract to provide technical assistance in construction of a logistic base at Vung Tao for offshore exploration and to set up an office in Ho Chi Minh City (Saigon) that would manage relations with foreign oil companies.[75] The Japanese companies, unhampered by restrictive legislation, continued to press for offshore concessions, and Norway agreed to provide an offshore rig and technical training in its use.[76] There was one report of an onland oil strike (Thai Binh province), but no further offshore drilling had been conducted by year-end 1977.[77]

It is still too early to assess the offshore petroleum prospects of Vietnam. Of four exploratory wells drilled in 1974 and 1975, one came in as a significant discovery—a far better ratio than had been achieved by any of the other countries drilling around the periphery of China's continental shelf. Vietnam's shelf areas are directly contiguous to China's, although this geographic continuity does not necessarily imply a close geologic analogy, since different portions of the shelf have different sedimentation environments and may have varying structural characteristics. The eagerness of foreign oil companies to return to exploration in Vietnamese waters might also indicate favorable results from earlier drilling. The motivation of the new government of Vietnam (now unified) is a mixture of commercial and political factors. Offshore oil discoveries would greatly benefit the reconstruction of Vietnam's war-torn economy. The country also has an interest in moving offshore as rapidly as possible, in order to strengthen its claims to contested portions of the continental shelf and to islands in the South China Sea.

Summary of Foreign Offshore Exploration Activities

This chapter has provided some details on the offshore exploration programs of countries bordering China's continental shelf or subsea areas

TABLE 7.1
Offshore Drilling Programs in East Asia

Year	Offshore wells	Offshore discoveries[a]	Year	Offshore wells	Offshore discoveries[a]
Japan:			Philippines:		
1972	10	5	1972	1	0
1973	11	4	1973	4	0
1974	9	5	1974	2	0
1975	2	0	1975	10	0
1976	4	0	1976	7	1
1977	5	0	1977	7	3
Total	41	14	Total	31	4
South Korea:			Cambodia:		
1972	3	0	1972	1	0
1973	2	0	1974	2	0
1975	2	0	Total	3	0
Total	7	0	Vietnam:		
Taiwan:			1975	4	1
1974	4	1	Total	4	1
1975	10	2			
1976	4	0			
1977	6	0			
Total	24	3			

Source: "Petroleum Developments in Far East," *AAPGB* (annual international report), Table 2.
[a] Discovery defined as minimum show of 1,000 BOPD or 3 MMCFD. No commercial evaluation implied.

claimed by the PRC. The brief histories of these offshore programs indicate a relatively high level of exploratory activity throughout the region, activity that is likely to continue and may increase if significant hydrocarbon discoveries are made (see Table 7.1). During the period under review, the countries around China's continental shelf (Korea, Taiwan, the Philippines, Cambodia, and Vietnam—excluding Japan) drilled 69 offshore exploration wells. They made a total of eight significant oil and gas discoveries through the end of 1977. At a conservative estimate of $2 million per well, the investment in drilling activities alone (excluding the costs of obtaining exploration concessions) was well over $100 million. There was a 13 percent success ratio in drilling programs that averaged a per discovery cost of more than $14 million. None of the finds were considered immediately commercial, although several might be activated at a commercial level by government investment. Japan's offshore program did much better, registering 14 discoveries in the near-shore areas out of 41 wells drilled between 1972 and 1977. Many of the Japanese discoveries were also subcommercial, and most were plugged and abandoned. None of the Japanese wells were drilled in the area south and west of Japan that is under dispute with Korea and China. Of the other contiguous countries, Vietnam chalked up the best discovery ratio, with one discovery in four wells drilled. The Philippines and Taiwan followed, both with a 13 percent discovery rate. These figures may be distorted somewhat by the lack of official test data from Taiwan, but the distortion is offset by the small production capacity of most of the discoveries in the region. Nothing in any of the drilling programs in areas explored so far would indicate vast, easily extractable crude petroleum reserves in the Chinese continental shelf. There is a somewhat greater indication of gas potential than oil potential, but none of the drilling programs are far enough advanced or extend out onto the shelf far enough to determine the likely ratio of future oil and gas discoveries. With the experience and data generated by these early drilling programs in mind, we are in a somewhat better position to evaluate conflicting foreign estimates of China's offshore oil potential. But it should also be kept in mind that none of the thicker and deeper sediment basins have yet been tapped by the drill, a test that will render the final verdict on hydrocarbons in the continental shelf.

Estimates of China's Offshore Hydrocarbon Resources

Estimating the ultimately recoverable oil and gas resources in the Chinese continental shelf under present information and exploration constraints lies somewhere between speculation and heresy in the lexicon of the petroleum geologist. For that reason, there have been very few systematic efforts to evaluate China's offshore oil and gas potential, and such efforts as have occurred are generally regarded with skepticism within the field and are usually excluded from regional and global resource estimates. Foreign exploration of shelf areas close to China reached only the most primitive stage—preliminary seismic and magnetic mapping—before it was cut short by Peking's objections to such activities and by the growing strength of political relations between China and the United States. By the end of 1970, the narrow window for geophysical exploration of the shelf had closed—before follow-up studies could be launched and three years before the sharp increase in petroleum prices that accompanied the Arab oil embargo and the onset of the energy crisis. The general extent and thickness of sedimentary deposits are the main types of data regarding the shelf available outside of China.

The great size of the sedimentary basins, coupled with indications that the shelf contains a number of "graben" structures that facilitate the migration of hydrocarbons in the sediments into economically exploitable traps, led initially to an optimistic assessment of the oil-bearing potential of the continental shelf.[78] The Chinese government, which had drilled only a few test wells in marginal areas around the shelf, dropped speculative hints to visiting foreign delegations that they thought the oil potential to be enormous. Peking was attempting to lure Japanese business into crude oil trade (and away from joint development projects in Siberia) at the time, and had a vested interest in stimulating Japanese dreams of a second Middle East on their own doorstep. And that was precisely the conclusion of the most speculative foreign guesses.[79]

More recently, however, geologists and ocean engineers have used two different methods to estimate the broad limits within which oil resources in the Chinese continental shelf may fall. One method, applied by Maurice Terman at the U.S. Geological Survey, was to locate the graben structures both onland and offshore and to evaluate the economically recoverable resources which could possibly be extracted from each graben, based on their specific depth, geologic history, and fracture characteristics. This approach yielded the general conclusion that economically recoverable resources from each of the 20 graben in the northeast onland and continental shelf areas would range around one billion barrels.[80] The total hydrocarbon content of each graben might be much higher. However, the tectonic crustal movements that formed the original basin structure also caused the basins to be highly fractured, once formed.[81] The graben that form Taching, Shengli, and Takang oilfields, contiguous to and at points continuous with the offshore basins, are known to be highly fractured. Western experts also believe the trap structures to be predominantly stratigraphic, analogous to the Uinta (Green River) Basin in Utah.[82] Highly fractured, stratigraphic traps would make the oil and gas reservoirs within the graben relatively small, dispersed in irregular patterns, and very difficult to locate with a drill. Thus the quantity of oil that may be economically retrieved from each graben is limited, placing total economically recoverable resources from onland and offshore areas at a maximum figure of 5–7 billion metric tons, of which only 1–2 billion tons would come from the offshore areas.[83] Terman had some doubt about the economics of recovery of even this quantity of offshore oil. Should the main deposits be discovered in deep-water areas or the yield prove to be primarily natural gas, the hydrocarbon potential of the continental shelf might become uneconomical to realize. Our review of the offshore exploration programs of neighboring countries suggests the type of economic limit that Terman has in mind. For example, the natural gas discovery on the Taiwan Bank lies 100 miles from the coast of Taiwan and will only be brought ashore if the size of the gas reservoirs

justifies the expense of the necessary subsea pipelines. Even a determined government development program faces the balance of cost and
return in offshore exploration.

A completely independent investigation by an ocean engineer at the
Massachusetts Institute of Technology yielded a somewhat more optimistic but still guarded result. Jan-Olaf Willums projected the likely oil
and gas yield of the sedimentary basins along the shelf through the use
of probability analysis and analogy to similar basins elsewhere in the
world.[84] Each projection was tied to a specific level of probability, and a
range of likely resources was thereby established. The median result was
that economically recoverable offshore resources might be around 4 billion metric tons (30 billion barrels). A. A. Meyerhoff and Willums more
recently published a paper supporting this estimate.[85] They added the
projected offshore resources to Meyerhoff's onland estimate to produce
a total estimate of ultimately recoverable crude petroleum resources of
about 10 billion metric tons (75 billion barrels).[86] Petroleum geologists
tend to be skeptical of probability-analogy estimates that have not been
confirmed by drilling programs. The difficulty stems from the choice of
analogous basins. Analogy with a high-yielding basin produces some
probability of a high yield in the resulting estimates. Analogy with a low-
yielding basin produces some probability of a pessimistic outcome. Willums himself provided a low estimate of about one million metric tons
and a high estimate of 40 billion tons in his original study, indicating the
extreme range of possibilities generated by the analog type of analysis.[87]
It should be noted, however, that despite their divergent approaches to
the problem, Terman and the Meyerhoff and Willums paper reached
total recoverable resource estimates of 5–7 and 10 billion metric tons,
respectively. These estimates provide a range of reasonable projections,
and neither should be rejected out of hand.

The upshot of these independent studies is that foreign experts (and
Peking itself) simply do not know how much oil and gas are likely to be
discovered in the Chinese continental shelf. Until further evidence from
drilling ventures begins to filter out of the PRC and other countries
around the shelf, a fairly conservative approach to the problem would be
warranted by the geological characteristics of the sedimentary basins in
the shelf, by China's own onland exploration experience, and by the preliminary drilling results from the contiguous countries. If this ambiguous result is somewhat distressing from the perspective of the scientific
criteria normally applied to the analysis of petroleum potential, it does
not really hamper our analysis. The function of estimates of recoverable
sources in the context of this study is simply to provide a reasonable
foundation for projections of growth in China's petroleum industry.

The projections provided in the Statistical Profile and the last chapter of Part I assumed a range of crude oil and natural gas resource scenarios, from total onland and offshore recoverable resources of 5 billion tons (35 billion barrels), to an optimistic 35 billion metric ton total resource (250 billion barrels). The seriously considered projections were all based on 8.5–20 billion metric tons of recoverable crude petroleum and 7.5–15 trillion cubic meters of natural gas resources. The oil resources were quadrupled to 35 billion tons and gas resources raised to 40 trillion cubic meters to provide a "what if" outer limit on the projections. This outer limit allows for the possibility that rumors circulated by Chinese petroleum officials in the early 1970's may have some validity. The outer limit would give China oil and gas resources in the range of U.S. recoverable resources, but not in the range of the Middle East.[88]

A number of nongeological factors further cloud the future potential of China's offshore oil development. The shelf is fairly shallow, increasing in depth to 150–200 meters as one moves southward along the sweep of the Chinese coastline and eastward toward the continental margin. Some of the most promising sedimentary basins are located in the deepest areas of the shelf, making extraction more costly. The seas along the shelf are normally quite placid, but subject to seasonal typhoons which sweep up from the Philippines, carrying winds of more than 100 miles per hour. Thus, particularly in the southern portions of the shelf, where the typhoon danger is greatest, offshore rigs will have to be sufficiently sturdy to withstand such gales.

Finally, the perversity of nature has located the thickest and most promising sediments precisely in the areas of greatest international contention—the Tiaoyutai region just north of Taiwan, and in the deep section of the East China Sea, midway between China and Japan. And so it is to the jurisdictional dispute that we turn next.

The Territorial Issue

Seven governments (eight before the unification of Vietnam) have laid claim to portions of the continental shelf—the People's Republic of China, Japan, both Korean governments, Taiwan, Vietnam, and the Philippines. Not only do the various governments disagree about the ownership of portions of the shelf, but they differ fundamentally regarding the international legal principles under which the jurisdictional dispute should be settled, or whether it should be settled within the framework of international law at all.

Peking has not stated the exact extent of its claim, but vociferous editorials in the Chinese press indicate that the PRC believes it owns the entire shelf from the Pohai Gulf to the remote island areas of the South China Sea, with the exception of narrow strips along the Korean and Vietnamese coasts.[89] The pattern of making the maximum conceivable initial claim, and then showing willingness to "compromise" over the most far-flung portions of the claim, is traditional in Chinese diplomacy and was used recently in border disputes with India, Burma, and the Soviet Union. In the Sino-Indian border dispute, China claimed the entire area of the Himalayas (in the eastern sector), right down to the smallest foothills, but defended claims only up to the McMahon Line (watershed) despite a demonstrated ability to penetrate to the farthest extent of the formal claim.[90] During the Sino-Soviet border dispute, China has claimed large chunks of Siberia, but is really concerned about limited areas of the border in Sinkiang and along the Amur River. These historical precedents would indicate that the maximum Chinese claim is not necessarily a statement of political intent. This observation should be tempered, however, by the recognition that China has exceedingly long time-horizons in its territorial claims, and clings tenaciously to a claim that the government considers essential to the maintenance of "historical boundaries" or to national pride.

The Chinese government has based its claim to contested areas of the shelf on a variety of principles that are only loosely related to the formal structure of international law. The public and formal Chinese position rests on the twin pillars of the natural prolongation of the shelf from the Chinese coastline and historical sovereignty over the islands on the shelf as expressed in various historical documents and by traditional use of the entire shelf area by Chinese traders and fishermen.[91] Peking was slow to lay formal claim to the shelf, but vociferous in the expression of those claims.

Japanese Claims

Tokyo is the most significant antagonist Peking faces over the issue of the ownership of the continental shelf. Japan's narrow continental shelf extends down the Ryukyu island chain and connects directly with the Chinese shelf south of Korea in the area of the Japan-Korea Joint Development Zone (see Map 7.2). Japan has implicitly claimed broad reaches of the East China Sea portion of the shelf that contains the thickest and most promising sedimentary deposits. The Japanese claim to the East China Sea shelf is based on the principle of the median line between the Japanese coast and the Chinese coast.[92] This position contrasts sharply with the rationale advanced by the Chinese government for its claims, a logic that leans toward the depth criterion and natural prolongation of the shelf.

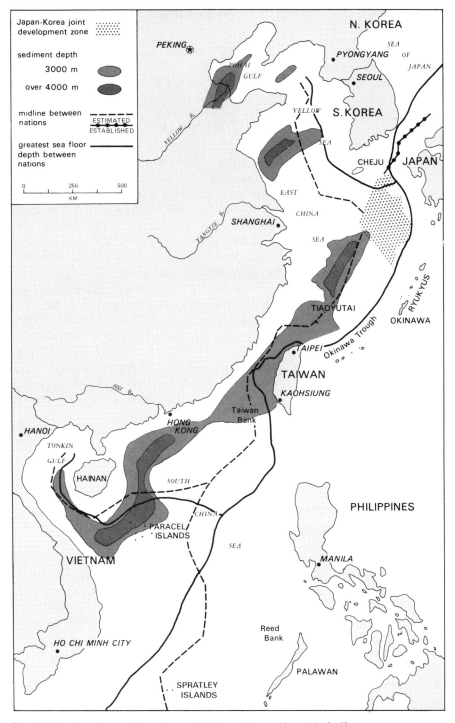

Map 7.2 Sediments and boundary criteria on the continental shelf.

Both governments have advanced complex historical arguments to support their claims, but such arguments tend to overlap and cancel each other out to a significant degree. Both Chinese and Japanese nationals have been active on the shelf area in fishing and other commercial ventures for centuries. Both governments can show documentary evidence of earlier control of or claims to sovereignty over some of the islands along the shelf.[93] None of these historical arguments are very convincing in view of the fact that the present dispute was stimulated by discovery of the hydrocarbon potential of the shelf areas. It is doubtful that any of the historical documents presented as evidence in official statements will have any bearing on the future exploration for oil and gas in the offshore sedimenatry basins. The image of one of the two most powerful governments in Asia giving up its political claims to an area of possible petroleum discoveries on the basis of a document unearthed in the archives of its opponent is ludicrous.

The Sino-Japanese territorial dispute over the continental shelf has been aggravated by an intense confrontation over ownership of the Tiaoyutai Islands, a cluster of microscopic islands situated off the northern tip of Taiwan over some of the thickest sediments in the entire shelf area. Japan claims the Tiaoyutai (or Senkakus in Tokyo's vocabulary) partly on the basis of the Okinawa Reversion Treaty signed with the United States in 1971.[94] The treaty included the entire Ryukyu chain, and Japan took the Ryukyus to include the Tiaoyutai. Taipei also claims the Tiaoyutai on the basis of proximity, and the overseas Chinese communities became emotionally involved in the nationalist aspects of the dispute. If Tokyo could establish its claim to the Tiaoyutai, it would open up a further jurisdictional dispute over the entire shelf in the southern portion of the East China Sea. Japan could then claim the median line on the shelf between the Tiaoyutai and the Chinese coast, assuming that international law (and practice) provides for such a magnificent shelf area connected to such small islands.[95] The Japanese claim to the Tiaoyutai is seriously damaged by a deep trench that runs north-south between the shelf belonging to the Ryukyus and the shelf connected with Taiwan and the Chinese coast. A successful midline claim based on the Tiaoyutai would be a most unlikely outcome, since the Tiaoyutai Islands lie to the west of the Okinawa Trough. However, China, Taiwan, and Japan have continued their active claims to the Tiaoyutai, and the issue must be considered far from closed.

A brief history of the confrontation between Tokyo and Peking over the shelf indicates that both governments have made efforts to sharply limit the intensity of the dispute in order to avoid disrupting the political accommodation that has been taking place since 1971. As early as March

11, 1971, the Japanese government stopped exploration activities in the East China Sea sections of its concession zone.[96] Only a few seismic surveys have been conducted by Japanese companies since that date, and no wells have been drilled in the contested shelf area or around the Tiao-yutai.[97] In April 1972, following a series of strong statements by the Chinese press, Japan's Defense Agency announced that the Tiaoyutai (Senkakus) would be included in Japan's air identification zone.[98] Japan's fishery agency sent patrol boats into the Yellow Sea in the late months of 1972 after Peking protested the violation of its own military surveillance zone in the Yellow Sea by some 360 Japanese fishing boats.[99] But the communiqué establishing diplomatic relations in September 1972 made reference to the negotiation of a fisheries agreement between the two countries, and both sides exercised considerable military restraint while attempting to maintain their verbal policy positions. There were some reports that China attempted to tie the Tiaoyutai issue to the first oil export agreement with Japan in 1973, but such efforts had no visible effect on the Japanese position.[100]

The Sino-Japanese fisheries agreement was negotiated in 1974, signed on August 15, 1975, and ratified on December 22, 1975.[101] Among other provisions, it included a Chinese assertion of a "military warning area" in the Pohai Gulf and the northern Yellow Sea and required Chinese permission for Japanese fishing boats entering this zone. The Japanese government "took note" of the Chinese position regarding this zone but declined to endorse it. The agreement also established a "trawl-free zone" along the Chinese coast in which fishing vessels with engine capacities of more than 600 horsepower were prohibited. This zone is essentially designed to protect the Chinese fishing industry from highly mechanized Japanese fishing ships. The outer edge of the "trawl-free zone" is of interest in the context of the Sino-Japanese subsea jurisdictional dispute over the continental shelf. The outer boundary of the fishing zone runs about 200 kilometers off the Chinese coastline from the edge of the "military warning area" in the northern Yellow Sea to the 27th parallel north of Taiwan.[102] This fishing boundary runs slightly west of the median lines, with both Korea's and Japan's median-line claim on the shelf (using the Ryukyus as the base for Japan's median). Peking deliberately avoided provoking the Japanese in establishing the line, leaving delineation of shelf claims to an unspecified future political settlement.

It should be pointed out that China's position vis-à-vis Japan on the continental shelf has been greatly weakened by recent developments in the law of the sea. The Japanese claim to East China Sea portions of the shelf must "jump" the deep Okinawa Trough that lies between the Ryukyus and the continental shelf proper. There has been a strong trend toward the acceptance of 200-mile "economic zones" outside of the territorial seas limit (12 miles) bordering coastal countries:

All evidence . . . indicates an established trend of opinion in most parts of the world towards a basic revision in the law of the sea in such a way as to provide new protections for the developmental interests of coastal states in extensive offshore areas. According to this view, what is needed is an extensive maritime regime or regimes under which the coastal state can exercise special rights or privileges and certain responsibilities with respect to the living and non-living resources of the sea and related activities affecting the environmental activities of these areas.

What is envisaged by many states is the establishment of a specific multifunctional zone which may extend as far as 200 miles from the base line of the territorial sea, the exact extent in each case to be determined by reference to agreed upon criteria.[103]

Many coastal countries have adopted 200-mile economic zones, and they have been incorporated in the negotiating text of the draft treaty of the United Nations Third Conference on the Law of the Sea. The zone includes subsea mineral rights and the control of hydrocarbon exploration and exploitation. The acceptance of the concept of the exclusive economic zone has direct relevance to demarcation of the continental shelf lying between China and Japan. The negotiating text defines "continental shelf" in terms of natural prolongation (the basis for the Chinese claim):

The continental shelf of a coastal State comprises the sea-bed and subsoil of the submarine areas that extend beyond its territorial sea throughout the natural prolongation of its land territory to the outer edge of the continental margin, or to a distance of 200 nautical miles from the baselines from which the breadth of the territorial sea is measured where the outer edge of the continental margin does not extend up to that distance.[104]

However, the negotiating text also provides for delimitation of the continental shelf between adjacent or opposite states on the basis of the midline criterion (basis for the Japanese claim), rather than the line of greatest depth:

The delimitation of the continental shelf between adjacent or opposite States shall be affected by agreement in accordance with equitable principles, *employing, where appropriate, the median or equidistance line,* and taking account of all the relevant circumstances.[105]

The negotiating text does not even mention the line of greatest depth or natural prolongation as suitable criteria for delimitation of the continental shelf when the baselines of two coastal states lie less than 400 miles apart. The People's Republic of China, moreover, is in the awkward position of having loudly supported development of the 200-mile exclusive economic zone:

Firmly safeguarding their sovereignty and jurisdiction over the 200-mile exclusive economic zone, many third world countries urged that no foreign activities in the economic zone should be detrimental to the independence and security of a coastal country and that no foreign military activities and installations should be permitted in the economic zone of a coastal country or on its continental shelf without the approval of the given country.[106]

Peking obviously supports the 200-mile economic zone for both security and economic reasons. But this support implies acceptance of a Japanese 200-mile exclusive economic zone reaching westward from the baseline established by the Ryukyus and thereby "jumping" the Okinawa Trough.

Acceptance of the "median or equidistance line" in the Yellow Sea or the East China Sea would seriously damage the Chinese claim to wide areas of the continental shelf. The PRC has not explicitly referred to the midline settlement criterion in its support for the 200-mile exclusive economic zone. Acceptance of the midline would mean relinquishing exploration rights in the thickest structures along the entire continental shelf, lying along the "Taiwan-Sinzi Folded Zone."[107] It would also mean relinquishing claims to the Tiaoyutai Islands and would establish a precedent for de jure separation of Taiwan from Chinese sovereignty. Peking, therefore, is most unlikely to accept the midline as the basis for delimitation of its continental shelf. China's legal position along the continental shelf has been greatly weakened by international acceptance of the 200-mile exclusive economic zone and the implied international acceptance of the midline criterion. Japan's claims have been correspondingly strengthened, as have the claims of the two Koreas in the Yellow Sea and Vietnamese claims in the Gulf of Tonkin. It would not be wise to overemphasize the functional importance of this legal development. China may very well refuse to sign any new convention on the law of the sea or may seek to disrupt its successful conclusion. There are many "anti-imperialist" arguments that could be advanced as rationale for rejecting one or another peripheral articles in the convention. In terms of the political realities of the region, China's naval strength has been growing steadily, especially in the type of small fast-attack craft that could be used to threaten or disrupt offshore exploration by any country along the shelf. A midline settlement will be impossible without at least tacit Chinese acceptance.

On the other hand, international acceptance of the 200-mile exclusive economic zone and the midline criterion has probably increased the determination of the Japanese government and other claimant governments to press for an equidistance settlement against China. The creation of a joint development zone for hydrocarbon exploration in the contested areas east of the midline represents the minimum Japanese demand, if experience in the settlement of the dispute between South Korea and Japan is any guide. Even the concept of joint development zones has been vigorously attacked in the Japanese Diet as a betrayal of the midline criterion. A further retreat to the line of greatest depth would be political hara-kiri for any Japanese administration.

This analysis leads directly to the conclusion that no immediate settlement is likely in the continental shelf dispute between China and Japan. Unless one government or the other changes tactics drastically, there will most likely be an extended period during which both governments will exercise restraint in exploration or development of contested areas of the shelf. The importance of smooth political relations to both parties greatly transcends the importance of short-term exploitation of unknown and possibly nonexistent oil and gas resources that are thought to lie hidden in the sediments of the Taiwan-Sinzi Folded Zone. A later section of this chapter will explore a third option—joint development—but only after the positions of other shelf claimants have been presented.

Korean Claims

Korean claims to the continental shelf have been complicated by the existence of two competing governments in the northern and southern halves of the country and by the establishment of the Japan–South Korea Joint Development Zone. Judging from the extent of Seoul's concession zones on the shelf, the South Korean claims must be based on the natural prolongation principle in the southern parts of the shelf under dispute with Japan and on the midline principle in the middle section of the western shelf under dispute with China.[108] Unlike Japan, South Korea has no political relations (except combative propaganda exchanges) with the People's Republic of China. Seoul has therefore pursued its offshore exploration program with considerable vigor, encouraging foreign oil companies to take high risks in drilling ventures in disputed waters. Unfortunately for Korea, the sediments along its coast are thinner than in other shelf areas, ranging around 1,000 meters in thickness over most of the area claimed by South Korea. Sediments of this thickness may still be productive, but initial drilling has done nothing to raise hopes of large petroleum potential along the southwestern Korean coastline.

Following initiation of its drilling program in 1973, Korea successfully negotiated an agreement with Japan for joint exploration of contested areas of the shelf lying between the two countries. The Japan–South Korea Joint Development Zone agreements were initialed in January 1974. Seoul had a substantial political and commercial stake in the agreement. It served to legitimize its claims in the more distant areas of the shelf and drew the Japanese government and major Japanese enterprises into joint participation in oil exploration with South Korea. Seoul therefore made every effort to ensure that the agreement would be ratified by the Japanese government as soon as possible. However, by early 1975 it became clear that the Japanese administration under Prime Minister Takeo Miki was going to have considerable political difficulty in gaining ratification from a reluctant Diet.[109] Resistance in the Diet to the joint development zone was based on a coalition of political groups on the left who opposed any measure that might seriously offend the People's Republic of China and groups on the right who were concerned that ratification of the treaty would represent relinquishment of the midline principle as the basis for Japanese claims along the Chinese continental shelf. (In fact, a second agreement accompanying the Joint Development Zone Agreement explicitly defined and accepted the midline as the line of demarcation on the shelf north from the joint development zone to a point at 35°18.2′N, 130°23.3′E.)[110]

China expressed opposition to the pact on numerous occasions. The Chinese position developed on the basis of two principles—that the agreement was an "infringement on China's sovereignty" and that it was reached "behind China's back."[111] Of these two Chinese arguments, the sovereignty position is the weaker. The zone lies much closer to South Korea and Japan than to China, and the hypothetical China-Japan midline runs through just the westernmost tip of the zone. Even if all the parties agreed to the midline principle, which they do not, China could be excluded by a marginal alteration of the boundaries of the zone. Furthermore, the precise location of the median line, itself dependent on prior agreement regarding baselines, is still in doubt. The Chinese press has used the midline argument with reference to the zone, but official statements of the Foreign Ministry have steered clear of the midline criterion.[112] Official reference to the midline would compromise China's insistence on the natural prolongation criterion. The exclusion argument is perhaps somewhat more realistic, since the PRC will obviously have long-range interest in any settlement along the shelf and Peking argues that Chinese representatives should participate in the conclusion of any shelf-related agreements. Unfortunately, this position leaves the Chinese government in the awkward dilemma that it is arguing on behalf of participation in negotiations with a government that it refuses to recognize at any level.

The Joint Development Zone issue came to a head in the Diet in the early months of 1977. Prime Minister Takeo Fukuda, who had inherited the issue from his predecessor, finally attempted to push the agreement through the Diet in a series of complicated parliamentary maneuvers. The Chinese government saw ratification coming and registered its disapproval, commenting freely on the nature of the Japanese political process.[113] Peking's protests, however, were futile, as Fukuda successfully delayed the end of the current Diet session, forcing a vote on the issue in June and ratification of the Joint Development Zone.[114] Instruments of ratification for the Japan-Korea Agreement on Joint Development of the Continental Shelf were exchanged on June 22, 1978, much to the annoyance of Peking. Joint exploration had still not begun at the end of 1978. The South Korean government, whose initial efforts to discover oil on the shelf have been frustrated by both politics and nature, is staking its remaining hopes on the Joint Development Zone. Regardless of whether or not exploration within the zone is successful, the establishment of the zone is an important political precedent in the context of the future of contested shelf areas.

North Korea is also engaged in a very low-key dispute with China in the offshore areas of the boundary between the two countries. The dispute first surfaced in the Asian rumor mill in 1974.[115] Neither side has commented publicly on these rumors, and China has never announced any principle for settlement of the dispute except that territorial matters should be negotiated by all parties to a dispute. North Korea unilaterally announced a 50-mile military control zone along both coasts on August 1, 1977.[116] This line is based on the midline principle known as the "lateral line" as the zone reaches the land boundary between China and North Korea. Farther from shore it delimits a relatively narrow band of North Korean control when compared to the midline. Like the Chinese "military warning area," the Korean zone may well be intended as a minimum claim made for security purposes and may not reflect the full extent of Pyongyang's final claims in the area. China has not responded in public to the establishment of the Korean military zone and was probably consulted in advance of the announcement. Both sides have a strong political interest in muting their offshore dispute. China is concerned about Soviet influence in North Korea and North Korea depends on China for many varieties of assistance, including petroleum exports. Neither side is likely to upset the balance, although China's vigorous exploration program in the Pohai Gulf could easily reach across the midline into North Korean claims.

North and South Korea have not agreed between themselves regarding any territorial matter and each government claims legitimacy as the future inheritor of Korea's unified political destiny. No agreement is likely concerning delineation of offshore oil exploration zones. The vicinity of the Demilitarized Zone should be considered an area of extreme risk for any foreign exploration venture in the Yellow Sea.

Taiwan's Claims

The political relationship between China and Taiwan represents a monumental barrier to further progress toward settlement of conflicting claims to the continental shelf. Taipei's formal claims to the shelf extend from a point just south and west of the Korean concession zone to the southern portion of the South China Sea. Maps of Taiwan's concession areas are intentionally exaggerated, extending the zones of potential concession westward to the Chinese coastline itself. Careful cartography indicates that the *actual* concessions granted by Taiwan and South Korea do not overlap, although there is some marginal overlap in the theoretical concession zones. There is broad conflict between the concession areas granted by Taipei and those offered to Japanese companies by Tokyo. Taiwan has even asserted its claims to the Spratley Islands in the South China Sea, garrisoning a small military force on the largest island.[117] Like the mouse that roared, these claims are a gross exaggeration of Taipei's ability to enforce its quixotic version of history. Taiwan does have large military capabilities relative to its size, thanks to two decades of American military aid. But this military force is largely defensive and engages most of its energies warding off hypothetical attacks by the PRC and maintaining Taiwan's beachhead across the Taiwan Strait on Quemoy.

Taiwan has also asserted its claim to the Tiaoyutai.[118] Indeed, on the basis of location alone, that claim would stand against the rather weak positions of Peking and Tokyo. The eight islands in the Tiaoyutai chain range in size from 0.02 to 0.07 square kilometers. They are located 125 kilometers northeast of the tip of Taiwan, 250 kilometers from the Chinese coastline, and 200 kilometers from the Ryukyus. They are separated from the Ryukyu shelf by the Okinawa Trough and lie on a shelf area that is continuous with Taiwan's shelf. Given their location, the Tiaoyutai were probably visited most frequently by fishing boats from Taiwan, although the written record of any such visits is far from established.[119] Taiwan is the only country that has conducted drilling operations in the vicinity of the islands. Gulf drilled one well in a Taiwan concession area in November 1973 about midway between Taiwan and the Tiaoyutai.[120] Three more wells in the same area were listed on a map of Taiwan's 1975 drilling program, but they were not reported.[121] Both Taiwan and Japan have avoided drilling right in the Tiaoyutai area in order to maintain the delicate political balance in their relationship.[122] There was a brief flare-up of the Tiaoyutai issue in April 1978 when Peking deliberately sent a fleet of 100 fishing boats into the area around the islands. Chinese fishermen displayed banners reiterating China's claim and precipitated a standoff with Japanese patrol vessels. The fishing fleet departed as rapidly as it had arrived and Peking apologized for the "accident," but not before the point had once again been made that China continues to challenge the Japanese claim to the area.

But the Taiwan issue itself is the real sticking point for the Tiaoyutai controversy. The government in Taipei not only claims the islands and contiguous shelf areas, but tenaciously clings to the proposition that it is the legitimate government of the whole of China. If this proposition lent the whole matter a certain air of absurdity in the mid-1970's, no one in Taipei, Peking, Tokyo, or Washington was laughing. Because of the broader issue of Taipei's residual claim that it is the government of China, and China's claim that Taiwan belongs under Peking's jurisdiction as a province of the PRC, Peking asserted its claim to the Tiaoyutai more forcefully than might otherwise have been warranted.[123] In May 1973, Chinese Premier Chou En-lai told the Canadian Minister of Mines that China would be willing to negotiate demarcation of the continental shelf.[124] However, there was no mention of the Tiaoyutai. As long as Peking perceives the Tiaoyutai to be linked to the issue of Taiwan's status, there can be little hope of any final agreement on the fate of these tiny islands. The intensity of China's feeling on this score may account for the alacrity with which the Japanese and American governments moved to discourage exploration activities in the area by home-based oil companies.

Philippine Claims

The territorial claims of the government of the Philippines in the South China Sea are only marginally important to the PRC. China has on several occasions fussed about Philippine offshore exploration ventures, but more at the level of intensity of claim maintenance than active concern. The Philippine government asserts an offshore claim that is somewhat vague, but one that extends to a zone at least 200 miles from the coastline of the Philippines proper. The South China Sea is sprinkled with tiny islets and shoal areas that lie atop high outcroppings from the floor of the China Basin. Manila has established defined exploration concessions on the Reed Bank area and has garrisoned military detachments on six islands nominally belonging to the Spratly archipelago.[125] Some of the islands have been formally included in Palawan province.[126] A direct confrontation between the Philippines and Vietnam is far more likely than entanglement with China in the South China Sea. China's claims formally include the Spratleys (Nansha Islands in Peking's lexicon), the Reed Bank, and areas as remote from the Chinese coastline as the Tsengmu Reef off Malaysia.[127]

As a consequence of the rather formal nature of Peking's interest in the area, the issue did not come to a head between the two governments until 1976, when the Philippine-Swedish consortium began drilling on the Reed Bank. Sino-Philippine relations were already suffering the results of a sudden Chinese cutback in crude petroleum exports to the Philippines in early 1976. Peking made its displeasure with the Reed Bank operation known through diplomatic channels in June 1976.[128] However, Manila not only refused to bend on the issue, but extended the protection zone covered by the Philippine Navy to the 200-mile limit, including the Reed Bank, and threatened to defend by force any rigs operating in the area.[129] There is little evidence that the PRC has pushed the issue any further. Peking considers its new relations with Manila sensitive and important in the context of its regional policies toward the Association of Southeast Asian Nations (ASEAN). Manila's continuing commercial ties with Taiwan are probably as great a concern to the PRC as the low-level offshore dispute in the South China Sea.

Vietnam's Claims

China's offshore dispute with Vietnam is far more serious than that with the Philippines. The South Vietnamese government incorporated 11 of the 33 islets in the Spratley group into Phuoc Tuy province in September 1973. China was strangely silent in the face of this move.[130] But in the following month China's response became entirely clear, as the PRC asserted its claims to the Paracels with the direct use of military force. Accounts of the fighting that occurred between Chinese and South Vietnamese forces between January 15 and January 20, 1974, vary, but all accounts agree that Peking used a relatively large combined land, air, and sea assault force to sweep the Vietnamese from the Paracel Islands.[131] China, which maintains a phosphate mining operation on the islands, claimed that Vietnamese vessels harassed fishing boats and fired on Duncan Island.[132] The Chinese responded in force, sinking at least one Vietnamese gunboat and capturing 48 soldiers. There were light casualties on both sides. This incident, which culminated in China's complete control of the Paracels, marks the only occasion when force has been used in pursuit of Chinese offshore claims. Within one month, China had quietly repatriated its Vietnamese prisoners and had withdrawn half of its naval force in the area.[133]

Occupation of the Paracels was widely reported in the foreign press as indicating a high level of Chinese concern with its claims in the South China Sea. However, there are some indications that once control had been established, Peking sought to reduce rather than increase the regional impact of the conflict. There was apparently concern that the incident might seriously damage China's new political relations with the ASEAN countries. China's diplomatic efforts in the wake of the seizure may have resulted in the assertion by Indonesian Foreign Minister Adam Malik (a presumably neutral party) that Indonesia and ASEAN accepted China's right to the Paracels under the San Francisco Treaty.[134] Some three years later, the *People's Daily* carried an article revealing that the handling of the military occupation of the Paracels had been a matter of policy debate at the highest levels in Peking.[135]

In 1975, Hanoi and the new South Vietnamese government inherited the offshore dispute with the PRC. Rumors had circulated for several years that there was no agreement on the issue between Peking and Hanoi.[136] In April 1975, before the communist victory in South Vietnam, a low-level border dispute along the land boundary between North Vietnam and China was reported in the area of Lao Kay and Lang Son.[137] This dispute apparently included some of the features of China's boundary disputes with the Soviet Union and India, albeit without the use of force by either side. The dispute was highly ritualized, with the daily movement of demarcation pegs back and forth at dawn and dusk.

Following the change of government in South Vietnam, the PRC publicly reasserted its claims in the entire area of the South China Sea in November and December 1975.[138] Extensive documentation was produced to demonstrate historical use and active development of the economic potential of the Paracels. The articles were no doubt intended as a warning to Hanoi that Peking still intended to press its offshore claims. However, the legalistic and relatively noncombative language would suggest that China wished, if at all possible, to continue a relatively low profile in its assertion of the claims, and was primarily interested in holding onto the Paracels.

Vietnam on its part has responded to the Chinese claims by a recent assertion of a 200-mile "exclusive economic zone" that if enforced would include the Paracels, the Spratleys, and other contested shelf areas in the Gulf of Tonkin.[139] No firm line is known to have been established in the Gulf area, a matter that may prove intractable even if the two parties accept a settlement principle, since Hainan Island extends the Chinese claim far to the south of Hanoi and Haiphong. American petroleum engineers, flown in to render technical assistance on a recently purchased Chinese jack-up rig, reported the rig operating in an area about 50 miles from Peihai in 170 feet of water.[140] If accurate, this report would indicate that China is actively exploring for oil in an area not far from the terminus of the land boundary with Vietnam (see Map 7.1). The implications of an oil or gas discovery in this area of the shelf might not be entirely propitious for the development of Sino-Vietnamese relations.*

The Soviet Factor

A final and less well-defined factor in the offshore territorial equation is Chinese fear of growing Soviet naval power in East Asia. This fear is not entirely unfounded. A Japanese report indicated as early as August 23, 1972, that Soviet bombers were passing over the Tsushima Strait into the East China Sea in a display of their ability to approach China from the sea.[141] Three Soviet warships passed through the Taiwan Strait in May 1973.[142] The Chinese spotted a Soviet submarine near the Paracels in September 1976.[143] These symbolic incursions reflect growing Soviet naval strength in the western Pacific and are probably conducted largely for intelligence-gathering purposes.

The Soviet naval presence near Chinese waters has the effect of pushing Peking toward stronger political relations with its immediate neighbors, even at the expense of its claims and interests in the region. The Chinese press, for example, has occasionally encouraged Southeast Asian countries toward greater vigilance over their offshore oil resources in the face of proffered Soviet technical assistance programs.[144] China will not relinquish its offshore claims, but may be willing to maintain a low profile under pressure from Soviet influence around its borders.

Midline and Depth Criteria

Our review of the claims and counterclaims of the People's Republic of China and the other countries that wish to explore on the continental shelf for hydrocarbons reveals a general pattern of great complexity. Historical use and control are difficult to document, produce a kaleidoscopic effect rather than well-defined areas of traditional sovereignty, and are largely irrelevant to the contemporary problems associated with offshore oil development. The claimant countries have not specified clearly delimited areas and boundaries for their claims, but have produced new claims on a completely ad hoc basis. Claims have frequently

---

*See Chapter 8 for a brief description of the recent conflict between China and Vietnam. This conflict, although not directly related to the offshore jurisdictional dispute, will doubtless rigidify positions on both sides. The fact that Sino-Vietnamese tensions have been expressed in an escalating conflict along their common boundary lends a territorial element to the dispute. There will be no prospect for cooperation or joint development in contested areas of the continental shelf as long as China and Vietnam continue their acrimonious dispute.

been defined solely in terms of concessions offered to foreign oil companies or in terms of innuendo. There is no agreement among the claimants regarding appropriate standards or principles for settlement, and some of the claimants offer contradictory rationales for claims made in different parts of the shelf. If there has been any progress at all in the disposition of the shelf since 1970, it has been in the direction of containing the political impact of offshore territorial disputes, rather than in the direction of settling the disputes themselves. The only exception has been the establishment of a Joint Development Zone between South Korea and Japan, a settlement disputed hotly by the PRC.

China itself has been a largely passive participant in the dispute. The Chinese have relied on formal statements by the Foreign Ministry and on press attacks to establish their position. There is an enormous difference between Peking's maximum implied claim area and the areas actually under Chinese control. As in other areas of foreign policy, the Chinese government tends to overstate its verbal position while maintaining a restrained political and military posture on the offshore issue. Even the brief conflict over the Paracels was conducted in a relatively restrained manner, with rapid deescalation after control had been established. From China's perspective, the one intractable issue is the status of Taiwan, an issue that appears inextricably entangled with any settlement that might be achieved on the continental shelf.

Japan and China are the main protagonists in the continental shelf controversy. Both countries are politically powerful within the region. Their respective claims overlap across an area hundreds of thousands of square kilometers in extent. Japan and China both have serious disputes with the smaller claimants, but the areas under dispute among the smaller claimants either do not overlap significantly (Taiwan and South Korea) or are located far from the coastlines (Vietnam and the Philippines). The main problem, therefore, lies in achieving a settlement between China and Japan. Unfortunately, the presence and political diversity of the smaller claimants greatly complicates the achievement of a central Sino-Japanese settlement. The presence of the serious disputes between both China and Japan and the smaller claimants will considerably slow any settlement between the two major protagonists. The role of the Taiwan issue in the Tiaoyutai dispute and the political division of Korea both illustrate this point. No political settlement between China and Japan is likely in the presence of these long-range regional problems.

The simplest way to project the future of the continental shelf area is in terms of a comparison of the two fundamental criteria that form the basis for most of the claims, however vaguely asserted. The two basic criteria are the midline principle and the depth criterion ("natural prolongation").* A careful plot of both the midline and the line of greatest depth (Map 7.2) reveals that the two lines converge in areas where the disputes are relatively muted and diverge in areas where the disputes are relatively severe. The greatest area of divergence between the midline and line of greatest depth lies in the zone contested between China and Japan along the outer edge of the shelf in the East China Sea. This area happens by nature to coincide with the region of thickest sedimentary deposit. Japan would obviously benefit from a midline settlement and China from a depth settlement. Other areas of sharp divergence between the midline and line of greatest depth lie between South Korea and China and between Vietnam and China. China would benefit from reliance on the line of greatest depth.

For this reason, a midline settlement of the type achieved in the North Sea is extremely unlikely along the Chinese continental shelf. China has thus far avoided pushing its line of actual control past the midline, except in the Paracels. But there have been no indications that the PRC would withdraw its more extensive claims and settle on the basis of the midline. This is particularly true in the East China Sea, because of the perception that the Okinawa Trough is a natural feature that separates the shelf from land areas under Japanese sovereignty, and additionally because acceptance of the midline in the East China Sea would set a precedent for the de jure separation of Taiwan from mainland sovereignty. The midline is likely to be a viable criterion only in the Gulf of Tonkin and the northern Yellow Sea, where it coincides with the line of greatest depth in any case. Japan, on the other hand, is unlikely to be satisfied with the line of greatest depth, a criterion that would leave the Japanese oil industry with no stake in future exploration of the richest sediments along the shelf, reaching as far south as the Tiaoyutai Islands. The political resistance in the Japanese Diet to relinquishment of the midline criterion was evident in the protracted ratification proceedings for the Joint Development Zone with South Korea.

If a simple midline division of the shelf is unlikely, joint development remains as a possible future solution to conflicting territorial claims. The PRC has a fairly clearly defined and well-established claim to exploration rights in the Pohai Gulf, the northwest Yellow Sea, and near-shore areas in the East China Sea and South China Sea. These areas will doubtless be the first parts of the shelf explored by China's growing fleet of offshore drilling rigs. The vast extent of these areas and the great expense of off-shore development in deeper water will help to buy time for the achieve-

---

*Natural prolongation and the depth criterion are not technically the same, but they have much the same effect and both are to be sharply distinguished from the midline criterion.

ment of an accommodation of claims in contested parts of the shelf. Japan has indicated its willingness to participate in joint development programs in the establishment of the Joint Development Zone with South Korea. If joint development programs were proposed in such a way as to maximize Chinese access to Japanese offshore exploration technology and minimize the perception that the PRC was relinquishing its cherished principle of resource sovereignty or its territorial integrity, Peking might well be drawn into a cooperative endeavor on the outer edge of the shelf.

Indeed, the Chinese government has at times mentioned the prospects for such a negotiated settlement in a favorable light. In early 1973, Premier Chou En-lai told the visiting Japanese Minister of Trade and Industry that there was no possibility of Sino-Japanese cooperation in development of the shelf. Then in May 1973, Chou reversed himself in a discussion with the Canadian Minister of Mines, indicating that China was willing to negotiate the offshore dispute with Japan.[145] During 1973, rumors also surfaced that Peking had expressed passing interest in a proposal by Broken Hill Proprietary of Australia for a joint offshore exploration program.[146] But on many other occasions from 1974 until 1977, China flatly rejected such proposals by foreign oil companies. Then in 1978, in a complete reversal of its earlier position, the Chinese government suddenly began inviting American, Japanese, and European petroleum companies to discuss the prospects for joint offshore development in both the Pohai Gulf and South China Sea exploration theaters (Chapter 8). At the end of 1978, no firm contracts for joint offshore development had been signed, but the prospects were looking good for such action in the next year or two. The initial joint development projects will be in near-shore areas clearly under Chinese control, but within a few years joint development projects may also be suggested in contested zones.

China's smaller neighbors have also sporadically shown signs of interest in joint offshore oil exploration. In 1974 it was reported that seven East Asian countries, including South Korea, South Vietnam, and the Philippines, and six industrial countries, including Japan and Australia, had agreed to a small ($5 million) joint offshore exploration program in the region under the auspices of ECAFE and the United Nations Development Program.[147]

If the political environment for joint offshore exploration and development in the region has not been entirely hostile, it is nonetheless the case that proposals for joint offshore programs must be carefully structured and cautiously written. Prospective zones for joint exploration should be well defined and should lie in the areas of divergence between the midline and the line of greatest depth. Any agreements forwarded to the Chinese government regarding joint development in the offshore areas should contain clear language deferring to Chinese defense requirements in the near-shore areas and should avoid any language that implies the establishment of territory or sovereignty. Titles and claims to the offshore areas are still sufficiently inchoate to permit intentional ambiguity regarding the jurisdictional status of the areas under joint development. Joint exploration endeavors should be organized in parallel fashion, with independent lines of organization and control and no effort to achieve integrated command structures. Chinese participants should of course be given equal authority in all matters, both technical and otherwise, and some means for resolving minor disputes should be established at the outset.

The main obstacles to joint development of contested areas of the continental shelf will of course be political. China and Taiwan will have great difficulty sitting at the same negotiating table for some time to come, let alone participating in any sort of joint venture. Yet the possibility of political accommodation between Peking and Taipei across a number of issues should not be overlooked. There is great pressure on both sides for accommodation. Time is running out on China's claims to sovereignty of any sort over Taiwan, as the island moves further down its own path toward economic development and as successive generations of Taiwanese and Taiwan-born mainlanders move into political power. For Taiwan, its many diplomatic disasters of recent years and increasing isolation are a powerful motivation to begin political discussions with Peking. The establishment of diplomatic relations between the United States and the People's Republic of China greatly increase the pressure on Taipei to enter such discussions. The Chinese government itself might prove willing to talk, for fear of a political liaison between an isolated Taiwan and the Soviet Union.

The division of Korea is another political stumbling block to any proposed joint development zone with China in the Yellow Sea. Peking has insisted on its own inclusion as well as the inclusion of North Korean authorities in the establishment of the Japan–Korea Joint Development Zone.[148] No bilateral agreement will be possible between China and South Korea without inclusion of Pyongyang, an event that appears unlikely under present circumstances. However, the sediments lying between China and Korea are not as thick as in other areas of the shelf and have not to date produced any significant discoveries. Settlement in the area could be put off for a while as long as both sides show constraint in their offshore drilling programs.

The active disputes in the South China Sea area are concerned with islands lying completely off the shelf in the deep China Basin. The China Basin sediments will not be drilled for some time to come because of technical and cost factors in deep-water drilling—even assuming adequate exploration technology. De facto division of control over the island groups has already occurred, with China holding the Paracels, the Philippines holding the Reed Bank and eastern islands in the Spratley archipelago, and Vietnam holding the predominant position in the western Spratleys. This de facto division will prevent any de jure settlement in the South China Sea for some time to come. Vietnam, for example, is unlikely to legitimize Chinese military control of the Paracels. Joint exploration and development might some day be possible in the contested areas of the Gulf of Tonkin between China and Vietnam. The two countries share (roughly) the same political and economic structures and would be organizationally compatible in a joint venture. Even assuming better political relations, Vietnam would be the more reluctant of the two partners, since assistance is available from other countries for offshore exploration in promising areas of the continental shelf off the Mekong delta. However, the territorial dispute with Vietnam will not seriously hamper China's offshore development program in most areas of its southern continental shelf, areas that have already been tested by the Chinese drill.

Regardless of the political desirability of doing so, the United States will not be able to extricate itself entirely from entanglement with the Chinese continental shelf controversy. The United States has strong military commitments in Japan, South Korea, and the Philippines, and remaining ties with Taiwan. The Vietnam debacle has brought a much lower American profile in East Asia and some military withdrawal. However, growing Soviet naval strength in the western Pacific will counterbalance the American inclination to cut losses and withdraw from the region entirely. All of the countries of the region, including the PRC, have urged the continuation of an American military presence. Regional instability introduced by conflict over the continental shelf would be inimical to the present low profile of the American presence, since the many military forces the United States supports in the region would be involved in any serious confrontation.

Offshore Constraints and Resource Conservation

Once again our analysis has suggested that China's international energy policies operate within a framework of energy-resource, economic, and political constraints. Perhaps more than any other area of energy development in the PRC, offshore oil and gas exploration will be limited by a combination of these factors. An extensive review of the offshore drilling programs of China's neighbors around the shelf revealed that the rate of discoveries in the area has been modest at best and disappointing at worst. Foreign oil companies have withdrawn from concessions in waters off South Korea, Taiwan, and the Philippines (Reed Bank area), and have been forced out of Vietnam's offshore exploration zones. Many millions of dollars have been spent on initial exploratory drilling programs with little return. The sweep of the Chinese continental shelf covers an enormous area, larger than Texas and Oklahoma combined. Only a few of the potential trap structures and none of the thickest sediments have been test-drilled. Despite the lack of early economic oil and gas discoveries, therefore, judgment must be suspended until far more exploration has been undertaken. Nonetheless, a conservative approach to the hydrocarbon potential of the Chinese continental shelf is warranted until such exploration programs materialize. The lack of knowledge regarding precise geological configurations along the shelf in itself constitutes a constraint on the pace of offshore development by any of the littoral states.

Political constraints operating in the offshore areas are at least as serious as resource and exploration constraints. Some aspects of the territorial dispute over the continental shelf appear intractable in the short term and difficult to resolve even in a longer frame of reference. It should be recalled that the Taiwan issue hampered the development of Sino-American relations for nearly three decades. The K rean War was fought more than 25 years ago. The war in Indochina lasted for more than 20 years. All of these subregional conflicts were related in one way or another to the extreme dislocations in East Asia associated with the Second World War. The instabilities that they reflected may have been largely resolved in the intervening years. However, undue optimism regarding the prospects for regional cooperation in the immediate future should be avoided. Here again, the effect of remaining political and territorial constraints will be to greatly slow the pace of offshore exploration and commercial development.

The limitations on offshore oil development should not necessarily be construed in a negative light. Their basic effect will be to greatly extend the amount of time that such development will require. Given the known and inferred ceiling on world oil and gas resources, such an extension of time horizons on offshore oil development in East Asia may be a blessing in disguise. The fossil resources in question have a long-term value that may greatly transcend their value as a source of energy. Petrochemical uses of both crude petroleum and natural gas are rising rapidly throughout the world, especially as a feedstock for the production of nitrogenous fertilizers. China is no exception to this general pattern. The Chinese petrochemical industry is growing at a rate that rivals the startling expansion of oil and gas production. Domestic chemical fertilizer production has been given high priority in the allocation of domestic capital and foreign exchange. (China spent more than $600 million on foreign nitrogenous fertilizer plants from 1973 to 1976.) The careful husbanding of fossil resources will ensure an adequate supply of feedstock for the petrochemical and fertilizer industries into the indefinite future. Constraints on rapid oil and gas development for energy purposes that may seem irksome in 1980 could well operate to conserve sufficient resources for long-range non-energy requirements. In this way, the constraints on offshore oil development could be thought of as a sort of natural resource conservation program.

Throughout this chapter, we have skirted the question of China's offshore development program, without addressing it directly. The pace of that program will be greatly influenced by the resource, economic, and political factors that affect offshore oil programs throughout the region. Because of the steady growth in China's population, and the determination of the leadership in Peking to achieve industrial modernization by the turn of the century, energy consumption requirements will press relentlessly on China's domestic energy production capacity. Fossil-fuel exports to the region are and will be directly affected by the balance of production capacity and consumption requirements. The presence and accessibility of offshore oil or gas would ease the production-consumption balance and would greatly increase China's ability to export energy commodities to the region. The offshore oil development program and China's regional trade will, therefore, be dealt with together in the next chapter.

Chapter 8

China's Energy Policies in Asia:
Offshore Development and Regional Energy Trade

The pace of China's offshore oil exploration and development program is inextricably related to the future role of the People's Republic as a regional supplier of energy commodities. The last two chapters have reviewed China's energy relations with Japan and the continental shelf controversy. It has been suggested that the Sino-Japanese relationship will play a central role in regional energy trade and development. Careful review of the exploration programs of neighboring countries and an evaluation of foreign estimates of China's offshore oil resources indicated that a cautious approach to the hydrocarbon potential of the continental shelf should be taken, in view of the many geological constraints on offshore development in the area. Finally, an examination of conflicting territorial claims to the continental shelf revealed that offshore oil development will be further complicated by long-range political constraints. Thus, serious uncertainties face any Chinese program for early or rapid exploration and development of oil and gas resources on the continental shelf.

This general conclusion should not be surprising or disconcerting when placed against the background of world offshore oil development. Increasing attention has been paid to the world's outer continental shelves (OCS) as a potential geologic zone for hydrocarbon extraction. By 1976, some 34 percent of the continental shelf areas bordering noncommunist countries was under lease for offshore oil exploration.[1] In the decade from 1965 to 1975, massive amounts of capital were invested in the construction and deployment of technically sophisticated offshore drilling rigs. At least 15 major offshore exploration theaters were identified, and five theaters (California, Gulf of Mexico, North Sea, Persian Gulf, and Indonesia) have proved rich and productive. To a great extent the exploration effort (not extraction or production) shifted from the Middle East to the world's OCS areas. By 1975 it was estimated that fully 40 percent of the world's undiscovered crude oil potential lay in the OCS areas.[2] Roughly 25 percent of the world's proved crude oil and natural gas reserves were located offshore.[3] Offshore crude oil production, however, has only gradually increased its share of total world oil production.

By 1960, offshore oil production was running about 10 percent of world total crude oil production.[4] The first offshore fields to be explored and developed were natural extensions of onshore discoveries. Relatively small drilling programs produced impressive results in these near-shore fields. However, the next phase of offshore exploration, drilling in areas not associated with onland discoveries, proved more expensive and difficult. Even the very rich deposits in the North Sea proved expensive to extract, with many unexpected delays, despite high incentives for rapid offshore development and a good background of technological capabilities. The contribution of offshore production to total crude oil production continued to grow at a rapid pace during the 1960's, to about 13 percent in 1965 and 15 percent in 1970. Offshore production increase was slower in the early 1970's, reaching 16 percent of world crude oil production by 1972, 18 percent by 1975, and about 19 percent by 1977.[5] Present indications are that, barring vast new offshore fields in the OCS areas, the offshore contribution to world crude oil production could level out at about 20 percent of the total. Speculative future deep-water production might again provide a surge in the relative contribution of offshore oil, but once again economic and political constraints on deep-water exploration should be kept in mind. One oil authority summarized the prospects for world offshore production in 1976 as follows: "Soaring expenditures for offshore drilling and for construction of producing facilities are raising the price of finding offshore oil, and activity can continue at a high level only if the price of oil remains high. Any thought of a flood of cheap new offshore oil is wishful thinking."[6]

The U.S. experience with offshore oil development is similar. The contribution of offshore oil to total U.S. crude oil production grew from 5 percent in 1960 to 9 percent in 1965 and 16 percent in 1970.[7] However, the offshore contribution leveled out after 1970 at about 16 percent of the total, under the pressure of rising exploration costs, greater difficulty of extraction, and new environmental constraints imposed in the wake of the Santa Barbara blowout. New offshore production in the Beaufort Sea (Alaska) or along the east coast of the United States will probably be balanced by depletion of existing fields in the Gulf of Mexico and along the California coast.

The general point implied by these comparisons is that the constraints facing China's offshore oil development program are by no means unique, and have been experienced in many other parts of the world. The People's Republic of China has just begun its offshore exploration efforts at the time of writing. Significant offshore discoveries and production may be just around the corner. If significant discoveries are made, considerable expansion in the offshore oil industry may occur during the 1980's. Each new discovery will bring a wave of foreign speculation about the oil and gas prospects of the Chinese continental shelf. As we enter a more detailed analysis of China's offshore oil program, the general constraints operating on offshore exploration and recovery should be kept firmly in mind. The existence of a vigorous exploration program, high capital outlays, and the purchase of foreign offshore drilling equipment do not necessarily imply an offshore oil bonanza. Even a sharp rise over the next few years in the offshore contribution to China's oil production should be treated with considerable caution in view of similar experience elsewhere in the world.

In the closing months of 1978, Peking began to take a series of public policy decisions that will directly affect the prospects and pace of offshore development. These decisions on joint offshore development ventures with foreign countries and corporations open a new horizon on both offshore oil and regional energy trade. In initiating contacts with foreign multinational corporations interested in participating in development of the hydrocarbon potential of the Chinese continental shelf, Peking has tipped its hand regarding its offshore oil and regional export strategy. For the first time, we are beginning to see the outlines of the Chinese scenario for the development of the continental shelf over the next several decades. The middle section of this chapter explores the prospects for joint offshore exploration agreements between the PRC and foreign multinationals. I believe that such joint development agreements, limited to the offshore basins, present the Chinese leadership with a master key that opens a number of political and economic doors without sacrificing the underlying structure of Chinese energy policy. By the same token, they do not relieve the basic constraints on China's future energy development and energy export potential. Nor will the existence of joint development agreements for the offshore areas in any way guarantee the discovery of large and commercially viable oil and gas deposits. If offshore oil and gas resources prove substantial, the joint development agreements could become an important part of Chinese energy development policy for the next two decades, without providing a magic cure for all of China's energy development problems.

As the People's Republic of China begins to enter the era of joint offshore development agreements, a direct link between offshore oil and gas development and regional energy commodity trade is becoming increasingly apparent. The final section of this chapter reviews the history of China's energy commodity trade with the Asian countries around its perimeter, other than Japan, which has already been dealt with in

Chapter 6. Regional energy commodity trade has important underlying political benefits for Peking and will continue to be contingent on political considerations. The PRC has also begun to purchase significant amounts of energy production equipment (offshore drilling rigs) from Singapore and may use Hong Kong as an operational base for foreign exploration of Chinese sections of the South China Sea. A final section of the chapter summarizes total energy commodity trade with all regions of the world and discusses the link between offshore development and future energy commodity exports.

China's Offshore Exploration Program

The development of China's offshore exploration program during the 1970's can be thought of in terms of three general development phases. In the first phase, Peking awoke to the potential of offshore oil and gas development and began a preliminary assessment of that potential. Phase I was stimulated by development of Takang oilfield along the margins of the Pohai Gulf and by the findings of the CCOP seismic surveys and the subsequent wave of concession agreements between China's neighbors and a number of multinational corporations. During Phase I, exploratory drilling was initiated in the Pohai extension of the Takang graben, and Peking began its own program of offshore surveys across broad areas of the continental shelf. Phase I began in 1969 with the first wells drilled in the Pohai Gulf, and was coming to a close in 1978 with the completion of a four-year magnetic and seismic survey of China's coastal waters.

The second phase of China's offshore program involves the construction and purchase of a fleet of mobile offshore drilling rigs and preliminary exploratory drilling at selected sites in the Pohai Gulf, East China Sea, and South China Sea. The emphasis in Phase II is on near-shore exploration of the most promising structures revealed in the seismic and magnetic profiles obtained in Phase I. No effort is being made to exploit initial discoveries, but extensive tests are being conducted in an attempt to confirm the commercial viability of oil and gas resources in the Pohai Gulf and South China Sea coastal areas. Phase II began in 1973 with the purchase of the first foreign drilling rig from Japan and reached a peak in 1976–78 with the acquisition of nine sophisticated foreign offshore drilling rigs and a variety of computerized survey and data-processing systems. Phase II gives Peking an independent capability for oil and gas resource assessment in the offshore areas, facilitating long-range planning while maintaining control of strategic resource information. The foreign equipment needed for Phase II cost China a total of about half a billion U.S. dollars through the end of 1978.

The third phase in offshore oil and gas development will consist of the initiation of offshore production (beyond Takang), the initial assessment of deeper, thicker, and politically contested basins, and an effort to link regional crude petroleum exports directly to the development of the continental shelf. Actual offshore production will be the point of emphasis in Phase III. It appeared that Phase III was just beginning as this book entered its final stages in late 1978. In a series of moves that startled foreign observers (and potential investors), Peking suddenly opened discussions with Japanese, European, and American oil companies about the potential for joint development of resources in the continental shelf—particularly in the Pohai Gulf and South China Sea coastal areas where Peking had already conducted initial test drilling. Oil samples from the South China Sea, reportedly lighter and less waxy than northeast crudes, were sent to Japanese laboratories for analysis. The implication of these moves is that China will soon seek large-scale foreign involvement in offshore development and will link the success of the new offshore production program directly to regional energy commodity trade.

It is important to recognize that the first three phases of China's offshore development program are intimately connected to each other, overlap in time, and will continue as the program unfolds. Phase I, the initial assessment of offshore potential, was drawing to a close at the end of the 1970's. But seismic and magnetic surveys, an important feature of Phase I, will be continued in Phase II as exploration of the shelf proceeds. Phase II and Phase III will also proceed in tandem as exploration and production accelerate. Despite the prospects for greater foreign involvement in Phase III, it would certainly be premature to write off active Chinese participation in development of the shelf. Massive rig purchases in the last several years indicate that Peking intends at minimum to control further exploratory drilling along the shelf. The balance of Chinese and foreign participation in the production phase has yet to be determined.

Takang Oilfield

Some authorities would argue that China is already producing offshore oil in significant quantities. In a strictly technical sense, this might be said to be the case. Out of the major oilfields developed in the PRC during the late 1960's and early 1970's—Takang, or "Big Harbor"—has been producing from structures located in an underwater extension of what is essentially an onland field, or series of fields.

Takang oilfield, like Taching oilfield, is an administrative unit encompassing a number of geologic oilfields located on several major structures. The two main areas of Takang are some 40 kilometers in length and run roughly northeast-southwest across barren coastal salt marshes and into the westernmost fringe of the Pohai Gulf.[8] The area lies immediately south of the Hai River and the twin cities of Tientsin and Tangku. Takang is administratively distinct from Shengli ("Victory") oilfield, which is a short distance to the south, at the mouth of the Yellow River. In contrast to Takang, oil production at Shengli does not presently extend offshore, although the structure at the extreme northeast end of Shengli is right at the water's edge. Discoveries in the Pohai Gulf immediately off the mouth of the Yellow River have recently been included in Shengli oilfield.

According to the Chinese press, Takang oilfield was discovered in 1964, if one dates discovery to the beginning of prospecting work in the area.[9] The first wells were drilled in 1966 or 1967 and commercial production began in 1967. Construction of oilfield facilities was intensive from 1967 through 1973 and has continued at a somewhat slower pace since 1973. Production increases were rapid during the first five years of commercial production, averaging over 60 percent per annum.[10] The growth rate then slowed to about 25 percent in 1974 and 16 percent in 1975.[11] Precise estimates vary, but most put 1975 production at about 4–4.5 million tons of crude petroleum and an unknown quantity of natural gas.[12] Pipeline facilities may already exist to move some of the natural gas to Tientsin. If natural gas comprises a large proportion of the discoveries at Takang, the oilfield could become an important regional supplier of gas to industry and urban areas in northeast China. By 1977 there were three refineries directly associated with the oilfield with a total capacity of 4.2 million tons.[13] Two nearby refineries provide an additional 2 million tons per year of refining capacity, and there are numerous other refining and petrochemical facilities in the region. Takang crude, like Taching crude, is known to be low in sulfur content and very waxy, with a specific gravity of about 0.8.[14] If accurate, these reported characteristics imply that any shift toward Takang oilfield as a source of export crude petroleum will present roughly the same refining problems as Taching crude.

Takang's general geological characteristics are interesting from the perspective of future oil development in the Pohai Gulf. Oil has been found in both sandstone and limestone Tertiary sediments at an average depth of nearly 3,000 meters. By 1976 there were at least eight producing structures, including "complexly faulted noses and anticlines."[15] Because of the highly fractured nature of the structures, exploration proved difficult in the early phases and may still be relatively expensive in terms of the ratio of meters of drilling to discovered reserves. No precise information is available on the origin of the sediments, although the waxy nature of the crude produced might suggest analogy to the lacustrine sediments at Taching. If the fracturing of the Takang structures and the possible lacustrine origin of the sediments extend far into the offshore province, there could be significant consequences for the economics of recovery in the Pohai Gulf. By February 1976, there were reported to be more than 50 rigs operating at Takang, with cumulative completion of 700 producing wells.[16] If accurate, this report would imply annual productivity of about 7,000 metric tons per well (140 bbl/day) plus associated natural gas.

The productivity of Takang wells is, therefore, comparable to or lower than average productivity at Taching. These figures are low by international standards, indicating that the number of producing wells has probably been inflated through reporting error. Normally a well producing at 500 bbl/day would be considered marginal. Wells are capped and abandoned as subcommercial in the Middle East at much higher productivity levels. But the relatively shallow reserves at both Takang and Taching might make onland low-productivity wells economic in the framework of the Chinese energy system. Assuming that half the "producing wells" were actually exploratory wells or water-injection wells, productivity would run at 300–500 bbl/day in the major Chinese oilfields. This is still a very low figure, indicating again the difficulty of locating and extracting oil from the highly fractured graben that comprise China's northeast oilfields. Similar levels of productivity in the offshore areas would be disastrous for the economics of recovery. As a point of comparison, commercial offshore discoveries in Indonesia test at 3,000–9,000 bbl/day, with some running as high as 20,000 bbl/day. Only one oilfield in northeast China has reported favorable per well productivity rates. The Jenchiu oilfield in central Hopeh reports average daily output per well at more than 1,000 metric tons (7,500 bbl/day), a level that would be commercial if achieved in the offshore areas.[17]

The most important feature of Takang's development is its extension into the offshore areas in the Pohai Gulf. The exact boundary between the onland and offshore provinces is indistinct, owing to the flat salt marsh that covers much of the main Takang area. But it is generally believed that drilling began from a fixed platform 16 kilometers offshore in 1969.[18] The entire Pohai Gulf area is very shallow, permitting drilling from causeways built out from shore, from relatively primitive drilling barges, and from fixed platforms. The Chinese have used all of these methods in the offshore extension of Takang. Occasional photographs of offshore platforms have been published in the Chinese press and a few foreign visitors have toured the oilfield.[19]

In addition, the outside world has fairly accurate information regarding the amount and types of offshore drilling equipment that have been sold to the PRC, at least by the industrial market economy countries. There is every indication from these sources that Peking is consciously using the Pohai Gulf as a giant laboratory for the development of its offshore capabilities. A wide variety of techniques have been employed in both the exploration and extraction phases, rather than adopting a single foreign model. In April 1973, three test wells were reported to have produced significant quantities of crude oil from the offshore province.[20] It is apparent that some offshore discoveries have been made and that the Chinese are engaged in defining areas with commercial potential and in establishing initial estimates of proved reserves in the offshore extension of Takang. As of 1977, the actual level of oil extraction from the offshore province was still marginal and experimental in nature. A commercially significant level of offshore production from the Pohai should not be expected before about 1980. Lacking precise information on the exploratory wells that have already been drilled, it is impossible to evaluate the hydrocarbon potential of the offshore province of Takang oilfield, or of the Pohai Gulf.

Scientific Research and Seismic Surveys

In contrast to the rather deliberate movement into the offshore province of Takang oilfield, the level already achieved in offshore scientific research and survey work confirms the impression that Peking was primarily interested in reconnaissance and preliminary exploration during the 1970's. Harrison documents a wide array of oceanographic capabilities in place by early 1977.[21] Several independent authorities agree that China's offshore research and survey technology has already reached the general level of Soviet capabilities and is hard on the heels of the most advanced American subsea measurement equipment.[22] The PRC has developed its offshore research and survey technology through an intensive program of domestic training, equipment development, and selective importation of cutting-edge foreign equipment. Oceanographic research and subsea geological reconnaissance is a very cost-effective way of assessing initial hydrocarbon prospects along the continental shelf. The entire cost of such a program might be comparable to the purchase of just one or two sophisticated offshore drilling rigs. As in its limited space program and several other areas of advanced research, China has the scientific ability to mount research efforts that achieve advanced international levels in a very short period of time. Peking has repeatedly shown a willingness to divert research funds and scientific personnel to specific tasks in narrowly defined areas of the technological spectrum, when it is anticipated that the research and development results will contribute directly to the short-term requirements of national defense or economic development.

Oceanographic and subsea geological research during the 1950's was confined to a low priority by the tremendous effort to map China's onland mineral resources. The onland geological surveys were conducted with considerable technical assistance from the Soviet Union and occupied the attention of the PRC's rapidly growing corps of geologists and its first institutes of geology. But the initial efforts in ocean research were probably directed more to the requirements of coastal transport, harbor systems, and fisheries than to marine geology. This situation began to change in the early 1960's. In February 1963 an article appeared in *Oceans and Lakes,* a Chinese journal published since 1959, reporting the results of a bathymetric study of the continental shelf.[23] This study established the surface area of different sections of the shelf, as well as average depth, slope, and width. It also reported that sediment samples had been dredged at different points along the shelf and analyzed in Chinese laboratories. The article indicated keen Chinese interest in foreign subsea geological research in areas near China. The first preliminary foreign surveys of the shelf were taking place at about the same time and had reached approximately the same level of research (bathymetric and dredged samples) as the Chinese work.

Further marine geological research probably continued throughout the 1960's, although the blackout on Chinese scientific journals after 1965 prevented information on the results of such work from filtering out of the PRC. The real explosion in Chinese interest in offshore survey research occurred after 1970. Our primary channel of access to this research has been through technical exchange delegations and via a series of Chinese equipment purchases that had offshore survey applications. Peking's decision to accelerate the pace of marine geology was a result of the confluence of three important events. First, China, like the other countries in East Asia, was directly stimulated by the results of the first CCOP reconnaissance survey of the sedimentary basins of the East China Sea and the Yellow Sea. While on the one hand the Chinese government publicly denounced foreign survey research on the continental shelf, on the other hand that very research challenged China's own offshore research program. Second, the subsea jurisdictional dispute with Japan and other littoral countries over the Tiaoyutai Islands, the South China Sea islands, and broad areas of the continental shelf began in 1970 and continued to intensify through about 1974. It appeared in the rush of conflicting claims and concessions that exploration activity might be an important basis for ultimate control of the disputed areas of the shelf. Survey research was an inexpensive and relatively quick way to mount an offshore exploration program that would help to establish the legitmacy of China's claims, particularly in areas remote from the Chinese coastline. A recent article reporting a Chinese survey of the South China Sea by the Institute of Oceanography confirms this impression.[24] The article details China's jurisdictional claims to each island group, mentions five previous surveys, speculates about the resource potential of the area for China's future development, and is accompanied by a map showing the outline of the extreme Chinese claim reaching as far south as Indonesia. It obviously implies a greater interest than scientific research.

The third factor stimulating the offshore surveys was that the PRC had begun to reach into the Pohai Gulf. Just as offshore exploration has proceeded in most of the world's promising subsea basins from onland fields, so China was drawn into the sea by oil-bearing structures discovered at Takang. Completion of most of the survey work at Taching and the shift in geological attention to Takang and Shengli oilfields in the early 1970's was accompanied by intensive survey research activity in the Pohai Gulf. This activity reached a crescendo in 1974, when China commissioned a seismic survey of the Pohai Gulf by the French Compagnie Général de Géophysique (CGG), the same company that has been active in survey work off Vietnam and in several other areas in East Asia.[25] During the same year the Chinese government purchased the CGG survey ship used to conduct this contract research, and negotiated for the purchase of a variety of other seismic, magnetometer, and data-processing equipment, as well as at least one Japanese ocean survey ship. The Pohai Gulf area is a prime target for geological survey research, located near existing oilfields, free of conflicting jurisdictional claims, and shallow enough to permit early drilling.

After 1974 the seismic and magnetic surveys began to reach out beyond the confines of the Pohai Gulf. From 1974 until the summer of 1978, China's General Administration of Civil Aviation and the State Geological Bureau conducted a mineral survey of the Yellow Sea, the East China Sea, and the South China Sea. The survey covered more than 250,000 line-kilometers by air, and an undisclosed amount of surface reconnaissance took place over broad areas of the Chinese continental shelf. The survey concluded that "Preliminary results show the geological structure under the coastal water areas and indicate petroleum and natural gas resources there."[26] This was the same conclusion reached by the CCOP surveys several years earlier. Survey activity was particularly intensive in the South China Sea, where a number of subsurveys were taken, concentrating in the vicinity of Hainan Island.[27]

In 1976 and 1977, China reached even farther out into the Pacific with its oceanographic research program. Two separate oceanographic voyages were reported, both using the 10,000-ton Chinese-built research ships "Hsiangyanghung 5 and 12." Research conducted on these trips included marine hydrology, meteorology, chemistry, gravitation, seabed geology, geomorphology, topography, telecommunications, and navigation.[28] The voyages were organized by the State Oceanographic Bureau and took about two months each. There is no information on the areas covered, but it was claimed that the research voyages reached far into the Pacific. This type of oceanographic research is not directly relevant to marine resources, but it does put China in the same class with the industrial countries that are concerned with the future potential of deep-ocean mineral resources.

China's Offshore Drilling Program

The pace of China's offshore exploration program is nearly impossible to gauge in terms of the rate and extent of wildcat drilling. No details have been reported in the foreign press regarding the number of offshore wells drilled each year, the nature of these test wells, or the preliminary results achieved in the offshore areas. All of this information is treated as a matter of national security by the Chinese government. We do have information suggesting that wildcat wells have been drilled in four areas (see Map 7.1). The Pohai Gulf is known to have been drilled extensively since at least 1973, and may be producing oil from near-shore platforms. At least one test well has been drilled in the Yellow Sea, off the coast of Kiangsu province in April 1975.[29] Land-based offshore drilling has occurred using the tiny Paracel islets as drilling platforms since 1973.[30] And sophisticated jack-up drilling rigs purchased in Singapore have been operating northwest of Hainan in the Gulf of Tonkin since late 1976. Of these four areas of drilling activity, only the Pohai Gulf and Gulf of Tonkin would rank as serious exploration efforts. Most of the drilling outside of the Pohai Gulf has been on training or equipment shakedown cruises. The general level of offshore drilling activity achieved by China in 1977 could be roughly compared to the offshore program mounted by Taiwan. It was certainly not in the same category as offshore exploration in Indonesia or the world's other major offshore theaters.

There are persistent reports of oil strikes along the Chinese coastline in the South China Sea, both in the Gulf of Tonkin near Hainan and at the mouth of a Pearl River estuary west of Hong Kong. These reports have come from Chinese officials at the national level and in Kwangtung province.[31] Furthermore, the American oil companies that are discussing joint development proposals with Peking are being encouraged to submit proposals for individual projects in the South China Sea zone. The Chinese, operating their two imported jack-up rigs from Robin Loh (Singapore), have taken samples of "Hainan crude" and "Pearl River crude" and shipped them to Japan for laboratory analysis. These crudes are lighter and less waxy than the crudes from northeast China, indicating possible marine origin, a development that would be favorable for the economics of offshore development in the South China Sea areas of the continental shelf. The Chinese government has not made public any data on the number of successful wells in the area or on the per-well test yield of the wells drilled so far. If foreign oil companies have access to this information, they are not talking about it publicly. But heightened interest of American oil companies in the area may be one measure of the commercial viability of China's initial offshore discoveries in the South China Sea. If foreign interest persists, the discoveries were probably commercial by Western standards. If foreign interest slackens, it would indicate that Peking was not able to deliver sufficiently convincing data from its first test wells.

This evaluation, however, does not do justice to the long-range potential of China's offshore exploration program. That program is obviously in its earliest stages—survey reconnaissance and preliminary test drilling. Perhaps a better yardstick than the number of test wells drilled so far would be the pace at which China has been constructing and acquiring offshore drilling equipment. Once again, the main obstacle to an accurate comparative analysis of China's offshore exploration capabilities is the paucity of information regarding the precise number and type of offshore rigs that have been built and imported for use in exploring the Chinese continental shelf. The information is fragmentary and foreign rig counts are notoriously contradictory. Even foreign equipment purchases are treated as proprietary information by both the Chinese and the company selling the equipment, making it difficult to trace the precise status of purchase contract negotiations. A number of "final" contracts have been prematurely reported, only to dissolve a few months later with no agreement on the price or other purchase conditions. Purchase contract negotiations with the Chinese should never be taken as an indication of final intent, and even a final signed contract is no absolute guarantee that delivery will be accepted.[32] As a result of these information constraints, there are a number of phantom offshore drilling rigs reported in foreign sources, spudding illusory wells on mythical subsea structures.

Careful sifting and cross-checking of available information on China's construction and import of offshore drilling rigs reveal some important features of the offshore program (Table 8.1). By year-end 1978, the PRC had built, purchased, or ordered at least 14 offshore exploration rigs of various types. The earliest rigs were drilling barges of Chinese construction designed for use in the shallow waters of the Pohai Gulf. They represented offshore conversion of onland drilling technology and were supplemented, in the early stages of exploration of the off-shore province of Takang oilfield, by fixed platforms and causeways built out from shore. The "Pohai 1" was China's first effort to build an offshore rig with technology explicitly designed for subsea hydrocarbon exploration. Patterned on early Western and Japanese jack-up designs, it was capable of drilling in somewhat deeper water (60–70 meters).[33] The "Pohai 1" was supplemented in 1973 with a Japanese jack-up, the "Fuji" (Japan Ocean Drilling, $8.4 million), renamed the "Pohai 2." The design and capabilities of the Japanese rig were similar to the first domestically produced jack-up. In 1974, Shanghai's Hutung Shipyard and the Shanghai Mine Drilling Equipment Plant joined forces to construct the "Kantan 1," a catamaran drill-ship with static positioning and relatively limited depth capabilities (about 75 meters of water).[34] Thus, early offshore-rig acquisition depended primarily on domestic construction and was sharply limited in water-depth capabilities. As a consequence, as of 1975 China's offshore exploration program was held to the near-shore areas and the Pohai Gulf. This represented a small gamble of domestic production capital and foreign exchange in return for some basic geological information obtained from the early drilling. China's offshore drilling program before 1976 should be thought of primarily as geological reconnaissance work, supplementing and extending the information obtained from seismic surveys.

During Phase I in the offshore program, however, Peking was laying the groundwork for the purchase of much more sophisticated offshore equipment and technology. Chinese offshore delegations and rig-purchase negotiating teams made contact with potential suppliers in Japan, Singapore, West Germany, Denmark, Poland, and Norway.[35] Negotiations were initiated in order to evaluate competing rig design, but contracts were repeatedly delayed or declined as Peking sought to buy time for its reconnaissance surveys and drilling. We have no information regarding the precise outcome of the reconnaissance phase of exploration. But the early results must have appeared encouraging to Chinese geologists, for a second batch of purchase contracts for more sophisticated rigs was signed beginning in 1975. This second phase in the offshore program appears to be relying heavily on the purchase of expensive foreign rigs loaded with the latest American offshore drilling equipment. Phase II also represented a gamble, since nine rigs were scheduled

TABLE 8.1
China's Confirmed Offshore Drilling Rigs, Year-End 1978

Name	Type	Delivery date	Water depth (meters)	Drill depth (meters)	Supplier	Cost (million dollars)
Pinhai 1	Barge	1967	30	2,000	Domestic	n.a.
Pinhai 2	Barge	1970	30	2,000	Domestic	n.a
Pohai 1	Jack-up	1972	70	2,500	Domestic	n.a
Pohai 2 (Fuji)	Jack-up	1973	54	4,575	Japan	n.a.
Kantan 1	Catamaran drill-ship	1974	75	n.a.	Domestic	n.a.
Nanhai 1	Robray 300 jack-up	1976	90	7,650	Singapore	30
Nanhai 2	Robray 300 jack-up	1976	90	7,650	Singapore	30
n.a.	Robray 300 jack-up	1977	90	7,650	Japan	30
Borgny-Dolphin	Aker H-3 semisubmersible	1978	185	9,200	Norway	40[e]
n.a.	National 1320 production rig	1978	n.a.	6,100	U.S.	15
n.a.	National 1320 production rig	1978	n.a.	6,100	U.S.	15
n.a.	Bethdrill JU-250 mat jack-up	1979	75	n.a.	Singapore	25
n.a.	Marathon 82-SD-S jack-up	1980	n.a.	n.a.	Singapore	23
n.a.	Marathon 82-SD-S jack-up	1980	n.a.	n.a.	Singapore	23
n.a.	Hitachi Zosen jack-up[a]	1980	n.a.	n.a.	Japan	26
n.a.	Hitachi Zosen jack-up[a]	1980	n.a.	n.a.	Japan	26

[a] Reported too late for inclusion in the analysis.　[e] Estimate.

for delivery between 1976 and 1980 at a total cost of some $230 million. This was roughly ten times the amount spent on foreign offshore-drilling equipment before 1976. Purchase commitments of this size must have rested on a favorable assessment of China's offshore potential. Furthermore, the rigs were designed for use in areas of the shelf outside of the Pohai Gulf. The first two Robray 300 jack-up rigs, delivered by a Singapore yard in 1976 (Robin Loh, $60 million), were towed to the Gulf of Tonkin and are beginning an exploratory drilling program along the South China Sea portion of the continental shelf. The destinations of the third Robray 300 (Hitachi, $30 million) and the Aker H-3 semisubmersible (Fred Olsen, $27–40 million) are unknown, but they are assumed to be in moderate- to deep-water areas of the shelf outside of the Pohai Gulf.[36] Delivery of the semisubmersible from Norway in 1978 was to extend China's offshore drilling capabilities to the very edge of its continental shelf and into the thickest sediments.

The pace of rig purchases led some observers to wonder if China had the necessary technical personnel to absorb properly the new exploration equipment into its offshore program. Indeed, the first Robray 300 rig was reported to have experienced technical difficulties during its first assignment. A team of technical experts from six American contractors was flown to the rig on location in the Gulf of Tonkin in September 1976, and quickly corrected lubrication and misalignment errors in its operation.[37] But there have been no reports of Chinese difficulties in handling the rigs since 1976, and judging from the discovery claims in the South China Sea areas where the Robray rigs were put to work, China's technicians appear to have quickly mastered their new assignment.

During 1977, the PRC ordered its first two offshore rigs directly from U.S. suppliers. The Armco Steel Corporation sold two National 1320 production rigs to Peking late in the year.[38] Unlike the mobile exploration rigs purchased from Japan and Singapore, the National rigs consist of equipment packages that are to be mounted on fixed platforms of Chinese construction. It is still too early to tell the likely destination of these rigs, but it is significant that they are for production rather than exploration purposes. This is another sign that Peking was moving into Phase III of the offshore program in 1978. It also indicates that Peking does not intend to delegate the responsibility for offshore production entirely to foreign oil companies.

During 1978, China ordered three additional advanced jack-up exploration rigs from Singapore shipyards, this time from Singapore subsidiaries of U.S. corporations. Marathon Le Tourneau received a Chinese order for two shallow-draft jack-up rigs, to be delivered in March 1980 at a total cost of $46 million.[39] In addition, Peking ordered a Bethdrill

JU-250 jack-up, already under construction in the Singapore yards of the Bethlehem Steel Corporation, for about $25 million.[40] The Bethdrill rig has a special feature that will help exploration in the soft sea-bed areas near Hainan Island. Its three legs are fixed to a steel mat that broadens the support base. The three 1978 orders for mobile exploration rigs signal strengthened interest in the exploration phase of Peking's offshore program. Once again, this might warrant speculation that the results of early exploration, particularly in the South China Sea, have been encouraging.

On the basis of these recent rig purchases, it should be anticipated that the PRC will embark on a drilling reconnaissance program across wide areas of the continental shelf between 1978 and 1980. This reconnaissance drilling program will still not constitute active offshore oil production. Once again, the primary effort will be directed at wildcat exploration, core drilling, geological analysis, and locating the most promising areas for commercial exploitation. Perhaps the Pohai Gulf has begun to move toward limited offshore oil and gas production. No such production should be expected before at least 1980 from any other offshore area. It appears from the expansion of China's offshore program during the 1970's that Peking regards the 1980's as the target decade for commercial offshore development.

On the other hand, it must also be recognized that even the current reconnaissance drilling program may have serious short-term political consequences. With delivery of the Norwegian semisubmersible, China has achieved the ability to drill anywhere it likes along the continental shelf, including areas claimed by other littoral states. In late 1978, there were rumors that the PRC was making inquiries for the purchase of a dynamically positioned drill-ship capable of drilling in 350 meters of water.[41] That would round out the Chinese fleet and bring even the deepest areas of the shelf within range. So far, Peking has exercised caution in the deployment of its drilling rigs, concentrating in areas of accepted Chinese jurisdiction. Regional political relations are highly sensitive to unilateral drilling in disputed waters. Particularly in its relationship with Japan, Peking might incure substantial political and commercial costs by an overextended offshore-drilling program. But a sudden "radical" phase in domestic Chinese politics or an active dispute with one of its neighbors might precipitate more reckless behavior, accompanied by efforts to enforce China's claims with its growing regional naval power. Peking may also attempt to substantiate its own claims by planting the flag with the drill bit. The risk of unilateral Chinese moves to resolve the offshore dispute exists, but should not be overstated.

How does China's 1978 rig capability compare with other Asian countries? About 40 offshore rigs of various types were reported active in Asian waters in July 1978. Another six rigs were idle and five were under construction. China owns or has ordered 14 offshore rigs, of which some are out of service at any given time.[42] In mid-1978, China's offshore activity (eight rigs or less) compared with the level of activity in Malaysian waters. By 1980, the Chinese exploratory program will compare to the offshore program in Indonesia, although offshore production will have just begun. Current Indonesian offshore production levels could not be achieved until at least 1982, even with participation by foreign oil companies. This pace of development conforms with the expectation that Peking has been gearing up for large-scale exploration of the shelf during the early 1980's, followed by growing production from discovered fields. If the wildcat drilling program is successful in locating commercial offshore resources, production from the offshore areas will be contributing a statistically significant proportion of crude oil and/or natural gas production by 1985.[43]

China's new offshore drilling fleet requires a wide range of support ships and equipment. Nearly all of the supplementary offshore equipment bought on the international market so far is related to exploration rather than production, although some of it can be used in both Phase II and Phase III. A complete list of the supplementary offshore-equipment purchases is difficult to compile from fragmentary reports. However, it is possible to identify several types of offshore support equipment imported since 1970. A number of rig supply ships have been purchased from Denmark, Norway, and Japan. The first was the 400-dwt work ship "Kuroshio" (Japan Ocean Drilling, $1 million) that was included along with a supply of spare rig parts with the first imported jack-up rig, the "Fuji." In 1973, the PRC ordered eight rig supply and towing ships from Denmark (Weco, $41.8 million) and five more from Japan (Hitachi, $10 million). These supply ships were received over a several-year period and the transactions have only recently been completed. Several more supply ships were reportedly purchased from Norway (Fred Olsen) in 1973 and 1974 at an unknown price, and from Norway (Sandoy) and Singapore during 1977. By 1978, the total cost of imported rig supply ships must have been approaching $100 million. China's fleet of rig supply ships will be supplemented by the addition of two Bo105 multipurpose helicopters ordered from West Germany in 1975 (Messerschmitt) and delivered with two Australian gas turbine engines (Hawker de Havilland, $0.3 million) in 1977.[44] The helicopters were specifically equipped for offshore work.

The PRC has also imported a wide array of offshore seismic exploration equipment, including at least four and possibly more complete survey ships.[45] Much of the imported seismic data-processing equipment, including the large American Cyber computers imported through a French company (CGG and Control Data, $7.0 million) may be used for both onland and offshore exploration. In June 1977, a Canadian company announced the sale of three small seismic survey aircraft to the PRC, complete with advanced aerial geophysical survey equipment (De Haviland, $6 million). These aircraft may be used for prospecting for a number of different mineral resources, including both offshore hydrocarbons and uranium deposits.[46] More recently, Shen Chen-tung, Director of China's Bureau of Oceanography, projected long-range plans for an integrated aerial, coastal, and oceanographic surveillance system to be developed over the next several decades.[47] The system would integrate marine prospecting with navigation aids, oceanographic research, and meteorology. It would also obviously have defense implications for China's long and exposed coastline. In all of its foreign seismic equipment purchases, China has insisted on the latest technology and has stipulated training in the supplying country as part of the contract.

A very important and seldom mentioned category of supplementary offshore equipment imported recently by the PRC is the sophisticated drilling and measurement gear carried by each of the offshore rigs. Equipment on the secondhand "Fuji" jack-up rig was apparently somewhat dated. But the three Robray 300 jack-ups delivered in 1976 and 1977 and the Aker H-3 semisubmersible scheduled for delivery in 1978 all carry the latest and most advanced American hardware. In the case of the Robray rigs built new to Chinese specifications, the value of American exploration equipment was estimated at $10–15 million per rig. As the Chinese become familiar with the advanced offshore exploration technology carried on their new rigs, they will be reaching for cutting-edge capabilities, much as they have already done with the seismic survey equipment.

Comparison to offshore development in the North Sea, if hazardous from a geological perspective, nonetheless gives some picture of the scale of infrastructure requirements generated by a significant level of offshore oil and gas production. Intensive seismic survey activity and the granting of offshore concessions in the North Sea began in 1963.[48] The first offshore gas field (West Sole) was discovered in 1965 and came online in 1967.* The first large oilfields (Ekofisk and Montrose) were discovered in December 1969, but major oil production did not begin in the North Sea until October 1975. By year-end 1977, reserves had reached about 23 billion barrels (3 billion metric tons) of crude oil and 30 trillion

---

*An oil or gas field comes "on-line" when it actually begins production.

cubic feet (850 billion cubic meters) of natural gas. In the same year, production from the North Sea reached 1 million barrels per day of crude oil (50 million metric tons per year) and 5 billion cubic feet per day of natural gas (50 billion cubic meters per year).

This production level would correspond roughly to China's crude oil output in 1973. The achievement of this level of output required intensive exploration and development activities stretching over a decade and a half, absorbing billions of dollars in investment capital, engaging the advanced engineering skills of half a dozen industrialized European countries, and including the laying of five major subsea oil pipelines and two gas pipelines to shore terminals. It was predicated on the smooth settlement of offshore boundary claims by consensual agreement of the littoral states, all of which accepted the midline criterion established for subsea exploration at the U.N. Law of the Sea Conference in Geneva in 1958. Well productivity in the North Sea varies enormously, from about 500 bbl/day to 25,000 bbl/day. Commercial discoveries routinely test at 5,000 bbl/day. (Well productivity at Taching and Takang is thought to average 300–500 bbl/day.) Even at this level of productivity, the North Sea discoveries are considered "economic" only within the framework of the international petroleum market-price increases effected by OPEC in 1974. North Sea development costs are high because of great water depth (100–200 meters) and because of the severe weather conditions in the region. (These factors are present in some areas of the Chinese continental shelf.)

There is nothing in the record of offshore development in the North Sea that would lead one to expect a significant level of Chinese offshore oil and gas production before 1985. Quite the contrary, the high level of infrastructure and political requirements for rapid offshore development in the North Sea would lead one to expect an even longer lead time in the Chinese case. As repeatedly argued in the preceding examination of other offshore development programs in East Asia, and documented in the case of China's own offshore exploration program, there are many persistent constraints operating on offshore hydrocarbon development along the Chinese continental shelf. These constraints operate at the level of the geologic information available regarding the hydrocarbon potential of the shelf. They operate at the level of the politics of conflicting claims to the shelf and to political legitimacy itself that are endemic to East Asia. And the constraints operate at the economic level as well, given the enormous cost of offshore development even within the structure of China's centrally planned economy. It must be recognized that China is a dynamic and increasingly powerful country determined to press toward industrial modernization by the turn of the century. But it must also be recognized that offshore oil development is just one of the various energy policy options facing the government in Peking. The time and cost constraints on that option must be carefully assessed to avoid massive miscalculations in projecting the likely course of China's energy development policy, energy production mix, and regional energy commodity export potential.

Joint Offshore Development and Phase III

During 1978, there were a series of dramatic developments in China's offshore program that indicate Peking's intention to move as swiftly as possible into offshore oil and gas production. It is still too early to assess the magnitude or likely success of Phase III of the offshore program. But we are quite certain that it has begun. Peking is seriously considering a joint offshore development program in Phase III that may involve participation by Japanese, American, and European oil companies. If the Chinese government exercises this option, the decision to do so will have important implications for the entire structure of China's international energy policy. Foreign production organization, as well as technology, will be introduced into an important growth sector of the Chinese oil industry. Offshore crude oil production will be linked more closely with China's regional energy commodity trade. China's territorial claims to contested parts of the continental shelf may receive international sanction, and at minimum the PRC will achieve production-sharing agreements in areas under dispute with Japan. Joint offshore development will further shift China's global political posture in the direction of the West and will strengthen the new regional partnership between the PRC and Japan. There is absolutely no geological guarantee that joint offshore development will result in new oil and gas discoveries in China's continental shelf. But even the exploration effort will have certain implications for Peking's international energy policies. Given the importance of this development, it is worth taking a detailed look at the sequence of events in 1978 that drew China toward the joint development option for Phase III.

Typically, Peking's inquiry into the potential of joint offshore development began with a series of Chinese delegations to Western petroleum industries and culminated in direct discussions with foreign oil companies and a cabinet-level visit to China by an American energy delegation. Chinese petroleum delegations visited several West European countries in 1977, emphasizing North Sea development, particularly in the technically difficult British sector.[49] In January 1978 a delegation of the "Chinese Petroleum Corporation" (a nonofficial cover for the Ministry of Petroleum and Chemical Industries), led by then Vice-Minister Sun

Ching-wen, visited the U.S. petroleum industry for three weeks at the express invitation of Secretary of Energy James R. Schlesinger.[50] Schlesinger gave the Chinese the red carpet treatment, taking them to production facilities in every phase of the U.S. oil industry, including the most advanced petroleum technology.[51] The delegation then stopped off in Japan on the way back to China to talk over their American trip with counterparts from government and industry. Upon their return to the PRC, the delegation held a three-day debriefing session with Minister of Petroleum and Chemical Industries Kang Shih-en and, according to the Chinese press, had an open discussion of the petroleum technology gap between China and other countries.[52]

In February, right on the heels of the Chinese petroleum delegation's visit to the United States, the long-expected Sino-Japanese trade agreement was completed and signed (Chapter 6). The trade agreement established a base line for trade of U.S. $10 billion in each direction, with the Chinese exporting increasing quantities of coal and crude oil to Japan, and expecting to accelerate the pace of plant and equipment purchases through 1982. The Chinese side made it clear throughout the treaty negotiations, and subsequently, that it hoped for a much higher level of trade than stipulated by the formal terms of the agreement. In essence, the trade agreement formalized and extended the existing exchange of Japanese technology for Chinese raw materials. It also set the stage for Peking's consideration of joint offshore development in the Pohai Gulf and East China Sea theaters with Japanese companies.

One result of the trade agreement and China's already accelerating pace of foreign equipment and plant deals was to stimulate some interest among foreign analysts in the PRC's balance of trade. During 1973 and 1974, Peking had incurred serious balance-of-trade deficits and a tightening of its foreign exchange position by accelerating plant and equipment orders without a concomitant acceleration of commodity exports. Analysts began to see higher crude oil exports as the only way to avoid a repeat experience.[53] But even higher oil exports would not completely alleviate the problem, since Peking wants to place its plant and equipment orders now, to lay the foundation of its ambitious Ten-Year Development Plan. For both production and market reasons, crude oil exports can increase only slowly, bringing additional revenues by the mid-1980's, if then. This creates a lag of at least several years between rising foreign exchange requirements and rising oil export revenues. The usual approach to this problem in dealing with analogous trade problems among the industrial market economy countries would be to seek credits and loans that permit short-term expansion of production capacity to be financed by long-term expansion of production.

It appears that Peking was immediately sensitive to the balance-of-trade and finance problems. It was quite clear that reliance on limited and expensive supplier credits would not suffice for an import program as ambitious as China's planners visualized. By July 1978, the trade finance problem had been discussed at the highest levels in the Chinese government. The Central Committee of the Chinese Communist Party convened a "National Finance and Trade Conference on Learning from Taching and Tachai," where both internal and external finance were discussed at length among 5,000 of the country's top finance and trade officials. The conference concluded:[54]

We should develop economic and technical exchanges with other countries in accordance with our national needs and the principles of equality and mutual benefit and supplying each other's needs provided these activities do not infringe on China's sovereignty or hamper her economic independence and provided they conform to Chairman Mao's line in foreign affairs. We should also apply common trade practices and handle our foreign trade flexibly and successfully. It is necessary . . . to give full play to China's immense labour power and certain surplus equipment to expand the work of processing raw materials, copying prototypes and assembling machine parts. Where techniques and equipment are inadequate, the method of importing them and repaying with their own products can be used. It is necessary to introduce advanced technology and equipment in a planned way.

Self-reliance, the vaunted principle of China's energy and economic development, was mentioned just once—in a speech by Vice-Chairman Li Hsien-nien.[55]

Meanwhile, the British government had picked up on China's reevaluation of its international finance policies, as Secretary of Trade Edmund Dell offered Ku Ming, Vice-Minister of China's State Planning Commission, access to London's extensive export credit facilities.[56] A British oil delegation followed up with a trip to Peking in May, emphasizing the advantages of North Sea technology. By July, there were reports that China was holding talks with Japanese companies over the prospects for joint offshore development.[57] The link between China's foreign exchange situation and the potential of joint offshore development schemes was becoming obvious to all concerned.

During the first six months of 1978, more than 30 U.S. companies gave technical seminars in the PRC, a substantial increase over the previous year. These seminars were not all concerned with the energy sector or offshore oil, but a list of the companies involved (Exxon, Union Oil, Chevron, Armco, N. L. Petroleum Services, etc.) leaves a strong impression that the seminars were not simply academic in nature.[58] Several of the companies invited to give seminars stayed for contract negotiations, and it may have been during these negotiating sessions that Peking first raised the prospect of joint offshore development. There may also have been a link between joint development proposals and Chinese orders for three more offshore exploration rigs from American subsidiaries in Singapore during April. Peking may have timed these orders to convince the oil companies of the seriousness of China's intent in offshore development.

During the summer of 1978, various Chinese officials began to drop obvious hints about the extent of China's petroleum reserves and export potential. Vice-Premier Teng Hsiao-ping was widely said to have placed China's oil resources at 400 billion barrels, which would rank the country with Saudi Arabia.[59] Chiao Lin-yi, executive secretary of the Kwangtung provincial Party Committee, took a somewhat more subtle approach by announcing plans for a "fairly large" offshore field at the mouth of the Pearl River, and then sending samples of "Pearl River crude" to Japan for laboratory analysis.[60] Meanwhile, five more U.S. companies (Pennzoil, Exxon, Union, Phillips, and Mobil) were formally invited to Peking to discuss joint offshore oil exploration and development.[61] Japan, represented by Japan National Oil Corporation, announced an agreement for joint development of oil resources in the Pohai Gulf at about the same time.[62] Chinese talks with British, French, and West German companies were also rumored, each country believing that it had the edge in the competition for participation in China's offshore development, which by the end of the summer was reaching magnificent if somewhat imaginary proportions.

In a not entirely unrelated development, Sino-Japanese political relations, which had improved steadily since the establishment of diplomatic relations in 1972, reached a new peak. Negotiations on the pending treaty of peace and friendship, formally ending the state of war (World War II) between the two countries and committing them to a common front against "hegemonism" (Soviet expansion), was initialed on August 12 in Peking and ratified on October 23 in Tokyo.[63] Taken together with the trade agreement signed in February, the peace treaty signaled a new political and economic alliance between China and Japan within the region. The successful conclusion of the treaty greatly accelerated the tempo of economic cooperation between the two countries and facilitated more detailed discussion of Peking's new joint development proposals for the offshore areas. Though not party to either the negotiations or the treaty, Washington encouraged both as a further step toward normalization of diplomatic relations with China and containment of the Soviet presence in the Western Pacific.

By Fall 1978, negotiation of joint development projects had begun to map out specific proposals. More U.S. oil companies (Gulf, Standard of

Indiana) entered the talks, and Peking suggested as many as ten different projects in the South China Sea and East China Sea.[64] Attention began to be focused on the type of contracts that would be most acceptable to both sides, preserving China's absolute control over the disposition of its hydrocarbon resources while granting the foreign oil companies the necessary degree of freedom of action to operate in an efficient (and profitable) manner. Several alternatives were suggested in the course of the discussions, which were linked to the general structure of Peking's finance and credit policies for the purchase of foreign plants and equipment. In early August, Jardine Matheson, a Hong Kong firm with a long history of investment and trade in pre-liberation China, brought back startling news from Peking.[65] China was ready to encourage the financing of imported equipment and technology with "pay back by product" arrangements with foreign companies. Under the pay-back contract, which has long been a feature of Soviet package deals with the West, complete factories, mines, and other production units may be imported with a specific provision for export of a certain percentage of the product for a specified period of time to finance the original capital cost of the imported technology. In essence, future production is used as collateral for current credit. Japanese projects for development of Siberian timber, coal, oil, and natural gas resources are being financed through pay-back contracts.[66]

The Hong Kong connection with a shift in Peking's finance policy was more than coincidental. Rumors began to circulate that China might go so far as to set up "export-processing zones" for factories operating under pay-back contracts.[67] Hong Kong firms had already begun experimenting with this type of arrangement, both inside the colony, where many businesses are owned outright by China, and along the border with Kwantung province on Chinese soil. The implication for a new Hong Kong role in offshore oil and gas development projects was too obvious to be missed. Just as Canton and other Chinese ports once functioned as an interface between Western barbarian traders and Chinese compradors, so Hong Kong might provide a base for foreign participation in China's joint offshore development projects in the South China Sea. The setting was perfect—a distinct geographic and political entity with defined borders, a free-swinging commercial structure, and powerful communist Chinese presence. Indeed, Chinese petroleum products had already deeply penetrated the Hong Kong market. Both sides took symbolic measures to reinforce conjecture that Hong Kong would be the operational base for foreign oil companies working under contract with the PRC. British Petroleum established an important office in the colony. Peking announced plans for new helicopter and airboat transportation services between Canton and Hong Kong. The deal was struck.[68]

During September and October, Peking began to move on all fronts to loosen its approach to foreign credit. Japanese Minister for International Trade and Industry Toshio Komoto and Yoshihiro Inayama, the president of the Japan-China Association on Economy and Trade who had been intimately involved in negotiations for the trade agreement, visited Peking in early September. They reached agreement with Chinese officials that Tokyo's Export-Import Bank would extend credit to the Bank of China for oil and coal development at an interest rate of 6.25 percent over 10 years.[69] Sino-Japanese plant and equipment trade had long been hampered by Peking's insistence on supplier credits but refusal to pay the higher interest rates on such credits (7.25–7.5 percent) established by an informal OECD agreement. Komoto and Inayama reciprocated by indicating that the volume of Sino-Japanese trade would be revised and extended beyond the levels set by the formal trade agreement.[70] By October, Peking had approached West German banks to arrange export credits for a $4 billion coal project, and was reassuring the EEC that syndicated bank credits were an acceptable practice in the China trade.[71] The United States then entered the act with renewed discussion of the frozen assets issue, which has hampered commercial relations between Chinese and American banks.

The basic Chinese objective in the credit discussions has been to convey the impression of greater flexibility regarding the financing of its capital imports from the industrial market economy countries. Peking has even dropped its objection to money from Japan's Overseas Economic Cooperation Fund, an official agency that dispenses soft loans to Third World countries for development projects.[72] The PRC has had justifiable public pride in its debt-free status since the remaining Soviet loans were paid off in the 1960's. But the pace of plant and equipment imports implied by China's drive for modernization requires a less rigid attitude toward financial policy. In a recent symbolic gesture, China was even seeking small aid projects from the United Nations Development Program and other U.N. agencies.[73] Many of these steps toward greater flexibility can be seen as a recognition that foreign support for China's modernization effort is a legitimate attitude, not a threat to Chinese sovereignty or national independence.

The political framework for these events must be kept firmly in mind when evaluating their commercial significance. In 1978, Peking seemed more preoccupied than ever with the Soviet threat. Moscow remains the one dark cloud on the horizon of China's modernization effort. The USSR could at a stroke d stroy China's chance of success, after 50 years of revolution and war and 30 years of domestic economic and political development. China has two responses to the Soviet menace. On the one hand, Peking continues to strengthen and broaden its own military forces, still no match in lightning warfare for the Soviet Red Army. On the other hand, Peking is seeking the widest possible framework of international alignments to frustrate and contain Soviet ambitions in Asia. The trade agreement and peace treaty with Japan must certainly be seen in this context. During 1978, Hua Kuo-feng traveled to Romania, Yugoslavia, and Iran (all "front line" states), while Teng Hsiao-ping went to Japan, Thailand, Malaysia, and Singapore—China's most important Asian neighbors. Peking also took steps to revive the dialogue with India and to continue the long-term relationship with Pakistan.[74] The big political setback for China in 1978 was its relationship with Vietnam. Relations began to deteriorate in 1977 with the flare-up of armed confrontation along the Vietnam-Cambodian border. China openly took the Cambodian side, wishing to avoid a unified Indochina under Hanoi's suzerainty. Hanoi responded by antagonizing Chinese citizens living in Vietnam, driving many to seek refuge by fleeing across the Chinese border. The smoldering border dispute along the Sino-Vietnamese boundary broadened and intensified. Vietnam, fearful of a war on two fronts with Cambodia and China, moved rapidly toward the Soviet Union, signaling its new position by entry into the CMEA. But the final blow, as far as Peking was concerned, was the sudden announcement on November 3, 1978, that Vietnam and Moscow had entered into a treaty of peace and friendship that echoed the Sino-Japanese peace treaty and established a de facto military alliance against China.[75] The treaty called for the "consolidation of the world socialist system" (anathema in Peking) and for mutual consultation in the event of a threat or attack directed against either country by an unspecified third party (China). This puts China in an extremely sensitive security position vis-à-vis Vietnam. In February and March 1979, the simmering dispute between China and Vietnam broke into open warfare as Peking sent troops deep into Vietnamese territory on a "punitive" mission. The Soviet Union threatened retaliation on China's sensitive northeastern border, but did not carry through on the threat.

Meanwhile, Hanoi had begun to take its case against China to the region. Vietnamese diplomats traveled to the ASEAN countries just prior to the Teng tour and both sides did some public sniping.[76] In addition, Vietnam has also been seeking the participation of foreign oil companies in its offshore development program and offers a somewhat broader range of contract options than the PRC.[77] This could have interesting consequences if the same companies bid for contracts on both Vietnamese and Chinese sectors of the continental shelf. It is obvious that Vietnam, like the PRC, will try to use foreign participation to strengthen its offshore territorial claims against China, Cambodia, and the Philippines.[78] Hanoi has also dropped its prior conditions for diplomatic relations with the United States and is actively pushing Washington toward normalization. Both the United States and the five members of ASEAN are reluctant to improve relations with Vietnam just as Hanoi shifts into the Moscow camp. There is considerable concern throughout the region about Vietnamese intentions toward Cambodia and Laos and fear that the Russians will be invited into the former American naval base in Cam Ranh Bay.

It was against the background of this realignment of political relations in the region (China-Japan and USSR–Vietnam) that Peking began to play its American card more seriously. The pro-U.S. tilt in Chinese foreign policy became increasingly visible during 1978. The Chinese petroleum delegation in January, the direct discussions with U.S. oil companies of joint offshore development projects, and a state visit to Peking by National Security Adviser Zbigniew Brzezinski in May set an upbeat tone. Brzezinski, known for his hard line on U.S.–Soviet relations, was a smash hit in Peking, contrasting sharply with the negative Chinese reaction to Secretary of State Cyrus Vance during his visit in August 1977.[79] By the summer of 1978, both sides were specifying sharply defined sets of conditions for the normalization of diplomatic relations. The conditions centered on remaining differences over the status of Taiwan, with Peking pressing for withdrawal of American military support for Taipei and Washington pressing for a Chinese promise not to use force to "liberate" the island.

The link between Sino-American energy relations and normalization of diplomatic relations was rendered explicit when U.S. Secretary of Energy James R. Schlesinger visited China from October 24 to November 5, 1978. A former Secretary of Defense, Schlesinger took a 23-member delegation of high-level assistants from the Departments of Energy and State. The delegation visited China's most advanced energy production units and engaged in a series of remarkably frank discussions of China's remaining energy development problems.[80] The Chinese plied their guests with the usual optimistic assessments of their oil and gas resources and requested expanded energy cooperation between the two countries.[81] Specific cooperative projects were identified in five areas—coal mining, hydroelectric power, oil and gas, renewable energy, and high-energy physics (nuclear).[82] Surprisingly, the talks did not center on joint offshore development proposals, and subsequent reports indicated that the Chinese tried to steer the discussion away from offshore cooperation. It is likely that Peking is still wary of American dominance in offshore oil exploration and prefers to deal individually with United States multinationals, rather than on a government-to-government basis. Schlesinger managed to please his hosts with the technical strength of his delegation while maintaining a low diplomatic profile. In a press conference in Japan following his visit, Schlesinger correctly identified the central mission of the exchange as political: "As a result of our discussions, a substantial agenda for cooperation between our two countries has been established. . . . This visit to China was a manifestation of an important step in the improvement of Chinese-American relations. . . . We achieved a clear understanding on mutual questions in the energy field. We identified energy projects of mutual benefit to both countries."[83] The political framework of the Schlesinger visit became clear just one month later when, on December 15, 1978, President Carter announced the normalization of diplomatic relations between China and the United States. Once again, Peking's energy diplomacy preceded the flag.

At year-end 1978, the final prospects for joint development of oil and gas resources along China's continental shelf were still uncertain. Peking is still hedging its bets and has yet to make a firm commitment to any foreign company. The Japanese may have moved further toward contract agreements for projects in the Pohai Gulf than have American and European oil companies. This would conform to the high priority Peking attaches to close commercial and political relations with Tokyo. It would also represent a first step toward solution of the still-outstanding jurisdictional dispute between the two countries in the East China Sea. In April 1978 there was a sudden flare-up of the Tiaoyutai Islands issue when 100 Chinese fishing boats suddenly appeared in the islands and began casting their nets for territory.[84] The incident infuriated Japanese public opinion and delayed the negotiation of the treaty of peace and friendship. There followed a wave of public confusion in Tokyo, as Peking then muted the issue and promised to negotiate the peace treaty with no reference whatsoever to the outstanding jurisdictional dispute along the continental shelf. No one was quite certain of the Chinese motive for such a blunt maneuver in the framework of the much more important peace treaty negotiations. My own interpretation of this and similar incidents is that Peking intends to express its continuing determination on the Taiwan issue, which ranks in China's hierarchy of foreign policy problems with relations with Japan, the United States, and the Soviet Union in terms of perceived importance. By showing the flag in the Tiaoyutai, Peking reminded Tokyo of its continuing concern with the status of Taiwan and with the unsettled jurisdictional dispute over broad areas of the continental shelf in the East China Sea. In moving toward closer relations with Japan, China has by no means sacrificed the underlying structure of its claims in the area. Peking and Tokyo may be able to alleviate or even avoid their jurisdictional dispute along the continental shelf through joint offshore development programs, to the extent that joint development does not impinge directly on the issue of Taiwan's status. However, the long-range solution to the Taiwan problem lies in direct discussions between Taipei and Peking, a fact of life that has not yet been accepted on either side of the Taiwan Strait.

What about the underlying issue of China's principle of self-reliance? The People's Republic has for 30 years been a champion of self-reliant energy and economic development and was really the first country to apply the concept explicitly to the process of rapid industrialization. It seems as though, in moving toward joint offshore development projects, Peking has been caught in an embarrassing position, like a priest in a red-light district, violating its own most hallowed morality. The foreign press, naturally enough, is delighted to note that the priest has been caught in a compromising and even hypocritical act. What, after all, are foreign technology, bank loans, and oil concessions, other than the very decadence for which the Chinese press has long pilloried the Soviet Union and hapless opponents in the Third World? (Perhaps the real moral of the story is that a controlled press reaps its own reward.)

There is little doubt that the Chinese Communist Party has recently undertaken a vigorous discussion of the concept of self-reliance. At minimum, the definition of self-reliance is shifting to permit a much greater level of foreign technology inputs into China's industrialization. For example, as recently as August 1976, Liu Shao-chi and Teng Hsiao-ping were accused of "plotting to import" a 250-MW foreign steam-generating set in the early 1960's, for an amount equal to the total capital invested in the Shanghai Steam Turbine Plant and the Shanghai Electrical Machinery Plant.[85]

This enraged the workers of the two plants who said, "That's not using imports to spur domestic development! It's bartering hens for eggs! Why pay so much money to import power-generating equipment and not use it to develop our own power machinery industry?" Resolutely opposed to worshipping things foreign, the workers decided to design and make a 300,000-kw steam turbo-generating set themselves. This attitude contrasts sharply with a recent article on the reasons for importing foreign technology and equipment.[86]

Seven big and fairly advanced imported chemical fertilizer plants have gone into production in the last two years and another six are under construction. . . . In the past, chemical plants in China were mainly small or medium-sized employing rather backward technology so that output fell below demand. We had to spend several hundred million U.S. dollars every year to import chemical fertilizer. So Chairman Mao and Premier Chou in 1973 approved importing 13 big chemical fertilizer plants.

A few years ago, it was taboo in China to even admit publicly that the country was using any imported plants or equipment. The following suggestion would have landed its author in a thought reform camp in 1976, but is now *de rigueur:* "We acknowledge our backwardness so as to swiftly change our backwardness. And how are we to bring this about? Mainly by relying on our own efforts and at the same time extensively importing advanced technology and equipment and absorbing everything that is good from abroad."[87] This statement still does not address the important matter of what is happening to the self-reliance ethic in Chinese development policy as successively greater amounts of foreign technology and perhaps some foreign capital are introduced into the energy system and the economy as a whole. The typical response to this problem in Peking is to fall back on definitional arguments.[88]

Self-reliance does not mean "closing our doors," nor does "maintaining independence and keeping the initiative in our own hands" mean blind rejection of foreign things. The "gang of four," however, exploiting vestigial feudal ideas of a number of comrades, came out against learning what is good from other countries, against importing advanced technology and equated self-reliance with closed-doorism, independence and initiative with blind rejection of foreign things.

What is going on in this and similar statements is a broadening of the concept of self-reliance to permit more open access to foreign technology. Thus modified, the term "self-reliance" will remain in the Chinese lexicon and will be widely used to rationalize a wide range of development strategies over the next several decades.

But what about the underlying reality? Is a country that invites foreign oil companies to produce and export crude petroleum discovered in the offshore areas truly "self-reliant"? It would appear that joint offshore development projects are the antithesis of self-reliant development and imply direct reliance on foreign technology, production organization, capital, and even marketing infrastructure. Reality can only bend any concept so far, before a different concept begins to apply.

In my own judgment, the Chinese are still fully entitled to wave the banner of self-reliance. First, it should be recognized that even if all offshore oil development had been undertaken by foreign companies with no Chinese participation except through regulatory agencies, the offshore theater is just one part of the Chinese energy production system, which is in turn just one part of the industrial infrastructure. Second,

Peking has engaged actively in the offshore theater in Phases I and II of oil and gas exploration along the continental shelf and has full control of the information that will be required in Phase III for successful offshore development. Third, the Chinese government has recognized that joint offshore development could lead to an erosion of its control over the energy system, and is taking measures to ensure continued capital control and proper absorption of foreign technology. Fourth, the offshore theater is the only part of energy industry within which China will likely participate in joint development projects on anything resembling an equal basis. Foreign plant and equipment will continue to be imported for other energy industries—coal mining, hydropower, and refining, to name a few. But little direct foreign participation will be permitted in the organization or control of onland energy industries. In a sense, the offshore oil projects are ideal as a means of preserving the independence of the Chinese energy system from outside penetration. The arms-length interface role suggested for Hong Kong symbolizes the type of insulation that Peking would prefer in its acquisition of foreign energy production technology. Fifth, even with relatively heavy industrial plant and equipment imports in every industry, China will continue to produce the bulk of the means of production itself. A recent article claimed that the PRC today makes 80 percent of the equipment used in its basic industries.[89] If true, one is hard pressed to think of any other Third World country that produces even half of its own industrial plant. Furthermore, most of the currently industrial countries went through a long period when they produced the bulk of their own capital goods.

For all of these reasons, it would be premature to dismiss the self-reliance ethic as a major factor in China's energy development policy. Indeed, the bad experience with dependency on the Soviet Union during the 1950's and the heavy policy emphasis on self-reliance since 1960 would lead one to expect continuation of this basic trend for some time to come. This expectation is reinforced by the observation that much of the ballyhoo over foreign technology in 1978 was a reaction to the narrow and sectarian attitude toward development policy that prevailed before 1976. There are also powerful political motivations in the international system (i.e. exacerbated relations with the Soviet Union and the Western tilt) that lead Peking to emphasize the prospects for cooperation with the West and Japan in virtually every field. It is no accident that discussions of joint offshore projects with Japan preceded the signing of the Sino-Japanese peace treaty, or that the Schlesinger visit preceded the normalization of relations with the United States. The close ties between Peking's international political position and energy policy have been noted in virtually all of the earlier chapters of this book.

Rather than dismissing continued reference to the self-reliance ethic as pure propaganda, we should expect that the PRC will in the future maintain the inward preoccupation of its energy policies with domestic control of domestic resources (resource sovereignty), absorption and internal application of foreign technology, growing capacity to produce capital goods in the energy sector, a high priority for domestic energy consumption requirements, and improvement in individual standards of energy consumption. All of these points of emphasis are quite consistent with the self-reliance ethic.

Regional Energy Commodity Trade

In 1978, it appears that the government of the People's Republic of China may make an effort to link expanding regional energy commodity exports to the success of joint development projects along the Chinese continental shelf. If this should happen, it will represent a departure from both China's historical pattern of energy commodity trade since 1949 and Peking's current approach to energy commodity exports. Roughly speaking, the history of China's energy trade may be broken into three periods. From 1949 to 1963, the PRC was a substantial energy commodity importer, relying on the Soviet Union for half of its annual consumption of refined petroleum products (Chapters 4 and 20). From 1963 until 1973, the PRC was basically self-sufficient in energy commodities, importing and exporting marginal quantities of particular commodities on a spot basis. In 1973 the PRC became a net energy exporter, with its first crude oil exports to Japan and some expansion in the level of annual coal exports. Exports of crude oil and refined petroleum products were then extended to include Hong Kong, Thailand, and the Philippines in Southeast Asia. So far, all of the petroleum exported to Asian countries has been produced on land, principally at Taching and Shengli oilfields. If current indications are correct, starting in the early 1980's China will begin exporting oil produced in offshore fields, depending of course on the scale of commercial oil and gas discoveries along the continental shelf.

The recent expansion of Japan's energy commodity trade with China has been dealt with in depth in Chapter 6. In addition, Chapter 20 in the Statistical Profile provides a detailed set of statistics for China's energy commodity trade, disaggregated by commodity, country, and year from 1949 to 1978. Chapter 21 summarizes these statistics, and Chapter 24 projects energy commodity export potential over the next two decades. Regional energy commodity trade is, therefore, a central theme throughout this book. Without repeating information provided in other chapters, this section will lay out in some detail the pattern of energy commodity trade with Asian countries around China's perimeter, particularly in Southeast Asia. We shall then be in a position to assess China's present and potential role as a regional energy commodity exporter.

Historical Patterns in Regional Energy Commodity Trade

It comes as something of a surprise to most foreign analysts to discover that China has been an active energy commodity exporter since the inception of the PRC in 1949. A careful examination of partner-country trade returns reveals that not only Japan but also Hong Kong, Malaysia, Pakistan, Singapore, Cambodia, and other Asian countries have had energy commodity trade with the PRC since the 1950's. The quantities involved in this trade were quite small by international standards, and thus scarcely noticed outside of China. Nonetheless, the early trade established a network of trade contacts throughout the region that was available when Peking began considering energy commodity exports on a larger scale in 1973.

Coal exports to Japan from Manchuria began long before 1949. Ejection of the Japanese from northeast China caused little disruption in this trade, and it resumed smoothly as early as 1950. By 1952 (possibly earlier), Hong Kong had also begun to import coal by rail from its huge northern neighbor. At first these coal imports were small, running about 15,000 to 25,000 metric tons (mt) per year (Table 20.11). But from 1956 to 1966, Hong Kong took annual shipments of 100,000–200,000 mt of Chinese coal. This trade then tapered off in the late 1960's and early 1970's. Meanwhile, Pakistan had begun importing Chinese coal in significant quantities in 1957, and continued this trade on a fluctuating basis through the present. Pakistan's imports of Chinese coal peaked at just under half a million tons in 1967 and then declined. Malaysia imported marginal quantities of coal from the PRC in the late 1950's, as did Cambodia in the mid-1960's. This coal trade with Asia was over and above the 200,000 mt per year that China exported to the Soviet Union from 1955 to 1965.

Coke trade is hard to quantify, because of the failure of trade returns from many countries to distinguish among steam coal, coking coal, and prepared coke. Hong Kong took marginal quantities of Chinese coke each year from 1956 until the present (Table 20.13). Pakistan began importing coke from China in 1971 and has taken about 30,000 mt per year since. Other countries importing marginal amounts of coke were Cambodia, Malaysia, Singapore, and Thailand, during certain years.

Crude petroleum trade really began in 1973 with the export of the first million tons to Japan (Table 20.2). However, there were persistent rumors that China had begun exporting some crude oil to Vietnam during the mid-1960's as part of that country's war effort.[90] Furthermore, it is known that North Korea was also taking some Chinese crude. Neither Vietnam nor North Korea publishes trade statistics, so there is no way of measuring these rumors. Neither do we have any idea what proportion of "crude oil" exports to China's communist neighbors were actually in the form of refined petroleum products. The Soviet Union also provided part of the petroleum imports of both Vietnam and North Korea before 1973. I doubt that the total amount of crude petroleum plus refined petroleum products that China exported to both countries exceeded half a million tons per year before 1972. Crude oil trade since 1973 will be discussed in more detail below.

China made small spot imports of the distillate fuels (gasoline, kerosene, and diesel fuel) from time to time from both Hong Kong and Singapore prior to 1970 (Table 20.3). These spot imports were only a tiny fraction of the regular distillate imports from the Soviet Union, upon which China depended until the early 1960's. The spot trade met shortfall in certain local Chinese markets, especially Canton. It is likely that the Canton city or Kwangtung province authorities felt the pinch early each time there was a national shortage of distillates, which occurred frequently. They simply bought what they needed from nearby Southeast Asian neighbors. Residual fuel oil has been relatively plentiful in China since 1949 owing to the heavy quality of Chinese crudes and the primitive state of refinery technology. It was not traded in significant quantities before 1970. Since 1970, China made spot purchases of residual from Kuwait and has recently been exporting 100,000–200,000 mt per year to Hong Kong (Table 20.34).

Hong Kong has been China's main Asian trading partner in lubricants since 1961. This trade moved in both directions, with exports of cheap, low-grade lubricants and imports of more expensive, high-grade lubricants not available from Chinese refineries. This lubricant trade, although quite marginal in quantitative terms, is vital to certain Chinese industries that required specialized lubricants. After 1970, as Chinese refineries began to make a wider range of lubricants, lubricant exports to the region increased. Total lubricant exports to Asian countries are now running about 10,000 mt per year.

Petroleum jelly (petrolatum) and wax (paraffin) have been exported to a variety of Asian countries, especially Hong Kong, since the mid-1950's. Wax is a plentiful by-product of Chinese crudes and is a good foreign exchange earner, even traded in relatively small quantities (Table 20.51). There is also marginal trade in other petroleum by-products (petroleum coke, asphalt, nonlubricating oils, shale, and bituminous mixtures) with a number of Asian countries, notably Japan. Most of the by-product exports to Japan consist of petroleum coke (Table 20.61).

The data for total refined petroleum products trade are somewhat more complete than disaggregated data for various petroleum products. China has had significant trade in refined petroleum products since the 1950's with Japan, Hong Kong, Malaysia, Pakistan, and Singapore. Refined products exports have jumped by an order of magnitude since 1973 and have been broadened to include Thailand (Table 20.71). Hong Kong is now the largest single importer of Chinese refined petroleum products, followed by Thailand and Japan. Total refined products trade in both directions with Asian countries ran less than 20,000 mt per year in the 1950's and less than 100,000 mt per year in the 1960's. By 1977, China's refined petroleum exports to Asia exceeded 1 million metric tons. The PRC may not become a large-scale petroleum products exporter within this century because of continuing limitations on domestic refinery capacity and growing domestic demand for refined petroleum products, particularly the distillates. Hong Kong and perhaps Thailand were exceptions to this rule in 1978, and it is possible that other Southeast Asian countries will seek to import Chinese refined petroleum products, especially diesel fuel. However, in order to compete with Japan and other countries for the Asian refined products market, China would have to build at least one major refinery totally dedicated to the production of export commodities. This may be part of the reason for the new refinery at Whampoa (Canton).[91] It is also possible that China would invite a foreign company to build a refinery on Chinese soil solely for the purposes of the export trade. But so far no proposals of this nature have surfaced. There are several advantages to refining Chinese oil before shipment, including the special nature of refinery equipment needed for northern crudes and the greater foreign exchange generated by selling refined products.

Energy Trade with Asian Market Economy Countries Since 1973

During 1972 and 1973, rumors began to circulate that Peking was interested in exporting crude petroleum or petroleum products to Hong Kong, Thailand, and the Philippines.[92] However, initial contacts between Chinese trade officials and their counterparts in Southeast Asia did not have any immediate effect. China did begin to expand non-energy trade in the region as early as 1971.[93] However, the grueling war in Indochina continued to disrupt political relations in the region, and the governments of Southeast Asian countries were inclined to move slowly in their China policy, waiting until the implications of new development in Sino–U.S. and Sino-Japanese relations became clearer. For its part, the PRC was preoccupied with meeting its new commitment to export one million tons of crude oil to Japan in 1973, and emphasized that "What we have to export is still a very small quantity."[94] Only Hong Kong benefited from China's new role as an oil exporter in 1973, receiving 27,000 mt of diesel fuel.

This situation changed radically in early 1974. China's crude petroleum production leaped upward at growth rates of 25 percent in 1973 and 20 percent in 1974, giving Peking a new surplus, perhaps beyond the initial expectations of Chinese energy planners. Thailand's Deputy Foreign Minister Chatichai Choonhavan visited Peking in the opening weeks of 1974 and returned with a Chinese commitment to export 50,000 mt of diesel fuel to Thailand at a special "friendship price."[95] There were political overtones to the visit, as the Major General made the obligatory "one China" statement in public to pave the way for normalization of relations. This maneuver caused an immediate strain between the communist Thai Patriotic Front and Peking.[96] The Front welcomed the diesel fuel, but wanted to have nothing to do with normalization. Actual deliveries of diesel fuel to Thailand in 1974 reached just 32,000 mt.

The Philippine government was not far behind. In July, Geronimo Velasco, president of the Philippine Petroleum Corporation, headed an oil mission to Peking.[97] Trade negotiations continued until September, when a two-year barter agreement was signed under which China would supply crude oil in return for sugar, lumber, copper, and coconut products. At the end of September, Imelda Marcos, the President's wife, left for an official visit to China with the authority to sign an oil purchase agreement.[98] The agreement called for the immediate initiation of crude oil trade at about 60,000 mt per month, starting in October 1974 and reaching one million tons total in 1975. President Marcos met the first shipment at the dock amid great fanfare on October 17. However, by November, Philippine refiners had discovered that their equipment could not handle waxy Chinese crude. There were rumors that the Chinese crude would be reexported or swapped for other crudes. The biggest potential user, the Manila Electric Company, had a previous contract with a U.S. supplier.[99] Actual deliveries in 1974 totaled just 123,000 mt.

In contrast to Thailand and the Philippines, the export of Chinese refined petroleum products to Hong Kong in 1974 exceeded everyone's expectations. Diesel fuel exports jumped to 190,000 mt, and residual fuel oil (50,000 mt) was sold to the colony for the first time, reportedly at

15 percent below the international market price.[100] Kerosene trade rose to 28,000 mt. China's interest in the Hong Kong market seems to have been predominantly commercial rather than political. Communist interests bought a parcel of land for the construction of oil storage facilities and began to extend their retail network for kerosene and diesel fuel. Total refined products exports to Hong Kong in 1974 reached 278,000 mt, up from 41,000 mt in 1973.

If China's energy commodity exports to Southeast Asian countries were initiated in 1974, 1975 was a year of great optimism about the prospects for Chinese oil in the region. (See Map 8.1.) Crude oil exports to Japan doubled in a single year to 7.9 million metric tons. Crude oil exports to the Philippines, disappointing in terms of the first contract and initial projections, were 482,000 mt. Refined products exports to Thailand increased to 58,000 mt, and Hong Kong took some 652,000 mt of Chinese petroleum products, including shipments of Chinese jet fuel to be sold at Kai Tak airport. The petroleum trade was linked to Premier Chou En-lai's ebullient assertion that "We can certainly build China into a powerful modern socialist country in another twenty years and more before the end of the century."[101]

China's forward energy export policy appeared to be having all of the political side-effects that Peking had hoped for. Diplomatic relations were achieved during 1975 with Malaysia, the Philippines (June), and Thailand (July). Oil diplomacy was certainly not the only reason for China's political successes in Southeast Asia. Peking's allies in Cambodia and Vietnam swept to successive victories over their opponents and drove the American presence completely out of Indochina. This left what China began to see as a power vacuum along its southern border, as the new Indochinese regimes struggled for internal order and pleaded for external aid. Since Washington refused to recognize Hanoi, to grant it reparation aid in any form, or to admit Vietnam to the United Nations, Soviet influence in Indochina began to grow. The PRC was extremely sensitive to this trend and warned its Southeast Asian neighbors against any form of cooperation with Moscow, attacking even the very limited Russian role in regional technical cooperation in offshore exploration and other energy technologies that was getting under way at the time.[102]

As the year progressed, it became apparent that not everything was rosy in China's regional energy trade. The waxy and heavy quality of Chinese crude continued to bedevil exports. Japanese refiners raised a storm of protest over what they considered the high price and low quality of Chinese crude and burned it in power plants and steel mills rather than refining it. The Thai government suspended trade in crude oil entirely in 1975, after experimental imports (12,000 mt) in 1974 had

Map 8.1 Petroleum exports, 1975.

proved disastrous for refineries equipped to handle lighter Middle East crudes.[103] Philippine refiners also complained, and began mixing Sheng-li crude with more expensive lighter crudes to get it through their refineries. The resistance to Chinese crude throughout the region caused some anxiety in Peking, which faced a serious balance-of-payments deficit in 1974 and again in 1975.[104] The concern of the Chinese centered on their ability to continue plant and equipment purchases at the swift pace established in 1974 and 1975. Critical demand for foreign technology and equipment, including the two sophisticated offshore drilling rigs ordered from Singapore in late 1975, had increased even faster than the oil trade, outstripping the estimated $500 million in oil revenues earned in 1974 and the $1 billion earned in 1975. Peking's problems with petroleum exports were compounded by a concurrent glut on the international oil market and some erosion of the international price structure from the peaks that followed the Arab oil embargo in early 1974. During 1974 and 1975 there were rumors that Peking had offered crude oil exports to Australia, Singapore, Sri Lanka, and Nepal, without success.[105]

If China's regional energy commodity trade grew at an unexpected pace in 1974 and 1975, that trade proved quite fragile and sensitive to domestic political disturbances in 1976. The problems in the crude oil trade that had begun to surface in the closing months of 1975 caused an intense policy debate within the Politburo of the Chinese Communist Party over the continuation of the technology-import, oil-export strategy that appeared to be racking up growing balance-of-payments deficits and dribbling away China's new-found oil wealth. A group of radical Politburo members based in Shanghai (later dubbed the "Gang of Four") made a frontal assault on Chou En-lai's modernization policy, even as the Premier lay dying of cancer in January.[106] The attack on Chou was couched as a domestic political campaign against "Confucius" and Chou's peppery political ally, Teng Hsiao-ping, who had already been dumped once during the Cultural Revolution and rehabilitated. The anti-Teng campaign continued throughout the spring and summer of 1976, and was directly linked to energy export policy.

As a consequence of this turn of political events, China's petroleum exports were seriously disrupted throughout the year. Monthly crude oil exports to Japan fell suddenly in the first quarter to a level substantially below the contract agreement. Crude oil shipments to the Philippines were cut off completely in April, despite the conclusion of a new oil trade agreement as recently as November 1975.[107] Manila had to scramble to make up the shortfall by importing expensive refined products on a spot basis from Japan. On June 2 crude oil shipments to the

Philippines were resumed, but the damage had been done, holding oil exports to Japan at 1.8 million metric tons below 1975 and to the Philippines at 567,000 mt, far below the original terms of the contract.[108] The disruption of Manila's oil supplies did nothing to improve the state of political relations between China and the Philippines. By June the two countries were wrangling over Philippine oil exploration in the Reed Bank and the continuing commercial ties with Taiwan. The oil trade with Thailand was damaged as well, as Bangkok delayed receipt of 312,000 mt of Chinese crude agreed on as part of a rice barter deal, taking only 193,000 mt during 1976.[109] The delay was officially laid to a modification program at one of Thailand's three refineries. Hong Kong's imports of refined petroleum products slipped slightly below 1975 levels to 607,000 mt. Net liquid fuel exports in 1976 were 1.1 million tons under 1975, resulting in a foreign exchange loss of about $100 million. The coal trade suffered as well, with exports to Japan falling 29 percent to 322,000 mt.

The energy trade decline in 1976 was also related to shortages in domestic energy supplies caused by the massive July 28 Tangshan earthquake and by political disruption of the industrial and transport infrastructure. Following Mao's death in September, a quick succession struggle ensued, which returned political power to the Politburo faction favoring rapid modernization and expanding trade. The "Gang of Four" was instantly purged and order was slowly restored to industry. There is some evidence that moderate elements in the government attempted to avoid total disruption of energy commodity trade throughout the year. Petroleum delegations were dispatched throughout the region, ostensibly for technical exchange, to reassure China's Asian trading partners that normalization of petroleum trade and future expansion were just around the corner.[110] These delegations could point to some favorable developments in China's oil industry, including a new oilfield in Kwangtung province, a new refinery in Canton, and expansion of China's port and tanker facilities.[111] A new large-bore (39 inch) pipeline was laid between the Maoming refinery and the port of Chankiang on the southern coast of Kwangtung province.[112] Construction continued on oil-handling and storage facilities at Shatin and Tsingyi in Hong Kong. All of these projects pointed toward expanding oil trade with Southeast Asia.

This expectation was realized only slowly. The year 1977 was basically one of consolidation and recovery in China's energy commodity trade. My energy commodity trade statistics for 1977 are still incomplete, because of a lag in the publishing of official trade returns. However, it appears that energy commodity trade was restored to 1975 levels, with marginal gains in some categories. Crude oil deliveries to Japan reached an estimated 6.8 million metric tons, still more than a million tons under 1975. This was compensated for by an increase of crude oil exports to the Philippines (884,000 mt) and to Thailand (about 500,000 mt), as well as by a jump in refined products exports to Hong Kong (876,000 mt). My current estimate of total 1977 liquid fuel exports is 10.7 million tons, about equal to 1975. It is still too early to judge the impact on coal trade.

The biggest story in China's energy trade with Asia during the year was continued penetration of the Hong Kong refined products market. By 1977 Peking was operating in the Hong Kong market through at least two well-heeled trade organizations, the China Resources Corporation, responsible for transport, storage, and bulk-handling facilities, and Far East Overseas Oil, Ltd. (FEOSO), responsible for the retail trade.[113] By July, an oil depot and 10,000-mt storage facility were opened at Fotan, near Shatin.[114] Chinese gasoline began to be offered at the stations operated by FEOSO, kerosene and jet fuel imports increased (about 170,000 mt), and diesel fuel imports exceeded half a million tons during the year. China controlled about 16 percent of the Hong Kong market and earned an estimated $100 million in the oil trade. By the end of the year, FEOSO was considering offering bunker fuel through new outlets in Singapore.[115] Foreign exchange earned in the Hong Kong oil trade exceeded the total trade deficit for 1977 with OECD countries ($91 million).[116]

Toward the end of the year, it appeared that the consolidation of the power of the modernizers in the Politburo was complete. The Shanghai radicals were excoriated by name at the Eleventh National Congress of the CCP in August 1977, as Hua Kuo-feng, Teng Hsiao-ping, and Li Hsien-nien moved into the spotlight with their ambitious plans for national development through the turn of the century. In foreign relations, Peking strengthened its ties with ASEAN countries and continued the close relationship with Pakistan, seeking everywhere in Asia to block any increase in Soviet influence.[117]

If 1977 was a year of consolidation and recovery, 1978 was a year of unprecedented energy diplomacy and a forward economic policy. There was little doubt in anyone's mind as to who had won the domestic political struggle to succeed China's revolutionary generation of leaders. At the Fifth National People's Congress in February, Hua Kuo-feng announced the resumption of the Ten-Year Plan (1975–85) for national development, calling for 85 percent mechanization of agriculture, expansion of the transportation network, construction of six regional industrial complexes, an average industrial production growth rate of 10 percent per year, heavy capital investment, and 120 large-scale projects, at least 48 of which were to be in the energy sector.[118] The government ministries were reshuffled, splitting the Ministry of Petroleum and Chemical Industries, and greatly strengthening the interministry state planning commissions.[119] Two major long-range trade agreements were signed in February, with the European Economic Community and with Japan, committing the PRC to rapid expansion in foreign trade with the industrial market-economy countries. The trade agreement with Japan established explicit coal and petroleum export commitments through 1982 (Chapter 6). A National Science Conference was convened in March that produced the "Outline National Plan for the Development of Science and Technology," pledging to unleash China's scientific community from the constraints imposed by the Cultural Revolution and to train 800,000 new scientists.[120] These events caused an obvious stir in Peking and in the foreign media and raised new hopes about China's prospective role as a regional energy commodity exporter.

By early 1978, it appeared that the initial difficulties in China's crude oil trade with the Philippines had been overcome. Imelda Marcos received an important Chinese petroleum trade delegation in Manila, and the two sides signed a long-term crude petroleum trade agreement on January 29. The new agreement called for annual crude oil sales to the Philippine National Oil Company of 6 million tons over five years, or an average trade level of 1.2 million metric tons per year.[121] Crude oil exports to the Philippines were expected to reach about 1 million tons in 1978, up 13 percent over 1977. Philippine refiners are reported to be less resistant to Chinese crude than their Japanese counterparts, largely because of the concessionary prices at which Peking offers its crude to Manila. The exact price of Chinese crude oil exported to the Philippines has long been a state secret. This secrecy is difficult to penetrate because of the complicated price structure and variations of the exact price with the international market. It has been speculated that the "friendship price" initially offered to Manila in 1974 was around $9 per barrel, well under market prices at the time. By 1978, it was reported that the Philippine National Oil Company (PNOC) was buying Chinese crude at about $11.50 per barrel and selling it at a 15–20 percent profit to Shell, Caltex, Mobil, and the Bataan Refinery Corporation at $13.68 per barrel.[122] Even at this price, Chinese crude is well under Arabian Medium ($15.99/bbl), Indonesian Walio ($16.53/bbl) and Malaysian Miri ($17.94/bbl) at the refinery in the Philippines. There are occasional rumors that PNOC still gets Chinese crude at $9–10 per barrel and makes a profit in excess of 50 percent on its paper transaction between the Chinese and the refiners. However, these rumors should probably be discounted and laid to confusion resulting from official reluctance to discuss the true price structure. No one seems to doubt that China still sells crude to the Philippines at a price well under that charged Japanese importers. Once it arrives at the refinery, Shengli crude is mixed at about 10–15 percent by volume with lighter crudes to facilitate handling and avoid costly refinery modifications. This practice will obviously place a tight ceiling on the quantity of Chinese crude that Manila will be able to import. By 1978, PNOC was already importing nearly 10 percent of total crude petroleum supplies from China. This explains the structure of the current oil trade agreement, which commits the two countries to a fixed quantity of crude-petroleum trade over a five-year period. Philippine refiners simply cannot accept much more Chinese crude without installing dewaxing and thermal cracking facilities. Even so, the trade will bring China about $100 million per year from 1978 until 1982.

Recent developments in the oil trade with Thailand are far less certain, but also promising. As with Japan and the Philippines, oil trade with Thailand is contingent on the state of political relations. During 1978, Peking came to view Thailand as the keystone to its foreign relations in Southeast Asia, providing an important avenue of approach to the Association of Southeast Asian Nations and a barrier against further Vietnamese expansion in Indochina. During April, Thai Prime Minister Chamanand Kriangsak paid a state visit to Peking, where the two sides discussed their mutual concern over domestic problems in Cambodia and the border conflict between Vietnam and Cambodia. Kriangsak also signed an oil trade agreement with Peking for an unspecified quantity of Chinese crude petroleum and refined petroleum products.[123] The Thai government later revealed that it would request imports of 500,000 mt of diesel fuel, 2 million tons of residual fuel, and 500,000 mt of crude.[124] This would represent a huge increase over the estimated 500,000 mt of crude and 125,000 mt of products imported from China in 1977. The Electric Generating Authority of Thailand has had trouble finding enough residual to fuel its power generators, and Bangkok is concerned about its rapidly rising oil import bill. Chinese residual, presumably at "friendship" prices, would ease both problems. China's exact commitment had not been revealed at the time of writing, indicating that it may have fallen short of Thai expectations. Peking probably does not have sufficient refined products on hand to fill such a sudden increase in the level of trade, although higher products exports to Thailand should be expected over the next few years. Political relations, meanwhile, continued to move forward, with Teng Hsiao-ping's November 1978 trip to Bangkok, during which he peppered his hosts with warnings about the Soviet presence in Southeast Asia, Vietnamese expansion in Indochina, and the new treaty between Moscow and Hanoi. Teng's comments fell on willing ears.[125]

Aside from the Philippines and Thailand, China's relations with the other ASEAN members are mixed. Kuala Lumpur is still quite sensitive about Chinese support for the Malaysian Communist Party and gave Teng a chilly reception.[126] Singapore, although benefiting from recent offshore rig sales to China totaling some $130 million, has no diplomatic relations with Peking and is concerned about competition with Chinese refined petroleum products in the Thai market.[127] Indonesia, another ASEAN member with no diplomatic relations with Peking, is worried about competition with Chinese crude oil in the Japanese market. Moscow has played directly on this fear, accusing Peking of ruining Pertamina by dumping oil at $0.60 under Indonesian crude, and offering $100 million for hydropower stations in Java.[128] Indonesian fear of Chinese competition was greatly intensified by the Sino-Japanese trade agreement. In addition, Malaysia, Singapore, and Indonesia are all concerned about China's continuing empathy for their large "overseas" Chinese populations. Nonetheless, even if there is some concern in ASEAN capitals over China's political intentions, the same countries tend to view Hanoi with emotions ranging from alarm to panic. Vietnam is also viewed as a stalking horse for Soviet power and interests in the region. Peking's virulent attacks on both are some comfort to a region constantly preoccupied with future security problems and the absence of the familiar American shield.

Hong Kong, meanwhile, remains politically neuter but commercially adventurous in its developing energy relationship with the mainland. On the basis of first-quarter trade returns, the PRC will sell Hong Kong at least 1.2 million metric tons of refined petroleum products in 1978, including 200,000 mt of kerosene and jet fuel, 750,000 mt of diesel fuel, 160,000 mt of residual, 4,000 mt of lubricants, and 8,500 mt of petrolatum and paraffin.[129] This represents a 25–30 percent increase over 1977. China Resources expanded the Tsingyi oil storage depot to a total capacity of 250,000 mt.[130] China rejected a proposal for a new refinery in Macao, but was reported to be considering integrating the southern Kwangtung electric power grid with Hong Kong. British Trade Minister Edmund Dell suggested a complex three-way deal in which Britain would export $600 million of coal-mining equipment to China, China would sell China Light and Power (Hong Kong) 3.5 million tons of coal each year for a new power plant at Tuen Men in the New Territories, and China Light would sell Canton cheap electric power during off-load hours.[131] Needless to say, this will take a while to complete, since the new power station will not come on line until at least 1982.

There have recently been numerous indications that Peking and Moscow are beginning to engage in what one could aptly call "cross-over diplomacy" throughout the region. This practice has long been part of Chinese foreign policy in Eastern Europe and Soviet policy toward North Korea and Vietnam. It consists of maintaining a steady drumfire of public criticism of the opponent's friends or client states, while quietly extending contacts with the same countries in the hope of driving a wedge between the two. The current round of crossover diplomacy involves Korea, Taiwan, the Philippines, and ASEAN. It may eventually affect the pattern of energy commodity trade within the region, although the energy consequences are still too remote to judge with any degree of accuracy.

Both Koreas, it seems, are caught in the web of Sino-Japanese relations. North Korea is upset about expanding energy trade and offshore cooperation that may eventually involve Seoul as at least a silent partner.[132] China tries to blunt any incipient North Korean discomfort over this prospect by accusing Moscow of receiving members of the South Korean cabinet and referring to South Korea as the "Republic of Korea."[133] South Korea is worried about new contacts between the North and both Washington and Tokyo.[134]

In Taiwan, stories have circulated that a well-known KGB agent visits the island from time to time, and was to return in June 1978, a not unlikely prospect in view of continuing progress in the normalization of diplomatic relations between Washington and Peking.[135] Taipei, of course, denies the entire business. Someone then floated a rumor, perhaps in response to the Taiwan-Soviet connection, that Peking and Taipei were secretly discussing coal and oil trade and the establishment of a port in Amoy, Fukien, that would serve the Taiwan trade.[136] Taiwan is, in fact, expecting to increase coal imports and currently faces a natural gas shortage.[137] But trade and diplomatic contact with the PRC is always strictly taboo in Taipei, since it would erode the myth of the Great Return.

As for the Philippines, Marcos keeps an open mind about the Russians and has encouraged contacts between Hanoi and ASEAN. Soviet Deputy Foreign Minister Nikolai Firyubin visited Manila in November.[138] Manila's Soviet card could be played in the event of greater Chinese pressure on Philippine claims in the Spratleys. It also gives Marcos some leverage in negotiations over the "rental" for U.S. military bases. Moscow, meanwhile, has shifted its policy position toward ASEAN from overt hostility to quiet support, much to the annoyance of Peking.[139]

Crossover diplomacy in the region is a sign of the continuing fluidity of regional political relations. It has been evident throughout our discussion of China's energy commodity trade with Asian countries that oil trade is contingent on the current state of political relations and is frequently used as an opening wedge for a new political initiative. Thus, the highly fluid political environment represents a shifting constraint on China's regional energy policies. Energy relations, if properly handled, could provide a catalyst for regional cooperation and even integration, rather than a continuing bone of contention for regional jurisdictional and political disputes.

Energy Trade with Asian Centrally Planned Economy Countries

Our knowledge of China's energy commodity trade with its Asian communist neighbors is conspicuous by its absence. Oil exports to North Korea first began in 1964 under the terms of a 1963 trade agreement, and North Vietnam followed suit in 1965.[140] No one knows how much oil this trade involved each year, but it could not have been a large amount, given the limits on China's domestic oil industry throughout the 1960's. It is also possible that some of the oil exported to Vietnam had actually been imported by spot purchases on the international market and then transshipped to Hanoi via Chinese ports.

During the early 1970's, as the war in Vietnam reached a peak and then a pause, China expanded its infrastructure for oil exports to Hanoi. A pipeline was constructed from Pinghsiang in Kwangsi province to Kep. It consisted of a double four-inch line with a carrying capacity of about 35,000 metric tons of refined petroleum products per month (420,000 mt per year). A single ten-inch line runs the final 30 miles to Hanoi.[141] During the same period, the refinery at Maoming, originally a shale-retorting center, was expanded to handle crude oil shipped by sea to the nearby port of Chankiang on the southern coast of Kwangtung province.[142] There are direct rail links from Chankiang to Maoming and Maoming to Pinghsiang. Thus, it appears that crude oil was brought from the north by rail or imported via Chankiang to be refined at Maoming. The refined products were then shipped by rail to the border at Pinghsiang and loaded into the pipeline for Hanoi. Some Chinese crude oil was probably also shipped direct to Vietnam's refineries by rail.

By 1974, with the rapid increase in China's crude petroleum production, there was almost certainly also some increase in the amount of crude petroleum and refined products exported to Vietnam and North Korea. Several sources agree that crude oil exports to North Korea reached about 1 million metric tons and that exports of refined products to Vietnam were in the neighborhood of half a million tons, although there are no official data on which to base this guess.[143] It is unlikely that either North Korea or Vietnam imported significant quantities of coal from China, since both countries have coal industries that are sufficient to their needs, with a margin for export. Vientiane Radio reported in August 1975 that the Shell Oil Company of Hong Kong would ship

7,500 mt of oil from China to Laos as part of an aid agreement with the PRC.[144] Cambodia had imported some Chinese coal from 1964 to 1968, but this trade was disrupted by the spreading war in Indochina (Table 20.11).

There were several signs of increasing energy cooperation between North Korea and China in 1975 and 1976. A delegation from the Chinese Ministry of Petroleum and Chemical Industries visited North Korea in November 1975. This was followed by an exchange of electric power technology delegations in January 1976. In January it was also announced that a "Friendship Oil Pipeline" had been completed as a joint project of the two countries.[145] The pipeline runs from a small refinery at Tantung, on the Chinese side of the border, to Anju. It appears that Taching crude is shipped by rail to the Tantung refinery, where it is at least partially processed before being piped to Anju in North Korea. No details are available on the size or capacity of the pipeline. The line does have political overtones in Sino-Soviet competition for North Korean support, as the Chinese announcement made perfectly clear: "The pipeline is not only a means of conveyance; still more important, it also is of political significance as a friendship bridge between the Chinese and Korean people."[146]

Trade relations with Vietnam, meanwhile, were not going particularly well. The two countries held trade talks in August 1975, during which China suggested that exports that had previously been given as aid be shifted to paid commodities, since the war was over.[147] Oil was probably one of the commodities that was to be shifted from aid to trade status. Hanoi objected vigorously to this change, in view of the reconstruction needs of the country. Peking, which had provided $10 billion in aid and low interest loans during the war, reduced the annual level of aid in 1976 and continued it at the lower level. This caused an acrimonious debate between the two countries that surfaced publicly in July 1978, when the PRC discontinued its aid to Vietnam altogether.[148] In addition to the oil shipments, China provided some technical assistance and construction equipment for work on several energy projects in Vietnam, including the 100-MW Ninh Binh coal-fired thermal power plant.[149] The PRC also gave Laos another 10,000 mt of petroleum products during 1976.[150]

The trend toward greater energy cooperation with North Korea and less with Vietnam continued and accelerated throughout 1977 and 1978. The Council of the Sino-Korean Yalu River Hydroelectric Power Corporation met in Pyongyang and signed a new protocol on February 8, 1977.[151] There are functioning hydropower stations along the Yalu River, which forms the border between China and North Korea. The electric power output from these stations is shared by the two sides, as are the costs of construction and maintenance. North Korea is known to be interested in offshore exploration and may have asked for Chinese assistance in this area.[152] In May 1978 Hua Kuo-feng visited North Korea, and there were rumors that China had offered to export crude petroleum at $4–5 per barrel, less than half the price North Korea pays for Soviet oil ($11.10).[153]

As of October 1977, energy relations between Vietnam and China were still quite regular. Dinh Duc Thien, Minister of Oil and Natural Gas, visited the PRC during that month and went on a tour of Chinese oilfields.[154] Refined petroleum exports to Vietnam therefore probably continued at about the half-million-tons-per-year level through 1977. But in 1978, the Sino-Vietnamese relationship came apart completely, as described above, and oil exports were almost certainly stopped. Hanoi joined the CMEA in June, casting the country's economic lot with the Soviet bloc. The Chinese press reported in September that the border conflict with Vietnam had spread to a number of locations, including the town of Pinghsiang, where the oil pipeline begins and crosses the Vietnam border.[155] It is unlikely that oil exports survived the increase in tension along the border. In July 1978, Laos joined Vietnam in attacking Chinese policies in Indochina.[156] This move was also probably accompanied by cessation of Chinese aid in the form of oil shipments. Cambodia, on the other hand, may have picked up the refined petroleum products no longer shipped to Vietnam. There was a sharp increase in Cambodian petroleum imports from Hong Kong and Singapore in 1977.[157] A high-level Chinese delegation visited Phnom Penh just after the signing of the Soviet-Vietnamese treaty of friendship in early November 1978.[158] One of the tasks of the delegation was to discuss further aid, including perhaps coal and petroleum shipments.

China may have carried on some energy commodity trade with Mongolia during the 1960's or 1970's, but again no data are available. The sensitivity of Sino-Soviet border relations and Moscow's firm grip on Ulan Bator may prevent more than token trade. The Chinese press regularly accuses the USSR of extracting Mongolian mineral resources under concessionary terms.[159]

This completes our brief review of China's energy commodity trade with its communist Asian neighbors. The increasingly close energy cooperation with North Korea and growing problems in the energy relationship with Vietnam reflect the impact of political changes. Once again, therefore, the political constraint appears as a critical determinant of China's international energy policies, easily overriding long-term commercial ties.

Offshore Development and Regional Energy Trade

The Chinese government has increasingly linked offshore oil and gas development to the country's drive for modernization and industrialization by the turn of the century. The equation is simple. Teng Hsiao-ping, with his characteristic candor, put the matter thus:[160]

We must adopt a new technology . . . to import, we must export more. The first to my mind is oil. We must develop oil production as far as possible and export as much oil as we can. We must export and obtain in return the best technology to accelerate the technical transformation of industry and raise labor productivity. . . . We must develop production as quickly as possible and increase our exports as much as possible. The external market is very important and we must not neglect it. To hasten the exploration of our coal and petroleum, it is possible that on the condition of equality and mutual benefit, and in accordance with accepted practices of international trade such as deferred and installment payments, we may sign long-term contracts with foreign countries and fix several production sites, where they will supply complete sets of modern equipment required by us, and we will pay for them with the coal and oil we produce.

The principal site that the Chinese now have in mind is the continental shelf. There are sharp constraints on oil and gas production from onland fields in China. The most important of these constraints is the still limited scale of reserves and resources in onland basins. Unless Peking has or will discover vast deposits of oil and gas in the western half of the country, production from onland fields will be sharply constrained by available resources within a decade. Meanwhile, the oil and gas consumption requirement, and energy demand generally, will rise swiftly and relentlessly as the PRC accelerates the development of its energy-intensive industries, and improves the energy available for individual consumption. To put the matter bluntly, the importation or construction of a high-technology industrial infrastructure in China will be a useless exercise unless there are adequate energy supplies to increase agricultural and industrial production across the broad base of the Chinese economy. Selling more oil will work only if more oil is available from domestic production, so that both domestic demand and the foreign market can be satisfied.

It is this perception that propels the Chinese leadership into its vigorous offshore development program. Offshore development must not only be accomplished, it must be accomplished as rapidly as possible within the natural constraints imposed by the discovery of resources and the economic constraints imposed by the cost of their extraction. Peking evidently believes that it will not have the available capital, technology, or equipment to achieve offshore oil and gas production within the necessary time frame. For this reason, at least as of late 1978, China was moving toward joint offshore development programs with foreign oil companies. In a sense, Peking is sacrificing self-reliance in the off-shore theater in order to preserve it on land. That does not mean that China will not participate actively in its own offshore program, or will grant exclusive exploration and production concessions to the multina-tionals. The structure of offshore contracts has yet to be revealed and will certainly entail preservation of China's resource sovereignty along the shelf and Chinese participation in all phases of the offshore pro-gram. The term "joint" is important in this context. Western and Japa-nese oil companies should approach Peking with a sound recognition of the determination of the Chinese government to preserve the coun-try's independence of action, self-reliant industrial development, and resource sovereignty. Only in this spirit can the joint development pro-grams be successful.

Peking intends a substantial proportion of future energy commodity exports to come from oil and gas production along the continental shelf. If the growth curve for onland production is already feeling the down-ward pressure of resource constraints, it is obvious that additional incre-ments of exported petroleum will have to come from the offshore the-ater. The exact balance of onland and offshore contributions to future exports is open to speculation. But it should be pointed out that the Chi-nese government has already committed itself to at least 15 million tons of oil exports in 1980 and perhaps 20 million tons in 1982. This amount could probably be met from onland fields without much difficulty. But a further increase to 40–50 million tons of oil exports by 1985–90 would require additional oil production from offshore fields. Furthermore, the pressure of domestic consumption requirements will push the home-take from onland production relentlessly upward, leaving less onland production available for export by 1985 or so. All of these arguments point toward a direct link between offshore oil production and petro-leum exports.

Joint offshore development is a key that fits a number of doors simul-taneously. It will help the PRC to overcome continuing constraints on capital availability and foreign exchange in the energy sector. It will alle-viate at least part of the high risk of offshore exploration and place that risk in the hands of companies that are structured to absorb it. Offshore development may help the PRC avoid escalating infrastructure costs for oil transport, since the oil can be pumped directly onto waiting storage tankers and shipped without port or pipeline construction. If the crudes in the South China Sea deposits are less waxy and lighter than the north-east crudes, offshore development may ease the refining constraint at the import end. Substantial offshore development would accelerate the timetable for oil exports and ease the export drain on limited onland oil and gas resources. None of these advantages, of course, will overcome natural constraints on the presence or economic viability of oil and gas resources in the continental shelf.

On the political side of the ledger, joint offshore development will further Peking's policy objectives throughout the region. The most important political effect will be to identify Japan and the Western industrial market economy countries more closely with China in the region. Japan has already leaned toward Peking and away from Moscow by signing the peace treaty and the trade agreement. American involvement in joint offshore projects would have a similar effect, regardless of disclaimers from Washington. A successful joint offshore program in the East China Sea would further isolate Taiwan, and joint development in the South China Sea would strengthen Peking's hand vis-à-vis Vietnam. A successful offshore program would bring China into the community of Southeast Asian countries that are heavily involved in offshore development, including all of the members of ASEAN. It would also accelerate the growth of China's influence in Hong Kong, where the PRC already seems intent on buying the colony back piecemeal.

More important than any of these unilateral political advantages, however, would be the effect of joint offshore development programs on the jurisdictional dispute along the Chinese continental shelf. Joint development raises the possibility, suggested already in Chapter 7, that these disputes could be solved in a different manner than in the North Sea. That is, instead of attempting to run a single line of division or control along the shelf between parties to a dispute in any sector of the shelf, an alternative approach would be to ignore the matter of sovereignty altogether and proceed on a joint basis in the contested zones. The maintenance of 200-mile economic zones would be compatible with this solution, but would require mutually agreed-upon free movement within the 200-mile zone for offshore drilling rigs and support vessels. The most delicate problem to resolve in the disputed areas would be the matter of contract arrangements and profit-sharing. One should not underestimate the remaining obstacles to joint offshore development agreements. But it appears that this option has the potential to both accelerate China's pace of energy development and contribute materially to peace and stability in the region.

Chapter 9

Energy Policies and International Organization

Peking's Organizational Hierarchy

China's international energy policies and energy relations with different countries and regions are affected by Peking's general level of political interaction with a wide range of international and transnational organizations. The People's Republic approaches these organizations on the basis of its own underlying principles of international conduct. A firm hierarchy of supranational organizations is established, in Peking's eyes, by these principles.

The first and most important principle is the primacy of state sovereignty. We have already seen the makers of China's foreign policy apply the concept of "resource sovereignty" to energy relations between the industrial countries and the Third World. But the emphasis on state sovereignty is wider than its application to energy and other resource issues. It implies that countries and governments should be the primary locus of decision and authority in the international arena.[1] In this sense, Chinese policy still retains a strongly nationalist cast. The authority, legitimacy, and decision powers of all organizations above the national level are considered subordinate to national sovereignty.

The second principle is the belief that "political sovereignty cannot be separated from economic independence."[2] This principle is rooted in the self-reliance guideline for both domestic development and industrial development throughout the Third World. It implies that penetration of the economic infrastructure of any country by that of another country is an act of imperialism that will result in unfavorable terms of trade and development for the penetrated country. The gradual extraction of wealth then leads to an erosion of domestic political sovereignty for the dependent partner and concentration of power in the hands of the penetrating country or its corporate agents. This outcome destroys political sovereignty and should be resisted at all costs.

The third principle is that the international system as presently constituted is inherently unjust and should be replaced with relations of equality and mutual benefit among all countries. According to this principle, the Third World has already lost its economic independence and suffered severe impairment of state sovereignty. The successive forces of colonialism, capitalism, imperialism, and now social imperialism have combined to create this condition of economic and political disequilibrium. Destabilization and rapid change are therefore to be valued, even if at the cost of temporary suffering. The third principle makes the People's Republic a structural revisionist in the international system, a member of the opposition, opposed to the hierarchical status quo. Following this principle, Peking is a vocal, if cautious, advocate of basic changes in organizational structure within universal multilateral organizations such as the United Nations.[3] China advocates organizational changes, such as expanding the powers of the General Assembly, which would increase the political power of Third World governments within the organization.

There is, therefore, an evident and strong ranking of competing organizations in energy distribution from the Chinese perspective. Governments have been placed first as the primary locus of decision-making responsibility for the achievement of a more equal world balance in resource distribution. Multilateral intergovernmental organizations, including raw materials organizations, regional organizations, and universal organizations, have ranked second. These organizations are acceptable within the framework of China's basic principles of foreign relations, insofar as each organization functions to reinforce government control and state sovereignty over domestic resources. Multinational corporations have been placed at the bottom of the list along with Soviet joint-stock companies. They are seen as responsible for resource disequilibria and as retarding the current movement toward resource redistribution. This ranking and orientation toward the three types of organization involved in global energy distribution are largely the result of perspectives gained by Chinese leaders in the context of their own domestic industrial development. They firmly believe that maximizing government control and state sovereignty over energy resources will simultaneously release the energy production systems of the Third World countries from foreign penetration and from the vicious cycle of poverty, institutional corruption, and further poverty.

OPEC and the Raw Materials Organizations

The Organization of Petroleum Exporting Countries (OPEC) ranks very high in Peking's hierarchy of supranational organizations. OPEC is an organization oriented almost exclusively to control from the governmental level. It therefore represents exactly the type of multilateral organization that the PRC favors from a structural perspective. And OPEC's function serves all of the basic principles of China's foreign policy: struggling with the multinationals for resource sovereignty, protecting the drive of its members toward nationalization of their oil industries and achievement of self-reliant industrialization, and redressing the injustices of global resource disequilibria.

OPEC is a functionally specific multilateral organization with a regional bias toward the Arab producing countries, but with members from Latin America (Venezuela and Ecuador), Africa (Nigeria and Gabon), and Asia (Indonesia) as well. OPEC is definitely country-dominant and functions primarily as a convenient forum for discussion and coordination of oil export and production policies. OPEC members differ widely in area, population, development policies, oil reserves, oil production growth rates, and political ideology. Therefore, the area of potential agreement is sharply limited to oil export questions, and consensus is difficult to achieve even in that single functional sector.[4]

The organizational structure of OPEC reflects and serves its member-government orientation. The OPEC Conference (which is member-oriented) dominates decision-making, and the board of governors and secretariat play interim and service roles only. The position of secretary-general rotates annually, keeping the secretariat firmly in the hands of the Conference. This structure provides a convenient vehicle for mobilization and unified pressure tactics once consensus has been achieved. But OPEC withdraws from any issue that seriously divides the membership, or waits until bargaining among member governments reduces differences to the level where a minimum common denominator policy is accepted by all.

OPEC's primary function has been in the area of price control for crude oil exports. OPEC was founded in 1960 to combat a reduction in the posted price of crude by the concerted decision of the "major" oil corporations.[5] OPEC was largely unsuccessful in preventing this price erosion until 1970, when Libya jolted the oil world by unilaterally raising the posted price, and then forced the oil companies operating in the country to accept the new price level. OPEC responded in January and February 1971 with a series of oil price talks among the exporting countries. The conference resulted in a new price agreement with the oil companies on February 14, 1971, breaking their traditional grip on the price structure.[6] The Libyan affair and the Teheran conference brought OPEC to the attention of the Chinese press, which cautiously praised the achievements of the conference.[7]

China's enthusiasm for OPEC successes rose rapidly in 1972, as the basic Teheran agreement was steadily expanded in scope to include price and tax escalator clauses that compensated the producing countries for currency losses owing to the falling value of the U.S. dollar. When six Persian Gulf oil-producing countries wrested 20 percent participation in the consortia operating in their countries from the oil corporations, Peking termed the achievement a "new victory in these countries' struggle to safeguard their national economic interests and oppose imperialist plunder and exploitation."[8]

In June and September 1973, OPEC scrapped the basic Teheran agreement by announcing two successive crude oil price increases.[9] Then in October 1973, Egypt crossed the Suez Canal, engaging Israel in yet another bitter struggle for territory and survival. On October 17 the Arab Organization of Petroleum Exporting Countries (OAPEC) voted to reduce oil production and cut exports, a move that created the oil embargo against Israel's Western supporters and Japan. The Chinese press vigorously applauded every Arab move during the embargo, which lasted until February 1974, considering it a stroke of great importance to the Third World struggle for political and economic justice.[10] The embargo took the final lid off the posted price of crude oil, which soared to more than $11 per barrel. And the effects of the embargo on the intermediate industrial countries—Japan and Western Europe—made it perfectly clear that this action had shifted the global distribution of political power as well.[11] China, which was just entering the world petroleum market seriously in 1974, tied the price of Taching crude to that of Arabian light (via the price of Indonesian Minas crude). This made the PRC more than a mere spectator in the proceedings, and the Chinese press began analyzing the roots of the energy crisis, OPEC's success, and the future course of crude oil prices in earnest.[12]

Meanwhile, during 1974, the industrial market-economy countries, operating within the organizational framework provided by the Organization of Economic Cooperation and Development (OECD), began the first efforts to mobilize the oil-consuming countries into a structure that would counterbalance OPEC's cartelization of the international petroleum market.[13] The Chinese government, less than enthusiastic about any such prospect, supported French opposition to such a group and called for "dialogue" rather than confrontation between OPEC and the oil-importing countries of the Second World.[14] Peking began attacking the International Energy Agency, a branch of OECD, as an expression of American imperialism soon after its formation in 1975.[15] China also attacked the American trade law of December 20, 1974, which stipulated that preferential trade status be denied the members of OPEC and other raw materials organizations.[16] And Moscow has been accused of resisting further OPEC price increases and general complicity with Washington.[17]

Once OPEC established firm control of the oil industries operating within the member countries, the next objective was to tighten control over the world market price of crude oil through a series of unilateral price increases. OPEC announced one such increase in September 1975 (10 percent), another in December 1976 (10 percent), and a third in July 1977 (5 percent). The latter decision split OPEC, with Saudi Arabia leading resistance to the new price hike, and resulted temporarily in a "two-tier" price structure, with some OPEC countries offering crude at prices substantially under the levels demanded by others. The two-tier price structure proved unstable and prices fell again to the baseline established by Saudi crude. Then, in December 1978, OPEC jolted the industrial countries once again with a massive 15 percent price increase.

Peking supported these price increases with strong verbal statements:

Under the heavy blows inflicted by the world capitalist economic crisis, the superpowers have attempted to exert pressure to force the oil-exporting countries to lower prices. At the same time the currency inflation in Western capitalist countries daily worsens, damaging the import position of the oil-exporting countries. Under these conditions, the 10 percent oil export price decided by OPEC is an important measure to counter the monopoly economic crisis and to protect the value of their own oil.[18]

From the perspective of Chinese policy, the issue was not simply the price of the oil itself, but the further matter of control over prices. The PRC considered OPEC's ability to unilaterally determine crude oil prices an important harbinger of the advent of a new economic order.

Peking was not enthusiastic about the two-tier price structure and was inclined to be sympathetic with Iran and the other OPEC members that were attempting to push higher price levels in 1977.[19] The Saudi victory (a modest 5 percent increase) represented a distinct embarrassment for the PRC line on OPEC and was generally ignored in the Chinese press. The stabilization of crude oil prices cuts into Chinese energy policy in two ways. First, it affects China's efforts to maintain relatively high prices for Taching crude in long-term negotiations with Japanese importers. The PRC may now be forced to offer some price concessions to compensate for the difficulty of transporting and refining its crude oil. Second, a plateau on world crude oil prices would indicate a new equilibrium between Third World raw materials producers and the industrial countries. If this equilibrium is sustained and extends to other mineral commodities, the position of international commodity cartels will be weakened, or at least will not be further strengthened. That would again delay the advent of the "new economic order" that was supposed to be arriving promptly, according to the Chinese press.

China's policies toward OPEC have not been entirely without internal contradictions and inconsistency with Peking's other Third World energy policies. The energy crisis and rising crude oil prices have had a deleterious effect on the economies of Third World oil-importing countries.[20] Many Third World countries have no domestic energy production base at all and depend entirely on imported oil for domestic energy consumption. On the average, Third World countries are about 65 percent energy-dependent on imported oil, based on the energy-equivalent ratio of oil imports to total energy consumption.[21] The consequence of rapid oil price rises on the balance-of-payments position of such countries has been devastating. China has had some difficulty explaining its position on the issue:

Some people say the current economic difficulties are caused by the increase in oil price. This is a specious statement. In the final analysis, the present economic difficulties are the inevitable outcome of the imperialist system; they are not due to increase in the prices of raw materials, still less to any alleged misdeeds on the part of the oil-producing countries. . . . Of course higher oil prices have caused non-oil-producing countries of the Third World some temporary difficulties, but this struggle and its great historic significance must not be negated on this account.[22]

The foundation of the Chinese position is that the additional suffering of oil-importing counries is more than compensated for by the progress of the oil-exporting countries toward resource sovereignty and economic justice. To be fair, Peking has encouraged OPEC aid projects in the Third World.[23] In 1975, Iran purchased a certain amount of Chinese industrial equipment for its foreign aid projects in oil-importing Third World countries.[24] But the PRC continues to support ever higher oil prices, a position that has more than a coincidental relationship with its own oil export position.[25]

As will be seen below in the section on China's energy-related United Nations policies, Peking also supports higher prices and market stabilization for non-energy raw materials.[26] Peking is enthusiastic about the other new raw materials organizations that have formed following OPEC's success with oil prices in an attempt to assert price control over commodities ranging from peanuts and cocoa to rubber, bauxite, and copper.[27] However, such organizations are not proving as viable as OPEC, at least in the mid-1970's, for they are seriously constrained by such factors as commodity substitution, lack of geographic concentration, preferential trade agreements, high levels of production in the industrial countries, and other factors that increase demand elasticity.[28]

Will China eventually join OPEC? The question is intriguing. This study takes the point of view that China will not export petroleum past a limited ceiling because of the scale of domestic energy end use requirements and because of the reluctance of the revolutionary Chinese leadership to subordinate domestic self-reliance to the international energy market. But Chinese crude oil export potential will reach the lower range of OPEC membership qualifications before 1985. And under certain sets of assumptions, China could be an important oil-exporting country within 10 to 15 years.

The only precedent for Chinese participation in a commodity cartel or agreement on a multilateral basis has been in recent cooperation with Bolivia and the U.N. Conference on Trade and Development in the Committee on Tungsten. This UNCTAD committee constitutes a de facto commodity cartel. It was formed in 1963, ironically in reaction to the market effects of Chinese tungsten exports. In July 1974, a high-level Bolivian delegation visited the PRC to discuss tungsten prices. This in itself was unusual, since the two countries did not have diplomatic relations at the time. Bolivia apparently persuaded the PRC to participate in Geneva meetings of the Committee on Tungsten as an observer.[29] As a result of this participation, Bolivia, China, and the Committee on Tungsten established a price stabilization agreement for tungsten exports that provided both minimum and ceiling prices (to prevent commodity substitution by molybdenum).[30] The agreement was formalized in July 1975, and a second Bolivian tungsten delegation visited China in February 1976.[31]

This one example shows that under certain circumstances Peking will modify its insistence on absolute control of its export commodity prices. It also demonstrates that China may be interested in multilateral commodity price control agreements under circumstances that permit significant Chinese participation in the shape of the final decisions. China and Bolivia together control more than a quarter of the world's tungsten output. However, the precedent should not be automatically applied to other commodities in assessing China's intentions. The tungsten agreement was actually arranged largely on a bilateral basis between Bolivia and China, and may have been extended by the two governments to antimony as well. The Chinese doubtless felt little sacrifice of resource sovereignty in agreeing to controls on the price of tungsten exports. Participation in OPEC would obviously be an entirely different matter.

Chinese membership in OPEC would present some interesting dilemmas to the leadership in Peking. Would the PRC be willing to regulate domestic production levels in accordance with OPEC norms, tightening the supply in order to raise or maintain prices? Would China cooperate in information-sharing projects with other OPEC members? Would the

OPEC members with a more traditional political structure welcome Chinese membership? How would Peking react to dissident leftist movements in such countries as Iran?

The main contradiction presented by China's entry into OPEC would be Peking's insistence on absolute domestic state political control over petroleum resources and production. But China might be willing to regulate petroleum trade relations as long as domestic production and consumption patterns were not shifted dramatically by the need for concerted action among the OPEC members. OPEC's member-oriented structure would permit Peking to resist any decisions it considered in violation of its own sovereignty and ignore or bypass decisions it found annoying. As China's energy export potential expands, the PRC may be increasingly tempted to try its hand at direct involvement. The alternative would be to remain a spectator in an important arena in world politics and to allow the world market price of oil and other conditions of energy trade to be set by other countries.

Whatever China's long-run response to OPEC, Peking's present policies toward the organization reveal important aspects of dominant attitudes toward change within the Chinese leadership. Peking views the international energy market as an unstable system with an underlying tendency toward resource distribution in favor of the industrial countries. According to this view, which is shared in many Third World capitals, the nonindustrial countries have been producing an increasing proportion of the world's energy resources while consuming a relatively stable and inequitably small proportion of those resources. This condition creates long-term disequilibria in global energy distribution, which will eventually be resolved in favor of the Third World countries as they move to seize control of their own energy and other mineral resources.

Who decides and how to decide the price of oil is a question of economic "order." In the past, the price was determined at will by big international monopolists who forced oil prices down to the lowest level to cruelly exploit the third world oil producing countries. The old order, however, has been smashed in the oil struggle. These third world countries, the owners of oil, have wrested back the right to determine prices and thus put an end to the situation whereby the imperialists could wantonly plunder cheap oil. The oil producing countries rationally adjusted prices which had been forced down for a long time. The third world countries waged a tit-for-tat struggle in 1975 against the superpowers over oil prices. The former wanted to maintain equitable prices and ensure the achievements in their struggle while the latter tried to force down prices again and restore superexploitation. With the support of the world's people, the oil producers stood up to the threat of one superpower, exposed the sabotage by the other, thus firmly defending their right to determine prices.[32]

The industrial countries, particularly the superpowers, will resist any such change at their expense and will seek to maintain the old order by slowing or stopping the shifting locus of authority over prices, production, export levels, and the energy resources themselves. Peking believes that the resolution of disequilibria in global energy distribution will be speeded by OPEC and similar organizations. Thus, in the Chinese view, OPEC operates as a catalyst to precipitate a new equilibrium in energy distribution patterns. The organization itself is not the essential change, but its presence introduces the conditions for change by increasing the bargaining leverage of the oil-producing Third World countries. The catalytic action of OPEC explains the great importance that China has attached to the international role of this organization, the members of which have so little in common politically with the PRC. That is why Chiao Kuan-hua considered OPEC's struggle more important than "temporary difficulties" caused by higher oil prices for Third World importing countries.

Regardless of what one thinks of the reality of this Chinese perspective, it can be distinguished quite sharply from the dominant attitude toward change in the international energy system among Western analysts. The reasons for the energy crisis and OPEC's success in the Chinese view have nothing to do with growth. Rather, these events are an expression of fundamental injustices in distribution, an underlying shift in the relative pace of development in the Third World and the industrial areas. Energy and organization are interactive. Chinese policy makers emphasize the organizational side of the interaction, perhaps at the expense of the limitations on growth imposed by the energy side. Western analysts emphasize the technical conditions for growth on the energy side, perhaps overlooking the importance of organization as a conditioning factor in the distributional outcome of growth.

Regional Organizations

The *People's Daily* and other organs of the Chinese press keep close track of the main functions of the various regional organizations around the world.* Peking has a generally supportive attitude toward these organizations, although they do not fit the Chinese model as well as OPEC. The Chinese government considers the regional organizations a means of resisting the penetration of each region by multinational corporations and by the direct influence of the superpowers. Peking also supports the

*China's developing relations with the Association of Southeast Asian Nations (ASEAN) are dealt with in Chapter 8.

cooperative functions of regional organizations in the area of energy development, although China is leery of integrative behavior that would encroach on the absolute sovereignty of the member states. China has also established a direct trade relationship and political relations with the world's largest and most cohesive regional organization, the European Economic Community.

China's relations with the EEC began to improve after the PRC established diplomatic relations with Italy (November 1970), Belgium (October 1971), West Germany (October 1972), and Luxembourg (November 1972).[33] The Common Market itself was going through some important changes at the time, enlarging its membership and establishing closer ties with Mediterranean and Third World raw-materials-producing countries. Peking believed that this process was increasing the independence of the EEC from American economic policy, particularly on monetary and energy issues.[34] In contrast to OECD, which China considers (at least rhetorically) the organizational agent of American imperialism, the EEC is an expression of the unity of the Second World in the face of superpower contention for hegemony in Europe.

This political assessment of the EEC fit conveniently with China's growing trade relationship with Western Europe, particularly in complete energy and petrochemical production plants. Early in 1975, rumors began to surface that Peking was interested in a direct trade relationship with the EEC.[35] The opening of official relations was announced on May 8, during a meeting between Chou En-lai and Christopher Soames, Vice President of the EEC Commission. [36] Official relations have practical implications for future energy equipment trade between China and the West European countries, establishing a firm basis for credit arrangements, some tariff concessions for Chinese products, and a viable communications network for large-scale transactions. China should, therefore, be expected to rely fairly heavily on the intermediate industrial countries of the EEC for future energy technology and equipment imports, particularly in the area of electric power equipment.

Following the establishment of formal diplomatic relations with the EEC, there was some disruption of the relationship in 1976 and trade agreement discussions were suspended. This was possibly the result of the succession crisis under way in Peking at the time. Warming relations with the EEC may have come under attack by the Shanghai radicals ("Gang of Four") during the political campaign against Teng Hsiao-ping in early 1976. In any case, the situation had improved by 1977 and the trade agreement talks were resumed. In July 1977, a high-level delegation from the European Economic Community visited China to lay the groundwork for the final agreement. The trade agreement was important to both sides. To the Chinese side, it provided a wider avenue of access to advanced European industrial technology. To the European side, it represented the first attempt to negotiate a formal trade agreement with a nonmarket country. The negotiations focused on European insistence that EEC safeguard clauses permitting intervention to stem the flow of specific imports be included. The other principal issue was Chinese concern that a two-way balance of trade be maintained. China had been running a deficit of about half a billion dollars a year with EEC countries.

The final trade agreement between China and the EEC was signed in Brussels on February 3, 1978, with an initial term of five years. It provides a general framework for trade, rather than a specific set of commitments or tariff preferences. Each side grants the other most-favored-nation treatment, outside of the preferences that operate within the EEC. The agreement also establishes an EEC–China Joint Committee for Trade, which meets once a year to monitor the agreement. The trade agreement came at a propitious time in the development of China's energy relations with Western Europe. It has greatly facilitated Chinese access to European centers of energy and industrial technology. It also provides a stable framework within which European banks and consortia can offer China long-term credits without fear of a sudden political disruption of such commitments. By the end of 1978, China was responding powerfully to this stimulus by negotiating large construction contracts in coal, steel, nuclear power, and other areas with European companies.

But China's relationship with the Common Market also has political overtones. Peking believes the EEC to be an effective bulwark against Soviet economic and political penetration of Western Europe. This Chinese attitude is quite clear from the contrasting treatment of the Council of Mutual Economic Assistance (CMEA). Peking castigates the CMEA as "Soviet revisionism's instrument for neocolonialism" in Eastern Europe, particularly in energy trade relations:

In the past, other CMEA members relied on imports from various sources to feed their industry with raw materials and for fuel. Under the pretext of "international division of labour" and "fraternal cooperation," the Soviet revisionists have in the past ten years and more gradually monopolized the supply of fuels and raw materials to these countries. As a result, these countries have been reduced to dependency on the Soviet Union for fuels, raw materials, and energy, which enables the Soviet revisionists to meddle in the economies of these countries at will and exert political pressure on them.[37]

China has probably experienced "political pressure" on its East European energy trading partners directly, in the form of restrictions on the type of commodity and technology that these countries may export to the PRC. But the CMEA has not been successful (if it has tried) in blocking significant energy trade relations between China and the more independent East European countries, particularly Romania.

The PRC has also accused the CMEA of acting as a cover for unilateral Soviet price control of energy commodities in Eastern Europe. According to the Chinese press, fuel and raw materials prices have risen sharply within the CMEA countries since 1975. Chinese sources claim that crude petroleum prices in the CMEA rose 130 percent in 1975, 8 percent in 1976, and 22 percent in 1977.[38] The Chinese do not relate these price increases to OPEC crude oil price controls and suggest that higher energy prices have led to severe energy shortages in Eastern Europe and to higher exports of manufactured commodities from the satellite countries to the USSR. Not only have price increases damaged the economies of the smaller CMEA members, but they have lost control over their own economic destinies: "In relations between nations and states, the 'joint ownership' and 'economic integration' introduced by the Soviet revisionists to the member states of the Council for Mutual Economic Assistance in a big way are virtual acts of annexation."[39] Here again, the Chinese treat organizational independence and economic self-determination as the critical issues at the heart of resource distribution and economic integration.

Energy relations with regional organizations in the Third World are more vicarious and less direct than the negative interactive relationship with the CMEA and the positive interactive relationship with the EEC. The Chinese press has been particularly attentive to regional energy relations in Latin America. In August 1972, the Latin American ministers of power and petroleum met in Caracas, Venezuela, to discuss the establishment of a Latin American regional energy organization.[40] On October 19 of the same year the ministers of eleven Latin American countries adopted a resolution asserting the right of all countries to control their natural resources.[41] On February 8, 1973, the Inter-American Economic and Social Council adopted a resolution opposing the interference of multinational corporations in the internal affairs of Latin American countries.[42] A similar resolution was adopted by the Third Session of the Organization of American States on April 15.[43] These various resolutions were more than pro forma restatements of old positions, given the context of Venezuela's steps toward nationalization of the petroleum industry and the general atmosphere created by the energy crisis. And China supported each resolution as an expression of growing Latin American restiveness about the multinationals.

Late in 1973, a number of steps were taken toward subregional organization and further economic integration in Latin America, including the formation of the Latin American Energy Organization in Lima at the end of October.[44] During 1974, the focus of regional energy relations shifted somewhat from resolutions criticizing the multinational oil companies to direct efforts at regional cooperation in development projects.[45] But Latin America has kept up the drumfire of criticism of U.S. penetration of the region's petroleum and energy infrastructure. This attitude fits comfortably within the framework of China's disequilibrium model.

China's relations with regional organizations in Africa, the Middle East, and Asia have been less concerned with energy matters. Peking took note of the January 1974 meeting between Arab oil ministers and African foreign ministers under the rubric of the Organization of African Unity.[46] But the impact of high oil prices on African economies is not a comfortable topic for the Chinese. Regional relations with the Middle East are dominated by OPEC and OAPEC and have already been discussed. Aside from these organizations, Middle Eastern regional organizations are not particularly vigorous, and are divided along multiple fracture lines according to the political differences of the various governments in the area. China does participate in the Economic and Social Council for Asia and the Pacific (ESCAP) and has encouraged ESCAP to take action to safeguard mineral resources in the region. But Chinese relations with ESCAP tend to be rather testy.[47] China resents ESCAP's long period of cooperation with Taipei and considers its data-gathering mission an invasion of sovereign privacy. Peking would also like to see ESCAP take much firmer positions against penetration of the region by both the United States and the Soviet Union.

The United Nations

If China finds the regional organizations a convenient forum for attacks on the control of world energy markets and resources by the multinational corporations, the United Nations provides a forum for Chinese views on energy issues at the level of state-to-state relations. China's entry into the United Nations in September 1971 followed 22 years of isolation, enforced by a powerful coalition of countries under U.S. leadership. China rode into the U.N. on the crest of its new political relationship with Washington and the votes of the Third World.[48] Following the initial success in the General Assembly, the PRC was quickly accepted into most U.N. agencies and other universal organizations.[49]

Peking has a number of important political objectives as a participant in the United Nations, most of which impinge in one way or another on China's energy policies and international energy relations. The forum function of the U.N. is the most vital to Peking, providing a rostrum for direct communication of its views on all topics of political and economic importance to the world. And U.N. diplomatic functions provide a convenient and inexpensive channel for regular contacts with more than 150 countries and territories. China's representatives may attack Washington and Moscow at will without risking the rupture of tenuous diplomatic contacts with the superpowers.[50]

China enthusiastically takes the side of the Third World in most political scraps in the United Nations and participates actively in the formation of Third World coalitions such as the "Group of 77."[51] Such coalition formation includes the objective of structural revision of the rules of the diplomatic game, in an effort to shift the locus of political authority toward the Third World and away from the industrial countries.[52]

Once it became a member of the United Nations and its agencies, Peking immediately turned its attention to the issue of trade relations between the industrial countries and the Third World. The U.N. Commission on Trade and Development (UNCTAD) held a series of meetings in the spring and summer of 1972 on the question of the conditions of trade for commodities produced by Third World countries. These meetings produced resolutions calling for a new equality in trade relations between the exporters of raw materials and the exporters of industrial products.[53] These resolutions were more pointed than usual because of the excitement generated by initial changes in the posted price of crude oil.

The UNCTAD meetings and resolutions were followed in 1973 by a series of challenges in all of the relevant U.N. agencies to the basic rules of the old economic order. The Economic and Social Council passed a resolution in April affirming "permanent sovereignty over natural resources," an almost perfect echo of China's resource sovereignty principle.[54] By July, the U.N. Trade and Development board was working on a "Charter of Economic Rights and Duties of States," to be placed before the General Assembly.[55] The Conference of Non-Aligned Countries held in September, meetings of the General Agreement on Tariffs and Trade (GATT) in Tokyo in the same month, and finally the Twenty-eighth Session of the General Assembly raised the issues of resource sovereignty, equal trade relations, and control over raw materials in a rising chorus.[56] It was as if Peking had suddenly been given some magic power over the agenda of the United Nations and all of its agencies.

But 1974 witnessed the zenith of Chinese influence on energy and resource issues in the United Nations. The Arab oil embargo had just shaken the industrial world to its roots, and the price of oil had climbed to levels so astronomical that journalists were questioning the survival of Western civilization. The U.N. General Assembly called the Sixth Special

Session (New York, April 1974) to consider the problem of natural resources and development. China sent Vice-Premier Teng Hsiao-ping, the highest available state official short of Chou En-lai, who was in the hospital with cancer. Teng delivered a long speech focusing on the theme that the Third World was rising up to confront imperialism, social imperialism, and contention between the superpowers for world hegemony: "At present, the international situation is most favorable to the developing countries and the peoples of the world. . . . International relations are changing drastically. The whole world is in turbulence and unrest. . . . This 'disorder' is a manifestation of the sharpening of all the basic contradictions in the contemporary world."[57]

Teng also restated the basic tenets of China's energy policies toward the Third World—the self-reliance development guideline and the principle of resource sovereignty—and asserted that the oil-producing countries had broken "the international economic monopoly" of imperialism over the world's resources. He attacked the Soviet Union for its energy trade policies in the Middle East and Eastern Europe. He identified China as a Third World country and renounced superpower status for the People's Republic. Finally, he called for unity and cooperation among Third World countries on energy and resource issues and in economic relations generally.

Teng evidently did well politically at the Special Session. He met with delegations from a number of Third World and East European countries after his speech.[58] And he was quoted by other delegations in the context of their own speeches, which included some references to the exact phrasing of the Chinese resource sovereignty and self-reliance policies.[59] The Special Session adopted a Declaration on the Establishment of a New Economic Order and a Programme of Action incorporating statements resembling the Chinese position.[60] China voted for the Declaration, after expressing some reservations about its mild wording and the inclusion of such terms as "the international division of labour" and "economic integration," which Peking considers encroachments on state sovereignty.[61]

In the period since the Sixth Special Session, Peking has used the Declaration and Programme as points of reference for its statements on international energy and resource distribution issues.[62] Peking continues to be adamant about the need for a new economic order based on self-reliance in domestic development and the establishment of a new international economic order:

There are two conflicting positions on the question of development. The position taken by the third world is for maintaining independence and self-reliance, transforming the old economic order of exploitation of the third world by a few big powers and establishing a new economic order on the principles of sovereignty, equality, and mutual benefit. The other position, taken by the superpowers, stresses "interdependence" or "international division of labour" between the exploiting and the exploited countries in an attempt to preserve the old economic order.[63]

This rather bald statement of the Chinese position does not preclude technological transfer in favor of the nonindustrial countries. Indeed, the PRC advocates precisely such a transfer of energy and other production technologies to the Third World, but always within the political and economic framework of self-reliance and the maintenance of resource sovereignty.[64] According to this view, there should be no sacrifice of domestic control over energy resources in exchange for energy technology. Peking does oppose large-scale technological aid projects controlled by the governments of the superpowers.[65] These by their very nature provide an entry for American and Soviet goods into Third World markets and capture the developing countries in a vicious cycle of credit and finance problems. But the PRC itself carries on limited aid projects in the field of energy technology.[66]

China has also been involved in recent law-of-the-sea developments that impinge on sea-bed energy resources and petroleum transport. China voted for the General Assembly resolution that convened the Third United Nations Conference on the Law of the Sea in Caracas, Venezuela.[67] The PRC participated actively in the conference in June and July of 1974, which gave China the first opportunity to spell out in public a policy regarding various law-of-the-sea problems.[68]

In general, Peking simply supported the Third World positions at the conference, insofar as those positions were cohesive and discernible. China does not take a firm position on the breadth of territorial seas, preferring to recognize whatever limits the coastal states set—another example of the transcendence of state sovereignty in Chinese policy. China itself operates with a modified 12-mile limit and an implied 200-mile economic zone. Peking vigorously supports the 200-mile limit set by certain Latin American countries for protection of their fishing industries. China has used discussion of territorial seas problems to argue with Japan over the ownership of the Tiaoyutai.[69]

As with the question of the breadth of territorial seas, Peking has retained maximum flexibility toward the issue of ownership of sea-bed resources. This issue, which could be very important in the controversy over ownership of the Chinese continental shelf, is related to the problem of exclusive economic zones and fishing rights. Here again, the PRC simply recognizes the right of the coastal state "to reasonably define" such zones.[70] Peking does seem to lean toward a definition of sea-bed resource rights based on "the depth and inclination of the coastal sea-bed" (i.e. the extension of the continental shelf), rather than the principle of the median line.[71] The natural prolongation definition of the shelf would give China the advantage in its dispute with Japan. Japan favors the median-line definition of sea-bed resource rights, at least in the context of the dispute over the shelf.[72]

The Chinese delegation has strongly supported the Group of 77 in its efforts to provide for an equitable distribution of mineral resources from the sea-bed. The Fifth Session of the Third U.N. Law of the Sea Conference debated the problem of control over manganese nodules (which lie over vast stretches of the ocean floor and are rich in a variety of minerals) in the summer of 1976. The United States locked horns with the Third World during this session over the extent of authority and resource control to be granted to a proposed international authority. The United States would like an agreement that would set aside half of the nodules for the international authority and would permit the multinationals to mine the other half, using their relatively advanced deep-sea mineral extraction technology. China believes that such an arrangement would simply open the door for unrestricted exploitation of the nodules by the industrial countries. The PRC has also accused Moscow of collaborating with the United States in monopolizing this potentially rich future source of minerals.[73]

As with special economic zones, territorial seas, sea-bed resources, and fishery protection, China recognizes the right of contiguous states to set their own regulations for navigation through narrow straits.[74] Thus, Peking denies the right of Japanese tankers to free passage through the Straits of Malacca, should Indonesia or Malaysia decide otherwise. As with the other issues, the critical problem from the Chinese perspective is the question of state sovereignty. Peking simultaneously supports the right of landlocked countries to "enjoy reasonable rights and interests in the economic zones of neighboring coastal states and have the right of transit through the territories and territorial seas of the latter and other sea areas."[75] It is still unclear whether China will remain consistent on this point if Mongolia should claim a portion of the oil reserves on the Chinese continental shelf and request rights of transit for the crude oil obtained therefrom.

China's position on energy-related international pollution problems is fairly complex. It would be an oversimplification to assert that the PRC either ignores international pollution problems or is highly conscious of the dangers of global pollution. China was represented at the First United

Nations Conference on the Human Environment, held in Stockholm in June 1972.[76] However, the PRC abstained on the Declaration on Human Environment adopted by the conference, again because of fear that it would imply some encroachment on state sovereignty.[77] Peking has taken a somewhat more positive attitude toward marine pollution from oil spills.[78] But in general the Chinese have tried to get away without committing themselves to any specific environmental protection measures, preferring to blame global pollution problems on the superpowers.

China has not to date participated in the International Atomic Energy Agency (IAEA), or any other organization concerned with nuclear power regulation. Peking is very sensitive about anything related to its nuclear infrastructure. The lack of Chinese interest in the IAEA does not necessarily preclude future participation, although Peking would be likely to insist on terms that could make its participation meaningless. The PRC is still far from permitting inspection of its own nuclear facilities. Chinese refusal to accede to such inspection under international safeguard regulations could very well slow importation of nuclear power equipment from the industrial countries. As an unregulated exporter of nuclear power equipment, China could represent a real danger to the international community. (See Chapter 12.)

Multinational Corporations and Joint-Stock Companies

A great deal has already been said regarding the Chinese attitude toward the multinational corporations and need not be repeated here. Peking finds its emphasis on Third World self-reliance and resource sovereignty entirely consistent with a steady verbal attack on the role of the multinationals in energy and other raw materials trade. Every move of the oil-exporting countries toward expropriation of corporate holdings is supported by the *People's Daily*, which relates such changes to China's own experience with Western capitalism and Soviet-style socialism. Thus, the attacks on the multinational corporations meet both the state sovereignty criterion and the socialist ideological criteria that condition the making of Chinese foreign policy.

This does not prevent the People's Republic of China and its government trading organizations from dealing directly with the multinationals. At one level, China simply cannot afford to avoid the multinationals completely. But at another level, trade with the multinationals fits Peking's disequilibrium model of global change. The forces of history are beyond the scope of the trade relations of any single country. Great revolutionary shifts in global energy distribution patterns will occur, regardless of the immediate consequences of trade with the multinationals.

It is better to preserve the state, safeguard national sovereignty, and develop the national economy than to go on quixotic crusades against the multinationals.

The energy crisis has strongly reinforced the Chinese ranking of organizations, since it has strengthened the governments of the oil-exporting countries at the expense of the multinational corporations. The oil corporations in a few years have lost accumulated control over the greater part of the world's remaining known crude petroleum reserves and over a part of the marketing structure for petroleum products in Third World countries.[79] In a sense, the multinational corporations dealing in oil are being pushed into the sea from both the export and import ends. Through higher prices in the industrial oil-importing countries, they have managed to maintain and expand profit margins, but the long-term effect on corporate control of the global energy distribution system may be to shift that control toward the governments of both exporting and importing countries.

If anything, Peking has become more vitriolic in its attacks on Soviet joint-stock companies than it is in its attitude toward the multinational corporations:

> The Soviet social-imperialists, to keep a continuous flow of profit from their expansion and plunder abroad, have tried their utmost, including the use of counter-revolutionary tactics, to thwart and undermine this struggle of the developing countries. While hypocritically denouncing such corporations, in the same breath the social-imperialists speak highly of their "advantages," alleging that the Soviet Union understands that in order to obtain capital and technology a number of developing countries "might be interested in knitting ties with transnational corporations." Meanwhile, the Soviet revisionists are peddling everywhere "joint-stock companies"—transnational corporations of the Moscow brand. . . .
>
> The form of direct investment is used by the Soviet Union to impose on the developing countries accepting its investment in a situation in which the Soviet Union provides the funds and technical equipment while the latter provide labour and raw materials [sic]. In this way, it subjects these countries to more ruthless exploitation and plunder. This kind of "joint-stock company" is exactly the same as the transnational corporation of the Western monopoly capital. In addition, as the capital exported from the Soviet Union is owned by that social-imperialist state, the areas where the investment goes, the projects to be undertaken and the spheres of activity are all selected strictly in accordance with the needs of the Soviet Government in aggression and expansion abroad. In this sense, the "joint-stock companies," the transnational corporations of the Moscow brand, have far outstripped their counterparts of the West in rapaciousness.[80]

According to Peking, there are several motivations for Soviet establishment of joint-stock companies in the Third World. They provide a convenient avenue of political infiltration into the partner countries. They control the production and trade of raw materials. They open markets for Soviet products that cannot be sold in Western markets. And they make available the vast human and natural mineral resources of the Third World to exploitation by Soviet industry. These Chinese accusations are politically motivated by the tension in state relations with Moscow. However, they may not be entirely without foundation in China's own experience with Soviet joint-stock companies and technical assistance during the 1950's.

Chapter 10

Domestic Energy Development
in Comparative Perspective

It was suggested at the beginning of Chapter 1 that the making of energy policy is fundamentally conditioned by a balance between perceptions of constraint and perceptions of change. Constraints on energy development are difficult to measure in absolute terms. Rather, constraints on the energy system are perceived by each government and each energy industry against a background of experience accumulated by other countries and other industries. China's energy system, like any other, must be evaluated relative to the energy development experience of other countries and regions. An annual production rate of 100 million tons of crude oil means nothing in and of itself. A petroleum production growth rate of 20 percent per year sounds high, but must really be evaluated in terms of the relative stage of growth of the oil industry in question, the likely resource constraints on further growth, and the early growth experiences of oil industries in other countries.

There are many other questions that may also be best answered against a comparative background of statistics from other countries and regions. How large is China's energy system? How fast has it been developing? How significant are recent oil and gas discoveries in the framework of global energy resources? How will China's particular energy resource base affect the future energy mix? Will China have an adequate resource base for commercial nuclear power development? Has China's form of centrally planned economy significantly accelerated the growth of primary energy production, above and beyond what would have been expected in any case? What has been the impact of the self-reliance energy strategy on energy commodity consumption patterns? Is there any way out of the paradoxes created in the Chinese energy system by its large and still-growing population? All of these questions have a comparative connotation or may be approached from a comparative perspective.

An analysis of China's energy balance against the background of energy balance statistics for other countries and regions also offers an opportunity to summarize a vast sea of energy data for China. The Statistical Profile provides a complete set of aggregate energy accounts for the

PRC, including resources, primary production, secondary production, consumption, and trade, disaggregated by year and fuel. It is appropriate that a summary of the major statistical results of the Profile be presented as part of the policy analysis in comparison with similar statistics for other countries and regions. Indeed, one of the central purposes of the Profile was to provide statistics that could be easily absorbed into the general framework of international energy accounts available through the United Nations and other organizations.

Finally, this comparative chapter offers the author an opportunity to comment in a general vein on the world energy situation. Cross-national research plunges one into an alien world of concepts, ideologies, and perceptions. Cross-national researchers are therefore prone to don the mantle of the objects of their study, in this case the Chinese *shihchiehkuan* (world view). This represents both a danger and an opportunity. The opportunity arises when fresh perspectives are gained on familiar or challenging problems.

Energy Reserves and Resources

There are two basic points that must be emphasized in comparing China's energy resource situation with that of other countries and regions. The first is that China has plentiful resources for energy development within the foreseeable future. The second is that China's energy resources are not incommensurately large, especially in view of the size of the Chinese population. The energy reserves and resources of the PRC are about what might be expected, considering the sheer size of the country and its geographical diversity. Furthermore, the energy resources are fairly evenly distributed among the various fuels and renewable energy resources such as hydropower potential. Thus China has the resource base for even and rapid domestic energy development over the next 20 years.

The measured and inferred coal reserves of the PRC rank third in the world after the United States and the Soviet Union. (See Tables 10.1 and 10.2.) At 100 billion metric tons, China has about 16 percent of the world's coal reserves, enough to last more than 200 years at current rates of production.[1] However, recoverable coal resources are thought to be 1–1.5 trillion metric tons, exceeding present identified reserves by an order of magnitude. There are vast untapped and still unmeasured coal basins stretching across Shensi and Shansi provinces and buried deep under the loess hills of north-central China. These deposits are comparable to the large bituminous coal resources of Montana and Wyoming in the United States. They will probably be the next theater for develop-

TABLE 10.1
Primary Energy Reserves and Resources by Region

Region	Coal (bmt) Reserves[a]	Resources	Crude petroleum (bmt) Reserves[b]	Resources	Natural gas (tcm) Reserves[b]	Resources	Hydropower (GW) Capacity[c]	Potential	Uranium (tmt) Reserves[d]	Resources
Market economies	283	3,769	8.9	65	12.6	56	259	570	1,023	3,585
North America	187	3,033	4.9	50	7.6	40	109	290	562	2,556
Western Europe	70	527	3.7	10	3.9	10	115	193	68	544
Oceania	25	200	0.3	5	1.1	5	9	37	390	485
Japan	1	9	0.01	1	0.02	1	26	50	3	n.a.
Planned economies	301	7,345	15.4	70	29.4	75	69	847	630[e]	n.a.
Soviet Union	137	5,714	10.3	40	26.1	50	43	269	500[e]	n.a.
Eastern Europe	62	127	1.0	5	0.3	5	8	22	20[e]	n.a.
China	100	1,500	4.0	20	3.0	15	15	500	100[e]	n.a.
Other Asian CPEs	2	4	0.1	5	n.a.	5	3	56	10[e]	n.a.
Third World	35	192	66.0	165	32.9	85	63	1,020	647	611
Africa	16	59	8.0	20	5.9	20	10	437	332	541
Asia	14	92	2.4	15	3.5	10	16	226	300[g]	n.a.
Central America	1	13	4.5	20	2.3	10	10	52	1	n.a.
South America	2	20	1.0	10	0.8	5	24	277	13	70
Middle East	2	8	50.1	100	20.4	40	3	28	n.a.	n.a.
World	619	11,306	90.3	300	74.9	215	391	2,437	2,300[e]	5,000[e]

[a] 1974 estimates from SER, 1974, pp. 52, 58, 61.   [b] Jan. 1, 1978, estimates from IPE, 1978, p. 270.   [c] 1976 on-line hydropower capacity estimates from WES 20 (1978), Table 18.   [d] Estimates for "reasonably assured U$_3$O$_8$ resources" at $30/kg from Ford Foundation, Nuclear Power: Issues and Choices (Cambridge, Mass.: Ballinger, 1977), p. 81.   [e] Author's estimate.   [f] Speculative estimates for U$_3$O$_8$ resources at $60/kg from Ford Foundation, Nuclear Power: Issues and Choices, p. 81, and SER, 1974, pp. 203–4.   [g] Estimate of India's ThO$_2$ resources at $30/kg from SER, 1974, p. 214.

TABLE 10.2
Distribution of World Energy Reserves and Reserves-Production Ratios

Region	Coal		Crude petroleum		Natural gas		Hydropower		Uranium	
	Percent[a]	Res./Prod.[b]	Percent[b]	Res./Prod.[b]	Percent[b]	Res./Prod.[b]	Percent[a]	Pot./Cap.[c]	Percent[d]	Res./Prod.[d]
Market economies	45.7%	245	9.8%	14.3	16.8%	15.4	23.4%	2.2	44%	
North America	30.2	288	5.4	9.2	10.2	11.9	11.9	2.7	24	30
Western Europe	11.3	217	4.1	53.3	5.2	22.4	7.9	1.7	3	30
Oceania	4.0	298	0.3	13.0	1.4	133.0	1.5	4.1	17	100+
Japan	0.2	55	0.01	16.1	0.03	6.2	2.1	1.9	neg.	neg.
Planned economies	48.6	205	17.0	23.0	39.2	77.9	34.7	12.3	28[e]	
Soviet Union	22.1	266	11.4	18.8	34.8	82.1	11.0	6.3	22[e]	50+
Eastern Europe	10.0	156	1.1	47.2	0.4	5.6	0.9	2.8	1[e]	
China	*16.2*	*200*	*4.4*	*44.3*	*4.0*	*63.4*	*20.5*	*33.3*	*4[e]*	*50+*
Other Asian CPEs	0.3	35	0.1	n.a.	n.a.	n.a.	2.3	18.7	1[e]	
Third World	5.7	233	73.2	37.9	44.0	265.7	41.9	16.2	28	
Africa	2.6	187	8.9	26.4	7.9	358.4	17.9	43.7	14	50+
Asia	2.3	115	2.7	21.2	4.7	148.3	9.3	14.1	13	
Central America	0.2	102	5.0	23.6	3.1	78.9	2.1	5.2	neg.	
South America	0.3	379	1.1	20.5	1.1	69.4	11.4	11.5	1	100+
Middle East	0.3	242	55.5	45.3	27.2	472.8	1.2	9.3	neg.	
World	100.0	223	100.0	29.6	100.0	58.0	100.0	6.2	100	

[a] 1974 estimates. [b] 1977 estimates. [c] Ratio of 1974 estimated potential to 1976 on-line capacity. [d] 1975 estimates. [e] Author's estimate.

ment in the Chinese coal industry. Large coal deposits are also found in the northeast, where the bulk of the current industry is located, and in Szechwan and Sinkiang, with scattered deposits across the entire eastern half of the country. In short, there is no real resource constraint on coal development in the PRC. The industry is already large, however, and its further growth is slowed by the capital cost of mechanization and further expansion, as well as by the limitations of the rail transport network.

Current coal reserves are incommensurately distributed in favor of the already industrialized regions of the world, in both the centrally planned and market economy countries. It is difficult to say, however, whether this distribution is the result of natural factors or the differential exploration effort conducted by countries at various stages in economic development. Coal has not been emphasized in the energy development programs of very many Third World countries. Even a marginal coal exploration effort in certain of these countries (e.g. Indonesia) has yielded rewarding returns. As the age of petroleum begins to reach its natural limits, one would expect more Third World governments to pay attention to locating and extracting coal for future energy needs.

China's crude petroleum reserves are extremely difficult to estimate with any degree of accuracy (Chapter 14). However, proved plus probable crude oil reserves in 1978 could reasonably be placed at 3–5 billion metric tons. This figure does not include any offshore oil, which would still fall into the category of economically recoverable resources rather than defined reserves. Economically recoverable resources may already be placed at 10–20 billion metric tons. I have used the upper estimate in this range in recognition of the fact that the Chinese oil industry is still in its infancy and has not reached into offshore sediments that are potentially petrolific. Ultimate recoverable crude petroleum resources could some day be demonstrated to be greater than 20 billion metric tons, but there is no evidence that would indicate the likelihood of resources larger than that figure at the present time, at least within acceptable probability limits and the characteristic uncertainty of such long-range speculations.

Based on my current estimate of proved plus probable reserves at 4.0 billion metric tons, the PRC had 4.4 percent of the world's crude oil reserves as of January 1, 1978. This would be nearly as much as the current reserves of North America (5.4 bmt) or Central America (5.0 bmt).[2] This figure would be only 40 percent of the current proved plus probable reserves of the Soviet Union and less than 10 percent of the current reserves of the Middle East. Thus it is obvious that, at least as of 1978, China was not "another Persian Gulf." On the other hand, China already possesses oil reserves that are significant on a regional scale and that exceed the combined reserves of the rest of Asia, including Indonesia (but not Siberia). From this set of comparisons one could conclude that, whereas China will be a significant regional energy commodity exporter, the PRC will not enter the world petroleum market unless there are very large discoveries in the offshore theater.

Comparative statistics are also provided for the reserves-production ratio, which is a good index of the growth prospects for the oil industry of any country. As of 1977, there were more than 40 years of remaining production at current reserve levels. The only other regions with such favorable reserves-production ratios were the Middle East, Eastern Europe, and Western Europe (the North Sea). This means that Peking can comfortably continue to push annual crude oil production up through at least 1985, although oil production growth rates have already declined from 20 percent per year to 10 percent, and this downward trend in the growth rate will continue, at least in onland fields. This comparative finding strengthens the computer projection, which indicates high primary energy production growth rates through the mid-1980's. Energy production will outstrip domestic energy consumption until sometime after 1990, generating a bubble of surplus energy commodities that will be available for export, but in limited quantities.

The situation in natural gas is pretty much the same as in China's crude oil production. Based on the materials in Chapter 14, I would place current natural gas reserves at about 3.0 trillion cubic meters, and economically recoverable resources at 15 trillion cubic meters, including the offshore theater. This would give China about 4 percent of current world natural gas reserves, comparable to Western Europe, Central America, or the rest of Asia combined. China's natural gas reserves are half the reserves of North America and about 10–12 percent of the huge gas reserves of the Soviet Union. Nonetheless, China has a comfortable gas reserves-production ratio and could easily expand natural gas production through 1985. If anything, Peking has paid less than commensurate attention to the role that natural gas could play in the energy economy, given the current reserves level. Offshore exploration could yield extensive new gas discoveries that could be used in coastal industries or liquefied and exported. China already has extensive gas reserves in the Tsaidam Basin and western provinces that are "locked in" by the lack of a long-distance pipeline network.

China has the largest hydropower potential of any country on earth, including the Soviet Union, which is often given credit for the record. Theoretical hydraulic potential is estimated in excess of 500 gigawatts by virtually all authorities, whereas usable potential at commercially viable sites is variously estimated at 300–500 gigawatts (Table 14.6). Commercially viable potential is toward the upper end of this range, since Peking has an unusual concept of "commercial" and has accelerated the installation of small-scale hydropower-generating stations in the last decade. Some of these stations are in the "micro-hydro" range, with as little as 25 kilowatts capacity. I have visited a small-scale hydro station in a Chinese commune that was running from falling water in a small stream. Intermediate-scale hydro stations are already commonplace. Small units may be built with a minimum of machinery and a maximum input of construction labor. China also has several large river basins with massive hydraulic potential, including the Yangtze River with 215 gigawatts potential and the Yalutsangpu with 115 gigawatts and the world's largest single-site potential (Table 14.7). As a rule of thumb, if China developed 100 percent of its hydraulic potential, it could run the entire U.S. electric power system on hydropower alone. This will not happen in reality because of environmental constraints and competing land use, but the comparison is illustrative of the scale of this renewable energy resource in China. But the PRC has developed only about 3 percent of its hydropower potential at the current time, in sharp contrast to the industrial market economy countries that have already developed about half of their hydropower resources.

For the sake of argument, I have also included an estimate of China's uranium reserves at 100,000 metric tons of uranium oxide.[3] This estimate is highly speculative, based on a few scattered pieces of information and comparison of the size of China's likely uranium mining industry to similar industries in other parts of the world. China has enough uranium to build a substantial nuclear weapons program. On the other hand, the Chinese government has occasionally shown interest in importing uranium from other countries (Chapter 12). This indicates that Peking may hedge its bets on a uranium supply for the civilian nuclear power program, choosing to import reactor-grade enriched uranium while saving domestic supplies for future weapons needs. It is unlikely, therefore, that current uranium reserves are as large as those of the United States or the Soviet Union. But the size of the enrichment and weapons program indicates that current reserves of easily available uranium ($30 per kilogram) are substantially larger than those of the world's small uranium producers. Unfortunately, it is difficult to distinguish the effects of uranium reserves from constraints imposed by the current level of exploration and mining or the size of China's gaseous diffusion enrichment plant. Current reserves could easily be smaller than my estimate by an order of magnitude (10,000 metric tons). They are unlikely to be larger, but I have chosen an estimate at the upper end of the range of possibilities to indicate the likelihood of new discoveries as China's nuclear industry moves forward. China may be producing uranium oxide at about the same rate as France or Niger, about 2,000 metric tons per year, but less than South Africa.[4] This would permit the PRC to continue production at current levels for 50 years or more. The introduction of a civilian nuclear power industry would of course raise the consumption requirement substantially, providing an incentive for further exploration and higher annual production.

On the whole, it might reasonably be argued that China has between 5 and 10 percent of the world's total energy resources. This represents a large energy resource endowment for any single country. It is a foundation for optimism regarding the viability of Peking's ambitious modernization program, at least from the perspective of energy development. The PRC is particularly strong in coal and hydropower resources and still only moderately strong in oil and gas resources. This indicates that Peking will be paying close attention over the next several decades to various alternative energy technologies, including nuclear power. China will also show increasing concern for energy use efficiency and resource conservation as the pressure of rising consumption requirements begins to be felt under the production curve by about 1990 (Chapter 12). China is obviously in no position to squander its fossil resources and will have to measure the appropriate level of oil exports very carefully to avoid exerting downward pressure on domestic economic growth. It should also be kept in mind that even if China had 10 percent of world energy resources, it also has more than 20 percent of the world's population. Available resources will therefore have to be rationed carefully and used efficiently. Over the long run, China will have to move with the rest of the world toward renewable or inexhaustible energy resources.

Primary Energy Production

There is little doubt that China is already among the world's largest primary energy producers. By 1976, the PRC ranked fourth in total primary energy production, behind the United States, the Soviet Union, and Saudi Arabia. Current Chinese levels of energy production are comparable to Saudi Arabia or Iran, the world's two largest oil-exporting countries. The gap between China and the superpowers is still substantial. In 1976, China produced about one-fourth the energy production of the United States, or one-third that of the Soviet Union. The PRC contributes about 20 percent of the energy output of the centrally planned economy countries, and 6 percent of world production. It is also true that from 1961 to 1977, China was among the world's fastest growing regions in primary energy production. At an average annual growth rate of 9 percent per year, the growth of China's energy system was comparable to that of Oceania, Africa, and the Middle East, areas that are riding the crest of the oil and gas era. China's primary energy production growth rate is more than triple that of the industrial market economy countries and higher than that of all centrally planned economy countries. On the other hand, the PRC grew at the same rate as the Third World. Based on the rapid expansion of crude petroleum production in the OPEC countries, the Third World is also moving forward rapidly in energy production. This rapid energy development is poorly distributed, however, so that the PRC's energy output is growing substantially faster than Latin America or the rest of Asia. In Asia, only the other centrally planned economy countries are close to keeping pace with the PRC. China's energy production growth rate is nearly twice that of the world as a whole.

This picture of high energy production and rapid growth rates is confirmed by a glance at the figures for each energy industry. (See Table 10.3.) The Chinese energy system is still largely coal-based. In 1976, the PRC was the world's third largest coal producer, close on the heels of the United States (600 mmt) and the Soviet Union (500 mmt). No other country is anywhere near the three coal giants. At current rates of expansion, the PRC would soon overtake the superpowers in coal production. China produces more coal than the rest of Asia combined and is growing faster in coal production than the other regions, except Oceania (Australia) and the other Asian centrally planned economy countries. The strategy in China's energy system has been to continue heavy capital investment in the coal industry while simultaneously accelerating the oil and gas industries. Thus, in contrast to the Western market economy countries, the coal base for China's energy system has not declined with the introduction of other fossil fuels, but has continued to expand. The PRC may be close to saturation of the domestic market for lump coal and is already generating some surplus for export. This export surplus will probably grow during the 1980's, reaching perhaps 20 million tons per year by 1985. Should oil and gas discoveries along the continental shelf prove disappointing, Peking will be in a good position to experiment with coal conversion technologies. The only shadow remaining for the Chinese coal industry is the primitive state of coal beneficiation facilities.* As a consequence, Chinese coal has less than standard energy value and must be discounted in the tabulation of total energy output by about 25 percent. The Chinese government is taking steps at the present time to correct this situation.

---

*Coal beneficiation is the removal of crude impurities from raw coal through washing and other processes.

TABLE 10.3
Primary Energy Production by Region, 1976

Region	Coal Mmtce	Coal Growth	Crude oil Mmt	Crude oil Growth	Natural gas Bcm	Natural gas Growth	Hydropower Bkwh	Hydropower Growth	Nuclear Bkwh	Nuclear Growth	Total Mmtce	Total Growth
Market economies	1,050.1	0.6%	594.7	2.4%	807.4	4.5%	984.1	4.1%	366.6	33.5%	3,152.8	2.8%
North America	622.2	3.1	527.9	1.8	623.7	3.0	503.6	5.0	207.5	38.8	2,308.5	3.2
Western Europe	329.8	-2.9	43.8	7.3	174.0	18.8	359.4	3.3	125.0	27.1	680.1	1.0
Oceania	80.1	6.8	22.3	104.5	6.8	81.1	32.4	6.8			126.0	10.2
Japan	18.4	-7.4	0.6	-1.4	2.9	5.5	88.7	2.1	34.1	32.0	38.2	-4.1
Planned economies	1,392.2	2.8	627.0	8.3	383.9	10.3	204.8	5.6	24.7	37.6[a]	2,730.9	5.4
Soviet Union	505.7	1.7	522.5	7.6	293.5	10.3	135.7	5.1	14.0	25.3[a]	1,674.1	5.9
Eastern Europe	386.0	2.1	20.8	2.3	52.0	9.9	19.5	8.8	10.7	82.9[a]	488.2	2.8
China	450.0	6.5	83.6	21.0	37.9	16.6	33.0	12.3			514.9	8.8
Other Asian CPEs	52.5	9.8	n.a.	n.a.	n.a.	n.a.	17.6	3.6			54.7	8.9
Third World	227.4	3.9	1,730.1	7.7	122.3	10.7	261.7	10.2	6.4	39.0[a]	2,966.6	8.9
Africa	81.2	4.2	291.3	14.9	16.5	30.4	40.4	10.4			536.7	13.1
Asia	123.5	4.0	102.7	9.5	22.9	13.2	61.1	10.0	3.9	27.5[a]	312.3	7.3
Central America	9.4	5.9	186.3	-0.3	29.8	4.6	43.1	10.7	0.02	neg.	328.5	1.5
South America	5.1	2.8	46.1	5.3	11.1	4.5	103.8	9.8	2.6	45.5[a]	100.6	6.3
Middle East	8.3	3.9	1,103.6	9.2	41.9	20.7	13.4	13.9			1,688.5	11.1
World	2,669.8	1.9	2,951.7	6.1	1,313.6	6.0	1,450.7	5.0	397.8	34.2	8,850.3	5.1

Sources: Production data are from WES 15 and WES 21. Average annual growth rates are from 1961 to 1977, using three-year end-point averages and the formula percent growth equals $[(x_2/x_1)^{1/t} -1](100)$.
[a] Log normal growth rate for 1972–76 only.

China's oil industry has also made substantial progress in the last two decades and must already be ranked among the world's intermediate oil producers. By 1976, the PRC ranked eleventh in crude oil production, comparable to Indonesia or the United Arab Emirates in petroleum output. By 1978, China ranked tenth. By 1982, Chinese oil production will exceed 120 million metric tons per year, Venezuela's current level of production, perhaps ranking as high as fifth in crude oil output. Nonetheless, the Chinese oil industry does not compare to the world's largest oil producers (the Soviet Union, Saudi Arabia, the United States, and Iran) and will not overtake them in the foreseeable future unless offshore discoveries are very favorable during the 1980's. In 1976, China produced just 3 percent of world oil output, roughly commensurate with China's proved plus probable crude petroleum reserves, which are about 4 percent of the world total.

The growth performance of the Chinese oil industry since 1961 is unique in the annals of the world oil industry. Based on a single large producing zone (Taching oilfield), Peking pushed oil production up at an average annual rate in excess of 20 percent over a 15-year period. The growth rate dropped to 10 percent per year between 1975 and 1978, still high by world standards. Further declines in the growth rate, however, will spell trouble for China's oil export program during the 1980's. This explains the urgency attached to further expansion of the oil industry in the current Ten-Year Development Plan, as well as Peking's recent inclination to allow joint offshore development projects with foreign oil companies. China's oil production growth rate will be higher than the world average for at least several years to come.

Production figures for China's natural gas industry are still characterized by a high degree of uncertainty. Estimates by different sources vary widely, and the Chinese press has provided only a few hints in the form of fragmentary or inferential data. By 1976, total marketed (i.e. not flared) natural gas production was in the vicinity of 40 billion cubic meters, containing less than half the energy value of crude petroleum output in that year. This production is substantial by world standards, ranking about sixth in 1976 with an output level identical to Romania and Britain. Soviet and U.S natural gas production is still an order of magnitude greater than Chinese ouput. In 1976, China produced more natural gas than the rest of Asia combined, and nearly as much as the entire Middle East.

At about 17 percent average annual growth, the Chinese natural gas industry outstripped world growth rates, but fell behind the pace of development in Western Europe, Oceania, Africa, and the Middle East during the period from 1961 to 1977. It must be concluded, therefore, that, given the relatively early stage of development of the gas industry in China, it has performed only moderately well against the background of experience in other countries and regions. The basic constraint on natural gas production in the PRC is the lack of a sufficient pipeline network rather than reserves. With some 70 years of remaining production at current levels, reserves are running well ahead of production. Many gas fields are locked in by the lack of long-distance pipelines. Even Szechwan, the largest provincial natural gas producer, must use all of the gas internally for lack of interregional pipelines. Even some of the gas produced at oilfields in the northeast in associated form is wasted for lack of an adequate distribution network. The Chinese natural gas industry is one area within which American production and transport technology could fruitfully be shared. It is also an industry ripe for institutional reform within China and a greater research effort by foreign analysts.

A country with 20 percent of the world's hydraulic potential, China produced just 2 percent of world hydropower output in 1976. This situation is largely a historical artifact. The People's Republic began its hydropower development in 1949 with a miniscule existing hydro capacity, much of which departed with the Russians from Manchuria at the end of World War II. A number of large hydropower projects were started with Russian assistance during the 1950's with mixed results. Several of the biggest projects were not completed until the early 1970's, and one dam on the Yellow River had to be reconstructed as the result of faulty engineering, which failed to provide sufficient runoff to prevent rapid siltation. After 1960, the Chinese switched to a hydro development strategy that has proved far more effective. It is based on a mix of large-, medium-, and small-scale projects, with each new dam fitted to the needs and construction capabilities of the surrounding area. This strategy resulted in average growth in hydropower output at 12 percent per year from 1961 to 1976, a high growth rate by world standards. The Third World has been developing its hydropower output at about 10 percent per year, a wise development strategy in view of the more than 40 percent of world hydraulic resources that are situated in Third World countries (60 percent including China).

At the present time, China has no commercial nuclear power production. Existing reactors are used for the manufacture of plutonium for weapons purposes and for research. Present indications are that this situation is about to change and that China will have its first nuclear power station on-line by about 1985 (Chapter 12). The world nuclear industry has grown at an average annual rate in excess of 30 percent per year since 1961. Between 1972 and 1976 it was still growing at more than 25 percent per year. Not all of this growth is due to the scale effect. The United States, with the world's largest nuclear industry and two decades of development in nuclear power generation, increased its nuclear generating capacity at an average annual rate of 20 percent per year from 1972 to 1978. New orders for nuclear plants did decline in the late 1970's in several industrial market economy countries, indicating that a decline in output growth rates may follow. But energy planners in the market economy countries are still banking heavily on nuclear power, and the downward trend in growth rates could be reversed under the pressure of further increases in the price of fossil energy commodities.[5] This point has obviously not been lost on Peking. Eager to advance to the forefront of world energy technology and concerned about long-range constraints on oil and gas development, the Chinese government is having a hard look at the nuclear option.

Aggregate Energy Consumption

Comparison of China's aggregate energy consumption levels to those of other countries and regions is rendered difficult both by the lack of any direct data on Chinese energy consumption patterns and by the inadequacy of consumption statistics in international energy data collections. Energy consumption statistics for the PRC must be inferred from primary energy production, energy commodity trade, and a series of assumptions about waste, inefficiencies, plant use, non-energy use of fossil fuels, and thermal electric power conversion (Chapter 18). This yields figures for energy end-use that are lower than "inland consumption," the statistics commonly used in international data collections. "Inland consumption" is simply production by commodity plus net imports. Inland consumption statistics contain an upward bias because of the failure to take the thermal electric power generation cycle into account. Electric power consumption figures are thereby either understated (including just hydropower), or double-counted by failure to discount coal, petroleum, and natural gas statistics for the amounts used in power generation. The comparative consumption figures for China in Tables 10.4 and 10.5 should therefore be handled with caution. Tabulation according to the United Nations accounting procedure would yield aggregate energy consumption for China of about 460 million metric tons coal equivalent, 14 percent higher than the figure given in the table. The different tabulation methods do not seriously affect comparative growth rates. United Nations statistics for coal, petroleum, and natural gas consumption are overstated by the amount of these fuels used in thermal electric power generation.

TABLE 10.4

Aggregate Energy Consumption by Region, 1976

Region	Coal		Petroleum		Natural gas[a]		Electricity[b]		Total	
	Mmtce	Growth	Mmt	Growth	Bcm	Growth	Bkwh	Growth	Mmtce	Growth
Market economies	1,086.9	0.4%	1,597.6	6.1%	837.8	4.1%	4,577.3	6.6%	4,809.8	4.1%
North America	569.9	2.7	796.4	4.0	627.0	3.2	2,416.6	6.2	2,716.2	3.6
Western Europe	394.2	-2.6	569.2	7.6	193.2	20.7	1,547.0	6.4	1,573.0	4.0
Oceania	43.8	3.0	31.7	7.2	6.8	80.1	101.9	7.7	105.7	5.7
Japan	79.0	1.7	200.3	13.4	10.8	15.4	511.8	10.0	414.9	9.0
Planned economies	1,159.6	2.8	458.9	8.5	374.8	10.3	1,619.8	7.9	2,384.8	5.0
Soviet Union	485.2	1.6	316.8	7.1	278.4	10.0	1,099.8	8.2	1,349.9	5.1
Eastern Europe	367.0	1.7	77.2	11.6	63.8	11.5	376.1	7.7	572.5	3.9
China[c]	*256.9*	*6.2*	*63.9*	*16.2*	*32.2*	*16.5*	*114.0*	*10.9*	*407.8*	*8.4*
Other Asian CPEs	52.2	9.7	2.1	14.2	n.a.	n.a.	29.9	6.5	57.4	9.7
Third World	225.8	3.8	362.1	7.2	95.0	9.4	691.6	10.2	938.8	6.9
Africa	76.9	3.9	47.2	7.4	7.4	22.5	139.4	8.3	164.1	5.8
Asia	120.8	3.8	92.9	9.5	13.9	9.3	211.9	12.1	288.8	6.6
Central America	9.9	6.1	84.4	5.2	30.0	3.7	128.1	10.0	184.5	5.6
South America	9.7	3.8	78.0	6.0	11.4	5.7	144.9	7.9	157.7	6.1
Middle East	8.5	4.0	59.6	9.4	32.3	19.7	67.3	12.9	143.7	11.0
World	2,472.3	1.7	2,418.6	6.6	1,307.6	6.4	6,888.7	7.2	8,133.4	4.6

Sources: Consumption data are from *WES* 15 and *WES* 21. Average annual growth rates from 1961 to 1976 are tabulated as in Table 10.3. [a]Excluding refinery gas and manufactured gas. [b]Total consumption, including thermal, hydro, and nuclear. [c]Energy end-use is not strictly comparable to U.N. data (see text).

With this caution in mind, it can still be concluded that China is already the world's third largest aggregate energy-consuming country. China and Japan have roughly the same annual energy consumption in aggregate terms. Given China's strength in energy resources and Japan's strength in energy technologies, energy parity between the two countries makes them equal trading partners, with a high motivation on both sides to expand the energy trade relationship.

Since 1961, China's aggregate energy consumption has been growing at about 8 percent per year, again roughly equivalent to Japan's energy consumption growth rate during the same period. Japan's annual consumption reached a peak in 1973 and has since declined somewhat under the impact of higher prices for oil imports. Growth of energy consumption in the Middle East is marginally higher than in China. Other Asian centrally planned economy countries (principally North Korea) have been expanding energy consumption at about the same rate as the PRC, but they rely on oil imports for part of the growth. In sum, then, the pace of China's energy consumption growth has been very high since 1961, despite the depression in the national economy caused by the Cultural Revolution, the succession crisis, and the Tangshan earthquake. This rapid expansion in commercial energy consumption has helped to stimulate industrial and economic growth. Continued rapid growth in energy consumption will occur for the next two decades, perhaps at a slightly more modest pace. This may be good news for the Chinese domestic economy, but will place a low ceiling on energy commodity export potential. Unlike the OPEC countries, China has a very large population. Rising living standards accelerate the consumption of commercial energy fuels and limit the availability of such fuels for export. One has only to visit a Chinese city and see streams of carters moving goods by hand in the noonday sun to understand the potential demand for petroleum in China.

Disaggregation of energy consumption statistics by fuel shows that a surprising 63 percent of commercial energy consumption in 1976 was in the form of lump coal (Table 18.6). The entire economy is still heavily dependent on coal, which is burned under boilers in factories, in locomotives, and in homes for heat and cooking. Coal consumption rose at more than 6 percent from 1961 to 1976, in sharp contrast to the industrial market economy countries, where coal consumption has remained relatively constant until recently. This pattern is quite atypical for Third World areas that tend to rely heavily on oil. Indeed, China consumes more coal each year than all the Third World countries combined. Oil and gas combined supplied about 34 percent of commercial energy consumption in 1976, up from 13 percent in 1961. This trend toward greater reliance on oil and gas, combined with still increasing coal consumption, will continue through at least the mid-1980's. The proportion of coal in aggregate energy consumption will continue to decline slowly.

Electric power consumption in China is low relative to the total, at about 3–5 percent in 1978.* Furthermore, the contribution of electric power to energy consumption has risen only slowly, from 2.6 percent in 1961. This situation is particularly serious in view of the relatively large proportion of energy consumed in the industrial sector of the economy. Electricity is a "high-grade" energy commodity, relatively easy to control, efficient in application, and essential to many industrial processes as well as to personal comfort. The addition of a single, low-wattage bulb in many Chinese households, for example, has extended the day and changed life-styles. Electric power consumption has grown at 11 percent per year since 1961, high by world standards, but about the same as the growth rate in various regions of the Third World. As a point of comparison, world electric power consumption represents about 10 percent of total energy consumption, twice the contribution of the Chinese electric power industry. This demonstrates that in order to achieve their modernization objectives, Chinese energy planners must invest heavily in the expansion of the electric power industry over the next several decades.

Beyond these rough inferential statistics, we know very little about energy consumption patterns in the Chinese economy, particularly at the micro-level. The U.S. Central Intelligence Agency has attempted a disaggregation of Chinese energy consumption statistics by sector.[6] The CIA figures suggest that, in 1974, industry and construction consumed 62 percent of commercial energy supplies, agriculture 6 percent, transportation 5 percent, and residential-commercial uses 27 percent. Even if this breakdown was approximately correct in 1974, patterns of energy consumption are changing rapidly, in unknown directions. For example, development policy has recently stressed agricultural mechanization and transportation. The impact on consumption patterns of agricultural mechanization would be substantial, since Chinese agriculture is at present very energy-nonintensive. A further CIA effort to disaggregate each consumption sector by the contribution of various energy fuels is fanciful at best and misleading at worst. The truth is that we lack an empirical

---

*Recent official claims place 1978 electric power consumption (excluding production and transmission losses) at 225 bkwh, some 60 percent higher than previous foreign estimates. The contribution of electric power to energy consumption and the electric power consumption growth rate may therefore be somewhat higher than indicated in Table 10.4. But even at the higher figure, electric power represented no more than 5 percent of aggregate commercial energy consumption.

foundation for firm analysis of Chinese energy consumption patterns beyond the most aggregate levels.

Our ignorance of real energy consumption patterns in Chinese society is a serious hindrance to accurate analysis of the Chinese energy system, and affects the reliability of energy balance projections as well. For example, some energy analysts have suggested that China is relatively inefficient in energy use, compared to other societies and the size of the Chinese economy, measured in dollars of gross national product.[7] The validity of this generalization, however, is contingent both on the accuracy of consumption statistics used for the PRC and on the validity of GNP as a measure of China's level of economic activity. The Chinese government has, as a matter of public policy, restricted the growth of the money economy, encouraging local barter systems and maintaining tight control of monetary expansion to prevent inflation. The PRC may, therefore, be a relatively efficient user of money, rather than an inefficient user of energy. The point is that the level of uncertainty overshadows the range of variation in such comparisons. The PRC has opened its doors to a new tide of foreign visitors and scholars and is rapidly loosening control on the information that may be released to foreigners or through the public media. Perhaps the next large study of China's energy system should concentrate on the problem of energy consumption.

Per Capita Energy Consumption

The same information constraints that apply to comparative analysis of aggregate energy consumption apply to per capita energy consumption as well. The statistics for per capita energy consumption are purely inferential averages derived from aggregate consumption divided by current population. The quantities of commercial energy commodities available to the "average" Chinese citizen are only a small fraction of average per capita consumption figures, since most of the energy used in Chinese society is consumed in industry and other production or commercial activities. Industrial consumption of energy does contribute indirectly to personal living standards. But the availability of commercial energy commodities at the individual level in Chinese society is still only marginally higher than it was in preindustrial society.

In contrast to the large aggregate scale of the Chinese energy system, on both the production and consumption sides of the energy balance the People's Republic is still very much a Third World country in terms of per capita energy consumption. In fact, in 1976, Chinese per capita energy consumption was closely comparable to average per capita energy consumption in the Third World as a whole, even allowing for discrepancies in the figures compared in Table 10.5. The fact that China consumes large quantities of noncommercial energy fuels (firewood, dung, straw, etc.) does not alter the validity of this comparison. Other Third World regions also still rely heavily on noncommercial fuels, particularly in the rural areas. The comparison illustrates most graphically that China is still a country with a "dual energy personality," large and growing in aggregate terms, but poor in per capita terms.

Comparative growth rates for per capita energy consumption do indicate that the PRC has made some progress on this score. From 1961 to 1976, China's average per capita energy consumption grew at 6.2 percent per year, faster than any other region except the Middle East, and just under the pace of the famous Japanese growth spurt. The PRC started in 1949 with one of the lowest per capita energy consumption figures in the world (37 kilograms coal equivalent per capita) and had multiplied this initial figure 15 times by 1978 (540 kgce/capita), an implied growth rate of 9 percent per year for the intervening period. China is now midway among Third World regions in per capita energy consumption, doing somewhat better than Africa or the rest of Asia. The PRC is still at the bottom of the heap among centrally planned economy countries, and will have to increase per capita energy consumption by another order of magnitude to achieve current Soviet levels. To achieve that objective would require an energy production infrastructure twice as large as any the world has yet witnessed, assuming that Peking wished to maintain energy self-sufficiency and avoid heavy energy commodity imports. Energy-efficient life-styles will obviously be important in China for some time to come, as will the family planning program.

A glance at the figures for per capita consumption by fuel reinforces this conclusion. The absolute consumption figures mean very little at the individual level, because of the heavy use of energy commodities in industry. But the relative growth rates are indicative that China has done well since 1961 in expanding per capita coal, petroleum, and natural gas consumption. Once again, the record in the electric power industry is less than encouraging. Even at a growth rate of nearly 9 percent per year during the period, by 1976 *average per capita consumption of electric power was lower than any other region.* I have argued throughout this book that during the 1980's and 1990's electric power must be one of the high-growth energy industries in China. The comparative per capita electric power statistics support this conclusion.

It might be pointed out that China's general perspective on world energy problems and the implications of the energy crisis are broadly supported by the tables in this chapter. Chinese analysts tend to view the world energy crisis in terms of the maldistribution of available energy

TABLE 10.5
Per Capita Energy Consumption by Region, 1976

Region	Coal Kgce	Coal Growth	Petroleum Kg	Petroleum Growth	Natural gas Cu m	Natural gas Growth	Electricity Kwh	Electricity Growth	Total Kgce	Total Growth
Market economies	1,507	−0.6%	2,101	5.0%	1,092	4.0%	6,077	5.6%	6,388	3.1%
North America	2,391	1.6	3,342	2.9	2,630	2.1	10,138	5.0	11,395	2.5
Western Europe	1,075	−3.3	1,552	6.9	527	20.1	4,218	5.6	4,289	3.3
Oceania	2,052	1.0	1,485	5.2	318	83.1	4,775	5.6	4,953	3.7
Japan	700	0.5	1,776	12.0	96	13.9	4,538	8.6	3,679	7.7
Planned economies	1,093	1.2	365	6.8	273	8.7	1,300	6.2	2,030	3.4
Soviet Union	1,890	0.6	1,234	6.0	1,085	8.8	4,285	7.1	5,259	4.0
Eastern Europe	3,362	1.5[a]	707	10.3[a]	582	9.0[a]	3,443	6.9[a]	5,240	3.6[a]
China[b]	*269*	*4.0*	*67*	*13.8*	*34*	*14.2*	*119*	*8.5*	*427*	*6.2*
Other Asian CPEs	822	6.0[a]	33	4.8[a]	n.a.	n.a.	470	3.9[a]	904	5.7[a]
Third World	78	1.2	175	4.5	48	6.7	305	7.5	426	4.2
Africa	186	1.1	114	4.5	18	19.3	337	5.4	397	3.0
Asia	105	1.3	81	7.0	12	6.6	184	9.5	251	4.1
Central America	68	3.0	579	2.1	206	2.6	878	6.8	1,265	2.5
South America	53	1.2	429	3.3	63	2.1	798	5.2	868	3.4
Middle East	69	1.2	485	6.4	263	16.5	548	9.9	1,169	8.0
World	671	−0.2	603	4.6	318	4.4	1,720	5.2	2,069	2.7

Sources: Per capita consumption data are from *WES* 15 and *WES* 21. Average annual growth rates are from 1961 to 1976, tabulated as in Table 10.3.
[a] Weighted average regional per capita consumption growth rates using simple exponential growth equation from 1961 to 1976, with single-year end-points.
[b] Energy end-use is not strictly comparable to U.N. data (see text).

commodities, rather than in terms of growth rates or a technological impasse (Chapter 2). A comparison of Tables 10.2, 10.3, and 10.5 lends considerable weight to this argument. World energy resources are about equally distributed among the industrial market economy countries, the centrally planned economy countries, and the developing countries. The Third World share of coal resources is disproportionately low, perhaps owing to a lack of adequate mineral exploration. But the Third World share of oil and gas resources and hydropower potential is roughly commensurate with the population of Third World regions. To be sure, these resources are not evenly scattered within the Third World. But developing countries do not face an unfair dearth of energy resources. This conclusion is reinforced by the comparative primary energy production statistics in Table 10.3. Developing countries already produce about one-third of world energy output, about half of which comes from the Middle East. At current growth rates, primary energy production in the Third World regions, even outside the Middle East, is overtaking the industrial market economy countries. Energy consumption, however, is quite another matter. The Third World consumes only 12 percent of the world's available energy supplies (17 percent including China and the other Asian centrally planned economies). This is not commensurate with the contribution of the developing countries to primary energy production or to their natural share of world energy resources. Average per capita energy consumption in the Third World is only 21 percent of the world average and 7 percent of average per capita consumption in the industrial market economy countries. The artificial differentials in consumption levels among various regions are placing enormous stresses on the global energy distribution system. OPEC and the energy crisis of 1973–74 are symptomatic of this stress. It should be expected that Third World countries will continue to exert pressure in the direction of a more equitable energy commodity distribution system throughout the remainder of this century. Furthermore, the solution of the energy problem in the industrial countries cannot be to move further in the direction of energy commodity imports, the trend that caused the stress to begin with.

Energy Commodity Trade

I have provided the statistics in Table 10.6 as a tonic for people whose blood pressure rises at the thought of Chinese oil exports. In 1976, the PRC exported just 3 percent of total primary energy production and about 10 percent of crude petroleum production. That represented one-half of one percent of the world energy market (by volume). Further-

TABLE 10.6
World Energy Commodity Trade by Region, 1976

Region	Coal		Crude oil		Refined oil[a]		Natural gas		Total[a]	
	Mmtce	Balance	Mmt	Balance	Mmt	Balance	Bcm	Balance	Mmtce	Balance
Market economies	39.2	3.6%	1,139.2	67.4%	46.5	2.9%	28.4	3.4%	1,822.9	37.9%
North America	-50.4	-8.1	278.1	37.4	71.1	8.9	-0.7	-0.1	464.3	17.1
Western Europe	60.6	15.4	623.9	93.5	-19.0	-3.2	21.2	11.0	976.0	62.1
Oceania	-31.3	-39.1	11.3	34.0	-0.2	-0.8	0.0	0.0	-15.1	-12.0
Japan	60.3	76.3	225.9	100.0	-5.4	-2.6	7.9	73.2	397.7	95.9
Planned economies	-41.6	-3.0	-36.8	-2.6	-41.8	-8.4	-1.1	-3.7	-161.2	-5.9
Soviet Union	-20.5	-4.0	-104.4	-20.1	-35.9	-10.2	-13.1	-4.5	-247.0	-14.8
Eastern Europe	-20.5	-5.3	76.9	78.9	-6.9	-8.2	12.0	18.8	98.6	17.2
China	*-0.3*	*-0.1*	*-8.2*	*-9.8*	*-0.9*	*-1.4*	*0.0*	*0.0*	*-14.0*	*-2.7*
Other Asian CPEs	-0.3	-0.5	n.a.	n.a.	2.1	n.a.	n.a.	n.a.	2.8	4.8
Third World	3.0	1.3	-1,127.3	-65.2	-171.0	-33.1	-27.3	-22.3	-1,923.2	64.8
Africa	-4.3	-5.3	-230.0	-80.2	-1.2	-2.6	-9.2	-55.6	-356.1	-66.4
Asia	2.0	1.7	16.4	13.9	-7.6	-7.5	-9.1	-39.5	2.9	1.0
Central America	0.5	5.4	10.0	5.4	-108.2	-56.1	0.3	0.8	-121.6	-37.0
South America	4.5	46.4	40.5	47.5	1.5	1.9	0.3	2.6	66.7	42.3
Middle East	0.3	3.3	-964.2	-88.1	-55.5	-48.2	-9.6	-22.9	-1,515.1	-89.7
World[b]	216.6	8.8	1,591.8	55.9	313.1	12.9	132.5	10.1	3,223.4	39.6

Note: Regional trade in energy commodities is expressed as net imports (i.e. minus equals net exports). The term "balance" refers to the percent of production exported or the percent of consumption imported. The table excludes net trade in electric power, which is negligible at the regional level. Net electric power trade is included in net total trade statistics. Net import figures are based on data in *WES 21*. All data for China are the author's estimates.

[a]Bunkers are counted as exports. Thus imports and exports do not necessarily balance.

[b]World trade is measured as imports only. Balance of world trade refers to the ratio of imports to world consumption.

more, the situation did not change much between 1976 and 1978. Most regions import or export in excess of 20 percent of the size of their domestic energy systems. World energy commodity trade across international boundaries represents about 40 percent of energy consumption. China still has a long way to go in developing energy commodity exports before it will affect the world energy market to any significant degree. This is the basic logic behind the argument that the PRC will be a significant *regional* energy exporter but will not be significant in the world market. Under the most optimistic projections offered in Chapter 24, Chinese energy commodity exports will peak at about 5 percent of the world market, significant at about the same level as Venezuela during that country's peak oil-export years. Venezuela exports about 85 percent of its energy trade to countries in the contiguous regions.

Coal, and perhaps natural gas, are just as likely as crude oil to be significant components of China's future export mix. The PRC still exports less than one percent of total coal production. If the coal industry continues to expand as projected, increasing quantities of coal will be available for export. The main difficulty facing coal exports will be finding the market. The Japanese government is planning expansion of coal imports in an effort to diversify its import mix. But Australia is also expanding coal production for export, and the competition for the Japanese market will be intense. In contrast to oil, there is no cartel arrangement in the international coal trade to ensure prices at a given level.

Natural gas is another Chinese energy industry with untapped export potential. Japan is also expanding its liquefied natural gas imports, and there has been talk of a deal in which Japanese companies would build an LNG plant at one of the coastal oilfields in China in return for a guaranteed annual export of gas (Chapter 6). However, a number of other Asian countries have LNG projects under way, with an eye to the potential Japanese and American gas markets.[8] Malaysia, Indonesia, Australia, and Siberia are all likely competitors for a market that is still limited by safety constraints and the high cost of transport and harbor facilities. There is some evidence of overbuilding in potential LNG exporting countries during the late 1970's. This situation could be reversed, of course, as world crude oil prices continue to rise, or in the event of a serious oil shortage. In contrast to the oil and coal trade between China and Japan, there has been no apparent movement toward LNG trade for the last several years.

The limits on coal and gas markets leave crude petroleum in a dominant position in the Chinese export mix. This is another argument for Peking to favor joint offshore development projects. If joint projects could open up significant offshore oil production, the PRC would be in a position to expand crude oil exports during the 1980's and 1990's, at little cost to the domestic energy system. Domestic oil needs would continue to be met by onland fields. Once again, this stengthens the link between joint offshore development projects and energy commodity exports. I would project that if no significant offshore development takes place, China's oil exports will remain at 10–15 percent of production, and the production curve itself will be seriously constrained by resource availability. The remaining 85–90 percent of China's onland oil production will be required for domestic consumption. The only other alternative would be to restrict economic and industrial growth, not a likely option, given the mood in Peking.

This concludes our discussion of China's energy balance within the context of the world and regional energy systems. The interested reader is referred to the Statistical Profile for detail on each energy sector and industry and for a complete statistical array. At the end of the 1970's, China had already achieved third rank among the world's national energy systems, counting both the production and consumption sides of the energy balance. The PRC has plentiful reserves and resources for continued and balanced growth in its energy industries. However, domestic consumption requirements and persistently low per capita energy consumption standards place heavy demands on available energy production. Production is currently rising somewhat faster than consumption, creating surplus energy commodities available for export. But the size of the surplus is limited by continuing consumption pressure and the early stage of development of the Chinese oil and gas industries. In terms of comparative growth rates, all sectors of the Chinese energy system have performed well since 1961 by world standards.

Chapter 11

Domestic Energy Development: Taching Oilfield

The Strategic Importance of Taching Oilfield

A comprehensive study of China's international energy policies requires some understanding of the constraints imposed by the organization and capabilities of the domestic energy production system. It would be impossible, without providing an additional volume on each energy industry, to provide an accurate and detailed organizational analysis of the entire domestic energy infrastructure in the PRC. Given the problems of data-gathering and access to organizational information, no foundation has yet been laid for an adequate summary analysis of the structure of the energy sector. For example, much more research will be required before adequate output statistics will be available for the electric power and natural gas industries, let alone the intricacies of organization—management, finance, labor force, planning, distribution network, and so on.[1]

Another approach to the problem of domestic constraints, and the one used for this study, is to choose a particularly strategic energy production unit for detailed structural analysis, drawing general if tentative conclusions about the constraints imposed by the domestic energy system. Taching oilfield provides a particularly convenient example for detailed analysis in this study. Located on the Sungliao Plain in Heilungkiang province, Taching is China's largest single energy unit in terms of output. (See Map 11.1.) According to recent CIA figures, Taching provided about half of China's annual crude oil production in the mid-1970's.[2]

Taching has occupied a central position in China's energy development since the early 1960's. It is located just to the north of China's industrial heartland, reducing the cost of transportation and facilitating flexible supply to refineries and industries in the Northeast and Manchuria. Crude oil production increases at Taching averaged about 25 percent per year for 15 years (1960–75), as discoveries raised reserves to the status of a "giant" field by international standards. The timing of its development was critical to the entire Chinese economy. The PRC had

Map 11.1 Taching oilfield and the energy infrastructure of northeast China.

been about 50 percent dependent on the Soviet Union for petroleum supplies and was threatened with disruption of its industrial and transport sectors by the Sino-Soviet split that developed in 1960. But the timing of Taching's development would have been important in any case, providing a launching platform for modernization of China's energy sector. Even if Taching declines in importance relative to offshore oil development, or perhaps gives way to oil and natural gas development in China's interior, its crude oil will have provided the basis for modernization of Chinese industry and agriculture—petrochemicals, fertilizer, transport fuel, electric power, and many other applications. And development of the field has also produced a reservoir of human talents for Chinese development—oil technology, skilled personnel, management experience, distribution networks, and geological knowledge.

Taching oilfield is also of direct strategic importance to the People's Republic of China at the international level. The oilfield is strategically vulnerable to attack by the Soviet Union. It lies very close to a sharply contested area of the Sino-Soviet border, where armed clashes have repeatedly taken place. Massive armies confront each other along the Amur River (Heilungkiang) border. Taching is vulnerable to Soviet attack from three sides (Mongolia, the Amur River, and the maritime provinces). China is said to maintain some 20 armies of 40,000 soldiers each in the northeast, while the Soviets have stationed 20 heavily mechanized divisions in this sector. The Soviet armaments include tactical nuclear weapons, and both sides are believed to have intermediate-range ballistic missiles (IRBM's) deployed in the area for strikes on airfields and critical industrial installations.[3] Some sources, including a Soviet pilot who defected to Japan in a MiG-25 in September 1976, have indicated that Moscow would employ blitzkrieg tactics in the area, with a sharp attack that would shut down Chinese industry throughout the northeast in a matter of a few days to a month.[4] Peking must, therefore, be highly sensitive to the vulnerability of Taching to direct attack in the event of open hostilities.

Earlier chapters have already indicated the importance of Taching crude oil in China's international political posture. Oil exports to Japan, critical in diverting Japanese attention from Soviet joint-development proposals in Siberia, have been principally Taching crude. Taching has thus represented a Chinese counterweight to Tjumen and Yakut oil and natural gas development for the Japanese market. Crude oil production at Taching grew so rapidly that it outstripped the capacity of Chinese industry to refine, distribute, and utilize the oil. Temporarily, at least, the crude oil surplus could be bargained directly for political influence (and hard cash) throughout East and Southeast Asia. Crude oil exports covered the cost of massive equipment and complete plant purchases from Japan in the early 1970's, smoothing the transition to close diplomatic and economic ties between the region's two most powerful countries. Petroleum exports to North Korea and Vietnam have strengthened Peking's influence vis-à-vis the Soviet presence in these countries. China has exported oil to Thailand and the Philippines, and appears to dominate the Hong Kong energy market. The Taching surplus was critical to all these regional political moves, either providing the exported oil directly, or substituting for oil exported from other fields. In political terms, therefore, Taching has helped ease China's transition to its new status as an Asian power rivaling its industrial neighbor Japan.

Finally, Taching has been important within China as an organizational model in industrial development. It exemplified the Chinese communist approach to industrialization. The construction of the oilfield was accomplished at breakneck speed, using the method of "concentrated attack" to relieve critical bottlenecks. It was built using the most primitive equipment at first, and constantly recycling its surplus directly into capital expansion and equipment modernization. It was built entirely with Chinese hands and primarily with Chinese technical knowledge, exemplifying the spirit of "self-reliance." The oilfield provided a proving ground for Chinese management techniques and a training ground for petroleum and energy specialists. Taching developed a flexible organizational style, permitting mutual adaptation among different levels in the planning apparatus. Oilfield management did prove vulnerable to vicissitudes in the political climate at the center, suffering serious political disruption of production during the Cultural Revolution, and again at the height of the succession crisis in 1976. But on the whole, Taching has proved very adaptive during its period of growth from a ragged band of ill-equipped workers to a complex industrial organization that absorbs the most advanced technologies; manages a large-scale integrated network of producing fields, refineries, and transportation facilities; and sends regular delegations of petroleum scientists abroad to consult, learn, and even advise. Taching's metamorphosis took just fifteen years. It is in this sense that the oilfield has been treated as an industrial model in the PRC.

Taching has proved, therefore, of strategic importance to Chinese energy development from a number of perspectives. Because of its importance, and because of its status as an industrial model, a relatively great amount of detail has been provided by the Chinese press on the development of the oilfield. This information has been supplemented by first-hand reports from foreign visitors who have inspected Taching and by technical information that has filtered out through the crude oil export network. The wealth of information on Taching provides a good background against which to assess the domestic constraints on China's international energy policies.

The History of the Oilfield

Taching is situated on a frigid and windswept plain in the northeasternmost corner of China in Heilungkiang province. Temperatures plunge to −10° centigrade or more in the dead of winter. Oil was initially discovered there in the late 1950's, probably in 1957.[5] Soviet technicians drew up the initial plans for development of Taching between 1957 and 1960, but virtually nothing happened beyond surveys and development planning before the withdrawal of Soviet technicians in 1960.[6]

Then in response to the withdrawal of technical assistance and under an imminent threat of the loss of petroleum product imports from the Soviet Union, China launched a massive development of Taching in 1960. At an emergency meeting, the Party Central Committee directed 100,000 oil workers to gather on the Sungliao Plain in February 1960.[7] The workers came by rail from China's established oilfields—Yumen in Kansu province and Karamai in Sinkiang. They brought with them a motley assortment of equipment. Some of the drilling rigs dated to the 1940's. The oil workers were moved in complete teams from other fields and disembarked at Anta from freight trains that rattled up an existing rail link to this otherwise deserted area. The workers brought with them virtually no housing accommodations and many lived in holes in the ground for the first few months.[8]

The bitterness of the Chinese government at the suddenness of the Soviet withdrawal has been retold in the Chinese press a thousand times:

China was being bullied by the imperialists and revisionists because of its dependence on foreign oil. It would not achieve economic independence and carry forward its industrialization if this situation was not changed. The great needs of China's economic development and the terrible weakness of its petroleum industry stood in sharp contradiction.[9]

The 1205 drilling team led by Wang Chin-hsi came to the new oilfield in the spring of 1960. On their way to Taching, they saw buses carrying large gas bags on top and tractors standing idle in the fields for lack of oil. This heightened their indignation against imperialism and modern revisionism which tried to bully China by imposing an oil blockade. Seeing a vast sea of oil in their mind's eye, they felt their strength surge. Wang Chin-hsi said, "I simply want to knock open the earth with my fist to let the black oil gush out, and dump our backwardness in petroleum into the Pacific."

The sixty-ton drilling machine arrived. But there was no hoisting gear. Wang Chin-hsi and other workers went into action and, by dint of physical effort, moved the whole derrick to the drilling site many kilometers from the railway station. They got the machine in working order before the water pipeline was laid. Nevertheless they began to dig. When the well water was used up, they fetched it from a distance. Through five days and nights of strenuous labor, they completed drilling the first well. The leadership at a higher level awarded the drilling team the honored title "iron drilling team" for their high sense of revolutionary responsibility and hard work and called on all the pioneering workers to learn from them. The call set the whole oilfield in motion, each group trying to overtake the other.[10]

The first well was completed at the oilfield on April 14, 1960, and the first oil shipment by rail was made on June 1.[11] These events preceded the recorded withdrawals of Soviet technicians in July, but the technicians may have ceased to function before their departure, and the Chinese government must have been aware of the impending withdrawal by as early as February. China has since claimed that the first oil refinery at Anta was completed in a single year and that the infrastructure for the oilfield was basically in place by 1963.[12] This would indicate that preparations were well under way for oilfield development before the departure of Soviet technicians. In any case, although some of the accounts of the opening of Taching may involve retrospective reporting and apocryphal tales, there is little doubt that it was done under adverse conditions.

Peking also claimed that China was "basically self-sufficient in petroleum" as early as 1963.[13] However, the trade statistics in Part II, Chapter 21, show that self-sufficiency in petroleum was not reached until 1965. Although the earliest self-sufficiency claims were not literally true, they did capture the spirit of the moment, for China was managing to beat the loss of petroleum imports from the Soviet Union. Taching production was climbing fast—perhaps faster than the wildest hopes of China's energy planners. The end of the Chinese energy crisis was in sight. Taching was mentioned by name for the first time in the Chinese press in May 1964.[14] The name means "Great Celebration," which may have reference to the fact that the oilfield was scheduled to be developed starting around the time of the October 1959 celebration of the tenth anniversary of the founding of the People's Republic. There was doubtless great celebration in official Chinese petroleum circles at the magnitude of oil discoveries at Taching, at the timeliness of its development, and at the great breakthrough it represented for the Chinese petroleum industry.

Taching became a model unit for all Chinese industry in 1964. References to Taching began to appear in the Chinese press on a regular basis, and by 1966 a campaign was under way throughout Chinese industry to study the Taching approach to industrialization.[15] (We shall return to discussion of the Taching model below.) The importance with which Peking viewed this advance in the petroleum industry was reflected in a new sense of confidence about the extent of China's energy resources. As early as 1964, Chinese trade officials made overtures toward Japan regarding the possible sale of Taching crude on the international market.[16] New production records kept rolling in from Saerhtu, and in 1966 Wang Chin-hsi and the number 1205 drilling team surpassed 100,000 meters of drilling in a single year, breaking the American record and nearly doubling the previous Soviet mark.[17] The refinery at Saerhtu was expanded considerably into an entire petrochemical complex, producing chemicals, synthetics, and fertilizer, as well as energy petroleum products.[18] Taching had arrived, and the stage was set for the Cultural Revolution.

The first event of political importance during the Cultural Revolution at Taching was that the Peking Petrochemical Institute moved there in 1966.[19] The move was made for a variety of motives, but it reflected the shift in the center of gravity of China's petroleum industry from the oldest oilfield (Yumen) to the newest and most successful. It also reflected the new political emphasis in education on direct contact with the masses and direct involvement in production. The result was to transplant a virulent strain of the new Peking student radicalism, with direct political ties to radical campuses such as Tsinghua University in Peking, into the heart of the Chinese energy industry. Although no foreigners visited Taching during the Cultural Revolution, and we have very little direct evidence of what occurred there, it is known that political activities at the oilfield were intense, that Taching was not effectively shielded from the storm center in Peking, and that massive numbers of oil workers (perhaps 10,000) dropped their jobs and climbed on trains heading for rallies in Tien An Men Square.[20] The result was that, in 1967, Taching's growth rate, which Peking earlier touted at over 30 percent per year, dropped sharply; this inflicted serious temporary setbacks on the entire petroleum industry.

Taching's production recovered as suddenly as it had dropped off in 1967. By the end of 1968 the oilfield was back to near-normal production schedules, and by 1969 rapid growth had resumed.[21] But the Taching leadership may have lost favor in the interim, for there was a temporary hiatus in Taching's status as an industrial model. No Taching leaders attended the Ninth Party Congress, in contrast to the rather prominent participation by Chen Yung-kuei from Tachai, China's agricultural model.[22] Evidently, Peking learned during the height of the

Cultural Revolution that political radicalism had to be directed toward promoting production ("grasp the revolution, promote production") rather than disrupting it, especially in the industries at the cutting edge of China's modernization. If China again experiences such intense political upheavals, the center may bend considerable effort toward the insulation of key sectors of industry from the effects of the political storm.

Sweeping changes in organizational structure were introduced at Taching during the course of the political upheavals of the Cultural Revolution. "Mao Tse-tung Thought propaganda teams" were organized to attack the existing administrative and party structure at all levels: "In response to Chairman Mao's great call: 'The working class must exercise leadership in everything,' Mao Tse-tung Thought propaganda teams organized by the Taching oil workers went to all the schools to lead struggle-criticism-transformation in the superstructure."[23]

As the existing administrative structure crumbled under this concerted attack, it was replaced by "three-in-one revolutionary committees," which became the core of a new management.[24] The oilfield itself came under the administrative jurisdiction of the Taching Oilfield Revolutionary Committee, and revolutionary committees were also introduced down through every administrative component, such as the refineries and living communities. After the Ninth Party Congress (April 1–14, 1969), the Party reasserted its leadership at all levels by the introduction of Party committees, which stood beside, and oversaw, the revolutionary committees. During 1978, as part of the new modernization drive, the revolutionary committees were completely disbanded and replaced once again by conventional administrative apparatus.

Petroleum production at Taching has boomed in the period since the Cultural Revolution, laying a foundation for the next stage in China's petroleum development, the exploitation of offshore oil reserves. From 1969 through 1975 the emphasis was placed primarily on production rather than on political struggle or organizational innovation. The Tenth Party Congress (August 24–28, 1973), and the anti–Lin Piao campaign of late 1973, which were the two main political events of the post-Cultural Revolution period, were dealt with in a ritualized manner at Taching and had little if any impact on production or management.

Taching's crude oil output grew at about 20 percent per annum from 1969 to 1975, racing ahead of refinery capacity and stretching the petroleum equipment and transportation industries to the limit. A new zone was opened for production in January 1973.[25] The capacity of the Taching General Petrochemical Plant was doubled in 1972.[26] A 1,152-kilometer crude oil pipeline was completed from Taching to the coastal port of Chinhuangtao (on the Pohai Gulf) between the winter of 1970 and September 1973.[27] A parallel line was built to Tiehling (in Liaoning) and began supplying a refinery there in 1974. This line was extended to the oil port at Dairen, where an oil dock with handling facilities for tankers of 100,000 deadweight tons (dwt) was constructed to facilitate the export of Taching crude oil to Japan.[28] An extension of the Taching–Chinhuangtao pipeline was laid to Peking, an additional 355 kilometers, where Taching crude is refined at the Peking General Petrochemical Works or diverted to the Shih-lou railway depot for shipment to refineries in other parts of China.[29] A small-diameter pipeline, possibly for refined products, was laid from the Dairen line directly to North Korea in 1975. By 1976, Taching's production had reached more than 40 million tons per year, the Taching refinery had expanded to a capacity of 5 million tons per year, and the pipeline network was capable of carrying some 24 million tons per year to coastal ports and refineries throughout the northeast.[30]

In 1976 and 1977, however, Taching's development was once again disturbed by a series of seismic and political events completely outside its control. A major earthquake (7.3 on the Richter scale) in February 1975 may have damaged some Taching facilities.[31] There were reports from Taiwan, since discounted, of serious fires and explosions at Taching in the spring of 1976. On July 28, 1976, tragedy struck northeast China in the form of an earthquake of magnitude 8 centered near Tangshan (Hopei province), which killed more than half a million people and seriously damaged the industrial infrastructure in the region. Direct earthquake damage at Taching was unlikely, but the pipeline to Peking may have been broken, and coastal oil ports were damaged.[32] The regional coal supply was disrupted, which may have caused some industries to shift to oil for process heat, straining the supply of petroleum and interrupting crude oil shipments to Japan and the Philippines.

Meanwhile, political turbulence in Peking reached the oilfield, disturbing management patterns and causing a succession of reevaluations of development policy in the petroleum industry. Subsequent events have shown that the political struggle in 1976 was part of the succession crisis generated by the deaths of Chou En-lai and Mao Tse-tung in a single year. Premier Chou died in January 1976, setting off an attack on Teng Hsiao-ping, a Vice-Premier who had been purged during the Cultural Revolution and then rehabilitated. The "radical" faction in the Politburo evidently used petroleum development, crude oil exports, and petrochemical plant imports as the basis for their attack on Teng (and by implication on Chou's development policies).[33] Minister of Petroleum and Chemical Industries Kang Shih-en dropped from public view during the anti-Teng campaign, and a wave of political-criticism meetings swept Taching and other major oilfields and refining centers.[34] Taching's status as an industrial model for China was under attack, as were policies that advocated greater interaction with Japan and other Asian countries in petroleum trade and development projects.

By the time of Mao Tse-tung's death (September 9, 1976), Taching's image had apparently been considerably tarnished.[35] But the political tables in Peking were quickly turned as Hua Kuo-feng, a Chou protégé, was appointed Party Chairman to succeed Mao in October.[36] The "Shanghai radicals" (Chiang Ching, Wang Hung-wen, Chang Chun-chiao, and Yao Wen-yuan, dubbed the "Gang of Four" by the Chinese press) were arrested, purged from the Politburo, and attacked for their "disruption" of Taching and other industrial projects. The counterattack began with a debate over the political merits of the film "Pioneers," which depicts the development of Taching oilfield.[37] By December 1976 there was renewed stress on Taching as an industrial model, and an elaborate conference in Taching was planned; the conference, held in April 1977, drew 7,000 delegates from all branches of Chinese industry to the oilfield.[38] Speeches at the "National Conference on Learning from Taching in Industry" emphasized production, modernization, the need to draw on foreign technology, the utility of crude oil exports, and other aspects of the Taching model. The Shanghai radicals were vigorously attacked for their opposition to Taching-style industrialization, and especially for their opposition to crude oil exports and petroleum equipment purchases abroad. In particular, Chou En-lai's objective of a modern socialist industrial society by the turn of the century was emphasized as the key development slogan at the conference.[39]

These political events appear to have had a direct effect on Taching's production and management in 1976. The growth rate of crude oil production declined to less than 10 percent for the first time since the Cultural Revolution. Crude oil exports to Japan and the Philippines were also seriously affected in the spring of 1976, dropping below 1975 levels for the entire year. Once again, Taching proved vulnerable to political turbulence at the center.

But this time there were other factors that clouded the picture and made it difficult to separate the impact of political events from other aspects of Taching's development. In particular, reports have reached the foreign media through recent visitors to Taching that the oilfield may be reaching its natural peak production capacity, and that downward pressure on Taching's growth rate may be as much a matter of a reserves constraint as of political disruption.[40] "Stripper wells" (secondary recovery) are being installed, some of the older wells may have been closed, and water injection ratios have apparently increased. Shengli oilfield's growth rate ran well ahead of Taching's in 1976.[41] A precise projection of the oilfield production curve is impossible without knowledge of Taching's reserves, but CIA figures indicate that 273 million metric tons had been extracted from Taching by the end of 1976.[42] If recoverable resources at Taching are in the one billion metric ton range, absolute annual production would theoretically peak at 400–500 million tons cumulative output and then decline. That peak would be reached in about five years, perhaps as early as 1980. Thus, some slowing of the annual production growth rate would be expected by 1976–77 on the basis of the assumed resource constraint. However, Taching's resources are a closely guarded secret and may be greater than one billion tons of recoverable crude petroleum.

Resources and Production

Taching's geological characteristics are of considerable interest because of the lack of Tertiary Period sea moraines, which have constituted the principal oil-bearing strata in the Middle East and other oil-rich areas. China's lack of sea moraine sedimentary structures led Western geologists to the mistaken conclusion that the area would be without substantial petroleum deposits.[43] However, Taching was formed by lake moraines, rather than by sea moraines. The oil-bearing strata are sandstone, permitting osmosis of the oil within the formations. The formations themselves have been fractured by earth movement into relatively small segments, making accurate drilling within 3° inclination of the intended target a standard requirement on the Taching fields.[44] The segmented nature of oil-bearing strata may also account for the rejection of the "spread the net widely" method of exploration and the adoption of what the Chinese call the method of "concentrated attack."[45] But despite the fractured nature of individual deposits, Taching covers a large aggregate area and should be counted among the world's large oilfields:

> The region in which the Ta-ching oil field is developing includes the area from Harbin westward to Mao-mao-ch'i, a large plain which includes the basins of the Nonni River (Nen-chiang) and Sungari River (Sung-hua-chiang). The distribution of oil formations encompasses the wide area centered around the Sha-erh-t'u station, which extends north toward Ssu-fang-t'ai, and south toward Lung Feng, Fu-yu, Ta-t'ung, Ta-lai, and Fu-lung-ch'uan.[46]

The Taching oil fields consist of many oil fields with relatively small oil formations scattered across the moraine basin. The characteristics of these relatively small oil formations are different. These conditions are quite different from the wide expanse of super-rich oil formations spreading in wide areas as seen in the

Mid-East. (In spite of this, if the sum total of the deposits is large, collectively the fields can be called a large oil deposit field.) Taching could be termed a structure with many oil strata. As such there were difficulties in its development.[47]

The average depth of oil pools at Taching is somewhere around 1,000 meters below the surface, but the fractured structures vary in depth from 300 to 1,400 meters.[48] In 1965, it was claimed that a record well of over 4,500 meters (nearly three miles) was drilled.[49] But on the whole, Taching deposits could not be considered deep by world standards.

Considering the importance of Taching's proved and ultimate recoverable reserves to the overall development of the Chinese energy system, remarkably little solid geological research has been done outside China to provide a reasonable range of reserves estimates for the oilfield. Far more work has gone into analogue estimates of China's potential offshore oil and gas resources. A. A. Meyerhoff published an estimate in 1970 of 0.6–1.2 billion barrels (100–200 million metric tons approximately), but the Chinese have already produced more than 300 million tons cumulatively from Taching and the annual production level is still rising.[50] Meyerhoff's original estimate was based on a rough determination of the extent of oil-bearing reservoir sandstone in the Taching structure. In 1976 Meyerhoff raised his original estimate to 3 billion barrels (400 million metric tons) of recoverable crude oil resources. The U.S. Geological Survey is reportedly working on a study of China's hydrocarbon sediments, with detailed estimates of sediment area and volume for each major basin in the PRC. But no results of such a study have yet been released.

Other guesses at the size of Taching's reserves have been published, but without any confirming evidence with which to judge their validity.[51] Ling reports that Chinese authorities released a figure of one billion metric tons "potential reserves" for Taching in 1961, but his source was a Hong Kong communist newspaper, not the official Chinese press.[52]

Given the lack of solid research on the likely range of Taching's crude oil resources, any final judgment would be foolhardy. However, the shape of the production curve at Taching should provide some clues regarding the ultimate scale of resources, or at least their lower limit. Several assumptions could be made about Taching that are not applicable to other Chinese oilfields. First, we may safely assume that Peking has a fairly good idea itself of the range of ultimate recoverable resources at Taching, and some very detailed data on proved reserves. Second, in view of the history of the oilfield, it is safe to assume that Taching has been developed at the maximum possible rate, with crude oil production growth rates reaching the limit of China's ability to provide the necessary equipment and personnel for oilfield development. If these two assumptions are correct, then the shape of the production curve should indicate the rate of resource depletion.

It appears from CIA estimates for Taching crude oil production that the growth rate has been declining in 1976–77 at Taching to something less than 10 percent per year. If this decline in the annual growth rate continues for another year or two, the conclusion must be that Taching has begun to approach peak absolute production levels.

Assuming, as we have, that Peking has full knowledge of the scale of Taching reserves and has pushed oilfield development to the limit, the peak production level should occur at about 30–35 percent resource depletion. Production would then decline over successive years as extraction became increasingly difficult. In other words, ultimate recoverable reserves at the oilfield would amount to more than twice the level of cumulative production at the point of peak output. This argument would lead to the conclusion that economically recoverable resources at Taching are probably in the range of one to two billion metric tons. Proved reserves were probably well below one billion tons in 1977, although the ratio of proved to ultimate resources could be very high, given the intensive exploration effort that the Chinese have lavished on the oilfield.

This conclusion could be upset by either of two considerations. First, Taching's decline in annual production growth rate could be the result of political factors and therefore temporary. If the oilfield growth rate rises again to 15–20 percent in any year between 1977 and 1980, it must be assumed that resources are larger than one billion tons. Second, the production curve at Taching could turn out to be unusually flat, owing to the stratified and fractured nature of the trap structures. In this case, the period of peak ouput would be relatively protracted, as Chinese drillers found each of the many traps and continuously added new structures to the field. The continuous discovery of new traps would extend the life of the oilfield and raise the final estimate of recoverable resources.

It has been known for some time that Taching's crude oil production capacity far exceeds the capacity of refineries at the oilfield, necessitating the shipment of Taching crude to refineries in Peking, Shanghai, Nanking, Lanchow, Maoming, and Chungking.[53] The three refineries at the Taching oilfield proper handled 2–3 million tons in 1966, 4 million tons in 1970, and 5 million tons in 1973.[54] A 1976 estimate put total refinery capacity at 6 million metric tons per year, including 4.2 mmt/year at Saerhtu, 1.0 mmt/year at Chingchiaweitzu, and 0.7 mmt/year at Lamatien. Refinery expansion at Taching has included some units of foreign construction. Output-to-capacity ratios are probably very high, owing to the ready supply of crude, China's overall shortage of refinery capacity, and the general tendency of Chinese energy industries to produce at the limits of equipment capacity.

Taching crude oil may be characterized as very waxy, high in residue, and very low in sulfur. (See Table 6.2.) The low-sulfur quality has made it appealing as an import crude in Japan, which has air pollution problems in the major urban areas. But the waxiness of Taching crude has caused a series of refining problems in Japan, Thailand, and the Philippines. Refinery equipment in these countries has desulfurization processes that were designed to handle high-sulfur, low-viscosity Middle Eastern crudes. The additional investment required by high-viscosity Taching crude has dampened what might have been a very enthusiastic seller's market for Chinese oil in Asia. Special handling equipment would include "coil" (heated) tankers, heated pipelines, and various wax-screening devices. The short-run solution has been to mix Taching crude with low-viscosity crude from the Middle East. In the long term, the waxiness of Taching crude and its high residual content may cause downward pressure on the price that the Chinese must accept on the international market. Direct burning of crude oil in steel mills and electric power plants is very wasteful of the lighter fractions and will also lead either to a lower price per ton or to partial refining.

The average productivity of oil wells at Taching is open to some question. One report claimed that average productivity was 500–700 barrels per day, or about 25,000–35,000 tons per year.[55] But this claim is open to some doubt, based on the number of wells and the estimated aggregate output of the oilfield. Although the exact number of wells is not known, it was estimated at 820 in 1965, 1,000 in 1968, 1,080 in 1969, and 4,069 in 1976.[56] That would put productivity closer to 10,000 metric tons per well per annum or less. The wells producing at 500–700 bbl/day were therefore unusually prolific for Taching, where the average is probably closer to 200 bbl/day. Low productivity could be the result of the fractured nature of the oil traps.

But the main mystery at the oilfield (at least for foreign observers) is its aggregate annual output. Wide consensus had been reached among U.S. observers that Taching's crude oil production was running about 20–25 million metric tons per year in the mid-1970's.[57] This figure had been reached through careful analysis of official claims in the Chinese press regarding the increase for each year over the previous year's production. However, as Table 11.1 shows, in 1976 the CIA released a study that showed Taching production at nearly twice the consensus figures.[58] Furthermore, the CIA figures fit the same set of annual increase criteria as the consensus series. That is, both sets of estimates were equally con-

TABLE 11.1

Alternative Estimates of Crude Oil Production at Taching Oilfield, 1960–76
(Million metric tons)

Year	Cheng (consensus)				CIA				Press reports		
	Million metric tons	Absolute annual % increase	Multiple of year given	Average annual % increase since 1960	Million metric tons	Absolute annual % increase	Multiple of year given	Average annual % increase since 1960	Absolute annual % increase	Multiple of year given	Average annual % increase since 1960
1960	0.5				0.8						
1961	1.1	120%			1.0	25%					
1962	2.0	82			2.7	170					
1963	2.7	35			4.4	63					
1964	3.4	26			5.8	32					
1965	4.2	23			7.1	22					
1966	5.4	29			8.8	24					
1967	5.8	7			9.0	2					
1968	6.2	7			9.2	2					
1969	8.5	37			12.8	39			37%		
1970	10.6	25	2.5 × 65	36%	17.7	38	2.5 × 65	36%		2.5 × 65	
1971	13.3	25	4.9 × 63	35	22.1	25	5.0 × 63	35	25	5.0 × 63	35.2%
1972	15.3	15		33	25.5	15		33	15		35
1973	17.0	11		31	28.3	11		32	11		
1974	20.7	22	4.9 × 65	30	34.6	22	4.9 × 65	31	22	5.0 × 65	
1975	22.5	9	5.4 × 65	29	40.1	16	5.6 × 65	30		5.5 × 65	30
1976	25.0	11	6.0 × 65	28	43.1	8	6.1 × 65	28		6.0 × 65	28

Sources: Cheng Chu-yuan, China's Petroleum Industry: Output Growth and Export Potential, p. 28; U.S. CIA, China: Oil Production Prospects, p. 9. Various issues of Peking Review, Far Eastern Economic Review, Economic Reporter, Ta Kung Pao, Joint Publications Research Service, and Hsin Hua She as listed in the two major sources and checked by the author.

Note: Calculation of average annual percent increases for the Cheng and CIA figures was based on the assumption that the Chinese government uses the formula

$$\log P_t = \log P_0 + t \times \log (1 + r).$$

sistent with statistics in the Chinese press for absolute and average annual increases and for multiples of previous years. This illustrates the hazards faced by foreign experts confronting China's statistical policies. There is no inherent reason to choose the CIA figures as more accurate than the Cheng (consensus) series. But it must be assumed that the CIA has inspection techniques (satellite surveys, well counts, etc.) not available outside the intelligence community. The CIA figures would also be more consistent with per well productivity estimates.

The critical years of divergence between the two data series are 1960 and 1965, which have been used repeatedly in the Chinese press as benchmarks for comparison with production levels in the 1970's. Cheng's estimates (and those of the other academic experts) for these two years were not well documented, owing to the paucity of information on Taching from the early 1960's.

In any case, it would appear that standard judgments regarding Taching's contribution to the Chinese oil industry must be radically revised upward. Taching has been producing half the crude petroleum output in China, rather than the one-third previously supposed. This means that the Chinese energy system is even more dependent than had been thought on the development of the Taching oilfield. And it lowers estimates of output from China's other main oilfields. If accurate, this revision would lay additional stress on the importance of proved reserves at Taching. If Taching resources are in the one billion metric ton range, then vigorous efforts will be required within the next five to ten years to develop other oilfields, particularly offshore. That would require high levels of investment in offshore oil exploration, or possibly in oilfields in the western part of the country (Tsaidam), or in nonfossil energy sources such as nuclear power.

The Organization of Taching Oilfield

In the preceding sections of this chapter, we have reviewed the history and technical characteristics of Taching oilfield. Now we turn to the more intangible aspects of the Taching model. Taching oilfield is unique in a number of ways that have very little to do with the fact that it is an oilfield, and much more to do with the Chinese communist approach to production organization in energy and related industries. The distinctive Chinese approach to production organization in turn affects the entire process of industrialization, and ultimately the direction of China's international energy policies.

The "self-reliance" guideline is particularly important in this regard. "Self-reliance" is a slogan that is applied both to individual production units like Taching, and to China's international energy posture as well. The Chinese press uses exactly the same phrase in both contexts. But the coincidence is more than purely verbal. "Self-reliance" represents a whole complex set of attitudes toward development that grew out of the extreme hardships faced by the revolutionary generation of Chinese leaders in their base areas during the war against Japan and the Chinese civil war. The communist base areas were isolated and surrounded by hostile forces. They developed a style of organization that permitted survival, recruitment, and growth even under such adverse conditions. This style of organization centered on the concept of "self-reliance." Each base area was expected to produce its own necessities—food, clothing, and even ammunition. A whole generation of Chinese revolutionary leaders was trained under these conditions and rose to control China after 1949.

After the end of the Chinese civil war in 1949, the communist leadership faced a whole new set of problems of development and survival in a hostile world. They applied exactly the same style of organization to these problems that they had learned during their days as "outlaws" in the revolutionary base areas. In 1949, China was a terribly poor country, with a shattered population that had suffered from a century of upheaval and foreign depredation, with scarcely enough food and clothing to provide for its enormous and largely illiterate population, and with only the barest beginnings of an industrial sector and no capacity to generate new capital or equipment for industrial growth. Under such conditions, each industry was expected to develop itself with minimum help from the central government and maximum local initiative and organization.

The same set of guidelines were applied to Chinese foreign policy, perhaps with some delay in the early years as China attempted unsuccessfully to enlist the full support of the Soviet Union for its development efforts. During the 1950's, Soviet technical assistance and imported Soviet equipment were welcomed on the assumption that the common ideological orientation of the two countries would bridge their cultural differences and distinctive interests. But the experiment in socialist internationalism failed, and Peking was forced to reconsider and reject the relationship with the Soviet Union and to fall back on the old strategy of "self-reliance." Equipment and technology imports were minimized as the country settled back into its own development pattern.

The organization of production at Taching should be understood against this background of historical conditions and experiences. Many characteristics of Taching's organizational style would strike the Western observer as arbitrary or even harsh.[59] The old drilling equipment, shoddy houses, low wages, and high labor intensity might appear odd in contrast to a modern and "efficient" oilfield in the West. But to the Chinese planner, they are simply another aspect of the self-reliance policy of building Chinese industry with the equipment, materials, and personnel at hand, rather than begging for foreign aid or trading needed resources and raw materials for foreign capital. Self-reliance doubtless has its dreary side, but the Chinese are intensely proud of the independence which this policy has produced. It is in this sense that Taching oilfield became a model for Chinese industrial development.

Political organization at Taching begins at the base level with the 60,000–100,000 workers and auxiliary personnel who engage in some form of oil-related production on the oilfield itself, or in one of the refineries, research institutes, or transportation networks that dot the area.[60] The mass of oilfield workers and their dependents are organized into work teams, production teams, or production brigades, the exact term varying according to the task. For example, in 1973, there were 29 drilling teams at Taching.[61] One such team (1205, a model team) has 124 skilled workers and 52 cadres.[62] The teams work a 24-hour schedule with rotating shifts.

In addition to the drilling teams, Taching also has a full complement of work teams at every stage in the oil exploration, extraction, and refining process. There are also a large number of teams engaged in support work such as social welfare, education, medicine, and logistics. The oilfield has been turned into a vast agricultural cooperative farmed by agricultural production brigades, which are primarily composed of the dependents of oilfield workers. One article claimed that 95 percent of the adult inhabitants of Taching are engaged in some form of production.[63] The team structure is central to the pattern of production organization, mobilizing the work force, organizing the details of daily production, keeping base-level production statistics and accounts, and coordinating with other units.[64]

Most of the articles on Taching in the Chinese press make some reference to the special living arrangements that have been provided there for the oilfield workers—or that, more accurately speaking, the workers have provided for themselves under the development plan for the entire oilfield. Living facilities for the workers and their dependents are intentionally not being developed into a large city, but into 60 "habitation points" (also called "worker-peasant villages") built on a decentralized basis around the oil wells.[65] These "habitation points" are themselves surrounded by 164 housing settlements sprinkled across the oilfield. Families of the workers farm the fields in and around the oil-producing areas. Living areas around factories and refineries have also been decentralized, with family members engaged in agriculture or some other "auxiliary industrial labor." A number of "habitation points" constitute a "living base" with a "central population point" directed by a "base administrative committee," which organizes "agricultural production, livelihood, and social management." The central population points each have welfare facilities such as a hospital or clinic, a primary school, a work-and-study middle school, a spare-time cultural school, shops, a post office, a barbershop, a bathhouse, a grain mill, a mess hall, a grain store, a vegetable depot, a sewing and mending group, a shoe repair shop, and a child-care center. The central population points also provide a social center of gravity. The mess hall, for example, may be used for meetings, dramas, and movies. Highway and bus lines connect the central population points with each other and to the oilfield administrative centers. The population points have electric lights, running water, and natural gas.

Dependents work during the busy seasons in agriculture and at other times on highway maintenance, housing construction, cottage industries, and trades. For example, one population point has six production teams—four agricultural, one housing, and one supply.[66] The housing construction team built 126 adobe houses and trained "women tile workers, carpenters, painters, electricians, etc." The supply team manages social welfare functions at the population point, has two carriages, two oxen carts, one mule cart, and has raised 86 cows, 17 horses, and 15 pigs. Taching family members work an eight-hour day, or six hours if they are weak or ill, or if they have "too many children." They work harder during the busy agricultural season and less hard at other times.

The school system at Taching was first organized in dining halls and warehouses. Later, adobe buildings were provided at the population points by the students themselves. Primary and junior middle school is now available generally in the Taching mining area. Taching has been experimenting with half work (farming) and half study education.

The petroleum mining area in which there is coordination between industry and agriculture and between urban and rural areas provides a broad arena for labor, thus creating favorable prerequisites for these two kinds of educational system. There are now in the mining area half a dozen semi-working (farming) and semi-studying special schools on the middle level (namely, geology, drilling, agricultural machinery, normal, finance and economics, and public health) and 10 junior middle schools and agricultural schools.[67]

Center and periphery, therefore, meet face to face at Taching, in a manner that could hardly be more direct. The oilfield has both the characteristics of a large industrial center and the characteristics of rural soci-

ety. "This arrangement of Taching oilfield is like both a city and a
village, possessing the merits of both. Thus, people say that Taching is a
rural type of city as well as an urban type of countryside."[68] When the
center has an opportunity to implement its version of an intentional
community, the result looks surprisingly like a traditional Chinese
village.

The Chinese press has given much less of a picture of the organizational superstructure at Taching than of its organizational base. We do
know that the Taching Oilfield Revolutionary Committee was organized
in 1968 and remained its central administrative organ, under the direction of the Taching Oilfield Party Committee until 1978.[69] Taching includes five subsidiary producing fields, each of which probably had its
own revolutionary and party committees. Other major installations include three refineries, a petrochemical plant, a drilling equipment factory, and a drilling explosive-charge factory.[70] This list is a mere beginning of a catalog of what must already be a major industrial center. The
entire oilfield is organized into a city ("city people's cooperative").[71]

Because of the size and importance of Taching in China's petroleum
industry, the oilfield is directly responsible to the Ministry of Petroleum*
in Peking, which in turn is part of the State Council and responsible to
the Premier and the Politburo of the Chinese Communist Party. The
lines of authority that run through the Taching Party Committee are less
clear. The Party Committee probably has direct ties both to the Heilungkiang Province Party Committee and to the Central Committee apparatus. An unusually large percentage of the Taching oilfield workers are
Party members, and the Party organization on the oilfield is doubtless
very strong, running right down to the base level in the production
teams. There are reported to be 50 Party committee headquarters (in
various factories, refineries, fields, etc.) and 2,600 Party branches.[72] This
would indicate that there are more than 2,000 production teams at the
base level in all aspects of work at Taching.

The research and development function has been very important at
Taching and is carried out through the Peking Petroleum Institute (now
the Oil Institute?), Drilling and Prospecting School, Taching Oilfield Development Research Institute, Design Research Institute, Mining Equipment Research Institute, Oil Drilling Research Institute, and the 1,202
Drilling Academy.[73] The use and development of technology lie at the
heart of what the Chinese refer to as the "Taching model." Although
technological innovation has been a constant part of every phase in oil

*In 1978 the Ministry of Petroleum and Chemical Industries was split into the Ministry
of Petroleum and the Ministry of Chemical Industries.

production at Taching, there are two areas—exploration and extraction—that have provided particularly rich fields for Chinese technological experimentation. The peculiar characteristics of the oil-bearing formations at Taching required a new approach to exploration and preparatory drilling of test wells. At the same time, Taching geologists, fresh from their encounters with Soviet colleagues and eager to prove their prowess, attacked the problem of defining a distinctive Chinese approach to oil prospecting with vigor. They were apparently convinced that Taching contained large quantities of crude oil, if it could only be located through a technology of exploration appropriate to local conditions. The first step in the new Chinese approach was the collection and collation of an enormous mass of raw data:

> When prospecting was started at Taching in 1960, the pioneers adopted a method different from that commonly used abroad. Some "authorities" abroad claim that one can get only a rough understanding of the oil formations buried deep underground. But the oilfield builders at Taching undertook a very large-scale investigation and obtained masses of primary data which enabled them to complete the prospecting work in an extraordinary short space of time.[74]

Starting in 1960, the workers at Taching collected data on every test well and every stratum penetrated by each test well. Data collection, like other tasks on the oilfield, was approached in a labor-intensive manner. When the literally millions of strata analyses and miles of tabulations were brought together by the research institutes at Taching, it was possible to develop a detailed three-dimensional map of the strata and to locate the fractured formations with a relatively high degree of accuracy.[75] In this way, oil exploration at Taching "combined revolutionary zeal with a strict scientific approach."[76] According to official Chinese commentary, once Taching workers had gained "a clear view of the geological formation of the oil fields," worked out a practical design for oilfield development, and developed the oilfield itself, they had effectively smashed the grip of the petroleum blockade imposed by imperialism and social imperialism.[77]

The exact process used at Taching for exploratory drilling reveals the "breakthrough" mentality that prevails in Chinese industrial planning. Taching prospectors, we are told, applied the thoughts of Mao Tsetung, particularly the theory of contradictions, to the analysis of "oil layers as a whole," including each layer that is oil-bearing, rather than relying on averages. They sought nothing short of discovery of "the original features of all the layers." However, they were faced with a contradiction between not knowing the conditions of the layers without drilling and obviating the ultimate exploitation design (wasting wells) by the drilling of many wells. In foreign oilfields, this problem is usually solved by using an average parameter for the various strata. And because of the use of these average parameters (according to the Chinese), many foreign oilfields have development plans that differ substantially from conditions of production in the field itself. This would not do at Taching, with its small formations.[78]

And so the Taching geologists and drilling teams, through studying Mao's theory of contradictions and method of application of theory to practice, made a breakthrough in their thinking to a new mode of oilfield exploration. The new mode of thought regarded prospecting work and test well-drilling as "a link and a phase of the whole process of development from practice to knowledge and back to practice." Citing Mao's teaching that "The two processes of acquiring human knowledge, that is, from the particular to the general and from the general to the particular, are interconnected," they designed a multistage development procedure for test wells. This procedure involved the following steps:[79] (1) drilling wells in the area of most reliable oil layers; (2) *not* putting these wells into operation after drilling; (3) comparing detailed changes discovered in the layers; (4) deciding upon a well network "in conformity with the oil layers"; (5) drilling, but not putting into operation, a second group of wells; (6) acquiring new stratification data; (7) repeatedly comparing the conditions of oil layers; (8) altering the original well network; (9) injecting steel pipe and concrete; (10) operating and injecting water. Apparently, the critical steps were numbers 2 and 5, in which wells were drilled but not put into operation until further data could be collected and analyzed.

"The victory in the geological work in Taching oilfield is a victory for the thought of Mao Tse-tung."[80] Mao's thought was the catalyst that broke a technical disequilibrium between the small oil formations at Taching and available exploration resources.

> Taching's achievement is due to the readiness of the people working there, inspired by Mao Tse-tung's thinking, to break away from foreign stereotypes and scale the heights of world technology. It is a triumph of Mao Tse-tung's approach to problems. Mao Tse-tung's words that "man's correct knowledge comes from social practice" spurred them to experiment and thoroughly investigate the laws of oil exploration at this oilfield.[81]

These words were written at the outset of the Cultural Revolution, accounting for the particular stress on the importance of Mao's thought to technological breakthrough. But the important point for our purposes is that the Chinese felt a breakthrough had occurred that brought a sudden change on the oilfield, releasing its productive force.

Other technological innovations have been attempted at Taching in the area of oil extraction, including several that the Chinese press claimed were unique in the history of oilfield development. In particular, the Chinese claim that their method of "early flooding" water injection, which helps maintain well pressure and sweeps a higher proportion of in-place reserves into the well, was an original contribution to oil extraction technology.

Petroleum experts here say that this has never happened at any oilfield of the same type anywhere else in the world. To the best of their knowledge, they said, at the big oilfields abroad a drop in the pressure within the oil formations usually ensues after a few years of extraction, many of the wells stop gushing and additional measures have to be taken to get any oil, with a consequent rise in production costs. Water injection at this stage is too late to insure the maintenance of the initial output.

The engineers and workers at the Taching oilfield have devised and developed a whole series of measures, including early water injection and simultaneously multiple-zone water injection, which have solved this awkward problem and raised China's production technology to a new level. This is not only of far-reaching importance for the Taching oilfield in particular, but is a great contribution to the science and technology of oil exploitation in general.[82]

With early water injection, the Taching wells maintain "a natural flow at about the original pressure of the sub-surface strata." Study groups among oil extraction teams are responsible for research into the relationship between the proper amount of water injection and the permeability of the formation. The team that originally developed the technique did 1,018 experiments over an eight-month period, balancing water injection and oil output. By 1965, each formation had been studied and regulated, achieving steady pressure conditions throughout the oilfield. It is not clear from the Chinese press sources just how long well pressure can be maintained in this fashion, or what the exact effect has been on recovery rates, but the press has claimed a high recovery rate and has often attributed it to the early water injection method.[83]

It is not entirely established that China has actually discovered a unique oil recovery method. Early water injection is practiced at many other oilfields in the world, and is used extensively in the Soviet Union.[84] One Canadian petroleum engineer, Dr. Necmattin Mungan, who has visited Taching and examined its water injection method, indicates that the Chinese used the "line drive" water injection pattern in the early phases of oilfield development.[85] In this system, a line of oil wells alternates with a line of water injection wells. The method injects a lot of water in a hurry and results in very rapid oil recovery. However, its disadvantage is that it sweeps a relatively low proportion of in-place reserves into the oil extraction wells before the injected water begins to penetrate to the extraction wells, thereby flooding the system and stopping production.

More recently, judging from the age of the wells, Taching has switched over to a "nine point" water injection method.[86] In this system, water is injected into a single central well surrounded by eight producing oil wells in a rectangular pattern. The result is that a higher proportion of in-place reserves is swept into the oil wells before water flooding occurs. However, the nine-point system results in a lower pace of recovery at each producing well than the line drive system. Thus, the recovery ratio is improved at the cost of a lower rate of production at each well.

If Mungan's observations are correct, it appears that in the early phases of development at Taching, the line drive system was used, increasing the daily yield of each well at the cost of lower ultimate recovery. Then, as the limits of reserves at Taching began to become evident, planners switched to a recovery system that maximizes the proportion of oil recovered at the cost of lower per-well production rates. This would help account for the very high annual rate of growth of Taching's crude oil output in the early years of its development. But it would also indicate that slower growth rates should be expected in the future.

Other technological innovations have been attempted at Taching, with unknown results. One article in 1974 claimed that Taching had accumulated 20,500 technological innovations since 1960, with 50 such innovations up to advanced international levels, including "extraction by separate zones, long-barrel coring, and identification of oil-bearing structures according to individual reservoir sandstone."[87] Taching has also experimented with the use of a "small oil collecting tree" which is lighter and easier to handle than standard oil-collecting equipment.[88] And Taching's refineries have been a target of self-conscious technological innovation. Technical innovation of eight sets of refining equipment at the Taching Petrochemical Plant was said to have doubled refinery capacity there in 1972, at 30 percent of the original cost of refinery construction.[89]

From an organizational perspective, technological innovation at Taching has "walked on two legs." At the base level within the production teams, the process of technological innovation is stimulated by wide publicity for worker innovations of all sorts. The "three-in-one teams" prevalent throughout Chinese industry are present on the oilfield as well, presiding over numerous aspects of intentionally introduced innovations. "Carrying out the 'three-in-one combination' of workers, cadres, and technicians relies on the masses for technological innovation."[90] The base-level team approach may or may not be formalized as a recognized three-in-one team. Individuals may make heroic sacrifices for the sake of data collection on a problem, but individual inventions are seldom attributed to the inventor.[91]

The self-conscious base-level development of technology at Taching has at times been carried to extremes. In one case, a team of workers and technicians was attempting to overcome transport difficulties posed by the waxiness of Taching's crude oil and the severity of winters in the area. To solve the problem, two technicians sat in an oil tank car on a trip of 10,000 kilometers, gathering data at the heat booster stations along the route, and measuring the ambient temperature and wind velocity every hour.[92] This rather direct approach to technical problems is quite common on the oilfield.

Resting on the other leg of technological innovation on the oilfield is a comprehensive array of research institutes that carry on the central data-gathering and data-processing function. These research institutes are under the direct management of the Ministry of Petroleum. They have access to modern data-processing equipment, including computer systems.

But they are also expected to be aware of base-level technological innovation and to encourage it. Technical cadres go directly to the work sites to practice the "four togethers" with the workers, taking part in labor, becoming workers, dropping pretenses, and acting as students.[93] For example, "the long tube rock core assault team of the Taching Research Institute on Mining Machinery moves equipment to the work sites, rather than relying solely on books, and takes 'the workers as instructors.' "[94] The Ministry of Petroleum may call periodic forums on such topics as "technical innovations and the technical revolution," where Taching innovators of every level gather and compare notes on progress in drilling, pumping, and refining, "to overtake world standards." They may also compare notes on political themes, innovating "under the great red banner of the thought of Mao Tse-tung" and maintaining a strict work style.[95]

The phraseology of these clauses ("the technical revolution," "assault team," etc.) is neither accidental nor purely rhetorical. Here again, as in the example of oil extraction technology, the breakthrough mentality prevails, revealing the underlying structure of the Chinese concept of change. The underlying message is the same—that given the proper ideological orientation and organizational stimulus, the struggle against nature will succeed, the catalytic event will occur, and a new production horizon will suddenly come to view. This is reminiscent of the Chinese view that the energy crisis is phony, and that energy resources are by nature unlimited. The Taching experience reinforced the perception that resource shortages are artificial and that a new political breakthrough will move a properly organized system to a new further stage of development whenever faced by such shortages. But then new contradictions will occur as "one divides into two," and the whole process begins again.

This concept that development depends on the release of latent forces of production through contradictions and struggle orients the Chinese theorist toward the base level of production organization—in Chinese parlance, toward the "masses." "Relying on the masses, ceaselessly releasing the latent force of the enterprise, and raising labor productivity are the main road of development of socialist enterprises."[96] The mass orientation of production organization introduces a political factor into the growth equation and sets up the production breakthrough as a political and organizational objective. This view is fundamentally dissimilar to the standard Western paradigm of exponential growth through the technological feedback loop (i.e. rising technology yields rising production, yields rising demand, yields rising technology).

Taching became the technological capital of the Chinese petroleum industry in 1966, when the Peking Petroleum Institute moved to the oilfield. It thereby replaced Yumen as the training center for oil workers and petroleum technicians. From its founding until 1977, Taching had sent 56,000 workers and cadres to other oilfields, including 15,000 in 1973 alone.[97] The workers and cadres from Taching serve a dual purpose at other fields. They establish a network among China's major oilfields for the sharing of technological innovation, and they establish a core of workers in new oilfields with experience at the cutting edge of the Chinese petroleum industry. Most of the 15,000 workers and cadres who left Taching in 1973 went to China's two new oilfields—Shengli and Takang. They retain personal ties to Taching from the formative years of their work experience and thereby facilitate coordination of output and technology transfer. They also help to carry the seeds of Taching's socialization process to other areas of China.

The four elements of political organization at Taching—base-level technological innovation, mobilization for production, political struggle, and political socialization—all center on the theme of self-reliance, which is the core of the Taching model. Under the slogan "*dulizizhu, ziligengsheng*" (self-reliance), the Taching experience has been expanded to the status of a model for all Chinese industrialization.[98] Although self-reliance appears to be a fairly simple set of slogans and concepts, it actually runs through all of the rather complex aspects of political organization at Taching. The motivation for self-reliance is simple—to free China from external dependence and maintain independence through the critical development years. But the implications of self-reliance are not so simple when it comes to implementation on the oilfield. Hard decisions must be made about the use of domestic and imported technology. Central control must be balanced by peripheral initiative. Political mobilization must be balanced by sustained production. Rapid expansion of production must be balanced by the minimization of waste. These dilemmas are very real, and they lend credibility to the thesis that the process of development is governed by the dynamics of internal contradictions and the movement from one set of contradictions to the next.

Domestic Constraints on Energy Policy

The development of Taching oilfield helps to illustrate a number of the constraints the domestic energy system places on China's international energy policies. Four major constraints could be distilled from the Taching case—strategic, political, resource, and organizational. Each functions in a manner that ties international energy policies directly to domestic energy development. Each could probably be discovered in a detailed analysis of any of China's major energy industries and enterprises.

The Strategic Constraint

Taching makes an enormous contribution to China's defense. Rapid development of the oilfield has liberated the PRC from dependence on imported petroleum products and has stimulated industrial and agricultural expansion in nearly every sector of the economy. And, of course, the Chinese military is directly dependent on Taching oil for its mobility and increasing mechanization. But Taching has also increased China's strategic vulnerability. The location and concentration of the oilfield infrastructure and its extreme fragility in the face of a concerted military attack must be factors that carry enormous weight in China's military posture vis-à-vis the Soviet Union. There is really little that can be done about Taching's vulnerability, other than attempting to develop other fields as rapidly as possible.

On balance, Taching may have strengthened Peking's hand in dealing with the Soviet Union because of the special oil export relationship that has developed with Japan. As this relationship develops further, the Chinese will be in a strong position to discourage Japanese participation in strategic development projects in Siberia. This would have both a political and a military payoff for China, and it would produce the obvious advantages of a strong trade relationship with Japan.

The Political Constraint

Taching represents the highest stage of development of China's style of industrialization, the political mobilization of production. That the oilfield developed as rapidly as it did is a tribute to the capabilities that can be brought to bear by a concerted and concentrated national effort coupled with root-level organizational innovation. But Taching has proved repeatedly that such a close tie to national politics can be disruptive as well as catalytic. Major national political competition and upheaval appear to have a direct effect on oilfield production and management, disturbing the operation of the oilfield and slowing its growth curve more than any other single factor. Such political disruptions have then in turn been echoed at the international level in China's foreign trade patterns. Crude oil export has been disrupted at least once, and equipment imports, which require long lead times and careful planning, have been interrupted by a domestic political debate over their utility. The political debate may have been required to preserve the independence of China's energy development, but the policy volatility that results is antithetical to long-range development planning.

The Resource Constraint

Taching's vast petroleum reserves have opened an entirely new page in China's industrial development. The oilfield was developed at a time that made it a launching platform for the entire energy sector. The size of Taching reserves permitted very high annual production growth rates. However, even the resource that Taching represents should be viewed as a constraint on international policy. Rapid production growth rates have also meant rapid depletion of the Taching resource. Although we are still not certain that the Taching oilfield production curve has begun to peak, maximum production levels will be reached in a few years unless the size of reserves is far greater than any foreign estimates would indicate.

Rapid energy resource development always represents a sort of gamble with time. The gamble is that the next resource—oilfield, natural gas, or future technology—will be developed before the exploited resource reaches critical levels of depletion. Furthermore, rapid production expansion can result in wasteful production techniques, transportation and refining bottlenecks, and distortion of machinery and equipment industries in the direction of a single line of development. Ironically, China has been critical of the West for precisely this type of development error in the expansion of energy industries and the subsequent energy crisis. But there are signs that the PRC itself may have followed a similar path of rapid growth, resource depletion (still at a very early stage), and subsequent problems of adjustment. There are very real questions whether Taching, the pillar of China's petroleum and energy industries, will be able to continue to support growing energy consumption and export levels without balanced development of other oilfields and other energy industries. The Taching miracle could turn out to be a development nightmare if peak production levels are reached before China is able to produce substantial petroleum output from its potential offshore fields.

The Organizational Constraint

The "self-reliance" policy guideline and all of the organizational innovations that have been produced in its name have greatly strengthened China's energy development. The PRC is today completely self-sufficient in energy commodities and has developed an energy export surplus. Chinese energy equipment industries have sprung up in most industrial centers in the country. China's level of technological expertise in petroleum extraction, refining, and transportation has risen with unprecedented swiftness toward world levels.

But in some areas, self-reliance may have hobbled China's international and domestic energy development policies. On the equipment import side, the PRC could probably benefit from imported technology for offshore oil exploration, electric power generation, and nuclear power development. But the technology transfer has frequently been delayed by concerns that the imported item might to some degree sacrifice the independence of China's equipment industries. Chinese planners appear at times naive about foreign technology and at times overly aggressive in seeking technology transfer without equipment purchases. On the export side, sales of Taching crude to Japan and other Asian markets have been hurt badly by inflexible Chinese pricing policies that fail to allow for the specific characteristics of the crude oil.

Here again, on balance, the self-reliance policy and the Taching model of energy development must be judged a success. China's energy development, when compared with that of the other large countries in the Third World (India, Indonesia, and Brazil), has been very swift. The PRC has achieved rapid growth rates on the basis of a domestic equipment industry and domestically nurtured technology. But the very real organizational and policy constraints that remain must be recognized as part of the framework within which China's international energy policies will be formulated for the next several decades.

Chapter 12

China's Future Energy Policies

> If we let Chinese ethics and famous teachings serve as an original foundation, and let them be supplemented by the methods used by the various nations for the attainment of prosperity and strength, would it not be the best of all procedures?
> —Feng Kuei-fen, 1860

> When we persist in self-reliance, we do not preclude learning advanced things from foreign countries; on the contrary . . . we must make this a condition of self-reliance.
> —Hu Chiao-mu, July 1978

My generation is privileged to witness the deliberate modernization of China, the world's most populous country. The magnitude of the task seldom fails to evoke awe from foreign visitors. One hopes that it can be accomplished without the degradation of Dickens's England, the callousness of Steinbeck's America, or the brutality of Stalin's Russia. Woe betide the government that seeks to use a temporary technological advantage over China to manipulate the process. Foolish indeed is the scholar who underestimates the determination of the Chinese to control their own destinies.

As of 1980, I believe that we are somewhere in the middle of this epic. China has already experienced a century of humiliation, 30 years of war and revolution, and another 30 years of reconstruction and consolidation. The outlines of China's industrial system are slowly becoming visible. The diet and basic security of China's massive agrarian population are assured. But in many ways the country remains in the shadow of the past. There is absolutely no reason why China, with its three millennia of cultural, political, social, and economic development, should not rival and lead, as well as follow and learn. If China could advance to the edge of modern science, to a broad and penetrating educational system, to industrial power and agricultural plenty, and even to personal ease and the occasional luxury, it would be an inspiration for every country in the Third World that bends its effort in the same direction.

Projecting China's Energy Future

There is a difference between anticipating the future and understanding it. This is particularly the case in efforts to project China's energy future. Simple extrapolation will not do. Certain general points should be made about the complex art of energy projections before proceeding to the Chinese case. First, *energy development rarely, if ever, takes place along a simple exponential curve.* Regardless of the energy industry or variable in question, a simple, fixed growth rate (which generates an exponential curve) seldom describes what occurs as the process of development takes place. Rather, the growth curve is dynamic, with variable growth rates at different points in time. For example, when an energy industry, such as the petroleum industry, first gets under way, growth rates are likely to be very high following initial discoveries and investment. If there is one oil well working, drilling another will double production—a 100 percent increase. The petroleum production growth rate then drops as production itself accelerates, eventually reaching zero, or even a negative value when the reserve begins to be depleted (Chapter 23). The rate of production growth is therefore related both to previous rates of production and to the size of current reserves and the rate at which new resources are located and defined. The curves generated by alternative reserves and resource assumptions are therefore neither linear nor exponential, but dynamic and complex.

A second point that is frequently missed by analysts projecting China's oil exports is that *energy systems are highly interactive.* That is, everything is connected to everything else. Even if one successfully projects the growth curve for petroleum production, that is only one of the many pieces of information needed to infer export potential. One also needs to know the entire framework of the energy balance within which petroleum production is growing. This is not just a way of making life more complicated or of rationalizing resort to computer models. We simply cannot discuss oil export potential in the absence of some understanding of the likely domestic demand for petroleum products, the pace of growth in the general economy, or the likelihood of substitution by other energy fuels for the exported oil. Once we have successfully projected export surplus or an import deficit, then further reference must be made to the state of the international petroleum market (and other energy commodity markets) at the time.

Another point that applies more generally to the art of projection is that *complex systems can be projected but not predicted.* When knowledge of the underlying conditions of growth is imperfect, as it always is with energy systems, each set of growth projections must be associated with an explicit alternative set of growth assumptions. Different sets of assumptions may or may not be further identified with explicit probabilities, but a prediction goes considerably beyond projection by choosing just one scenario and attaching to it a probability of 1.0. The conditions of growth in energy systems are never known with complete certainty. For example, even in advanced oil and gas exploration programs, reserves figures are estimates, not measurements, and resource figures are themselves projections. The same point could be made regarding the assumptions underlying projections of economic growth and energy consumption. This study, therefore, provides a range of alternative projections, rather than a single set of figures for each energy variable. We can define a reasonable range of possible or even likely alternative energy futures for China. And further efforts will be made to narrow the range as new information becomes available. But it would be silly to try to choose which of the many alternative futures will actually occur.

With these general observations in mind, it would be possible to dismantle the logic of each of the many projections of various aspects of the Chinese energy balance that have been made by foreign analysts in recent years. I do not intend to engage in that exercise, both because the weakness of some projections has already been demonstrated by the course of events and because my own work has benefited so greatly from previous efforts. I would, however, make the general comment that projections to date, particularly for crude petroleum production and export potential, have almost universally been on the high side. A few examples will illustrate this point.

Very few authors have attempted projections of China's future coal production. Such projections tend generally to be more reasonable than projections of crude petroleum production, but are usually made on the basis of fixed growth rates. Projections are usually in the range of 550–600 million metric tons of raw coal output in 1980.[1] My projected range was slightly more optimistic at 624–666 million tons (Tables 24.2 and 24.7). Park and Cohen, Smil, and the CIA all based their coal projections on fixed assumed growth rates of about 5–7 percent per year. Smil's 1980 projection is a very conservative 440–470 mmt (raw coal), but by 1990 his fixed-growth rates yield output levels of 810–950 million tons. This figure would equal or exceed current production levels of the United States, the world's largest coal producer and would approximately double China's 1976 raw coal production. I assumed gently declining growth rates for coal production, given the already large scale of the Chinese coal industry. I modeled three coal production scenarios by varying the assumed level of measured coal reserves from 100 to 150 billion metric tons. Under the three assumptions, raw coal output would reach 1 billion tons per year in successively shorter time spans (Tables 24.2, 24.6, and 24.7). I believe it most likely that the billion ton mark will be reached between 1995 and the year 2000, although with heavy investment the Chinese coal industry could conceivably reach this level by 1990. Our experience with large coal industries is limited, but for a variety of reasons one should expect a decline in growth rates after a level of about 500 million tons per year. The reasons for the decline include the capital requirements of proportional expansion at high production levels, the stress introduced in the rail transportation system, and limits on the internal market for lump coal. It is possible that all three of my coal production forecasts are too optimistic. But I consider it highly unlikely that raw coal output will exceed 1.2 billion metric tons by 2000 under any circumstances.

Oil production is a much more notorious arena than coal for the guessing game. Many of the earliest projections of Chinese crude oil production were of the pin-the-tail-on-the-donkey variety. One source reported in 1975 that Japanese officials expected China to be producing 400 million metric tons of crude petroleum by 1980, a figure that either would have implied an annual growth rate of 34 percent per year in the interim, or was simply a mistaken identification of the decade in question.[2] A more common early projection for 1980 was 200 million tons.[3] This represented an exponential extrapolation of the 20 percent growth rate that had characterized the Chinese oil industry from 1961 to 1975. But in 1976, the crude oil production growth rate fell to about 10 percent per year, where it remained through the end of 1978. Actual production in 1980 will be 110–120 million tons, judging from our now nearer vantage point.

More recently, a commonly heard crude oil production figure for 1985 is 335 million metric tons, and the Chinese government is said to have established a production goal of 400 million tons by the year 1990.[4] The 1985 figure is absurd, since it would require sustained growth from 1978 to 1985 of 17 percent per year, in view of recent growth rates reported publicly by the Chinese press.[5] Another source suggested 278 million tons by 1985, a figure that could have been reached if China's recoverable oil resources were four times the best recent estimate, but would require a sustained 15 percent growth rate, unlikely in view of the current situation (Table 24.7). My own figures suggest 1985 crude oil production of 145 million metric tons without substantial offshore production, and up to 175 million tons with substantial offshore production (Tables 24.2 and 24.6). In the former case, the growth rate will have dropped to about 4 percent in 1985, in the latter case to about 6 percent.

What about the reported 1990 production target of 400 million metric tons?[6] It would require a sustained growth rate of 11–12 percent per year from 1978 to 1990, a possible outcome but not a likely one, judging from the development experiences of other large petroleum industries, with the exception of the Middle East. It would be a remarkable feat to sustain current growth rates, still very high by international standards, at this phase in the development of the Chinese oil industry. Even substantial offshore recovery would only bring 1990 production to the upper end of my projected range of 160–240 million tons. The CIA study points out that at current estimated levels of onland economically recoverable crude oil resources (not reserves) and a sustained growth rate of 10 percent per year, 50 percent depletion would occur before 1992, an event that would precipitate a zero or negative growth rate in the early 1990's and a serious crisis in the Chinese oil industry.[7] It is axiomatic, therefore, that achievement of the reported production target of 400 million tons by 1990 would require enormous production from the offshore theaters. Under my highest resource projection, which assumes recoverable oil and gas resources in the range of the recoverable resources of the United States (including Alaska), China might reach 300 million tons of crude oil output by the early 1990's (Table 24.7). But I consider this outcome unlikely, since it would require quadrupling our current best estimates of China's oil and gas resources and an enormous capital investment in the offshore theaters. If the petroleum production growth rate slips below 10 percent in the early 1980's, then this outcome would be precluded. But it cannot be completely ruled out at the present time. If production at onland fields continued to rise steadily, joint development projects moved very rapidly, and offshore oil and gas discoveries were very large in the early 1980's, then the production goal of 400 million tons would be attainable by 1995 (five years late). I do not consider this combination of fortuitous events highly probable.

Few authors have attempted to project China's total primary energy production or aggregate energy consumption. In their second study of China's oil policy, Park and Cohen offer some cautious arithmetically derived projections for total primary energy production and energy demand as a vehicle for their further projection that the PRC will be exporting about 25 million tons of oil in 1980.[8] The CIA, in a 1975 study of the Chinese energy balance, projected alternative series for energy supply and demand in the year 1980, on the basis of fixed growth rate assumptions in the various energy industries and for the economy as a whole.[9] Both of these studies were useful in that they recognized the importance of the link between China's energy consumption requirements and the constraints on export potential. Professor Vaclav Smil is the only other author I am aware of who has attempted long-range energy balance forecasts for the PRC.[10] Smil used alternative fixed growth rates for the primary energy industries, and introduced an energy/GNP regression coefficient as a measurement of demand elasticity. Smil's projections are generally higher than my own, with a low limit that corresponds roughly to my median projection for the year 1990. Or, viewed from a different angle, I would expect the Chinese energy balance to reach Smil's projected range for 1990 in about 1995, with some remaining differences. My projections also introduced a number of innovations that could make them more reliable, including (a) dynamic oil and gas production growth rates tied to the resource depletion curve; (b) decaying energy/GNP regression coefficients that allow for improvement in energy end-use efficiency; (c) the effect of population dynamics on energy consumption requirements; (d) introduction of the thermal electric power production cycle, which shifts the consumption mix and reduces energy availability; (e) introduction of a growth curve for future energy production technologies, including nuclear (Chapters 23 and 24). Nonetheless, many of my qualitative and quantitative judgments regarding the likely constraints on the Chinese energy balance agree with Smil's.

It is hard to dignify most statments about China's future energy commodity export potential with the term "projection." Most talk about how much oil China will export and when is pure conjecture, based on the mood of the moment and the wishes of the speaker, rather than on any combination of analytic techniques. In the early days of oil exports to Japan, Chinese officials deliberately exaggerated their hints about oil resources and future exports (Chapter 6). The Japanese were remarkably gullible in those days, or perhaps had their own reasons for public optimism. The Japan External Trade Organization, an institution that surely has access to advanced economic projection methodologies, in 1975 was projecting 50 million tons of oil exports for 1980 and 200 million tons for 1985.[11] This projection fell rapidly, as Japanese refiners discovered the problems associated with importing Chinese crude. The less the Japanese business community wanted Chinese crude oil, the lower became the projections of China's export potential. The current forecast by prominent members of the Japanese Zakai (big business) is that China will be exporting 40–50 million tons of crude oil in 1985.[12] This range lies within the ceiling on energy commodity export potential indicated by my projections. The Chinese themselves are apparently somewhat more cautious, projecting their own oil export capacity at about 30 million tons in 1985.[13] The projections of energy commodity export potential are the last step, or the "payoff" of a successful energy balance projection. I shall return to this subject below, after a quick review of the major constraints operating to limit the energy commodity export potential of the PRC.

Constraints on Energy Development

Energy balance projections for China, as well as for other countries, are best understood in terms of a set of definable constraints. Capital investment, equipment imports, technical training, and other inputs into the growth potential of energy industries may be viewed as efforts to deal with long-term constraints. Furthermore, the set of constraints operating on different countries varies enormously. Some countries have a small hydrocarbon resource base but a developed industrial infrastructure (Japan). Some countries have resource potential, but lack adequate mineral surveys or resource development programs. Some countries have all the other necessary components for rapid energy development, but lack an appropriate organizational structure to mobilize national resources and technical talent in a coordinated fashion. Identification of the critical constraints operating on a country's energy development is the first step toward an adequate set of energy balance projections.

Resource Constraints

Energy production is basically constrained by the availability or lack of resources. Under some conditions, certain energy industries may be relatively free of resource constraints on development, but only in the short term. For example, the Chinese coal and hydropower industries will not be seriously restricted by resource considerations within the time frame of our projections. Coal and hydropower resources are enormous, both on the scale of current production and in terms of comparative world standards. The growth of these industries in China is therefore restricted by other factors—capital availability, technology, competing land uses, the size of the internal market, and so on. If one were to project Chinese energy development over two centuries instead of two decades, then coal and hydropower would also be resource-constrained energy industries. But in the short term the resource constraint is not important.

On the other hand, there is mounting evidence that the Chinese oil and gas industries are and will increasingly be restricted by the availability of resources and the economics of resource recovery. Current evidence indicates that oil and gas industries that grow under conditions of resource constraint will feel a steady downward pressure on the annual growth rate, beginning at about the time 10 percent of ultimate economically recoverable resources have been produced (Chapter 23). Figure 12.1 shows what would happen to the Chinese oil and gas industries if resources were limited to current estimates of onland recovery (i.e. 5 billion metric tons of crude petroleum and 5 trillion cubic meters of natural gas). I have intentionally chosen a pessimistic projection to better illustrate the dynamics of the model within a 20-year time span. As increasing quantities of oil and gas are produced each year, the remaining resource (not current reserves) slowly declines. But this decline in turn puts downward pressure on the production growth rate until production flattens out at zero percent increase and then begins to decline (negative growth rate). Under pessimistic resource assumptions for the Chinese case, crude petroleum production would peak in 1988 or so, with about two-thirds of recoverable resources still in the ground. Peak gas production would be reached about a decade later. Enhanced recovery techniques might flatten and extend the top of the production curve, putting off the day when production begins to decline.

Meanwhile, the balance of energy commodity trade (export potential) has shifted twice, moving from an energy deficit in the early 1970's to an increasing surplus. Peak export potential would be reached in the mid-1980's, and then the curve plunges down, crossing back over into a net import deficit in the early 1990's. This is what I have referred to elsewhere in the text as China's "export bubble." Note that the export potential curve peaks well before either oil or gas production. The constraint operating on export potential is not simply current production. Rather, as production growth rates gently decline, energy consumption, necessary for the burgeoning Chinese economy, continues to press relentlessly upward. It is the upward pressure of consumption, as much as the slowing of rapid production growth rates, that constrains energy commodity exports and would eventually return China to the position of an energy importer. The consumption constraint is present in the energy balance of other oil-exporting countries (e.g. the Soviet Union), but it is seldom as strong as in the Chinese case.

For the sake of argument, I also included an unspecified future energy production curve in the model, which varies inversely with the depletion of oil and gas resources. Under conditions of limited oil and gas resources, there would be high motivation for rapid introduction of future energy production technologies, particularly as the export boom turned into a nagging energy deficit, or import requirement. This scenario shows the energy trade curve bending upward again slightly at the end of the century, with the rapid introduction of energy production from future technologies (nuclear power, geothermal, solar, biomass, etc). The shape of the future technologies production curve is hypothetical, but necessary to account for a likely shift in the energy production mix away from the conventional primary fuels, should oil and gas resources be very small.

Once again, I do not think this low resource projection is likely to occur, but it illustrates the basic dynamics of the model over a narrow time

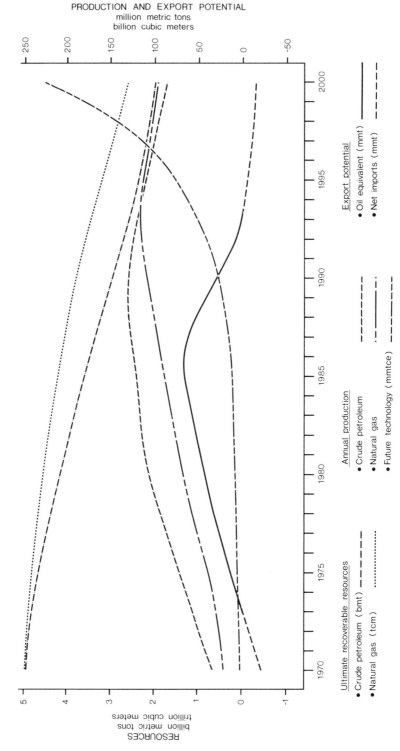

Fig. 12.1 Dynamics of resource depletion. Low projection data are from Table 24.5.

horizon. The important point is that the production curves for crude petroleum and natural gas will be restricted by resource availability. (As
with all parts of the projections, the interested reader is referred to
Chapters 23 and 24 for a complete technical discussion.)

The projection model allows for an infinite range of reserve and resource assumptions. Total resources are broken down into two categories—reserves (proved plus probable) and resources (additional discoveries). Resources move into the reserves category through a discovery
function and then into the energy system through a production function. The rate of discovery and the rate of production vary according to
the size of assumed resources and the stage of development in the industry (Chapter 23). I chose four basic reserves-resource projections to define a range of production curves for the Chinese oil and gas industries.
Reserves were set to constant initial values—5 billion metric tons of
crude petroleum and 5 trillion cubic meters of natural gas. These figures
are on the high side for proved plus probable reserves and allow for a
lag in foreign estimates. My initial reserves value corresponds roughly to
CIA estimates of onland recoverable resources.[14] The low projection was
constructed with just this basic reserve and no additional discoveries.
The "baseline" projection assumed a set of resource assumptions that
correspond to the best available current foreign estimates. Recoverable
crude petroleum resources were assumed to be 8.5 billion metric tons
and recoverable natural gas resources were set at 7.5 trillion cubic meters. (Additional crude oil discoveries would therefore be 3.5 bmt and
additional natural gas discoveries 2.5 tcm.) This set of assumptions,
labeled R_1 for short, is just a shade under the Meyerhoff-Willums estimates, which include moderate offshore discoveries.[15] The "median"
resource projection (R_2) more than doubles the Meyerhoff-Willums estimates to 20 bmt of recoverable crude oil and 15 tcm of recoverable natural gas. The median projection is at the upper range of what I would
consider reasonable conjecture for ultimate oil and gas recovery in the
PRC. Reaching R_2 would require greater than expected onland discoveries and substantial offshore discoveries as well. Finally, a high projection
(R_3) was constructed, using oil and gas resource assumptions four times
as large as the Meyerhoff-Willums estimates. Ultimate crude petroleum
recovery was assumed to be 35 billion tons (250 billion barrels) and ultimate natural gas recovery was set at 40 trillion cubic meters. These figures correspond to what would happen if China discovered the original
recoverable oil and gas resources of the United States (including Alaska),
according to the best available current estimates. There is no demon-
strable reason at the present time to believe that Chinese oil and gas resources will be anywhere near this range. But the high resource projec-

tion (R_3) provides a statistical hedge on the possibility of windfall discoveries either onland or offshore.

Production Constraints

As argued above, I believe that the basic constraints operating on future primary energy production will be crude petroleum and natural gas reserves and resources. The oil and gas industries are the high-growth sectors of China's energy system, and are also directly related to the pattern of energy commodity trade. The faster the oil and gas industries grow, the greater will be the quantity of petroleum and petroleum products (and possibly LNG) available for export after domestic consumption requirements have been satisfied. Accurate projection of the growth curves for crude petroleum and natural gas production is therefore essential to an accurate projection of the energy balance as a whole and of energy export potential.

Three sets of crude petroleum and natural gas production curves are projected in Figure 12.2. Each set of curves is identified according to a resource projection (R_1, R_2, R_3). The low one was excluded, since it has already been presented in Figure 12.1 and because in my judgment its resource assumptions have already been superseded. The "baseline" projection (R_1) is an extrapolation of what appeared to be happening in 1978. Under the Meyerhoff-Willums resource assumptions, crude petroleum production will peak at about 165 million metric tons per year (more than 3 million barrels per day) in about 1990, and then decline slowly to 140 million tons in the year 2000. Natural gas output would peak in the late 1990's at about 140 billion cubic meters per year. The peak years for crude oil production could be extended by enhanced recovery techniques, but the production curve would not be significantly raised. This is not an optimistic outcome, considering the ebullience of early projections that were based on much smaller reserves and resource assumptions. It illustrates graphically the importance of tying oil and gas production growth rates to the resource depletion curve. The outcome of this projection, incidentally, is not all that surprising. At one-fourth of the recoverable oil and gas resources of the United States, the production curve peaks at one-third the historical peak for U.S. crude petroleum production.

The production curves for the median projection (R_2) are much more optimistic and represent a more common assessment (largely unfounded) of what will occur in the Chinese oil and gas industries over the next two decades. Oil production grows rapidly during the early 1980's, reaching 175 million tons per year (3.5 million barrels per day) in 1985. Output then rises to 240 million tons in 1990, 290 million tons in 1995, and flattens out at over 300 million metric tons at the turn of the century. This is an optimistic crude oil production curve for China, given what is known about oil reserves and resources. And yet it completely eliminates the possibility of China's achieving the purported production target of 400 million tons in 1990. The natural gas production curve follows the oil curve up at a lower level, reaching 100 billion cubic meters in 1985 and flattening out at over 200 bcm per year by 2000. (For purposes of comparison, 1 bcm equals 0.9 mmtoe.) The production curves generated by the baseline and median resource scenarios represent a reasonable range of oil and gas projections for the PRC. There is a high probability that the actual production curves will fall somewhere between R_1 and R_2. Meyerhoff has already increased his 1976 estimate of economically recoverable crude petroleum resources to about 10 billion metric tons.[16] The consensus of foreign opinion is moving slowly toward a round figure of 100 billion barrels (13.7 bmt) of recoverable crude oil, including the offshore theaters. It does not require a stretch of the imagination to foresee a doubling of Meyerhoff's current assessment over the next ten or twenty years, based on new information or new discoveries by the Chinese. Certainly a large strike in any offshore theater would raise foreign estimates. Nonetheless, given the history of fantasy in projections of China's future oil and gas production, the lower curves (R_1) should be kept in mind as a conservative but possible outcome.

In addition to the reasonable range of production curves bounded by R_1 and R_2, I have provided one unreasonably high set of production curves (R_3). This is more than just a hedge against the reliability of my own projections. It provides a heuristic device for a further argument, given below, about the long-range constraints on energy commodity export potential. The high oil and gas projection should satisfy the wildest hopes of those who are optimistic about China's future as a crude petroleum exporter. It is based on the ultimate recoverable oil and gas resources of the United States, including past as well as future production. Chinese officials sometimes drop hints to foreign delegations that this is what they are hoping for. Crude oil production races upward to 220 million metric tons in 1985 and 310 million tons in 1990. By 1995, China's oil industry would have broken the 400 million ton mark, sometimes cited as a target for 1990. By the end of the century, crude petroleum production would have surpassed 500 million tons per year (10 million barrels per day) and would be headed for a peak level of less than 550 million tons per year, comparable to the 1977 crude oil output level of the Soviet Union. Natural gas output would reach 120 billion cubic meters in 1985, 200 bcm in 1990, and would still be growing fast at 400 bcm in the year 2000. (U.S. natural gas output peaked at over 600 bcm per

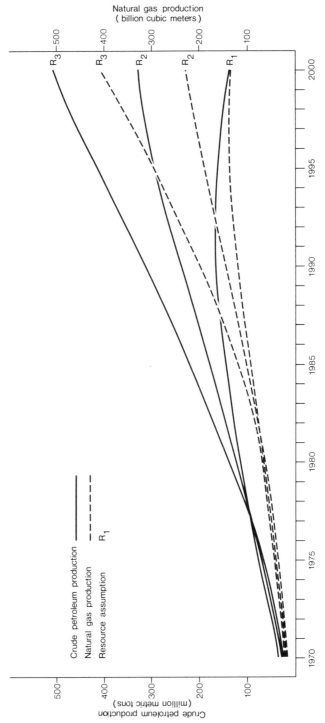

Fig. 12.2 Projected crude petroleum and natural gas production, 1970–2000. The scales for crude petroleum and natural gas are not energy-equivalent.

year.) This would give China, in combination with further growth in the coal and hydropower industries, a giant energy production system by the end of the century, presuming that the necessary capital and industrial infrastructure could be mobilized in the short period of two decades. It took the United States twice as long (1930–70) to move from China's current production levels to peak production, but Saudi Arabia will make the same transition in about 15–20 years (1965–85), proving that it can be done. One would not want to attach a high probability to the fantasy that China could match Saudi Arabia's pace of development in crude oil production. Perhaps this sheds some light on the hope that China will produce 400 million tons per year by 1990.[17]

Consumption Constraints

In a rapidly developing society, rising energy consumption requirements (energy demand) are a function of population growth, rising standards of living, industrial growth, general trends in economic growth, and the efficiency with which energy is used. The projection model for China's energy balance is flexible to variation in assumptions regarding all these growth factors on the consumption side of the model (Chapter 23). The impact of all these variables can be conveniently thought of in terms of alternative consumption scenarios (S_1, S_2, S_3) that provide a reasonable range of outcomes in the form of various projected curves for the energy end-use requirement (Figure 12.3). These curves in turn were generated by differential sets of assumptions for (a) growth in per capita GNP and (b) energy/GNP elasticities (expressed as regression coefficients). Per capita GNP is useful as a growth parameter, since it captures the likely effect of variable population growth as well as economic expansion. At this stage in the development of the model, I assumed a range of fixed per capita GNP growth rates from 3.0 percent per year to 5.0 percent per year. In combination with the likely population expansion (to about 1.3 billion by 2000), this yields slowly declining growth rates for GNP that are initially (1970–80) in the range of 5–7 percent per year. By the 1990's, with slowing population growth, the GNP growth rate drops to the 4–6 percent per year range. This is not an extreme set of economic growth assumptions. China's GNP grew at 6.7 percent per year from 1949 to 1978 and at 5.5 percent from 1970 to 1978 (Table 19.1).

I also established a range of energy/GNP elasticities, in the form of regression coefficients for various historical periods in China's energy development. Energy consumption (end-use) and a constant were regressed against GNP to produce a set of linear equations describing the relationship (Table 23.1). The energy/GNP coefficient projecting the

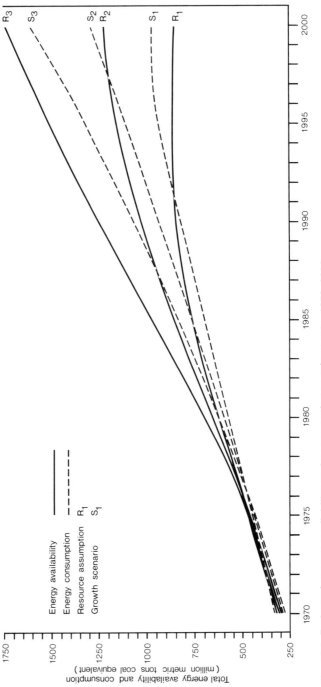

Fig. 12.3 Projected energy availability and consumption requirements, 1970–2000.

Total energy availability and consumption
(million metric tons coal equivalent)

Energy availability
Energy consumption
Resource assumption R_1
Growth scenario S_1

R_3
S_3
S_2
R_2
S_1
R_1

future pattern of energy consumption was set at the same initial value (1.5) as the most efficient value of the reliable historical coefficients. This initial projection coefficient was then allowed to decay over time to reflect gradual improvements in energy end-use efficiency. Roughly translated, this means that all my projected energy consumption scenarios are more conservative (i.e. energy-efficient) than historical experience over the last 30 years. This was done to avoid overstating future energy end-use requirements.

The energy availability curves (supply) projected in Figure 12.3 were derived from total primary energy production, minus conservative estimates of petrochemical use, plant use, loss in the thermal electric power cycle, and other inefficiencies that occur in the process of delivering energy commodities to the user. The three curves for energy availability (R_1, R_2, R_3) correspond to the three sets of oil and gas reserves and resource assumptions and the projected production curves discussed in the last section. It should be recalled that R_1 and R_2 represent a reasonable range of estimates, while R_3 is an extremely high projection. Here again, I ignore the low projection as unlikely at the conservative end of the total projected range.

The vertical distance between the projected energy availability curves and the projected consumption curves (R_1-S_1, R_2-S_2, R_3-S_3) represents the theoretical energy commodity surplus available for export. When the difference is negative, it implies an energy deficit or import requirement. Note that this surplus is a *maximum* figure for export potential, or a minimum figure for import requirements. In practice, few countries export at 100 percent of their theoretical surplus because of marketing difficulties, government export policy, contract delays, and the like. I term the theoretical surplus the "export potential" to distinguish the projected figure from a projection of actual energy commodity exports. In other words, the Chinese government could choose to export at less than its export potential, but could not export energy commodities at greater than its export potential without damaging domestic economic growth. Let us now look at the three projected scenarios for the PRC.

The energy consumption curve for the base-line projections (S_1) was projected on the basis of an assumed annual per capita GNP increase of 3.5 percent and a decaying energy/GNP coefficient with an initial value of 1.5. This represents an extrapolation of the per capita GNP growth rate that has been typical of the period since 1970 (3.5 percent) and a moderate improvement in energy use efficiency over the current situation. The baseline consumption curve reaches about 700 million metric tons coal equivalent (end-use) in 1985, 800 mmtce in 1990, and 1,000 mmtce in 2000. This would give China about the current energy consumption level of the Soviet Union (1976) at the turn of the century. From the perspective of energy export potential, the energy availability curve crossed over the projected curve for consumption requirements in the early 1970's. This created an "export bubble" of surplus energy commodities available for export. If the energy balance continues on its present course, energy availability will outstrip China's energy consumption requirement until the early 1990's, when slowing oil and gas production and relentlessly rising consumption requirements will once again meet and cross over, creating a net energy deficit or import requirement. The deficit will then increase sharply until rising production from future energy technologies causes another inflection in the energy availability curve, sometime in the early decades of the next century.

Under the growth assumptions of the median projection (R_2-S_2), per capita GNP was permitted to grow at 4.0 percent per year, just half of one percent higher than the growth rate in the baseline projection. The initial value of the energy/GNP coefficient was once again set at 1.5, somewhat more efficient than historical experience, and allowed to decay slowly as energy conservation measures are introduced into the Chinese economy. Under the assumptions of the median projection, energy consumption will approach 750 mmtce in 1985, 900 mmtce in 1990, and 1,300 mmtce in the year 2000. Once again, under the optimistic reserves and resource assumptions of the median scenario, energy availability outpaces consumption requirements over a 25-year period, yielding a net energy commodity surplus for export. Crossover would be reached in the mid-1990's, producing a moderate energy deficit or import requirement by 2000.

The high scenario (R_3-S_3) shows what would happen if everything went extremely well in the Chinese economy over the next two decades. The discovery of enormous oil and gas deposits in the western basins and the offshore theaters produces a series of upward shocks in the energy balance, analogous to the oil booms in Texas, Oklahoma, and California. The government in Peking, recognizing that it is sitting on a sea of potential oil wealth, invites the foreign multinationals to engage in massive joint-development projects along the Chinese continental shelf. Peking meanwhile mobilizes its capital resources and throws them into rapid development of the western fields and a huge network of oil and gas pipelines and refineries. This boom in the energy sector, coupled with rising crude oil exports and large-scale imports of foreign plants and equipment, precipitates rapid growth throughout the Chinese economy, particularly in the industrial sector. Per capita GNP expands at a full 5.0 percent per year, 1.5 percent higher than the baseline projection.

As a result of this fanciful sequence of events, energy consumption (end-use) would exceed 800 mmtce in 1985, reaching 1,000 mmtce in 1990 and 1,600 mmtce by 2000, the level the United States achieved in the early 1960's. Energy availability, meanwhile, would leap upward at an even higher rate, outstripping consumption requirements through the entire projected period until crossover occurred at about the turn of the century, when economic growth would have to be restricted to avoid an energy deficit. Meanwhile, a substantial energy commodity export potential would have been generated over a period of 30–35 years.

There are several points that should be made about this analysis. The growth curves in Figure 12.3 are neither exponential nor linear. Rather, they are subtly inflected by long-range growth trends aggregated across a number of variables. The curves are most sensitive to alternative resource and economic growth assumptions and relatively insensitive to changes in most of the other variables in the model. But given the subtlety of the inflections, some range of error is possible. The general conclusions would probably survive a wide range of projection error in the curves, but precise values would not.

A second important point is that, given the necessary oil and gas discoveries, the Chinese government might consciously restrain domestic economic development in order to generate a higher energy commodity surplus for export. For example, energy availability might grow along the curve generated by R_2, while economic growth was constrained to a 3.5 percent average annual increase in per capita GNP (S_1). This would yield a higher energy commodity surplus for export ($R_2 - S_1$). There is no theoretical reason why the curves should be paired in the manner I have suggested. However, I believe that this outcome, while possible, is not likely. The Chinese government would be hard pressed to prevent some economic expansion in the event of higher oil and gas discoveries. The foreign exchange revenues generated by slightly higher crude oil exports would bring higher levels of plant and equipment imports, which would feed back into a growth effect on the Chinese economy. In addition, the faster pace of industrial growth would generate higher internal energy consumption requirements. Even marginal increments in the growth rate for the economy as a whole generate large increases in energy consumption requirements. Furthermore, the present Chinese administration appears firmly committed to rapid industrial and economic growth. No miracle will prevent this growth from generating new energy consumption requirements. Some economic growth might be sacrificed to prevent an energy deficit, but it is unlikely that Peking will sacrifice its modernization program on the altar of its oil export program.

Export Constraints

We are finally in a position to deal adequately with the problem of long-range constraints on China's energy commodity exports. Figure 12.4 outlines the outcome, in terms of energy commodity export potential, of the alternative aggregate energy balance projections discussed in the last section. Three curves for export potential are shown, which illustrate the general range of projections in the export sector generated by the energy balance model. The last two or three years have, perhaps, been a slow period for China's energy commodity exports. In fact, total 1978 energy commodity exports will be only slightly higher than 1975 exports. But I believe that this situation will not be typical of the 1980's and was due largely to an internal political struggle over oil export policy and more generally over modernization policy. At the time of writing, all signs pointed in the direction of higher energy commodity exports over the next few years at least.

The alternative projections of energy commodity export potential reveal that export potential is surprisingly insensitive to wide variations in the overall framework of the energy balance. Under all three projections, including the extremely optimistic growth projections, export potential will be sharply limited by the inexorable rise in domestic energy consumption requirements. All three projections overstate export potential during the late 1970's by a factor of about 1.5 to 2.0. This exaggeration was the result of relatively conservative growth parameters for energy consumption that were introduced to avoid an exaggeration of the long-range projections of the consumption requirement. The export potential curves may, therefore, rise too swiftly and peak a bit early, but I believe that the peak export level is accurately defined for all three.

Under the resource and economic growth assumptions of the baseline projection, total energy commodity export potential will rise swiftly through the mid-1980's, reaching 50 million metric tons of oil equivalent by 1985. If Peking were able to export this entire potential to Japan in the form of crude petroleum, it would satisfy less than one-fourth of Japan's current (1976) crude oil import requirement. The Chinese government will probably choose to export at a level somewhat below its theoretical surplus. Furthermore, some of the energy exported will be in the form of coal, refined petroleum products, and possibly liquefied natural gas. And China has already developed a number of other energy commodity customers in Asia. Thus, it is unlikely that the PRC would be able to satisfy more than 10–15 percent of the Japanese crude petroleum market at peak export levels. Under the limiting assumptions of the baseline projection, energy export potential will decline as rapidly as it rose, reaching crossover by the early 1990's, and declining into a substantial energy deficit thereafter. The introduction of enhanced oil and gas recovery technology at the peak of the crude petroleum curve would extend peak production for a number of years. But this would have only marginal effect on the energy deficit and would not significantly raise the export curve.

The median energy balance scenario (S_2) is remarkably similar to the baseline projection. Export potential will peak a few years later, in the late 1980's, at 75 million metric tons oil equivalent, only 1.5 times the peak level reached under the baseline projection. The median export potential projection then declines under the pressure of rising consumption requirements, crossing over into a net deficit or import requirement in the late 1990's. This would occur regardless of the fact that crude oil production continues to rise through the year 2000 in the median projection, although at declining rates of increase (Figure 12.2). By 1995, the median crude oil production curve is nearly twice the baseline projection of crude petroleum production. Yet energy commodity export potential still declines rapidly under the pressure of rising consumption induced by continued industrial and economic growth.

The export situation is only marginally better under the absurdly optimistic assumptions of the high-growth scenario. Net export potential (S_3) rises fast during the early 1980's, reaching 100 million tons oil equivalent by 1985. Export potential then continues to grow, although more slowly, to a peak level of 135 mmtoe (2.7 million barrels per day) in the early 1990's. Even this high export projection then succumbs to falling oil and gas growth rates and rising consumption requirements, and drops off in the closing years of the century, crossing over into an import requirement sometime after the year 2000. However unrealistic the high-growth scenario, it does demonstrate that the "bubble" shape of China's future energy commodity export potential is a persistent characteristic of the projected energy balance, under a wide variety of assumed growth projections. It is unlikely that the PRC will ever be a crude petroleum exporter on the order of Iran or Saudi Arabia. The sheer size of the population and the pace of domestic economic growth preclude this outcome. Under maximally favorable—and very unlikely—growth conditions, China might reach Venezuela's peak level as a crude petroleum exporter. But assuming that Peking exports at less than theoretical potential and that part of the energy commodity exports are in the form of coal, the PRC will not reach Venezuela's crude oil export position in the international market under any conditions.

Under a variety of alternative resource and economic growth assumptions, my projections indicate that China's theoretical energy commodity

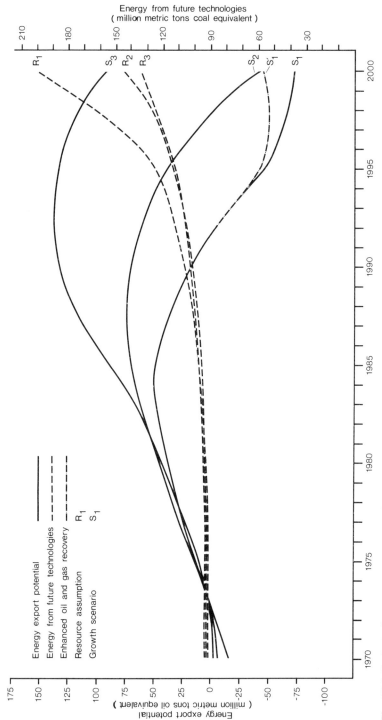

Fig. 12.4 Projected energy export potential and production from future technologies, 1970–2000. The scales for energy export potential and production from future technologies are not energy-equivalent.

Energy from future technologies
(million metric tons coal equivalent)

210 180 150 120 90 60 30

R₁ S₃ R₂ R₃ S₂ S₁' S₁

Energy export potential
(million metric tons oil equivalent)

175 150 125 100 75 50 25 0 -25 -50 -75 -100

Energy export potential ⎯⎯⎯⎯⎯
Energy from future technologies ⎯ ⎯ ⎯
Enhanced oil and gas recovery ⎯⎯ ⎯⎯
Resource assumption   R₁
Growth scenario   S₁

TABLE 12.1
Projected Export Commodity Mix

Year	Coal (mmtce)	Crude petroleum (mmt)	Refined products (mmt)	Total energy (mmtce)
1978	0.5	9-10	1.5	16-18
1980	3.0	15-20	2-3	30-35
1985	10-15	25-40	3-5	50-80
1990[a]	15-20 (20)	25-40 (60-80)	3-5 (5)	55-85 (120-150)
1995[a]	10-20 (20)	10-20 (60-80)	0-3 (5)	25-50 (120-150)
2000[a]	0-20 (20)	0 (30-50)	0 (5)	0-20 (70-100)

[a] Figures in parentheses assume high growth scenario.

export potential will peak within a realistic range of 50–75 million metric tons oil equivalent (75–100 mmtce, or 1.0–1.5 million bbl/day) during the period between 1985 and 1990. Peak export potential will be maintained over about five years and will then decline. If my statistics are correct, Peking currently exports at about 75 percent of theoretical energy commodity surplus (Chapter 24). The exact commodity mix within this export ceiling will be a matter of policy and market conditions. Based on historical patterns of energy commodity trade and on China's current plans for expansion of the coal and oil industries, I project what I believe will be the export situation over the next several decades (Table 12.1). Naturally enough, the further into the future this projection moves, the more hazardous it becomes.

All the projections for the Chinese energy balance show a rapid expansion of energy commodity exports in the early 1980's. As this expansion occurs, it will generate considerable interest in China's energy development, and perhaps some speculation regarding China's future as an energy exporter to world markets. The highest growth in energy commodity exports should occur between 1980 and 1985, as export potential doubles over current levels. Japan will not be able to absorb all of the Chinese coal and oil offered for export during this period, since Tokyo already has a defined network of energy commodity trade commitments with the Middle East, Indonesia, the Soviet Union, and China itself. Consequently, Peking will be looking hard for new markets for its coal and oil. Energy commodity trade agreements with Southeast Asia will grow from current levels to whatever these regional trading partners can absorb without major investments in new refinery equipment to handle Chinese crude. Peking will also try to break into the U.S. and West European import markets. But actual exports to these areas will be small in comparison to their total import needs.

The most dramatic increase could very well be in coal exports, rather than crude petroleum. China currently exports about half a million tons of coking coal and steam coal each year (Table 20.1). Most of this goes to Japan, some to Pakistan, and small amounts to other trading partners in Southeast Asia. The current Sino-Japanese trade agreement commits both sides to increase coal trade to more than 3.5 million metric tons in 1982. About half of this will be coking coal and about half steam coal. Japan is currently building a series of large coal-fired thermal electric power plants that will greatly increase imports of steam coal. A number of countries are competing for the 15–30 million tons per year of additional coal trade that this development will stimulate, including Canada, the United States, the Soviet Union, Australia, and now China. Coking coal imports, which have traditionally represented the bulk of the Japanese coal market, are steady or declining somewhat because of a depression in the steel industry that is expected to last into the 1980's. Japan's additional coal imports will therefore be predominantly steaming coal for the large power plants and other industries. Japan's total coal imports are projected to rise from the current level of 60 million tons per year to 90–100 million tons in 1985.[18] Peking will be directing its coal export drive toward that increment of new Japanese coal imports, as will other countries, notably Australia. This could cause some jostling and price-cutting on the Asian coal market, a prospect that greatly concerns Australian companies that are currently expanding capacity to meet the expected increase in Japan's imports of steam coal.

China, meanwhile, is also expanding its coal production capacity from the already high levels achieved by the mid-1970's. In 1978, China may have reached 600 million tons of raw coal output. The coal production increase in the first half of 1978 was reported at nearly 20 percent over the corresponding period of 1977.[19] This figure includes capacity that was restored to production after the Tangshan earthquake and the political disturbances of 1976. But a final 1978 coal production growth rate of anywhere near 20 percent would be a sign that the industry is still expanding at a healthy pace. China has recently contracted with West German and British firms for equipment and technical assistance for the further expansion of its basic coal-mining capacity. The United States recently agreed to provide technical assistance to China in the field of open-cast coal mining.[20] In January 1978, Chinese Minister of Coal Hsiao Han forecast a sharp increase in coal exports over the next ten years.[21] My own analysis suggests that China's internal market for coal is nearing saturation and will expand only slowly over the next 20 years. All these indicators point in the direction of higher coal exports. I project that Peking will attempt to market 10–15 million metric tons of coal by 1985, an event that could have considerable impact on the world coal market, particularly in Asia. Coal exports could reach 15–20 million tons by 1990, and will be in the upper part of this range if new oil and gas discoveries are very large during the 1980's. Coal exports will be hurt less by the general decline in China's energy commodity export potential than will crude oil exports. China will probably export at least 10 million tons of coal per year from 1985 until 2000. This will require a considerable improvement in coal beneficiation and transport facilities.[22]

For the distant future beyond 1990, there is some possibility that China will be exporting coal to Japan for gasification and liquefaction. The Japanese government is interested in coal conversion technologies and recently signed a $10 billion research and development agreement with the U.S. Department of Energy for a program that will lay heavy emphasis on gasification and liquefaction plant designs.[23] The economics of coal conversion are still a matter of conjecture, but these technologies could become competitive as crude petroleum prices continue to rise on the international market. Even if China's crude oil exports were sharply restricted by internal demand by the year 2000, coal could be made available for export to a gasification or liquefaction plant in Japan.

The situation for crude petroleum exports is far less optimistic. China's 1978 crude oil exports were in the range of 9–10 million metric tons, depending on the amounts that Romania and North Korea took. Of this quantity, Japan was committed to import 7 million tons under the terms of the trade agreement.[24] Japan's imports will then rise to 8 million tons in 1980 and a projected 15 million metric tons in 1982. It is unlikely that Japanese refiners will be willing to take more than this amount of Chinese crude in the short run, given their resistance to the terms of the trade agreement.[25] The Japanese Ministry of International Trade and Industry would like to import about 40 million tons of Chinese crude in 1985. But imports on this scale would imply an investment of as much as $10 billion in specialized hydrocracking refinery plants to handle the heavy northeast China crudes.[26] MITI could take one of two approaches to the problem. Either the government could subsidize the construction of the necessary refinery facilities or it could seek to shift oil-fired thermal power plants and other heavy industries toward the use of Chinese heavy oil, importing lighter crudes from the Middle East for refining. The second option would be cheaper to implement, but involves rearranging long-term supply contracts and threatening the continued import of Indonesian crude, which is comparable in some respects to the heavy Chinese crudes. The Indonesian government, naturally enough, does not savor this prospect.[27] Japan's crude oil imports have actually declined from the peak level reached in 1973, and there is little prospect that Japan will experience another big surge in crude petroleum imports. This means that the introduction of new crude oil imports from any source tends to displace previous suppliers and introduce rancor into Japan's trade relations. The political motivation for a shift in the direction of Chinese crude is very high, however, and further increases should be expected.

On the whole, my projections indicate that China's crude petroleum exports could reach 15–20 million tons by 1980, and 25–40 million metric tons per year by 1985. Because of the short-term limits on the Japanese market for Chinese crude, for a few years this will create a situation in which Peking looks for new trading partners to mop up its surplus crude export capacity. One American company has reported a contract for the import of about a half-million tons of Chinese crude in 1979.[28] Coastal States Gas Corporation will refine the Chinese crude into a low-sulfur fuel oil that meets California's strict environmental laws. But the American majors seem to be shying away from Chinese crude. During the summer of 1978, Gulf denied rumors that it was considering buying Chinese oil, citing the high price.[29] But the majors are probably equally concerned with the current glut of oil on the West Coast as Alaskan production increases. This would leave China with marginal access to the U.S. market via the smaller oil companies.*

The market situation for Chinese crude oil could change dramatically if the PRC is able to produce significant quantities of lighter crudes from Kwangtung province and the South China Sea. Such crudes would have easier access to Japanese refineries, and have already been tested in Japan.[30] But it may be some time before production levels warrant use in international trade. Ironically, the PRC itself would probably like to have greater quantities of light crude oil for its own refineries. Other export strategies that Peking could employ include expanding crude oil trade with Southeast Asia and lowering the price of Chinese crudes to give them a greater competitive edge. The northeast crudes are now priced at about $0.50 per barrel below Indonesian crude, a price that most refiners consider high because of handling difficulties. The Philippines are already taking about as much Chinese oil as their refineries can successfully mix with lighter crudes. Thailand may expand its purchases of Chinese crude, but is more interested in refined products, particularly fuel oil. Peking may, therefore, have to consider price cuts, if the government wishes to expand crude oil exports in the short term. This could cut into foreign exchange earnings and will be stoutly resisted by Peking.

*The revolution in Iran, which occurred while this book was in press, significantly tightened the supply of crude oil on the world market. If the tightness continues or accelerates, it may affect the international market demand for Chinese crude.

Long-range projections of crude petroleum exports are extremely difficult to make with any degree of certainty without resorting to an absurdly broad range of estimates. If the Chinese energy balance grows at rates somewhere between the baseline and median projections, crude oil exports should level out between 1985 and 1990 at 25–40 million metric tons per year. By 1995, slowing oil and gas growth rates and continuing growth in internal consumption requirements will put downward pressure on crude oil exports, curtailing them to half the peak levels that are attained between 1985 and 1990. Crude oil exports will then drop to zero by the turn of the century, while coal exports continue at a fairly constant level. Even this pessimistic long-range projection would require slowing the growth of the domestic economy below the levels in the median projection. The figures in parentheses in Table 12.1 indicate what would happen to crude oil exports in the event of the large oil and gas discoveries of the high-growth projection. China could, perhaps, export as much as 60–80 million tons of crude petroleum in 1990 under these conditions. Exports would then drop to 30–50 million tons under pressure of rising domestic demand by 2000. Even this level would require restraining the growth of domestic energy consumption. Under all projections, therefore, we should expect a decline in crude petroleum exports during the 1990's. This situation will parallel what happened in the United States in the 1950's, as net oil exports were replaced by imports made necessary by continued expansion in the domestic economy.

China's trade in refined petroleum products will continue to be sharply constrained by available refinery capacity throughout the period of the projections. Exports of refined products, currently running around 1.5 million metric tons per year, are mostly targeted at the limited market in Hong Kong. Thailand would like to import significant quantities of Chinese diesel fuel and residual fuel, albeit at concessional prices. Thus we should expect a modest increase in annual exports of refined products through 1985, reaching a plateau at about 3–5 million tons per year in the late 1980's. Exports of refined products will then decline during the 1990's under the pressure of rising domestic consumption requirements. Even a plateau figure of 5 million metric tons per year of refined products exports would require the construction of one or two refineries dedicated to the export trade, an expensive proposition, particularly at a time of short refinery capacity for domestic consumption.

In terms of total energy commodity trade, we should expect China's energy commodity exports to rise from less than 20 million metric tons coal equivalent in 1978 to 30–35 mmtce in 1980 and 50–80 mmtce by 1985. This represents an average annual growth rate of 15–20 percent per year in the intervening years, which if achieved will cause a stir in regional energy markets. Assuming that Peking exported at about 75 percent of capacity and maximum growth conditions occurred, energy commodity exports would peak at 120–150 mmtce in 1990–95 and then decline. Under every projection, exports of total energy commodities will peak at between 5 and 10 percent of primary energy production, continuing the traditional balance between production and consumption in the Chinese energy system.

Under favorable conditions, China will be an energy commodity exporter on the scale of Indonesia. These exports, however marginal in terms of the world market, will be a significantly earning force in China's balance of trade. Assuming an average return of about $75 per metric ton coal equivalent exported, the PRC will earn $2–2.5 billion in 1980 and $4–6 billion per year in energy export revenues between 1985 and 1990. Even assuming the high-growth scenario and hefty price increases, peak earnings from China's energy commodity trade will not exceed $10–15 billion per year, about one-fourth of the figure that the United States is currently spending on oil imports. This warrants some caution in Peking about the size of its plant and equipment import programs. In 1978 alone, China already placed more than $5 billion in new orders from Japan. That exceeds 1978 revenues from energy commodity exports by a factor of three. This disparity helps explain the more relaxed attitude currently prevailing in Peking toward long-term credits and loans to finance the import program.

Energy Production from Future Technologies

China, like many countries faced with long-range resource constraints on the development of their energy systems, is showing some signs of interest in future energy production technologies. In the PRC, research and development of energy production technologies fall loosely into what is referred to as "science and technology policy." Energy technology innovations are under the direction of the State Scientific and Technological Commission, rather than being the responsibility of one of the energy ministries. At a national conference in March 1978, Fang Yi, Minister of Science and Technology, called for acceleration of China's energy-related research and development effort. Fang Yi admitted that the PRC lags by 15–20 years in many important energy technologies and suggested that the country set itself the objective of reaching advanced world levels in some areas by 1985 and in all branches of industry by the year 2000.[31] He mentioned a number of existing technologies that require updating in the PRC, including petroleum geology, oil and gas recovery, oil-processing, coal-mine mechanization, coal transport, mine safety, coal gasification and liquefaction, large-scale hydropower engineering, mine-mouth thermal power generation, and high-voltage electric power transmission. In addition, however, he called for advanced research on future energy technologies of unproved value, including solar energy, wind energy, tidal power, geothermal energy, biomass, oil shale, and low-calorie coals. These are all areas of energy research and development that have generated interest in the United States. China has already developed some research programs and applications for exotic energy sources (Chapter 14). But if implemented, Fang Yi's program would greatly accelerate the pace of research on these future energy technologies. He also expressed interest in high-energy physics, particle research, commercial nuclear power, and controlled thermonuclear fusion, subjects we will return to in a moment.

In order to account for the possibility of the introduction of future energy production technologies into the Chinese energy balance, I included an unspecified variable in the model for energy production from such technologies. It is known that China already produces some energy from oil shale, geothermal electric power generation, and small rural biogas generators. This type of energy production has already reached significant proportions and will continue to grow over the next several decades. In addition, Peking is showing increasing interest in commercial nuclear power, and has already agreed to import one or two large French reactors.[32] These reactors should be working by the mid-1980's, producing energy that is classified in the model as production from future technologies.

Successfully modeling the introduction of future energy technologies is problematical. A simple exponential growth curve based on some reasonable estimate of the pace of technological development overlooks the direct link between the depletion of oil and gas resources and the motivation for investing heavily in nonfossil technologies. I therefore tied variation in the growth rate for production from future technologies directly to the crude petroleum resource depletion curve (Figure 12.4). The greater China's oil and gas resources and production, the less will be the motivation for investment in costly alternative energy production technologies. On the other hand, the greater the resource constraint on oil and gas production, the higher the motivation for accelerated development of future technologies. The hypothetical production curves under various projections for energy from future technologies were therefore identified by the oil and gas resource curves in question (R_1, R_2, R_3). The future technology curves are inversely related to the growth of the Chinese energy balance. Under the sharp resource constraints of the baseline projection (R_1), energy production from future technologies will grow rapidly, exceeding 150 million metric tons coal equivalent by

2000. Under the median projection, future production will reach about 75 mmtce in the year 2000, and under the high projection about 60 mmtce. The absolute figures in these comparisons are meaningless, but the structure of the growth curves should be roughly correct relative to each other. Figure 12.4 also illustrates a relationship between downward pressure on the potential export curve and the growth of production from future technologies.

There are current indications that China will seek cooperation in the development of advanced energy technologies from the United States. As I have argued in other parts of this book, both Japan and Western Europe are strongly competitive with the United States for China's energy equipment market, and for a variety of reasons have led U.S. energy plant and equipment sales to China by a wide margin. China is already leaning heavily on American offshore exploration technology in its rig purchases, but still prefers to deal through intermediaries in Singapore and elsewhere when possible. If U.S.–based multinationals are permitted a role in joint offshore development programs, Peking will try to hold them at arm's length by stationing them in Hong Kong. To China, the United States represents an overwhelming industrial power, which requires a certain shielding or distance for proper management of commercial relations. This gestalt in trade relations between the two countries may persist even beyond the point when full diplomatic relations have been achieved. China is far more comfortable with Japan as its primary trading partner, and still looks to Europe for big purchases such as the French nuclear power plants—which are American technology, licensed to French companies by Westinghouse.

On the other hand, the United States retains its edge in research on advanced or future energy production technologies. Washington is already sponsoring the world's largest energy research and development program in response to what it perceives as its "energy crisis." When Secretary of Energy James R. Schlesinger visited China in the fall of 1978, the package of proposals he carried to the Chinese sounded more like a technical assistance program than a trade package. He offered technical help with such conventional technologies as open-cast mining, hydropower, and oil and gas recovery. But the American delegation also stressed renewable energy sources, including geothermal, solar, and wind power.[33] Chinese experiments with shale oil, coal conversion, and biomass were of particular interest to American specialists on the trip. The United States even offered to help China design, build, and test a 50-billion-electron-volt synchrotron for theoretical research in high-energy physics.

The United States could, therefore, have a relatively free hand in cooperative advanced energy research and development projects with the PRC, taking advantage of natural American strength in cutting-edge technologies. This type of cooperation will be particularly important in the event that China's oil and gas resources are relatively limited on the scale of foreign estimates. Sino–U.S. relations in the nuclear field are bound to be characterized by a certain degree of ambivalence, as Washington tries to entangle Peking in the net of international nuclear control agreements and the Chinese government tries to elude the net. And so it is to the subject of China's commercial nuclear development prospects that we turn next.

China's Nuclear Option

China's nuclear development program, like those of the United States, the Soviet Union, Britain, and France, began with the acquisition of nuclear weapons. Every aspect of nuclear science and technology in the PRC was initially tied to the weapons program. Over the years, however, China has moved gradually in the direction of nonmilitary applications of nuclear technology. Today we see the culmination of this trend in the announced plans to purchase one or two pressurized water nuclear power reactors (PWR) from France. At the end of the 1970's, we were at the beginning of China's commercial nuclear power development program. The "nuclear option" in the Chinese case is not an opportunity to acquire materials for the construction of nuclear weapons, which the Chinese have long possessed, but an opportunity to apply nuclear technology to the development of civilian nuclear power. The nuclear weapons and nuclear power technologies, although closely related, are not instantly interchangeable. The PRC faces a long period of learning and building before nuclear power could possibly contribute significantly to the Chinese energy balance. If Peking chooses to exercise its nuclear option in the field of commercial nuclear energy, it will raise important questions for the international community. To what extent should the industrial market economy countries share their nuclear advances with a country that has only signed one international nuclear control agreement? How can Peking be induced to participate in international agreements, such as the Non-Proliferation Treaty and the Strategic Arms Limitation Talks, or in organizations dedicated to the control of civilian nuclear technology, such as the International Atomic Energy Agency (IAEA)? A brief review of the history of China's nuclear development program provides a basis for understanding Peking's current thrust into the development of commercial nuclear power.

Early Nuclear Development

The leaders of the Chinese Communist Party were aware of the strategic importance of the atomic bomb as soon as it had been exploded over Hiroshima in August 1945. In an interview with Anna Louise Strong in August 1946, Mao Tse-tung called the atomic bomb "a paper tiger."[34] But this very assertion underlined its impact on Mao, who was fond of expressing himself in conundrums. In fact, the bomb had defeated Japan very suddenly, leaving the CCP in a good position to begin its drive for power in all China. The Soviet Union exploded its first atomic bomb on September 23, 1949, one week before the proclamation of the People's Republic of China. Britain followed on October 3, 1952, and the United States tested its first hydrogen bomb one month later, on November 1. Moscow tested a thermonuclear fusion device on August 12, 1953. On December 8, 1953, President Eisenhower proposed his atoms-for-peace program to the General Assembly of the United Nations, and in April of the following year Indian Prime Minister Nehru called for the suspension of all tests by the nuclear powers. This rush of events on the world scene kept Peking's attention focused on the strategic implications of nuclear development, but the Chinese leadership, burdened with the problems of reconstruction, recovery, and the establishment of a socialist state, deferred any decision on nuclear problems throughout the early 1950's.

It is difficult to pinpoint with any degree of accuracy the date when the Chinese government decided to develop nuclear weapons, but it appears to have been sometime in 1955 or perhaps even earlier. A speech by Mao Tse-tung made in April 1956 refers to the acquisition of the bomb as if the decision had already been made to include nuclear development as part of the Second Five-Year Plan.[35] Peking thereupon moved quickly to establish the foundation for its nuclear weapons program. The program was built around a core of nuclear scientists and engineers who had been trained in the United States and other Western countries. A fundamental technical assistance agreement with the Soviet Union was signed on October 15, 1957, under which Moscow agreed to provide a wide range of basic nuclear research equipment and to train an additional cadre of Chinese scientists at the Dubna Institute for nuclear research.[36] Peking initiated a number of nuclear research institutes within China during 1957 and 1958, including the nuclear physics department at Futan University, and the Institute of Atomic Energy in Peking.[37] These institutes were given Soviet Van de Graaff accelerators, cyclotrons, a 10-megawatt experimental reactor, and other equipment for the Chinese nuclear research program. (See Chapter 14 for technical details.) Czechoslovakia provided assistance in setting up the first Chinese uranium mines and an ore concentration plant in Chuchou, Hunan province.[38] Czechoslovakia was also reported to have processed some Chinese uranium in exchange for half of the uranium, but the dates and amounts involved are still hidden in official secrecy.[39] Ironically, the Soviet Union also helped China launch its missile program in 1958, a program that was later effective in providing China with intermediate-range ballistic missiles, which are now used as a strategic deterrent against the Soviet Union.

Sino-Soviet nuclear collaboration came crashing to a halt on June 20, 1959, when Moscow refused to provide China with a prototype atomic bomb, which Peking later claimed had been part of the 1957 nuclear assistance agreement.[40] This event marked the turning point toward a completely independent Chinese nuclear development policy. China was also beginning to experiment with its own strategic nuclear policy. In February 1958, Chou En-lai had endorsed Nehru's proposal for an Asian nuclear-free zone, but the Chinese resisted Russian interpretation of the zone in a manner that might have restricted Peking's own weapons development program.[41] China was also rumored to have turned down a Soviet request to station nuclear-armed missiles on its soil.[42]

The Period of Isolation (1960–70)

Complete withdrawal of Soviet nuclear technical assistance in 1960 must have seriously damaged the Chinese program. But the PRC moved ahead with its weapons development at a remarkable pace, considering this setback. It is still unclear precisely how China managed to move forward with the construction of the Lanchow Gaseous Diffusion Plant and two plutonium reactors near Paotaw, Inner Mongolia, in the absence of Soviet assistance.[43] Perhaps much of the equipment for these plants had already been received from the Soviet Union by the time of the break in 1960. It is unlikely that any such equipment was delivered after 1960. In any case, it is widely believed that the gaseous diffusion plant began its initial operation in the early 1960's and that the plutonium reactors followed.[44] Even more obscure is the manner in which China obtained the highly enriched uranium for its first test of a fission device on October 16, 1964. Some sources argue that Czechoslovakia may have provided China with weapons-grade uranium, but this is unlikely in view of the lack of isotopic separation facilities in Czechoslovakia.[45] If the weapon used enriched uranium rather than plutonium, then the logical conclusion is that the enrichment was conducted at the Lanchow plant.[46] This again implies a high level of initial Soviet assistance in the construction of the diffusion plant. The PRC is known to have begun construction on the Liuchiahsia hydropower station, China's largest, in 1958 to provide the great quantities of electric power required in the diffusion process.[47] In any case, the pace of development in the Chinese nuclear program was remarkable, even against the background of such efforts as the Manhattan Project.

It was also during the early 1960's that Peking rejected all Western efforts to reach adequate international nuclear control agreements. As early as January 1960, the PRC renounced the binding force of any disarmament agreement that was reached without direct Chinese participation.[48] During the final stages in the negotiation of the nuclear Test Ban Treaty in 1963, nuclear disarmament became a subject of debate in the acrimonious ideological dispute between the Chinese and Soviet communist parties, greatly hardening the Chinese position regarding international nuclear control. Peking felt itself caught between two colossal nuclear powers, either one of which could have initiated a surgical strike against its fledgling nuclear weapons facilities. Furthermore, accession to any aspect of the Test Ban Agreement would have crippled China's atomic weapons program at birth.

In order to avoid damaging its international political position among prominent Third World advocates of nuclear disarmament, Peking began circulating its own proposals in 1963. These were based on total dismantling of Soviet and American arsenals and were largely ignored by the international community. In its announcement of the first Chinese atomic test, however, Peking declared a unilateral policy renouncing the first use of atomic weapons, and called on the other nuclear powers to do likewise.[49] The non-first-use proposal became the backbone of the Chinese position on disarmament, which was followed without deviation until at least the mid-1970's. The apparent rigidity of the Chinese position rejecting international nuclear control agreements dates to an early period in its own nuclear development program. This rigidity has important implications for commercial nuclear power development over the next two decades. It is closely associated with the extended period of international isolation that Peking experienced from 1960 until the early 1970's.

By the end of the 1960's, it was apparent that China's nuclear weapons program had succeeded beyond all expectation. China exploded at least ten test devices from 1964 through 1969, including five or six fusion weapons.[50] Medium-range ballistic missiles were tested from 1966 on and achieved ranges of up to 1,000 miles, sufficient to reach deep into Soviet Siberia. Work on an intercontinental ballistic missile was initiated as early as 1965, although deployment of ICBMs in the 1970's was slower than expected.[51]

Reemergence and Nuclear Outreach

The end of China's international isolation, which began in 1971 and has continued at an accelerating pace since, brought with it renewed interest in foreign nuclear technology. The first few steps toward nuclear collaboration with the industrial market economy countries were tentative and couched in the framework of scientific exchange, particularly in the field of high-energy physics. In 1972, Premier Chou En-lai placed high-energy physics at the top of the list of priorities for the Chinese National Academy of Sciences.[52] This may have caused a revival of theoretical nuclear physics, and subsequent reports have indicated a high level of activity in nuclear research organizations throughout China at about this time. Some new research equipment was built or converted from obsolete devices from the early 1960's.[53] By 1975 the nuclear research program was experimenting with such exotic technologies as controlled thermonuclear fusion.[54] The Chinese press also reported wide experimentation with new uses for radioactive isotopes.[55]

Thus rehabilitated and fortified, China's community of nuclear scientists initiated an extensive round of delegation diplomacy that continues today. The first Chinese nuclear delegation may have been the high-energy physics group that was reported to have visited the United States in 1973.[56] The United States sent a return delegation in 1974 that discussed the development of Sino-American cooperation in the development of atomic energy.[57] During the same year, Chinese delegations visited nuclear power plants in Japan, Canada, and Western Europe, and some Chinese nuclear specialists were reported to have undergone advanced training at Britain's Atomic Energy Authority Centre in Hartwell.[58] In November 1975, a 12-member delegation of the European Organization for Nuclear Research visited China and reported rising interest in technical cooperation with Western scientists.[59] A Chinese delegation with special competence in high-energy accelerators followed up by attending the May 1976 meetings of the European Organization for Nuclear Research in Geneva.[60] Contacts established at this meeting may have led to the October-November 1976 uranium mining and geology study group from France's Commission of Atomic Energy.[61] The French group, which had been invited by the Atomic Energy Bureau of the Chinese Academy of Sciences, refused to be photographed, immediately broadcasting its importance. The group may have been permitted to visit uranium mines and is thought to have initiated the dialogue between Peking and Paris that culminated in the sale of two French nuclear power reactors to China in 1978.

During 1977, Peking further broadened its range of international contacts in fields associated with nuclear science and technology. At least three American nuclear scientists went to China on separate trips, including J. R. Nix (Los Alamos Scientific Laboratory), John Rasmussen (Berkeley), and George Temmer (Rutgers).[62] An Iranian nuclear power delegation visited Peking in May at the invitation of Kuo Mo-jo, president of the Chinese Academy of Sciences.[63] A Chinese "academic" exchange delegation including Chien San-chiang, a prominent nuclear physicist, went to Australia in June 1977, generating a wave of rumors that China was interested in importing Australian uranium.[64] A Chinese high-energy physics group visited Japan in August, and two European delegations, one from France and one from West Germany, toured Chinese nuclear research establishments in September.[65] Meanwhile, nine Chinese high-energy physicists were reported to have taken up residence in Hamburg, West Germany. The Chinese can evidently give as well as receive in the nuclear field. North Koreans were reported working on nuclear physics in Urumchi and Chinese may have been dispatched to help repair a heavy-water facility in Pakistan in September 1977.[66] Few of these many delegations were important in and of themselves. But in aggregate they vividly illustrate China's growing interest in foreign nuclear science and technology.

In the midst of the resurgence of Chinese interest in theoretical nuclear physics and the round of nuclear delegation diplomacy, the Chinese government has displayed direct interest in the development of commercial nuclear power since the early 1970's. One report at the end of 1973 indicated that Peking was discussing the feasibility of a nuclear power reactor in Kwangtung province that would have supplied electric power to Hong Kong.[67] This idea was evidently dropped in favor of a coal-fired thermal power station inside Hong Kong that will supply power to Canton. A year later, in December 1974, an article in a Chinese scientific journal discussed the comparative advantages of nuclear power.[68] In 1976, an Italian company signed a contract to provide China with centrifugal compressor technology that could be related to the nuclear fuel cycle (Nuove Pignone, ENI, $8 million).[69] China has apparently discussed uranium imports with both Australia and Gabon, with the long-range prospect in mind of a burgeoning nuclear power industry.[70]

Meanwhile, China continued to move forward with its nuclear weapons program. New weapons tests are reported every year, to the dismay of nearby neighbors who must absorb the fallout. At least four nuclear detonations were reported in 1976 alone, and the tests continued in 1977, reaching a grand total of 22 by September.[71] By 1976, the PRC had deployed 200–300 nuclear warheads, carried by a variety of delivery vehicles, including 65 intermediate-range bombers, 30–50 medium-range ballistic missiles (700 miles), 20–30 intermediate-range ballistic missiles (1,750 miles), and a small number of ICBM's with a limited range (3,000–3,500 miles).[72] Although not comparable to the strategic arsenals of the United States or the Soviet Union, this force is sufficient to make the Soviet Union extremely uncomfortable in the event of armed hostilities.

The Chinese government continues its intrasigent opposition to any form of international control agreement acceptable to either the Soviet Union or the United States. During the period under consideration, Peking attacked the provisions of the Non-Proliferation Treaty, the ban on underground nuclear weapons tests, the interim strategic arms limitation agreement, and every phase of the SALT negotiations.[73] China initially opposed the convening of a special session of the United Nations General Assembly to deal with disarmament, but then participated in the special session.[74] There were very few signs in the early 1970's that Peking had changed its fundamental position on arms control or international nuclear control agreements. China did sign Protocol II of the Treaty of Tlatelolco in April 1973.[75] The treaty itself establishes a nuclear weapons free zone in Latin America, and the Protocol commits nuclear powers outside of the region not to introduce nuclear weapons into the zone. By 1976, 97 countries had signed the Treaty or one of its protocols, but some important Latin American countries (Brazil) did not sign, greatly limiting its effectiveness. Neither did the Soviet Union, a point that the Chinese press has raised on more than one occasion.[76] The Chinese signature on the Treaty of Tlatelolco may seem like a minor concession in the context of the broader framework of international nuclear control agreements. But it does demonstrate that China is interested in *regional* nuclear control agreements, particularly if they are cast in a form that condemns outside interference. China has at times expressed interest in an Asian nuclear weapons free zone that would remove U.S. nuclear weapons from South Korea, a move that Washington seems to be taking in any case.[77] The point is that China might be induced to join a regional agreement inhibiting the use of commercial nuclear technology for weapons development, particularly if the initiative for such an agreement were to come from within Asia itself rather than from one of the superpowers.

As for strategic weapons limitations, if anything, the Chinese position has hardened. Peking has adopted Western deterrence theory and now decries any softening of NATO's strategic posture vis-à-vis the Soviet Union. China may even be moving away from its non-first-use position, and condemned Soviet pressure on Italy to sign a non-first-use agreement.[78] The issue is academic in any case, since Italy lacks a nuclear force.

Early Nuclear Power Development (1978–85)

By 1978 it had become obvious to all concerned that China was about to launch upon the course of commercial nuclear power development. The first stage in this development will coincide with China's current Ten-Year Development Plan, which runs until 1985. During that period, we should expect to see the installation of China's first commercial nuclear power reactor. My projections indicate that at 10 percent of total energy production from future technologies, nuclear electric power production would reach 2–3 billion kilowatt-hours by 1985, about 1 percent of total electric power production (Table 24.3). That would require only a single nuclear power station of moderate capacity. Current plans call for the purchase of at least two nuclear reactors from France. But there is no guarantee that both would be on-line and operational by 1985. In any case, during the period from 1978 to 1985, the PRC will seek to master the basics of nuclear reactor technology and design. This will be comparable in some ways to China's initial efforts to master offshore oil and gas exploration in the early 1970's.

Every evidence indicates that China intends to continue and intensify its development in the various fields of nuclear science and technology through the mid-1980's. Hua Kuo-feng reiterated Peking's commitment to basic nuclear research at the Fifth National People's Congress in February 1978.[79] Minister of Science and Technology Fang Yi strengthened this commitment in March when he called for the construction of a 30–50 billion electron-volt proton accelerator within five years.[80] Construction of an even larger accelerator is planned for the next five years, with completion ambitiously scheduled for 1987. By June 1978 construction of a model for the first accelerator had already begun.[81] American energy officials believe that Peking would like to involve U.S. experts in the design and construction of the first accelerator.[82] During the year, the Chinese press also reported the establishment of a society for nuclear science and technology in Shanghai, further radioisotope research, especially in agricultural applications, more work on controlled fusion, and a new journal entitled *High Energy Physics and Nuclear Physics*.[83] China would clearly like to establish itself as a leader in theoretical nuclear research.

One of the implications of this effort will be far greater scientific exchange with the market economy countries in nuclear research. But during 1978, most of the nuclear exchange was on the technical rather than scientific side, and focused on the impending purchase of foreign commercial nuclear power plants, technology, and possibly fuel. In January, French Premier Raymond Barre visited Peking, taking along high executives of Alsthom-Atlantique and Creusot-Loire, two French companies involved in reactor construction.[84] A high-level Chinese electric power delegation visited West Germany and France in January-February 1978 to discuss nuclear power.[85] The delegation, which included Vice-Minister of Water Conservancy and Electric Power Chang Pin, spent a full three weeks in France, working out the details for the purchase of French-built nuclear power plants. Another delegation of Chinese experts visited Italy in March to attend the "Electronic, Nuclear, and Aerospace Fair." This team toured the Trino Vercellese nuclear energy center, which includes a pressurized water reactor.[86]

It was evident by April, when China signed its new trade agreement with the European Economic Community, that Peking preferred a European supplier for nuclear power plants rather than a U.S. or Japanese company. The Chinese government views Europe, and particularly France, as relatively independent in nuclear policy and unlikely to burden the transaction with the framework of international nuclear controls. The Japanese are already in one tangle with Washington over reprocessing technology, and were probably not eager to start another row about the sale of a sensitive U.S.-licensed technology to the PRC. Hitachi and several other Japanese companies had held discussions of nuclear power plant sales with Chinese officials, but the Japanese were evidently not able to compete successfully with the advanced European nuclear industry.[87] U.S. companies were unable even to bid on the deal, because of the lack of diplomatic relations, tight U.S. export controls on nuclear technology, and the frozen-assets issue. In May 1978, Vice-Premier Ku Mu returned Barre's call and engaged in further discussions with the French government to pin down precise conditions for the sale.[88] Ku Mu also visited the advanced high-temperature gas-cooled reactor (HTGR) project at Hinkley Point in Great Britain.[89] A delegation from the American Nuclear Society that went to China in May reported that Peking was in the market for a 600–700-megawatt pressurized water reactor (PWR).[90] China would like a reactor that could be paired with its own large water-cooled turbines and the Chinese power transmission network. As part of the trip, American experts and company officials gave as series of lectures on reactor design. Here again the emphasis seemed to be on acquiring familiarity with advanced American technology without contracting with American companies directly for the plant construction work. A return Chinese nuclear delegation is expected soon in the United States.[91]

In late November 1978, the news finally broke that China would import one or two PWRs in the 900-megawatt class from a French consortium. The first announcement was made, paradoxically enough, in Washington. On November 24, the Carter Administration announced tentative approval of a request by France to sell China the reactors, which are under license from Westinghouse.[92] The plants will be produced by Framatome, a corporation owned by Creusot-Loire, the French government, and Westinghouse (15 percent), and Alsthom-Atlantique.[93] Under the 1958 Atomic Energy Act, the United States must approve all nuclear exports of technology under American license. The Carter Administration is apparently pressing for some sort of inspection system, but has not subjected the deal to normal IAEA safeguards provisions. Washington is not expected to submit the sale to the Coordinating Committee for Export Control (Cocom), which normally oversees sales of sensitive technology to communist countries. This follows the precedent set by U.S. restraint in not obstructing the sale of European military hardware to the PRC, a policy that enrages Moscow. On December 4, 1978, as an anticlimax, Foreign Trade Ministers Jean-François Deniau and Li Chiang signed a Sino-French long-term trade agreement that included the two reactors.[94] Teng Hsiao-ping later placed the price tag of the nuclear plants at $1.1 billion each. The trade agreement also includes two conventional 600-megawatt thermal power stations and unspecified petroleum equipment.

At the time of writing, a number of details remained to be worked out in the Sino-French nuclear power deal. No contracts had yet been signed.* It remains to be seen just how Peking will finance the purchase, where the plants will be located, what specific safeguards provisions will apply, how long construction will take, how the plants will be integrated with China's limited transmission network, how the fuel rods will be fabricated and from what uranium sources, and what will be done with the nuclear waste and plutonium generated by the plants along with the electric power output. A number of other countries may be able to take advantage of the French project. Another trade agreement with Sweden, signed just days after the Sino-French agreement, calls for cooperation in the nuclear power field.[95] A British electric power delegation was in China in December 1978, visiting power plants, research institutes, and electric power equipment plants.[96] The achievement of Sino-

---

*The Sino-French nuclear deal was canceled in July 1979 as part of the general retrenchment of foreign technology acquisition programs under the Ten-Year Development Plan that occurred in the first half of 1979. Peking had discussed the purchase of an additional four nuclear reactors from France prior to the cancellation. This indicates that China's nuclear power plans are in flux. Cancellation of the French deal will reopen the Chinese market to competitive bidding from other nuclear supplier countries, should Peking decide to resume the program.

American diplomatic relations on January 1, 1979, greatly improves the prospects for American participation in China's nuclear power development program. And the Japanese companies Hitachi and Mitsubishi cannot be counted out of long-range competition, since they are also under license with Westinghouse for construction of the type of reactors that China apparently prefers.

China's acquisition of power reactors raises an important question regarding the likely source of enriched uranium to fuel the French plants. Reports circulated in February 1978 that a Chinese trade mission, including Chien San-chiang, who had been to Sydney just a year before in June 1977, would go to Australia during the spring of 1978 for direct discussions of uranium purchases.[97] The delegation did reach Australia, but was kept completely out of public view. The uranium mining and export business is an extremely sensitive political issue within Australia and seriously affects the course of national politics. There was another story in October 1978 that China has discussed the export of uranium to Japan in return for nuclear technology.[98] This would contradict the Australian story. China is thought to have extensive indigenous uranium resources. Uranium mining is concentrated in the south in three principal mines in Kwangtung and Kwangsi provinces.[99] Additional deposits are thought to be located in Sinkiang, Manchuria, Inner Mongolia, and Chinghai.[100] Total production of uranium ore was estimated by one source in 1974 at 2,500 metric tons per day.[101] Depending on the grade of the ores in question, this would yield 1,000–2,000 metric tons of U_3O_8 per year, about 10 percent of current United States production.[102] This figure corresponds to what one would expect from international comparisons, giving the PRC about the same annual uranium production as France or Niger, but less than Canada or South Africa.[103] China's uranium enrichment capacity is limited to a single gaseous diffusion plant in Lanchow. Given the country's weapons requirements, the PRC may require additional enriched uranium for the French nuclear power plants. Australia, however, is not in a position to provide enrichment facilities. This raises the possibility that Peking would like to ship Australian ore to Japan for enrichment and fabrication into fuel rods for the new reactors. Japan itself imports all of its enriched uranium from the United States and Western Europe, and has adequate supply contracts for its nuclear power plants through at least 1990. A Japanese pilot enrichment plant (gas centrifuge) is scheduled to come into operation in 1981, and a commercial enrichment plant will presumably follow.[104] The timing coincides neatly with the construction schedule for China's new reactors. It remains to be seen whether the Japanese government would be enthusiastic about dedicating part of its new but limited enrichment capacity to China's needs.

The prospect of China moving into a triangular uranium supply agreement with Australia and Japan should not alarm Western governments. To the contrary, it should be encouraged as a means of drawing the People's Republic into a network of commercial contracts for nuclear fuel within the region. This might well be a step toward relaxation of Peking's attitude toward regional nuclear control commitments. Which brings us to the broader issue of China's current attitudes toward international control of commercial nuclear technology.

Nuclear Control Agreements and Long-Range Nuclear Development

China's commercial nuclear development program raises serious questions for the international nuclear control system. On the one hand, China insists on its own sovereignty and complete independence in determining the direction of its own nuclear development. On the other, every phase of the Chinese program would be delayed by a failure to obtain access to foreign commercial nuclear technology. In some ways, China is very different from the other countries that are interested in purchasing advanced nuclear plants and technology. The PRC, after all, already possesses a considerable arsenal of nuclear weapons and a growing force of delivery vehicles. Thus, there can scarcely be much fear of direct proliferation consequences, and even minimum safeguards would deter China from diverting imported nuclear fuel for weapons purposes. But the great danger is that China, still untrammeled by international nuclear control agreements, would in turn pass sensitive, proliferation-prone technologies to other countries. China would thereby become a giant loophole in the safeguards system.

There is considerable evidence that this fear is not entirely academic. Peking has on occasion itself attempted to accelerate its own weapons program by importing Western technology. For example, in 1965 the PRC tried unsuccessfully to obtain a large IBM computer via France for its nuclear weapons program.[105] The Chinese press consistently supports the efforts of Brazil, Argentina, Pakistan, and Libya to obtain plutonium-reprocessing facilities and other plants that are easily converted to weapons purposes:

The small and medium-sized countries are fighting against the superpowers' bid for nuclear control and monopoly, turning a deaf ear to what the Soviet Union and the United States are advertising. . . . In recent years, contracts on the peaceful utilization of nuclear energy have been concluded between West Germany and Brazil, between France and Pakistan. . . . The President of the Argentinean Commission on Atomic Energy said: "We refuse to sign the nuclear nonproliferation pact because of its discriminative character." . . . As a result of its steadily growing ability and need to develop nuclear industry, the third world is strengthening its co-operation with the second world in this field. Common interests in the struggle against the nuclear control and monopoly of the Soviet Union and the United States have led to a daily strengthening of the unity between the second and the third worlds against hegemony. Gone for ever are the days when the two superpowers can maintain their nuclear monopoly.[106]

If China's position on the issue were purely verbal, just one more attack on the "superpowers," the matter would be of less concern than if Peking moves in the direction of supplying sensitive technology or equipment to foreign countries without appropriate safeguards. Unfortunately, there is initial evidence that the PRC is considering doing just that. Pakistan, a long-time friend and ally of the PRC, signed a contract in January 1976 for the purchase of a plutonium-reprocessing plant from a French company.[107] The country currently has only two reactors, a tiny research reactor and a 137-megawatt-power reactor, hardly enough to justify a complete fuel cycle on economic grounds. The government of Pakistan was obviously concerned to respond to India's 1974 test of a nuclear device by acquiring its own nuclear weapons capability. Under tremendous pressure from Washington and the other members of the Nuclear Suppliers Group, France finally canceled the deal on August 20, 1978. There are persistent rumors that China is considering supplying Pakistan with the plutonium extraction technology, which may have been offered to Pakistan during a visit by Vice-Premier Keng Piao.[108] If this report is correct, it means that the Chinese position on control of weapons-sensitive technology is not merely verbal. Any of a number of other countries could become involved in the acquisition of reprocessing technology from the PRC. Peking vigorously supports Brazil's efforts to purchase reprocessing technology from West Germany, again in the face of U.S. opposition.[109] Foreign Trade Minister Li Chiang recently praised Argentina's policy of nuclear independence.[110] Libya's Prime Minister Abdul Salem Jalloud, during a visit in August 1978, directly requested nuclear weapons technology from China in exchange for advanced conventional weapons technology that Libya has obtained from Western Europe and the Soviet Union.[111] Peking allowed him to look around its nuclear industry, but made no commitments.

Any Chinese export of uncontrolled or weapons-sensitive nuclear technology would certainly result in a review of European nuclear export commitments to the PRC. Even though China already possesses plutonium extraction technology, the Nuclear Suppliers Group would be reluctant to accelerate the pace of China's nuclear development in the face of a major violation of the international safeguards system or their basic export restraints. Regardless of its verbal position on the matter, the Chinese government must maintain a prudent nuclear export and technical assistance policy. The sword, after all, cuts both ways. By 1978, Taiwan has three nuclear power plants on-line or under construction.[112] The government plans to have six large nuclear plants operational by 1988. Only a delicate balance of American and Japanese pressure, international safeguards and luck, restrains Taipei from developing nuclear weapons technology, and the government has made at least one false start in the direction of plutonium extraction facilities. Vietnam has one small research reactor left over from a U.S. program in the south that is being started up again with Indian technical assistance and Soviet uranium.[113] Vietnamese acquisition of plutonium extraction technology might make China very uncomfortable indeed. Vietnam also, incidentally, has its own uranium resources near the Chinese border, which it has accused China of trying to steal.[114] China is also vulnerable to nuclear proliferation in South Korea.

The Chinese position on nuclear arms limitation and disarmament is still less than encouraging. China used the Special Session of the United Nations General Assembly on Disarmament in May 1978 to attack once again the prohibition of nuclear weapons tests, nonproliferation agreements, and the strategic arms limitation agreements between the Soviet Union and the United States.[115] The substance of the Chinese criticism is that the superpowers are simply legitimizing their own strategic arms race while monopolizing nuclear weapons for themselves. Peking places all the blame for the arms race on the superpowers and refuses to consider constraining its own weapons development until the superpowers disarm first.[116] This position is hardly calculated to influence the course of global nuclear disarmament, but provides a rationalization for China's continuing expansion of its own weapons capabilities in an effort to overtake the giants and protect itself from the Soviet Union. It is obvious that Peking would never accede to a set of nuclear weapons control agreements in which it had no voice. If China is to be included in future arms limitation or disarmament negotiations, the framework within which those negotiations take place must be considerably broadened, perhaps to include all of the nuclear weapons powers.

The industrial market economy countries cannot move forward in their nuclear cooperation with the PRC heedless of China's response. They must at all times remain sensitive to the Chinese spirit of independence, sovereignty, self-reliance, and pride in the achievement of their own development goals. This sensitivity may provide the necessary environment for the reciprocal development of a responsible Chinese nuclear policy. But sensitivity to China's needs must be balanced by firmness in the face of any Chinese effort to dismantle or circumvent the existing framework of international nuclear control agreements. In the long run China's own security is at stake.

Increasingly as we move toward the turn of the century, China will be able to participate as an equal partner in the community of nations possessing nuclear technology. That community itself is expanding rapidly. According to my long-range projections, admittedly tentative in the case of future energy production technologies, China will have 10–15 gigawatts of nuclear electric power generating capacity by the year 2000 (Chapter 24). This is a minimum figure, based on a variety of oil and gas discovery projections. If Peking should decide to move heavily in the direction of nuclear energy and invest in a domestic nuclear plant and equipment construction industry, then the growth rate for nuclear power could be much higher. Furthermore, my projections end in the year 2000, but the world goes on. Commercial nuclear development between now and the end of the century will provide the foundation for a much larger nuclear industry in the early decades of the next century, assuming, of course, that all goes well for the technology itself. I would expect China to experiment with various nuclear technologies and the construction of a complete nuclear fuel cycle in the next 20 years. Expensive breeder technology will be largely an academic matter in the PRC until sometime in the 1990's. But China will continue to expand its scientific and technical exchanges with other countries in theoretical physics, high-energy physics, controlled thermonuclear fusion, and a number of other advanced and related fields. China will never be satisfied with a lagging position in the nuclear field. And, indeed, Chinese contributions to world nuclear science and technology should be only a matter of a few years.

Part Two

Statistical Profile

Chapter 13

Introduction to the Statistical Profile

China as a Special Energy Data Problem

The People's Republic of China presents special difficulties in gathering and analyzing a comprehensive set of energy data for the period since the founding of the People's Republic in 1949. The Chinese government published comprehensive energy production data through the end of the 1950's.[1] However, during the aftermath of the Great Leap Forward, as China experienced a wave of statistical overreporting and the embarrassingly obvious chasm between official production claims and the reality of faltering production in all sectors, Peking simply stopped reporting any production statistics for either industry or agriculture. The sudden rupture with the Soviet Union and reports by Soviet technicians of the transport and production failures of the Great Leap reinforced the new statistical silence of the Chinese government. The Chinese press developed an entirely new style of statistical reporting, printing only scattered statistics for individual production units that had continued to achieve well even in the backwash of the Great Leap. Thus, by 1961 or 1962, foreign analysts were faced with official silence on the critical indices of China's industrial and agricultural development.

This situation has continued with little or no relaxation until the present. Chinese foreign policy makers have apparently found nonreporting of domestic production statistics a more comfortable retreat than overreporting proved to be. Consequently, the only energy "statistics" available since about 1961 have been the statistics published by foreign observers. These foreign estimates have not been entirely without foundation. Peking has usually provided disguised claims for energy production in the form of annual rates of increase in the primary energy production sector. Especially if a given unit or industry does well, production increase estimates have been provided on a quarterly and annual basis in the Chinese press. However, in off-growth years, only certain enterprises within an industry—the successful units—report their rate of increase. The press is silent regarding the rest and the industry as a whole. This situation, for example, has occurred over the past year or two in press reports of the coal industry.

The difficulty presented by a lack of official statistical reporting has been even more pronounced in the foreign trade sector than for domestic production statistics. China has never published data on energy trade and has not followed the example of the Soviet Union and East European countries, which provide annual trade books with statistics by commodity and partner country. Thus the only access to China's international energy trade has been through the statistical reports of partner countries. And the task of collecting data by partner country has proved so overwhelming that foreign estimates of China's energy trade by other authors have been limited to China's largest energy trade partners—principally the Soviet Union and Japan.

The difficulty of collecting statistics on China's domestic energy production and energy trade has been the fundamental limit on our understanding of the Chinese energy system since the founding of the People's Republic. Before 1970, there was only a single book-length study of China's energy development.[2] And the latter study was constructed from a combination of pre–Great Leap statistics and a massive sifting of the Chinese press for bits and pieces of information. The Chinese press is full of articles on the various producing units in the coal and petroleum industries, and contains a substantial amount of reporting on natural gas and hydropower. The press articles usually provide everything but statistical information on production. So the limit to our understanding has been fundamentally statistical in nature.

The result was that until recently, the world has treated the Chinese energy system as a large blank space. Despite the fact, known for some time, that China ranks as the world's fourth largest energy producer, most collections of world energy statistics ignored China completely, assigned China the production statistics of the tiny island of Taiwan, or lumped China with the Soviet Union, giving a common total statistic to both under the politically inept category of the "Sino-Soviet" bloc. The inability to deal with China's energy system statistically introduced roughly a 5 percent error into world energy accounts. In the case of world coal statistics, the missing China factor introduced an error of nearly 15 percent.

Therefore, any study of the broader structure of China's domestic or international energy policies, whether from an economic or from a political perspective, must still begin with the arduous task of establishing a firm statistical point of reference. This has been the case since at least 1960 and has seriously hampered the cumulative progress of research on Chinese energy policy. Tremendous time and effort must be devoted to minute data and statistical problems, leaving little research time for closer scrutiny of the important policy issues raised by China's distinctive pattern of energy organization and development.

This Statistical Profile addresses the energy data problem directly in a manner that it is hoped will clear the decks of the most rudimentary tasks of data-gathering and analysis for both specialist and general reader. It provides in compact and standardized form the most basic measures of primary energy resources and reserves, primary energy production, secondary energy production, aggregate consumption, per capita consumption, trade, and projective analysis. With adequate and regular revision over the years, it will continue to provide a general statistical point of departure for those interested in China's energy policies and will help to overcome the endless repetition of basic statistical research. The policy analyst should be able to move directly to policy issues on the basis of these tables, rather than spending time reconstructing the tables themselves.

The limits on a general statistical compendium of Chinese energy data should be mentioned to avoid any misunderstanding of the objective of the Statistical Profile. First, and perhaps most important, the Profile does not seek to settle all the data problems associated with the precise value of any bit of data. Given the serious constraints on data-gathering in the Chinese case, any claim to ultimate accuracy would be ridiculous. The Chinese government itself must deal with data that may contain serious reporting error as it filters upward from the base production units. The Chinese press has obvious propaganda as well as informational objectives in reporting on various energy production sectors. And many foreign guesses have been made on the basis of intuition and experience as much as on the basis of the Chinese press itself. Thus, for years to come, we will be faced with further detailed research on each energy sector, on each energy production enterprise, and on such technical matters as appropriate energy conversion factors.

Second, the Statistical Profile is an energy profile, not an economic analysis. The reader will find no reference to monetary flows associated with the energy sector. There is no analysis of labor efficiency, value added, price structure, or other economic indexes. Even China's energy trade has been dealt with in terms of energy units rather than foreign exchange. Projective analysis has also ignored such fundamental issues as the impact of world petroleum prices on China's energy exports. The treatment of economic matters as a secondary stage of analysis follows the precedent set by major statistical collections on domestic and international energy flows.[3]

Third, the Profile includes only data on commercial energy flows, which commonly exclude fuels produced in the agricultural sector, such as wood and dung. Noncommercial agricultural fuels constitute a substantial proportion of China's total energy consumption and would considerably raise our estimates of per capita energy consumption. However, the detailed information required for an analysis of noncommercial energy consumption is not available to Peking, let alone to foreign observers. Furthermore, nonagricultural fuels are gradually being replaced by commercial fuels, even in the Chinese countryside, and represent a diminishing proportion of domestic energy consumption. Neither should agricultural fuels be considered significant for China's international energy policies. The greater proportion of such fuels are consumed on the spot, and such minor trade in wood as has occurred does not warrant opening the Pandora's box of data problems raised by introducing noncommercial energy flows. These reasons for excluding agricultural fuels should not be taken as a derogation of their importance to the Chinese energy economy, but simply as a limit on the extent of this study.

Within these broad limits, the Statistical Profile has a number of rather specific objectives: (1) to provide a single, comprehensive collection of alternative foreign estimates; (2) to evaluate these estimates on the basis of internal consistency, technical energy considerations, and reference to the Chinese press; (3) to provide a technically adequate set of inferential data on end use and per capita consumption; (4) to provide a comprehensive set of energy trade data from partner country sources; (5) to arrange the data in a format that meets minimum international energy analysis standards; (6) to provide ready access to the data in standard international energy units; (7) to provide a reasonable range of production, consumption, and export potential projections based on explicit alternative growth and resource assumptions.

Within the framework of these objectives, hard choices have been made regarding a number of technical problems and the reliability of various foreign estimates. These choices will be open to scrutiny and criticism by other experts on the Chinese energy system, as well as by the general reader who notices certain obscurities in the manner in which the statistics were presented. Every aspect of the Statistical Profile will be open to revision. The author hopes to republish the Statistical Profile on a regular basis and to narrow the range of controversial choices over a period of years, based on new information from the Chinese government, on the objections of other specialists, and on new research into the individual Chinese energy industries.

Methods of Analysis

The basic methods of analysis used for the construction of the Statistical Profile included both special data-gathering techniques fitted explicitly to the problems of the Chinese case and data-processing techniques borrowed from the literature on energy statistics. Different approaches were used for domestic energy data and energy trade data collection. Two different processing methods were used for the historical data collection and the projective analysis.

The "data wash" or "alternative series" approach to China's domestic production statistics was developed some time ago by economists interested in measuring China's pace of industrial development.[4] Rather than initially attempting to list a single authoritative data series through time, they would provide alternative estimates for each production index. These alternative estimates are usually drawn from both secondary and primary sources. The advantage of the alternative data series approach is that it refuses to establish any a priori criteria for data accuracy and simply looks at the range of available estimates. Once the range of estimates has been established, a rather obvious picture of their likely accuracy appears of its own accord. If there is a narrow range of difference over a substantial time series for independent estimates of the same variable, and if known Chinese government statements are not inconsistent with the resultant "data wash," a median determination can be achieved with a fair degree of certainty. If, on the other hand, the estimates vary widely and there is no primary source that would establish confidence in any single series, then the data must be set aside as inconclusive.

The alternative series approach to domestic Chinese energy data has several serious disadvantages that should not be overlooked. First, the foreign experts may all be wrong despite their apparent agreement. A case in point was the low estimates of China's crude oil output that prevailed in the late 1960's until Premier Chou En-lai startled the experts with the announcement that China had produced more than 20 million metric tons of crude in 1970.[5]

A second disadvantage of the alternative estimates approach is that it may lead to a median production figure for a given year that is inconsistent with a percent increase announced in the Chinese press when compared with the median estimate for the previous year. This particularly rankles the China specialist concerned with the precise conditions that led to a given increase during a given year. Some caution must be exercised, therefore, not to simply take an arithmetic average of the available estimates. However, it still remains the case that the wider the range of available estimates, the greater the prima facie uncertainty of any given estimate.

Finally, some authors have simply been more careful than others in compiling their estimates. An estimate that differs wildly from both the increases indicated in the Chinese press and other expert opinion measures the carelessness of the researcher, not the uncertainty of the other estimates. Weight must be given, therefore, to the level of documentation achieved by each estimated series.

After all of these problems with the alternative series approach have been acknowledged, this method still remains the most efficient way to provide access to statistics on China's domestic energy development. By admitting the level of uncertainty for any given series, the alternative estimates method provides a basis for further cumulative research. The cumulative effect of the method is two-edged. It indicates which estimates and energy industries require further research. And it provides base-point estimates that permit the statistical incorporation of Chinese energy production into regional and global estimates.

China's international energy trade has presented at least as severe a data problem to the energy analyst as domestic energy production. The Peking government does not publish foreign trade statistics in any area, let alone detailed energy commodity trade statistics. The only resort, therefore, has been to trade statistics published by partner countries. Partner country data sources present a number of difficulties. A number of countries publish trade commodity data by monetary value rather than by weight. Trade books are usually published in the language of the country in question, introducing uncertainty regarding the exact specification of commodity categories. Trade books may omit transactions beneath a certain level of monetary value, or may omit politically sensitive commodities.

A number of these problems have been overcome through the use of regional commodity trade series published under the auspices of the regional organizations of the United Nations. Regional commodity series are available for the industrial market-economy countries, and for some nonindustrial market-economy countries of Asia and Africa. They provide energy trade data by weight or volume, by commodity, by country, by region, and by year. They have been arranged according to the numbered and explicit categories of the Standard International Trade Classification (SITC).[6]

The detailed characteristics and limits of each of these publications will be described in some detail in the section on energy trade. Since the collection of energy commodity trade data from these sources represents a new data contribution of this study, some care has been taken to establish the precise boundaries of the data collection. In general, it could be said that in combination with the Soviet, East European, and Asian trade books, the SITC series has provided well over 90 percent of China's energy trade for most commodities in most years. The main cautions that should be taken in the use of the trade data are as follows: (1) The totals for more specific classifications (e.g. mineral jelly plus mineral wax) may be less than the listing for a more general category (e.g. mineral jellies and wax), owing to the statistical peculiarities of reporting countries. When presented with a choice, always refer to the broader category. (2) Data are still largely missing for Latin America and the Middle East. (3) Important countries in Africa (Egypt) and Asia (Indonesia) are missing for some years. (4) Transactions under a certain minimum trade value (usually $10,000 in a single year) have not been recorded in the SITC publications.

If these limitations are kept in mind, this new collection of trade data should prove useful to both the energy analyst and the China scholar interested in the development of trade relations between the PRC and partner countries. It also indicates that access to other commodity trade data is not as impossible as has traditionally been thought. Even the use of regional data collections entails considerable scanning to reconstruct China's trade in any particular commodity. However, the standard classification system, the availability of these data in English-language format, and the collection into regional aggregates makes the task manageable within the time frame of a normal research project.

Once gathered, the production and trade data form the basis of a time series analysis of China's historical energy balance from 1949 through 1978. Internally consistent production series for the primary fuels (coal, crude petroleum, natural gas, and hydropower), and some secondary fuels (coke and thermal power), as well as trade data for general commodity categories (solid fuels, crude petroleum, and refined petroleum products) were entered as base data in a program specially constructed for the analysis of Chinese energy statistics. The program was written for Stanford's IBM 370/168 using the Time Series Processor (TSP) package developed at Princeton and Harvard. The program consisted primarily of arithmetic transformation statements, covariance statements, and ordinary least squares statements.[7] In short, it was designed in relatively simple format in a manner readily amended for new data, new common energy units (e.g. BTU, Q), or new variants on the regression analysis.

The program output consisted of the following types of tabulation: (1) transformation of energy production and consumption data into common energy units (million metric tons coal equivalent, million gigajoules, and million barrels oil equivalent per year); (2) annual percent increase for primary energy production (all fuels), secondary energy production (coke, thermal power, total electric power), aggregate energy consumption (all fuels), and exogenous variables (population and GNP); (3) annual energy mix (in percent contribution) for primary energy fuels and the electric power mix; (4) coal consumption for coke and thermal power production; (5) inferred estimates of refined petroleum product output, consumption, refinery capacity, and the principal refinery products (gasoline, kerosene, diesel, residual, lubricants, and other); (6) inferred estimates for plant use for coal, petroleum, natural gas, electric power, and total energy production; (7) inferred estimates of chemical use of fossil fuels (including fertilizer) for coal, petroleum, natural gas, and total energy products; (8) inferred estimates of fuel and power consumption (end use) for coal, petroleum, natural gas, electric power, and aggregate energy consumption; (9) inferred estimates for per capita consumption of commercial fuel and power for coal, petroleum, natural gas, electric power, and energy; (10) analysis of covariance for energy production, energy consumption, per capita energy consumption, GNP, and per capita GNP; (11) regression analysis for energy production, energy consumption, per capita energy consumption, GNP, and per capita GNP.

Several general features of the historical time series analysis should be emphasized. Neither the data nor the inferred estimates should be taken seriously beyond the third significant digit. Fuel and power consumption estimates should not be confused with "inland consumption," which refers to production minus net exports. Rather, fuel and power consumption estimates refer to an approximation of "end use" for each fuel and for total energy. The end-use statistics eliminate double counting (e.g. subtracting the coal used for thermal power generation from coal consumption), nonenergy use (petrochemical), and inefficiencies (e.g. plant use, transmission loss, etc.). Per capita consumption estimates were also based on end use.

The correlation and regression analyses were important in themselves, demonstrating that China's general pattern of commercial energy development and the relationship between total product and energy consumption are roughly what one would expect from experience with the energy development of other countries. But beyond confirming our general historical expectations regarding the relationship between GNP and energy consumption, the regressions provided a statistical basis for the projective analysis. For example, the regressions show that the commercial energy intensity of GNP growth has *increased* over the past decade and a half. In other words, each additional increment of GNP in 1975 cost a higher input of energy than the same increment would have cost in 1955. This indicates that the energy/GNP elasticity for the PRC not only is quite high when compared with other countries but has been getting even higher. This result is probably related to the declining percentage contribution of noncommercial agricultural fuels in the Chinese countryside. It may also have been precipitated by the rapid growth of energy-intensive industries such as cement, aluminum, and petrochemicals.

Whatever the historical reasons for the increasing Chinese energy/GNP elasticity, it provides information necessary for the projection of energy production, consumption, and trade through the turn of the century. The detailed structure of the projection model is discussed in Chapter 23. The basic projective technique was to divide the model into two sectors—the production side and the consumption side. Potential export capability then remains as a residual category. Energy production is pushed by historical growth rates and limited by reserve availability. Energy consumption ("energy end-use requirement") is pulled by the per capita GNP growth rate and the energy/GNP elasticity.

The projective model was written explicitly for the Chinese case. It included all the basic variables present in the historical time series analysis, permitting the coupling of the projections with the historical pattern of development. The computer program for the projected series was written in the language of a separate statistical package—DYNAMO II$_F$.[8] DYNAMO was written for resource development projections involved in the *Limits to Growth* studies at the Massachusetts Institute of Technology.[9] It is a flexible and dynamic projective language that uses integrated-level equations and provides ready format for projections based on alternative growth assumptions. The dynamic feature ensured that different parts of the model were fully interactive (e.g. the interaction of resource depletion and production growth rates). The alternative-assumptions feature provided for easy modification of multiple assumptions within a single run (e.g. varying both petroleum reserves and natural gas reserves).

Once the basic program had been written, over 200 alternative projected series were produced, varying assumptions for reserves of each of the fossil fuels, alternative conservation policies, alternative coal conversion ratios, alternative per capita GNP growth rates, alternative birth rates, and alternative energy/GNP elasticities. Thus none of the projected series represents a single claim regarding the exact outcome of China's energy development over the next 25 years. On the other hand, taken together, the alternative projections provide a range of likely energy futures for the PRC, or a set of statistically defined limits within which Chinese policy makers must make development decisions over the next quarter century.

The Statistical Profile can provide only a few of the most interesting projections, owing to space limitations. But the level of detail achieved by the model could also provide order-of-magnitude estimates for individual variables (e.g. thermal power production) not included in the general alternative projections simply by altering the print statement. In other words, it is possible to inquire of the program what would happen to a specified variable, given certain general growth assumptions.* This feature permits sensitivity analysis for any single variable under alternative sets of assumptions. This type of analysis has proved particularly important for projections of China's energy export potential.

Recent foreign interest in China's petroleum industry has been sparked by the combination of the global energy crisis and the prospect that the PRC may be a significant oil exporter in the near future.[10] Thus, China's energy export potential, expressed in terms of crude oil export capabilities, represents the most critical variable in the projective model from the standpoint of international energy problems. The projective program treated China's energy export capability as the difference between possible energy production levels (under different resource assumptions) and domestic energy consumption requirements (under different economic growth assumptions). This residual category refers to the upper bound on what China *could* export. The projections of China's energy export capability make no statement about the PRC *will* actually export.

The latter caveat represents more than simply a clever way of escaping responsibility for the projections. In preliminary discussions of these projections, economists have raised the objection that the projective model ignores the price elasticity of oil exports. Obviously, if the world market price of crude oil dropped to pre-energy-crisis levels, China would be less motivated to export significant quantities of oil, and would probably retain domestic production for domestic use, or would simply deemphasize investment in the petroleum industry to the degree required to bring production into line with domestic consumption. On the other hand, if the price of oil goes through the ceiling as a result of protracted global shortages (say in 1985), the Chinese government would be tempted to push investment in petroleum production, to constrain domestic consumption, and to export the maximum feasible amount. These two extreme possibilities illustrate the impact of the world petroleum market on what China will actually export. Thus the projections provided by this model refer to the ceiling on energy export capabilities, not to actual exports. The projections describe the limits within which Chinese policy makers are working, not the necessary outcome of their policy decisions.

Another feature of the energy export capability projection should be noted. The projections refer to total energy exports, not just petroleum exports. The model was constructed in a way that permitted the free

---

*A list of program variables is provided in Tables 24.1–24.4.

substitution of one fuel for another, *before* the determination of energy export capability. In other words, it provides for the possibility that Peking may substitute coal, natural gas, hydropower, or an unspecified "future energy technology" for petroleum in the domestic sector. Similarly, natural gas exports could be substituted for petroleum exports without affecting the limits set by the model. For the sake of convenience and to permit comparison with current exports and the oil exports of other countries, energy export capability was expressed in units of millions of metric tons of oil equivalent per year. But it could just as easily have been expressed in terms of barrels of oil equivalent, tons of coal equivalent, tons of LNG, or any other energy-equivalent unit.

The free substitution feature of the program was intended as more than just a convenient statistical device. It helps to answer in advance questions such as "What would happen if Peking doubled investment in the natural gas industry to cover domestic energy demand and permit larger oil exports than indicated by the limits determined in the projections?" China could presumably emphasize the development of fuels other than petroleum for domestic consumption, leaving more oil for export at high prices. The model has taken account of this by looking at the maximum possible rates of development for the entire energy production sector under different growth projections for the primary fuels. An aggregate energy requirement statistic has also been provided on the consumption side, avoiding the specific issue of just how China will choose to utilize any particular fuel (e.g. whether agricultural mechanization will begin to demand a significant quantity of petroleum products). The aggregate energy features of the model avoid the treatment of petroleum as an independent sector and tie petroleum exports to overall energy capabilities and requirements.

The results of the sensitivity analysis of energy export capabilities have been expressed as a series of projected limits on oil exports under different growth assumptions. When these limits are compared over time, the impact of different resource projections, alternative GNP growth rates, alternative birth rate dynamics, alternative energy/GNP elasticities, alternative conversion ratios, and alternative conservation policies may be assessed for the relative degree of export sensitivity to each set of growth projections. In addition, a general band of likely oil export potential can be determined, using upper and lower bounds for each set of assumptions. For example, it is possible to demonstrate the upper and lower bounds on possible oil exports determined by China's ultimate recoverable crude oil resources beginning with very conservative estimates of proved onland reserves, and moving through very high potential resources in the continental shelf area.

These comments provide an introduction to the basic techniques of historical and projective analysis used in the construction of the Statistical Profile. More detailed theoretical and empirical discussions follow in each section of the Profile. The objective throughout has been to present and analyze the available data in a form that could easily be assimilated into more general analysis of international energy problems. The focus of the entire project has been upward, in the direction of comparative and international energy analysis, rather than downward into the exciting but empirically overwhelming task of reconstructing each Chinese energy industry and consumption sector. Therefore, this is a dependent project—dependent on the accuracy of foreign estimates of China's domestic energy development, and dependent on the comprehensiveness of indirectly collected trade data.

Conversion to Common Energy Units

One specific methodological problem remains. Aggregate energy analysis depends on common units. There have been nearly as many systems for classifying and aggregating the various forms of primary and secondary energy production in the energy literature as there have been data collections. Data collections in this country have tended toward the barrel of oil (42 gallons) as the common volumetric unit, and the BTU (British Thermal Unit) as the common unit of heat content. Because American energy consumption relies heavily on petroleum products, barrels of oil (bbl) provide a convenient unit, expressed either in barrels per day, barrels per year, or, in the case of reserves, in billions of barrels. The anomalous BTU and its derivatives have apparently been adopted by the American engineering establishment because of traditional links to British units—feet, miles, short tons, and so on.* However, these units do not correspond to common international usage or to the standard set by international organizations. United Nations data collections, for example, use the metric ton (10^3 kilograms) as the basic unit of weight, the cubic meter (m^3) as the basic unit of volume, the kilowatt-hour (kwh) as the basic unit of electric power, and the gigajoule (10^9 joules) as the basic unit of work.†

---

*A BTU is defined as the quantity of heat required to raise the temperature of a pound of water one degree Fahrenheit. Never mind the derivation of the pound or the degree Fahrenheit. A derivative energy unit, the "Q" or "Quad" (10^{15} BTU), has become increasingly popular in American energy analyses. It is much too large for the Chinese case.

†A joule is a meter-kilogram-second of work. The watt is defined as a joule per second of power. A kilowatt-hour is equivalent to the energy expended in one hour by a thousand watts of power.

In order to maximize the ease of integration of the Chinese energy statistics with international data collections, the metric system has been adopted in this study. The only concession to British-American units was the conversion of energy production and consumption figures into million barrels of oil equivalent per year. Million barrels per day would have been too large a unit for the Chinese case. The common unit of energy used for tabulations in the Statistical Profile was million metric tons coal equivalent (mmtce). The "metric ton of coal equivalent" or "standard metric ton of coal" has been defined precisely in terms of the combustion of a standardized average grade of coal. The exact conversion factor to mmtce for other fuels (and for coal itself) varies, but has been determined within close limits by the combustion of standard average grades of energy fuels in a calorimeter. Table 13.1 presents the conversion factors adopted in this study. The quantity in million metric tons coal equivalent was calculated by multiplying the datum in question by the given conversion factor. These conversion factors were consistently used throughout the computer programs and in all of the tables of the Statistical Profile. They have not, therefore, been repeated in each chapter. Besides the conversion of output data, all common energy transformations and calculations internal to the historical and projective programs were carried out in coal equivalents.

Primary and secondary energy production and aggregate energy consumption statistics were also provided in million gigajoule (10^6 GJ) units. The gigajoule tabulations were made on the basis of a standard 28.8 GJ per metric ton coal equivalent.

There are a number of considerations in designating energy conversion factors for the People's Republic of China that transcend mere technical dimensions and become vital methodological issues. China is an unusual case in this regard because of the lack of firm government information and because of the difficulties of foreign observation in what would otherwise be routine investigation. A series of difficult choices must be made which affect our understanding of the entire Chinese energy balance.

The designation of an appropriate coal conversion factor is the first and most serious of these methodological problems. Though there is a relatively high degree of agreement among foreign observers about the general range of Chinese raw coal output, there is no consensus regarding the average energy content of a metric ton of Chinese coal. Most international energy data collections have not even raised the issue, and simply count the energy content of Chinese raw coal at 1.0 mtce/mt.[11] Studies of the Chinese coal industry before the Great Leap Forward discounted Chinese raw coal at the rate of more than 0.7 mtce/mt.[12] During

TABLE 13.1
Common Energy Unit Conversion Factors

Fuels	Original units	Mmtce	10^6 GJ	10^6 bbl/y
Solid:				
Raw coal	mmt	0.75	21.6	3.7
Trade coal	mmt	1.0	28.8	4.9
Coke	mmt	0.9	25.9	4.4
Liquid:				
Crude petroleum	mmt	1.47	43.24	7.3
Refined petroleum	mmt	1.47	43.24	7.3
Gaseous:				
Natural gas	bcm	1.333	38.4	6.6
Electric power:				
Hydropower	bkwh/y	0.123	3.6	0.6
Thermal power	bkwh/y	0.123	3.6	0.6

Abbreviations: mmt–million metric tons; mmtce–million metric tons coal equivalent; GJ–gigajoules; bbl/y–barrels per year; bcm–billion cubic meters; bkwh/y–billion kilowatt-hours per year.

the Great Leap, raw coal production statistics were obviously greatly inflated and probably included massive amounts of rock and debris, especially from the new small-scale coal-mining operations. Official silence followed the Great Leap and made new estimates a matter of conjecture. During and after the Cultural Revolution (1967), the contribution of small-scale mining operations once again began to grow, although the wild claims of the Great Leap era were not repeated. The entire situation has been considerably complicated by the fact that Soviet coal statistics always refer to raw coal, which should be discounted for energy content at approximately 0.7 mtce/mt (excluding peat).[13] It is difficult to judge the degree to which Chinese accounting methods were modeled on Soviet experience during the formative years of the Chinese statistical system. Finally, without some direct information it would be impossible to specify the ash content or the contribution of brown coal and peat to the Chinese production total. All these factors taken together leave us in the dark regarding an appropriate coal conversion ratio for the PRC.

Lest the coal conversion ratio be deemed a trivial consideration worthy only of the attention of the specialist, it should be pointed out that the difference between a 0.7 conversion factor (the ratio of metric tons coal equivalent per metric ton of raw coal) and a 0.9 conversion factor has a larger impact on analysis of China's historical energy balance than would omission of the other three primary energy industries (petroleum, natural gas, and hydropower) taken together. This margin of error would extend to critical measures of total energy production, the energy production mix, aggregate and per capita energy consumption, growth rates, and so on. The coal conversion ratio also has some impact on projections of energy export capability. The greater the energy content of a ton of Chinese raw coal, the more energy should be available for export.

Foreign researchers are now aware of the coal conversion factor problem in Chinese energy statistics and have suggested discounting raw coal at two different ratios, depending on the size of the producing units.[14] These sources use the general argument that raw coal produced in China's small-scale mining operations has a lower energy content and a higher content of ash and rock per ton than raw coal produced by modern methods in the large-scale mining operations. Since the percentage contribution of small-scale mining operations to total raw coal output has been increasing steadily for the past decade, the average discount ratio for both small- and large-scale operations taken together may have declined somewhat. Small-scale operations, discounted at 0.6 mtce/mt, now account for about one-third of total raw coal output. Large-scale operations, discounted at 0.8 mtce/mt, account for about two-thirds of raw coal output. This would give an average discount ratio of just over 0.7 mtce/mt.

Whereas such a two-track coal conversion system may be useful in the context of some studies, it has not been adopted here for several reasons. Data on small-scale coal-mining operations are still fragmentary and are not reliable. Even estimates of total raw coal production vary widely enough to make the distinction between small- and large-scale mining operations insignificant in the context of appropriate conversion factors. I have chosen to use a single conversion factor for total raw coal production (0.75 mtce/mt) that is based on the average calorific content of raw coals from a variety of Chinese mines and for a variety of periods.* This conversion factor implies that every four metric tons of raw coal production reported by official Chinese sources or estimated by foreign observers contains the energy equivalent of three metric tons of standard coal (coal equivalent).

Trade coal, which in the Chinese case has been primarily in the form of coking coal exports to a number of Asian countries and anthracite exports to Japan, has been rated at 1.0 mtce/mt. The high-quality Chinese

---

*The CIA estimates that the average calorific content of Chinese raw coal was 5,400 kilocalories per kilogram in 1965 and 5,200 kilocalories per kilogram in 1975. Since a kilogram of standard coal is rated at 7,000 kilocalories, an overall conversion factor of 0.75 mtce/mt is reasonable. This conversion factor is also consistent with the calorific content of washed coals from a broad spectrum of Chinese mines that Ikonnikov derived from Russian sources. See U.S. CIA, *China: The Coal Industry*, p. 14; Ikonnikov, chap. 2.

export coal may in fact have slightly more or less energy content than a standard ton, but, on the average, it comes to about the calorific content of standard coal (7,000 kilocalories per kilogram).

The conversion factor for both crude petroleum and refined petroleum products was set at 1.47 mtce/mt, the standard United Nations conversion factor for crude petroleum. Chinese crude was assumed to have an average specific gravity of 0.86, which meets international criteria for crudes with standard calorific content, and is consistent with the reported specific gravity of crude petroleum exported by the PRC from the oilfields of the northeast.[15] The choice of a single conversion factor for crude petroleum and refined petroleum has several advantages. It permits the inclusion of non-energy residuals in the total. It allows for consistency between domestic production statistics and petroleum trade statistics. It compensates for the lack of precision in the commodity composition of petroleum products in trade with certain countries. It avoids double-discounting for plant use, loss, and petrochemical use. Finally, the single petroleum conversion factor greatly simplifies the tabulation of total energy trade statistics and the structure of the projection program. And all of these advantages are accomplished with no significant loss of precision, given the range of available estimates and other sources of error in the basic petroleum production and trade data.

The natural gas conversion factor (1.333 mtce/10^3 cubic meters) was simply adopted from the standard United Nations factor. Gases other than natural gas, including "city gas," coke oven gas, marsh gas, and refinery gas, are all produced and used in various urban and rural localities in China. They would normally have widely varying energy content per cubic meter. However, no production statistics exist for these gases. Furthermore, except for marsh gas (produced from small biogas generators in the countryside), manufactured gases are all secondary-energy products and would not, therefore, change the primary-energy production balance significantly. Finally, the margin of error in natural gas production estimates is greater than the error introduced by ignoring the calorific losses incurred by the production of manufactured gas from primary energy fuels.

Another conversion problem that warrants attention is the matter of electric power conversion factors. Some statistical series convert hydro-electricity (in billion kilowatt-hours) into the heat content of the amount of coal that would have been burned in a thermal plant to generate an equivalent amount of electricity.[16] Other statistical series simply convert the bkwh of hydropower output directly into the heat equivalent of burning coal. The former conversion could be referred to as an "input conversion," whereas the latter could be referred to as an "output conversion." The two types of conversion are useful for different research tasks. For example, if the researcher wants to know how many metric tons of coal will be required on an annual basis to generate the same amount of electricity as a certain hydropower project, the input conversion would be more convenient. On the other hand, if one wishes to compare the total energy production of Norway and Britain, the output conversion is required, since Norway uses a high proportion of hydroelectricity and its electric power production would be overstated in relation to Britain by the input conversion. This study has relied exclusively on the output conversion factor (0.123 mtce/bkwh/y) except for the calculation of coal consumption for thermal power generation. The input conversion factor for the coal consumption of thermal power generation was estimated on the basis of a thermal efficiency curve specific to the Chinese case rather than on a fixed conversion factor.

If this discussion of the conversion of China's primary energy fuels to common units seems elaborate or overdrawn, it simply reflects the rather primitive stage of research that has been achieved to date on Chinese energy production. The failure to be explicit about the form in which Chinese energy data are presented has led to considerable confusion in comparing one set of estimates with another. It has also prevented the easy assimilation of energy data on the PRC into international statistical compilations. Several authors have made no distinction between raw coal and clean coal, leading to serious overstatements of China's aggregate energy consumption. The other conversion problems are less serious, but continue to nag at a cumulative research effort.

Summary

The chapters that follow present a comprehensive tabular review of China's internal and external energy flows. No effort has been made in the text to repeat the findings of the tables, which should be self-evident. Footnoting has been minimized and maximum use of abbreviations should provide the reader with adequate documentation while reducing the burden of repetitious referencing on both reader and writer. Specific abbreviations have been chosen on the basis of easy recognition value and are presented in Table 13.2. A single abbreviation may refer to several related documents. For example, "Hoover" refers both to the work of Yuan-li Wu and to that of H. C. Ling, two individual authors who have worked closely together and have relied on one another's estimates. This convenient code is not intended to imply total agreement among the authors listed under a single term. It simply reduces the number of alternative estimates that must fit on a single table. Specialists involved in primary research on China's energy policies should make direct reference to the documents in question.

TABLE 13.2
Abbreviations List for Data Sources

Abbreviation	Source	Abbreviation	Source
BOM	Bureau of Mines, U.S. Dept. of the Interior	Myrhf	A. A. Meyerhoff
Chang	Chang Kuo-sin	NCUSCT	National Council for U.S.–China Trade (U.S.–China Business Review)
Cheng	Cheng Chu-yuan		
CIA	Central Intelligence Agency (U.S.)	OGJ	Oil and Gas Journal
		PNSEA	Petroleum News: Southeast Asia
Dnthrn	Audrey Donnithorne	PRC	People's Republic of China (official data)
ECAFE	Economic and Social Council for Asia and the Far East[a]	Rawski	Thomas G. Rawski
FEER	Far Eastern Economic Review	SD	State Department (U.S.)
Hrsn	Selig S. Harrison	SER	Survey of Energy Resources (World Energy Conference)
Harvard	Harvard University (Choon-ho Park and Jerome Alan Cohen)	Smil	Vaclav Smil
		Terman	Maurice Terman
Hoover	Hoover Institution (Yuan-li Wu and H. C. Ling)	Tregear	Thomas R. Tregear
		URI	Union Research Institute (Robert Carin)
Iknkv	A. B. Ikonnikov		
IOESB	Impact of Oil Exports from the Soviet Bloc (U.S. Natl. Petroleum Council)	UNSY	United Nations Statistical Yearbook
IPE	International Petroleum Encyclopedia	USGS	U.S. Geological Survey, U.S. Dept. of the Interior
JEC	Joint Economic Committee, U.S. Congress	WES	World Energy Supplies (United Nations Statistical Office)
JETRO	Japan External Trade Organization	Willums	Jan-Olaf Willums
		WO	World Oil
Kmbr	Tatsu Kambara	WPD	World Power Data (U.S. Federal Power Commission)
Koide	Yoshio Koide		
Kudo	Kochu Kudo	WCT	World Coal Trade (U.S. Natl. Coal Association)

Note: See Bibliography for complete references.

[a] Economic and Social Council for Asia and the Far East (ESCAP) after 1975.

The principal objectives of this Statistical Profile are, once again, to present the available data on China's domestic and international energy flows in a single package, to make that package statistically compatible with international energy data collections, and to provide the empirical basis for analysis of China's international energy policies. Though each energy industry has been reviewed, no attempt has been made to analyze each domestic Chinese energy industry in detail. The purpose of the broad-brush text in each chapter is to guide the reader through the jungle of information provided by the tables. Finally, the policy analysis is left to Part I, rather than being repeated in the context of the statistical material.

Chapter 14

Primary Energy Reserves and Resources

Methods

The different concepts and definitions that confuse the science of estimation of energy reserves have complicated an already difficult data collection situation for the energy reserves of the People's Republic of China. Such overlapping categories as reserves, resources, proved reserves, total reserves, inferred reserves, estimated reserves, in-place resources, theoretical resources, and economically recoverable resources are to be found in the energy literature. The categories that have been applied to one fuel, such as coal, may have a different nomenclature than those applied to another fuel, such as petroleum. These differences are based both on the nature of the particular fuel in question and on the precise measurement techniques used for estimation. Therefore, for the purposes of this study, four technically simple but relatively consistent energy reserve categories have been selected and applied to coal, petroleum, natural gas, and hydropower reserves.[1] The four reserves categories, with their consistently used classification numbers (listed under "class" in each table) are as follows:

Class 1, proved reserves
Class 2, proved plus probable reserves
Class 3, ultimately (economically) recoverable resources
Class 4, ultimate in-place resources

Many authors who have made reserves estimates for China have not identified their estimates according to category. It has been necessary to assign these unclassified reserves estimates on the basis of the degree to which they fit the general range of the classified estimates available at roughly the same period. Thus, for example, an unclassified coal resource estimate of one trillion metric tons would be assigned to category 3 on the basis of similar estimates of the same period that carried an explicit classification.

Another confusion has occurred in assigning a year to each reserves estimate. Some authors provide the year of estimate, others do not. In cases where the year of estimate has been provided by the author, the estimate was listed under that year. In other cases, the estimate was simply assigned the year of publication of the document from which the estimate was taken. Thus, for example, Ikonnikov assigned the year 1957 to the data on which he based his estimate of proved coal reserves. But his estimates of ultimate recoverable and in-place coal resources were not identified by year and were assigned to the year of publication—i.e. 1975. (See Table 14.1.) This convention proved to be much more important for petroleum and natural gas reserves estimates than for coal and hydropower reserves estimates. Coal and hydropower reserves estimates have been stable for more than a decade, owing to the lack of updated information and the fact that these resources had been relatively well surveyed by 1960, when the Chinese government stopped providing official estimates. Estimates for natural gas and petroleum reserves, on the other hand, have continued to climb, owing to more intensive research by Western scholars and presumably to further discoveries by the Chinese government, which have been hinted but not quantified in the Chinese press.

Offshore and shale oil resources and Szechwan natural gas reserves were so identified in the table only when the original document made an explicit identification. All offshore estimates in the tables also include onshore, with separate offshore estimates identified in the text. Shale resources include only the oil content, not the weight of the shale rock itself. The shale category includes natural crude petroleum plus shale oil. Separate estimates of shale have been provided in the text.

The reserves categories for hydropower were identified slightly differently than for the fossil fuels, but the categories are generally consistent with the fossil fuel categories. The criterion for "proved" hydraulic reserves was strict, including only already developed potential. "Proved plus probable" added new hydropower facilities under construction. "Exploitable potential" includes estimates of what China could develop with a maximum hydropower component in the energy production mix. Theoretical potential includes the total theoretical energy in average rainfall years of all the watersheds in China. In comparing hydraulic and fossil-fuel reserves, it should be recognized that hydraulic reserves are nondepletable and represent a much larger increment of total energy reserves than a common energy unit conversion would indicate. Thus, to obtain a true estimate of the energy value of Class 1 hydropower potential, one should multiply the in-place production capacity by the expected lifetimes of the dams.

Coal Reserves

Proved coal reserves should be rated at over 100 billion metric tons, ranking China third in coal resources.[2] At current rates of production, the PRC would be assured enough coal to last for at least 200 years. However, ultimately recoverable resources were estimated 20 years ago at one to one and a half trillion metric tons, enough to last 2,000 years at current rates of production. The one trillion ton estimate was provided by numerous official Chinese reports during the 1950's, but was based on exploration and estimates that antedated the People's Republic by decades as well as on Soviet and Chinese exploration after 1949. Soviet geologists confirmed that resources were at least one trillion tons and possibly much higher.[3] The estimates of ten trillion tons cited in Hoover publications were announced by the Chinese government at the height of the Great Leap Forward and must be considered euphoric. (See Table 14.1.)

At any rate, China's coal production has not been limited by reserves considerations during the historical period under study and will not be so limited in the foreseeable future. The main constraints on coal production have been and will be capital requirements, the transportation system, and the consumption requirement for lump coal.

Largest known coal deposits are located in three areas—the northeast corridor stretching from Liaoning province (Fushun, Fushin, and Anshan mining districts) northward toward Harbin; the enormous Shensi Basin in north and north-central China; and the entire Szechwan Basin. Large portions of the rest of China are pockmarked with coal deposits of a smaller scale, but still economically exploitable, at least in the context of Peking's coal production policy, which has promoted local exploitation of small seams over wide areas of the country, including the previously coal-poor regions south of the Yangtze River. A general breakdown of coal deposits would put 6 percent in northeast China, 37 percent in north China (Shansi, Hopeh), 38 percent in the north-central area (Shensi), 12 percent in the central south (Szechwan), 5 percent in the east, 2 percent in the southwest, and 6 percent in other areas.[4]

China's main coal deposits could be characterized as flat and relatively deep.[5] The depth of the deposits prevents low-cost open-pit mining in most areas. The flatness of the coal seams (with some famous exceptions in the northeast) makes shaft mining more economical than open-cast mining. But even in areas with steeply inclined seams, the depth and amount of overburden have increased the relative cost of strip mining. Thus, to date, China's coal-mining technology has focused on shaft-mining machinery, hydraulic mining, conveyor belts, and long-wall mining rather than the development of equipment for strip mining. Recent imports of American strip-mining shovels may indicate some rethinking of development policy.[6]

China's coal deposits are predominantly bituminous (78 percent), with

TABLE 14.1
Coal Reserves, 1953–77
(Billion metric tons)

Year of estimate	Class	Quantity	Source	Class	Quantity	Source	Class	Quantity	Source	Class	Quantity	Source
1953							3	400	URI			
1954												
1955										4	1,500	Hoover
1956												
1957				2	280	Iknkv	3	450	URI			
1958	1	80	Hoover				3	1,200	URI	4	9,000	Hoover
1959	1	100	Hoover	1	80	Iknkv	3	1,500	URI	4	9,600	Hoover
1960							3	1,500	FEER	3	1,115	WCT
1961												
1962	1	70	SER				3	1,011	SER			
1963												
1964												
1965	1	100	FEER									
1966												
1967	1	80	JEC				3	1,500	JEC			
1968							3	1,011	SER			
1969												
1970												
1971												
1972												
1973												
1974	1	80	SER	1	100	Kmbr	3	1,000	SER			
1975							3	1,991	Iknkv	4	5,555	Iknkv
1976	1	80	CIA	1	100	Smil	4	1,500	CIA	4	1,500	Smil
1977	1	99	CIA									

Note: For full forms of abbreviations, see Table 13.2. Class: 1–measured; 2–measured plus inferred; 3–ultimate recoverable; 4–ultimate in place.

the remainder mostly anthracite (19 percent) and a relatively small proportion of lignite (2 percent).[7] The carbon, ash, sulfur, and moisture content vary considerably but on the average give Chinese bituminous coal an energy rating somewhat lower than North American coal. On the whole, Chinese coal could be rated at between 6,500 and 7,500 kilocalories per kilogram after processing.[8] This would make a rating of Chinese clean coal at 1 mtce/mt a reasonable approximation. But further work should be done to analyze the calorific content of coal from China's different mining centers. There is a considerable amount of coal suitable for coking purposes, perhaps as much as 35 percent of the total.

Petroleum Reserves

Despite intense foreign interest and considerable research by foreign scholars, proved crude petroleum reserves are difficult to estimate because of the necessary precision of the required information and the reluctance of the Chinese government to disclose the exact results of its extensive petroleum exploration efforts. Proved plus probable onland reserves could be estimated in 1978 at between 3 and 5 billion metric tons (20–35 billion barrels). Ultimate recoverable crude petroleum resources are probably within the general range of 10–20 billion metric tons (70–140 billion barrels), including the offshore basins. (See Table 14.2.)

Offshore resources in the continental shelf are still completely unmeasured and highly speculative. An optimistic guess might place recoverable offshore resources in the general range of onland reserves, or 3–5 billion metric tons. There is some controversy over the economics of recovery of even this amount (Chapters 7 and 8). However, based on seismic exploration of the extent and volume of potentially petrolific sediments in the continental shelf, the figure could go much higher, once extensive test drilling has occurred. There is absolutely no indication in the results of early survey and drilling exploration along the continental shelf that would justify comparison with the crude petroleum resources of the Middle East.

The Chinese government recently announced the results of a survey of oil shale that indicate resources of 100 billion metric tons of shale for the country as a whole.[9] Depending on the oil content of the shale and the economics of recovery, this could yield 10–20 billion metric tons of shale oil, comparable to China's recoverable crude petroleum resources.

Because of the relatively early stage in the development of China's petroleum industry and the cloak of official secrecy, there remains a wide range of estimates of both current petroleum reserves and ultimate recov-

TABLE 14.2
Crude Petroleum Reserves, 1949–77
(Million metric tons)

Year of estimate	Class	Quantity	Source	Class	Quantity	Source	Class	Quantity	Source	Class	Quantity	Source
1949				2	200	Cheng						
1950												
1951				2	210	Harvard						
1952												
1953	1	30	JEC				3	1,700	Hoover	3	2,750ᵃ	Hoover
1954												
1955												
1956												
1957	1	100ᵃ	JEC	3	1,700	Cheng	3	1,700	Iknkv	3	1,700	FEER
1958	1	900ᵃ	Iknkv	3	4,200ᵃ	Cheng	3	1,700	Harvard	4	60,000ᵃ	Iknkv
1959							3	9,000ᵃ	Iknkv	3	5,900ᵃ	Hoover
1960	1	200	JEC				3	2,000	Hoover			
1961												
1962												
1963												
1964												
1965												
1966	2	1,000	Kmbr	2	1,000	Hoover	3	6,000	Hoover	3	6,000	Harvard
1967				2	2,000	JEC						
1968	1	770	Myrhf	2	950	Myrhf	3	2,650	Myrhf	4	6,900	Myrhf
1969							3	2,000	BOM			
1970							3	2,800	IPE			
1971	1	2,000	BOM	3	2,700	BOM	3	4,100ᵃ	BOM	4	13,700ᵃᵇ	BOM
1972	2	1,700	UNSY	2	1,700	WO						
1973	2	1,800	Kmbr	2	2,700	Chang	3	6,500	Smil			
1974	1	1,100	JEC	2	1,700	SER	3	7,600	JEC			
1975	2	3,400	Smil	3	4,500	BOM	3	12,000ᵇ	BOM	3	10,500ᵇ	JETRO
1976				2	3,000ᵇ	Cheng	3	4,600ᵇ	USGS	3	9,508ᵇ	Myrhf
1977	1	2,740	CIA				3	5,500ᵇ	CIA			

Note: For full forms of abbreviations, see Table 13.2. Class: 1 – proved; 2 – proved plus probable; 3 – ultimate recoverable; 4 – ultimate in place.
ᵃIncludes shale oil. ᵇIncludes offshore resources.

ery. This range should be reduced as drilling proceeds on the Chinese continental shelf, and as the government releases discovery and reserves data. At current rates of exploration, China will establish a relatively clear map of recoverable fossil resources over the next two decades. A high rate of discovery should be expected through 1985, declining somewhat after 1990. Thus China's proved reserves should outstrip production for 10 to 15 years, maintaining a reserves-to-production ratio at well over 10:1. Unless offshore resources prove to be insignificant or subeconomic, an absolute reserves limit on annual production will not appear before 1985 at the earliest.

Onland Reserves

China's onland reserves of natural crude petroleum are distributed among roughly seven major oilfield groups and eight oilfield groups that are still little understood outside of the People's Republic. It has been asserted by some authors that the present pattern of petroleum development, which is heavily weighted toward China's northeastern provinces, was determined by the pattern of industrialization and by the transportation difficulties posed by rapid development of the western basins (Tsaidam, Tarim, and Dzungarian basins). However, Table 14.3 indicates that Chinese oilfields produce roughly in proportion to their contribution to total proved onland reserves. This observation does not invalidate the argument that transportation difficulties have had some impact on the pattern of oilfield development, but it may temper that finding to some degree.[10] It may be that the western oilfields have a higher proportion of ultimate recoverable resources than the proved reserves figures would indicate. However, offshore oil prospects will certainly balance any western reserves in determining future oilfield planning and the long-range distribution of oilfield development. It should be expected that the big thrust in oilfield development for the next 25 years will be eastward onto the continental shelf rather than westward. The geographic distribution of oilfields will coincide with and reinforce the tendency to develop the northeast as China's major industrial base.

Taching oilfield has a disproportionately large share of current production based on proved reserves. This could reflect several factors in the development of Taching. Taching's proved reserves may be somewhat larger than generally conceded by foreign experts, especially if one includes the reserves of the new northern Taching formation which has been under development since about 1973.[11] Taching's crude oil production growth rate may also have been pushed disproportionately by Peking's planners in an effort to overcome the impact of the loss of Soviet refined products imports during the early 1960's. Once under way,

TABLE 14.3
Distribution of Crude Petroleum Reserves and Production by Field, 1974–75

Field	Discovery (year)	Depth (km)	Location	Class	Reserves (mmt)	Source	Production (mmt/year)	Year	Source	Pct. of reserves	Pct. of production
Karamai	1955	0.2	Sinkiang	1	100	IPE	1.0	1974	JEC	7%	1–11%
				2	100	Kmbr	1.1	1975	CIA		
				2	120	Myrhf	8.1	1975	NCUSCT		
Shengli	1962	2.7	Shantung	1	100	IPE	11	1974	JEC	19%	16–20%
				3	1,500	Hoover	14.9	1975	CIA		
				2	300	Myrhf	12.3	1975	NCUSCT		
Szechwan	1958	4.2	Szechwan	1	100	IPE	1.3	1970	Hoover	8%	2–3%
				2	134	Myrhf	2.6	1975	NCUSCT		
Taching	1959	1.5	Heilungkiang	2	400	Kmbr	19.2	1974	JEC	25%	33–54%
				3	1,000	Hoover	40.1	1975	CIA		
				2	410	Myrhf	25.3	1975	NCUSCT		
Takang	1964	1.5	Hopeh	2	400	Harvard	3.7	1974	JEC	19%	5–6%
				2	300	Myrhf	4.3	1975	CIA		
							4.1	1975	NCUSCT		
Tsaidam	1955	2.7	Tsinghai	1	150	JEC	0.5	1974	JEC	15%	1–6%
				2	250	Kmbr	0.6	1975	CIA		
				2	236	Myrhf	4.3	1975	NCUSCT		
Yumen	1939	0.9	Kansu	1	100	Kmbr	0.7	1974	JEC	5%	1–4%
				2	85	Myrhf	0.8	1975	CIA		
				3	540	Cheng	3.3	1975	NCUSCT		
Other[a]				2	20	Myrhf	12.5	1975	CIA	1–2%	17–22%
							16.7	1975	NCUSCT		

Note: For full forms of abbreviations, see Table 13.2. Class: 1–proved; 2–proved plus probable; 3–ultimate recoverable.

[a]Includes Panshan (Liaoning); Fuyu (Kirin); Ankuang (Kirin); Ordos Basin (Shensi-Kansu); Tushantzu (Sinkiang); Tarim Basin (Sinkiang); Chienchiang (Hupeh); and other scattered fields, as well as shale oil fields. Estimates do not include offshore potential or the new oilfield in Nanhai county (Kwangtung) near Canton or the new Jenchiu oilfield in central Hopeh.

Taching became an industrial model with an imperative for high annual production growth rates, possibly even at the expense of proper extraction management.[12] In any case, based on Taching's reserves, some slowing of the annual production growth rate should appear before 1980 and may already have been indicated by slower growth rates in 1976 and 1977.

Karamai's production may also be proportionately high, based on estimates of proved reserves by foreign observers. If true, this would be explained by the relatively early development of Karamai oilfield in the late 1950's with extensive Soviet technical and material assistance. Karamai's early development may also cast further doubt on the argument that distances determined oilfield development strategies. The oil-bearing potential of the Sungliao Plain (Taching) was known to the Chinese government at least as early as 1956, one year after the first strike at Karamai. The development of Karamai included large investments in transportation equipment—a short pipeline and a long rail line—as well as the construction of refineries at Karamai, Tushantzu, and Lanchow. Karamai may also have been developed early because of its shallow oil formations and because of Soviet interest in joint exploitation of its oil resources.[13]

Takang, on the other hand, is an oilfield with a disproportionately low contribution to total crude oil production, based on foreign estimates of its proved reserves, which should be on the same order of magnitude as Taching and Shengli. It could be that foreign estimates of Takang reserves are on the high side, but this appears unlikely in view of Peking's determined efforts to develop the field despite early difficulties with its highly fractured oil-trap structure.[14] A more likely explanation is that Takang was more easily explored than developed. Takang straddles the coastline of the Pohai Gulf and extends out into the salt-marsh perimeter of the coastline. Thus, in addition to complex fault lines in the trap structure of its single graben, the developers of Takang must cope with adverse surface exploration conditions. Takang represents China's first offshore attempt, grappling with production problems in a marine environment. Even shallow-water offshore technology represents a quantum jump in the required level of skills and capital equipment. So Takang's oil production growth rate has been restricted by the situation and geological structure of the oilfield itself, rather than necessarily by a reserves ceiling. Takang's production growth rate may provide a critical measure of the pace at which China may expect to develop offshore oil reserves, and of the economic costs of doing so.[15]

In contrast to Takang, the growth rate for crude oil production at Shengli oilfield indicates that its extensive reserves will be tapped immediately and used to take some of the burden of growth off Taching, easing the transition toward large-scale production from offshore fields.[16] Shengli consists of two fields, north and south, each based on a distinct graben. Its formations are also highly fractured and relatively deep.[17] Like both Taching and Takang, it developed from hydrocarbon deposits in a lacustrine sedimentary environment.[18] Some estimates have placed Shengli's reserves at a level even higher than Taching's, with claims for ultimate recoverable resources running as high as 1.5 billion metric tons (10 billion bbl).[19] The surface environment at Shengli is also favorable to rapid development, and the field lies within easy pipeline distance of Tientsin and Peking, and quite close to the coastline, permitting port construction and export shipments to Japan in the near future.

Foreign estimates have put the oil potential of the Tsaidam Basin at a very high level, perhaps approaching the ultimate recoverable resources of Taching.[20] These estimates may be somewhat overstated, but in general, the constraint on the development of the Lenghu and other fields in Tsaidam has been a combination of very difficult transport problems and an extremely harsh surface environment. The Tsaidam Basin lies at around three thousand meters above sea level and combines the conditions of dry desert, high mountain, and extreme temperature environments. Crude oil must be transported out of the basin entirely by truck.[21] Finally, the formations lie at considerable depth. It is the combination of these factors, rather than any single factor or a low reserves limit which has probably inhibited the development of crude oil production in the Tsaidam Basin.

China's other oilfields, including the older fields at Yumen and Yenchang, may face serious reserves limits. Yumen and Yenchang were China's first oilfields and now seek to maintain rather than increase annual production rates.[22] Tushantzu (Sinkiang) and the various Szechwan oilfields are less well reported in the Chinese press than other fields, despite their relatively early development. The Szechwan fields produce at about one million tons per year, primarily for consumption within the province.[23] Reports from China's other fields are scattered and often indirect. Tushantzu supplements Karamai production, but at much less than one million metric tons per year. There is at least one small oilfield each in Hupeh, Kirin, Liaoning, Hopeh, and Kwangtung provinces. A single oil strike was reported in the Tarim Basin in the late 1950's, which was evidently developed into the remote Tasharik oilfield on the northern edge of the basin. In October 1978 the government reported a new oilfield (Jenchiu) near Peking on the central Hopeh plain.[24] The field was reported to have 12 producing wells, each with a daily output of about 1,000 metric tons, much higher than is typical for the oilfields of the northeast. Two large-caliber pipelines were laid a distance of 200 kilometers to the Peking General Petrochemical Works, which locates the field somewhere near the small refinery at Paoting in central Hopeh. The new field was reported to be sufficiently productive to supply the crude oil requirements of the Peking refinery, a fact that indicates, in combination with well productivity data, that 1978 output was in the 4–5 million ton range, or about 5 percent of total crude oil production. The Chinese government also has high hopes for new oilfields in the Pearl River delta region of Kwangtung province and has already sent samples of crudes from the area to Japan for analysis.

Offshore Resources

China's offshore resource situation and offshore development program have been dealt with in detail in Chapters 7 and 8. Suffice it here to re-peat the principal findings of that discussion: (1) Large areas of the con-tinental shelf, including the most promising from a geological point of view, are under intense jurisdictional dispute. (2) China must build an inventory of capital equipment and skills for offshore exploration from scratch, relying on expensive domestic machine and ship-building in-vestments and expensive foreign technology imports. (3) Initial indica-tions are that the trap structures containing hydrocarbons may be highly stratified and fractured, making mapping, exploration, and exploitation difficult. (4) The marine environment is inherently more costly and slower to develop than comparable onland fields, such as Taching and Shengli, which have spurred China's rapid oil production growth rate. (5) The nature, composition (oil, gas, or tar sands), and extent of hydro-carbon deposits have yet to be determined by exploratory drilling over wide areas of the continental shelf.

No Western scholar would today enjoy being caught in the embarrass-ing position of the legendary geologists who once predicted that China would always be oil-poor. Indeed, a consensus of informed opinion would indicate the presence of at least 3 to 5 billion metric tons (20–35 billion bbl) of recoverable resources in the Chinese continental shelf. (See Table 14.4.) However, the five constraints listed above may well slow China's overall pace of petroleum development to a rate of growth considerably less than the spectacular leaps that have occurred since 1965. Onland production will continue to grow for at least a decade, but also at a slower pace, as extraction methods shift to maximize the recov-ery rate in already explored fields rather than the pace of expansion in new fields. A declining rate of growth would not be atypical for petro-leum industries at China's level of development—i.e. at production lev-els of over 100 million tons per year. That is not to suggest, however, that China will not be a major producing country within this century.

TABLE 14.4
Estimates of Offshore Recoverable Resources

Source	Pohai Gulf (bmt)	(bbbl)	Yellow Sea (bmt)	(bbbl)	South China Sea[a] (bmt)	(bbbl)	East China Sea (bmt)	(bbbl)	Total (bmt)	(bbbl)
1. Oil & Gas J.									7	50
2. JETRO	6-9	44-66								
3. Terman									2.7	20
4. Meyerhoff	0.8	5.6	0.8	5.6	1.1	8.0	1.8	12.8	4.2	31
5. Willums:										
Pessimistic	0.2	1.3	0.2	1.6	0.3	2.0	0.5	3.8	1.2	8.7
Middle	0.5	3.5	0.6	4.2	1.2	8.8	1.7	12.5	4.0	29.0
Optimistic	1.8	13.1	2.2	15.8	2.7	19.7	32	235	39	284

Sources: (1) John Cranfield, "Mainland China Gearing Up to Boost Oil Exports," *Oil and Gas Journal* 73, no. 32 (Aug. 11, 1975): 22; (2) Japan External Trade Organization, quoted in CIA, *China: Oil Production Prospects,* p. 5; (3) Dr. Maurice Terman, comments to Workshop on China's Energy Policy, Stanford University, June 2, 1976; (4) Quoted by Harrison, "China, the Next Oil Giant," p. 6; (5) Willums, *China's Offshore Oil,* p. 66.
Note: bmt = billion metric tons; bbbl = billion barrels.
[a] Includes Taiwan area.

Natural Gas Reserves

China's proved natural gas reserves could be conservatively placed at over 1 trillion cubic meters, including at least 0.6 tcm of nonassociated gas and perhaps another 0.4 tcm of associated gas. (See Table 14.5.) Very few authors have hazarded a guess in the area of natural gas reserves, and only onshore reserves have been included in the proved reserves estimates. Only one of the estimates has included possible associated gas discoveries in the petrolific northeast, where we know that China has already begun shipping natural gas into industrial and urban areas.[25] An order of magnitude estimate that included proved plus probable reserves of both associated and nonassociated gas in all onshore areas might be in the general range of 3–5 trillion cubic meters. Inclusion of the offshore areas would perhaps double this to an order of magnitude estimate of 10 tcm of ultimately recoverable resources. Exploration of the offshore areas and of lightly explored onshore areas such as the Tarim Basin could push the estimate of ultimately recoverable natural gas resources even higher during the next two decades, to perhaps 20–40 trillion cubic meters. However, as of 1978, such an estimate would be pure speculation.

Foreign experts really know very little about China's natural gas industry. The big fields in Szechwan had only begun to be developed when

TABLE 14.5

Natural Gas Reserves, 1967–77

(Billion cubic meters)

Year of estimate	Class	Quantity	Source	Class	Quantity	Source	Class	Quantity	Source	Class	Quantity	Source
1967	1	500	Hoover									
1968				2	529[a]	Myrhf	2	610	Myrhf			
1969												
1970												
1971	1	100	BOM							4	25,000	BOM
1972	1	99	UNSY	1	113	IPE						
1973	1	595	IPE	1	600	Rawski						
1974	1	680	SER							4	11,000	SER
1975	1	700	Smil	1	850[a]	BOM				4	30,000	Smil
1976	1	708	IPE	3	4,286[a]	Myrhf	3	5,714	Myrhf	3	8,571[b]	Myrhf
1977	1	708	CIA									

Note: For full forms of abbreviations, see Table 13.2. Class: 1–proved; 2–proved plus probable; 3–ultimate recoverable; 4–ultimate in place.
[a]Szechwan only.
[b]Includes offshore resources.

the Soviet technicians left China in 1960–a useful source of information on China's coal, petroleum, and electric power industries. And at about the same time, Peking completely stopped reporting official production statistics (and never had reported them for natural gas). Japan, a critical source of information on the Chinese petroleum industry, had little interest in China's natural gas (LNG) export potential until just recently, and so has not provided the same wealth of information on natural gas as on the Chinese petroleum industry.

The major natural gas fields could be conveniently categorized by geographic area into four groups—the Szechwan Basin, the Tsaidam Basin, the Shanghai area (Kiangsu and Chekiang), and the northeast. Meyerhoff's original study (1968) listed three fields in Tsaidam, one in Kiangsu, and ten in Szechwan. But his original reserves estimate of 0.6 trillion cubic meters was very conservative and did not include either the northeast or the offshore areas. In 1976, Meyerhoff and Willums placed ultimate gas recovery an order of magnitude higher, at 8.6 trillion cubic meters, including 5.7 tcm onshore and 2.9 tcm offshore.[26]

Szechwan, certainly China's largest known onland natural gas area, has been producing since at least 221 B.C. from small surface seeps and shallow wells drilled with bamboo. Perhaps the most vivid (albeit not statistical) portrayal of the scale of Szechwan's natural gas deposits has been provided by the Chinese press:

> The province's gas industry entered a new historical period after liberation. In the 1950's, the local oil-workers prospected for natural gas resources throughout the basin and located underground oil and gas structures that are counted by the hundred. They started to tap natural gas in the province on a large scale.
>
> Braving the rain, the Chinese people's great leader Chairman Mao inspected the Lungchang gas field on March 27, 1958. This gave the workers great encouragement. They located over 30 oil and gas fields out of 60 structures, giving the lie to the fallacy spread by some foreign experts that Szechwan Province has no oil and little gas.
>
> In the Cultural Revolution, the workers criticized Liu Shao-chi's and Lin Piao's revisionist lines and launched a new mass campaign to prospect for natural gas in a revolutionary spirit and soaring enthusiasm.
>
> Tens of thousands of oil-workers worked hard for several years in the rolling country in the south and covered over 3,000 square kilometers of land by seismic prospecting. After a comparative study and conscientious analysis of the more than 2,000 metres of core samples and 100,000 data they had collected and 150 geological cross sections, the prospectors finally confirmed a big gas structure. Helped by the data provided by the prospectors, many drilling teams struck gas in one well after another. This further confirmed abundant natural gas deposits in the area.
>
> Northwest Szechwan has rich natural gas deposits, but recovery was limited in

the past for lack of geological analysis. Working at grassroots unit, leading members of the party committee of the Kuangning petroleum prospecting command in charge of gas recovery in the area made comprehensive analyses of the available data on 72 occasions last year. A big force was concentrated and a number of new wells were drilled on the basis of confirmed underground structures. They struck gas for industrial use at different structures and formations. This opened broad vistas for tapping oil and gas resources in this area.

The Shihyukou gas fields have been worked for many years. Some people thought that one of the fields was nearly exhausted. In the movement to criticize Lin Piao and Confucius, the party committee of the fields upheld the materialist theory of reflection and mobilized the workers to conduct investigations and study. They extended the scope of prospecting to water-bearing beds, which used to be regarded as "forbidden areas." They located six new gas formations. The field's gas output is eight times that of 1965, the year preceding the Cultural Revolution.

After eight years of efforts, people in the province have gradually deepened their knowledge of underground geological formations and constantly enlarged the scope of prospecting. They offer inspiring prospects. Gas fields formerly regarded as hopeless are now dotted with new high-pressure, high-yield wells.[27]

This rather bullish report on natural gas prospecting indicates that the materials Meyerhoff based his original reserves estimates on were already out of date. For example, Meyerhoff listed Shihyukou, treated here as an old field, as the major producer and one of the largest single fields, with about 200 billion cubic meters of reserves. It could be generally stated that before 1970, Szechwan natural gas was treated by Peking as a regional rather than national energy resource. However, this and other reports indicate that, since 1970, the wider potential for Szechwan gas has been realized in Chinese planning circles. One report, based on a Japanese source, even indicates that China may now be considering the construction of a major natural gas line from Szechwan to Wuhan, Nanking, and Shanghai (the most likely coastal destination).[28]

Shanghai also has access to its own natural gas fields, according to numerous reports in the Chinese press.[29] The fields reported to date include one area south of the city in either Kiangsu or Chekiang province or straddling the provincial boundary. In addition, natural gas operations have been reported in a number of counties and municipalities in Chekiang province, some of which may have been linked to the Shanghai supply system.[30]

Very little is known about the natural gas deposits in the Tsaidam Basin, other than their existence and the fact that they are "locked in" by the lack of pipeline transport to industrial centers. Some of the natural gas may be used on the spot to provide a cheap form of energy for the active oilfields in the basin. Meyerhoff's estimates put the Tsaidam natural gas reserves at nearly 100 billion cubic meters, doubtless a conservative figure.[31]

The northeast, with its large petroleum reserves, probably also contains substantial quantities of associated natural gas, either in solution with the crude oil or in traps at different levels. A single well drilled into the appropriate structure may go through alternating petroleum- and gas-bearing structures, producing each in succession. Takang, in particular, probably has substantial natural gas reserves, a fact substantiated by Sino-Japanese discussions of the import of Japanese LNG technology in exchange for an export agreement for the gas from Takang.[32] Some sources have indicated that Takang has already begun production with a natural gas pipeline to Tientsin.[33]

Hydropower Potential

China's hydropower resource is the largest of any single country in the world, with the possible exception of the Soviet Union, exceeding the hydraulic potential of North America and that of the whole of Africa. (See Table 14.6.) South America is the only continental region with a hydraulic potential approximating that of the People's Republic of China.[34] In 1955, the Chinese government estimated total hydropower potential at 540,000 megawatts. That estimate was based on initial surveys of the major river systems throughout China. At the level of the 1955 estimate, China could run the entire 1975 American electric power industry on hydropower alone.[35] Thus, as in the case of China's coal reserves, hydropower resources will not represent a limit on hydroelectric development for generations to come.

On the basis of Soviet estimates made prior to 1960, Smil has suggested that the hydropower potential that could actually be developed under a maximum capital allocation program would be closer to 300,000 MW.[36] This more conservative estimate has also been adopted by the *Survey of Energy Resources*.[37] In addition, the development of China's hydropower potential involves overcoming several major obstacles. First, a large potential is situated in Tibet, a region with a small population located far from the more populous and industrial regions. The installation of high-tension lines to carry Tibet's hydropower to the coastal regions, or even to Szechwan (which has its own hydro potential), would be very capital-intensive and would involve substantial transmission losses. Second, the Yellow River, which has a high theoretical potential and has already been the target of Peking's largest hydro projects (Liuchiahsia and San Men), also has the highest silt content of any river in the world, making hydraulic engineering difficult and reservoir lifetimes relatively

TABLE 14.6

Hydropower Potential, 1949–77
(Gigawatts)

Year of estimate	Class	Quantity	Source	Class	Quantity	Source	Class	Quantity	Source	Class	Quantity	Source
1949	1	0.25	Smil									
1950	1	0.27	Smil	2	1.87	Hoover						
1951	1	0.27	Smil									
1952	1	0.34	Smil	2	1.96	Hoover						
1953	1	0.35	Smil									
1954	1	0.40	Smil									
1955	1	0.60	Smil				3	300	Smil	4	540	URI
1956	1	0.80	Smil									
1957	1	1.07	Smil	2	4.49	Hoover						
1958	1	1.30	Smil							4	580	URI
1959	1	1.71	Smil									
1960	1	2.00	Smil	2	13.70	Hoover						
1961	1	2.20	Smil									
1962	1	2.40	Smil							4	2,000	IOESB
1963	1	2.50	Smil									
1964	1	2.60	Smil									
1965	1	3.00	Smil	2	15.00	Hoover						
1966	1	3.20	Smil									
1967	1	3.40	Smil							4	535	JEC
1968	1	3.60	Smil									
1969	1	4.00	Smil									
1970	1	4.40	Smil							4	500	Tregear
1971	1	5.40	Smil									
1972	1	6.90	Smil									
1973	1	9.00	Smil							4	535	Rawski
1974	1	10.00	Smil				3	330	SER			
1975							3	500	BOM	4	1,000	BOM
1976	1	13.5[a]	NCUSCT									
1977	1	15.5[a]	NCUSCT							4	500	NCUSCT

Note: For full forms of abbreviations, see Table 13.2. Class: 1 – current capacity; 2 – current capacity plus planned additions to capacity; 3 – exploitable potential; 4 – theoretical potential.
[a] Inferred.

short. Third, the Yangtze River, with the largest potential of any river basin in China, also has high fluctuation in runoff rates, requiring large reservoirs to stabilize the flow.[38] Such reservoirs would have to be built in very populous areas, involving the dislocation of millions from rich farm country.

Although the available estimates make it obvious that hydropower represents China's largest nondepletable energy resource, the difficulties in utilization and development of that resource should not be understated. At present, China has developed only about 5 percent of hydropower potential, even under restrictive assumptions regarding the extent of that potential. Production statistics indicate that hydropower development has moved rather slowly, keeping hydro at a constant percent (about 1 percent of total energy production).

The slow pace of hydro development holds true on an aggregate basis, despite the recent effort Peking has expended in the development of small-scale hydropower stations in the rural areas. The widespread diffusion of hydropower has spread the availability of small amounts of electric power throughout the rural areas. The total capacity of the 26 small hydro stations operating in 1949 was 2 megawatts. There were 9,000 small stations by 1960, 35,000 by 1971 with 16 percent of total generating capacity (about 1,000 MW), and 50,000 by 1975.[39] Particular attention has been paid to development of small stations in Kwangtung, Szechwan, Hopei, Honan, Chekiang, Shansi, and Sinkiang.[40] Many stations have been built in conjunction with pumping and flood-control projects. Other major applications have included home lighting in rural villages, threshing, small-scale rural industry, and similar uses requiring diffusion but not high voltages. Although the total hydro contribution to energy production has remained stable at 1 percent, the hydro component of electric power capacity, as well as the small-scale hydro component of total hydropower capacity, has increased steadily over the past 15 years.*

Recent large-scale hydropower installations include the completion of the Liuchiahsia Station (1,200 MW) in Kansu on the Yellow River; the reconstructed San Men Gorge project (200 MW), also on the Yellow River near Sian; the Chentsuen Station in Anhwei (150 MW); and a large station in Kwangtung (75 MW).[41] Total developed capacity on the Yangtze River was about 3,000 MW by 1975, that of the Yellow River about 2,000 MW.[42] (See Table 14.7.)

---

*An official report in July 1979 placed the total number of small hydropower stations at 88,000, with another 12,000 under construction. Total capacity of these stations was placed at 5,380 megawatts and 1978 output at 10 billion kwh. This would indicate a utilization ratio of about 2,000 kwh/kw, a reasonable figure in view of high variation in runoff rates in small streams.

TABLE 14.7
Hydrological Characteristics of Major River Basins, 1976

River basin	Length (10^3 km)	Basin area (10^6 km^2)	Discharge (10^9 m^3/y)	Potential[b] (gigawatts)	Current capacity[c] (gigawatts)	Developed potential
Yangtze	5.8[a]	1.8[a]	1,020[a]	214	2.888	1.3%
Yellow	5.5[a]	0.75[a]	48[a]	32	2.010	6.3%
Fuchun	0.4[b]	0.03[b]	n.a.	8	1.282	15.6%
Yalu	n.a.	n.a.	n.a.	n.a.	1.000	n.a.
Pearl	2.2[a]	0.42[a]	356[a]	28	0.939	3.4%
Sungari	1.7[b]	0.44[b]	30[b]	2	0.626	31.3%
Min	0.6[b]	0.06[b]	n.a.	3	0.273	9.1%
Hai	1.1[a]	0.26[a]	15[a]	1	0.228	22.8%
Liao	1.4[b]	0.12[b]	n.a.	1	0.177	17.7%
Huai	1.0[a]	0.26[a]	42[a]	10	0.111	1.1%
Tarim	n.a.	n.a.	n.a.	17	0.100	0.6%
Han	n.a.	n.a.	n.a.	n.a.	0.060	n.a.
Mekong	n.a.	n.a.	n.a.	15	0.050	0.3%
Yalutsangpu (Brahmaputra)	n.a.	n.a.	n.a.	115	0.0	0.0%
Total				450[d]	9.744[d]	2.2%[d]

[a] Ms. Chu, spokesperson of the Chinese Society of Hydraulic Engineering, in comments to the Water Resources Delegation to the PRC, Sept. 12, 1974, according to a transcript of notes by Richard T. Shen.

[b] Vaclav Smil, "Exploitating China's Hydro Potential," *International Water Power and Dam Construction* 28, no. 3 (Mar. 1976): 19–25; Vaclav Smil, *China's Energy: Achievements, Problems, Prospects* (New York: 1976), p. 70.

[c] William W. Clarke, "China's Electric Power Industry," *USCBR* 4, no. 5 (Sept.–Oct. 1977): 30–31.

[d] Approximate. Capacity figures exclude hydropower plants under 30 megawatts generating capacity.

Nuclear Power

Estimation of China's nonconventional energy resources even to a reliable order of magnitude remains an impossible task for the foreign observer. Essentially all we know is that the PRC has been experimenting with a number of alternative future energy technologies, any one of which could be developed into a producing future energy industry. Because of the uncertainties regarding both the extent of China's nonconventional energy resources and the likely future mix of alternative future energy technologies, each nonconventional technology will be treated briefly in this section on energy reserves, rather than being included among the active commercial energy production statistics.

Although no specific data are available in this sensitive area, it has generally been thought that China has extensive deposits of economically recoverable uranium ore. Uranium was believed to have been discovered in Sinkiang province in 1949.[43] On March 27, 1950, the Sino-Soviet Non-Ferrous Rare Metals Joint-Stock Company was established in Sinkiang, presumably to extract uranium ore. The company was dissolved in 1955 and transferred to Chinese control.[44] China entered into an agreement to supply the Soviet Union with uranium ore in exchange for Soviet technical assistance with atomic energy technology. Uranium and thorium were extracted from Chinese ores by 1957 on a laboratory scale and on a larger scale by 1964.[45] We know that the PRC is currently producing uranium ore in several locations outside of Sinkiang, notably Chusan (Kiangsi) and Weiyuan (Kwangtung). In Chapter 12, I estimate China's current production of U_3O_8 at 1,000–2,000 metric tons per year. This guess is based on a 1974 report that China was producing a total of 2,500 metric tons per day of uranium ore at three mines, and on a comparison to the uranium production of other countries and to the concentration of uranium oxide in American ores.[46] I have also estimated China's current uranium reserves at 100,000 metric tons of U_3O_8 at the 1976 price of $30 per kilogram (Table 10.1). The reserves estimate is highly speculative, an order of magnitude guess based on the size of the Chinese nuclear weapons program and a comparison to other uranium-producing countries.

The uranium ore from Chinese mines is processed at a beneficiation plant in Chuchou (Hunan) and at a gaseous diffusion plant in Lanchow (Kansu).[47] There were rumors in 1965 that Czechoslovakia had processed some Chinese uranium ore into highly enriched U-235. Apparently the Chinese sent partially processed ore from the Chuchou Uranium Ore Concentrating Plant to a plant in Czechoslovakia for further processing or chemical conversion. The Chinese paid roughly half of the processed uranium in return for this service.[48] There is some speculation that the arrangement with Czechoslovakia accelerated the Chinese atomic weapons program prior to the explosion of the first Chinese fission device in 1964. But Czechoslovakia lacks isotopic separation facilities, and the details of the construction of China's first atomic weapon remain shrouded in official secrecy.

One would expect, with the attention that China has paid to geological survey work, especially since the departure of the Soviet geologists in 1960, that the PRC has discovered many additional uranium deposits in its vast territory and has considerably developed the technology for uranium extraction, isotopic separation, and ore concentration. Depending on the size of the uranium reserves discovered and the scale of uranium requirements in the nuclear weapons industry, China may already have laid the resource base for a commercial nuclear power industry.

The production base for such an industry, however, has not yet been established. China ignored the development of the American nuclear power industry in the early 1950's, but expressed considerable enthusiasm over the commissioning of the first Soviet plant in July 1954.[49] On January 18, 1955, the Soviet Council of Ministers announced that the Soviet Union would supply China with a 6.5 megawatt experimental reactor. The reactor was completed by 1957 and started up in 1958. It had 2 percent U-235 uranium rods and a heavy-water moderator/coolant. Reports of its final capacity were raised from 6.5 MW to 7.0 MW and then to 10 MW. Under the same agreement, the Soviet Union also provided a 25 million electron-volt alpha-particle cyclotron for experimental research.[50] The reactor itself still does not produce significant quantities of electric power and is probably used entirely for experimental and educational purposes.[51] Foreign visitors have been permitted to see the reactor, indicating that if China is actively pursuing nuclear power plant design or development, any significant units would be at other, undisclosed locations.[52]

Interestingly, Chinese professional journals have shown an interest in reactor safety problems. Chinese scientists stress the production potential of nuclear power, but admit serious health and safety problems:

Although man has mastered and is mastering many kinds of energy sources such as coal, petroleum, wind force, hydraulic power, terrestrial heat, solar energy, nuclear energy, most of them have not been satisfactorily developed and utilized. For coal, which has the earliest development history, its known world reserves are more than enough to meet human demands for at least many thousands of years. As to the nuclear energy in matter, it is even more inexhaustible.

Naturally, every type of energy source has its specific characteristics, advantages, and disadvantages. To meet the multiple demands of industrial and agricultural production as well as people's living needs, all types of energy sources must be developed and utilized. Nuclear power, more commonly called atomic energy, is one of those with great prospects.[53]

There is also the problem of safety and environmental protection. Although radioactive pollution may occur in atomic boiler incidents, so long as sufficient safety measures are adopted, such incidents can be prevented. As to environmental protection, pollution created by atomic boilers is less than that created by burning coal or petroleum under normal operational conditions, and in that sense is much cleaner. Of the present environmental pollution around the world, the proportion of radioactive pollution is not too high.[54]

Although the tone of these comments regarding nuclear hazards is highly defensive, Chinese scientists have obviously been considering the problems of nuclear safety, possibly in connection with the design of their own experimental units. This impression is strengthened by the fact that China has shown some commercial interest in American emergency core-cooling systems.[55] The Lanchow Physics Laboratory has also done research on the medical effects of uranium radioactivity absorbed in connection with atomic energy–related employment (probably mining).[56]

The Soviet nuclear power and atomic science aid commitment in 1955 evidently stirred up both intense interest in the Chinese scientific community and priority funding of atomic energy programs by the Chinese government. On July 30, 1955, the National People's Congress listed the peaceful uses of atomic energy as a high-priority area of development. The Academy of Sciences was reorganized and expanded during the same year.[57] In his July 14, 1956, report to the National People's Congress, Chou En-lai laid stress on the development of atomic energy and nuclear technology as a high-priority objective for China's intellectual community.[58] By 1973, China had developed medical, industrial, and agricultural uses for radioactive isotopes, including the following:[59] (1) generation of new high-yield crop varieties; (2) increases in silkworm output; (3) sterilization of insect pupae; (4) tracing the environmental impact of pesticides; (5) phosphate fertilizer experiments; (6) quality control for continuous-cast steel billets; (7) synthesis of polyacetal polytrifluorochloroethylene and "organic glass," using polymerization; (8) density, thickness, and volume measurements; (9) metering of Yellow River silt content; (10) stratification analysis in coal and petroleum exploration; (11) tumor diagnosis; (12) thyroid diagnosis and treatment; (13) cancer treatment.

Whereas these various applications demonstrate Peking's scientific and technological interest in relatively inexpensive applications of nuclear engineering, until recently China had not moved toward the more expensive applications, especially commercial nuclear power generation. This situation, however, has changed radically since 1975. There is mounting evidence that China intends to develop a nuclear power industry as rapidly as possible and is planning to import one or two prototype power reactors as part of the new Ten-Year Plan for the Development of the National Economy (1976–85). Chapter 12 examines in detail the evidence that China has embarked on the road toward a nuclear power industry, the rationale for doing so, and the international implications of such a development. In 1976, 1977, and 1978, China sent a series of technical delegations abroad to study high-energy physics and to compare various nuclear power fuel cycle options. Party Chairman Hua Kuo-feng specifically mentioned nuclear power research and development as a key technological objective in his report to the Fifth National People's Congress on February 26, 1978.[60] Fang Yi, Minister of the State Scientific and Technological Commission, reiterated this objective in a speech to the National Science Conference on March 18, 1978.[61] The first prototype reactors will be imported, and Peking has already ordered two pressurized water reactors, with the construction design under license from Westinghouse, from a consortium of French companies (Chapter 12).[62]

The Chinese press has also recently emphasized the resumption of scientific programs in high-energy physics. In June 1978 it was reported that construction of China's first 30–50 billion electron volt (bev) proton accelerator had begun in Peking.[63] A much larger proton accelerator will then be built between 1980 and 1985. High-energy physics has been listed as one of eight "key disciplines" by the March 1978 National Science Conference.

If the broad assessment in Chapter 12 is correct, China will have its first full-scale nuclear power reactor operating by about 1985. The PRC will also develop a domestic nuclear power-generating equipment industry in the 1980's and should be producing nuclear power plants of domestic design and construction by 1990. Development of the nuclear power industry will then accelerate during the 1990's to provide significant additions to thermal electric power-generating capacity. Total nuclear power-generating capacity may reach between 5 and 15 GWe by the year 2000, depending on the ultimate size of petroleum and natural gas discoveries in the intervening years. Thus, over the next two decades, China's nuclear power industry could reach one-third of the 1975 U.S. nuclear power capacity and could surpass the 1975 nuclear power-generating capacity of the Soviet Union. The total contribution of nuclear power to China's energy balance would still be a marginal 5 million metric tons coal equivalent at the turn of the century. But China may have mastered commercial nuclear power technology and laid the foundation for construction of a large nuclear power industry in the decades that follow. During the two decades between 1980 and 2000, China may also explore advanced fuel cycles and reactor designs, including both high-temperature reactors and fast breeder reactors, as well as a variety of isotope-separation and spent-fuel-reprocessing technologies. In short, by 2000 China could be as much a part of the nuclear scene as the United States, the Soviet Union, Great Britain, France, West Germany, and Japan were in the mid-1970's.

Solar Power

The Chinese press has evidenced a considerable degree of interest in the development of solar power technologies. Wide areas of western China would be appropriate for the use of solar energy. The Tibet Industrial Architectural Surveying and Designing Institute has already experimented with solar bathhouses, a solar cooking stove, and a solar water boiler. "The slant-surfaced box-type solar energy stoves are now introduced widely in farming and pastoral areas of the autonomous region by the departments concerned."[64] The same article reports the construction of ten solar-heated bathhouses in Lhasa, including one unit with a 280-square-meter collector. Sunshine averages 3,000 hours per year in Lhasa at high average radiation levels. Other parts of the country also report experiments with solar energy. Shanghai's No. 15 Radio Factory produced 1,000 umbrella-shaped collapsible solar stoves in 1974 for rural cooking purposes.[65] The Peking Technical Exchange Center has been promoting the use of solar water boilers for bath water in the Peking area and solar stoves for use on the nearby communes.[66] Tientsin University has experimented with a small device for solar electric-power generation.[67]

These specific bits of information indicate that small-scale solar power technology may follow the small-scale coal mines and small hydropower plants in the development of China's rural energy system. Solar technology is particularly adaptable to small-unit production because of the diffuseness of the energy source and the steep capital requirement curve as one moves to larger units. High levels of solar radiation are available in precisely the areas that lack hydropower resources (Tibet has both). All these considerations might make the development of small-scale solar technology a particularly attractive option in certain areas of the PRC, especially for process heat and home use. Small-scale solar technology also lends itself to construction from local materials and a high degree of labor intensity, characteristics that have already made the small-scale coal mine and small hydropower station attractive development alternatives in the Chinese countryside.

Geothermal and Tidal Power

The PRC has been experimenting with geothermal electric power generation for at least eight years. By 1971, a geothermal power station operating on a hot-water system had been installed in Fengshun county (Kwangtung). The plant runs on a well 800 meters deep and includes a number of technical innovations developed in China.[68] Its generating capacity has not been reported, but judging from the technical description, it would be on the scale of an experimental unit rather than a medium or large power generation unit.

As with solar power, Tibet will be an important future area for geothermal development. Tibet is reported to have extensive geothermal steam resources and more than 100 hot spring districts, indicating that the magma is relatively close to the surface under wide areas of Tibet. Specific promising geothermal fields are located near Lhasa and at Ngamring, 5,000 meters above sea level in the upper reaches of the Yalu Tsangpu River. The Academy of Sciences has sponsored a geothermal group of the Chinghai-Tibet Plateau Multipurpose Scientific Survey Team since 1973. A geothermal greenhouse and swimming pool have been constructed in Shadthongmon county, and surveying and prospecting were under way near Lhasa in 1975 for the construction of China's first geothermal steam electric power station.[69]

China presumably has a number of other potential steam and hot-water geothermal sites at unknown locations. Nothing in the Chinese press would indicate that the PRC has been working on a technology for dry-rock geothermal power, a technology that will require drilling to great depths and as yet undetermined water injection systems.

Several foreign delegations have been taken to visit the Shunte county tidal hydroelectric project at Kanchu rapids on an estuary of the Pearl River (Kwangtung).[70] This station might be characterized as a "semi-tidal" hydropower generating plant. It has a 5-megawatt total generating capacity and runs on low waterhead generators which take advantage of the tidal drop at low tide. The station does not, however, run on tidal power in both directions and uses the river flow at high tide. Therefore, it could not be considered a full-scale tidal power generating station, but represents a mixed technology. There is no indication of whether or not China has many sites suitable for such a unit.

Biomass Energy

As with many predominantly agricultural societies, China for centuries depended primarily on biomass energy as the chief energy supplement to human and animal labor. Heating, lighting, and cooking fuel were all provided by the burning of firewood and crop residues. The use of these traditional biomass fuels continues today in China, but on a lower per capita level because of the increasing use of coal, electricity, and other commercial energy fuels in the countryside. One recent estimate of China's total annual consumption of firewood was 130 million cubic meters, or 45–50 million metric tons coal equivalent in energy consumption from firewood. Another 30–35 million metric tons coal equivalent in energy was said to be obtained annually from the burning of crop residues.[71] These are obviously order of magnitude estimates and should not be taken as absolute values.

China has also recently adopted what appears to be a new form of biomass energy utilization which could prove important in the countryside over the next 25 years. The Chinese press refers to the new biomass energy technology as "marsh gas" production. It consists of the fermentation of organic wastes in simple covered pits that generate gas containing about 50 percent methane and 45 percent carbon dioxide. The gas pits are connected directly with village houses: "The marsh gas pits are of many shapes and sizes. They have an inlet and an outlet, with a gas pipe leading out through the center of the cover. Plastic pipes insulated with mud lead from pit to the interior of a house."[72]

The pits serve a dual purpose, since the fermented residues make excellent organic fertilizers, continuing the ancient Chinese cycle of waste management, organic fertilizer, crop, and waste. The fermentation raises the temperature of the waste to a point where natural sterilization occurs, reducing the hazards of the traditional night-soil fertilizer. The gas from the pits is used for cooking (not heating, since fermentation stops in cold weather), lighting in areas without electricity, water pumps, small-scale electric power generation, rice threshing, flour mills, and so on.[73] Smil estimated that the total number of pits in China grew from 30,000 in 1973 to 200,000 in 1974, 410,000 in 1975, and some 4.3 million by May 1977.[74] The main area of development has been Szechwan, which has the proper temperature conditions for most of the year. But other areas such as Shanghai have joined the experiment.[75]

Controlled Fusion Experiments

China has been experimenting with thermonuclear fusion devices, which could lead toward electric power applications in the distant future. The PRC has constructed a small "Tokamak" apparatus for magnetic confinement of deuterium-tritium plasma as a basis for initial controlled-fusion-reaction experiments. The unit includes a ring-shaped magnetic bottle and a specially designed bank of storage capacitors.[76] No results have been reported from the Chinese experiments, but they would doubtless parallel the findings of the initial stages of fusion power research in this country, Europe, and the Soviet Union. No laser fusion experiments have been reported, although China has developed commercial lasers for other purposes.[77] Peking has been open about the nature of its fusion experiment, but so far has not offered to join the group of countries now sharing fusion power discoveries.

Chapter 15

Alternative Estimates of Energy Production

As with primary energy reserves and resources, the estimation of production statistics for China's primary and secondary energy industries presents some unique problems. Under normal conditions, governments publish annual production statistics for coal, crude petroleum, natural gas, and electric power output. These simple statistics provide a skeletal framework within which energy balance analysis takes place. In addition, many governments publish detailed data on each of the primary and secondary industries, including econometric and physical output statistics. Unfortunately for the foreign analyst, the government of the People's Republic of China published such statistics only sporadically during the 1950's and ceased publishing any production data in 1960. This added an entirely new layer of research and estimation to the already difficult problem of analyzing China's energy balance. A data-collection task that should take a few hours in the library mushroomed into years of elaborate research and guesswork.

At the time of writing, it appears that the new government in Peking is finally modifying the long-standing policy of official statistical silence. In recent weeks, annual production statistics have been published for the steel and coal industries for the first time in nearly 20 years. There is reason for optimism regarding the publication of other energy and economic production statistics as well. The availability of official data assists the foreign analyst in several ways. It helps reduce the margin of uncertainty surrounding patchwork estimates. It fixes end-points for production data series, facilitating the choice among alternative estimates by various foreign sources. And it releases the researcher from the tedious task of piecing together production estimates from fragmentary and unreliable information in the Chinese press.

This chapter provides alternative estimates of production data for China's primary and secondary energy industries. It represents a collection of the work of many other authors and institutions over two decades. None of the estimated series are completely accurate. The running text in the chapter provides an analysis of the accuracy of various estimated data series and also discusses the state of technological development in each Chinese energy industry. It should be kept in mind that this is a simple overview of China's energy production system. As with the book as a whole, the focus is upward, in the direction of China's international energy policies, rather than downward into the structure of the individual energy industries. Far more research should be done on each energy industry, especially now that China has opened its doors to a wave of foreign visitors and is beginning to open statistical windows on its own industrial development.

Coal Production

Estimates of Chinese coal production have been plentiful both in the international energy literature and in economic studies specific to Chinese industry. The statistical series from the PRC's *Ten Great Years* have usually been taken as the benchmark data for raw coal production during the 1950's. However, starting in 1958, the official PRC estimates took such gigantic leaps that only the most credulous foreign observers believed them at the time. For 1958 alone, Peking claimed to have doubled coal production, a most unlikely event, given the five-year lead time usually required for construction of new shaft or pit mines. The 1958 figure was claimed to have included some 50 million metric tons of coal from newly developed "native mines," or small-scale local mining operations. Even if this were the case, it would be extremely unlikely that the Chinese actually increased the output of large mines by the remaining 90 mmt in a single year, even if they were able to exceed the capacity of some mines. Given what is known about overreporting during the Great Leap, the conclusion could safely be drawn that the official claims for raw coal production were seriously exaggerated.[1]

In fact, many foreign observers not only discounted coal production claims made at the height of the Great Leap Forward, but also estimated that China's coal industry lagged seriously in the early 1960's, with little new mine construction and low levels of output for existing mines.[2] Peking was evidently embarrassed by the aftermath of the Great Leap and the withdrawal of Soviet assistance and ceased publishing production statistics in 1961. The ambiguities surrounding the coal industry in the early 1960's led to a divergence of opinion in the foreign literature regarding the true level of raw coal output. (See Table 15.1.) Two basic series were constructed by different branches of the American government starting with 1961. These two series were estimated by an expert on the Chinese coal industry (K. P. Wang) publishing through the Bureau of Mines (BOM) and by the U.S. Central Intelligence Agency, publishing through the Joint Economic Committee of Congress (JEC). The

TABLE 15.1
Estimates of Raw Coal Production, 1949–78
(Million metric tons)

Year	BOM	CIA[a]	CIA[b]	Dnthrn	ECAFE	FEER	Hoover	Iknkv	JEC
1949	15			32		31	32.4	32.4	32.4
1950	37						42.9	42.9	42.9
1951	44						53.1	53.1	53.1
1952	64	66		66			66.5	66.5	66.5
1953	67						69.7	69.7	69.7
1954	80						83.7	83.7	83.7
1955	94						98.3	98.3	98.3
1956	108						110	110	110
1957	130	131		130			130	130	131
1958	270			270		270	270	270	230
1959	350			348		348	348	348	300
1960	420		280	425	429	425	425	425	280
1961	250				254	380		300	170
1962	250			200	254	240		200	180
1963	270			210	275	200		210	190
1964	290			220		240		220	204
1965	300	220	240		304	240		230	220
1966	325	248			332		325	250	248
1967	225	190			232				190
1968	300	205			304				205
1969	330	258			282				258
1970	360	310	338		304		330		310
1971	390	335	365				356		335
1972	400	357	389						356
1973	430	377	411						377
1974	450	389	417						389
1975	465	427	480						
1976		440	463						
1977			519						
1978									

[a] Early CIA series from *China: the Coal Industry*, Nov. 1976, p. 5.
[b] Later CIA series from National Foreign Assessment Center, *Handbook of Economic Statistics, 1978*, Oct. 1978, p. 91.

TABLE 15.1 *(continued)*
Estimates of Raw Coal Production, 1949–78
(Million metric tons)

Year	JETRO	PRC	Rawski	SD	SER	Smil	UNSY	URI	WES
1949	32.4	32.4				32.4	32.4	32.4	
1950	42.9	42.9				42.9	41.1	42.9	
1951	53.1	53.1				53.1	53.1	53.1	
1952	66.5	66.5	65		63.5	66.5	64.5	66.5	
1953	69.7	69.7			66.6	69.7	69.7	66.7	
1954	83.7	83.7			79.9	83.7	83.7	83.7	
1955	98.3	98.3	67		93.6	98.3	98.3	98.3	
1956	110.4	110			106	110	110	110.4	
1957	130.1	130				130	130	130	
1958	230	270				230	270	270	
1959	300	348	300			300	348	347	
1960	280	425				280	425	400	
1961	170					170	250		254
1962	180					180	250		254
1963	191					190	270		275
1964	200					200	290		295
1965	220		219			220	299		304
1966	240			240		240	327		332
1967	190			190		190	227		232
1968	200			200		200	300		305
1969	250			250		250	325		325
1970	310			300		300	360		360
1971	335		324	325	410	320	390		390
1972	357					340	400		400
1973	378					365			430
1974	382					390			450
1975						425			470
1976		450				440			490
1977		500							
1978		600							

two series began with divergent estimates of raw coal production for 1961 and 1962 and then constructed data for subsequent years on the basis of annual rates of growth reported in the Chinese press. Consequently, the two series are consistent with figures from the Chinese press, and are parallel to each other, being about 60–70 mmt apart. With the exception of the series constructed by Ikonnikov (which lies between the BOM and JEC estimates), most other sources have relied on one or the other of the two basic American government estimates.

The thesis version of this study adopted the higher Bureau of Mines series for raw coal production. The higher series initially appeared to reflect more accurately the steady growth in small coal-mine output that is frequently mentioned in Chinese press accounts. However, a recent study by the CIA publicly documented the empirical basis for their estimates for the first time.[3] The documentation for the CIA series was relatively thorough, built on three separate levels of aggregation—the individual mines, regional and provincial data, and national coal production growth rates. Estimates for some of the large mines may also have been confirmed by satellite photography.

At the end of 1978, the Chinese government itself finally provided data that establish fairly firm estimates of raw coal production for the period 1976–78. An article published in *Hong Qi* (*Red Flag*) in January 1978 claimed that coal production had increased "more than 15 times" when compared with 1949.[4] That would put 1977 raw coal output at 490–500 million metric tons. This figure was confirmed at the end of 1978, when the Chinese government claimed that 1977 raw coal production had been 500 million tons and that 1978 production would be 600 million tons by the end of the year.[5] A subsequent article confirmed the 600 million ton estimate for 1978 and revealed that production for 1977 was 50 million tons higher than for 1976, a figure compatible with an earlier claim that 1977 production increased by more than 10 percent over 1976.[6] The implied increase of 100 million metric tons in a single year, from 1977 to 1978, was a complete surprise to foreign observers, but consistent with claims during the year that coal production was increasing by some 20 percent.[7]

These new data from the Chinese press evidently caused a reevaluation of the early CIA series, which was raised by 9 percent in a CIA publication of October 1978.[8] The two series are exactly parallel, so that both are consistent with the same information on annual coal production increases culled from the Chinese press. But the new series is more compatible with data available from 1958–60 and with official claims for 1976–78. Chinese raw coal production suffered absolute declines in 1961 (aftermath of the Great Leap), 1967 (Cultural Revolution), and 1976 (Tangshan earthquake). But the magnitude of these declines has been difficult to assess, since the Chinese press was silent on the subject during the years of decline. It is likely that the earlier CIA-JEC series overstated the production decline in 1961, thereby understating coal output in subsequent years. The new series corrects this downward bias and brings the data closer to other foreign estimates.

Furthermore, the high CIA series helps explain the big jump in coal production that was claimed in 1978. According to the new CIA data,

1975 production was about 480 million tons, up from the previous estimate of 427 million tons. Output then declined in 1976 to 450 million tons, the official Chinese figure for that year. It has been known for some time that 1976 was a poor year for the coal industry because of the destruction of the Kailuan coal mines by the massive Tangshan earthquake in July 1976, and because of political disruptions during the year of the deaths of Mao Tse-tung and Chou En-lai. During 1977, coal output recovered to 500 million tons, registering a modest 4 percent increase over 1975. The 20 percent increase in 1978 to roughly 600 million tons reflected the reconstruction of Kailuan, the introduction of new capacity that had been under construction since 1975 or earlier, and the stretching of available capacity under the impetus of the program for modernization.

Assuming that raw coal production did indeed reach 600 million metric tons in 1978, another such increase in a single year will be very unlikely. Capacity can be stretched into a sudden boom once, but it will be difficult to maintain the boom level of production without adding new capacity, let alone stretching it further. In addition, all of the contracts with European, Japanese, and American companies signed or rumored in late 1978 for the construction of new coal mines in China, taken together, will add less than 100 million tons of new capacity, and will require at least five years for completion. China's machine-building industry makes equipment for collieries of up to 2.2 million tons per year capacity.[9] That implies the installation of 40–50 individual mines for every 100 million tons of new capacity. This and the relatively primitive state of open-cast mining technology in China have led Peking to seek mine construction contracts with foreign companies. It also places serious constraint on the pace at which new capacity can be introduced.

China's new leadership would obviously like to substitute coal for petroleum in satisfying the requirements of growing domestic energy consumption over the next several decades. This would release additional crude and refined petroleum for export. This strategy, however, faces a number of constraints, similar to those experienced by the coal industries of other industrial countries. The addition of new coal-mining capacity is both time- and capital-intensive, regardless of the size of the coal resource base. There are also serious market constraints on the use of coal in a modern industrial economy. These factors will limit Peking's high-coal-energy option.

Size and Distribution of Coal Mines

China's active coal mines now number in the thousands. By 1974 there were at least seven major coal complexes, each with an annual output of over 15 million metric tons and ranging in output to 25–30 mmt.[10] If the big seven produced an average of 20 mmt per year, they accounted for about 30 percent of production in 1975. An additional 25 percent was provided by medium-range mines (5–15 mmt/year), 20 percent by small mines (1–5 mmt/year), and the remaining 25 percent by very small local mines (less than 1 mmt/year).

Anthracite accounted for about 25 million tons in 1975, or 5 percent of total output. Coking required about 50 million tons of raw coal in 1977, or 10 percent of total coal production.[11]

Technology in the Coal Industry

Peking has sought to modernize coal-mining technology as rapidly as possible, within the limits set by the domestic machine-building industries and capital constraints. Long-wall mining has been adopted at some of the larger mines.[12] Hydraulic cutters and mining machines have been introduced to the most modern mines. China received early assistance with coal-mine construction from the Soviet Union and Poland. More recently, mining equipment has been imported from British, German, and American companies.[13] Coal-washing equipment has been produced primarily by China's own machine-building industries and has lagged far behind total raw coal output.[14] It has been estimated that as much as 40 percent of China's rail traffic is engaged in moving coal, motivating the search for small-mine coal supplies for the areas south of the Yangtze River.[15]

One of the principal objectives of mine technology development has been to sustain the output of the older mines in the industrial northeast. The mines associated with the Kailuan combine are among the oldest in the country and have become a model unit in the coal-mining industry as a whole because of successful efforts to sustain and further increase output.

In order to compensate for remaining weaknesses in coal-mining technology, Peking is engaging a number of foreign mining corporations and organizations in construction contracts and technical exchange programs. The British National Coal Board has agreed to serve as a special technical consultant to the Chinese Ministry of Coal during the current ten-year development plan. A West German mining consortium agreed in September 1978 to construct more than 20 million tons of new coal-mining capacity in a $4 billion arrangement. The United States Department of Energy is encouraging the American National Coal Association to participate in the construction of two surface mines in China with capacities of 20 million tons per year each.[16] In addition, the Department of Energy would like to have American mining firms submit bids on development of five new deep mines, upgrading of three existing mines, construction of six coal preparation plants, and construction of factories in China to produce advanced coal-mining equipment. The United States is also collaborating with the PRC in technical research on fluidized bed coal gasification. China already has some coal gasification plants, operating since the days of the Japanese occupation.

Crude Petroleum Production and Transportation

It is impossible within the framework of this study to provide a detailed analysis of the Chinese petroleum industry. Chapter 8 examined China's offshore oil and gas exploration program. Chapter 11 looked at Taching oilfield, the nation's largest single energy-producing unit. Chapter 14 summarized what is known outside of China regarding crude petroleum reserves and resources. The foreign literature on China's petroleum industry is far more extensive than for any other Chinese energy industry.[17] Furthermore, Peking has encouraged international exchanges in petroleum exploration, extraction, transportation, and refining technology and has made heavy purchases of foreign equipment for each part of the petroleum industry. Much more, therefore, is seen through the window provided by such exchanges in the petroleum industry than has been seen by foreign visitors to coal, natural gas, or electric power production facilities. Multinational oil corporations and petroleum equipment suppliers have a direct interest in information of commercial importance regarding the Chinese oil industry. Finally, knowledge of China's petroleum industry is of strategic importance to certain foreign governments, including the United States and Japan. The CIA, for example, has collected and recently published detailed information on each of China's major oilfields and on national oil reserves and production statistics.[18] The uncertainties regarding China's oil industry have thus diminished as the tide of information available to foreign observers has risen. This brief synopsis will limit itself to an evaluation of alternative foreign estimates of China's crude petroleum output, a discussion of crude oil transport and storage facilities, and an overview of the "state of the art" in Chinese petroleum production technology. A later section of this chapter will summarize information on China's oil-refining industry.

Alternative Estimates of Crude Petroleum Production

Many estimates have been made by foreign observers of China's crude petroleum output. Indeed, only the more important have been listed in Table 15.2. There is a relatively high degree of consensus regarding crude petroleum output levels for the 1950's, when Peking supplied official statistics, and for the 1970's, when the Chinese government again provided firm clues about the country's crude oil growth rate and production levels. Virtually the only remaining area of disagreement concerns production levels from 1966 through 1969, the years of the Cultural Revolution. Most of the differences reflected in the alternative estimates were the result of errors (e.g. attaching a production level to the wrong year), or the omission of shale oil production from the total. This study adopted the CIA series for the years 1949 through 1977, because of the somewhat better documentation provided for this series than the others and because of the assumption that covert as well as documentary sources were used to make the estimates. The Chinese press often uses multiples of 1965 production to report petroleum production for later years. A recent article revealed that 1965 production was 94 times the 1949 production level, which in turn had been given in official statistics published in the 1950's.[19] The CIA estimate for 1965 (10.96 mmt) was close to the official figure for that year (11.37 mmt). This indicates that the CIA series is close to reality, perhaps a shade low.

My crude petroleum estimate for 1978 (100.2 million metric tons) was based on extrapolation from the CIA figure for 1977 (90.3 mmt), plus the 11 percent increase reported for January–August 1978 by the Chinese press.[20] The exact figure for 1978 has not yet been reported.* But whatever the precise production figure for 1978, it is evident that the decline in oil production growth rates since 1975 is a trend rather than an anomaly. Such a decline in annual growth rates to below 10 percent per year is a normal pattern that can be readily identified in the petroleum development experiences of other countries (Chapter 23). It by no means indicates that Chinese oil is "drying up," as some Western press reports have suggested.[21] Indeed, the absolute annual addition to crude petroleum production capacity has held constant since 1970 at about 8–10 million tons per year, and continues to be roughly in that range. But this rate of additions to production capacity costs increasing inputs of capital, exploration, and drilling effort each year, as new oilfields become more difficult to discover, deeper, or more remote from industrial centers. The rising cost trend per unit of added capacity will accelerate as China moves the petroleum industry into the offshore provinces. Thus the opening of "ten Tachings" by 1985, a stated goal of the current Ten-Year Development Plan, will prove an arduous and costly effort, if indeed the PRC has discovered sufficient reserves to support such an ambitious petroleum development program. This is the main reason

---

*The final official crude petroleum output figure reported for 1978 was 104 mmt, 4 percent higher than the estimate used throughout the Statistical Profile. The official production target set for 1979 was just 106 mmt, indicating serious difficulty in efforts to expand output.

TABLE 15.2
Estimates of Crude Petroleum Production, 1949–77
(Million metric tons)

Year	BOM	Chang	Cheng	CIA	Dnthrn	FEER	Hrsn	Harvard
1949	0.10	0.12		0.12	0.12	0.12		
1950	0.11	0.20		0.20		0.20		
1951	0.12			0.30				
1952	0.14			0.44	0.44	0.44		
1953	0.21			0.62				
1954	0.41			0.79				
1955	0.48			0.97		0.97		
1956	0.64			1.16				
1957	0.68			1.46	1.5	1.4		
1958	0.82			2.26	2.3	2.3		
1959	3.7	3.7		3.7	3.7	3.7		
1960	5.5			5.1	4.5	5.5		
1961	6.2		6.0	5.19		5.5		6.2
1962	6.8		6.7	5.75	5.3	6.9		6.8
1963	7.5	7.0	7.5	6.36	5.9	7.5	6.4	7.5
1964	8.5		8.5	8.65	8.4	8.5		8.5
1965	10		11.0	10.96		10		10
1966	13		14.0	14.07				13
1967	11		11.0	13.9				11
1968	15		15.4	15.2				15
1969	17		20.7	20.38				20
1970	28	25	29.1	28.21			20	26
1971	37	36	37.5	36.70				31
1972	43	43	45.0	43.06				50
1973	54	50	53.0	54.80				70
1974	65		63.0	65.76		65.8	70	
1975				74.26		74.5		
1976				83.61		84.5		84.7
1977				90.30				

(continued)

TABLE 15.2 *(continued)*
Estimates of Crude Petroleum Production, 1949–77
(Million metric tons)

Year	Hoover	Iknkv	IPE	JEC	JETRO	Kmbr	Koide
1949	0.12	0.12		0.12	0.12	0.12	
1950	0.20	0.20	0.1	0.20	0.20	0.20	
1951	0.31	0.30		0.30	0.31	0.30	
1952	0.44	0.44		0.44	0.44	0.44	
1953	0.62	0.62		0.62	0.62	0.62	
1954	0.79	0.79		0.79	0.79	0.79	
1955	0.97	0.97	0.5	0.97	0.97	0.97	
1956	1.2	1.16		1.16	1.16	1.16	
1957	1.5	1.46	1.4	1.46	1.46	1.46	
1958	2.3	2.26		2.26	2.26	2.26	
1959	3.7	3.70		3.7	3.70	3.70	
1960	5.5		5.2	5.5	5.50	4.50	
1961	6.5			5.3	5.00	5.26	
1962	7.0			5.8	5.65	5.83	
1963	8.0	7.5		6.4	7.50	6.50	
1964	8.5	9.0		8.7	8.48	6.90	
1965	10	10.0	7.8	10.8	10.50	8.67	10.60
1966	13	11.0	10	13.9	14.00	12.37	13.00
1967	11		8.5	13.9	13.00	10.40	14.90
1968	15		9.7	15.2	16.00	12.40	16.50
1969	18		10.4	20.3	18.00		18.00
1970	20		19.7	28.5	28.32		26.40
1971	31		25.2	36.7	36.42		36.45
1972	37		29.6	43.0	42.25		42.39
1973	50		42.4	54.5	53.00	40	50
1974			59.2	65.3	63.60		
1975			79.0				
1976							
1977							

TABLE 15.2 *(concluded)*
Estimates of Crude Petroleum Production, 1949–77
(Million metric tons)

Year	Myrhf	NCUSCT	PRC	Rawski	SD	SER	Smil	WES
1949	0.12		0.12				0.12	
1950	0.20		0.20				0.20	0.20
1951	0.30		0.30				0.31	0.31
1952	0.43		0.44	0.5			0.44	0.44
1953	0.62		0.62				0.62	0.62
1954	0.79		0.79			0.79	0.79	0.79
1955	0.97		0.97	1.2		0.97	0.97	0.97
1956	1.16		1.16			1.2	1.16	1.16
1957	1.41		1.47				1.47	1.46
1958	2.26		2.26				2.26	2.26
1959	3.70		3.7				3.7	3.7
1960	5.50		5.5				5.2	5.5
1961	5.30						5.4	6.2
1962	5.83						6.0	6.8
1963	6.40						7.0	7.5
1964	8.70						8.5	8.5
1965	10.80		10	5.4			10.6	10.0
1966	13.50				10		13.0	13.0
1967	13.00				10		14.9	11.0
1968	15.20				11		16.5	15.0
1969	20.30				14		18.0	14.6
1970	28.50	28.5	20		18		26.4	20.0
1971	36.70	36.7		26	23		36.5	36.65[a]
1972	43.00	43.0				29	42.3	42.95[a]
1973	54.70	54.5	50				53.0	51.25[a]
1974	65.30	65.3					63.6	65.0
1975	76.70	76.7					76.3	80.0
1976		83.4					85	91.0
1977		90.1						

[a]Revised estimate.

why Peking's energy planners are now willing to discuss joint offshore development programs with foreign multinational corporations.

Estimates of China's crude oil production include (or should include) annual output of petroleum from oil shale retorting. China has two shale oil-mining and retorting facilities, one in Fushun (Liaoning) and one in Maoming (Kwangtung). The Fushun facility was inherited from the Japanese occupation of Manchuria, but the Maoming shale oil unit was constructed by the Chinese themselves. By 1975, the two centers were probably producing about 4–5 million metric tons of retorted shale oil each year.[22] Insignificant amounts of synthetic crude have been produced from coal since before 1949. But the comparative cost per unit of added capacity is much higher for shale oil and synthetic crude than for natural crude oil, and Peking has therefore avoided heavy investment in these supplementary industries in recent years.

Crude Oil Transport and Storage

Peking has been channeling increasing amounts of capital, labor, and steel into the construction of transportation equipment for its burgeoning oil industry. As pointed out in Chapter 6, the new oil transport facilities are directly related to the expansion of China's crude petroleum exports to Japan and other countries. But the pipeline, rail, and tanker network is also important to the movement of petroleum and petroleum products within China. Most of China's refineries are located either at the major oilfields or near the major urban points of consumption (Peking, Shanghai, Nanking, and Canton). The older refineries were constructed at the sites of the oilfields to reduce the volume of petroleum products that had to be shipped by rail. New additions to refinery capacity, however, have been primarily in the major cities, with crude petroleum shipped in by pipeline or coastal tanker at lower cost than by rail.

China was slow to begin constructing crude oil pipelines and initially depended almost entirely on rail transport for crude. The first pipeline, completed with Soviet assistance in 1958, was a double line (one 16 inches and one 24 inches in diameter) from Karamai to Tushantze in Sinkiang, a distance of 300 kilometers. It was intended to move crude from the Karamai oilfield to the Tushantze refinery and to a railhead from which the bulk of the crude was shipped to the Lanchow refinery.[23] A second line was reported completed in 1965 from Yumen to Lanchow (about 880 km), but this line does not appear on CIA petroleum maps.[24] Given that a pipeline of that length would be readily visible by satellite photography and that the original report came from Taiwan, the line in question should be deleted from the literature. A pipeline for transport of Taching crude from Shenyang to Dairen (500 km) was built sometime during the 1960's.[25] But the loss of Soviet technical assistance and the Cultural Revolution kept oil pipeline construction at a virtual standstill until the early 1970's.

From 1970 until 1974, China undertook the construction of major trunk lines (24 inches) from Taching oilfield to various industrial centers in the northeast. A double line was constructed from Taching to Tiehling (Shenyang) to feed the existing line to Dairen and a new pipeline to Chinhuangtao on the Pohai Gulf. The Chinhuangtao line was then extended by May 1974 to the Peking General Petrochemical Works.[26] During the same period, two four-inch pipelines were constructed across the southern border with Vietnam from Pinghsiang to Kep, 50 kilometers north of Hanoi. Then an additional ten-inch line was built from Kep to Hanoi.[27] From 1975 through 1978, oil pipeline construction continued to accelerate. Short lines were built to connect Shengli and Takang oilfields with the coast and with nearby refineries and cities. A long line was completed from the Tsaidam Basin to Lhasa, Tibet, a distance of some 1,100 kilometers over rugged terrain. The cost of this pipeline could only be justified by strategic considerations, and the line is used to fuel divisions stationed throughout Tibet and along the sensitive Sino-Indian border. Another "friendship" pipeline was completed in 1976 from Tantung across the Korean border to Anju. A 1,000 km crude oil pipeline from Shengli oilfield south to the city of Nanking was completed in 1978. At the end of 1976, China had built 3,500 kilometers of crude oil pipeline, with another 2,000 kilometers under construction, most of which had been completed by mid-1978.[28]

Much of the large-diameter pipeline construction during the 1970's was based on the importation of Japanese seamless steel pipe. By 1977, China was still able to produce only small-diameter seamless pipe (10–12 inches) with small carrying capacity.[29] As the output of crude steel increases from 1980 to 1985 and the volume of petroleum requiring transport rises, Peking could opt for the construction or purchase of a plant for the domestic production of large-diameter oil and gas steel pipe. The acquisition of subsea pipeline technology will also be necessary, although the pipe required for offshore collecting networks need not be of such large diameter.

China has also been making progress in marine transport facilities for crude oil shipment. A number of small tankers were built and commissioned for coastal and inland waterway use before 1970.[30] Then, in 1971, China began to accelerate its tanker construction, completing a 10,000- and a 15,000-deadweight-ton tanker in that year and a pair of 24,000-dwt tankers at the Dairen shipyard.[31] In early 1977, construction of the 50,000-dwt tanker "Hsihu" was reported.[32] A number of foreign tankers have been purchased since 1970, including at least 12 tankers in the 50,000- to 100,000-dwt range (Chapter 22). The heaviest tanker purchases occurred in 1975–76, bringing China's oil-carrying fleet to about 100 tankers with a total of 2.2 million dwt by year-end 1976, still far short of the needs of China's coastal and international oil trade.[33] The PRC will require additional tanker tonnage during the early 1980's and may begin constructing tankers in the 100,000-dwt range.

The size and number of oil ports are another constraint on China's coastal and international petroleum trade. New port facilities have been under construction all along the Chinese coast since 1973. At the end of 1976 the maximum tanker capacities of the major ports were as follows: Dairen—100,000 dwt (Nienyu Bay); Chinhuangtao—50,000 dwt; Huangtao—70,000 dwt; Tientsin—25,000 dwt; Shanghai—unknown; Chankiang—70,000 dwt.[34] Storage tanks are available at Dairen, Huangtao (110,000 mt), and Shanghai. Shanghai and Chankiang have been used primarily as receiving ports for their respective refineries. Intelligence reports indicate that Chinese coastal tankers do not pass Taiwan and that crude oil received at Chankiang comes from the Middle East and Africa.[35] It is also possible that crude oil received at Chankiang was refined at Maoming for shipment by rail to Pinghsiang and thence to Vietnam by pipeline. If offshore oil is developed in the South China Sea, Chankiang and Maoming will become key petroleum handling and refining centers for the whole of southeastern China.

Assessing China's Oil Production Technology

General assessments of the "state of the art" in China's petroleum industry are a hazardous undertaking, owing to the extremely wide range of technologies in current use in the PRC and the number of countries from which that technology has been borrowed or bought. Professor Smil has given one of the more pessimistic assessments of China's petroleum technology:

In fact, contemporary Chinese deficiencies in the field of hydrocarbon drilling and production are very similar to the Soviet problems, only more widespread. Lack of sophisticated geophysical equipment (such as modern seismic devices and computerized field units) limits the capability of locating deep structures; inefficiencies in field operations are due to shortages of high-quality drilling and casing pipes, continued reliance on old turbodrills, poor drill bits and mud pumps, and lack of gas-treating facilities. The PRC's offshore oil-drilling technology is, of course, especially rudimentary.[36]

This contrasts sharply, of course, with the official Chinese view of its technological growth in the petroleum industry. The petroleum industry, and particularly Taching oilfield, is considered technologically advanced within the framework of China's overall industrial development. Frequent claims are made regarding innovations in exploration or production technology, while at the same time officials of the Chinese petroleum industry frequently admit in general terms that much needs to be done to achieve "advanced world levels." Technically competent visitors to China's oil facilities give the most objective assessment of the Chinese oil industry, and it is usually a mixed review.[37]

In my own technically untutored view, China's petroleum technology is analogous to a volcanic island chain. The pressure of rapid industrial development backed by the massive force of China's large aggregate capabilities pushes petroleum and other technology toward selective achievements (the tips of the island chain) in very limited sectors. At the same time, the basic structure of the oil industry, usually hidden from public view, incorporates production technologies that would be considered antiquated and uneconomical in the world petroleum industry. From my general review of the literature, I believe that the state of the art is particularly advanced in geological and geophysical exploration. China's geologists have managed to locate sizable reserves under difficult natural circumstances—lacustrine sediments, stratigraphic trap structures, complex faulting, and so on. Furthermore, the Chinese oil industry has recently absorbed a large dose of sophisticated computerized seismic and magnetic exploration equipment from foreign suppliers (Chapter 22). Drilling and extraction technologies, on the other hand, were based largely on Soviet and East European equipment prototypes and equipment imports. This equipment tends to be heavier, less efficient, and less sophisticated than the Western equivalents. It is also within the range of the Chinese steel and petroleum equipment industries to build drilling rigs and production systems along Soviet lines, but difficult to achieve Western materials and tooling standards. Peking showed interest in American drilling and extraction technology in 1977 and 1978, but the broad base will remain East European for some time to come. This limitation has a serious impact on recovery ratios, as Chinese visitors to the U.S. petroleum industry have evidenced by their interest in advanced secondary and tertiary recovery technology.

Offshore exploration technology, however, is another area where China can move right to the frontiers of world capabilities by the judicious selection of offshore drilling rigs purchased on the international market and by sending Chinese petroleum engineers abroad for specialized training in the use of advanced equipment. After experimenting with a few simple rigs of domestic design and a secondhand Japanese jack-up rig, the PRC has begun ordering new offshore drilling rigs from Singapore shipyards that carry advanced American exploration equipment. The five rigs ordered from Singapore so far are all jack-up rigs for operation in relatively shallow coastal waters. China has purchased just one semisubmersible rig for operation in deeper waters. Thus the new fleet of Chinese drilling rigs and support vessels was carefully designed to meet realistic short-term objectives. And the equipment chosen for the rigs is up to "advanced world standards." The basic difficulty that China will experience in incorporating the new offshore drilling technology will be training a sufficiently large group of technicians to handle the new equipment effectively. Peking has sent numerous teams of engineers and technicians to the United States, Norway, Singapore, Japan, and elsewhere for advanced training in the use of the new technology. There is no reason to believe, therefore, that the Chinese will lag at all in the use of offshore exploration technology by the time the first commercially significant offshore fields are discovered. China will be on the cutting edge of offshore technology in its exploration program, but will have trouble producing advanced offshore equipment domestically for some time to come. On the other hand, Peking may decide to produce much of the heavy infrastructure for offshore production—production platforms, subsea pipelines, etc.—in domestic factories.

Refined Petroleum Production

Although petroleum refining is an integral part of the petroleum industry and is usually controlled by the same organizations or corporations that manage crude petroleum exploration and extraction, the refining process is most often classified as a form of "secondary" energy production. This is the case because petroleum refining involves the conversion of a primary energy fuel (crude petroleum) into secondary products (liquid fuels, feedstock, and by-products), rather than the extraction of energy directly from the physical environment. To illustrate this difference, it should simply be recalled that crude petroleum need not be refined in order to be burned. Certain Chinese electric power plants and industries burn crude petroleum directly under boilers. Even in advanced industrial societies, thermal power plants are sometimes set up to burn crude oil directly in the event of shortages of refined residual fuel oil. But the classification of refinery output as "secondary" energy production is a relatively minor distinction that helps avoid double energy accounting or the statistical loss of energy used in the refining process itself. The exact location of the boundary between primary and secondary energy production is as arbitrary in the petroleum industry as in other energy industries. For example, it might well be asked whether coal beneficiation or natural gas separation should not be classified as secondary energy production. Clean coal and pipeline gas are usually considered primary energy products. So the distinction between crude and refined petroleum is a matter of convention and statistical convenience, rather than a matter of generic differences between different points in the petroleum production stream.

Alternative Estimates of Refinery Capacity and Output

For at least a decade, foreign observers of China's petroleum industry have been struggling with the mystery of the missing refinery capacity. Many sources that have accurately estimated crude petroleum output have underestimated refinery capacity and then gone on to generalize about the strictures that the shortage of refinery capacity was imposing on China's energy balance. However, most estimates of refinery capacity in the mid-1970's are low, and estimates of actual refinery output are low as well. The low estimates of refinery capacity were based on Chinese press reports in the early 1970's that indicated annual growth in refinery capacity as only 10–15 percent per year, compared with annual crude petroleum production increases of 20–25 percent per year. But my analysis of the Chinese refining industry indicates underestimation of baseline refinery capacities for the mid-1960's, from which the later low estimates were extrapolated. (See Table 15.3.)

Various efforts have beem made to explain the evident contradiction between crude petroleum production levels and refinery capacity.[38] These explanations have been based on the existence of a hypothetical secret refinery, the burning of crude oil under boilers, and storage in underground reservoirs. It should be recalled, however, that even modern refineries operate at only 80–90 percent of capacity and must allow "down time" for periodic maintenance. Even the CIA estimates of refinery capacity, which lie at the top of the range of alternative estimates, must assume a 5 percent loss and the use of 12 percent of crude oil production under boilers to bring capacity utilization figures into a reasonable range.[39] My compilation of estimates for individual refineries, however, shows that China's current refinery capacity is at least as high as the CIA series and probably appreciably higher.

My method of estimating 1976 refinery capacity was to list all the available estimates for each refinery that could be identified both in the literature and on the recent CIA petroleum map of the PRC (Table 15.4). An estimate of 1976 capacity for any refinery was based on the higher of competing 1975 reports, whenever the 1975 reports were within 1 million tons of each other and there was no outside evidence to confirm one of the reports independently. CIA estimates were used whenever available for the larger refineries, since it was assumed that these estimates were based on aerial photography. This method was conservative in several regards. First, it excluded refineries not indicated on the CIA petroleum map of the PRC (e.g. the "Chungking refinery" and several other refineries reported by Kudo in 1966).[40] Second, it excluded refineries for which no capacity estimates existed in the literature (i.e. Anching,

TABLE 15.3
Estimates of Refinery Capacity and Output, 1949–78
(Million metric tons)

Year	Refinery capacity						Refinery output			
	Cheng	CIA	FEER	IPE	NCUSCT	WES	BOM	Hoover	IOESB	WES
1949	0.16							0.13		
1950				0.1				0.21		
1951								0.31		
1952	1.00						0.3	0.42		
1953								0.65		
1954								0.85		
1955				0.5				1.16	1.0	
1956								1.34	1.2	
1957	2.20						1.3	1.58	1.5	
1958								2.52	2.2	
1959	4.00							3.73	3.7	
1960	5.50			4.9				5.52	5.0	
1961								6.19		
1962							6.5	6.88		
1963								8.00		
1964	16.00							8.60		
1965		13.6						8.60		
1966		17.8		10.4				11.18		
1967		20.0						9.46		
1968		22.8		7.5				12.90		
1969		26.0		9.5				15.48		
1970	28.50	31.5		15.0	28.5		21.0	17.20		
1971	33.00	38.0		21.0	34.3	33.5		27.09	25.0	27.47
1972	38.00	45.6		24.0	40.8	37.0		31.56		32.39
1973	42.00	54.4		25.9	46.0	40.0		43.00	35.0	36.50
1974	47.50	58.7	54.0	30.0	53.1	52.0	60.0			48.0
1975		66.5	67.0	47.5	61.4	65.5				61.1
1976			73.0	50.0						
1977			78.0							
1978		85.0								

Chilin, Loyang, Panshan, and Tantung refineries), even though these refineries were shown on the CIA map of the PRC petroleum industry. Third, it excluded the large new refinery in Canton, even though this refinery may have been partly functioning in 1976. Fourth, the estimate of total refinery capacity assumed that refinery capacities last estimated in the mid-1960's were still roughly the same as indicated by the last estimate (i.e. Chinchou, Karamai, Kangchou, Urumchi, and Yenchang refineries). Even allowing these conservative assumptions, 1976 average refinery capacity totaled 76 million metric tons per year, a 14 percent increase over the 1975 CIA estimate. Relaxing the four conservative as-

Estimated Petroleum Refinery Capacities, 1976
(Million metric tons per year)

Refinery	Province	Reported capacity Cap.	Reported capacity Year	Reported capacity Source	Est. 1976 capacity
Anching	Anhwei	n.a.			n.a.
Anshan	Liaoning	2.5 / 3.0	1975 / 1975	BOM / NCUSCT	3.0
Canton[a]	Kwangtung	n.a			n.a
Chinchou	Liaoning	0.75	1966	Hoover	1.0
Chinhsi	Liaoning	3.0 / 3.5	1975 / 1975	BOM / NCUSCT	3.5
Chilin	Kirin	n.a			n.a.
Chingmen	Hupeh	2.0	1976	CIA	2.0
Dairen	Liaoning	5.0 / 4.0	1975 / 1975	BOM / NCUSCT	5.0
Fushun[b,c]	Liaoning	6.5 / 7.0	1975 / 1975	BOM / NCUSCT	5.0
Fuyu	Kirin	2.0	1976	CIA	2.0
Hangchow	Chekiang	1.3	1975	NCUSCT	1.3
Karamai	Sinkiang	1.0	1966	Hoover	1.0
Kangchou	Sinkiang	1.0	1966	Hoover	1.0
Lanchow	Kansu	5.0 / 6.6	1975 / 1975	BOM / NCUSCT	6.5
Lenghu	Tsinghai	0.3 / 1.1	1976 / 1975	CIA / NCUSCT	0.3
Linhsiang	Hupeh	2.5	1976	CIA	2.5
Loyang	Honan	n.a.			n.a.
Maoming[c]	Kwangtung	2.5 / 3.0	1975 / 1975	BOM / NCUSCT	3.5
Nanchung	Szechwan	0.8	1975	NCUSCT	0.8
Nanking	Kiangsu	3.0 / 3.0	1975 / 1975	BOM / NCUSCT	3.0
Panshan	Liaoning	n.a.			n.a
Peking	Peking	4.0 / 5.0	1975 / 1975	BOM / NCUSCT	5.0
Shanghai[b]	Shanghai	5.0 / 5.0	1973 / 1975	Kambara / NCUSCT	5.0
Shengli[b]	Shantung	3.5 / 7.2	1975 / 1976	BOM / CIA	7.2
Taching[b]	Heilungkiang	6.0 / 6.4 / 6.0	1975 / 1975 / 1976	BOM / NCUSCT / CIA	6.0
Takang[b]	Hopeh	2.0 / 6.5	1975 / 1976	BOM / CIA	6.5
Tantung	Liaoning	n.a			n.a
Tushantzu	Sinkiang	1.5 / 2.0	1976 / 1975	CIA / NCUSCT	1.5
Urumchi	Sinkiang	0.5	1966	Hoover	0.5
Wuhan	Hupeh	1.7	1976	CIA	1.7
Yenchang	Shensi	0.2	1966	Kudo	0.2
Yumen	Kansu	2.0 / 1.0 / 4.0	1975 / 1976 / 1975	BOM / CIA / NCUSCT	1.0

[a]Under construction in 1976. [b]Includes several associated refineries. [c]Includes shale oil retorting.

sumptions somewhat, I would put 1976 average refinery capacity at 80 million metric tons per year or higher. This would make the CIA series low and would only be consistent with the estimates provided by the *Far Eastern Economic Review.*[41] As a conservative hedge, however, the computer program used data consistent with the CIA series.

Refined Products Mix

If estimating refinery capacity is like groping about in a dark room, analyzing China's refined products mix is like trying to find the thread of Ariadne in the labyrinth. There are plenty of false leads and no empirical data. Not only is the proportion of each of the refined products completely unreported, but the products mix shifted radically from the 1950's to the early 1970's. During the early years of the People's Republic, domestic refineries had no catalytic cracking capability and simply distilled the higher petroleum fractions. This means that domestic production included a high proportion of residual fuel oil and a low proportion of the higher fractions, especially gasoline. During the 1950's, China imported large amounts of gasoline, kerosene, and diesel fuel, but no residual fuel at all. The higher fractions required by China's liquid fuel consumption sector were coming primarily from Soviet refineries, while the heavy fractions were coming from Chinese refineries.

This situation changed rapidly after 1960, under the pressure of declining petroleum products imports from the Soviet Union. China was suddenly thrown back onto its domestic refinery capacity. The result was a domestic energy crisis of serious proportions from 1961 through 1963. Spot imports of refined products were sought from other sources, and Peking turned to the serious task of modifying the refineries that had been built with Soviet aid in the 1950's to produce a higher proportion of the lighter fractions through the introduction of catalytic cracking techniques. The first achievement was to raise the proportion of diesel fuel.[42] The Lanchow refinery was chosen as the first to undergo modernization in the early 1960's.[43] A new refinery was constructed at Taching, and plans were drawn up for several large petrochemical complexes, one for each of the major cities, which would provide the entire range of necessary products, from high-grade gasoline to specialized lubricants. In the interim, certain foreign cracking and processing equipment was imported from Western Europe to supplement existing refineries. In 1968, construction began on an integrated petrochemical complex—the Peking General Petrochemical Plant—which came into operation with 2.5 million tons capacity in 1973.[44] Constructed largely with Chinese-built machinery, it produces the whole range of petroleum

TABLE 15.5
Estimates of Refined Products Mix
(Percent of total refinery output)

Estimate	Year	Gasoline	Kerosene	Diesel	Lubricants	Residual	Other
Hoover[a]	1952	26%	10%	4%	2%	58%	—
Hoover[a]	1955	22	10	4	3	60	—
Hoover[a]	1957	24	11	5	4	55	—
Hoover[b]	1960	24	8	26	1	16	25%
Hoover[b]	1965	24	8	33	3	8	24
Hoover[b]	1970	24	5	35	5	8	23
Hoover[b]	1972	24	5	35	5	8	23
Kambara	1973	20	20	20	10	20	10
World[c]	1973	22	8	22	1	36	11
Industrial[c]	1973	25	7	23	1	30	14
Third World[c]	1973	14	9	18	1	51	7
This study	1949–78	15	10	20	1	40	14

[a] Quoting a series from CIA, *The Economy of Communist China, 1958-61*, Jan. 1960, p. 66.
[b] Quoting a second series from Ono Hideo, "The Turning Point of China's Petroleum," *Chagoka Keizai Kenkyu Geppo*, Feb. 1973, p. 29.
[c] *World Energy Supplies* 18 (1975), Tables 8, 9, 12-14.

products required by industry, agriculture, transportation, and domestic commerce. It also achieves modern cuts of the high fractions through catalytic reforming. Several other major plants are either under construction or newly completed with the same capabilities in Shanghai, Maoming, Taching, Nanking, and perhaps other locations. They will provide the backbone of China's future refinery capacity.

As beneficial as these developments have been for China's petroleum industry, they have enormously complicated the task of estimating the domestic refined products mix. By 1975, the mix was quite different than it had been in the early 1950's. But the exact nature of the shift is impossible to judge. The estimates in Table 15.5 are so far out of line with world averages for every period that they must be considered imaginary. They placed Chinese production of gasoline in the early 1950's at proportions that would have required the capability of modern refineries in industrial societies. They probably understated diesel output for the 1950's and overstated it for the 1960's. Kambara's estimate of kerosene production was twice too high and of lubricants ten times too high.

In view of the lack of any data and any reasonable foreign estimates, this study has simply chosen to apply the general pattern of Third World refined products mix to the entire 27-year period, with minor adjustments. Gasoline, kerosene, and diesel were placed slightly higher than Third World averages to allow for the high level of potential domestic consumption of these products. Residual was placed at a lower proportion to reflect the catalytic cracking capabilities of newer Chinese refineries—but not as low as the world average. The "other" category, which includes approximately 5 percent naphtha for petrochemical production, was also adjusted upward to reflect the high paraffin content of Chinese crude.

Unfortunately, until further empirical data become available, it will be impossible to provide an accurate estimate of the shift in refined products mix. For the same reason, no effort has been made to break down the projection of future total refinery output into a projection for each products category. Analysis of the products mix should move cautiously until further information becomes available.

Petrochemical and Fertilizer Production

The production of naphtha for petrochemical and fertilizer (ammonia) production is another area for which there has been little or no foreign research. There are Chinese petrochemical plants attached to refineries at Taching, Shanghai, Shenyang, Fushun, Peking, Tientsin, Lanchow, Maoming, Nanking, and possibly other locations. Estimation of the total amount of petroleum required for petrochemical and fertilizer production is an extremely hazardous undertaking. Again, there is no data base, since domestic Chinese petrochemical production was developed in the period after the departure of Soviet technicians, and Peking has been silent on this score. Moreover, China's petrochemical production from petroleum is difficult to infer from output statistics on the petrochemical industry, because of the unusually high contribution of both coal and natural gas to the total petrochemical output. Finally, Chinese energy requirements for petrochemical production would not necessarily conform to world or Third World patterns, since China's petrochemical and fertilizer industries are larger than usual relative to the domestic petroleum and natural gas industries.

China's total 1975 production of nitrogen fertilizer was about four million metric tons (in terms of nitrogen content).[45] On the basis of Brazilian energy requirement statistics for nitrogenous fertilizer production, each metric ton of nitrogen content in ammonium nitrate required 1.7 metric tons of ammonia input.[46] Each metric ton of ammonia in turn required 0.66 metric tons of naphtha and 0.725 metric tons of fuel oil, if produced in plants of 500 metric tons or less capacity. Since most Chinese ammonia plants are probably not in the giant range (1,000 mt/day capacity), efficiencies would be about the same as for Brazilian plants. This would yield an input requirement of 1.12 metric tons naphtha per ton of nitrogen output. If one-third of China's total nitrogen output was derived from petroleum (the other two-thirds from coal and natural gas), *the refined petroleum requirement for nitrogenous fertilizer in 1975 was about 1.5 million metric tons.* If half of China's petrochemical production from petroleum consisted of ammonia, *the total petrochemical input requirement for petroleum was about 3 million tons in 1975.* This thumbnail inferential estimate coincides with an estimate of petrochemical use of petroleum based on an assumption that 5 percent of total refined petroleum output was used for petrochemical production.

Refinery Technology

Considering the reticence of Peking's planners to discuss refinery capacity or output statistics, they have been remarkably open in various technical journals and even in the popular press about the design and functioning of individual refineries, as well as about the domestic refinery equipment manufacturing industry. The Peking General Petrochemical Plant, for example, has been discussed in some detail, including a complete history of its construction, technical details of its design and layout, and photographs of its components.[47] The plant is said to include 1,000 pieces of machinery manufactured in China, 70 large and medium tanks, 200 kilometers of piping, and three basic refining sets. Products include 15,000 tons per year of synthetic rubber, all petroleum fuels, specialized lubricants, and a variety of synthetic raw materials. Its start-up capacity was revealed to be 2.5 million tons per year.

Similar details have been provided for technical refining procedures and for the structure of other refineries.[48] With careful primary materials research, therefore, it should be possible to reconstruct a more adequate picture of China's hydrocarbon-processing industry.

Articles on the domestic petroleum machine-building industry began appearing as early as 1961.[49] This industry, which is based in Shanghai, may have been started in 1955, when the Shanghai Petroleum Machinery Parts Plant was established.[50] A number of preexisting plants, such as the Hsinchien Machine Works and the Ssufang Boiler Plant, were incorporated into the new plant and began making such refinery equipment as fractional distillation towers, heat exchangers, and silicon furnace frames. This incorporation of existing plant and conversion to new functions became a standard pattern in the petroleum machine-building industry. In 1963, the industry was placed under the direct control of planning ministries in Peking, owing to the expansion of crude petroleum output and the loss of Soviet refined-products imports, both of which precipitated a sudden demand for domestic refinery equipment. The manufacture of petroleum machinery was said to have grown 60 percent in 1963, and then another 100 percent in 1964![51] If true, the scale effect was operating, as well as the effect of new refinery requirements. But by 1970, the Chinese petroleum refinery equipment industry was on its feet and producing whole sets of refinery equipment for large-scale modern plants.

China has also imported a number of large pieces of foreign refinery equipment from Japanese and West European sources. In 1963, Peking purchased a complete refinery set from Snam-Projetti, an Italian corporation.[52] In 1964, orders were placed with Lurgi Gesellschaft for cracking and olefins units.[53] Petrochemical plant purchases from 1963, when the import program was initiated, until 1966, when it was ended by the Cultural Revolution, totaled about $150 million in value (Table 22.2). A second petrochemical and refinery plant import program began in 1972 with the purchase of synthetic-fiber and other equipment from Japan ($150 million). This program peaked in 1973 ($650 million) with contracts for a complete refinery, petrochemical, and synthetic-fiber complex from France's Technip-Speichem and a group of associated West European countries. This petrochemical complex was China's single largest energy plant purchase. The plant, scheduled for completion in Shenyang in 1977–78, will produce 65,000 metric tons per year of gasoline, 74,900 mt/year of ethylene, and 87,000 mt/year of polyester resins, among other products.[54] Foreign exchange shortages in 1974 and 1975 reduced the petrochemical plant imports to about $115–120 million in each year. This doubled to $240 million in 1976.

Data for 1977–78 are still incomplete, but indicate some decline in the importation of petrochemical equipment. The largest components for refineries produced in China are designed for units in the 2.5 million ton per year category. China will continue importing some refinery components and specialized petrochemical equipment for the foreseeable future, primarily from Japan (Chapter 22).

That China is capable of manufacturing and installing basic refinery components is evident from Chinese participation in the construction of the Ballsh oil refinery in Albania.[55] China was also reported to have aided in reconstruction of the Viet Tri chemical plant in Vietnam and may have assisted North Korea in refinery construction.[56]

Natural Gas Production

The information constraints on foreign analysis of China's natural gas industry are more serious than for any of the other energy industries. We know only that substantial natural gas production occurs in Szechwan and in the oilfields of the northeast, that the Tsaidam Basin may have substantial untapped natural gas reserves, that there may be natural gas potential in the offshore areas, and that limited amounts of natural gas are produced from fields near Shanghai. Accounts of the natural gas industry in the Chinese press are infrequent and relatively vague, giving few clues of a statistical nature. The U.S. Central Intelligence Agency has not released a public analysis of China's natural gas industry. Foreign analysts have dealt with natural gas only within the context of publications directed primarily toward examination of China's petroleum industry. The estimates of China's annual natural gas production are few and widely divergent. Thus there is very little to go on in assessing the contribution of natural gas to China's current or future energy balance.

Alternative Estimates of Natural Gas Production

The estimates listed in Table 15.6 diverge widely from one another. If all were taken at face value, 1975 natural gas output would lie somewhere between 25 billion cubic meters per year (JETRO series, Japan) and 65 bcm (JEC series, United States). The highest estimates can be eliminated by comparison to the overall energy balance. If accepted, the Joint Economic Committee estimate of 60 bcm/year in 1974 would have implied that the natural gas industry was making an equally large contribution to the Chinese energy balance as crude petroleum—an unlikely proposition in view of the importance that China has attached to the petroleum industry, development of Taching oilfield, offshore oil prospects, and foreign petroleum equipment purchases. The apparent source of error in the JEC series was overestimation of natural gas output in the mid-1960's. Thus, the median range of estimates, which would put the energy contribution of the natural gas industry at about half the energy contribution of the petroleum industry, would appear more reasonable in view of the relative treatment of the two industries in Chinese energy policy.

This impressionistic method of evaluating the general level of development of the natural gas industry has been reinforced by a second, much stronger, line of argument. In January 1975, several important articles on the Szechwan natural gas industry appeared in the Chinese press. These articles pinned down the scale of Szechwan natural gas production to a fairly close approximation: "The province now has 3.3 times as many gas wells as it did in 1965, the year preceding the Great Cultural Revolution. Daily output rose 3.2 fold by the same comparison or was more than two times the annual output before liberation."[57] The last sentence in this paragraph is the operative one. We know on the basis of fairly reliable data that Szechwan's annual natural gas production was 50–60 million cubic meters in 1949 and the years immediately preceding Liberation.[58] That would place Szechwan's 1974 year-end production of natural gas at 100 million cubic meters per day, or about 36 bil-

TABLE 15.6
Estimates of Natural Gas Production, 1949–77
(Billion cubic meters)

Year	BOM (gross)	BOM (marketed)	CIA	FEER	Hoover	IPE	IOESB
1949							
1950							
1951							
1952							
1953							0.04
1954							0.05
1955					0.26		0.06
1956					0.34		0.07
1957			0.06		0.74		0.13
1958					1.5		0.19
1959					3.9		
1960			3.1		3.9		
1961					3.9		
1962					4.0		
1963					7.7		
1964					11.5		
1965			9.2		11.8		
1966					12.1		
1967					10.3		
1968					14.0		
1969					16.8		
1970			20.7		18.6	4.2	
1971	18.46	15.62	23.6		23.3	4.2	
1972	24.99	21.30	27.0		27.0	4.0	
1973	31.24	26.98	27.6			4.5	
1974	39.76	34.08	28.8	55.2		5.3	
1975	45.44	39.76	34.6	58.4		36.4	
1976			37.9	64.8			
1977			47.3				

TABLE 15.6 *(continued)*

Estimates of Natural Gas Production, 1949–77
(Billion cubic meters)

Year	JEC	JETRO	Meyerhoff	PNSEA	PRC	Rawski	SER	Smil
1949								0.0
1950								0.0
1951								0.0
1952		0.06				0.06		0.0
1953		0.10						0.01
1954		0.11						0.01
1955		0.11	0.11			0.11		0.11
1956		0.23	0.23					0.23
1957	0.06[a]	0.33	0.33	0.6				0.33
1958		0.94	0.94					0.94
1959		1.42	1.4					1.42
1960		1.98	2.0					1.98
1961		2.83	2.8					2.83
1962	10.2[a]	3.27	3.3	10.2				3.27
1963	11.9[a]	5.66	5.7	11.7				5.66
1964	14.0[a]	10.90	10.9	13.5				10.90
1965	16.3[a]	11.32	11.3	15.8	11[a,b]	11.3		11.32
1966		11.01	11.0					11.01
1967		10.47	10.5					10.47
1968		11.32	11.3					11.32
1969		12.64	14					12.70
1970		14.12						16.00
1971		15.78				52.1		19.50
1972	49.0[a]	17.62		42.3			21.0	24.50
1973	55.8	19.69		48.6				30.60
1974	60	22.64		55.2	36[a,b]			35.00
1975				58.4				40.50
1976				64.8				45.00
1977								55.00

[a] Szechwan province natural gas production only.
[b] Inferred.

lion cubic meters per year. The same quote would fix 1965 natural gas output at 11 bcm/year. Assuming that the stated figures were peak daily output for Szechwan, and that natural gas production in the rest of the country was no more than one-quarter that of Szechwan, an order-of-magnitude estimate of about 35–40 billion cubic meters for year-end 1974 would be roughly correct.

This estimate is satisfactory in a number of ways. It is based on a direct announcement in the Chinese press. It would place the energy contribution of natural gas at about half that of petroleum. And it conforms neatly to the median range of estimates from foreign sources, including a recently revised estimate by the U.S. Bureau of Mines.[59] This study has, therefore, adopted the conservative CIA series through 1976, with some adjustments prior to 1955 and extrapolation to about 50 bcm/year in 1978. The Smil and Bureau of Mines estimates may be somewhat closer to Chinese claims, but here, as with coal and petroleum data, I have opted for the lower CIA series to avoid overstating the output of any Chinese energy industry.

Natural Gas Pipelines

Pipeline construction capacity is even more critical to the Chinese natural gas industry than to the petroleum industry, since there are no alternative transportation methods other than liquefaction, which is even more capital-intensive and expensive per unit of gas delivered than pipeline construction. Szechwan, the largest province in terms of natural gas production, also has the most extensive pipeline system. There is at least one trunk line from Nanchung to Chungking, supplying Chungking's industries with gas from western Szechwan. In addition, there are thousands of kilometers of small-gauge pipelines for local distribution of natural gas within the province.[60] Shanghai also reports an extensive network of natural gas and manufactured gas pipelines for local distribution.[61] Some 31 cities throughout China are said to be providing some level of gas service and must, therefore, have at least limited local pipeline networks.[62] Many of the latter networks provide manufactured rather than natural gas, unless regional pipelines connect them to natural gas supplies.

The most obvious gap in the Chinese natural gas industry is in interprovincial gas pipelines. Until such lines are constructed, natural gas will remain a regional energy resource and some fields (e.g. the Tsaidam Basin) will remain totally locked in, despite extensive natural gas discoveries. First indications have surfaced that Peking has begun planning such interprovincial gas transport networks. The Takang Design Institute is reportedly designing pipelines to carry associated gas from the

Takang oilfield to industrial centers in northeast and east China.[63] One rumor from a Japanese source indicates that China may soon build a natural gas pipeline from Szechwan to the cities of eastern China.[64] Given the new petroleum pipeline construction capability, such developments would not be surprising. And if much of the hydrocarbon content of the continental shelf turns out to be natural gas, undersea pipelines will be required—an expensive and difficult technology.

Liquefied Natural Gas (LNG)

There has been no indication from the Chinese press that the PRC currently possesses any liquefied natural gas production capacity. Some experimental units may have been constructed for limited production, meeting specific industrial needs. China has shown some interest in an LNG deal with Japan, whereby Japanese companies would provide an LNG plant at Takang oilfield, for the manufacture of liquefied gas to be shipped in cryogenic tankers to Japan. The Japanese have reportedly offered to build a 300,000 metric ton per year plant, but Peking is holding out for an even larger unit, hoping to divert some of the LNG to domestic consumption or other foreign markets.[65] Whatever the outcome of this protracted negotiation, China may export LNG as well as crude petroleum over the next quarter-century. Depending on the exact balance of natural gas and petroleum reserves in the continental shelf, LNG could play a relatively important role in energy exports. But LNG exports require a more capital-intensive infrastructure than crude petroleum exports and would be slower to develop. The development of a domestically oriented LNG industry will also be slowed by the capital constraint.

Manufactured Gas

Several articles have indicated that China has been introducing manufactured gas service in some cities. The gas varies from city to city and includes refinery gas, liquefied petroleum gas, coke oven gas, and coal gas.[66] Synthetic gas is produced in some locations by high-pressure gasification of low-grade coal and by "splitting heavy oil."[67] Among the cities that have some manufactured gas production, the press has mentioned Peking, Shanghai, Tientsin, Shenyang, Chengtu, Nanking, Tsinan, Urumchi, and Lanchow. Some additional 25 cities have gas service of some type, probably including all of China's major industrial cities. Manufactured gas may be displaced by cheaper natural gas as regional and interprovincial gas pipelines develop.

There is still no way to evaluate statistically the contribution of manufactured gas to the Chinese energy economy. Since it represents secondary energy production, most of the energy value of manufactured gas has probably been captured by statistics on the coal and petroleum industries.

Electric Power Production

Electric power production statistics for the PRC may be roughly broken down into three data series—hydropower production, thermal power production, and total electric power output. Alternative estimates exist in the foreign literature for all three data series. Furthermore, the three series are interdependent and must be rendered mutually consistent. On the whole, information constraints operating on the estimation of China's electric power production statistics are more severe than for the petroleum industry, less severe than for the natural gas industry, and comparable to information constraints that still hamper foreign analysis of China's coal industry. The electric power industry is an area of the Chinese economy that is ripe for a thorough book-length study. A vast sea of empirical information on the Chinese power industry is available through the Chinese press and still largely untapped.[68] Peking spent a great deal of capital during the early 1970's expanding the domestic electric power production equipment industry and is producing an ever wider array of generators, transformers, transmission cables, and switch gear. The electric power industry is justifiably considered a "weak link" in the overall energy economy, and 30 new power stations are planned as part of the Ten-Year Plan ending in 1985.[69] Finally, if China adopts nuclear power technology during the next two decades, a compatible generating and transmission network must be prepared to comfortably receive nuclear power stations with generating capacities in the range of 1 gigawatt for each new plant. This study will provide only the broadest overview of the electric power industry.

Alternative Estimates of Hydropower Production

Considering the amount of information published in China about the hydropower industry, there is a surprisingly low level of agreement among foreign observers regarding the level of hydropower output—especially for the period since 1961. Again, as with the coal production statistics, observers could generally be divided between the pessimists and the optimists, depending on their evaluation of what happened to the Chinese hydro industry immediately after the Great Leap Forward. The Hoover series was based on a careful analysis of statistics provided by the Chinese government before 1960, and has generally been accepted as authoritative. But several authors have fallen prey to a remarkably unreliable set of data for the period since 1961. Table 15.7 reveals that the

TABLE 15.7
Estimates of Hydropower Production, 1949–78
(Billion kwh)

Year	CIA	Hoover	IOESB	JEC	NCUSCT	Rawski	SER	Smil	URI	WES	WPD
1949				0.7				0.70	0.7		
1950								0.70			
1951								0.70			
1952	1.3	1.3		1.3		1.3		1.26	1.3		
1953		1.5						1.54	1.5		
1954		2.2						2.18	2.2		
1955		2.4				2.4		2.36	2.4		
1956		3.5		3.5				3.46	3.5		
1957	4.7	4.7	4.8	4.7				4.71			
1958		6.7		5.5				6.68			
1959		8.8		7.8				8.80			
1960		11.9		9				9.0			
1961				8				8.0		14.3	8
1962			29.6	6				6.0		14.2	6
1963				6				6.0		16.9	6
1964				7				7.0		22.4	7
1965	9.0	33.8		8		16.5		8.0		27.6	8
1966		45.9						9.0		32.7	10
1967		26.2						8.0		27.6	10
1968		36.2						8.0		28.9	13
1969		57.4						10.0		26.0	11
1970	14.0	60.5						12.0		27.0	
1971	15.0	71.3				29.8	38.1	14.0		30.0	
1972	20.0							18.0		33.0	
1973	23.0							21.0		34.5	
1974	24.0							26.0		35.0	
1975								29.0		37.0	
1976				32[a]				30.0			
1977								33.0			
1978								34.0			

[a] Inferred.

Joint Economic Committee (JEC) data, the CIA data, and Smil's data all derived from a tiny annual publication of the Federal Power Commission, entitled *World Power Data (WPD)*. *WPD*, begun in 1961 and defunct since 1969, was a brief statistical summary of the annual capacity and output statistics for the electric power industries of the world's largest industrial countries. No evidence is presented for the *WPD* estimates, which are very low for both the hydro and thermal power industries of China. Some estimates were simply repeated from the previous year for lack of further information. And the whole series seems to have been based on China's large electric power plant capacity alone, ignoring plants under some minimum capacity and extrapolating output from capacity.

The U.S. Joint Economic Committee of Congress apparently picked up electric power production statistics for China from *World Power Data*.[70] The CIA and Smil use the JEC statistics with no further explanation.[71] Although the exact sequence of events is impossible to trace, it appears that the initial estimates were made by an anonymous researcher in the Federal Power Commission, with a data slot to fill and no information! The FPC may itself have gotten the China data from the CIA, so that the final origin of this series remains obscure. What is clear, however, is that the data have never been publicly documented and must therefore be considered unreliable. Unfortunately, the only alternative data series for hydropower production, that estimated by the United Nations publication *World Energy Supplies,* is equally undocumented, and 25–30 percent higher than the JEC series. This study, once again following a conservative strategy, has adopted the Smil series, despite its lack of documentary base. The Smil series has the advantages of internal consistency, consistency with Smil's estimates of China's hydropower-generating capacity, and consistency with the Hoover series for the 1950's. But extensive further research is necessary in this area. China's total hydropower output and capacity could be much higher than indicated by the Smil series.*

Hydropower Production Technology

China produces a wide range of hydropower equipment and imports some equipment as well. The largest unit of domestic construction reported to date was the 300 MWe generator with water-cooled rotor produced for the Liuchiahsia station in 1974 by the Harbin Electrical Machinery Plant.[72] The smallest was a 1.5 kw "miniturbogenerator" designed especially by the Tientsin Electric Transmission Designing Institute as a prototype for use in remote areas or on tiny streams.[73] Most provinces by now have substantial hydropower equipment industries, concentrating on the production of machinery, transmission lines, transformers, switch gear, etc., for small-scale hydro plants.

The diffusion of small-scale hydro plants should not be underesti-

---

*This analysis was confirmed in official electric power data reported during 1979 while this book was in press. Electric power output was officially reported at a figure 60 percent higher than the total given in most foreign estimates for the years 1976 and 1978. This indicates that foreign estimates for the base years in the early 1960's were also substantially too low. Hydropower may have accounted for a major proportion of the disparity between foreign estimates and recently released official figures. See the section below on total electric power output.

mated. Hainan Island, for example, has already constructed 803 medium- and small-sized hydro plants, supplying electric power to all of the cites and towns, 50 percent of the communes, and 30 percent of the production brigades. The island also has 11 factories producing electric power equipment. The hydropower is used for small industry, chemical fertilizer, sugar refining, cement production, farm machinery, and agricultural mechanization, as well as home use.[74]

This type of development, even in China's most remote areas, will produce electric power for about half of China's rural villages by 1980, judging from provincial reports.[75] By 1985–90, the rural areas should reach almost complete electrification. Electric power production, and particularly hydropower, has apparently been judged a key to rural development of all types. It provides a visible index of development to the people, who are being asked to stay in the countryside rather than migrate to the industrial cities. It relieves the most burdensome physical labor tasks such as water pumping or threshing. It conforms closely to the self-reliance ethic.

Alternative Estimates of Thermal Power Output

Few sources have made separate estimates of China's thermal electric power production. Several of the estimates shown in Table 15.8 were inferred from the difference between total electric power production estimates and estimates of hydropower production. Once again, following a conservative strategy has led to the adoption of the Smil series, which is a median-to-low estimate in the field of alternatives and has the additional advantages of internal consistency, general consistency with the authoritative Hoover series for the 1950's, and consistency with the other Smil series for hydropower and total electric power output. The Smil data for the 1960's were a modified version of the *World Power Data* series first published by the Federal Power Commission of the United States. This does not speak well for the level of documentation in the Smil series, and further analysis will be necessary before any level of certainty can be achieved regarding thermal power production statistics for China. Again, the series originally published by the Federal Power Commission (*WPD*) was probably low, excluding plants below a limiting capacity and excluding thermal power produced in industry for direct plant use. Since this latter type of power generation unit, either one using process heat or a small thermal plant in isolated factories, is fairly common in China, which lacks integrated transmission networks, exclusion of industrial thermal power would cause a relatively serious downward bias in the estimates of thermal power production. A close analysis of the thermal power industry for the 1960's and 1970's would result in a

TABLE 15.8
Estimates of Thermal Power Production, 1949–76
(Billion kwh)

Year	Hoover	IOESB[a]	JEC	NCUSCT[a]	Rawski[a]	Smil	URI[a]	WES	WPD
1949	3.7		3.6			3.61	3.6		
1950	3.9					3.85			
1951	4.9					5.05			
1952	6.1		6.0		6.0	6.00	6.0		
1953	7.8					7.65	7.7		
1954	9.1					8.82	8.8		
1955	10.1				9.9	9.92	9.9		
1956	13.4		13.1			13.13	13.1		
1957	14.9	14.5	14.6			14.63			
1958	21.3		22.0			20.85			
1959	33.4		33.7			32.70			
1960	44.1		38			37.0			
1961		40	23			23.0		39.9	21
1962			24			24.0		45.7	22
1963			27			27.0		48.2	25
1964			29			29.0		48.7	27
1965			32		35.5	34.0		50.0	29
1966						38.0		52.9	34
1967						33.0		41.0	39
1968						36.0		46.2	31
1969						40.0		45.2	39
1970						48.0		50.3	
1971					76.4	57.0		59.3	
1972						67.0		66.3	
1973						79.8			
1974						82.0			
1975						95.0			
1976				97		108.0			

[a]Inferred from estimates of total electric power production minus estimates of hydropower production.

higher series than indicated by the Smil estimates. If total thermal power production in China was about 100 billion kwh in 1975, the PRC ranked eighth in the world but produced less than 7 percent as much thermal power as the United States.[76]

Thermal Power-Generating Technology

During the 1950's, much of China's thermal power-generating capacity was based on equipment manufactured in other countries. The Japanese had constructed a number of thermal plants in northeast China prior to 1945. Much of this equipment was removed by the Soviet Union between 1945 and 1949, but then restored under an agreement with the new government after 1949.[77] During the 1950's, China received substantial construction, equipment, and technical assistance from the Soviet Union, East Germany, Czechoslovakia, and perhaps other East European countries.[78] Meanwhile, China had begun a domestic thermal power equipment industry, which was providing about 50 percent of added thermal-generating capacity in 1960.[79] There was a serious lag in the installation of new capacity in the early 1960's, owing to the loss of Soviet and East European equipment imports, reducing the growth rate of thermal power capacity to half what it had been before the Great Leap. The disruptions of the Cultural Revolution again slowed the expansion of thermal capacity, and actually reduced the output of existing plants.

Since 1970, thermal electric-generating capacity has once again been increasing at a steady pace. By 1977, thermal power capacity had reached about 25 gigawatts.[80] China now produces a wide range of thermal power equipment, including standardized generating sets of up to 300 megawatts, transmission and switch gear, transformers, insulating equipment, and so on. The PRC may be working on design of a 600 MWe steam-generating set, which would bring the country up to "advanced world levels."[81] Most domestically produced generating equipment was designed for steam-powered plants, but China has also experimented with the manufacture of gas turbines.[82]

In addition to the expansion of thermal capacity using domestically produced equipment, Peking imports thermal-generating equipment of a technically advanced type from the industrial market economy countries and from the Soviet Union (Table 22.5). Imports during the 1950's were entirely from the Soviet bloc countries. China then switched to West European and Japanese sources for the purchase of high-technology transmission and generating equipment during the 1960's. After 1970, the size of the purchased units grew to include complete plants and advanced gas turbine generators.[83] It is interesting to note that China has also become an exporter of low-technology thermal-generating and transmission equipment to some countries in the Third World, and occasionally to certain West European countries.[84] This trend could accelerate if China's intermediate-level thermal power technology proves compatible with the needs of other developing countries.

Thermal Efficiency

Peking's awareness of thermal efficiency problems in its power-generating industry dates to the earliest days of the People's Republic.[85] The technically obsolete plants inherited from the Japanese in Manchuria and from European colonists in China's coastal cities were easily improved. The new equipment from the Soviet Union and Eastern Europe was reasonably efficient, and each new plant designed and constructed in China was built with thermal efficiency considerations in mind. The Great Leap Forward (1958–60) placed heavy emphasis on output increases, often exceeding the designed capacity of individual plants and causing equipment failures. This led to a temporary setback in the trend toward modern thermal efficiencies.[86] The coal shortage in the early 1960's, also precipitated by the Great Leap Forward, eventually reversed excess enthusiasm for total output. A coal economy campaign in the electric power industry was extensively reported in the Chinese media and lasted at least until 1965.[87] This campaign reflected a general tightness in the energy economy, owing to the loss of Soviet oil imports. The coal conservation campaign once again stimulated greater concern for thermal efficiencies in China's power plants. More recently, there are continuing signs of concern for improvement in average levels of thermal efficiency. Efficiency measures include the use of waste process heat to preheat water in the steam cycle, a measure only recently considered economic in Western thermal power plants.[88]

Estimates of thermal efficiencies in electric power plants are statistically important for the analysis of coal and petroleum consumption statistics (Chapter 17) and for the projection of future trends in the energy balance (Chapter 24). The only empirical data available on average thermal efficiencies in Chinese power plants are now more than 20 years out of date. For the purposes of this study, I have adopted the Hoover Institution's estimates of average thermal efficiencies for the 1950's and have then simply extrapolated a linear trend for efficiency improvement for the 1960's and 1970's.[89] If the extrapolation is generally correct, the average heat rate reached 0.54 in 1960, 0.51 in 1965, 0.48 in 1970, and 0.43 in 1975.[90] Modern average efficiency (0.40 kgce/kwh) would have been achieved in Chinese power plants by about 1978–80. (The thermal efficiency series may be too optimistic and was not, therefore, included as a confirmed statistic in the tables of this Statistical Profile.)

Alternative Estimates of Total Electric Power Output

The data base for foreign estimates of China's total electric power output is much better than for either hydropower or thermal power. Indeed, most estimates of hydro and thermal power production were derived by inference from growth rates of total electric power output given annually in the Chinese press. There is near consensus among various American sources (and Smil) that the PRC produced roughly 120 billion kilowatt-hours of electric power in 1975. The Japanese (JETRO) and U.N. (WES) series are somewhat higher than the usual American estimates, and may be closer to reality, if my observations are correct regarding the likely underestimation of hydropower and thermal power statistics by these sources. Since Chinese press sources give only annual growth rates and no absolute data, a higher series could be constructed that would be consistent with official reports. Nonetheless, I have chosen the Smil series for this study on the basis of the conservative strategy of estimation. (See Table 15.9.)*

Since 1970, there have been many indications that the electric power industry is moving into a growth spurt after more than a decade of mixed-to-poor performance. The Chinese press reported that total power generation in 1971 was 20 percent higher than in 1970 and that 1973 power-generating capacity rose some 30 percent in a single year.[91] A number of large hydroelectric stations began production in the 1970's, including China's largest (1.2 GWe) at Liuchiahsia on the Yellow River.[92] We also know that Peking has been purchasing major generating components abroad (Table 22.6) during this period. Finally, 30 new electric power stations have been included among the 120 large-scale industrial projects to be completed during the Ten-Year Development Plan (1976–1985).[93] The indications are, then, that Peking is pushing hard for rapid growth in the electric power industry during the 1970's.

Electric Power Transmission Technology

Electric power transmission grids will be a key area of technological and production development for the next several decades. Regional integrated power grids have been developed in the principal industrial areas, including the northeast, the north (Peking and Tientsin), east-central (Shanghai, Nanking), and probably Wuhan, Canton, and areas of Szechwan.[94] There is a limited, but important, grid in the upper reaches of the Yellow River, supplying industry at Lanchow, including the gaseous diffusion plant, which has a high electric power requirement.[95]

Most electric power equipment manufactured in China is designed for power grids operating with 110 or 220 kilovolt high-tension lines.[96] China recently announced completion of its first 330 kv line in Kansu-Shensi, which is a total of 534 kilometers in length and has a transmission capacity of 420 megawatts.[97] It took two years to build (April 1970–June 1972) and carries power from the Liuchiahsia hydropower station into the Lanchow grid. This line might indicate that China is ready to

*Total electric power output was officially reported in mid-1979 at 203 bkwh for 1976 and 256 bkwh for 1978, figures that are about 60% higher than foreign estimates for those years. This indicates that the series reported in Table 17.3 is too low from 1961 on.

TABLE 15.9
Estimates of Total Electric Power Production, 1949–77
(Billion kwh)

Year	CIA-JEC[a]	ECAFE	FEER	Hoover	IOESB	JETRO	NCUSCT
1949	4.308			4.4	4.3	4.31	4.3
1950	4.550			4.7		4.55	
1951	5.750			5.9		5.75	
1952	7.261			7.4	7.3	7.26	7.3
1953	9.195			9.3	9.2	9.20	
1954	11.001			11.2	11.0	11.00	
1955	12.278			12.5	12.3	12.28	
1956	15.593			16.8	16.6	16.59	
1957	19.340			19.7	19.3	19.34	19.3
1958	28.0			28.0	27.5	27.53	
1959	42.0		41.5	42.2	41.5	41.50	
1960	47.0	62.3	55	56.0	55.5	47.00	
1961	31.0	64.2	43			31.00	31.0
1962	30.0	66.8	30		74.0	30.00	
1963	33.0	69.2	30			34.00	
1964	36.0	72.1				38.00	
1965	42.0	74.6				44.00	42.0
1966	50.0	77.5				50.00	
1967	45.0	78.6				44.00	
1968	50.0	80.0				51.00	
1969	60.0	76.4				58.00	
1970	72.0	87.2				71.82	72.0
1971	86.0					85.82	86
1972	93.0					95.00	93
1973	101.0					100.80	101
1974	108.0					114.00	108
1975	121.0						121
1976	128.0						129
1977	141.0						145

[a]Identical estimates.

TABLE 15.9 (continued)
Estimates of Total Electric Power Production, 1949–77
(Billion kwh)

Year	PRC	Rawski	SD	SER	Smil	WES	WPD
1949	4.3				4.31		
1950	4.5				4.55		
1951	5.7				5.75		
1952	7.3	7.3			7.26		
1953	9.2	9.2			9.19		
1954	11.0	11.0		11.0	11.00		
1955	12.3	12.3		12.3	12.28		
1956	16.6	16.6		16.6	16.59		
1957	19.3	19.3			19.34		
1958	27.5	27.5			27.53		
1959		41.5			41.50		
1960					46.0		
1961					31.0	54.2	29
1962					30.0	59.8	28
1963					33.0	65.2	29
1964					36.0	71.1	34
1965		52.0			42.0	77.6	37
1966			47		47.0	85.5	40
1967			41		41.0	68.6	49
1968			44		44.0	75.0	44
1969			50		50.0	71.2	50
1970		88.9	60		60.0	77.0	
1971		106.2	70		70.8	91.0	
1972					85.0	102.0	
1973					100.8	112.0	
1974					108.0	118.0	
1975					122.0	126.0	
1976					128.0		
1977							

move to a new stage of transmission technology, and possibly toward more broadly integrated power grids within the next decade. As with pipeline technology, Chinese industry may now have laid the foundation for rapid expansion of electric power transmission equipment production. The large size of China's 1975 electric power output would make the greater efficiencies of integrated grids an attractive option within the near future. However, China will for decades continue to build and operate thousands of unintegrated grids in the rural areas, serving the villages and agriculture from low-capacity generating units.

Growth of the Electronics Industry

The electronics industry is not directly part of the electric power infrastructure, but is closely linked to it on both the production and consumption sides of the energy balance. China has established an impressive and rapidly expanding electronics industry. Accounting for about 1 percent of GNP, the Chinese electronics industry manufactures a wide array of equipment suitable to the needs of domestic industry and communications.[98] Chinese computers with substantial memory capacity, high operating speeds, and solid-state circuitry are not available. The fastest Chinese computer handles 1 million operations per second (ops), still behind the standard IBM model 370/168, which was introduced in 1971 and handles 2.4 million ops.[99] China has been swifter in the development of computer hardware than program software, interface systems, disk storage, and access languages. Computers are used in energy production for on-line control of petroleum refineries and power plants and for processing geological exploration data, among other uses.[100]

Aside from computer hardware (actually a small industry in aggregate terms), China also manufactures many electronic components and products for use in industry, communications, and instrumentation. A Peking factory manufactures Large-Scale Integrated (LSI) circuits with a reported capacity of 10,000 transistor elements, comparable to Japanese and American LSI circuits.[101] Domestically produced color television is available in still limited but expanding numbers of sets. All provinces have radio-manufacturing industries, and black-and-white television has been produced in 26 provinces.[102] The instrumentation industry, the largest single part of the electronics industry, produces measuring equipment for routine application and some highly specialized and technically advanced measuring devices.

China has long imported part of its electronic equipment requirements and exported some electronics products. Prior to 1960, nearly all electronics imports and production prototypes came from the Soviet Union and Eastern Europe. But since the Sino-Soviet break, China has moved increasingly toward West European, Japanese, and, recently, American equipment, both for imports and for design prototypes.[103] There is some speculation that China may become a significant electronic equipment exporter. Several conditions are present in the Chinese electronics industry that provide the foundation for electronics trade in the world market. China has a huge captive domestic market for electronic components and consumer products, so that research and development costs are easily justified and produce a visible return within short time horizons. For example, Chinese transistor radios (260 varieties) are common in villages and households throughout the country and the PRC is already the third largest annual producer of radios in the world.[104] Chinese labor and materials costs are lower than similar costs in the United States or Japan. If Chinese electronics products could be made aesthetically palatable to Western consumers, they could easily become sharply competitive on the international market. China already exports electronics components and equipment to a number of Third World countries.

Chapter 16

Primary Energy Production

Chapters 14 and 15 have established estimates for China's primary energy reserves and for primary and secondary energy production. They have also provided a brief overview of the current state of technology in each Chinese energy industry. Careful empirical work is fundamental to the construction of a computerized historical energy profile (Chapters 16–19) and to the trend analysis and energy balance projections (Chapters 23–24). This avoids the risk of "garbage in, garbage out" computerization and provides a foundation for further cumulative research and correction of these estimates by future studies. The statistical description of China's energy balance is a plastic art, not an exact science. Computerization provides the flexibility for continuous data revisions, as long as no single set of statistics is taken as final. Several generations of computerized statistics preceded this version of the Statistical Profile, and more generations of energy profiles for the PRC will certainly follow its publication. For this reason, the statistics in Chapters 16–19 are seldom valid beyond one or two significant digits and rarely accurate to even a single decimal place. None are valid to the four or five extraneous decimal places provided gratuitously by the computer.

Tables 16.1–16.6 provide primary energy production statistics for coal, crude petroleum, natural gas, hydropower, and total energy—the conventional energy fuels. These fuels are "primary" in the sense that they involve the direct exploitation of energy reserves, not the reprocessing of previously extracted fuels. The series presented here exclude both noncommercial energy production (firewood, dung, grass, etc.) and nonconventional energy production (solar power, biomass methane generation, etc.). The exclusion of noncommercial energy fuels in the rural sector is particularly significant, since largely agricultural economies sometimes consume as much traditional biomass as they consume the products of modern energy industries.

For ease of access, primary energy production statistics are provided in original units of measurement for each fuel, and in several different common energy units. Tables are provided for conversion of the primary energy production sector into coal equivalents, gigajoules, and oil

TABLE 16.1
Primary Energy Production in Original Units, 1949–78

Year	Raw coal (mmt)	Crude petroleum (mmt)	Natural gas (billion cu m)	Hydropower (billion kwh)
1949	32.4	0.1	0.05	0.7
1950	42.9	0.2	0.05	0.7
1951	53.1	0.3	0.06	0.9
1952	66.5	0.4	0.08	1.3
1953	69.7	0.6	0.1	1.5
1954	83.7	0.8	0.2	2.2
1955	98.3	1.0	0.3	2.4
1956	110.0	1.2	0.4	3.5
1957	131.0	1.5	0.6	4.7
1958	230.0	2.3	0.9	5.5
1959	300.0	3.7	1.4	7.8
1960	280.0	5.1	2.0	9.0
1961	185.0	5.2	3.0	8.0
1962	200.0	5.7	5.0	6.0
1963	210.0	6.4	6.0	6.0
1964	220.0	8.7	7.0	7.0
1965	240.0	11.0	9.2	9.0
1966	270.0	14.1	12.0	10.0
1967	210.0	13.9	10.0	10.0
1968	225.0	15.2	15.0	12.0
1969	280.0	20.4	18.0	15.0
1970	338.0	28.2	20.7	18.0
1971	365.0	36.7	23.5	21.0
1972	389.0	43.1	26.9	23.0
1973	411.0	54.8	27.6	25.0
1974	417.0	65.8	28.9	27.0
1975	480.0	74.3	34.6	30.0
1976	450.0	83.6	37.9	33.0
1977	500.0	90.3	47.3	36.0
1978	600.0	100.2	54.0	40.0

equivalents. The conversion factors for each fuel are discussed in Chapter 13.

Primary Energy Production Growth Rates

The annual production growth rate for each energy fuel and for total energy production indicates that China has experienced rapid, if uneven, growth in its primary energy sector for the past 30 years. The

TABLE 16.2
Primary Energy Production in Million Metric Tons Coal Equivalent, 1949–78

Year	Coal	Petroleum	Natural gas	Hydropower	Total
1949	24.3	0.2	0.07	0.09	24.6
1950	32.2	0.3	0.07	0.09	32.6
1951	39.8	0.4	0.08	0.1	40.5
1952	49.9	0.6	0.1	0.2	50.8
1953	52.3	0.9	0.1	0.2	53.5
1954	62.8	1.2	0.3	0.3	64.5
1955	73.7	1.4	0.4	0.3	75.8
1956	82.5	1.7	0.5	0.4	85.2
1957	98.3	2.1	0.8	0.6	101.8
1958	172.5	3.3	1.2	0.7	177.7
1959	225.0	5.4	1.9	1.0	233.3
1960	210.0	7.5	2.7	1.1	221.3
1961	138.8	7.6	4.0	1.0	151.4
1962	150.0	8.4	6.7	0.7	165.8
1963	157.5	9.3	8.0	0.7	175.6
1964	165.0	12.7	9.3	0.9	187.9
1965	180.0	16.1	12.3	1.1	209.5
1966	202.5	20.7	16.0	1.2	240.4
1967	157.5	20.4	13.3	1.2	192.5
1968	168.8	22.3	20.0	1.5	212.6
1969	210.0	30.0	24.0	1.8	265.8
1970	253.5	41.5	27.6	2.2	324.8
1971	273.8	53.9	31.3	2.6	361.6
1972	291.8	63.3	35.8	2.8	393.7
1973	308.3	80.6	36.8	3.1	428.7
1974	312.8	96.7	38.5	3.3	451.2
1975	360.0	109.2	46.1	3.7	518.9
1976	337.5	122.9	50.5	4.1	514.9
1977	375.0	132.7	63.0	4.4	575.2
1978	450.0	147.3	71.9	4.9	674.1

growth rate was faster for coal, oil, gas, and hydro during the 1950's than during the 1960's. Coal and hydro had higher growth rates during the 1970's than during the sluggish middle decade. The petroleum and natural gas industries both averaged annual increases of more than 20 percent over the entire 30-year period—a remarkably sustained and rapid pace of development in the annals of global hydrocarbon development. But it should be noted that the "scale effect," capital requirements, infrastructure constraints, and perhaps reserves constraints reduced oil

TABLE 16.3
Primary Energy Production in Million Gigajoules, 1949–78

Year	Coal	Petroleum	Natural gas	Hydropower	Total
1949	699.8	5.2	1.9	2.5	709.5
1950	926.6	8.6	1.9	2.7	939.9
1951	1,147.0	13.2	2.3	3.4	1,165.9
1952	1,436.4	18.9	3.1	4.5	1,462.9
1953	1,505.5	26.9	3.8	5.5	1,541.8
1954	1,807.9	34.1	7.7	7.8	1,857.6
1955	2,123.3	41.8	11.5	8.5	2,185.1
1956	2,376.0	50.3	15.4	12.5	2,454.1
1957	2,829.6	63.0	23.0	17.0	2,932.6
1958	4,968.0	97.9	34.6	19.8	5,120.3
1959	6,480.0	160.0	53.8	28.1	6,721.8
1960	6,048.0	220.5	76.8	32.4	6,377.7
1961	3,996.0	224.2	115.2	28.8	4,364.2
1962	4,320.0	248.5	192.0	21.6	4,782.1
1963	4,536.0	275.0	230.4	21.6	5,063.0
1964	4,752.0	374.2	268.8	25.2	5,420.2
1965	5,184.0	474.0	353.3	32.4	6,043.6
1966	5,832.0	608.6	460.8	36.0	6,937.4
1967	4,536.0	601.0	384.0	36.0	5,557.0
1968	4,860.0	657.2	576.0	43.2	6,136.4
1969	6,048.0	881.1	691.2	54.0	7,674.3
1970	7,300.8	1,219.8	794.9	64.8	9,380.3
1971	7,884.0	1,586.9	902.4	75.6	10,448.9
1972	8,402.4	1,862.1	1,033.0	82.8	11,380.3
1973	8,877.6	2,369.7	1,059.8	90.0	12,397.2
1974	9,007.2	2,843.7	1,109.8	97.2	13,057.8
1975	10,368.0	3,211.0	1,328.6	108.0	15,015.7
1976	9,720.0	3,615.2	1,455.4	118.8	14,909.4
1977	10,800.0	3,904.6	1,816.3	129.6	16,650.5
1978	12,960.0	4,332.6	2,073.6	144.0	19,510.2

and gas growth rates to less than 15 percent per year after 1975, a trend that will be more pronounced in the decade to come. Total primary energy production grew at an average annual rate of 11 percent from 1949 to 1978—20 percent from 1949 to 1960, 4 percent from 1960 to 1970, and 9 percent from 1970 to 1978. Rapid growth during the 1950's could be traced to the scale effect (high growth rates are likely when absolute production levels are relatively low) and to the impact of direct assistance in all of China's energy industries from the Soviet Union and Eastern Europe. The sluggish rate of growth in energy production during the

TABLE 16.4
Primary Energy Production in Million Barrels Oil Equivalent, 1949-78

Year	Coal	Petroleum	Natural gas	Hydropower	Total
1949	119.9	0.9	0.3	0.4	121.5
1950	158.7	1.5	0.3	0.4	161.0
1951	196.5	2.2	0.4	0.6	199.7
1952	246.1	3.2	0.5	0.8	250.5
1953	257.9	4.5	0.7	0.9	264.0
1954	309.7	5.8	1.3	1.3	318.1
1955	363.7	7.1	2.0	1.4	374.2
1956	407.0	8.5	2.6	2.1	420.2
1957	484.7	10.6	4.0	2.8	502.1
1958	851.0	16.5	5.9	3.3	876.8
1959	1,110.0	27.0	9.2	4.7	1,150.9
1960	1,036.0	37.2	13.2	5.4	1,091.8
1961	684.5	37.9	19.8	4.8	747.0
1962	740.0	41.9	33.0	3.6	818.5
1963	777.0	46.4	39.6	3.6	866.6
1964	814.0	63.2	46.2	4.2	927.6
1965	888.0	80.0	60.7	5.4	1,034.1
1966	999.0	102.7	79.2	6.0	1,186.9
1967	777.0	101.5	66.0	6.0	950.5
1968	832.5	111.0	99.0	7.2	1,049.7
1969	1,036.0	148.8	118.8	9.0	1,312.6
1970	1,250.6	205.9	136.6	10.8	1,604.0
1971	1,350.5	267.9	155.1	12.6	1,786.1
1972	1,439.3	314.4	177.5	13.8	1,945.0
1973	1,520.7	400.1	182.2	15.0	2,117.9
1974	1,542.9	480.1	190.7	16.2	2,229.9
1975	1,776.0	542.1	228.4	18.0	2,564.5
1976	1,665.0	610.3	250.1	19.8	2,545.3
1977	1,850.0	659.2	312.2	21.6	2,843.0
1978	2,220.0	731.5	356.4	24.0	3,331.9

1960's reflected the impact of two massive political disruptions (the Great Leap Forward and the Cultural Revolution) and the withdrawal of Soviet technical assistance and material aid. During the 1970's, the Chinese energy industries recovered and resumed a pattern of steady growth based on the twin pillars of domestic energy equipment manufacture and equipment imports from the industrial market economy countries.

China's energy production growth rate has proved highly volatile over the three decades since the establishment of the PRC. Total primary en-

TABLE 16.5
Annual Percent Increase of Primary Energy Production, 1950–78

Year	Coal	Petroleum	Natural gas	Hydropower	Total
1950	32.4%	65.3%	0.0%	5.2%	32.5%
			20.0		
1951	23.8	52.5		26.6	24.0
1952	25.2	43.0	33.3	33.6	25.5
1953	4.8	42.7	25.0	22.2	5.4
1954	20.1	26.8	100.0	41.6	20.5
1955	17.4	22.4	50.0	8.3	17.6
1956	11.9	20.4	33.3	46.6	12.3
1957	19.1	25.4	50.0	36.1	19.5
1958	75.6	55.3	50.0	16.8	74.6
1959	30.4	63.4	55.6	41.8	31.3
1960	-6.7	37.8	42.9	15.4	-5.1
1961	-33.9	1.7	50.0	-11.1	-31.6
1962	8.1	10.8	66.7	-25.0	9.6
1963	5.0	10.7	20.0	0.0	5.9
1964	4.8	36.1	16.7	16.7	7.0
1965	9.1	26.7	31.4	28.6	11.5
1966	12.5	28.4	30.4	11.1	14.8
1967	-22.2	-1.2	-16.7	0.0	-19.9
1968	7.1	9.4	50.0	20.0	10.4
1969	24.4	34.1	20.0	25.0	25.0
1970	20.7	38.4	15.0	20.0	22.2
1971	8.0	30.1	13.5	16.7	11.3
1972	6.6	17.3	14.5	9.5	8.9
1973	5.7	27.3	2.6	8.7	8.9
1974	1.5	20.0	4.7	8.0	5.3
1975	15.1	12.9	19.7	11.1	15.0
1976	-6.3	12.6	9.5	10.0	-0.8
1977	11.1	8.0	24.8	9.1	11.7
1978	20.0	11.0	14.2	11.1	17.2

ergy production fell about 40 percent during the aftermath of the Great Leap Forward (1961–62) and 20 percent at the height of the Cultural Revolution. Although China's political leadership in the post-Mao period seems to have rejected the type of political upheaval that characterized the late 1950's and 1960's, there is absolutely no guarantee that energy development will proceed smoothly for the next two decades. Total primary energy production growth rates will probably average between 5 and 10 percent through the turn of the century, depending on domestic political conditions and the continued expansion of China's fossil-fuel resource base. Use of alternative energy resources, such as nuclear fuel, solar power, or biogas, will have to grow rapidly during the 1990's to maintain total energy production growth rates in the 5–10 percent range.

Primary Energy Production Mix

The contribution of coal to China's total energy production mix declined steadily from 99 percent in 1949 to about 67 percent in 1978. Thus, while coal is still the backbone of the Chinese energy system, its growth rate has not kept pace with petroleum and natural gas. Furthermore, the decline in the relative importance of coal has been swifter in the 1970's than in the 1960's, and was faster in the 1960's than the 1950's. Production data indicate that the coal industry, although still vital and expanding at 5–7 percent per year, is beginning to feel constraints imposed by escalating capital requirements, transportation limits, and saturation of the domestic market for lump coal. Market considerations may be paramount during the late 1970's, judging from the pressure that China's trade officials have exerted on the Japanese to take more Chinese coal imports during the 1980's. Future expansion of the coal industry will also be contingent on the pace of construction of coal-fired thermal power stations and on growth in the steel industry. Petroleum and natural gas, on the other hand, are not competing with coal as a source of industrial process heat. The transportation sector has been moving increasingly toward petroleum fuels, which now have penetrated rail transport, the traditional province of the coal-fired steam locomotive. The rapidly expanding road network and agricultural mechanization are also increasing the demand for petroleum fuels, but not for coal. Peking will probably take steps through the planning process to maintain the coal industry. The use of coal will therefore continue to grow slowly through the turn of the century, rather than declining in absolute terms, as it did in Western Europe, Japan, and North America.

The contribution of hydropower to energy production is another interesting result of statistics on the primary energy production mix. Hydro increased its contribution slightly during the 1950's, but remained about half a percent of total energy output until the mid-1970's. In energy equivalent terms, hydro still constitutes a very small energy industry, despite China's enormous hydraulic potential and Peking's concerted efforts to promote the installation of vast numbers of small-scale rural hydropower stations. It should be recalled that the PRC could theoretically run the entire U.S. electric power system of 1975 on hydropower alone (Chapter 14).

The reasons for the low relative energy contribution from hydropower are not immediately evident. Hydro is more capital-intensive per

TABLE 16.6
Primary Energy Production Mix, 1949–78
(Percent contribution to total energy production)

Year	Coal	Petroleum	Natural gas	Hydropower
1949	98.7%	0.7%	0.3%	0.4%
1950	98.6	0.9	0.2	0.3
1951	98.4	1.1	0.2	0.3
1952	98.2	1.3	0.2	0.3
1953	97.7	1.7	0.2	0.4
1954	97.4	1.8	0.4	0.4
1955	97.2	1.9	0.5	0.4
1956	96.9	2.0	0.6	0.5
1957	96.5	2.1	0.8	0.6
1958	97.1	1.9	0.7	0.4
1959	96.5	2.3	0.8	0.4
1960	94.9	3.4	1.2	0.5
1961	91.7	5.0	2.6	0.7
1962	90.4	5.1	4.0	0.4
1963	89.7	5.3	4.6	0.4
1964	87.8	6.8	5.0	0.5
1965	85.9	7.7	5.9	0.5
1966	84.2	8.6	6.6	0.5
1967	81.8	10.6	6.9	0.6
1968	79.4	10.5	9.4	0.7
1969	79.0	11.3	9.0	0.7
1970	78.1	12.8	8.5	0.7
1971	75.7	14.9	8.7	0.7
1972	74.1	16.1	9.1	0.7
1973	71.9	18.8	8.6	0.7
1974	69.3	21.4	8.5	0.7
1975	69.4	21.0	8.9	0.7
1976	65.5	23.9	9.8	0.8
1977	65.2	23.1	11.0	0.8
1978	66.8	21.8	10.7	0.7

unit of installed capacity than thermal-generated power. However, hydro has been increasing its contribution to total electric power output in China, while thermal has declined in relative terms (Table 17.3). Thus, the thermal power industry has been expanding even more slowly than hydro, relative to the growth of total energy output. In the Chinese case, it would be difficult to write off the slow pace of hydro development to capital costs alone. Furthermore, many small hydro plants have been constructed with local labor and materials, significantly lowering the initial capital costs of installation.

Smil has argued that hydro has other high social and economic costs that have deterred Chinese planners.[1] Large reservoirs would have to be constructed in densely populated and agriculturally rich rural areas, displacing masses of rural people. Smil also argues that great distances between potential hydropower sites in the mountainous west and industrial sites in the densely populated east have restricted development of the hydropower industry. Irregular flow and heavy silting are also problems faced by China's hydraulic engineers.[2]

Whereas these factors help explain some of the difficulty Peking has faced in developing its hydraulic wealth, they are not entirely convincing. The Yangtze River, with a potential of some 200 GWe, flows through a basin that is both heavily populated and undergoing rapid industrial growth (the Szechwan Basin). So far only about 3 GWe of hydropower-generating capacity has been installed along the entire length of the Yangtze. Intensive development could supply the electric power needs of both rural and urban areas across a wide belt in central China without incurring unusual transmission losses. The Yangtze has numerous separately exploitable tributaries and moderate silting rates. The loss of agricultural land to reservoirs would indeed be serious in the densely populated Yangtze region, but could be minimized by locating reservoirs in the many hilly and mountainous parts of that region. Furthermore, flood control and irrigation could be greatly increased by the same reservoirs that produce electric power, thereby compensating for the loss of agricultural land through the introduction of high-yield, all-weather agricultural production zones.

A more likely explanation for the slow pace of hydro development might be that China was simply not able to manufacture enough hydropower-generating equipment and transmission equipment during the 1960's to substantially increase the contribution of hydro to total energy output. Before 1960, much of China's newly installed hydro capacity was constructed using Soviet and East European generators. A domestic hydro equipment industry began tooling up after 1960, and has surfaced in many provinces since 1970 (Chapter 15). That machine-building industry, particularly suited to manufacture of small-scale hydro-generating equipment but capable of producing generating sets of up to 300 MWe, is now in place. It could easily start an upswing in the contribution of hydro to the energy balance within five to ten years. Hydro is evidently a "sleeper" industry with large potential but a slow initial pace of development, the reverse of the pattern of development in the petroleum and natural gas industries.

Chapter 17

Secondary Energy Production

Secondary energy production can most easily be defined as the conversion of one energy fuel to another. As such, it is a catch-all category that can be used to provide a cluster of statistical energy production series that do not easily fall into either primary production or energy consumption categories. The number and variety of secondary energy production statistics could be multiplied indefinitely by an ever sharper differentiation of substages in the flow of energy commodities through society. I have chosen to include just a few forms of secondary energy production in this analysis—coke production, thermal electric power generation, total electric power generation, total refined petroleum production, the differentiated production of petroleum fuels, plant use of energy in energy production, and the use of hydrocarbons in the production of petrochemical and fertilizer feedstocks. These were statistics that were available for the Chinese case or could be generated by inference from primary energy data and a few oversimplified assumptions. All the secondary energy production statistics presented in this section were generated by the computer and then rounded to a reasonable level of approximation. All the statistics presented for various forms of secondary energy production are general estimates, and none have been tested directly against whatever data exist in the Chinese press. Validation of the statistics would require separate in-depth analysis of each secondary energy production industry—a task far beyond the means of this book. These statistics, therefore, should be taken as a point of reference, not the final word.

Coke Production

Only two sets of estimates are available in the foreign literature on China's coke production. The two available series were published by the U.S. Bureau of Mines (BOM) and the U.S. Joint Economic Committee of Congress (JEC).[1] The JEC series was based on a careful statistical analysis of the Chinese iron and steel industry. Coke requirements were inferred from steel output at large and small steel mills. The JEC series ran high during the Great Leap years (1958–60) and then dropped very

TABLE 17.1
Secondary Energy Production: Coke from Coal, 1950–78

Year	Coke production			Annual percent increase	Coal consumption for coke	
	Mmt	Mmtce	Million GJ		Mmtce	Pct. of total coal output
1950	1.0	0.9	25.9	233.3%	1.5	4.8%
1951	1.1	1.0	28.5	10.0	1.7	4.3
1952	1.9	1.7	49.2	72.7	2.9	5.9
1953	2.1	1.9	54.4	10.5	3.2	6.2
1954	2.8	2.5	72.5	33.3	4.3	6.9
1955	3.1	2.8	80.3	10.7	4.8	6.5
1956	3.8	3.4	98.4	22.6	5.9	7.1
1957	4.5	4.1	116.6	18.4	6.9	7.1
1958	11.3	10.2	292.7	151.1	17.4	10.1
1959	18.1	16.3	468.8	60.2	27.9	12.4
1960	24.1	21.7	624.2	33.1	37.1	17.7
1961	6.8	6.1	176.1	−71.8	10.5	7.5
1962	6.7	6.0	173.5	−1.5	10.3	6.9
1963	7.5	6.8	194.3	11.9	11.6	7.3
1964	8.8	7.9	227.9	17.3	13.6	8.2
1965	10.1	9.1	261.6	14.8	15.6	8.6
1966	12.0	10.8	310.8	18.8	18.5	9.1
1967	9.6	8.6	248.6	−20.0	14.8	9.4
1968	11.2	10.1	290.1	16.7	17.2	10.2
1969	12.6	11.3	326.3	12.5	19.4	9.2
1970	16.2	14.6	419.6	28.6	24.9	9.8
1971	20.1	18.1	520.6	24.1	31.0	11.3
1972	22.4	20.2	580.2	11.4	34.5	11.8
1973	24.3	21.9	629.4	8.5	37.4	12.1
1974	22.6	20.3	585.3	−7.0	34.8	11.1
1975	24.3	21.9	629.4	7.5	37.4	10.4
1976	21.5	19.4	556.9	−11.5	33.1	9.8
1977	25.0	22.5	647.5	16.3	38.5	10.3
1978	30.0	27.0	777.0	20.0	46.2	10.3

low in the wake of the Great Leap. The Bureau of Mines estimates were in general higher than the JEC series, perhaps justifiable in terms of a lower level of efficiency than usual in the Chinese coking industry, requiring more than the standard 1.54 metric tons of coal to produce a single ton of coke. This study adopted the JEC series on the basis of the conservative strategy of estimation, although the JEC series is itself probably too high for the Great Leap years. Note that the coal requirement for coke production was stated in terms of tonnage of standard coal, not

Chinese raw coal. The percentage of coal consumption for coke was also based on standard coal. (See Table 17.1.)

The coke production estimates for 1976–78 were provided by the author on the basis of steel output data from the CIA and extrapolation. If the CIA figures are roughly correct, China produced about 23 million metric tons of steel from 30 million tons of pig iron in 1976, requiring 21.5 million tons of coke. The steel production figure for 1976 was down from 26 million tons in 1975. In my extrapolation, I assumed that 1977 steel production recovered to 1975 levels and that 1978 steel production would be at least 3 million tons higher than in 1977. Thus, the 1978 coke requirement could be conservatively estimated at 27 million metric tons. That would require 42 million metric tons of standard coal, or about 11 percent of China's total coal production in 1978.[2] The average growth rate of the coking industry, highly sensitive to the growth pattern in the steel industry, reached 30 percent per year during the 1950's, dropped to zero from 1960 to 1970, and then recovered to an average rate of 8 percent per year between 1970 and 1978. The proportion of coal output required for coking purposes has remained fairly steady at 9–12 percent since 1966, indicating that the coking industry has grown at the same pace as the coal industry itself. This pattern could shift in the decades ahead, as the Chinese coal industry levels out and the steel industry continues to grow. There may, therefore, be a shift in coal consumption toward coking coal. Such a shift would be easily absorbed, since China has large reserves of coking coal and because of the displacement of coal by petroleum and natural gas in transport and other sectors.

Thermal Electric Power Production

The basic data series for thermal power output was derived from the alternative estimates listed in Table 15.8 and described in the accompanying text. During the 1950's, nearly all of China's thermal power generation was coal-based and only a negligible proportion was generated by burning residual fuel oil or crude petroleum. As China's oil industry began to grow rapidly in the mid-1960's, however, petroleum began to be burned in some power plants. This trend accelerated until 1976, when about 25 percent of thermal electric power generation was oil-based.[3] We know that some natural gas was also burned in thermal power plants by the mid-1970's, but have no estimates of how much.[4] Table 17.2, therefore, divides thermal power generation into just two categories—coal-based and oil-based. The estimated series for thermal power production from petroleum was based on a linear growth assumption, starting from 1 percent of total thermal power output in 1963 and projected

TABLE 17.2
Secondary Energy Production: Thermal Electric Power Generation, 1950–78

Year	Thermal electric power production (billion kwh)			Coal consumption for thermal power production		Petroleum consumption for thermal power production	
	From coal	From petroleum	Total	Mmtce	Pct. of total coal output	Mmt	Pct. of total petroleum output
1949	3.6		3.6	3.6	14.8%		
1950	3.8		3.8	3.5	11.0		
1951	4.8		4.8	4.1	10.3		
1952	6.0		6.0	4.4	8.8		
1953	7.7		7.7	5.3	10.1		
1954	8.8		8.8	5.9	9.4		
1955	9.9		9.9	6.4	8.7		
1956	12.1		12.1	7.5	9.1		
1957	14.6		14.6	8.8	8.9		
1958	22.5		22.5	12.4	7.2		
1959	34.2		34.2	18.5	8.2		
1960	38.0		38.0	20.5	9.8		
1961	23.0		23.0	12.4	9.0		
1962	24.0		24.0	13.0	8.6		
1963	26.7	0.3	27.0	14.2	9.0	0.1	1.5%
1964	28.1	0.9	29.0	14.6	8.9	0.3	3.6
1965	31.4	1.7	33.0	16.0	8.9	0.6	5.2
1966	37.2	2.8	40.0	18.6	9.2	1.0	6.8
1967	31.9	3.2	35.0	15.9	10.1	1.1	7.7
1968	33.8	4.2	38.0	16.9	10.0	1.4	9.4
1969	39.2	5.9	45.0	19.2	9.1	2.0	9.6
1970	45.9	8.1	54.0	22.0	8.7	2.6	9.4
1971	54.0	11.1	65.0	25.4	9.3	3.5	9.6
1972	56.7	13.3	70.0	26.1	8.9	4.2	9.7
1973	60.0	16.0	76.0	27.0	8.8	4.9	8.9
1974	62.4	18.6	81.0	27.4	8.8	5.6	8.5
1975	68.3	22.8	91.0	29.3	8.2	6.7	9.0
1976	72.0	24.0	96.0	30.2	9.0	6.9	8.2
1977	78.8	26.3	105.0	32.3	8.6	7.3	8.1
1978	90.0	30.0	120.0	36.0	8.0	8.2	8.1

to 25 percent in 1976. The oil-based proportion of thermal power generation was estimated to have remained steady at 25 percent in 1977 and 1978, owing to political pressure to conserve crude oil for export rather than burn it under boilers.[5] China discovered at about the same time as the West that burning petroleum is an expensive way of producing electric power.

The coal consumption and petroleum consumption requirements for thermal power generation were estimated on the basis of annual thermal efficiency estimates (Chapter 15). Thus, in 1950, a billion kilowatt-hours of thermal power required twice as much coal input as a billion kwh generated in 1975.[6] In 1976, the thermal power industry required about 30 million standard tons of coal, or 9 percent of China's coal output in that year. The coal consumption requirement for thermal power production has remained a constant proportion of total coal production (9–11 percent) since the early 1950's. Petroleum consumption for thermal power production reached 7 million tons in 1976, including both residual fuel oil and crude petroleum burned under power plant boilers. This represented 8 percent of China's crude petroleum production in 1976. Again, the proportion of petroleum burned to generate electric power has remained constant at 8–10 percent since 1967, indicating that oil-based power generation has grown at the same rate as crude oil production.

Total Electric Power Production

Basic data for thermal power production, hydropower production, and total electric power production were derived as described in Chapter 15 from alternative estimates in the foreign literature. (See Table 17.3.) It must be emphasized that these data are conservative estimates and that further analysis of the Chinese electric power industry could produce significantly higher series for these production variables. China's total electric power production reached at least 120 billion kilowatt-hours in 1975 and 140 billion kwh in 1977. Thus China ranked ninth in total electric power output in 1975.[7] China's electric power industry will be the world's third largest by the year 2000, at more than 1 trillion kwh per year, half as much as 1975 U.S. power output and roughly equivalent to 1975 Soviet output (Chapter 24).*

There has been a slow trend in the electric power mix toward hydropower, which reached 25 percent of total power output in 1976. This contrasts sharply with the proportion of generating capacity in hydropower plants, which was about 36 percent at the end of 1976.[8] Current analyses suggest that this discrepancy is due to the relatively low utilization of hydropower capacity caused by high fluctuation in run-off rates and the priority given to irrigation requirements during certain sea-

---

*Official data reported in mid-1979 indicate that total electric power output was 203 bkwh in 1976 and 256 bkwh in 1978, substantially higher than these estimates. If the official claims are correct, China's electric power output in 1976 matched that of France and ranked seventh. The 1950–78 growth rate for electric power production was 14.4 percent per year.

TABLE 17.3
Secondary Energy Production: Electric Power Mix, 1950–78
(Billion kwh)

Year	Thermal power production			Hydropower production			Total electric power production	
	Amount	Pct. of total	Percent increase	Amount	Pct. of total	Percent increase	Amount	Percent increase
1950	3.8	83.6%	5.7%	0.7	16.4%	5.2%	4.6	5.6%
1951	4.8	83.6	26.3	0.9	16.4	26.6	5.8	26.4
1952	6.0	82.6	24.8	1.3	17.4	33.6	7.3	26.3
1953	7.7	83.3	27.6	1.5	16.7	22.2	9.2	26.6
1954	8.8	80.2	15.2	2.2	19.8	41.6	11.0	19.6
1955	9.9	80.8	12.4	2.4	19.2	8.3	12.3	11.6
1956	12.1	77.8	22.3	3.5	22.2	46.6	15.6	27.0
1957	14.6	75.6	20.6	4.7	24.4	36.1	19.3	24.0
1958	22.5	80.4	53.8	5.5	19.6	16.8	28.0	44.8
1959	34.2	81.4	52.0	7.8	18.6	41.8	42.0	50.0
1960	38.0	80.9	11.1	9.0	19.1	15.4	47.0	11.9
1961	23.0	74.2	−39.5	8.0	25.8	−11.1	31.0	−34.0
1962	24.0	80.0	4.3	6.0	20.0	−25.0	30.0	−3.2
1963	27.0	81.8	12.5	6.0	18.2	0.0	33.0	10.0
1964	29.0	80.6	7.4	7.0	19.4	16.7	36.0	9.1
1965	33.0	78.6	13.8	9.0	21.4	28.6	42.0	16.7
1966	40.0	80.0	21.2	10.0	20.0	11.1	50.0	19.0
1967	35.0	77.8	−12.5	10.0	22.2	0.0	45.0	−10.0
1968	38.0	76.0	8.6	12.0	24.0	20.0	50.0	11.1
1969	45.0	75.0	18.4	15.0	25.0	25.0	60.0	20.0
1970	54.0	75.0	20.0	18.0	25.0	20.0	72.0	20.0
1971	65.0	75.6	20.4	21.0	24.4	16.7	86.0	19.4
1972	70.0	75.3	7.7	23.0	24.7	9.5	93.0	8.1
1973	76.0	75.2	8.6	25.0	24.8	8.7	101.0	8.6
1974	81.0	75.0	6.6	27.0	25.0	8.0	108.0	6.9
1975	91.0	75.2	12.3	30.0	24.8	11.1	121.0	12.0
1976	96.0	74.4	5.5	33.0	25.6	10.0	129.0	6.6
1977	105.0	74.5	9.4	36.0	25.5	9.1	141.0	9.3
1978	120.0	75.0	14.3	40.0	25.0	11.1	160.0	13.5

sons.[9] If the estimates in Table 14.6 are correct, the average utilization of hydropower capacity in China was less than 2,500 kilowatt-hours per kilowatt (kwh/kw) in 1976. Since average utilization for all electric power plants in China is estimated to have been 3,750 kwh/kw in 1976, utilization rates in thermal power plants must have been running well over 4,000 kwh/kw in that year.[10] China's utilization of installed capacity is quite respectable by world standards but could be sharply improved in the hydropower industry. U.S. utilization figures run 4,000–5,000 kwh/kw in both the thermal power and hydropower industries.[11]

The growth rate for total electric power production in China averaged 12 percent per year from 1950 to 1978, an impressive rate of expansion for the electric power industry of any country. However, the growth rate was much higher in the 1950's (23 percent) than in the 1960's (4 percent) and the 1970's (10 percent). The Sino-Soviet split has a serious delaying impact on the development of China's electric power industry, depriving the PRC of its primary source of imported generating equipment and technical assistance. The Great Leap and the Cultural Revolution also caused negative growth rates in at least three years, lowering the average rate of increase. Growth in the electric power industry has been impressive in recent years, integrating new equipment of Chinese manufacture with imported generating units. China has an enormous potential electric power requirement, only partially satisfied by current production levels. Expansion should continue at a rapid pace for the next two decades, generating high capital requirements for added capacity. Hydropower will continue to increase relative to thermal power output, and some nuclear power should be generated by the mid-1980's.

Refined Petroleum Production

Data for China's annual production of refined petroleum were estimated as the sum of crude petroleum production and net imports of crude petroleum (minus net exports) minus the plant use of petroleum in refineries and minus the generation of electric power by burning crude petroleum. (See Table 17.4.) Lacking information on the relative quantities of crude oil and residual fuel oil in thermal power plants, it was simply assumed that all petroleum burned in power plants was crude petroleum. The use of petroleum as a petrochemical feedstock was included in figures for refined petroleum production, since naphtha is normally counted as a refined product. Refinery capacity estimates were based on the alternative series presented in Table 15.4. Annual consumption of refined petroleum products was tabulated as the sum of domestic refined petroleum production and net imports of petroleum products.

TABLE 17.4

Secondary Energy Production: Refined Petroleum, 1950–78

	Refined petroleum production				Annual percent increase	Est. refinery capacity[a] (mmt/y)	Consumption of refined petroleum products[b] (mmt)
Year	Mmt	Mmtce	Million GJ	Million barrels			
1950	0.3	0.4	13.1	2.2	113.3%	0.3	0.5
1951	0.4	0.5	15.6	2.6	18.8	0.5	1.0
1952	0.5	0.8	22.1	3.7	41.8	1.0	1.0
1953	0.7	1.0	28.2	4.8	27.5	1.3	1.4
1954	0.9	1.4	40.1	6.8	42.2	1.5	1.6
1955	1.3	1.9	55.2	9.3	37.5	1.8	2.5
1956	1.5	2.2	64.1	10.8	16.1	2.0	2.8
1957	1.7	2.6	75.5	12.7	17.8	2.2	3.1
1958	2.8	4.1	120.6	20.4	59.7	3.0	4.6
1959	4.1	6.1	178.6	30.1	48.1	4.0	6.5
1960	5.4	7.9	233.7	39.5	30.9	5.5	7.8
1961	5.0	7.3	215.3	36.4	−7.9	6.0	8.0
1962	5.5	8.1	238.6	40.3	10.8	8.0	7.4
1963	6.1	8.9	261.9	44.2	9.7	10.0	7.5
1964	8.0	11.7	345.1	58.3	31.8	12.0	8.5
1965	9.7	14.3	419.3	70.8	21.5	13.6	9.9
1966	12.2	17.9	526.7	88.9	25.6	17.8	12.1
1967	11.9	17.5	514.4	86.8	−2.3	20.0	11.8
1968	13.0	19.1	562.1	94.9	9.3	22.8	13.1
1969	17.6	25.8	759.2	128.2	35.1	26.0	17.6
1970	24.5	36.1	1,061.0	179.1	39.7	31.5	24.5
1971	31.2	45.9	1,350.6	228.0	27.3	38.0	31.5
1972	36.1	53.1	1,562.5	263.8	15.7	45.6	36.6
1973	45.6	67.0	1,971.4	332.8	26.2	54.4	45.6
1974	52.4	77.0	2,265.9	382.5	14.9	58.7	52.1
1975	54.8	80.5	2,368.5	399.9	4.5	66.5	54.0
1976	64.8	95.2	2,800.1	472.7	18.2	75.0	63.9
1977	69.7	102.5	3,014.1	508.9	7.6	88.0	68.5
1978	77.6	114.1	3,356.8	566.7	11.4	95.0	76.2

[a]Estimated refined petroleum production exceeded refinery capacity in 1950 and 1959. This either reflects errors in the estimates or indicates that crude petroleum stocks were held over for refining in slack years. For the sake of statistical simplicity, it was assumed that all crude petroleum was refined and consumed in the year of production or import. Utilization of refinery capacity was within a normal range under this assumption except for the years 1950 and 1958–1960.

[b]Includes imported refined petroleum products.

China's output of refined petroleum products reached about 75–80 million metric tons in 1978. Utilization of refinery capacity has varied widely from one period to another. Utilization ran between 50 and 80 percent of capacity in the 1950's, excluding the years when crude petroleum must have been stockpiled for lack of sufficient capacity or when crude petroleum production claims by the Chinese government may have been exaggerated (1950 and 1958–60). Utilization ratios hovered around 65 percent in the 1960's and improved to about 80 percent in the 1970's. China produced only about half of the refined petroleum products consumed in the country during the 1950's, relying on the Soviet Union for the balance of domestic requirements. Complete self-sufficiency in refined petroleum was achieved in 1965 and has continued ever since. Expansion of China's refined petroleum production averaged 20 percent per year between 1950 and 1978, an impressive growth rate for any country to achieve over a sustained period. Growth was faster in the 1950's (29 percent per annum) than in the 1960's and 1970's (15 percent per annum), but high and steady overall. Refinery capacity has obviously "lagged" only behind crude oil output growth rates, not behind world standards. There is still no serious shortage of refinery capacity, as some authors have suggested. Nor is there any evidence for the widespread belief that "China must be stockpiling her crude oil in massive amounts."[12] Some crude petroleum may have been stockpiled for military purposes, but it is unlikely that this represents a significant proportion of crude oil output. China, after all, has probably not developed its underground crude oil storage technology beyond that of the United States, which would be happy to find a way of conveniently storing a few million tons of oil against the event of a new Middle East oil embargo. In any case, there is nothing in refinery capacity and output statistics that would lead us to suspect that the PRC has been unable to handle its new abundance of crude petroleum and must therefore store 10–15 million tons per year.[13]

Estimated Refined Petroleum Products Mix

Very little can be said on behalf of the breakdown of refined petroleum products presented in Table 17.5. Not a scrap of data exists in the Chinese press regarding the petroleum products mix other than scattered pieces of information on single refineries. Some data could possibly be collected by screening the notes of foreign visitors to China's major refineries. But even the venerable CIA avoids making a detailed estimate in this area. Table 15.5 demonstrates that previous estimates of the refined products mix in the foreign literature are way out of line with

TABLE 17.5
*Secondary Energy Production: Estimated Refined Petroleum
Product Mix, 1950–78*
(Million metric tons)

Year	Gasoline	Kerosene	Diesel	Residual	Lubricants	Other
1949	0.02	0.01	0.03	0.06	0.001	0.02
1950	0.05	0.03	0.06	0.1	0.003	0.04
1951	0.05	0.04	0.07	0.1	0.004	0.05
1952	0.08	0.05	0.1	0.2	0.005	0.07
1953	0.1	0.07	0.1	0.3	0.007	0.09
1954	0.1	0.09	0.2	0.4	0.009	0.1
1955	0.2	0.1	0.3	0.5	0.01	0.2
1956	0.2	0.1	0.3	0.6	0.01	0.2
1957	0.3	0.2	0.3	0.7	0.02	0.2
1958	0.4	0.3	0.6	1.1	0.03	0.4
1959	0.6	0.4	0.8	1.7	0.04	0.6
1960	0.8	0.5	1.1	2.2	0.05	0.8
1961	0.7	0.5	1.0	2.0	0.05	0.7
1962	0.8	0.6	1.1	2.2	0.06	0.8
1963	0.9	0.6	1.2	2.4	0.06	0.8
1964	1.2	0.8	1.6	3.2	0.08	1.1
1965	1.5	1.0	1.9	3.9	0.1	1.4
1966	1.8	1.2	2.4	4.9	0.1	1.7
1967	1.8	1.2	2.4	4.8	0.1	1.7
1968	1.9	1.3	2.6	5.2	0.1	1.8
1969	2.6	1.8	3.5	7.0	0.2	2.5
1970	3.7	2.5	4.9	9.8	0.2	3.4
1971	4.7	3.1	6.2	12.5	0.3	4.4
1972	5.4	3.6	7.2	14.5	0.4	5.1
1973	6.8	4.6	9.1	18.2	0.5	6.4
1974	7.9	5.2	10.5	21.0	0.5	7.3
1975	8.2	5.5	11.0	21.9	0.5	7.7
1976	9.7	6.5	13.0	25.9	0.6	9.1
1977	10.5	7.0	13.9	27.9	0.7	9.8
1978	11.6	7.8	15.5	31.1	0.8	10.9

world averages, and usually skewed in the wrong direction—i.e. toward overestimation of the distillates. Table 17.5 was generated directly from Table 15.5 and total annual refinery output, through the use of fixed percentages for the output of each refinery product. The "other" category includes petrochemical feedstock and wax, as well as asphalt, petroleum coke, nonlubricating oils, and bituminous mixtures of various kinds. It is obvious that the proportion of different petroleum products has shifted in the refinery mix since the early 1950's. These statistics, therefore, must be taken as order-of-magnitude guesses rather than as defined estimates.

Estimated Plant Use of Energy in Energy Production

An inferential series for plant use of energy was constructed using fixed-percent plant-use requirements for each fuel. (See Table 17.6.) Energy

TABLE 17.6
Estimated Plant Use of Energy in Energy Production, 1949–78

Year	Coal (mmtce)	Petroleum (mmt)	Natural gas (billion cu m)	Electric power (billion kwh)	Total (mmtce)
1949	0.6	0.008	0.003	0.2	0.6
1950	0.8	0.02	0.003	0.2	0.9
1951	1.0	0.02	0.003	0.3	1.1
1952	1.2	0.03	0.004	0.4	1.3
1953	1.3	0.03	0.005	0.5	1.4
1954	1.6	0.05	0.01	0.6	1.7
1955	1.8	0.07	0.02	0.6	2.0
1956	2.1	0.08	0.02	0.8	2.3
1957	2.5	0.09	0.03	1.0	2.8
1958	4.3	0.1	0.05	1.4	4.8
1959	5.6	0.2	0.07	2.1	6.3
1960	5.3	0.3	0.1	2.4	6.1
1961	3.5	0.3	0.2	1.6	4.2
1962	3.8	0.3	0.3	1.5	4.7
1963	3.9	0.3	0.3	1.7	5.0
1964	4.1	0.4	0.4	1.8	5.5
1965	4.5	0.5	0.5	2.1	6.2
1966	5.1	0.7	0.6	2.5	7.2
1967	3.9	0.7	0.5	2.3	5.9
1968	4.2	0.8	0.8	2.5	6.6
1969	5.3	1.0	0.9	3.0	8.3
1970	6.3	1.4	1.0	3.6	10.3
1971	6.8	1.8	1.2	4.3	11.6
1972	7.3	2.1	1.3	4.7	12.8
1973	7.7	2.7	1.4	5.1	14.1
1974	7.8	3.1	1.4	5.4	14.9
1975	9.0	3.2	1.7	6.1	16.8
1976	8.4	3.8	1.9	6.5	17.3
1977	9.4	4.1	2.4	7.1	19.4
1978	11.3	4.5	2.7	8.0	22.5

plants—coal mines, oilfields, refineries, electric power plants, etc.—use energy just like any other industry. The plant use of energy could be thought of as built-in inefficiency. The energy used in energy production is included in total energy production data but not in statistics for energy end-use or consumption. Plant use requirements for China's energy industries were calculated at 2.5 percent of total output for the coal industry and 5 percent of total output for the petroleum, natural gas, and electric power industries. The 5 percent plant use for electric power production is in addition to thermal inefficiencies and transmission losses, and refers to the use of electric power within the power plants themselves. The plant use percentages for the various energy industries were general estimates based on experience in other countries and on previous analysis of the Chinese energy industries by other foreign specialists.[14] The result was an order-of-magnitude estimate that Chinese energy industries consumed about 15–20 million metric tons coal equivalent of energy in various production processes in the mid-1970's. Inferred plant use requirements were subtracted from consumption statistics for each fuel and thereby from aggregate and per capita energy consumption estimates (Chapter 18).

Non-Energy Use of Hydrocarbons

The use of hydrocarbons as petrochemical feedstock should not technically be included in energy consumption statistics. Coal, oil, and gas are typically used in plants of various sizes in China to fix nitrogen in the form of ammonia. Coal is used as a feedstock in small plants at the commune or county level throughout the PRC. Naphtha and natural gas are used in much larger fertilizer plants located near major cities or associated with particular oil refineries. (See Table 17.7.) Peking's agricultural planners have encouraged both small-scale fertilizer production and large-scale production in central plants. China still lacks sufficient chemical-fertilizer production facilities and annually imports large quantities of fertilizer from Japan and other countries. Even with substantial imports of both nitrogen and phosphate fertilizers, however, the PRC still lags behind world standards in the per acre use of chemical fertilizers.[15] The PRC imported a number of complete ammonia and urea plants in the mid-1970's in an effort to ease the fertilizer shortage (Table 22.3). The new imported fertilizer plants have caused rapid growth in chemical fertilizer output since 1976.[16] In addition, nonfertilizer petrochemical plants for the production of plastics, chemical fibers, synthetic rubber, and other chemical products have also been imported on a large scale since 1972 (Table 22.2). The new petrochemical plants have usually

TABLE 17.7

*Estimated Hydrocarbons Used in the Production of
Petrochemicals and Fertilizers, 1949–78*

Year	Coal (mmtce)	Petroleum (mmt)	Natural gas (billion cu m)	Total hydrocarbons (mmtce)
1949	0.6	0.008	0.005	0.6
1950	0.8	0.02	0.005	0.8
1951	1.0	0.02	0.006	1.0
1952	1.2	0.03	0.008	1.3
1953	1.3	0.03	0.01	1.4
1954	1.6	0.05	0.02	1.7
1955	1.8	0.07	0.03	2.0
1956	2.1	0.08	0.04	2.2
1957	2.5	0.09	0.06	2.7
1958	4.3	0.1	0.09	4.6
1959	5.6	0.2	0.1	6.1
1960	5.3	0.3	0.2	5.9
1961	3.5	0.3	0.3	4.3
1962	3.8	0.3	0.5	4.8
1963	3.9	0.3	0.6	5.2
1964	4.1	0.4	0.7	5.7
1965	4.5	0.5	0.9	6.5
1966	5.1	0.7	1.2	7.7
1967	3.9	0.7	1.0	6.3
1968	4.2	0.8	1.5	7.3
1969	5.3	1.0	1.8	9.2
1970	6.3	1.4	2.1	11.2
1971	6.8	1.8	2.4	12.7
1972	7.3	2.1	2.7	14.0
1973	7.7	2.7	2.8	15.3
1974	7.8	3.1	2.9	16.2
1975	9.0	3.2	3.5	18.4
1976	8.4	3.8	3.8	19.0
1977	9.4	4.1	4.7	21.6
1978	11.3	4.5	5.4	25.1

been attached to existing petroleum refineries and have caused rapid growth in the output of various petrochemical products. National production of chemical fibers, for example, was reported to have doubled in the first six months of 1978.[17] The production of chemical fertilizer and petrochemicals should be expected to continue rising sharply into the 1980's as more new plants begin production.

As with plant use estimates, non-energy use of hydrocarbons was estimated inferentially, using fixed percentages of total production for each fossil fuel. Petrochemical use of coal (including fertilizer production) was estimated at 2.5 percent of total output. Petrochemical use of petroleum and natural gas was set at 5 percent each. The petrochemical-use statistics do not include energy used in production of petrochemicals and fertilizers. For example, the typical fertilizer plant uses as much fuel oil as naphtha in the production of ammonia. The fuel oil would be counted as energy consumption, while the naphtha would be counted as non-energy use of hydrocarbons. These rough estimates are consistent with the known size of the Chinese fertilizer industry (Chapter 15), but should be taken as order-of-magnitude estimates, since no data are available on the precise production of petrochemical feedstocks. The net result of these estimates is that China was using about 20 million metric tons coal equivalent per year of hydrocarbon output for petrochemical and fertilizer feedstocks by 1976–77. Petrochemical use of the three fossil fuels was subtracted from aggregate and per capita energy consumption statistics (Chapter 18).

Chapter 18

Aggregate Energy Consumption

"Energy consumption" is a surprisingly ambiguous term. Is energy "consumed" when oil leaves the ground or when it is pumped into gasoline tanks or when it is actually burned in internal-combustion engines? The dilemma is that the further down the energy stream one travels, the more diffuse it becomes, complicating the already difficult problems of estimation. The simplest definition of energy consumption is "inland consumption," a term used in statistics published by the United Nations and by other sources. "Inland consumption" refers to production plus net imports minus bunkers.[1] It is a crude but convenient way of estimating energy consumption which ignores inefficiencies, losses, non-energy use of hydrocarbons, and the transformation of one form of energy into another. "Inland consumption" therefore creates a serious upward bias in energy consumption statistics.

This study has made an effort to move "downstream" toward actual energy end-use in tabulation of energy consumption statistics. There is no way to collect data on energy end-use in various sectors of the Chinese economy. An approximation of end-use statistics, however, can be generated by inference from energy production, trade, and processing data. The energy consumption statistics presented in Tables 18.1–18.8 could be thought of as net domestic energy production minus transformation inefficiencies and non-energy use of hydrocarbons plus net energy commodity imports (minus net exports). There are still a number of transport and use inefficiencies that have not been eliminated from these statistics. But gross losses, such as the Carnot cycle in thermal power generation, have been subtracted.

Energy consumption statistics were provided in the original units for each fuel, in coal equivalents, in gigajoules, and in barrels of oil equivalent for the convenience of users working in different systems. (See Tables 18.2–18.4.) Note that coal consumption statistics are always presented in tons of standard coal, not in tons of raw coal, and are not, therefore, directly comparable to coal production data. The conversion factors for different fuels were identical to those used for energy production statistics. This may slightly skew petroleum consumption statis-

TABLE 18.1
Aggregate Energy Consumption in Original Units, 1949–78

Year	Coal (mmtce)	Petroleum (mmt)	Natural gas (billion cu m)	Electric power (billion kwh)
1949	19.0	0.3	0.04	2.9
1950	25.0	0.5	0.04	3.5
1951	32.1	1.0	0.05	4.6
1952	40.1	1.0	0.07	6.0
1953	41.0	1.4	0.09	7.7
1954	49.4	1.6	0.2	9.3
1955	58.2	2.5	0.3	10.5
1956	64.1	2.8	0.3	13.3
1957	76.5	3.1	0.5	16.5
1958	133.4	4.6	0.8	24.4
1959	166.9	6.5	1.2	36.6
1960	141.4	7.8	1.7	40.9
1961	108.7	8.0	2.6	27.0
1962	118.6	7.4	4.3	26.1
1963	123.4	7.5	5.1	28.8
1964	127.9	8.5	6.0	31.5
1965	138.4	9.9	7.8	36.8
1966	154.0	12.1	10.2	43.9
1967	117.2	11.8	8.5	39.5
1968	125.5	13.1	12.8	43.9
1969	160.5	17.6	15.3	52.7
1970	193.3	24.5	17.6	63.3
1971	203.3	31.5	20.0	75.8
1972	216.3	36.6	22.9	82.1
1973	228.1	45.6	23.5	89.2
1974	234.4	52.1	24.6	95.4
1975	274.8	54.0	29.4	106.9
1976	256.9	63.9	32.2	114.0
1977	285.0	68.5	40.2	124.5
1978	344.9	76.2	45.9	141.4

Note that aggregate consumption has been defined here as aggregate energy end use, and excludes waste, conversion inefficiencies, petrochemical use, plant use, etc. Fossil fuels used to generate electric power in thermal power plants have been subtracted from coal and petroleum consumption figures. Electric power consumption includes both hydropower and thermal power.

TABLE 18.2
Aggregate Energy Consumption in Million Metric Tons Coal Equivalent,
1949–78

Year	Coal	Petroleum	Natural gas	Electric power	Total
1949	19.0	0.4	0.06	0.4	19.8
1950	25.0	0.7	0.06	0.4	26.1
1951	32.1	1.5	0.07	0.6	34.1
1952	40.1	1.5	0.09	0.7	42.4
1953	41.0	2.1	0.1	0.9	44.1
1954	49.4	2.4	0.2	1.1	53.2
1955	58.2	3.6	0.3	1.3	63.4
1956	64.1	4.1	0.5	1.6	70.4
1957	76.5	4.6	0.7	2.0	83.8
1958	133.4	6.8	1.0	3.0	144.2
1959	166.9	9.6	1.6	4.5	182.6
1960	141.4	11.5	2.3	5.0	160.2
1961	108.7	11.7	3.4	3.3	127.1
1962	118.6	10.9	5.7	3.2	138.4
1963	123.4	11.0	6.8	3.5	144.8
1964	127.9	12.5	7.9	3.9	152.2
1965	138.4	14.5	10.4	4.5	167.9
1966	154.0	17.8	13.6	5.4	190.7
1967	117.2	17.4	11.3	4.9	150.8
1968	125.5	19.2	17.0	5.4	167.1
1969	160.5	25.8	20.4	6.5	213.2
1970	193.3	36.1	23.4	7.8	260.6
1971	203.3	46.3	26.6	9.3	285.5
1972	216.3	53.8	30.5	10.1	310.7
1973	228.1	67.0	31.2	11.0	337.3
1974	234.4	76.5	32.7	11.7	355.4
1975	274.8	79.4	39.1	13.1	406.5
1976	256.9	93.9	42.9	14.0	407.8
1977	285.0	100.7	53.6	15.3	454.6
1978	344.9	112.0	61.1	17.4	535.4

tics, since the sum of the calorific value of all refined petroleum products is not identical to the calorific value of crude oil and varies with the petroleum product mix. But the impact of this inaccuracy is marginal compared to other sources of error.

China's precise rank as an aggregate energy consumer is difficult to establish because of the difference between energy end-use consumption statistics and "inland consumption." By 1973, the PRC probably ranked third in the world in aggregate energy consumption, behind the

TABLE 18.3

Aggregate Energy Consumption in Million Gigajoules, 1949–78

Year	Coal	Petroleum	Natural gas	Electric power	Total
1949	547.9	11.1	1.6	10.3	570.9
1950	718.7	20.1	1.6	12.5	752.9
1951	923.1	43.9	2.0	16.4	985.4
1952	1,153.7	44.0	2.6	21.5	1,221.9
1953	1,180.3	61.5	3.3	27.7	1,272.7
1954	1,421.6	71.2	6.5	33.5	1,532.8
1955	1,675.0	107.3	9.8	37.7	1,829.9
1956	1,847.1	121.9	13.1	47.8	2,029.7
1957	2,202.1	136.1	19.6	59.6	2,417.3
1958	3,843.1	199.4	29.4	87.9	4,159.8
1959	4,808.1	282.8	45.7	131.6	5,268.2
1960	4,071.8	339.2	65.3	147.3	4,623.5
1961	3,130.7	344.0	97.9	97.1	3,669.8
1962	3,417.0	319.6	163.2	94.0	3,993.9
1963	3,553.5	324.7	195.8	103.6	4,177.7
1964	3,683.9	368.5	228.5	113.3	4,394.2
1965	3,986.9	426.2	300.3	132.5	4,845.8
1966	4,433.9	523.5	391.7	158.0	5,507.1
1967	3,375.9	510.6	326.4	142.2	4,355.0
1968	3,614.7	565.3	489.6	158.0	4,827.6
1969	4,622.6	760.2	587.5	189.6	6,160.0
1970	5,567.0	1,060.8	675.6	228.0	7,531.5
1971	5,854.7	1,362.8	767.0	273.0	8,257.4
1972	6,228.9	1,583.8	878.0	295.5	8,986.2
1973	6,568.4	1,970.9	900.9	321.2	9,761.4
1974	6,750.9	2,251.5	943.3	343.5	10,289.3
1975	7,913.3	2,334.8	1,129.3	384.9	11,762.3
1976	7,400.1	2,762.3	1,237.1	410.3	11,809.7
1977	8,208.3	2,963.4	1,543.9	448.5	13,164.0
1978	9,933.0	3,294.4	1,762.6	508.9	15,498.9

United States and the Soviet Union, but almost identical to Japan at about 425 million metric tons coal equivalent (inland consumption).[2] China's energy parity with Japan is important to the development of energy trade relations between the two countries. Aggregate energy consumption correlates closely with GNP, across all countries for any year and through time for any country. Thus, aggregate energy consumption is a partial measure of growth and political power in the international arena. China's strength in energy resources is neatly balanced by Japan's strength in energy technology. This makes them equal but differentiated energy trade partners.

TABLE 18.4
Aggregate Energy Consumption in Million Barrels Oil Equivalent,
1949-78

Year	Coal	Petroleum	Natural gas	Electric power	Total
1949	93.2	1.9	0.3	1.7	97.1
1950	122.3	3.4	0.3	2.1	128.0
1951	157.1	7.4	0.3	2.7	167.5
1952	196.3	7.4	0.4	3.6	207.8
1953	200.8	10.4	0.6	4.6	216.4
1954	241.9	12.0	1.1	5.6	260.6
1955	285.0	18.1	1.7	6.3	311.1
1956	314.3	20.6	2.2	8.0	345.0
1957	374.7	23.0	3.4	9.9	410.9
1958	653.9	33.7	5.0	14.7	707.2
1959	818.0	47.7	7.9	21.9	895.6
1960	692.8	57.3	11.2	24.5	785.8
1961	532.6	58.1	16.8	16.2	623.7
1962	581.4	54.0	28.1	15.7	679.0
1963	604.6	54.8	33.7	17.3	710.3
1964	626.8	62.2	39.3	18.9	747.1
1965	678.3	72.0	51.6	22.1	824.0
1966	754.4	88.4	67.3	26.3	936.4
1967	574.4	86.2	56.1	23.7	740.4
1968	615.0	95.4	84.2	26.3	820.9
1969	786.5	128.3	101.0	31.6	1,047.4
1970	947.2	179.1	116.1	38.0	1,280.4
1971	996.1	230.1	131.8	45.5	1,403.5
1972	1,059.8	267.4	150.9	49.2	1,527.3
1973	1,117.5	332.7	154.8	53.5	1,658.7
1974	1,148.6	380.1	162.1	57.3	1,748.1
1975	1,346.4	394.2	194.1	64.1	1,998.8
1976	1,259.0	466.3	212.6	68.4	2,006.4
1977	1,396.5	500.3	265.4	74.7	2,236.9
1978	1,690.0	556.2	302.9	84.8	2,633.9

It is beyond the scope of this study (and stretching the data in any case) to provide a detailed breakdown of energy consumption statistics by sector and fuel. A few scholars have attempted such a consumption analysis for China, with mixed results.[3] In general terms, industry and construction consumed about 60 percent of aggregate energy consumption in 1975, agriculture consumed 6 percent, transportation consumed 5 percent, and residential and commercial use of energy was about 29 percent.[4] China's energy economy is balanced heavily toward the industrial sector. The energy consumption requirement of the rural areas is understated by these figures, for two reasons. First, the statistics do not include the traditional agricultural fuels used commonly throughout the Chinese countryside. Second, rural household consumption is included under "residential and commercial." The rural areas of China actually consume at least 25 percent of China's commercial energy supplies and at least 40 percent of total energy supplies, including traditional fuels. Even so, considering the distribution of the population (70–80 percent rural), urban energy consumption is twice rural energy consumption on an average per capita basis. This is one of the main reasons for the large disparity in living standards between the cities and the countryside. Even energy consumption by urban industry further skews the energy consumption pattern in favor of the cities. Industrial occupations are less labor-intensive and more energy-intensive than agricultural occupations. Urban residents also have first chance at consumer products manufactured in energy-intensive industries. In China, industries themselves often generate electricity or manufactured gas that is distributed to worker settlements in the immediate vicinity. Urban dwellers have a much higher home use of commercial energy than do residents of rural villages. They also have access to public transportation. Peking's current emphasis on mechanization of the countryside through the introduction of small farm machinery such as walking tractors, treshing machines, and irrigation pumps may help to redress the urban-rural energy consumption balance a bit, but we should expect the general disparity to continue for some time to come.

Aggregate Energy Consumption Growth Rates

China's aggregate energy consumption has advanced at a respectable pace since 1949, growing at an average annual rate of 11 percent. (See Table 18.5.) Growth was far greater each year during the 1950's (19 percent) than during the 1960's (5 percent) or after 1970 (9 percent). The aggregate energy consumption growth rate will probably be 5–10 percent per year for the remainder of the century, higher than the sluggish pace of the 1960's, but lower than the takeoff growth rates of the 1950's. Petroleum consumption led all other fuels in its growth rate since 1950 (18 percent per year). Petroleum consumption has grown faster (14 percent per annum) than natural gas (12 percent) since 1970, but in general the two industries move in tandem. Coal consumption grew at just 3 percent per year in the 1960's, but has recovered to 7 percent since 1971. Coal consumption is constrained by saturation of the domestic market, as well as by the usual capital cost of further expansion.

TABLE 18.5
Annual Percent Increase in Energy Consumption, 1950–78

Year	Coal	Petroleum	Natural Gas	Electric power	Total
1950	31.2%	81.0%	0.0%	21.4%	31.9%
1951	28.4	118.5	20.0	31.4	30.8
1952	25.0	0.3	33.3	31.5	24.0
1953	2.3	39.7	25.0	28.4	4.1
1954	20.4	15.8	100.0	21.2	20.4
1955	17.8	50.8	50.0	12.5	19.4
1956	10.3	13.5	33.3	26.6	10.9
1957	19.2	11.7	50.0	24.7	19.1
1958	74.5	46.6	50.0	47.6	72.1
1959	25.1	41.8	55.6	49.7	26.6
1960	-15.3	19.9	42.9	11.9	-12.3
1961	-23.1	1.4	50.0	-34.0	-20.7
1962	9.1	-7.1	66.7	-3.2	8.9
1963	4.0	1.6	20.0	10.2	4.6
1964	3.7	13.5	16.7	9.3	5.2
1965	8.2	15.6	31.4	16.9	10.3
1966	11.2	22.8	30.4	19.3	13.6
1967	-23.9	-2.5	-16.7	-10.0	-21.0
1968	7.1	10.7	50.0	11.1	10.8
1969	27.9	34.5	20.0	20.0	27.6
1970	20.4	39.6	15.0	20.3	22.2
1971	5.2	28.5	13.5	19.7	9.6
1972	6.4	16.2	14.5	8.3	8.8
1973	5.5	24.4	2.6	8.7	8.6
1974	2.8	14.2	4.7	6.9	5.4
1975	17.2	3.7	19.7	12.0	14.4
1976	-6.5	18.3	9.5	6.6	0.3
1977	10.9	7.3	24.8	9.3	11.5
1978	21.0	11.2	14.2	13.5	17.8

Considering the importance of the electric power industry for industrial growth, the electric power industry has not done unusually well. Initially very high (24 percent per year) from 1949 to 1960, the growth rate for total electric power consumption from 1960 to 1978 averaged 10.2 percent per year, above the growth rate for aggregate energy consumption (6.7 percent) during the same period. Industrialized societies with large-scale electric power industries commonly experience 7 percent electric power consumption growth rates. Electric power consumption in the Third World is growing at an average rate of 10 percent per year.

China's total industrial production grew at 11 percent from 1961 through 1974, above the growth rates for electric power during the same period.[5] By 1975, many Chinese industries may have faced electric power shortages. If allowed to persist, such shortages could slow the entire pace of industrialization. China's electric power consumption is already skewed heavily toward industrial use, at the expense of rural and household consumption and other uses.*

It comes as no surprise, therefore, that the electric power industry has high priority in Peking's economic planning through 1985. An electric power consumption growth rate in excess of 10 percent per year through the year 2000 would be required to supply the burgeoning power needs of China's rapid industrial growth while maintaining steady increases in household consumption and rural electrification. Both hydropower capacity and thermal power capacity must grow rapidly to meet these new demands for electric power in all sectors of the Chinese economy. Hydro will be the base for rural electrification, whereas thermal, faster to install and more flexible in location, will be important in industrial and urban electric power supplies. Growth in the electric power industry may outstrip even the oil and gas industries for the next two decades. Given the needs of China's continued growth, a high level of investment and equipment manufacture in the electric power industry could drain off needed capital resources from other energy industries and shift the overall energy balance. The PRC is as likely to be an "electric power giant" as an "oil giant" by the turn of the century.

The People's Republic of China has been well over 95 percent self-sufficient in energy supplies since its establishment in 1949. Even during the period of highest petroleum imports from the Soviet Union and a slump in domestic energy production (1961), imports accounted for less than 4 percent of aggregate energy consumption (Chapter 21). Imports averaged about 50 percent of liquid fuel consumption from 1950 to 1960, making China heavily dependent on Soviet petroleum products within the framework of overall energy self-sufficiency (Table 21.2). There were certain periods during which self-reliance was not easy, from an energy consumption standpoint. Energy consumption lagged seriously in the early 1960's, following the Sino-Soviet break. This was due not only to the loss of direct petroleum imports, but also to disruption of development planning and construction in the domestic energy industries. From 1961 through 1965 or so, China had an "energy crisis" of its own. The shortages were sharply felt in petroleum supplies, forc-

---

*These electric power growth rates are based on official data released in mid-1979 and are slightly different than reported in Table 10.4.

ing emergency measures such as curtailment of industrial use, substitution in transport, and austerity programs of all sorts. Coal shortages were also severe, compounding the substitution problem. This Chinese energy crisis contributed to an industrial recession and may have been instrumental in precipitating the political upheavals of the Cultural Revolution. It may also help explain the bitterness of Chinese resentment of Soviet "sabotage" of their economic system, a bitterness that was turned against some domestic political figures for their cooperation with earlier Soviet assistance programs.

When China became a net energy exporter in 1973, self-reliance continued to be the foundation of Peking's international energy policy. In 1975, a peak year of petroleum exports, the PRC exported only 3 percent of total energy production, equaling just 4 percent of domestic aggregate energy consumption. (Indonesia, by contrast, exported 75 percent of total energy production in 1975, more than three times the amount of energy consumed within the country itself.[6] Both Indonesia and China produced 74 million tons of crude petroleum in 1975.) Even if Peking expands exports at the maximum feasible rate, net energy exports will peak at under 10 percent of total energy production sometime in the late 1980's. The PRC will never export more than 10–15 percent of the amount of energy that is consumed within the country. At a root level, the self-sufficient character of the Chinese energy economy is based on the energy needs of a large population undergoing rapid modernization. But self-reliance is also a matter of deliberate policy choice. Peking could, after all, have settled for energy development in a few major cities and simply exported the balance of its new oil wealth. That pattern is not uncommon among Third World energy-exporting countries. But as long as there is a deliberate choice to meet the needs of China's domestic growth first and its foreign exchange needs second, the self-reliance policy will continue to be sound and energy exports will be held to a small proportion of domestic energy production and consumption.

Aggregate Energy Consumption Mix

A glance at the aggregate energy consumption mix statistics establishes several features of the Chinese energy balance (Table 18.6). Clearly that balance is still characterized by heavy reliance on the burning of lump coal. Even after subtracting coal used for exports, coke, petrochemical feedstock, plant use in coal mines, and thermal electric power generation, the direct consumption of lump coal amounts to roughly 60 percent of the Chinese energy balance. This again points to a market ceiling on the consumption of lump coal within the PRC and indicates that fu-

TABLE 18.6
Aggregate Energy Consumption Mix, 1949–78
(Percent of Aggregate Energy Consumption)

Year	Coal	Petroleum	Natural gas	Electric power
1949	96.0%	1.9%	0.3%	1.8%
1950	95.5	2.6	0.2	1.6
1951	93.8	4.4	0.2	1.6
1952	94.5	3.5	0.2	1.7
1953	92.9	4.7	0.3	2.1
1954	92.9	4.6	0.4	2.2
1955	91.7	5.8	0.5	2.0
1956	91.1	5.9	0.6	2.3
1957	91.2	5.5	0.8	2.4
1958	92.5	4.7	0.7	2.1
1959	91.4	5.3	0.9	2.5
1960	88.2	7.2	1.4	3.1
1961	85.5	9.2	2.7	2.6
1962	85.7	7.9	4.1	2.3
1963	85.2	7.6	4.7	2.4
1964	84.0	8.2	5.2	2.5
1965	82.5	8.6	6.2	2.7
1966	80.7	9.3	7.1	2.8
1967	77.8	11.5	7.5	3.2
1968	75.1	11.5	10.2	3.2
1969	75.3	12.1	9.6	3.0
1970	74.2	13.8	9.0	3.0
1971	71.2	16.2	9.3	3.3
1972	69.6	17.3	9.8	3.2
1973	67.6	19.9	9.3	3.3
1974	66.0	21.5	9.2	3.3
1975	67.6	19.5	9.6	3.2
1976	63.0	23.0	10.5	3.4
1977	62.7	22.2	11.8	3.4
1978	64.4	20.9	11.4	3.2

ture consumption patterns will move away from solid fuels in relative but not absolute terms. Petroleum and natural gas are still increasing their contribution to energy consumption, but more slowly than a decade ago. The percent contribution of electric power to the energy consumption mix confirms what was said in the last section regarding the pace of development of electric power relative to the energy balance as a whole. Peking has been unable to move the contribution of electric power up from 3–4 percent of aggregate energy consumption since 1960. This contrasts sharply with average world electric power consumption statistics. In 1975, 10 percent of world energy consumption was in the form of electric power, using the output conversion ratio (0.123 kgce/kwh).[7] Electric power contributed 9 percent to Third World energy consumption, 12 percent to the energy consumption of the industrial countries, indicating that the importance of electricity in the energy balance usually increases as industrialization proceeds. Electric power contributes 8 percent to India's energy balance, a country with just one-third China's aggregate energy consumption. Japan's electric power industry contributed 15 percent of aggregate energy consumption. These figures establish that if China is relatively energy-rich, it is relatively electricity-poor. Current demands on China's electric power supply must be heavy indeed, and the electric power industry will require large equipment, labor, and capital imports in the near future.

Estimated Consumption of Petroleum Products

Estimated consumption of the various petroleum products listed in Table 18.7 was based on domestic production plus net imports of these commodities (Tables 17.5, 21.3, and 21.4). The statistics are only valid to an order of magnitude because of uncertainties in the estimates of the petroleum products mix.

Despite rapid development of the petroleum industry in China, the absolute level of petroleum products consumption remains very low for each product. On a per capita basis, access to petroleum products is microscopic. In 1975, if all the gasoline produced in the country had been distributed equally (it was not), an average Chinese citizen would have had access to about 3–4 gallons of gasoline, enough to ride 50–75 miles by car or 300 miles by public transport. That is about one-third the average per capita consumption of gasoline in the Third World and is nowhere near world standards (50 gallons per capita).

This simple observation demonstrates that the Chinese energy economy will look quite different from the energy economies of other countries, if for no other reason than because of the already staggering size of China's population. Private automobiles are obviously out. Only strict conservation and careful distribution will bring the Chinese energy consumer anywhere near the levels of comfort and convenience now prevalent in the West, even after another 20 years of vigorous energy development.

TABLE 18.7
Estimated Consumption of Petroleum Products, 1949–78
(Million metric tons)

Year	Gasoline	Kerosene	Diesel	Residual	Lubricants	Other
1949	0.07	0.01	0.08	0.06	0.001	0.03
1950	0.1	0.03	0.1	0.1	0.003	0.05
1951	0.3	0.1	0.3	0.1	0.05	0.05
1952	0.3	0.1	0.3	0.2	0.06	0.08
1953	0.4	0.3	0.3	0.3	0.06	0.1
1954	0.4	0.3	0.4	0.4	0.06	0.1
1955	0.8	0.4	0.5	0.5	0.08	0.2
1956	0.9	0.4	0.7	0.6	0.09	0.2
1957	0.8	0.5	0.7	0.7	0.1	0.2
1958	1.1	0.6	1.2	1.1	0.2	0.4
1959	1.9	0.8	1.4	1.7	0.3	0.6
1960	1.9	0.9	1.8	2.2	0.3	0.8
1961	2.1	1.0	1.8	2.0	0.3	0.7
1962	1.6	1.0	1.5	2.2	0.3	0.8
1963	1.4	1.1	1.5	2.4	0.2	0.9
1964	1.5	0.9	1.7	3.2	0.1	1.2
1965	1.5	1.0	2.0	4.0	0.1	1.3
1966	1.9	1.2	2.4	4.9	0.1	1.6
1967	1.8	1.2	2.4	4.8	0.1	1.6
1968	1.9	1.3	2.7	5.2	0.1	1.8
1969	2.6	1.8	3.5	7.0	0.1	2.5
1970	3.7	2.5	4.9	9.9	0.2	3.4
1971	4.7	3.1	6.5	12.6	0.3	4.4
1972	5.4	3.6	7.6	14.5	0.3	5.1
1973	6.8	4.5	9.1	18.3	0.4	6.4
1974	7.8	5.0	10.4	20.9	0.5	7.3
1975	8.1	5.0	10.8	21.9	0.5	7.7
1976	9.6	6.0	12.8	25.9	0.5	9.1
1977	10.3	6.3	13.7	27.9	0.6	9.7
1978	11.4	6.9	15.3	31.0	0.7	0.9

Inland Energy Consumption

In order to facilitate comparisons of energy consumption statistics for China with those of other countries, I have provided a statistical series for inland energy consumption (see Table 18.8). These statistics have not been used anywhere in the text and are only provided for the convenience of the reader who is attempting comparisons between my China data and standard international energy data collections. In my own comparisons

TABLE 18.8
Inland Energy Consumption, 1949–78

Year	Coal (mmtce)	Petroleum (mmt)	Natural gas (billion cu m)	Electric power[a] (billion kwh)	Total[b] (mmtce)
1949	24.3	0.3	0.05	4.3	24.8
1950	31.6	0.5	0.05	4.6	32.5
1951	39.8	1.0	0.06	5.8	41.5
1952	49.9	1.0	0.08	7.3	51.7
1953	52.1	1.5	0.1	9.2	54.6
1954	62.7	1.7	0.2	11.0	65.7
1955	73.1	2.5	0.3	12.3	77.5
1956	81.6	2.9	0.4	15.6	86.8
1957	97.1	3.2	0.6	19.3	103.2
1958	171.8	4.8	0.9	28.0	180.7
1959	224.5	6.8	1.4	42.0	237.3
1960	209.5	8.1	2.0	47.0	225.2
1961	138.5	8.2	3.0	31.0	155.6
1962	149.4	7.7	5.0	30.0	168.1
1963	157.0	7.9	6.0	33.0	177.4
1964	164.3	9.3	7.0	36.0	188.2
1965	179.0	11.0	9.2	42.0	208.5
1966	201.2	13.8	12.0	50.0	238.6
1967	155.8	13.6	10.0	45.0	190.3
1968	168.1	15.3	15.0	50.0	212.0
1969	209.6	20.6	18.0	60.0	265.6
1970	253.0	28.6	20.7	72.0	324.8
1971	273.3	36.9	23.5	86.0	361.4
1972	291.4	42.9	26.9	93.0	393.2
1973	307.9	53.1	27.6	101.0	425.9
1974	312.3	60.7	28.9	108.0	443.3
1975	359.5	63.9	34.6	121.0	503.2
1976	337.2	74.5	37.9	129.0	501.2
1977	374.5	79.9	47.3	141.0	559.4
1978	449.6	88.9	54.0	160.0	657.1

Note: Inland energy consumption is defined as production plus net imports.
[a] Including hydro and thermal electricity.
[b] Including hydro, but not thermal electric power.

(Chapter 10), I prefer to use some approximation of final energy use rather than inland consumption. But this does create an uncomfortable discontinuity with the United Nations data for energy consumption in other countries and regions. In addition, my per capita energy consumption statistics are based on energy end-use, not inland consumption.

Inland energy consumption is formally defined as production plus net imports minus bunkers. In the Chinese case, there is no way to estimate bunkers (sales to international transport), so that inland consumption is simply equal to production plus net imports. This is an entirely meaningless concept in the Chinese case because of the close balance between energy production and energy consumption. Much more interesting problems are posed by the estimation of energy end-use in the PRC.

The reader should note that the columns in Table 18.8 are nonadditive. Each column is independently correct. However, the column for electric power consumption includes thermal power generation, whereas the column for total inland energy consumption excludes electricity generated at thermal power stations. Inland consumption of hydropower in China is equal to hydropower production (Table 16.1).

Chapter 19

Per Capita Energy Consumption

From an energy perspective, per capita energy consumption statistics are among the most important results of an accurate analysis of China's energy balance. These statistics reveal fundamental characteristics of the Chinese energy system which help to explain past performance and to project China's future pace of energy development. Per capita energy consumption is a master key that unlocks both the door to an understanding of the Chinese energy life-style and the door to an understanding of the relationship between the energy system and the rest of the Chinese economy. In addition, some important characteristics of China's international energy policies may also be explained in terms of per capita energy consumption constraints.

Per capita energy consumption is defined as total fuel and power consumption (energy end-use) divided by the current population, yielding an average amount of commercial energy consumed by or theoretically available to each Chinese citizen. Distribution differentials, such as rural-urban differences and the concentration of energy use in the industrial sector, imply that most Chinese citizens do not "consume" the per capita quantity of energy assigned to them by these statistics. However, per capita energy consumption still reflects the average standard of living in any society and is sometimes used as a standard of comparison more reliable than per capita income, for cross-cultural comparisons. Per capita energy consumption is not subject to the vagaries of international monetary exchange rates, inflation, government fiscal policy, and so on. Therefore it provides a solid foundation for standard-of-living comparisons.

Per capita consumption statistics were calculated for each of the four fuels, plus total per capita fuel and power consumption. Although the terms "energy consumption," "fuel and power consumption," and "per capita end-use" are used interchangeably, the statistics were derived from aggregate energy consumption statistics in the last chapter. Per capita energy consumption as defined here is somewhat lower, therefore, than standard per capita energy consumption statistics used in most international compilations, which are based on "inland consumption" of energy. The per capita fuel and power statistics in Table 19.2 are estimates of energy end-use per capita, not inland consumption per capita. For example, China's 1975 inland per capita energy consumption was about 530 kilograms coal equivalent—22 percent higher than per capita energy end-use (435 kgce/capita). Per capita energy end-use figures were used throughout the study, including the regression analysis and the structure of the projection model (Chapter 23).

Population and Gross National Product

Gross National Product (GNP) was chosen as the basic indicator of economic growth. The author is aware of the greater accuracy of other measures of economic activity such as Industrial Product and Net National Product. However, in the Chinese case, the problems of estimation are such that a relatively simple indicator is more reliable. The U.S. Central Intelligence Agency provides annual estimates of China's GNP that are widely, but not universally, accepted by foreign analysts.[1] The CIA figures are relatively conservative and have therefore been adopted for purposes of this study. GNP data were used in the tabulation of per capita income, energy/GNP elasticities, and energy/GNP regression coefficients (Chapter 23). (See Table 19.1.)

Population data are also important for per capita energy consumption tabulations and for alternative projections of future energy end-use requirements. Growth in per capita energy consumption will be highly sensitive to variations in the Chinese birth rate over the next 20 years. In one sense, the most cost-effective investment that Peking could make in its energy infrastructure would be to increase production and dissemination of birth control devices. Peking is sensitive about the large size and continued growth of the Chinese population and publishes no national population data. Foreign evaluation of the size and various growth parameters of the Chinese population is an ongoing and fluid area of inquiry, not a hard demographic science. Dr. Judith Banister has recently prepared a new statistical evaluation of both historical and future growth patterns in the Chinese population.[2] Banister integrated a mass of fragmentary vital rates data available in the Chinese press and from foreign visitors to China into a composite analysis of population dynamics at the national, provincial, and local levels. The Banister series is close to, but more refined than, previous estimates by the U.S. Bureau of the Census and provides a better foundation for projections of China's future population dynamics.

TABLE 19.1

China's Population and Gross National Product, 1949-78

Year	Gross National Product[a]		Population[b]		Per Capita GNP	
	Billion dollars	Percent increase[c]	Million	Percent increase[c]	Dollars	Percent increase[c]
1949	49.0	—	538.0	—	91.1	—
1950	59.0	20.4%	547.0	1.7%	107.9	18.4%
1951	69.0	16.9	558.0	2.0	123.7	14.6
1952	82.0	18.8	570.0	2.2	143.9	16.3
1953	87.0	6.1	583.0	2.3	149.2	3.7
1954	91.0	4.6	595.0	2.1	152.9	2.5
1955	100.0	9.9	608.0	2.2	164.5	7.5
1956	108.0	8.0	623.0	2.5	173.4	5.4
1957	115.0	6.5	638.0	2.4	180.3	4.0
1958	137.0	19.1	654.0	2.5	209.5	16.2
1959	129.0	−5.8	672.0	2.8	192.0	−8.4
1960	129.0	0.0	687.0	2.2	187.8	−2.2
1961	99.0	−23.3	701.0	2.0	141.2	−24.8
1962	113.0	14.1	713.0	1.7	158.5	12.2
1963	125.0	10.6	727.0	2.0	171.9	8.5
1964	142.0	13.6	742.0	2.1	191.4	11.3
1965	163.0	14.8	759.0	2.3	214.8	12.2
1966	177.0	8.6	777.0	2.4	227.8	6.1
1967	172.0	−2.8	794.0	2.2	216.6	−4.9
1968	173.0	0.6	812.0	2.3	213.1	−1.6
1969	192.0	11.0	829.0	2.1	231.6	8.7
1970	219.0	14.1	847.0	2.2	258.6	11.6
1971	236.0	7.8	865.0	2.1	272.8	5.5
1972	246.0	4.2	883.0	2.1	278.6	2.1
1973	272.0	10.6	901.0	2.0	301.9	8.4
1974	283.0	4.0	919.0	2.0	307.9	2.0
1975	299.0	5.7	937.0	2.0	319.1	3.6
1976	310.0	3.7	956.0	2.0	324.3	1.6
1977	320.0	3.2	974.0	1.9	328.5	1.3
1978	340.0	6.3	992.0	1.8	342.7	4.3

[a]In 1975 U.S. dollars, from U.S. Central Intelligence Agency, *People's Republic of China: Handbook of Economic Indicators* (Washington, D.C., Aug. 1976), Table 2, p. 3. GNP figures for 1976-78 are the author's estimates.

[b]Midyear population figures (preferred series) from Judith Banister, "The Current Vital Rates and Population Size of the People's Republic of China and Its Provinces," Ph.D. dissertation (Stanford University, Food Research Institute, Sept. 1977), Table 4B, p. 521.

[c]Absolute annual percent increase over previous year.

Per Capita Energy Consumption by Fuel

China's population will cross the one billion mark in 1979 or 1980. In 1978, per capita energy consumption (end-use) in the PRC was about 500 kilograms coal equivalent—one-half ton of standard coal per person per year. These two facts are inextricably related. (See Tables 19.2 and 19.3.) Despite the enormous growth in the energy infrastructure since 1949, China is still a Third World country in terms of average per capita energy consumption standards. This confirms statistically what has been asserted throughout this book—that China has a "dual energy personality." China has the world's third largest energy system, but ranks with average Third World countries in terms of improved public access to energy commodities. China's 1975 per capita energy consumption (inland consumption equals 530 kgce/capita) compares closely with the average for the rest of Asia, but is double that for Asia excluding Japan.[3] The PRC started in 1949 somewhat behind the rest of Asia in per capita energy consumption. In the past three decades, China has been able to draw ahead of the rest of Asia in its energy living standard. China's 1975 per capita energy consumption was also 25–30 percent higher than the average level in the developing countries. But in 1975, China was still very much a Third World country, comparing closely to Zambia, Ecuador, Syria, or Malaysia in per capita energy life-style.

China would have to construct an energy production infrastructure of unprecedented size in order to provide its people with an energy lifestyle at the per capita level of the industrial countries. China's industrial neighbor Japan has seven times the per capita energy consumption. In order to achieve Japanese living standards, China would have to produce one and a half times more energy than current production levels in the United States. In order to achieve American per capita energy consumption standards, China would have to produce at five times current U.S. energy consumption levels. Since the most optimistic estimates of China's oil and gas resources are comparable to original in-place U.S. reserves, an energy system of the required order of magnitude would not be possible under current technology. Clearly the PRC must look in other directions for its energy development pattern.

The pattern of development in per capita energy consumption has an important bearing on the issue of China's potential as a petroleum-exporting country. No analysis or projection of China's export potential is complete without some reference to the constraint imposed by high domestic energy end-use requirements, generated at root by low per capita energy consumption levels. Even if the petroleum and natural gas industries continued to grow at extraordinary rates (the growth rate was drop-

TABLE 19.2
Per Capita Energy Consumption in Original Units, 1949-78

Year	Coal (kgce)	Petroleum (kg)	Natural gas (cu m)	Electric power (kwh)	Total (kgce)
1949	35.4	0.5	0.08	5.3	36.8
1950	45.6	0.8	0.08	6.3	47.8
1951	57.4	1.8	0.09	8.2	61.2
1952	70.3	1.8	0.1	10.5	74.4
1953	70.3	2.4	0.1	13.2	75.7
1954	83.0	2.8	0.3	15.7	89.3
1955	95.7	4.1	0.4	17.2	104.3
1956	102.9	4.5	0.5	21.3	112.9
1957	119.8	4.9	0.8	25.9	131.4
1958	204.0	7.1	1.2	37.3	220.6
1959	248.4	9.7	1.8	54.4	271.8
1960	205.8	11.4	2.5	59.5	233.2
1961	155.1	11.3	3.6	38.5	181.3
1962	166.4	10.4	6.0	36.6	194.1
1963	169.7	10.3	7.0	39.6	199.1
1964	172.4	11.5	8.0	42.4	205.2
1965	182.4	13.0	10.3	48.5	221.2
1966	198.1	15.6	13.1	56.5	245.5
1967	147.6	14.9	10.7	49.8	189.9
1968	154.6	16.1	15.7	54.1	205.8
1969	193.6	21.2	18.5	63.5	257.2
1970	228.2	29.0	20.8	74.8	307.7
1971	235.0	36.4	23.1	87.7	330.1
1972	244.9	41.5	25.9	93.0	351.8
1973	253.1	50.6	26.0	99.0	374.4
1974	255.1	56.7	26.7	103.8	386.7
1975	293.2	57.6	31.4	114.1	433.8
1976	268.8	66.8	33.7	119.2	426.6
1977	292.6	70.4	41.3	127.9	466.8
1978	347.7	76.8	46.3	142.5	539.7

ping to about 10 percent per year in the late 1970's), oil exports would be limited by domestic consumption requirements. It is extremely difficult to predict how much Peking will actually choose to export. But it is possible to project an export ceiling based on various growth and reserves assumptions. The most important single constraint in setting that ceiling on oil exports is China's low per capita energy consumption level. I assume that the Chinese government is firmly committed to its domestic development priorities. Given the simple logic of these priorities, there is

TABLE 19.3
*Per Capita Energy Consumption in Kilograms Coal Equivalent,
1949–78*

Year	Coal	Petroleum	Natural gas	Electric power	Total
1949	35.4	0.7	0.1	0.7	36.8
1950	45.6	1.2	0.1	0.8	47.8
1951	57.4	2.7	0.1	1.0	61.2
1952	70.3	2.6	0.2	1.3	74.4
1953	70.3	3.6	0.2	1.6	75.7
1954	83.0	4.1	0.4	1.9	89.3
1955	95.7	6.0	0.6	2.1	104.3
1956	102.9	6.6	0.7	2.6	112.9
1957	119.8	7.3	1.1	3.2	131.4
1958	204.0	10.4	1.6	4.6	220.6
1959	248.4	14.3	2.4	6.7	271.8
1960	205.8	16.8	3.3	7.3	233.2
1961	155.1	16.7	4.8	4.7	181.3
1962	166.4	15.2	7.9	4.5	194.1
1963	169.7	15.2	9.3	4.9	199.1
1964	172.4	16.9	10.7	5.2	205.2
1965	182.4	19.1	13.7	6.0	221.2
1966	198.1	22.9	17.5	6.9	245.5
1967	147.6	21.9	14.3	6.1	189.9
1968	154.6	23.7	20.9	6.6	205.8
1969	193.6	31.2	24.6	7.8	257.2
1970	228.2	42.6	27.7	9.2	307.7
1971	235.0	53.6	30.8	10.8	330.1
1972	244.9	61.0	34.5	11.4	351.8
1973	253.1	74.4	34.7	12.2	374.4
1974	255.1	83.3	35.6	12.8	386.7
1975	293.2	84.7	41.8	14.0	433.8
1976	268.8	98.2	44.9	14.7	426.6
1977	292.6	103.4	55.0	15.7	466.8
1978	347.7	112.9	61.6	17.5	539.7

a statistical limit on China's energy export capacity that will be set by the
annual output of domestically produced energy commodities minus the
domestic energy end-use requirement. Domestic energy end-use requirements will in turn be pushed relentlessly upward by industrialization and economic growth in every sector. China has achieved visible increases in the level of personal income and personal energy consumption in the last 30 years. This trend will continue in the next two decades,
generating ever higher levels of energy consumption and limiting the

availability of energy commodities for export. China's population and Peking's self-reliance policies differentiate the PRC from the other Third World oil-exporting countries.

Per Capita Energy Consumption Growth Rate

From 1949 to 1978, China achieved an overall per capita energy consumption growth rate of 9 percent. (See Table 19.4.) This must be judged an excellent performance in terms of world energy development standards. It is especially remarkable in view of the primitive state of the commercial energy infrastructure inherited by the People's Republic in 1949. In addition, this pace of energy development was achieved over and above an average population growth rate of 2.1 percent. This does not mean, of course, that personal consumption of energy commodities has risen in the PRC at an annual rate near 10 percent. Most of the new energy supplies have been channeled to industrial growth, urban development, the transportation infrastructure, and more recently to agricultural mechanization. Personal consumption of energy commodities has grown slowly, perhaps at 3–5 percent per year. That is just fast enough to make the growth visible to the Chinese population—the coal briquets used for cooking, the single dim electric light bulb in village homes, the village radio system, the commune tractor, or the new city bus route.

There are two instruments for limiting personal consumption of energy commodities and expanding the energy supplies available to industry, transport, and agriculture—the price structure and the state planning apparatus. Coal prices are reasonable at 10–30 *jenminpih* (jmp), or U.S. $5–15 per metric ton of bituminous coal at the mine head. Coal in the cities used for cooking purposes in briquet form is far more expensive (0.90 jmp per catty in Shanghai), reflecting Peking's efforts to minimize personal consumption of commercial energy fuels.[4] Petroleum prices range according to fuel and use, but are quite high compared with Western petroleum product prices. Diesel fuel for agricultural use is the cheapest fuel for internal combustion, at 250–300 jmp per metric ton, or $0.40–0.50 per gallon. Gasoline for agricultural use costs 750–1,000 jmp per metric ton, or about $2.50–3.20 per gallon. Gasoline for transportation purposes (taxis, official cars, etc.) in Canton runs 1.42 jmp per liter, or about $2.70 per gallon.

Electric power prices range from 0.03 jmp to 0.08 jmp per kilowatthour ($0.02–0.04/kwh), depending on the area and use. These power prices are low by American standards ($0.06/kwh on my last electricity bill), not particularly high relative to other Chinese energy commodities, and certainly not commensurate with the low per capita availability

TABLE 19.4
Annual Percent Increase in Per Capita Energy Consumption,
1950–78

Year	Coal	Petroleum	Natural gas	Electric power	Total
1950	29.0%	78.0%	−1.6%	19.4%	29.7%
1951	25.9	114.1	17.6	28.8	28.2
1952	22.3	−1.9	30.5	28.7	21.4
1953	0.02	36.6	22.2	25.5	1.8
1954	18.0	13.5	96.0	18.8	18.0
1955	15.3	47.5	46.8	10.1	16.8
1956	7.6	10.8	30.1	23.5	8.2
1957	16.4	9.0	46.5	21.8	16.3
1958	70.2	43.0	46.3	44.0	67.9
1959	21.8	38.0	51.4	45.7	23.2
1960	−17.2	17.3	39.7	9.5	−14.2
1961	−24.6	−0.6	47.0	−35.4	−22.2
1962	7.3	−8.7	63.9	−4.9	7.0
1963	2.0	−0.4	17.7	8.1	2.6
1964	1.6	11.2	14.3	7.1	3.0
1965	5.8	13.1	28.5	14.3	7.8
1966	8.6	20.0	27.4	16.5	11.0
1967	−25.5	−4.6	−18.5	−11.9	−22.7
1968	4.7	8.3	46.7	8.6	8.4
1969	25.3	31.7	17.5	17.5	25.0
1970	17.9	36.6	12.6	17.7	19.6
1971	3.0	25.8	11.2	17.2	7.3
1972	4.2	13.8	12.1	6.0	6.6
1973	3.3	22.0	0.6	6.5	6.4
1974	0.8	12.0	2.7	4.8	3.3
1975	15.0	1.7	17.4	9.9	12.2
1976	−8.3	16.0	7.4	4.5	−1.7
1977	8.9	5.3	22.5	7.3	9.4
1978	18.8	9.2	12.1	11.4	15.6

(scarce supply) of electric power. Personal consumption is evidently controlled by the pace at which household transmission networks are installed and by output rationing, rather than through the price structure.

Aside from the price structure, energy supplies are channeled to the production infrastructure directly through the planning apparatus. This occurs both by the assignment of priorities to various types of energy end-use in national, provincial, and local economic plans and by attaching energy production units directly to consuming units through contract arrangements. Most factories in the PRC have direct supply contracts with producing units or regional outlets for the purchase of fuel, power, and materials. This facilitates planning and rationing under conditions of shortage. But it also makes factories and other energy-consuming units compete for available supplies and further mitigates against personal consumption.

Many rural areas in the remote parts of China are still virtually untouched by the dramatic growth of average per capita energy consumption in the PRC. The first intrusion of the commercial energy system may be in the form of a battery-powered radio or loudspeaker system. The next contact is the construction of a dirt road, which may miss the village completely, but be within walking distance. Most rural areas continue to rely heavily on traditional noncommercial energy—firewood, rice stalks, dung, animal power. Dirt roads are used first by animal-drawn carts and bicycles, then by a few tractors and trucks. A single bulldozer may serve an entire county. The foreign visitor will still catch glimpses of irrigation water being lifted by a walking treadle. The use of traditional noncommercial energy in China would perhaps add another 200–300 kilograms coal equivalent to the average per capita energy consumption figures. But the shift to commercial energy fuels is already well under way and should be largely complete by the end of the century.

Per Capita Fuel and Power Mix

The per capita fuel and power mix statistics are nearly identical to the statistics for the aggregate energy consumption mix (Table 18.6). In terms of average per capita energy consumption, coal is still by far the most plentiful commercial energy commodity (65 percent). Petroleum and natural gas (20 percent and 10 percent, respectively) are available, but in strictly limited quantities. Natural gas availability is regionally concentrated in Szechwan, the northeast, and Shanghai. Electric power is scarce, and in most areas additional electric power for any producing industry must be obtained through a process of negotiation with various levels of the planning and management apparatus, not simply purchased at the going rate from existing transmission networks. For this reason, many factories and an increasing number of rural communes are constructing electric power-generating facilities for internal use. This greatly complicates the task of estimating China's true electric power-generating capacity and power output. Decentralization of the electric power system has mixed effects on generating efficiencies. On the one hand, factories are encouraged to use waste process heat in the steam cycle for power generation. On the other hand, diesel generators are common in the remote areas, a costly way of producing electric power. Small-scale hydropower has greatly benefited the rural electrification program, despite small unit capacities and low utilization ratios.

The next 20 years should witness a continued sharp rise in the domestic demand for petroleum products in China. Growth in the use of oil will be particularly spectacular in the transportation and agriculture sectors. The PRC has only begun to expand its road network and is building an increasing number of trucks, diesel locomotives, and buses. The transportation system will be heavily oriented toward commodity transport and public transport, with little or no room for vehicles for personal use except for official purposes. The military will consume an increasing share of petroleum products as it modernizes and mechanizes. The aviation network is expanding as rapidly as the road system, linking the most remote parts of a vast and geographically diverse country. Agricultural mechanization, currently a high-priority planning item, will rely on increased access to petroleum fuels and electric power. Industrial-process heat will continue to be coal-based, but the industrial demand for specialized petroleum products continues to rise sharply. All these indicators point toward higher petroleum consumption requirements within China. It seems clear that domestic energy consumption requirements must be given priority in order for China to achieve industrial and agricultural modernization by the turn of the century. The priority of domestic development objectives implies a sharp limit on the availability of oil for export.

Chapter 20

Energy Trade by Commodity and Country

The People's Republic of China, like some centrally planned economy countries and a few Third World countries, publishes no official trade returns. On the other hand, accurate information on energy commodity trade is essential for a full understanding of China's international energy policies. Chapters 20 and 21 represent the first effort to gather and present in a coordinated data series China's annual foreign trade in energy commodities. The data were gathered over the course of several years, from a variety of partner-country sources. The general method of data collection and processing was as follows: (1) search regional compilations of commodity trade data published by regional and central offices of the United Nations; (2) search the annual trade returns of the Soviet Union and other East European countries; (3) search the annual trade returns of certain critical countries, especially in Asia, to confirm and complete the data compiled from international sources; (4) combine estimates from different sources, different classification schemes (Standard International Trade Classification [SITC] and Brussels Tariff Nomenclature), and different units of measurement (weight, volume, English system, metric system, etc.); (5) estimate remaining discrepancies or missing data on the basis of other foreign sources, the value of recorded transactions, and current prices for the commodity in question; (6) exclude all foreign estimates not documented by government sources; and (7) present data in standard units of weight and energy content.

This careful method of search, screening, organization, and combination of thousands of bits of scattered data produced a comprehensive trade data series by commodity and partner country. There is a conservative bias in the data because of the exclusion of most unofficial foreign estimates. The rigidity of this criterion was necessary in order to avoid the incorporation of arbitrary interpolations or guesses that some authors have constructed for missing years. Once started, rumors about China's energy trade tend to persist. For example, a rumor that China imported more than a million metric tons of crude oil annually from Romania from 1962 through 1965 has bounced around in foreign estimates for a number of years.[1] The rumor began in an intelligence agency of the government of Taiwan, which may have had extraneous motivations in making the "information" public. There has never been confirmation of the rumor from any official source and it was not recorded in Suez Canal transit records. The trade does not appear in official Romanian trade returns. China would probably not have imported crude oil at the time, because of the tight situation in the early 1960's with refinery capacity. This is but one example of persistent rumors about China's energy trade that were discounted for lack of official confirmation. The criterion of official documentation was relaxed somewhat for very recent years and for countries like North Korea and Vietnam, which do not publish trade returns.

Although the scale of the data bits recorded in this collection may not seem impressive relative to world petroleum trade or China's domestic energy system, they do provide clues about underlying patterns in China's international energy trade. These patterns, or trading habits, reveal important features of Peking's nascent international energy policies toward different regions of the world. Trade in such peripheral commodities as mineral wax (a by-product of the Chinese petroleum industry) has often appeared very early in the development of China's political and diplomatic relations with Third World countries. Import of other commodities, such as high-grade lubricants, was important to the PRC during the period immediately following the rupture with the Soviet Union. Therefore, the significance of these data bits may transcend their monetary value or energy equivalent weight.

These tables are limited to energy commodity trade in units of weight (metric tons). Two other types of data were collected but have not been presented here. A parallel data series on the monetary value of each energy transaction was collected for each weight value recorded in the tables in this chapter. The monetary trade data were useful for estimation of missing weight data on the basis of current prices. However, it was impossible to include a table of trade by monetary value at this stage in the research, because of difficulties presented by a multitude of currencies and annual exchange rates. This task should be within the scope of future research. Meanwhile, the raw monetary trade data for energy commodities are available on request from the author.

A second type of data was collected but not used. Data on energy production equipment trade are available from the same sources and through the same screening process as energy commodity trade data. Data were collected for China's trade in engines, mining equipment, and electric power equipment. These data have permitted certain generalizations in the text. They were not presented in tabular form, however, because of the difficulty of using the SITC classification system for energy machinery. Such equipment has been broken down into components and then combined with other components that may have no energy function but have a similar industrial production process or physical structure. For example, petroleum refinery equipment is not listed under a single category, but broken down into boilers, pipes, valves, etc. and combined with other such components for non-energy-related equipment. The result was to render the SITC series less useful for an evaluation of China's energy machinery trade than a simple listing of the major purchases and major types of export in the body of the text.

The reader should be warned again of other limits on this collection of China's energy commodity trade data. Because these data were collected from an incomplete series of trade returns published by partner countries, certain gaps will obviously remain. Some countries (e.g. Romania) published trade data during some years but not other years. Some transactions fell below the recording limit of the country in question or the United Nations agency that collected the data. Some transactions were intentionally kept secret. Some trade returns were listed by month rather than year, making collection a lifetime task. The various issues of SITC publications were collected as a first priority from nearly every university library in California. It is believed that all in-print editions were searched. Trade publications for the Soviet Union and Eastern Europe were obtained from the Hoover Library and the U.S. Bureau of Mines. The trade returns of individual countries were obtained from the Stanford University library system and from the Asia Collection of the University of Hawaii library. The most serious remaining gaps were for certain Middle Eastern and East European countries. Data on oil exports from the Middle East to China tend to get lost, like dust in the cracks, in miscellaneous categories such as "other countries." The CIA reports that China imported 1 million tons of crude oil per year from 1974 through 1976 from "Africa, the Middle East, and Albania" via the southern oil port at Chankiang.[2] I have not been able to trace this trade through partner-country sources.

A brief note should be added regarding the format of the trade data tables. All data were presented in energy import values by weight or energy-equivalent weight. Thus, a minus sign ($-$) preceding the value of trade for any given commodity, country, and year indicates an export of the commodity. The commodity left China, and was therefore subtracted from domestic energy consumption. Conversely, an import is designated as a positive value ($+$), since the commodity entered China. Occasionally, both a negative and a positive quantity have been listed, indicating that China both exported and imported the commodity in trade with the same partner in the same year. The plus-minus convention permits the listing of both import and export data in the same tables.

The designation "e" always refers to an estimate by the author. These estimates were based on available monetary-value trade data that had not been listed in energy weight units. The monetary units were transformed into an estimate of trade in energy units by using current prices for the commodity in other Chinese trade transactions as a point of reference. Occasional estimates were made on the basis of fragmentary data, particularly for recent transactions that have been recorded in numerous reliable sources but have not yet appeared in official government trade returns. No estimates were made on the basis of inferential, interpolated, extrapolated, or rumored transactions except where explicitly noted in the text. The establishment of reliable trade data sources should provide the basis for cumulative research on China's energy commodity trade. This was the reason for the conservative bias in all my estimates. It will be easier to add new transactions as reliable information becomes available than to weed out the spurious transactions.

Coal Trade

Coal has been an important commodity in China's international energy trade since as early as 1950. Japan, the Soviet Union, and Hong Kong were China's earliest markets for coal, followed by Pakistan, Malaysia, and Cambodia. (See Tables 20.11 and 20.12.) Sino-Japanese coal trade was interrupted from 1959 to 1960 owing to a variety of political factors, including the Nagasaki Flag incident, the Taiwan Strait crisis, and domestic shortages of coal during the Great Leap Forward. Coal exports to the Soviet Union were used as a source of foreign exchange to pay part of the costs of petroleum imports. Coal exports to the USSR ceased after 1965, when petroleum product imports and other trade dwindled to insignificant levels. Peking made an unsuccessful effort in the late 1950's to find markets for its coal in Western Europe, probably in an effort to sell some of the coal originally destined for Japan.

The coke trade statistics are highly unreliable, since trade in coke is frequently reported simply as "solid fuels" or lumped together with coal (Table 20.13). Much of the coal exported to Japan was for coking purposes rather than steam coal. I have not been able to identify the reason for marginal but fairly steady coke exports to Hong Kong. Minor amounts of Chinese coke were exported to Pakistan in the late 1960's and early 1970's.

There is little doubt that China will seek to increase its coal exports, as well as crude petroleum exports, during the early 1980's. Japanese elec-

(Metric tons)

Year	Burma	Cambodia	Hong Kong	India	Japan	Malaysia	Pakistan	Singapore	Sri Lanka	Thailand
1950					-531,634					
1951										
1952			-15,798	+1,016						
1953			-24,763		-137,122					
1954			-6,873		-47,358					
1955			-19,730		-117,894					
1956			-118,317		-526,658	-7,000[e]	-297,760			
1957			-180,000[e]		-483,063	-2,000[e]	-64,089			
1958			-183,747		-190,135	-6,000[e]	-89,456	-1,338		
1959			-151,302				-73,957[a]			
1960			-189,105		-4,051	-3,292				
1961			-6,850		-12,636	-91	-9,453[b]			
1962			-184,495		-174,380	-30	-15,201[b]			
1963			-144,062		-127,398	-140[e]	-64,249			
1964		-12,000	-132,366		-228,252/+2,554		-75,000[e]			
1965		-28,056	-113,349		-590,456		-80,000[e]			
1966	-46,151	-35,010	-109,477		-885,762		-310,000[e]			
1967	-10,362	-14,000	-71,623		-1,081,597		-482,524[b]			
1968		-36,218	-44,302		-268,403		-280,000[e]			
1969			-39,948		-201,702	-1	-160,000[e]			
1970			-17,473		-226,945		-282,831[b]			
1971			-21,299		-344,353	-1	-74,000[c]		-483	
1972			-13,463		-250,522		-13,188[b]			
1973			-7,339		-293,622					
1974			-4,931		-405,127		-21,438[b]			
1975			-3,246		-455,784					-3,000
1976			-5,141		-321,959/+241					
1977			-3,010		-300,000[e]					
1978			-4,000[e]		-400,000[e]					

[a] Jan. 1960–June 1961 data. [b] Fiscal year data. [e] Estimate.

TABLE 20.12
Coal Trade by Country and Year: Non-Asian Areas
(Metric tons)

Year	Australia	Belgium-Luxembourg	France	West Germany	Ireland	Italy	Netherlands	Soviet Union	Tanzania	United States
1955								-520,000		
1956								-209,000		
1957								-201,900		
1958								-208,000		
1959			-9,822	-301	-439	-1,488		-204,000		
1960				-999		-9,600	-945	-200,000		
1961								-186,000		
1962								-201,000		
1963	+18,000[e]	-15,477						-205,000		
1964	+18,000[e]	-10,204	-10,469					-202,000		
1965								-201,000		
1966										
1967										
1968										
1969										
1970										
1971	+11,158								-5	
1972										
1973										
1974										
1975										
1976										
1977										-150,000[e]

[e] Estimate.

TABLE 20.13
Coke Trade by Country and Year
(Metric tons)

Year	Brunei	Cambodia	Hong Kong	Japan	Malaysia	Pakistan	Sarawak	Singapore	Thailand	Tanzania
1956			-5,784					-271		
1957			-2,400[e]					-584		
1958			-4,945							
1959			-2,551					-305		
1960			-2,807		-636					
1961			-1,452		-241					
1962		-70			-30					
1963		-30	-145		-80					
1964		-30	-777		-278					
1965	-20	-16	-441		-181		-10	-55		
1966	-1	-236	-1,142		-133			-20		
1967	-37	-1,497	-1,497							-5
1968			-4,748							-11
1969			-2,599		-1				-2,455	-937
1970			-3,304		-45	-14,111[a]				-1,939
1971			-1,788			-31,489[a]			-4,500	-2,000[e]
1972			-730[e]			-29,579[a]				-4
1973			-700[e]	+2,058	-203	-32,792[a]				
1974			-814			-29,520[a]				
1975			-775							
1976			-499							
1977			-406							

[a] Fiscal year data.   [e] Estimate.

tric power and steel companies began to discuss increased trade in steam and coking coal as early as 1975.[3] The Sino-Japanese long-term trade agreement signed in early 1978 specified that Japan would take 300,000–500,000 metric tons of Chinese steam and coking coal (about equally divided) in 1978.[4] Coal exports to Japan are expected to rise steadily to 700,000 mt in 1979, 1.5–1.6 million metric tons in 1980, 2.5–2.7 mmt in 1981, and 3.5–3.7 mmt in 1982. China would like to export even more coal to Japan than specified by the agreement, perhaps 5 mmt by 1981, but Japanese steel and electric power interests are resisting such a rapid acceleration in coal trade because of previous contracts for Australian and American coal. The Japanese have already identified specific plants that will take the new Chinese coal. Japan's Electric Power Development Company will import 1.2 mmt of Tatung steam coal starting in 1981, to fuel a 1 GWe coal-fired thermal plant still under construction at Matsushima, Kyushu.[5] Two more coal-fired thermal plants are now in the planning stage and could be supplied by Chinese coal. The Ministry of International Trade and Industry (MITI) would like to shift in the direction of diversified coal imports to relieve future dependence on scarce crude oil in the world market. More coal-fired thermal plants, as well as coal gasification and liquefaction centers, would fit neatly with China's desire to export more low-sulfur coal to earn foreign exchange and supplement its growing crude petroleum exports. Other countries in Southeast Asia may also be interested in Chinese coal, as the price of crude petroleum continues to rise on the world market.

Crude Petroleum Trade

Foreign trade in crude petroleum was not critical to China's energy development until quite recently. During the 1950's, the PRC imported crude oil from the Soviet Union on a regular basis to supplement limited domestic production. However, these imports were limited to about half a million tons per year by the state of China's refining industry. Not only were refineries few and relatively small; they produced mostly heavy residual oil and had little cracking capacity, further limiting the value of imported crude. Peking therefore imported refined products from the Soviet Union rather than crude petroleum. There must have been some demand for imported crude, since China switched to Albania as a source of crude oil after the Sino-Soviet break in 1960. There is firm evidence that the PRC imported crude petroleum as late as 1969–71 from Egypt. Spot purchases from Egypt and Nigeria may have been reexported to Vietnam, possibly after refining at Maoming in Kwangtung province.

China did export minor quantities of crude petroleum and refined petroleum products to its Asian communist neighbors starting in 1964 or 1965 (Tables 20.21 and 20.22). There is no precise way to measure this trade, since neither North Korea nor Vietnam publishes trade statistics. Nor is there any way to tell what proportion of the early petroleum exports consisted of crude petroleum and what proportion of refined petroleum products. I have attempted order-of-magnitude estimates by using an indirect method. I examined statistics for petroleum trade between the Soviet Union and North Korea and Vietnam. I then reconstructed total petroleum (crude plus products) import curves for both North Korea and Vietnam, smoothing the curves between peaks in Soviet oil trade with the two countries. There was a readily identifiable dip in Soviet oil exports to North Korea and to Vietnam at just about the right time (1964–67), indicating that China took up the difference. Taking some subjective factors into account (e.g. the war in Vietnam), it was possible to provide reasonable guesses regarding the scale of Chinese petroleum exports to these two countries during the mid-1960's.

A similar method was used to evaluate previous estimates of petroleum exports to North Korea and Vietnam during the 1970's. In general, I found that previous estimates were somewhat on the high side, and inconsistent with published Soviet trade statistics.[6] I therefore reconstructed what I consider a reasonable data series for petroleum trade with North Korea and Vietnam, taking into account the Soviet trade data, intelligence reports, and reports in secondary sources (Table 20.21). It should be kept in mind that a substantial proportion of the petroleum trade with these countries was in the form of refined or partially refined petroleum products. The data have all been included in the series on crude petroleum in order to avoid overstating the accuracy of the available information. The same general comments apply to the data on crude petroleum trade with Romania, Laos, and Cambodia (Kampuchea). I used a variety of sources to make the estimates, including previous trade patterns and projected import requirements for each country. In general, therefore, the responsibility for the estimates of China's petroleum exports to other communist countries rests here. There is little point in attempting to document these estimates to other sources, since the official data are not publicly available and the estimates are my own.

Data on crude petroleum trade with the Philippines, Iran, and Brazil were all from secondary reports based on official data or information.[7] Manila, oddly enough, has treated the oil trade with China as an official secret, and there are several different estimated series available. The series I used was obtained from the *China Trade Report,* a usually reliable source. The data for Iran and Brazil were based on official trade agreements with the PRC. All the oil in such cases is not necessarily delivered

TABLE 20.21
Crude Petroleum Trade by Country and Year: Asia
(Metric tons)

Year	Cambodia	Japan	Laos	North Korea	Pakistan	Philippines	Thailand	Vietnam
1964				$-50,000^{a,e}$	-300^e			
1965				$-100,000^{a,e}$				$-50,000^{a,e}$
1966				$-150,000^{a,e}$				$-100,000^{a,e}$
1967				$-200,000^{a,e}$				$-50,000^{a,e}$
1968					-100^e			
1969								
1970								
1971				$-200,000^{a,e}$				$-200,000^{a,e}$
1972				$-500,000^{a,e}$				$-200,000^{a,e}$
1973		$-969,888$		$-500,000^{a,e}$				
1974		$-3,898,406$		$-500,000^{a,e}$		$-123,000^e$	$-12,008$	$-200,000^{a,e}$
1975	$-50,000^{a,e}$	$-7,863,579$	$-7,500^{a,e}$	$-900,000^{a,e}$		$-482,000^e$		$-300,000^{a,e}$
1976	$-100,000^{a,e}$	$-6,058,002$	$-7,500^{a,e}$	$-500,000^{a,e}$		$-567,000^e$	$-193,277$	$-500,000^{a,e}$
1977	$-100,000^{a,e}$	$-6,827,000^e$	$-7,500^{a,e}$	$-500,000^{a,e}$		$-884,000^e$	$-200,000^e$	$-500,000^{a,e}$
1978	$-100,000^{a,e}$	$-7,000,000^e$		$-1,000,000^{a,e}$		$-1,000,000^e$	$-200,000^e$	

[a] Includes an unknown quantity of refined petroleum products. [e] Estimate.

Crude Petroleum Trade by Country and Year: Non-Asian Areas

(Metric tons)

Year	Albania	Australia	Brazil	Egypt	Iran	Italy	Nigeria	Romania	Soviet Union
1949									+29,000
1950									+120,000
1951									+75,000
1952									+103,000
1953									+65,000
1954									+188,000
1955									+377,000
1956									+397,800
1957									+380,400
1958									+672,000
1959	+11,000[e]								+635,000
1960	+21,000[e]								+567,600
1961	+56,000[e]								
1962	+105,000	-42,000[e]							
1963	+117,000								
1964	+158,000	-36,000[e]							
1965									
1966									
1967									
1968						-19,441			
1969				+158,532					
1970				+400,991					
1971									
1972				+97,132			+53,860		
1973									
1974									
1975		-45,000[e]			+200,000			-150,000[a,e]	
1976					+200,000			-500,000[a,e]	
1977					+300,000			-500,000[a,e]	
1978			-90,000[e]					-500,000[a,e]	

[a]Includes an unknown quantity of refined petroleum products. [e]Estimate.

during the year in which the agreement is signed, although my estimates assign the data to the year of the agreement. Official trade returns will eventually provide a precise data series in each case. Data for crude petroleum trade with Japan and Thailand were based on official trade returns and should be highly reliable.

Detailed analysis of China's crude oil trade has been provided in the relevant chapters of Part I, and need not be repeated here. Suffice it to say that crude oil exports grew rapidly from 1973 to 1975 and then flattened out under the pressure of rising domestic demand. There was a serious disruption in crude oil exports in the early months of 1976, partly because of internal political factors and partly because of unexpectedly sharp increases in the domestic use of petroleum for industrial process heat. Crude oil exports recovered in the second half of 1976 and ran at about 9–10 million metric tons per year in 1977 and 1978 (Table 21.2).

China's exact earnings from the crude oil trade would be even more difficult to establish than the commodity trade data. Price data are somewhat easier to pin down, but still ambiguous. Crude oil exported to Japan started at $3.75 per barrel in 1973, rose to $14.80/bbl in the early months of 1974, then dropped to $12.85/bbl in the third quarter of 1974.[8] The price fell again in 1975, bottoming out at about $12.10/bbl. By early 1976, the upward trend had resumed and Chinese crude was costing Japanese importers $12.65–12.68/bbl.[9] By year-end 1976, the price had reached $13.15/bbl, where it remained relatively steady through mid-1978 at around $13.20/bbl (FOB).[10] Chinese crude sold to the Philippines went for about $9.00/bbl in 1974, and rose to $11.50/bbl by early 1978, still a concessionary price. Price concessions for political purposes are common in the early stages of China's energy commodity trade with any country and have been granted over extended periods in the oil trade with Vietnam and North Korea. In the absence of special concessions, Peking prices its crude oil just under Indonesian crude.

On the basis of these price figures and statistics on the annual volume of crude petroleum exports (Table 21.2), it is possible to construct a rough estimate of China's earnings from crude petroleum trade. Earnings were $40–50 million in 1973, depending on the price of crude oil sold to Vietnam and North Korea. Net crude oil exports earned $400–500 million in 1974, about $850–900 million in 1975, dropped to $700–750 million in 1976, rose again to $850–900 million in 1977 and to $900 million–$1 billion in 1978. Earnings from the crude oil trade covered 1 percent of China's import bill in 1973, 5 percent in 1974, and about 10 percent since 1975. Petroleum (including refined products) has become China's largest single export commodity and has already earned the country more than $4 billion in foreign exchange (1973–78). That amount would more than pay for all of China's imported energy production plant and equipment since 1960—petroleum exploration and production equipment, refineries and petrochemical plants, chemical fertilizer plants, coal-mining equipment, electric power equipment, and China's new fleet of oil tankers (Chapter 22). China's crude petroleum exports are marginal by the standards of the world energy market. But the earnings generated by those exports are a powerful tool in the hands of Peking's energy planners, giving them access to advanced energy plant and equipment of foreign manufacture and to the technology that naturally accompanies energy equipment imports.

The government in Peking has already committed China to a slow but steady increase in crude petroleum exports through 1982, and further increases are likely in the annual crude oil export level until the late 1980's, when the pressure of rising domestic consumption requirements will begin to impose a ceiling on the oil available for export. After several years of negotiation, Peking and Tokyo signed a long-term trade agreement in February 1978. The agreement calls for a total of $20 billion in trade between the two countries from 1978 through 1982.[11] Fully half of the value of China's exports to Japan ($4.5–5.0 billion) will be generated by crude oil sales. The agreement provides for the export of 7 million metric tons of crude oil in 1978, 7.6 mmt in 1979, 8 mmt in 1980, 9.5 mmt in 1981, and 15 mmt in 1982. This constitutes a slow pattern of expansion through 1981, followed by a sudden jump in 1982. The sudden increase in crude oil trade scheduled for 1982 was the result of a compromise between the Japanese oil-refining industry, which seeks to limit its importation of Chinese crude, and the Keidanren, the steel industry, and the Ministry of International Trade and Industry, which seek to expand the oil trade with China (Chapter 6). Peking would like to see oil exports to Japan grow as rapidly as possible in the short term and will probably seek to exceed the levels agreed to in the long-term trade agreement. If the agreement operates like the memorandum trade agreements of the 1960's, additional trade could be added in each year of the agreement through private deals with individual Japanese firms. A large margin of additional oil trade would be surprising, however, in view of the resistance of Japanese refiners to Chinese crude, which has high wax and residual oil content. In any case, Peking will almost certainly press for higher oil trade levels between 1983 and 1985.

In addition, it should be recognized that crude oil exports to Japan constitute the largest market for Chinese oil, but by no means the only market. China has steadily increased crude oil exports to the Philippines, Thailand, Romania, Vietnam, and North Korea. This trend will continue (with the exception of Vietnam), coupled with Chinese efforts to find new trading partners for the crude oil trade and to expand the export of diesel fuel and other refined petroleum products. I would expect to see total Chinese oil exports in the range of 10–15 million metric tons per year in 1980 and 15–20 million tons in 1982, on the basis of current trends and agreements. The projections in Chapter 24 show that China's total energy export potential may expand rapidly between 1978 and 1985, to 50–75 million metric tons oil equivalent. There may be a considerable volume of market propaganda intended to attract new oil markets for Chinese crude, as well as marginal expansion into the American market. Chinese officials will cite reserves figures at highly speculative levels and will hint at massive Chinese markets for foreign goods.[12] The trick, from Peking's perspective, will be to sell just the right amounts of crude oil without making significant price concessions based on the waxiness and heaviness of Chinese crudes. Petroleum export potential, however, will peak between 1985 and 1990 unless offshore oil discoveries significantly increase foreign estimates of China's economically recoverable oil resources. In other words, China will be an oil exporter on about the scale achieved by Indonesia.

If this scenario is generally correct, China will be earning at least $1.5 billion per year in oil revenues by 1980, more than $2 billion per year by 1982, and $3–5 billion per year in oil revenues alone by 1985. The figures could go much higher, to the $4–6 billion range by 1985, if Peking chose to export oil up to the projected potential limits, leaving no margin for slippage in the domestic energy system. If the higher range of oil export earnings were attained, China would be earning as much in 1985 from oil exports alone as the country earned from total exports in 1975 and 1976. Crude oil exports will give China access to an increasing number and variety of foreign plants, equipment, and technology. The oil trade, therefore, will be a significant factor in China's modernization program between now and 2000. Caution should be taken, however, to avoid overstating the earning potential of crude oil exports. Peking's energy planners will be searching hard for a way out of the development-trade dichotomy in the allocation of available petroleum supplies. Coal and hydropower production will be emphasized in an effort to meet domestic energy consumption requirements without cutting into the petroleum trade. But my projections indicate that the solution will not be easy.

Trade in Liquid Fuels

In addition to its crude petroleum exports and coal trade, China has carried on a limited trade in liquid fuels (Tables 20.31–20.35). The overall balance of liquid fuels trade follows the pattern in crude petroleum trade. That is, the PRC was a net importer of liquid fuels (from the Soviet Union) in the 1950's, achieved self-sufficiency in the late 1960's, and has recently become a net exporter of liquid fuels to the countries of Southeast Asia. The information on trade in liquid fuels is not highly reliable. That presented in these tables is all accurate, in that it came directly from official trade returns. However, much of the data is still missing, especially for the 1960's. China imported refined petroleum fuels from the countries of Eastern Europe and possibly from the Middle East during that decade. Only part of the data on those imports shows up in the tables, since official trade returns were missing for several of the countries concerned (e.g. Albania) and for certain years for other countries (e.g. Romania and Egypt). Furthermore, part or all of the oil exports to Vietnam reported in Tables 20.21 and 20.22 as crude oil exports were actually refined petroleum fuels. Refined products may also have been included in the oil trade with North Korea. Finally, a number of market economy countries, particularly in the Third World, reported figures for total trade in refined petroleum products with the PRC, but did not break down the figures by fuel (Tables 20.71–20.74). I believe that most of China's trade in liquid fuels appears somewhere in the trade data reported in this chapter. Some distortion remains, however, in the disaggregation by fuel.

Gasoline Trade

China supplemented its meager domestic production of gasoline in the 1950's and early 1960's with heavy imports of Soviet gasoline. According to my estimates, the PRC imported more than 75 percent of its gasoline consumption in 1955 and more than 55 percent of gasoline consumption in 1960. Gasoline imports from the Soviet Union peaked at over one million metric tons per year in 1960 and 1961. As imports of Soviet gasoline tapered off between 1962 and 1967, Peking attempted to supplement the gasoline supply from East European sources. Imports from Romania alone may have been over 20,000 metric tons per year between 1965 and 1969. Even this amount, however, was trivial compared to earlier imports from the USSR. Domestic gasoline consumption continued to rise even as gasoline imports declined, owing to the new flow of crude oil from Taching oilfield and the accelerated gasoline production capacity of Chinese refineries (Table 18.7). Peking chose not to export gasoline at significant levels in the 1970's, reserving the high petroleum cuts for domestic use. China does supply its own retail outlets in Hong Kong with gasoline, which began to show up in Hong Kong trade statistics in 1977.

TABLE 20.31

Gasoline Trade by Country and Year

(*Metric tons*)

Year	Cambodia	W. Germany	Hong Kong	Japan	Laos	Romania	Singapore	Soviet Union	Tanzania	Yugoslavia
1955								+634,000[e]		
1956								+641,400		
1957								+573,100		
1958			+4					+640,400		
1959			+2,809					+1,256,000		
1960			+149				+33,842	+1,055,200		
1961			+5,280				+25,726	+1,325,200		
1962			+191					+764,700		
1963			+102					+455,400		
1964		-529	+95					+269,900		
1965			+122		-147	+25,700		+31,700		
1966	-2		+123	+4,518				+28,000		
1967	-1		+39					+3,900		
1968										
1969										
1970						+900			-100	
1971										
1972										+6
1973						+1,100				+17
1974										
1975										
1976										
1977			-4,577							
1978			-20,000[e]							

[e] Estimate.

TABLE 20.32
Kerosene Trade by Country and Year
(Metric tons)

Year	Hong Kong	Kuwait	Laos	Malaysia	Nigeria	Pakistan	Romania	Singapore	Soviet Union
1955									+263,800
1956	+22								+240,100
1957	+5								+372,800
1958	+8								+332,800
1959	+1								+380,100
1960	+8								+386,200
1961	+33							+2,642	+512,100
1962	+10								+488,300
1963	+13								+476,000
1964	+4								+139,100
1965	+7						+28,000		+2,000
1966	+4								
1967			−27						+4,000
1968									+400
1969									
1970				−1		−1[a]	+6,500		
1971	−18,101	+5,595							
1972	−3,032				−183	−38[b]	+1,500		
1973	−7,005								
1974	−28,294								
1975	−86,533[a]								
1976	−139,247[a]								
1977	−200,247[a]								
1978	−200,000[a,e]								

[a] Includes jet fuel.   [b] Fiscal year data.   [e] Estimate.

TABLE 20.33
Diesel Fuel Trade by Country and Year
(Metric tons)

Year	Cambodia	Egypt	Hong Kong	Iran	Japan	Kuwait	Pakistan	Romania	Singapore	Soviet Union	Thailand	Yugoslavia
1955										+233,000		
1956										+376,800		
1957										+380,200		
1958										+662,900		
1959			+845						+10,338	+556,600		
1960			+3						+11,139	+708,800		
1961			+6,989							+841,000		
1962			+45							+378,400		
1963			+216							+333,200		
1964			+239							+79,500		
1965	+70							+54,300		+3,600		
1966	+100		+2							+7,000		
1967				+53						+1,900		
1968		+120,210										
1969		+74,379										
1970								+10,400				+132
1971					-11,144/+3	+23,670	-20					
1972								+1,800				+350
1973			-27,432		-168			+2,300				+30
1974			-190,006					+7,300			-32,042	+691
1975			-413,909					+2,359			-56,340	+2,359
1976			-324,629								-118,371	
1977			-486,956								-150,000e	
1978			-700,000e								-200,000e	

e Estimate.

512

TABLE 20.34

Residual Fuel Trade by Country and Year
(Metric tons)

Year	Cambodia	Ghana	Hong Kong	Iran	Japan	Kuwait	Mexico	Pakistan	Singapore	Yugoslavia
1957					-20					
1958			+1					-88		
1959			+1					-90[e]		
1960										
1961			+53		+1,500[e]				+3,048	
1962										
1963	+100									
1964										
1965	+200[e]	+85,477			-9					
1966	+130[e]			+12,103	+217					
1967					-3/+10[e]					
1968					-261					
1969					-108					
1970								-1[a]		
1971					-28	+291,833		-152[a]		+745
1972						+420,320		-5[e]		+222
1973							+11			+1,705
1974			-50,044		-159					+3,786
1975			-144,825							
1976			-132,108		-35,567					
1977			-207,420							
1978			-200,000[e]							

[a] Fiscal year data. [e] Estimate.

TABLE 20.35
Liquefied Gas Trade by Country and Year
(Metric tons)

Year	Japan	Thailand	Year	Japan	Thailand
1957	+40[e]		1967		
1958			1968	+18[e]	
1959			1969		
1960			1970		
1961			1971	+13,557	
1962			1972		
1963			1973		
1964			1974		
1965			1975	+100[e]	
1966			1976		
			1977		−5[a]

Note that trade includes both liquefied natural gas and liquefied petroleum gas.

[a] Coal gas.

[e] Estimate.

Kerosene Trade

China imported about 50 percent of domestic kerosene consumption from the Soviet Union until 1961, after which kerosene imports tapered off, with some supplement continuing from Romania. Kerosene has strategic importance to China's fleet of military jet aircraft. Kerosene was the first liquid fuel to be exported at significant levels to Hong Kong. Kerosene exports to the colony began in 1971 and were expected to reach some 200,000 metric tons in 1978. Since 1975, kerosene exported to Hong Kong has included jet fuel for commercial flights fueled at Kai Tak Airport. This illustrates both the growing sophistication of China's refining industry and the growing energy symbiosis between China and Hong Kong.

Diesel Fuel Trade

China's trade in diesel fuel ("gas oil") follows the pattern of the other liquid fuels. Diesel fuel imports from the Soviet Union ran about 40–50 percent of domestic consumption until 1962, after which the trade declined and was partially supplanted by diesel imports from Eastern Europe and the Middle East. The PRC began exporting diesel fuel to Hong Kong in 1973, and by 1977 this trade had reached more than half a million tons per year. Hong Kong's transportation system runs largely on diesel fuel and China has already captured a significant proportion of the Hong Kong market. Diesel fuel exports to Thailand began in 1974 and reached more than 100,000 metric tons in 1977. The PRC prices its diesel fuel under world market levels to gain entry to the target market.[13] Diesel fuel imports from China are far more convenient for Third World Southeast Asian countries than importing China's waxy crudes. China's own industry, agriculture, and transportation sectors are also relatively diesel-oriented. This may place a tight ceiling on future diesel fuel exports.

Residual Fuel Trade

In contrast to the pattern for the distillate fuels, China has not been a significant importer of residual fuel oil, except in 1971 and 1972, when residual was imported from Kuwait. Chinese crudes have high heavy oil content. During the 1950's, China's infant refining industry was capable of satisfying the country's residual fuel oil requirements, eliminating the need for imports from the Soviet Union. Nor has China been a significant residual fuel exporter. Residual has not appeared at significant levels in China's oil trade with Japan and is only about 20 percent of liquid fuel exports to Hong Kong. The PRC evidently consumes most of its annual production of 25–30 million metric tons of residual fuel in its own factories and electric power plants. Here again, as with so many other examples in China's energy commodity trade pattern, we see the primacy of domestic consumption requirements reflected in the trade statistics.

Liquefied Gas Trade

China's only trade in liquefied gas (both petroleum gas and natural gas) consisted of marginal imports from Japan in 1957, 1968, 1971, and 1975. The amounts are so small that the liquefied gas must have been imported solely for the specialized needs of some industrial process.

Peking has for several years been sounding out the Japanese regarding possible liquefied natural gas exports to Japan. A consortium of Japanese companies headed by Bridgestone Liquefied Natural Gas Company has offered to construct a 300,000 ton annual capacity LNG plant at Takang oilfield, the entire output of which would be exported to Japan under a 20-year contract.[14] In November 1975 a Japanese delegation, including Japan Gasoline, Kawasaki Heavy Industries, Ishii Iron Works, and C. Itoh, were invited to China to discuss the exchange of distillation, liquefaction, storage, and transport facilities for guaranteed LNG exports.[15] The Japanese are looking for LNG imports to replace or supplement future imports from Siberia. The Chinese government would like to obtain a large plant in order to retain some of the output for domestic industrial uses. The talks continue from time to time, but so far nothing has materialized. LNG exports could become a significant part of China's energy trade if hydrocarbon deposits in the continental shelf proved to be primarily natural gas rather than crude oil.

Petroleum By-Products Trade

The statistics for China's trade in petroleum by-products—lubricants, mineral jelly and wax, and miscellaneous by-products such as asphalt and petroleum coke—are presented in Tables 20.4–20.6. The absolute quantities of these commodities in trade between the PRC and other countries are quite insignificant compared to China's energy balance. However, they reveal some interesting patterns in Peking's general approach to energy commodity trade. China trades with a much larger number of countries in nonfuel petroleum products than in liquid fuels. Some of the nonfuel commodities, particularly lubricants, have been of strategic importance to the PRC during certain periods. Others, like mineral jelly and wax, are solid foreign-exchange earners. Peking developed export markets for petroleum by-products long before China initiated crude oil exports to Japan. The by-products trade reveals some of the "trading habits" that have carried over into the crude oil trade and energy equipment trade as well.

Lubricants Trade

The PRC has imported a variety of lubricant products since the early 1950's. (See Tables 20.41 and 20.42.) The industrial value of lubricant trade is not evident from the commodity weight statistics. Some of the lubricants, especially those imported in recent years, were expensive, ranging in cost up to $5,000 per metric ton. The exact nature of these high-cost lubricants was not specified in the trade returns, but they were probably high-grade greases for specialized industrial application. Although lubricant prices were highly variable, the average was at least $500 per imported ton of lubricant. The average price of Chinese lubricant exports, on the other hand, was around $200 per metric ton. This price differential between imports and exports illustrates a general feature of China's energy commodity and equipment trade. China tends to import expensive high-technology energy commodities and equipment from the industrial countries and to export low-priced intermediate-technology energy commodities and equipment to Third World countries. The dual import-export pattern in China's energy trade may become increasingly important over the next quarter-century. The PRC will be dependent for some time on the importation of high-technology energy equipment from the industrial countries. But China could also become a major source of intermediate-technology energy commodities (e.g. low-grade lubricants) and energy equipment (drilling equipment, refinery components, power generators, transmission equipment, and the like) for Third World areas. Intermediate-technology energy commodities and equipment may suit Third World needs more closely than expensive high-technology commodities and equipment imported from the industrial countries. Particular items, such as Chinese diesel engines, have already become popular in some Third World countries. China's level of energy production technology will have appeal in countries and regions that have been nationalizing the domestic energy production and marketing structure. The new national energy industries in these countries cannot afford high-cost industrial technology imports and must develop domestic industrial capacity with intermediate-technology equipment. Chinese aid programs in the various branches of energy technology may also be highly effective because of the close match between China's intermediate-technology energy industries and the development needs of energy industries throughout the Third World.

The PRC imported large amounts of lubricants from the Soviet Union

TABLE 20.41

Lubricants Trade by Country and Year: Asia

(Metric tons)

Year	Cambodia	Hong Kong	Indonesia	Japan	Malaysia	Pakistan	Singapore	Thailand
1954		+1						
1955		+1						
1956		+2						
1957		+6						
1958		-12/+3						
1959		-12/+23		+18				
1960		-10/+13					-2	
1961		+128		+116				
1962		+164		+3				
1963		+39		+15^e				
1964		-25/+61						
1965		-263/+118		+15		-10^e	-5^e	
1966	-12	-129/+23		+33	-12	-20^e	-15^e	
1967	-11	-631/+5		+40^e	-15^e	-35^e	-20^e	
1968		-141/+167	-15	+1,468			-25^e	
1969		-845		+1	-487		-163^e	
1970		-171/+40			-440	-6^a	-372	
1971		-350/+4		-7	-24	-3^a	-281	
1972		-2,036			-92	-1^a	-711	
1973		-2,388			-247		-1,937	
1974		-4,267/+43		-4,171/+76	-963		-2,698	
1975		-3,168/+30		-86/+1,896	-797			-1,066
1976		-4,771/+136		-21				-2,213
1977		-5,957/+892						-4,800^e
1978		-3,800^e/+1,200^e						-5,000^e

Note that trade includes both lubricating oil and grease.
^{a} Fiscal year data. ^{e} Estimate.

TABLE 20.42
Lubricants Trade by Country and Year: Non-Asian Areas
(Metric tons)

Year	Great Britain	Equatorial Customs Union	West Germany	Iraq	Kuwait	Puerto Rico	Romania	Somalia	Soviet Union	Sudan	Tanzania	United States
1955									+71,800			
1956									+73,800			
1957									+95,300			
1958				-11					+198,500			
1959									+216,100			
1960									+219,000			
1961									+221,800			
1962									+213,400			
1963									+140,700			
1964	+460[e]								+16,300			
1965							+2,100		+500			
1966									+1,000			
1967		-27	+75						+700	-9		
1968					-34							
1969					-68							
1970					-204		+61,600					
1971	+644		+136		-88		+62,400	-17			-5[e]	
1972							+81,600					
1973			+363				+22,900					
1974			+38		-236						-40[e]	+33
1975						-170[e]						+400[e]
1976												+200[e]
1977												+200[e]

Note that trade includes both lubricating oil and grease.

[e] Estimate.

until 1964 and then switched to Romanian and other East European sources for lubricants. Chinese industry may have been importing as much as 80 percent of its lubricant requirements during the 1950's, making it highly dependent on continuing Soviet supplies (Table 18.7). Starting in the 1960's, China imported high-grade lubricants from Japan and Western Europe in limited volume but at very high cost per metric ton. The Chinese have imported some lubricants from the United States since 1974.

China's lubricant exports have gone primarily to Malaysia, Singapore, Thailand, and Hong Kong. Lubricant exports are mostly oil rather than grease. By 1977, the volume of lubricant imports and exports was probably about equal, although lubricant trade data for Romania stopped in 1974 and does not appear in Tables 20.41 and 20.42. No data are available for lubricant exports to Vietnam and North Korea.

Trade in Petroleum Jelly and Wax

If China's lubricant trade is serious business for Chinese industry, trade in mineral jelly and wax (petrolatum and paraffin) is Peking's comedy act. China has managed to export wax to at least 47 countries (Tables 20.51–20.53), including several countries that themselves produce wax as a by-product of the petroleum industry. In China itself, the paraffin content of crude oil is an enormous headache. At room temperature, Chinese crudes look like brown hand soap. (Relatively wax-free crudes look more like black coffee.) Chinese crudes are variously reported at between 16 percent and 20 percent paraffin by weight, indicating that China produces several million tons of paraffin each year.[16] Part of the paraffin is removed by special dewaxing screens at the wellhead. Part is removed at the refinery. The bulk of the paraffin is probably burned under boilers in residual fuel or crude oil used in factories and power plants. Only a tiny percent of the total paraffin content of Chinese crudes ever finds its way into international trade (Table 21.5).

The wax trade does bring China a profit. The price for Chinese paraffin ran around $125 per ton in the 1960's and reached $200 per ton in the early 1970's. Earnings from trade in paraffin peaked at about $12 million in 1974. The added cost of handling waxy crudes must be many times the export earnings.

The wax trade, like trade in lubricants, provides some interesting clues to China's approach to energy trade policy. Wax appears in the trade statistics of partner countries early in the trade relationship. Peking often gives a "friendship price" to get the trade started. Wax provides a low-bulk, low-cost, high-value export item that is imported by a number of countries in small quantities. It therefore serves as a wedge in

TABLE 20.51

Petroleum Jelly and Wax Trade by Country and Year: Asia

(Metric tons)

Year	Cambodia	Hong Kong	India	Indonesia	Japan	Laos	Malaysia	Pakistan	Singapore	Sri Lanka	Thailand
1956		+10			+84				-251		
1957		-400[e]/+108			+810				-5		
1958		-176/+38			+10			-6	-2		
1959		-162/+16			+10				-4		
1960		-44/+17	-2,199				-1	-6[a]			
1961		+92			+8		-2		-1		
1962	-5	-90/+25				-15	-1		-25		
1963		-132					-25	-9[b]	-225		
1964	-105	-127/+1					-414	-80[e]	-451		
1965	-121	-308			-1		-73	-1,130[e]			
1966		-1,272			-204		-92	-310[e]	-448	-1	
1967		-1,380			-2,370			-3,730[e]	-629	-5	
1968		-3,004			-1,448			-1,000[e]	-207	-3	
1969		-2,596		-175	-123/+70		-1,599	-2,000[e]	-825		
1970		-1,439					-357	-1,203[b]	-574		
1971		-1,830			-30		-451	-1,582[b]	-1,126		
1972		-3,974			-10		-1,645	-3,218[b]	-1,554		
1973		-4,300			-332		-2,298	-3,683[b]	-1,890		
1974		-5,744			-3,484		-369	-7,935[b]	-4,246		
1975		-3,448			-757/+5		-1,791				-730
1976		-6,734/+16			-1,735						-3,792
1977		-8,386/+3									-4,350[e]
1978		-10,000[e]									-4,500[e]

[a] Includes January 1960 through June 1961.　　[b] Fiscal year data.　　[e] Estimate.

TABLE 20.52
Petroleum Jelly and Wax Trade by Country and Year: Europe
(Metric tons)

Year	Belg.-Lux.	Britain	Denmark	Finland	France	W. Germany	Italy
1966		−1,010				−536	−2,050
1967		−1,866	+423			−1,651	−2,187
1968		−574				−575	−1,098
1969						−639	−1,410
1970		−722				−920/+591	−950
1971		−429		−759	−345		−3,831
1972	−730	−332	−745	−1,786		−387	−4,151
1973			−1,572	−1,303		−715	−4,433
1974	−355		−2,426	−2,267	−604	−3,159	−10,675
1975				−2,282		−1,710	

Year	Netherlands	Norway	Soviet Union	Spain	Sweden	Switzerland	Yugoslavia
1955			+2,000				
1956			+2,200				
1957							
1958			+500				
1959			+3,200				
1960			+2,900				
1961			+2,400				
1962			+2,500				
1963			+2,400				
1964	+548		+100				
1965							
1966	+400						
1967	+300				−584		
1968		−508					
1969		−612					
1970		−450				−530	−51
1971					−386		−65
1972		−476				−672	
1973				−969		−1,417	
1974	−797	−450		−3,093	−409	−1,212	
1975		−628		−555	−665	−445	

trade relations. Peking prefers to export wax to nearly a third of the countries of the world in small quantities, rather than singling out a few countries and capturing the whole market by price-cutting. Peking prefers a dispersed market structure for political reasons. It offers a chance for annual trade with many countries that are geographically or politically remote from the PRC. The annual trade agreement becomes a topic of diplomatic discourse and public proof of "friendly" relations. In

TABLE 20.53

Petroleum Jelly and Wax Trade by Country and Year: Africa and Other Areas
(Metric tons)

Year	Egypt	Ethiopia	Ghana	Kenya	Madagascar	Mauritius	Morocco	Nigeria	Sierra Leone	Sudan	Tanzania	Tunisia	Zambia
1965	-414			-5									
1966				-53			-229	-100[e]		-18	-24		
1967	-135			-56		-255	-859	-870[e]		-24			
1968			-152	-55		-28		-200[e]		-10			
1969		-152	-102	-45				-260[e]					
1970	-817			-25		-145		-10[e]			-20	-100	
1971	-2,596			-70		-371		-2,150[e]			-99		
1972	-1,308	-190		-265				-1,000[e]	-153	-20			
1973	-2,604	-695		-335							-38	-375	
1974	-1,142				-1,057								-1,200

Year	Australia	Brazil	Chile	Colombia	Ecuador	Iran	Iraq	New Zealand	Turkey	United States
1965							-68			
1966	-295					-546[a]				
1967	-570					-217[a]	-69	-10		
1968	-626				-152					
1969	-1,446							-202		
1970	-2,124				-370			-801		
1971	-3,305			-25						
1972	-1,621		-567		-182	-1,701[a]			-622	-2
1973	-2,317	-10				-998[a]				-1,700
1974	-6,555	-500	-3,680					-306		-554

[a] Fiscal year data. [e] Estimate.

TABLE 20.61

Petroleum By-Products Trade by Country and Year: Asia

(Metric tons)

Year	Burma	Cambodia	Hong Kong	Indonesia	Japan	Malaysia	Pakistan	Singapore	Sri Lanka	Thailand
1956			+9		+500					
1957					-24,168			-72		
1958			-3,891		-4,758					
1959			-4,827							
1960			-356/+8			-6	-5[a]			
1961										
1962	-270[e]		+9		+10	-5				
1963					-9,438/+5	-30[e]				
1964					-15,320	-80				
1965					-50,054					
1966		-299	+1		-111,404/+4,300	-83		-40[e]		
1967		-20	+1		-86,412/+100[e]			-230[e]	-3	
1968		-8			-46,499/+30			-20[e]		
1969				-131	-47,223/+1	-210				
1970			-117		-73,782	-262				
1971					-55,938	-257		-201		
1972					-60,877	-325	-2[b]	-2		
1973					-76,595	-112		-1		
1974					-71,123	-193		-62		
1975					-61,109/+152	-34				
1976			-3		-105,167/+582					-72
1977					-100,000[e]					-18
1978					-100,000[e]					

Note that trade includes petroleum coke, asphalt, nonlubricating oils, shale, and bituminous mixtures.
[a] Includes January 1960 through June 1961.   [b] Fiscal year data.   [e] Estimate.

TABLE 20.62
Petroleum By-Products Trade by Country and Year: Non-Asian Areas

(Metric tons)

Year	Australia	Belg.-Lux.	Ethiopia	Fiji	France	Ghana	Kuwait	Mauritius	Netherlands	Nigeria	Soviet Union	Tanzania
1958											-6,200	
1959											-3,900	
1960												
1961												
1962												
1963												
1964		-11,849			-9,906				-9,358			
1965					-28,216	-69						
1966					-1,901							-71
1967	-1,140^e						-63					-320^e
1968	-12			-3			-159	-90^e				
1969	-162							-40^e		-1,700^e		-260^e
1970							-63			-1,000^e		
1971												-70^e
1972			-1									
1973												-50^e
1974							-32					

Note that trade includes petroleum coke, asphalt, nonlubricating oils, shale, and bituminous mixtures.

^{e} Estimate.

the long run, if China decides to export more important energy commodities to countries outside of Asia, the trade network will be in place and operating, even if it presently carries only a few tons of petroleum jelly and wax.

Miscellaneous By-Products Trade

The Standard International Trade Classification (SITC) groups a variety of petroleum solids into a single category (SITC number 332.9). (See Tables 20.61 and 20.62.) These by-products include petroleum coke, asphalt, shale tailings, bituminous mixtures, and nonlubricating oils for leather tanning and other applications. The bulk of China's trade that falls into this category consists of petroleum coke exports to Japan. The value of these exports runs about $20–40 per metric ton, so that China has never earned more than a few million dollars from its annual petroleum coke exports. The regular exports to Malaysia are mostly nonlubricating oils and bituminous mixtures.

Total Trade in Refined Petroleum Products

Data for China's total trade in refined petroleum products by country and year are provided in Tables 20.71–20.74. These data are not necessarily the sum of the data contained in Tables 20.3 through 20.6. Many countries list total refined petroleum products trade data without providing disaggregated data by fuel and by-product. The totals listed here therefore frequently exceed the sum of data provided above, but should never be less than the sum of the petroleum products trade listed in Tables 20.3–20.6. Even these summary tables are not 100 percent accurate, since data may still be missing for some countries and years. The degree of completeness increases as the tables become more aggregated and less detailed. Thus, there is a direct empirical trade-off between detail and accuracy, although all of the tables are complete enough to be used as general indexes of Chinese energy trade.

Asia is currently the most important region in China's trade in petroleum products, having displaced the Soviet Union and Eastern Europe in that role in the early 1960's. China has been a net exporter of refined petroleum products to the rest of Asia except during the period immediately after the Great Leap Forward. Until recently, Japan was first among foreign markets for Chinese petroleum products, although figures are missing for Vietnam and North Korea. (Petroleum products trade with these two countries is listed as crude petroleum trade in Tables 20.21 and 20.22.) Hong Kong has recently displaced Japan as the biggest market for Chinese refined petroleum, followed by Thailand.

Malaysia, Pakistan, and Singapore are regular customers, although data for very recent years have not yet been reported in official trade returns. Singapore has frequently provided the PRC with spot purchases of unspecified petroleum products, probably bunker fuel for Chinese ships. Exports of diesel fuel and residual fuel oil to Thailand may increase significantly by 1980.[17] Exports of total refined products to Asian countries in 1978 will be about 1.5 million metric tons, only about 13 percent of total trade in liquid fuels. Thus China's new regional trade is predominantly crude oil, with coal and petroleum products in secondary roles.

China's petroleum trade with Europe, on the other hand, has been predominantly in refined petroleum products, both petroleum fuels and petroleum by-products. The Soviet Union and Eastern Europe have dominated trade in petroleum fuels. China imported nearly 3 million tons of refined petroleum fuels from the USSR as oil trade between the two countries peaked in 1961. This represented roughly 40 percent of petroleum products consumption in that year. As imports of Soviet refined petroleum products began to dry up, Peking switched to Albania and Romania for new supplies of foreign petroleum fuels. The new trade with Eastern Europe, however, did not replace the loss of imported Soviet oil. Rather, the Chinese petroleum industry itself, spurred by the development of Taching oilfield, was required to take up the slack.

Refined petroleum trade with Western Europe has traditionally consisted of petroleum by-products, particularly mineral jelly and wax. China exported by-products to 13 West European countries during the period under review. Britain also exported small quantities of by-products, mostly lubricants, to the PRC.

China has also maintained regular trade exchanges with 25 Third World countries in Africa, the Middle East, and Latin America. Aside from a few spot purchases of petroleum fuels from Egypt, Ghana, and Kuwait, this trade has all been in by-products, mostly mineral jelly and wax. Once again, one is struck by the small size of these transactions, their regularity, and the large number of countries involved. This confirms the hypothesis that petroleum by-products trade is used politically to help maintain formal trade relations at small volume with a large number of Third World trading partners.

China's petroleum products trade with the United States and Oceania is microscopic in terms of the scale of the energy balances of those countries. The PRC is shut out of Australian markets by Indonesian and Middle Eastern crude and out of the American market by Alaskan crude. This would only change if Peking offered substantial price concessions on its crude oil—unlikely in view of the country's limited export

TABLE 20.71
Refined Petroleum Products Trade by Country and Year: Asia
(Metric tons)

Year	Burma	Cambodia	Hong Kong (exports)	Hong Kong (imports)	India	Indonesia	Japan (exports)	Japan (imports)
1954				+1		+953		
1955				+1				
1956			-400[e]	+43				+500
1957			-4,079	+199			-24,188	+124
1958			-5,001	+54			-4,758	+810
1959				+3,695				+28
1960			-410	+199	-2,199			+10
1961				+12,584				+1,518[e]
1962	-270[e]	-5	-90	+435				+116
1963		+100	-132	+370			-9,438	+8
1964		-105	-152	+400			-15,320	+20
1965		-121/+270[e]	-571	+247			-50,064	+15
1966	-1,000	-313/+230	-1,401	+153			-111,608	+9,068
1967		-32	-2,011	+45			-88,785	+150[e]
1968		-8	-3,145	+167		-73	-48,208	+1,516[e]
1969			-3,441				-47,454	+72
1970			-1,727	+40		-313/+362	-73,782	
1971			-20,281	+4			-55,997	+13,557
1972			-9,042				-72,038	+3
1973			-41,125				-76,931	
1974			-278,355	+43			-79,105	+76
1975			-651,883	+30			-61,952	+2,153[e]
1976			-607,492	+152			-142,490	+582
1977			-913,543	+895			-100,000[e]	
1978			-1,133,800[e]	+1,200[e]			-100,000[e]	

Advantage of data are noted in Tables 20.1–20.6

TABLE 20.71 (continued)

Refined Petroleum Products Trade by Country and Year: Asia

(Metric tons)

Year	Laos	Malaysia	Pakistan	Singapore (exports)	Singapore (imports)	Sri Lanka	Thailand
1956				-323			
1957				-5			
1958			-6				
1959		-7	-88	-4	+10,338		
1960			-101[e]	-4	+44,981		
1961		-7		-1	+31,416		
1962	-15	-1					
1963		-25	-9[a]	-25			
1964		-444[e]	-80[e]	-225			
1965	-174	-153	-1,140[e]	-456			
1966		-187	-330[e]	-503[e]		-1	
1967		-15[e]	-3,785[e]	-879[e]		-8	
1968			-1,000[e]	-252[e]		-3	
1969		-2,296	-2,000[e]	-988			
1970		-1,060	-1,211[a]	-946			-1,000[e]
1971		-733	-1,739[a]	-1,608			
1972		-2,079	-3,282[a]	-2,267	+46,169		-500[e]
1973		-2,657	-3,683[a]	-3,863	+80,323		
1974		-1,525	-7,935[a]	-7,006	+86,325		-32,054
1975		-2,622					-58,208
1976							-124,394
1977							-159,155[e]
1978							-209,500[e]

Note that totals may exceed the sum of data reported in Tables 20.3–20.6.
[a] Fiscal year data.   [e] Estimate.

529

TABLE 20.72
Refined Petroleum Products Trade by Country and Year: Europe
(Metric tons)

Year	Albania	Austria	Belg.-Lux.	Britain	Denmark	Finland	France	W. Germany	Italy	Netherlands
1954				+1,100^e						+823
1955				+100^e						
1956				+160^e				+180		+472
1957				+125^e				+2,009		+619
1958				+700				+1,720		
1959							-9,789	+363		+955
1960								-99/+889	+1,000	
1961				+850^e						+2,450^e
1962	+16,000									
1963	+48,000									
1964	+77,000		-11,849	+460^e			-9,906	-529		-9,358/+548
1965				+116^e			-28,216			
1966				-1,548	-225		-1,921	-536	-2,050	-248/+515
1967		-302		-1,866/+109	-424			-1,651/+153	-2,187	-417/+390
1968				-574/+892				-575	-1,098	+377
1969				-320				-639	-1,410	+220
1970				-722				-924/+612	-950	-180
1971				-429/+651	-745	-759	-345	-392	-3,831	
1972			-730	-332		-1,794		-387/+436	-4,161	
1973					-1,572	-1,318		-715	-4,433	
1974			-335		-2,426	-2,304	-604	-3,159/+151	-10,675	-797/+189
1975						-2,282		-1,710		

Note that totals may exceed the sum of data reported in Tables 20.3–20.6.
^{e}Estimate.

TABLE 20.72 (continued)
Refined Petroleum Products Trade by Country and Year: Europe
(Metric tons)

Year	Norway	Poland	Romania	Soviet Union	Spain	Sweden	Switzerland	Yugoslavia
1949				+114,100				
1950				+160,500				
1951				+653,700				
1952				+505,200				
1953				+768,800				
1954				+716,300				
1955				+1,204,600				
1956				+1,335,000				
1957				+1,422,200				
1958				+1,835,200/−6,200				
1959				+2,412,300/−3,900				
1960				+2,395,200				
1961				+2,928,200				
1962				+1,856,400				
1963		+7,700		+1,408,100				
1964		+6,539		+504,900				
1965		+5,809	+110,400	+37,900				
1966	−250			+40,000		−275		
1967	−442			+6,800		−584		
1968	−508			+7,600		−270		
1969	−612	+1,443		+10,300		−259	−201	
1970	−450	+2,352	+84,400			−291	−530	−51/+132
1971		+2,840	+70,900					
1972	−476	+14,200	+87,500			−386	−672	−65/+1,095
1973		+9,000	+46,600		−1,002		−1,417	+258
1974	−450	+18,000	+2,359		−3,146	−409	−1,212	+2,413
1975	−628				−555	−665	−445	+6,145

TABLE 20.73

Refined Petroleum Products Trade by Country and Year: Africa and the Middle East
(Metric tons)

Year	Egypt	Somalia	Sierra Leone	Sudan	Equatorial Customs Union	Ethiopia	Ghana	Kenya	Madagascar	Mauritius	Morocco	Nigeria
1965	-414						-65/+85,477	-5				
1966								-53			-229	-100[e]
1967								-56		-345	-859	-870[e]
1968	+120,210/-135				-27	-19		-55		-68[e]		-200[e]
1969	+74,379					-16	-152	-45			-400	-1,960[e]
1970	-1,219					-152	-102	-25		-145	-200	-1,010[e]
1971	-2,853							-70			-2,333	-2,150[e]
1972	-1,494					-191		-265		-371		-1,183[e]
1973	-2,930					-695		-335				
1974	-1,233								-1,057			

Year	Sierra Leone	Somalia	Sudan	Tanzania	Tunisia	Zambia	Iran	Iraq	Kuwait	Turkey
1959								-11		
1960										
1961										
1962										
1963										
1964								-68		
1965										
1966			-18	-95			-546[a]	-69	-63	
1967			-33	-320[e]			-217[a]/+12,156		-193	
1968			-10					-68	-68	
1969				-260[e]				-98	-204	
1970				-120	-100				-63	
1971		-17		-174					-88/+291,833	
1972	-153		-20				-1,701[a]		+449,585	
1973				-128		-1,203	-998[a]			
1974					-375				-267	-622

Note that totals may exceed the sum of data reported in Tables 20.3-20.6.

TABLE 20.74

Refined Petroleum Products Trade by Country and Year: The Americas and Oceania

(Metric tons)

Year	Brazil	Chile	Colombia	Ecuador	Mexico	Puerto Rico	United States	Australia	Fiji	New Zealand
1966								−295		
1967								−1,720^e	−3	−10
1968				−152				−638		
1969								−1,608/+5		−202
1970				−370				−2,124/+10		−801
1971								−3,305		
1972	−10	−567	−25					−1,621		
1973	−500	−3,680		−182	−11		−2	−2,317		
1974							−1,700	−6,555/+100		−306
1975						−170^e	−587 / +400^e			
1976							+200^e			
1977							+200^e			

Note that totals may exceed the sum of data reported in Tables 20.3–20.6.

^{e}Estimate.

potential. Peking did sign a contract with Coastal States, a west coast U.S. refinery, for the export of a half million tons of Taching crude during the first half of 1979. There was some prospect that the contract might be renewed or expanded during 1979. Coastal States will use the Chinese oil, which is low in sulfur, to produce residual fuel oil for California plants. But so far this trade remains marginal for both the PRC and the United States.

This completes the analysis of China's energy commodity trade by country and year. It is my hope that these data will provide a significant addition to our understanding of China's energy trading habits and a realistic picture of the country's energy export potential. I would like to solicit additions to these data from other scholars and officials working with similar information, since I believe this to be the only reasonably comprehensive and accurate data series on China's energy trade extant outside of the PRC. These data will be revised and republished from time to time.

Chapter 21

Total Energy Trade by Commodity

Summary statistics on China's total energy trade include aggregated series for imports, exports, and net imports of solid fuels, liquid fuels, and total energy (Tables 21.1–21.6). Component trade series are provided for coal, coke, crude petroleum, and refined petroleum products. Trade in refined petroleum products is broken down by fuel (gasoline, kerosene, diesel, residual, liquefied gas) and by by-product (lubricants, mineral jelly and wax, miscellaneous by-products). These series render the Chinese energy trade data compatible with international energy trade data collections and provide a useful tool for more closely tabulating China's energy consumption and total energy balance. Energy trade has been important to China in the past as a source of critically needed petroleum products and as a market for surplus coal and by-products. Energy trade will continue to be important to the PRC in the future as a source of critically needed foreign exchange. Future energy exports will probably dwarf the historical record of energy imports.

It should be understood that the statistics in these tables are highly fluid and subject to further revision as data become available through the official trade returns of partner countries. These statistics and the data on which they are based were collected over the course of several years. It is my experience that each year new data are added for partner countries and years previously unrecorded. On the other hand, it is to be hoped that these statistics do not contain a large amount of spuriously reported data, since an effort has been made throughout the collection process to eliminate unsubstantiated reports of energy commodity trade between the PRC and various countries. The tabulations in this chapter were done by hand on tabletop calculators rather than by computer. This introduces another potential source of error. However, a cross-tabulation system was used, whereby imports, exports, and net imports were tabulated separately and then checked for consistency, a procedure that should have eliminated most errors of tabulation. I will be most grateful for indications of error in these statistics—either in the data base itself or in the tabulation—from other researchers. I see no reason, incidentally, why Peking should not publish trade returns as other coun-

TABLE 21.1
Total Annual Trade in Solid Fuels, 1950–78

Year	Coal (mt) Imports	Coal (mt) Exports	Coal (mt) Net imports	Coke (mt) Imports	Coke (mt) Exports	Coke (mt) Net imports	Solid fuels (mtce)[a] Imports	Solid fuels (mtce)[a] Exports	Solid fuels (mtce)[a] Net imports
1950		−531,634	−531,634					−531,634	−531,634
1951									
1952	+1,061	−15,798	−14,737				+1,061	−15,798	−14,737
1953		−161,885	−161,885					−161,885	−161,885
1954		−54,231	−54,231					−54,231	−54,231
1955		−657,624	−657,624					−657,624	−657,624
1956		−860,975	−860,975		−5,784	−5,784		−866,181	−866,181
1957		−1,164,723	−1,164,723		−2,671	−2,671		−1,167,127	−1,167,127
1958		−653,309	−653,309		−5,529	−5,529		−658,285	−658,285
1959		−457,753	−457,753		−2,551	−2,551		−460,049	−460,049
1960		−481,004	−481,004		−3,748	−3,748		−484,377	−484,377
1961		−215,030	−215,030		−1,693	−1,693		−216,554	−216,554
1962		−575,106	−575,106		−100	−100		−575,196	−575,196
1963	+18,000	−540,849	−522,849		−255	−255	+18,000	−541,079	−523,079
1964	+20,554	−675,564	−655,010		−1,140	−1,140	+20,554	−676,590	−656,036
1965		−1,023,065	−1,023,065		−668	−668		−1,023,666	−1,023,666
1966		−1,340,249	−1,340,249		−1,532	−1,532		−1,341,628	−1,341,628
1967		−1,695,895	−1,695,895		−3,036	−3,036		−1,698,627	−1,698,627
1968		−639,285	−639,285		−4,759	−4,759		−643,568	−643,568
1969		−401,651	−401,651		−3,537	−3,537		−404,834	−404,834
1970		−527,249	−527,249		−21,854	−21,854		−546,918	−546,918
1971	+11,158	−440,141	−428,983		−39,777	−39,777	+11,158	−475,940	−464,782
1972		−277,173	−277,173		−30,313	−30,313		−304,455	−304,455
1973		−300,961	−300,961	+2,058	−33,695	−31,637	+1,852	−331,287	−329,435
1974		−431,496	−431,496		−30,334	−30,334		−458,797	−458,797
1975		−462,030	−462,030		−775	−775		−462,728	−462,728
1976	+241	−327,100	−326,859		−499	−499	+241	−327,549	−327,308
1977		−453,010	−453,010		−406	−406		−453,375	−453,375
1978		−404,000	−404,000					−404,000	−404,000

Total Annual Trade in Liquid Fuels, 1949–78

[Metric tons]

Year	Crude petroleum			Refined petroleum products			Liquid fuels		
	Imports	Exports	Net imports	Imports	Exports	Net imports	Imports	Exports	Net imports
1949	+29,000		+29,000	+114,100		+114,100	+143,100		+143,100
1950	+120,000		+120,000	+160,500		+160,500	+280,500		+280,500
1951	+75,000		+75,000	+653,700		+653,700	+728,700		+728,700
1952	+103,000		+103,000	+505,200		+505,200	+608,200		+608,200
1953	+65,000		+65,000	+768,800		+768,800	+833,800		+833,800
1954	+188,000		+188,000	+718,354		+718,354	+906,354		+906,354
1955	+377,800		+377,800	+1,205,524		+1,205,524	+1,583,324		+1,583,324
1956	+397,000		+397,000	+1,336,195		+1,336,195	+1,733,195		+1,733,195
1957	+380,400		+380,400	+1,425,311	-24,911	+1,400,400	+1,805,711	-24,911	+1,780,800
1958	+672,000		+672,000	+1,837,909	-15,048	+1,822,861	+2,509,909	-15,048	+2,494,861
1959	+646,900		+646,900	+2,428,379	-18,793	+2,409,586	+3,075,279	-18,793	+3,056,486
1960	+588,600		+588,600	+2,442,279	-2,820	+2,439,459	+3,030,879	-2,820	+3,028,059
1961	+56,000		+56,000	+2,976,168	-7	+2,976,161	+3,032,168	-7	+3,032,161
1962	+105,000	-42,000	+63,000	+1,873,801	-367	+1,873,434	+1,978,801	-42,367	+1,936,434
1963	+117,000		+117,000	+1,464,278	-9,914	+1,454,364	+1,581,278	-9,914	+1,571,364
1964	+158,000	-86,000	+72,000	+589,867	-47,968	+541,899	+747,867	-133,968	+613,899
1965		-150,300	-150,300	+240,234	-81,447	+158,787	+240,234	-231,747	+8,487
1966		-250,000	-250,000	+49,966	-122,864	-72,898	+49,966	-372,864	-322,898
1967		-250,000	-250,000	+20,327	-108,617	-88,290	+20,327	-358,617	-338,290
1968		-19,541	-19,541	+130,762	-57,127	+73,635	+130,762	-76,668	+54,094
1969	+158,532		+158,532	+86,781	-64,878	+21,903	+245,313	-64,878	+180,435
1970	+400,991		+400,991	+87,546	-90,255	-2,709	+488,537	-90,255	+398,282
1971	+97,132	-200,000	-102,868	+380,880	-98,451	+282,429	+478,012	-298,451	+179,561
1972	+53,860	-700,000	-646,140	+598,151	-105,824	+492,327	+652,011	-805,824	-153,813
1973		-1,669,888	-1,669,888	+138,336	-149,225	-10,889	+138,336	-1,819,113	-1,680,777
1974		-4,733,414	-4,733,414	+113,388	-446,227	-332,839	+113,388	-5,179,641	-5,066,253
1975	+200,000	-9,798,079	-9,598,079	+2,583	-780,950	-778,367	+202,583	-10,579,029	-10,376,446
1976	+200,000	-8,425,779	-8,225,779	+934	-874,376	-873,442	+200,934	-9,300,155	-9,099,221
1977	+300,000	-9,518,500	-9,218,500	+1,095	-1,172,698	-1,171,603	+301,095	-10,691,198	-10,390,103
1978		-9,890,000	-9,890,000	+1,200	-1,443,300	-1,442,100	+1,200	-11,333,300	-11,332,100

TABLE 21.3
Total Annual Trade in Petroleum Distillates, 1955–78
(Metric tons)

Year	Gasoline			Kerosene[a]			Diesel fuel		
	Imports	Exports	Net imports	Imports	Exports	Net imports	Imports	Exports	Net imports
1955	+634,000		+634,000	+263,800		+263,800	+233,000		+233,000
1956	+641,400		+641,400	+240,122		+240,122	+376,800		+376,800
1957	+573,100		+573,100	+372,805		+372,805	+380,200		+380,200
1958	+640,404		+640,404	+332,808		+332,808	+662,900		+662,900
1959	+1,258,809		+1,258,809	+380,101		+380,101	+567,783		+567,783
1960	+1,089,191		+1,089,191	+386,208		+386,208	+719,942		+719,942
1961	+1,356,206		+1,356,206	+514,775		+514,775	+847,989		+847,989
1962	+764,891		+764,891	+488,310		+488,310	+378,445		+378,445
1963	+455,502		+455,502	+476,013		+476,013	+333,416		+333,416
1964	+269,995	−529	+269,466	+139,104		+139,104	+79,739		+79,739
1965	+57,522	−147	+57,375	+30,007		+30,007	+57,970		+57,970
1966	+32,641	−2	+32,639	+4,004		+4,004	+7,102		+7,102
1967	+3,939	−1	+3,938	+400	−27	+373	+1,953		+1,953
1968							+120,210		+120,210
1969							+74,379		+74,379
1970	+900	−100	+800	+6,500	−2	+6,498	+10,532		+10,532
1971				+1,500	−18,284	−16,784	+2,150		+2,150
1972	+6		+6	+5,595	−3,070	+2,525	+26,003	−11,164	+14,839
1973	+1,117		+1,117		−7,005	−7,005	+7,991	−27,432	−19,441
1974					−28,294	−28,294	+4,718	−222,216	−217,498
1975					−86,533	−86,533		−470,249	−470,249
1976	−4,577	−4,577	−4,577		−139,247	−139,247		−443,000	−443,000
1977	−20,000	−20,000	−20,000		−200,247	−200,247		−636,596	−636,596
1978					−200,000	−200,000		−900,000	−900,000

[a]Includes jet fuel.

tries do, thereby enlightening all of us and setting the record straight to the last decimal point.

As the statistics in these tables stand, I believe that they contain less than 10 percent reporting error for most commodities in most years. As suggested in Chapter 20, the more disaggregated the series in question, the higher the likely reporting error. There may be a greater-than-10 percent reporting error for trade in petroleum fuels for certain years in the 1960's. There is almost certainly a greater-than-10 percent error in the data on energy commodity trade with Vietnam and North Korea, although this error is reduced to less than 10 percent in aggregate with trade in energy commodities with other partner countries. There is obvious error in the estimates for 1978, and the data for certain commodities and countries are thin since 1975. This simply reflects a normal delay in the publication of official trade statistics.

China has been a net solid fuels exporter since the inception of the People's Republic. Solid fuel exports exceeded one million tons in 1957 and 1965 through 1967, but have never constituted more than one percent of China's coal production. Under the long-term trade agreement with Japan, solid fuel exports will reach about 4 million metric tons in 1982, still less than one percent of annual coal production. Crude petroleum imports were marginal during the 1950's, owing to the limits on domestic refinery capacity. Crude petroleum is and will continue to be the principal energy export commodity, perhaps supplemented by liquefied natural gas exports if offshore hydrocarbon deposits turn out to be predominantly natural gas rather than crude oil. Refined products imports were important in the early years of China's industrial development, providing about 50 percent of domestic supply in some years. China may export limited quantities of refined petroleum products to small Asian neighbors, but will reserve most refinery output for domestic consumption. Liquid fuel exports peaked in 1975 at 10.6 mmt and then declined under the pressure of a domestic political debate over the efficacy of oil exports (Chapter 6). Recovery in 1977 was followed by a record oil export year in 1978, with total exports reaching more than 11 million metric tons of crude petroleum and refined petroleum products. Exports constituted about 11 percent of China's 1978 crude petroleum production, which was expected to pass the 2 million barrels per day mark (100 mmt/year) sometime late in the year. In 1978, the PRC was expected to rank about fifteenth in liquid fuel exports, behind all of the OPEC countries except Gabon and Ecuador. China's current oil exports are comparable to the annual oil exports of Syria, Brunei, Norway, or Trinidad. If my projections are correct, China's future export potential will resemble Indonesia's role in the world oil market.

TABLE 21.4

Total Annual Trade in Miscellaneous Petroleum Fuels, 1949–78

(Metric tons)

Year	Residual fuel			Liquefied gas [a]			Unspecified petroleum products [b]		
	Imports	Exports	Net imports	Imports	Exports	Net imports	Imports	Exports	Net imports
1949							+114,100		+114,100
1950							+160,500		+160,500
1951							+653,700		+653,700
1952							+505,200		+505,200
1953							+768,800		+768,800
1954							+718,353		+718,353
1955							+923		+923
1956							+1,352		+1,352
1957		−20	−20	+40		+40	+3,668		+3,668
1958							+1,946		+1,946
1959	+1	−88	−87				+2,318	−9,789	−7,471
1960	+1	−90	−89				+24,989	−99	+24,890
1961	+4,601		+4,601				+28,150		+28,150
1962							+25,950		+25,950
1963	+100		+100				+56,100		+56,100
1964							+83,544		+83,544
1965	+85,667	−9	+85,658				+6,335	−23	+6,312
1966	+347		+347				+115	−1,556	−1,441
1967	+12,113	−3	+12,110				+278	−2,164	−1,886
1968		−216	−261	+18		+18	+8,869	−415	+8,454
1969		−108	−108				+12,330	−1,301	+11,029
1970		−1	−1				+7,383	−2,077	+5,306
1971	+292,578	−180	+292,398	+13,557		+13,557	+7,911	−3,301	+4,610
1972	+420,542	−5	+420,537				+64,405	−404	+64,001
1973	+1,716		+1,716				+104,249	−423	+103,826
1974	+3,786	−50,203	−46,417				+104,694	−205	+104,489
1975		−144,825	−144,825	+100		+100			
1976		−167,675	−167,675						
1977		−207,420	−207,420		−5	−5			
1978		−200,000	−200,000					−360	−360

[a] These were so reported liquefied gas exports.

[b] The trade returns of certain countries do not disaggregate trade statistics for refined petroleum products.

TABLE 21.3

Total Annual Trade in Petroleum By-Products, 1954–78
(Metric tons)

Year	Lubricants			Petroleum jelly and wax			Other by-products[a]		
	Imports	Exports	Net imports	Imports	Exports	Net imports	Imports	Exports	Net imports
1954	+1		+1						
1955	+71,801		+71,801	+2,000		+2,000			
1956	+73,802		+73,802	+2,210		+2,210	+509		+509
1957	+95,306		+95,306	+192	-651	-459		-24,240	-24,240
1958	+198,503	-12	+198,491	+1,348	-187	+1,161		-14,849	-14,849
1959	+216,141	-25	+216,116	+3,226	-164	+3,062		-8,727	-8,727
1960	+219,013	-10	+219,003	+2,927	-2,254	+673	+8	-367	-359
1961	+221,928		+221,928	+2,500	-2	+2,498	+19	-5	+14
1962	+213,680		+213,680	+2,525	-97	+2,428		-270	-270
1963	+140,742		+140,742	+2,400	-206	+2,194	+5	-9,438	-9,433
1964	+16,836	-25	+16,811	+649	-951	-302		-46,463	-46,463
1965	+2,733	-278	+2,455		-2,571	-2,571		-78,419	-78,419
1966	+1,056	-188	+868	+400	-7,257	-6,857	+4,301	-113,861	-109,560
1967	+820	-782	+38	+723	-17,263	-16,540	+101	-88,377	-88,276
1968	+1,635	-249	+1,386		-9,623	-9,623	+30	-46,579	-46,549
1969	+1	-1,699	-1,698	+70	-12,084	-12,014	+1	-49,686	-49,685
1970	+61,640	-989	+60,651	+591	-11,862	-11,271		-75,224	-75,224
1971	+63,184	-768	+62,416		-19,450	-19,450		-56,468	-56,468
1972	+81,600	-2,847	+78,753		-27,129	-27,129		-61,205	-61,205
1973	+23,263	-4,616	+18,647		-32,991	-32,991		-76,758	-76,758
1974	+190	-12,505	-12,315		-61,394	-61,394		-71,410	-71,410
1975	+2,326	-5,117	-2,791	+5	-13,011	-13,006	+152	-61,215	-61,063
1976	+336	-7,005	-6,669	+16	-12,261	-12,245	+582	-105,188	-104,606
1977	+1,092	-10,757	-9,665	+3	-12,736	-12,733		-100,000	-100,000
1978	+1,200	-8,800	-7,600		-14,500	-14,500		-100,000	-100,000

[a] Includes petroleum coke, asphalt, nonlubricating oils, shale, and bituminous mixtures.

TABLE 21.6
Total Annual Trade in Energy Commodities, 1949–78
(Metric tons coal equivalent)

Year	Imports	Exports	Net imports
1949	+214,650		+214,650
1950	+420,750	−531,634	−119,884
1951	+1,093,050		+1,093,050
1952	+913,361	−15,798	+897,563
1953	+1,250,700	−161,885	+1,088,815
1954	+1,359,531	−54,231	+1,305,300
1955	+2,374,986	−657,624	+1,717,362
1956	+2,599,793	−866,181	+1,733,612
1957	+2,708,567	−1,204,494	+1,504,073
1958	+3,764,864	−680,857	+3,084,007
1959	+4,612,919	−488,239	+4,124,680
1960	+4,546,319	−488,607	+4,057,712
1961	+4,548,252	−216,565	+4,331,687
1962	+2,968,202	−638,747	+2,329,455
1963	+2,389,917	−555,950	+1,833,967
1964	+1,142,354	−877,542	+264,812
1965	+360,351	−1,371,286	−1,010,935
1966	+74,949	−1,900,924	−1,825,975
1967	+30,491	−2,236,553	−2,206,062
1968	+196,143	−758,570	−562,427
1969	+367,969	−502,151	−134,182
1970	+732,806	−682,301	−50,505
1971	+728,176	−923,617	−195,441
1972	+978,016	−1,513,191	−535,175
1973	+209,356	−3,059,957	−2,850,601
1974	+170,082	−8,228,259	−8,058,177
1975	+303,875	−16,331,272	−16,027,397
1976	+301,642	−14,277,782	−13,976,140
1977	+451,643	−16,490,172	−16,038,529
1978	+1,800	−17,403,950	−17,402,150

Note that trade includes petroleum by-products. Liquid fuels trade is tabulated at 1.5 mtce/mt average energy value.

China's net energy imports peaked at about 4.3 million metric tons coal equivalent in 1961, about 4 percent of aggregate consumption. Net energy exports in 1978 equaled about 17–18 mmtce, or 3 percent of total energy production. Thus, even at the height of its petroleum dependency on the Soviet Union, China was 96 percent self-sufficient in energy, a remarkable development feat for a country of China's size and stage of industrialization. My projections indicate the overall balance between energy production and consumption in the PRC will continue, with export potential expanding to a maximum of about 10–15 percent of total energy production in the late 1980's. China's energy trade experience contrasts sharply with energy trade patterns in both the oil-importing and oil-exporting countries of the Third World. Third World oil-importing countries, on the average, are more than 75 percent dependent on foreign oil for their commercial energy supplies. Third World oil-exporting countries commonly export more than 75 percent of total energy production. China's energy trade pattern does have two precedents—the United States and the Soviet Union—both large countries that achieved rapid industrialization on the basis of domestically produced energy supplies, and both countries that for many years kept trade in energy commodities intentionally limited to the margins of their energy balances.

Two factors contributed to the maintenance of China's energy self-reliance—the large size of the domestic coal industry (and its rapid development with Soviet assistance), and stringent economy measures that sharply curtailed personal consumption of commercial energy commodities, channeling all available energy supplies into end-uses that would expand production capacity. The power of the Chinese energy development model lies in the fact that each additional increment of domestic energy consumption was earned by an equal increment of domestic energy production. Thus, by the time the PRC's aggregate commercial energy consumption began to reach modern levels, the country had already created an energy production infrastructure commensurate with its needs. China may still be a poor country on the basis of per capita energy consumption standards, but the PRC is totally free of dependency on foreign energy supplies or markets, an important motivation for continuation of Peking's self-reliant development policies. There are powerful development reasons why China refuses to consider consuming more energy than it produces, or offering energy resource concessions as the price of energy technology imports. If there is any feature of the Chinese energy development model that I consider relevant to the energy development problems of Third World countries, particularly large Third World countries like Indonesia, India, or Brazil, it is the lesson of self-reliance. Limited domestic energy resources should not be recklessly released to foreign control or squandered in nearsighted trade. Energy consumption must be earned by development of the domestic energy production infrastructure; it cannot simply be imported in oil tankers. In short, the energy balance of each Third World country must be made to fit as closely as possible to the contours of the domestic energy resource base.

Chapter 22

Energy Plant and Equipment Imports

The tables in this chapter provide a single listing of data on China's imported energy plants and production equipment. The tables are disaggregated according to the type of plant and equipment imported. Except for Table 22.4 (oil tanker imports), information is provided for each purchase on the contract year, exporting country, exporting company, price, number of units, and equipment type. The transactions were arranged chronologically by contract year and within each year alphabetically by exporting country. Individual transactions of importance have been discussed at length in the chapters of Part I; that discussion will not be repeated here.

As with energy commodity trade and other energy statistics, a relatively conservative strategy has been adopted in the compilation of these tables (Tables 22.1–22.6). The data were compiled largely from secondary sources. Previous compilations, including the complete plant purchases compiled by Dr. Hans Heymann for the U.S. Joint Economic Committee of Congress and by the National Council for U.S.–China Trade, were combined, checked for internal consistency, and greatly simplified.[1] Work by these other researchers was then supplemented by a line-by-line search of the *U.S.–China Business Review*, the *China Trade Report*, the *Far Eastern Economic Review*, the *Asia Research Bulletin*, and the English-language articles and books listed in the Bibliography. Data on China's purchases of oil tankers were taken primarily from the work of George Lauriat, published in a number of periodicals, and were supplemented from scattered reports from other sources.[2] Information on trade in high-technology energy production equipment is often considered proprietary information by the companies selling the equipment. Companies are particularly hesitant to reveal exact prices for equipment that may be traded at various prices under different market conditions. In many instances, the company will refuse to report the transaction to any source and to identify itself as the selling agent. Peking, on the other hand, is not particularly eager to talk about its equipment dependences, for both commercial and political reasons. These factors introduce a serious downward bias into the data as presented in these tables. Official trade returns are of little use in rectifying this situation, since in most cases they break the plants and equipment down into component parts (valves, transformers, pumps, and the like) that are aggregated with non-energy equipment in the trade returns. For these reasons, I chose to report only those data that had a clear energy function, a confirmed contract date, and a known country of origin.[3] Many reported transactions were eliminated as rumors or as duplicate reports of earlier transactions.

Extrapolating from transactions of known value to total transactions in each equipment category, I would estimate that total expenditures on energy production and transportation equipment (including chemical fertilizer plants) between 1960 and the first quarter of 1978 were at least $3.75 billion. Allowing for inflation and unreported transactions, the total would be in the vicinity of $4 billion in 1978 U.S. dollars. It is interesting that China's total expenditures on energy plants and equipment almost exactly equal the country's earnings from crude petroleum exports (Chapter 20).

Breaking the plant and equipment purchases down by equipment type, refineries and petrochemical plants led with 40 percent ($1.5 billion) of the total. Chemical fertilizer plants followed with 20 percent ($750 million) of the total. Petroleum exploration and production equipment, far and away the most popular topic of conversation among China trade experts, ranked third with 16 percent ($600 million) of total energy equipment imports. Electric power equipment constituted 13 percent ($500 million) and coal-mining equipment 8 percent ($300 million). No price figures were reported for most of the tanker purchases, but the total would not be in excess of $100 million, or 3 percent of the Chinese energy equipment market.

Based on current patterns in China's energy development, as reported throughout this Statistical Profile, I would expect electric power equipment to do particularly well on Peking's energy equipment shopping list between now and 1985. The purchase of a single commercial-scale nuclear power plant, for example, would cost on the order of $1 billion. Some of the equipment purchases related to the electric power industry will be heavy industrial machinery for China's own electric power equipment factories. Peking may also be interested in high-tension transmission technology.

In petroleum production equipment trade, we should expect continued emphasis on cutting-edge oilfield equipment, particularly secondary or tertiary extraction technology for China's maturing onland oilfields. The exact pattern of purchases is difficult to predict, but I would expect less emphasis on exploration equipment and more emphasis on produc-

TABLE 22.1
Petroleum Exploration and Production Equipment Imports, 1964–78

Contract year	Country	Company	Price (million $)	No. of units	Equipment type
1964	Japan	Nishijima	—	26	LPG pumps
1965	France	—	4.86	—	Oil-drilling equipment
1965	Romania	—	—	2	Oil-drilling rigs[a]
1966	Britain	Stanhope-Seta	—	—	Testing equipment
1967	Britain	Mannesmann	—	—	Steel pipe
1971	Romania	—	—	37	Oil-drilling rigs[a]
1972	Japan	Mitsubishi	9.8	1	Jack-up offshore drilling rig "Fuji"
1972	Japan	Nippon Kaiyo Kussaku	—	1	Workship "Kuroshio"
1972	Japan	Marubeni	13.0	6	Dredge boats (for harbor construction)
				8	Hopper barges
1972	Romania	—	—	37	Oil-drilling rigs[a]
1973	Britain	RHF	—	—	Lubricant-testing equipment
1973	Denmark	Weco	41.8	8	Rig supply and towing vessels
1973	Japan	Hitachi	10.0	5	Supply and service ships
1973	Japan	—	16.7	2	Tugboats
1973	Japan	—	—	—	Large-bore oil pipeline
1973	Japan	Nippon Kokan	56.6	8	Self-propelling bucket dredges
1973	Japan	Teikoku Oil	—	1	Shallow-water drilling unit ("jacket type")
1973	Japan	Mitsui	6.7	2	Crane ships (for harbor construction)
1973	Netherlands	NVIHC	39.3	4	Trailer suction hopper dredges
1973	Norway	Solstad Rederi	8.7	4	Supply ships
1973	Norway	Norse Petroleum	—	2	Supply ships
1973	Norway	Fred Olsen	—	2	Supply ships
1973	U.S.	Geospace	5.5	—	Seismic survey and computer equipment
1973	U.S.	—	0.5	—	Oil-drilling equipment

[a] Romania has exported an unknown number of drilling rigs to China each year since 1965. Only years for which reliable data exist have been reported here.

TABLE 22.1 (continued)
Petroleum Exploration and Production Equipment Imports, 1964–78

Contract year	Country	Company	Price (million $)	No. of units	Equipment type
1973	U.S.	Rucker	2.0	20	Blowout preventers
1974	France	CGG	–	1	Seismic survey ship ("Isabel")
1974	Japan	Komatsu	1.0	12	Pipelayers
1974	Norway	Fred Olsen	–	2	Supply ships
1974	U.S.	Control Data	7.0	2	Cyber 172 computers
1975	Canada	–	0.7	–	Steel casing for drilling operations
1975	Japan	San-Netu	–	–	Oil filter equipment
1975	Japan	Nichimen	–	–	Safety equipment for drilling
1975	Japan	Sumitomo Shoji	–	1	Ocean survey ship with diving spheres
1975	Singapore	Robin Loh	60.0	2	Robray 300 jack-up drilling rigs
1975	U.S.	Interdata	23.0	–	Computerized well-logging equipment
1975	U.S.	Cameron Iron	0.75	–	Well heads and gate valves
1975	U.S.	Caterpillar	3.8	38	Pipelayers
1975	U.S.	Dowell Schlumberger	3.0	8	High-pressure hydraulic fracturing equipment (truck-mounted)
1976	Britain	John Brown	–	1	Gas pipeline turbine pump
1976	W. Germany	Messerschmidt	–	2	Offshore supply helicopters
1976	Japan	Hitachi Robin Loh	22.0	1	Robray 300 jack-up offshore drilling rig
1976	U.S.	Digital Resources	1.7	2	Computerized seismic exploration systems
1976	U.S.	Stewart and Stevenson	5.8	20	Mobile oil-well servicing units
1976	U.S.	–	1.5	3	Truck-mounted seismic units
1977	Australia	Hawker de Havilland	0.318	2	Offshore helicopter engines
1977	France	Marep	2.3	–	Drilling pipes
1977	France	CGG	1.7	–	Cables for prospecting ships

(continued)

TABLE 22.1 (continued)
Petroleum Exploration and Production Equipment Imports, 1964–78

Contract year	Country	Company	Price (million $)	No. of units	Equipment type
1977	France	Cri-Dan	5.0	11	Drilling-pipe threaders
1977	W. Germany	Mercedes-Benz	3.0	115	Oil pipe trucks
1977	Norway	Fred Olsen	27-40[e]	1	Aker H-3 semisubmersible offshore drilling rig "Borgny Dolphin"
1977	Norway	Sandoy	–	2	Offshore rig supply ships
1977	Singapore	–	–	5	Offshore rig supply ships
1977	U.S.	Armco	15-20[e]	2	National 1320 offshore drilling rigs for production platforms
1977	U.S.	Caterpillar	–	120	Drilling-rig power units
1977	U.S.	Baker Trading	2.0	2	Hydraulic workover rigs
1977	U.S.	Otis Engineering	2.0	1	Hydraulic workover rig and testing equipment
1977	U.S.	Digital Resources	3.7	1	Seismic exploration system
1977	U.S.	Daedalus	2.0	–	Infrared survey equipment
1977	U.S.	Bowen Tool	0.5	–	Oil-well pipe recovery equipment
1977	U.S.	–	–	16	Hydraulic vibrators for exploration
1977	U.S.	International Harvester	2.85	3	Oil-rig moving systems (onland)
1977	U.S.	Hughes Tool	2.5	–	Drill bits
1977	U.S.	Smith International	–	–	Oil-drilling equipment
1978	Austria	Teufelsberger	–	–	Oil-drilling rig cables
1978	Canada	Proline Pipe	0.7	–	Pipeline construction equipment
1978	France	CGG	–	1	Seismic survey ship
1978[b]	France	Société d'Etudes de Recherches	15.0	–	Petroleum exploration laboratory materials
1978	Japan	Mitsui	18.8	2	Seismic survey ships
1978	Japan	Mitsui	–	2	Offshore rig supply ships

[b] Reported too late for inclusion in the text or the analysis.   [e] Estimate.

TABLE 22.1 (concluded)
Petroleum Exploration and Production Equipment Imports, 1964–78

Contract year	Country	Company	Price (million $)	No. of units	Equipment type
1978[b]	Japan	World Ocean Systems	6.9	5	Oil-skimming ships
1978[b]	Japan	—	6.9	1	Geophysical survey ship
1978[b]	Japan	Hitachi	53.0	2	Jack-up offshore drilling rigs
1978	Norway	Geco-Statex	2.2	—	Marine seismic equipment
1978	Singapore U.S.	Bethlehem Singapore	20-25[e]	1	Bethdrill JU-250 jack-up offshore drilling rig
1978	Singapore U.S.	Marathon Le Tourneau	46.0	2	Marathon 82-SD-S jack-up offshore drilling rigs
1978	Singapore U.S.	Hughes Tool	1.0	—	Oil pipe tool joints
1978	U.S.	Hughes Tool	10.0	—	Drill bits and cutters
1978	U.S.	Hughes Tool	4.5	—	Drill bits
1978	U.S.	B. J. Hughes	0.5	—	Offshore well-cementing equipment
1978	U.S.	Analog Devices	0.5	—	Integrated circuits for petroleum
1978	U.S.	B. J. Hughes	0.1	—	Petroleum-handling tools
1978	U.S.	Grant Geophysical	—	1	Geophysical research ship
1978[b]	U.S.	Reda Pump	1.25	—	Submersible pumps for oilfields

[b] Reported too late for inclusion in the text or the analysis.   [e] Estimate.

TABLE 22.2

Petroleum Refining and Petrochemical Equipment Imports, 1963–78

Contract year	Country	Company	Price (million $)	No. of units	Equipment type
1963	France	Speichem	8.5	2	Ethylene plants
1963	Italy	Snam-Projetti (ENI)	5.0	1	Oil refinery
1963	Japan	Kurashiki	20.0	1	Vinylon fiber plant
1963	Japan	Dai Nippon	30.0	1	Vinylon fiber plant
1964	Britain	Simon Carves	12.6	1	Polyethylene plant
1964	Britain	—	7.3	1	Polypropylene plant
1964	W. Germany	Uhde	1.75	1	Synthetic fiber plant (Perlon)
1964	W. Germany	Lurgi-Gesellschaft	12.5	1	Heavy oil-cracking plant
1964	Japan		3.0	1	Acetylene gas plant
1965	Britain	Scott Bader	—	1	Polyester resin plant
1965	Britain	Prinex	8.4	1	Acrylic resin plant
1965	W. Germany	Lurgi-Gesellschaft	11.0	1	Acrylonitrile plant
1965	Italy	Snam-Projetti (ENI)	9.0	1	Oil refinery
1965	Norway	—	14.0	1	Naphtha cracking plant
1966	Italy	Snam-Projetti (ENI)	5.5	1	Aromatic chemical plant
1972	Japan	Kuraray	—	1	Vinylon fiber plant
1972	Japan	Kurashiki	18.9	1	Synthetic fiber plant
1972	Japan	Toray	90.0	1	Synthetic fiber plant
1972	Japan	Kaisha	—	1	Acetic acid plant
1972	Japan	Mitsubishi	34.0	1	Ethylene and polyvinyl alcohol plant
1973	France	Speichem	90.0	1	Vinyl acetate plant
	Britain	Humphrey & Glascow		1	Methanol plant
	W. Germany	Lurgi, BASF			
1973	France	Technip-Speichem	282.0	1	Petrochemical and synthetic fiber complex
1973	W. Germany	Uhde	4.0	1	Acetaldehyde plant
1973	Japan	Toyo, Mitsui, Itoh	46.0	1	Ethylene plant
	U.S.	Lummus		1	Butadiene plant

TABLE 22.2 (continued)

Petroleum Refining and Petrochemical Equipment Imports, 1963–78

Contract year	Country	Company	Price (million $)	No. of units	Equipment type
1973	Japan	Kuraray	26.0	1	Ethylene plant
	W. Germany	Bayer		2	Polyvinyl alcohol plants
1973	Japan U.S.	Asahi, Niigata, Asaki Sohio	37.0	1	Synthetic fiber plant
1973	Japan	Toray, Mitsui Toatsu	49.0	1	Polyester polymerization plant
1973	Japan	Sumitomo	5.7	1	Aromatic chemical plant
1973	Japan	Mitsubishi	22.0	1	Polyethylene plant
1973	Japan	Sumitomo	47.0	1	Polyethylene plant
1973	Japan	Mitsui, Itoh, Kosho	26.0	1	Polypropylene plant
1973	Japan U.S.	Hitachi, Nisso Scientific Design	15.0	2	Ethylene plants
1974	Denmark	Haldor Topsoe	—	1	Reformer catalyst plant
1974	France	Rhone Poulenc	10.0	1	Nylon-spinning plant
1974	W. Germany	Uhde	19.0	1	Vinylchloride monomer plant
1974	W. Germany	Uhde	15.7	1	Polyethylene plant
1974	Italy U.S.	Snam-Projetti (ENI) Standard of Indiana	16.0	1	Polypropylene plant
1974	Japan	Itoh, Toho, Kosho	4.7	1	Polypropylene catalyst plant
1974	Japan	Teijin, Toray, Nissho	16.7	1	Polyester spinning plant
1974	Japan	Kuraray	19.0	1	Polyvinyl alcohol plant
1974	Japan	Nisso	14.0	1	Synthetic fiber plant
1975	France	Speichem	—	1	Acetylene plant
1975	W. Germany U.S.	Linde Houdry	20.0	1	Benzene and xylene plant
1975	Italy	Eurotecnica	30.0	1	Benzene plant
1975	Japan	Toyo	—	1	Petrochemical plant (unspecified)
1975	Japan	Toyo	—	1	Petrochemical plant (unspecified)
1975	Japan	Mitsubishi	31.5	1	Ethylene plant
1975	Japan	Itoh, Japan Gasoline	36.0	1	Benzene and tuolene plant

(continued)

TABLE 22.2 (*concluded*)

Petroleum Refining and Petrochemical Equipment Imports, 1963–78

Contract year	Country	Company	Price (million $)	No. of units	Equipment type
1976	W. Germany	Krupp-Koppers	50.0	1	Dimethylenephthalate (DMP) plant
1976	W. Germany	Uhde	20.0	1	Ethanol
1976	W. Germany	Kraus-Maffei	–	9	Polyester fiber centrifuges
1976	W. Germany	BASF	25.9	1	Diethylhexanol plant
1976	Italy	Nuovo Pignone	10.0	–	Centrifugal compressor technology
1976	Japan	Japan Synthetic Rubber	26.6	1	Synthetic rubber plant
1976	Japan	Toray	66.4	1	Polyester polymerization plant
1976	Japan	Ube, Unitika, Maruzen	–	1	Caprolactam-nylon plant
1976	Japan	Teijin	40.1	1	Polyester polymerization plant
1977[a]	W. Germany	Lurgi Zimmer	39.1	1	Terephthalic plant Polyester fiber plant
1977	Japan	Mitsubishi	0.75	3	Centrifugal gas compressors
1977	Japan	Mitsubishi	3.8	10	Hydrogen gas compressors
1977	Japan	Kurita	0.72	12	Dewaxing filter presses
1977	Japan	Chiyoda	16.9	1	Natural gas refining plant
1977[a]	Japan	Aka Okano	0.3	–	Petrochemical valves
1978[a]	Britain	Davy International	74.5	2 1	Oxo-alchohol plants Methanol plant
1978[a]	W. Germany	Lurgi Gesellschaften	275.0	1 1	Ammonia plant Methanol plant
1978[a]	W. Germany	Uhde	–	1 1 3	Ethanol plant Polyethylene plant Acetaldehyde plants
1978	Japan	Ishikawajima	4.2	4	Gas compressors
1978	Japan	Mitsubishi	9.4	1	Ethylene plant
1978[a]	Japan	Japan Gasoline	35.0	1	Synthetic leather plant (MDI)
1978[a]	Japan	Marubeni	125.0	1	Ethylene plant
1978[a]	Japan	Yamatake-Honeywell	0.36	–	Petrochemical valves

tion equipment between 1980 and 1985. In offshore exploration technology, the Chinese market is still wide open to foreign equipment. The PRC has already purchased a basic fleet of exploration rigs. Peking might be interested in one or two more semisubmersible rigs for deepwater work. The emphasis between 1980 and 1985 will be on exploratory drilling across a wide area of the continental shelf. China has already acquired the bulk of its seismic equipment needs and a considerable amount of remote sensing technology, so that purchases should decline in this category. Offshore production equipment purchases (production platforms, subsea pipelines, etc.) will begin in earnest before 1985 and will accelerate thereafter, depending on the volume and ease of access to reserves located offshore in the exploration phase. There are recent indications that Peking may choose to buy exploration services in the offshore zones through contract arrangements or some sort of joint venture with foreign firms.

In the refinery and petrochemical industries, I would expect a sharp decline from the levels of foreign equipment purchases recorded in the 1970's. Basic refinery capacity will have to keep pace with the expansion of the petroleum industry, but the PRC may be able to construct much of the additional capacity from domestically manufactured refinery components. Some petrochemical and synthetic-fiber plant purchases will continue into the 1980's, but China is slowly mastering this technology as well and will be able to substitute domestically produced components in some categories. The same general plan—lower foreign equipment imports and higher domestic equipment manufacture—will be evident in the chemical fertilizer industry. It is interesting to note that refineries, petrochemical plants, and chemical fertilizer plants were not mentioned in the explicit goal of 120 large-scale projects in the Ten-Year Plan, despite obvious needs for further expansion in these industries.[4] Some of the nonenumerated projects in the list were doubtless in these industries, but they have a lower priority than oilfield development or the steel industry.

It appears that Peking is planning substantial purchases of coal-mining equipment over the next few years and that British companies have a clear lead in the Chinese market. Technologically advanced equipment such as long-wall mining systems and hydraulic cutters will continue to be featured in this trade. But the emphasis may shift in the direction of surface mining equipment and beneficiation plants. China has enormous untapped coal reserves in the north-central part of the country (Shensi and Shansi provinces) that total more than a trillion metric tons.[5] The main deposits are generally deeper than 50 meters, making surface mining costly and difficult.[6] Furthermore, these deposits are remote

TABLE 22.3
Chemical Fertilizer Plants and Equipment Imports, 1963–78

Contract year	Country	Company	Price (million $)	No. of units	Equipment type
1963	Britain	Humphrey & Glascow	8.4	1	Ammonia plant
1963	Italy	Montecattini	14.2	1	Ammonia plant
1963	Italy	—	3.6	1	Ammonia plant
1963	Netherlands	Stork-Werkspoor	7.0	1	Urea plant
1965	Britain	Humphrey & Glascow	23.52	4	Ammonia plants
1965	Italy	Montecattini	7.5	1	Chemical fertilizer plant (unspecified)
1972	Japan	Kagaku, Mitsui	—	2	Chemical fertilizer plants (unspecified)
1973	Japan	Toyo, Mitsui	42.0	1	Ammonia plant
				1	Urea plant
1973	Netherlands	Kellogg Continental	34.0	3	Urea plants
1973	Netherlands	Kellogg Continental	56.0	5	Urea plants
1973	U.S.	Kellogg	75.0	3	Ammonia plants
1973	U.S.	Kellogg	130.0	5	Ammonia plants
1974	Britain	Scama	0.053	—	Urea plant monitoring equipment
1974	Denmark	Haldor Topsoe	13.0	1	Ammonia catalyst plant
1974	France	Heurtey	118.0	2	Ammonia plants
	Netherlands	Dutch State Mines		1	Urea plant
1974	Netherlands	Dutch State Mines	35.0	3	Urea plants
1975	France	Heurtey	127.0	3	Ammonia plants
	Denmark	Haldor Topsoe		1	Ammonia catalyst plant
1976	Japan	Nippon Kokan	—	1	Ammonia synthesis converter
1976	U.S.	—	7.5	—	Engines and turbines for ammonia plants
1976	U.S.	—	5.6	—	Gas compressors for ammonia plants
1976	U.S.	—	3.2	—	Steam boilers for ammonia plants
1978	France	Heurtey	21.0	—	Spare parts for fertilizer plants

TABLE 22.4
Oil Tanker Imports, 1974–76

Construction					
Country	Year	Year of purchase	Original name	Present name	Weight (dwt)
Britain	1952	—	Santa Fortuna Sandalwood	Taching No. 15	15,400
Britain	—	1976	Curlew	—	16,000[e]
Britain	—	1976	Gannet	—	16,000[e]
Britain	—	1976	Kestrel	—	16,000[e]
Britain	—	1976	Trust	—	16,000[e]
Britain	—	1976	Fulmar	—	16,000[e]
Denmark	1960	—	Gjertud Maersk	Chinshakiang	27,930
Denmark	1964	1974	Vesthav	Jianhu	59,115
Japan	1966	—	Viborg	Bingjiang	20,307
Japan	1951	—	Maru	Nisshin	27,169
Japan	1975	1975	Sanyo Maru	Xinhu	10,826
Japan	1972	—	Ocean Trader	Yanhu	8,749
Japan	—	1975	Tatsuta Maru	—	92,000
Japan	—	1976	—	—	32,280
Norway	1967	—	John Knudsen	Baohu	74,300
Norway	1963	1975	Berge Bergesen	Danhu	96,140
Norway	1957	—	Anella Amica	Laoshan	14,500
Norway	1957	—	Horn Crusader	Nanyang	20,307
Norway	1966	—	—	Quinghu	63,000
Norway	1952	—	Barbo	Taching No. 16	18,400
Norway	1958	—	Anne Belstar	Taching No. 34	15,970
Norway	1958	—	Horn Clipper	Taching No. 35	15,925
Norway	1957	—	Vivi	Taching No. 36	16,070
Norway	1957	—	Pet Norse Viking Farmland	Taching No. 37	17,260
Norway	1962	—	Dansborg Kindvil	Taching No. 38	13,428
Norway	1960	—	Gorthon Vinstra	Taching No. 41	18,885
Norway	1965	1974	Beauregard	Taihu	74,480
Norway	1966	—	Vanja	Yuhu	74,740
Norway	1966	—	Anna Knudsen	Zhinhu	74,300
Poland	1962	—	Prof. M. T. Huber	Taching No. 17	19,350
Spain	1968	—	Stolt Heron Tomaco	Sunniao	25,423
Sweden	1965	—	Anne Acina	Changhu	50,920
Sweden	1966	—	Beaumont	Gaohu	74,480
Sweden	1965	—	Bralinda	Honghu	56,525
Sweden	1963	—	Wanyia Antilla Tigre	Jinhu	45,725
Sweden	1965	—	—	Linghu	63,630
Sweden	1962	—	Gunilla Billner	Nanjiang	20,840
Sweden	1964	—	Guldren Regina Nova	Pinghu	46,045
Sweden	1950	—	Anco Sallor Sandefjord	Taipieng	8,820
Sweden	1937	—	Bramoa Brovig	Taching No. 13	14,820
Sweden	1945	—	Pieniny Tankland	Taching No. 14	12,837
Sweden	1964	—	Anmaj Belmaj	Wuhu	50,210
Sweden	1964	—	Harwi	Yinhu	58,555
Yugoslavia	1959	—	Ostrava	Honghu	20,195

[e]Estimate.

TABLE 22.5
Coal Mining Equipment Imports, 1973–78

Contract year	Country	Company	Price (million $)	No. of units	Equipment type
1973	Britain	Anderson Mavor	6.0	21	Longwall shearers
1973	Britain	Gullick Dobson	13.36	1,000	Longwall roof supports
1973	Britain	Baldwin & Francis	—	—	Controls for face machinery
1973	Britain	Hawker-Siddley	—	—	Transformers for coal mines
1973	Britain	John Davis	—	—	Face communications equipment
1973	Britain	Dowty	29.52	1	Powered roof-support systems
1973	Britain	Dowty	—	—	Conveyors and loaders
1973	Britain	Dowty	5.0	4	Narrow seam mining equipment
1973	U.S.	Bucyrus-Erie	20.0	25	Blast-hole drills
				5	Power shovels
1974	Britain	Dobson Park	35.0	1	Pit prop factory
1974	France	Ernault-Souma	2.1	4	Drilling machines
1974	W. Germany	Guttenhoffnungshuette	7.5	23	Power shovels
1974	W. Germany	G. H. H. Sterkrade	5.0	23	Conveyors
1974	Japan	Kawasaki	0.35	40	Mechanical shovels

TABLE 22.5 (continued)
Coal Mining Equipment Imports, 1973–78

Contract year	Country	Company	Price (million $)	No. of units	Equipment type
1974	U.S.	McNally Pittsburg	0.025	4	Coal samplers
1977[a]	W. Germany	Ritz Pumpenfabrik	0.5	—	Submersible pumps for coal mines
1977	Japan	Japan Iron and Steel	—	10,000	Light rails for coal mines
1978[a]	Britain	Dowty	133.7	25	Roof support systems
1978[a]	Britain	Anderson Strathclyde	26.0	—	Coal cutters and face conveyors
1978[a]	W. Germany	Orenstein & Koppel	42.0	10	135-ton hydraulic drag-lines for open-cast coal mining
1978[a]	W. Germany	Krupp-Demag	630.0	—	Equipment and services for open-cast mine in Kirin province
1978[a]	W. Germany	Westfalia Superator	200.0	35	Longwall equipment sets
1978[a]	W. Germany	Eickoff	30.0	35	Shearers
1978[a]	W. Germany	Gullick-Dobson	15.0	6	Longwall hydraulic support sets
1978[a]	W. Germany	Hermann Hemscheidt	100.0	30	Longwall face supports
1978[a]	Japan	—	9.9	—	Mine conveyor belts
1978[a]	Japan	Mitsui Miike	63.2	8	Coal-mining equipment sets
1978[a]	U.S.	Bucyrus-Erie	6.0	7	45-R blast-hole drills
1978[a]	U.S.	Joy Manufacturing	6.0	—	Continuous coal-mining equipment

[a]Reported too late for inclusion in the text or the analysis.

from the main industrial centers, and opening them up would cause transportation problems in the region's limited rail network. However, the ultimate incentive for developing the North China coal beds will be high, particularly in the late 1980's as the reserve limits on petroleum and natural gas become more evident. Peking might be interested in purchasing large shovels that could deal with the overburden problem and reach some of the North China coal beds in surface mining operations. The need for washing and beneficiation plants in the Chinese coal industry is obvious from the low calorific content of raw coal and the low percent of coal production that is currently treated at the mine to remove impurities. Coal beneficiation saves transportation costs and plant maintenance costs. This is another industry in which China could develop its own equipment-manufacturing capacity, but may be interested in some plant and technology imports between now and 1985.

The Chinese market for foreign oil tankerage is spotty and unpredictable. The limitations of harbor facilities and depth problems along the China coastline will make supertankers impractical as carriers of the Chinese oil trade. The PRC can already build its own tankers in excess of 50,000 dwt—about the appropriate range for the oil trade with Japan. Furthermore, Peking has so many options—lease arrangements, used tankers purchased at bargain rates, etc.—that orders for new foreign-built tankers are unlikely.

Using the recorded figures for the value of trade in energy plant and equipment with various regions and countries as a sample, it is possible to reconstruct a rough percentage distribution of the Chinese energy equipment market among the PRC's trading partners. Japan was first among countries trading in energy equipment with China, with about 30 percent of the total market. However, Western Europe as a whole captured 50 percent of the Chinese energy equipment market and therefore ranked first among regions trading with China. Western Europe accounted for 92 percent of coal equipment exports to China, 94 percent of tanker sales (by tanker capacity), 64 percent of chemical fertilizer plant exports, 48 percent of refinery and petrochemical plant exports, and about 27 percent of petroleum exploration and extraction equipment exports. Japan was strong in refineries and petrochemical plants (52 percent), in petroleum production equipment (28 percent), and in electric power equipment (24 percent).

North America (the United States and Canada) captured only about 10 percent of the market value of Chinese energy equipment trade, if that trade is allocated by primary contractor to the exporting countries. The qualifier is important, since American companies were secondary contractors in the sale of energy equipment through deals that had been arranged through subsidiaries in Japan, Western Europe, and Singapore. If trade through American subsidiaries were counted as American exports, or if package deals were broken down by the country of origin of equipment components, the U.S. share of the Chinese energy equipment market would rise to 10–15 percent. For example, three offshore jack-up drilling rigs recently built in Singapore shipyards for the PRC were constructed by American subsidiaries and loaded with American components. A high percentage of the total value of the three rigs probably found its way back into U.S. accounts. Nonetheless, the impact of this type of deal should not be overemphasized in the general energy equipment picture, and, even using the most generous assumptions, it is unlikely that the United States has captured more than 20 percent of the market, well behind Western Europe and Japan.

It is important to realize that despite its successes in sales of chemical fertilizer plants and petroleum exploration equipment, the United States missed the refinery and petrochemical plant market completely, was shut out of tanker sales and electric power equipment sales, and captured a meager 8 percent of the coal equipment market, at least through the beginning of 1978. American companies did very well indeed selling petroleum exploration equipment to the PRC in 1977 and 1978 and may be moving toward predominance in this market. But the prospects are not good for U.S. equipment manufacturers in sales to the other energy industries. American companies suffer from certain intractable political disadvantages in dealing with the PRC (Chapter 5). But a vigorous sales effort would probably produce results for aggressive U.S. electric power equipment manufacturers. The United States will probably get shut out of any Chinese market for nuclear power plants by government export constraints and the diplomatic situation. But there is no inherent reason why U.S. manufacturers should not be competitive in the sale of coal-fired thermal plants or hydropower equipment, or in potential exports of heavy machine tools required for the manufacture of advanced electric power generators, etc. American companies should also be taking a longer look at the Chinese market for hydrocarbon-processing components and coal-mining equipment—particularly for open-cast mining. Whatever the type of energy equipment in question, U.S. exporters should emphasize cutting-edge technology—design, efficiency and recovery factors, integrated control systems, and so on. Nor should American companies be shy about licensing advanced processes for use in the PRC, any more than they are shy about licensing technology to their competitors in Western Europe and Japan.

Companies in Southeast Asia (Singapore) did surprisingly well in equipment sales to the PRC, with about 4 percent of the total energy

TABLE 22.6

Electric Power Generating and Transmission Equipment Imports, 1972–78

Contract year	Country	Company	Price (million $)	No. of units	Equipment type
1972	Britain	John Brown	8.2	5	Gas turbine generators (25 MW)
1972	France	Alsthom	10.0	2	Hydro turbines
		Ste Creusot-Loire		2	Hydro generators (75 MW)
1972	Italy	GIE	9.7	1	Thermal generator (125 MW)
				3	Thermal generators (100 MW)
1972	Japan	Mitsubishi, Hitachi	13.0	1	Steam turbine
		Toshiba		1	Thermal generator
				1	Oxygen generator
1972	Japan	Hitachi	30.0	2	Steam turbines
				2	Thermal generators (125 MW)
				—	Control gear
1972	Sweden	Karlstade Mekaniska	4.0	3	Hydro generating sets
1972	USSR	—	9.3	4	Steam turbines (75 MW)
1973	Britain	John Brown	8.2	5	Gas turbine generators (25 MW)
1973	Britain	Thirst Mouldings	50.0	—	Hydro shaft seals
1973	Czech.	—	—	3	Turboalternators (110 MW)
1973	Italy	GIE	86.2	1	Thermal power plant, including:
				2	Steam turbogenerators (325 MW)
1973	Japan	Hitachi	72.0	1	Coal-fired thermal power plant, including:
				2	Steam turbines
				2	Thermal generators (250 MW)
				—	Control gear
1973	USSR	—	16.38	7	Steam turbogenerators (100 MW)
1974	Belgium	ACEC	5.0	3	Gas turbines
	Canada	Westinghouse		3	Thermal generators
1974	Britain	BICC	0.228	—	High-voltage transmission capacitors

TABLE 22.6 *(continued)*
Electric Power Generating and Transmission Equipment Imports, 1972–78

Contract year	Country	Company	Price (million $)	No. of units	Equipment type
1974	France Switzerland	CEM Sulzer	40.0	1	Coal-fired thermal power plant (300 MW)
1974	France	Electromécanique	41.4	1	Thermal power plant
1974	W. Germany	Brown, Boverie, Cie	59.0	—	Electric power equipment (unspecified)
1974	W. Germany	Brown, Boverie	5.0	—	Power substations for steel mill
1974	USSR	—	2.8	1	Steam turbine (200 MW)
1975	W. Germany	Siemens A.G.	6.0	—	Steam turbine manufacturing technology
1975	Japan	Hitachi	5.0	2	Gas turbine generators (25 MW)
1975	USSR	—	6.7	2	Steam turbines (200 MW)
1976	Britain	Yanmar Diesel	0.52	2	Marine diesel power generators
1976	Britain	Flexibox	—	—	Turbine test equipment
1976	USSR	—	7.0	2	Steam turbines (200 MW)
1978[a]	France	Framatome	2,200.0	2	Pressurized water power reactors (900 MW)
1978[a]	Hong Kong	Hong Kong Electric	2.0	5	Used thermal power generators (30 MW)
1978[a]	Italy	Nuove Pignone	8.0	—	Nuclear centrifugal compressor technology
1978[a]	Japan	Mitsubishi	300.0	2 1	Thermal power plants (150 MW) Thermal power plant (300 MW) (for Paoshan steel complex)
1978[a]	Japan	Tokyo Electric	2.1	—	Design and engineering services for Paoshan thermal power plants

[a]Reported too late for inclusion in the text or the analysis.

equipment market value but 25 percent of the petroleum equipment market. The good showing in petroleum equipment was entirely due to the order of five offshore drilling rigs from Singapore shipyards. Eastern Europe and Oceania were marginal exporters of energy equipment to the PRC, although Eastern Europe's position was grossly understated in the reported transactions.

Disaggregation of the energy equipment trade by contract year is instructive in establishing trends for the Chinese market. Total recorded trade for 1960 through 1978 in energy plants and equipment was about $3.75 billion, or roughly $4 billion after adjusting for inflation and other downward biases. Of this, about $250–300 million consisted of contracts signed in the 1960's. West European refinery components and petrochemical plants dominated China's energy equipment imports between 1960 and 1966. Energy plant and equipment import declined to zero during the Cultural Revolution. By 1972, the PRC had again initiated imports of foreign energy production equipment, at about $300 million for contracts signed during the year. The 1973 figure jumped to $1.5 billion, the peak year for energy plant and equipment imports contracts. Japan and Western Europe led the trade during the 1960's and reopened it in 1972. The United States joined them in 1973 with the sale of chemical fertilizer plants valued at some $200 million. In 1974, energy equipment trade declined to $500 million in new contracts under the pressure of China's rising balance-of-payments deficit. Energy plant and equipment trade remained at about the $250–300 million level from 1975 through 1977, with Japan and Western Europe splitting the bulk of the sales. U.S. energy equipment exports to the PRC were in the $30–40 million range each year from 1975 through 1977, or about 10–12 percent of the market. In 1975, Singapore weighed in with the sale of two Robray 300 offshore drilling rigs at a total price of some $60 million. The figures for 1978 are still only partially complete, at about $150 million for the first half of the year. That would indicate that the 1978 trade level in energy plants and equipment will resemble the 1975–77 period, at about $300 million in new contracts. The direct U.S. share will once again be in the $30–40 million range, unless there are some large sales in the last few months of the year. Singapore contracted for three more offshore rigs (with American equipment) in 1978 at a total value of $70 million.

Future trends in the Chinese energy plant and equipment market are notoriously difficult to predict. There may be some increase in contracts for energy plants and equipment as crude oil exports increase between 1978 and 1985. This outcome, however, is far from certain. Oilfields, natural gas fields, coal mines, and electric power plants constitute some

48 of 120 large-scale industrial projects planned for the 1976–85 period. If this plan is carried through to completion, it will require acceleration of imports of foreign equipment for these industries. But the exact pace of acceleration is impossible to predict. It depends on the rate of growth of China's own energy equipment manufacturing industries, on the level of technology introduced in the new producing units, and on international market conditions. If experience is any guide, Peking's planners and foreign trade officials will make every purchase only after careful consideration within the framework of their overall objectives and careful testing of the market alternatives. This means a lot of sales effort for each contract for the selling companies.

In addition, the Ten-Year Plan also specifies other priorities, such as the steel industry, for heavy capital investment. Not all of the oil revenues will be available for expansion of China's energy industries. As crude oil (and coal) exports rise, the energy plant and equipment share of the revenues will decline. From the early 1960's until the present, oil revenues and energy plant and equipment imports have just about balanced at $4 billion. But there is nothing automatic about this equation. It is much more likely that Peking will attempt to use oil revenues to satisfy its plant and equipment import needs across a wide range of industries.

As far as the distribution of new energy plant and equipment contracts goes, I have already speculated regarding the sectoral distribution of imports that it will favor the petroleum and electric power industries, with some decline in refineries, petrochemical plants, and chemical fertilizer plants, and an ambiguous situation for coal equipment trade. There are obvious reasons for believing that Japan will remain China's most important trading partner in energy plants and equipment. Aside from the historical pattern, the Japanese and Chinese governments in early 1978 signed a long-term trade agreement specifying that each side would import about $10 billion worth of goods from the other between 1978 and 1982. About half of China's exports to Japan will be crude oil. There is no way of predicting the proportion of Japan's exports to China that will be comprised of energy plants and equipment. But one would speculate that at least $1 billion of the total, a figure equivalent to the sum of energy equipment trade between Japan and China to date, will be available for further contracts in the energy sector. The figure could obviously go much higher.

Western Europe will also continue to do well in the Chinese energy equipment market. Britain and West Germany are working hard on new contracts for coal-mining equipment. Development of the North Sea gives several West European countries an edge in the type of offshore technology that Peking will be interested in for the next phase of work along the Chinese continental shelf. France is leading in the competition to sell the PRC its first nuclear power plant. Based on past experience, it will be a fair guess that Western Europe will sell half again as much energy plants and equipment to the PRC as Japan. That would indicate at least $1.5–2.0 billion in sales through 1985 for West European energy companies. The figure could go higher if a West European company or consortium gets a final contract for a nuclear power station.

Where does that leave the United States in China's energy future? If present trends continue, American companies can expect an increasing proportion of new contracts for petroleum exploration and extraction equipment. Beyond this proved area of strength, there is no certainty. American companies will find rough sledding in breaking into the pattern of energy equipment trade that has emerged between China and Western Europe and Japan. The best that can be hoped for from the American perspective is that U.S. firms will take advantage of any expansion in the Chinese energy equipment market that is induced by rising revenues from crude oil exports during the early 1980's. In approaching the growth portion of the Chinese energy equipment market, American corporations should work from their natural strengths, especially in advanced technology and integrated control systems.

Chapter 23

Trend Analysis and Projection Methods

The analyst projecting energy balance trends is faced from the outset with the disconcerting realization that there is no way to adequately convey to the reader all of the complex decisions that went into the structure of the projection. This fact is as true in projecting a country's future energy balance as in predicting any element of its future social structure. Projections are notoriously subjective. Futurists must shield themselves behind semantic devices, such as the distinction between "projections" and "predictions," to avoid taking sole responsibility for the wide margins of error that inevitably appear in their results. On the other hand, they are propelled forward by the realization that solutions to problems like the energy crisis increasingly call for long-range projections and long-range planning. In the final analysis, the computer does little to relieve this anxiety. It simply extends the range of possible alternative assumptions and the complexity of abstract models. Projection is, therefore, a highly interactive and subjective process—the principal interaction lying between the analyst and successive generations of his own projections. This particular set of projections of China's future energy balance has already been through at least four generations of computer modeling: (1) hand tabulation of future energy consumption and export potential based on fixed elasticities and fossil-fuel reserves assumptions; (2) computerized simulation of the production-consumption balance, based on variable growth-rate elasticities between energy consumption and Gross National Product; (3) dynamic computerized modeling, based on regression analysis of the energy/GNP relationship, disaggregated production and consumption sectors treating export potential as a residual sector of the model, and alternative assumptions regarding fossil-fuel reserves, GNP growth rates, population trends, conservation policies, electric power production growth rates, and the fuel mix; and (4) the current stage of the model, which simplifies the range of alternative assumptions and projections, and adds an important reserves discovery variable to petroleum and natural gas production subsectors of the model, permitting a range of alternative assumptions regarding the future rate of new reserve discoveries.

Each new generation of the model was integrated with historical data on China's energy balance from 1949 to the mid-1970's. And each new generation of the model introduced a new set of theoretical assumptions about relationships among production and consumption sectors in the energy balance. This chapter describes the structural assumptions upon which I built the projection model. The next chapter (Chapter 24) provides the statistical analysis itself and the results of the projections. Many hidden assumptions must remain the responsibility of the author. (Other researchers are invited to examine the computer program for the model, which is available on request.) The second, third, and fourth generations of the model developed through semi-interactive programming as much as through formal flow charts. Hundreds of projection runs were made, each having output containing the statistical results of a variety of resource and consumption parameters. Each printout contained thousands of estimates that had to be examined for internal consistency, plausibility, and conformity to past trends before adjusting the program for the next run. It would therefore be impossible to provide all of the adjustment decisions (each representing an assumption) that were made.

If this introduces an arbitrary element into the projections, the range of possible assumptions was radically reduced by a simple methodological ploy. I started the projection series in 1965 and ran it through the present to test the validity of hundreds of program decisions. This procedure has two advantages. First, it allows the model to get "warmed up" before it takes off into the future. There are certain programming awkwardnesses in DYNAMO (and I suspect other projection compilers) that make it hard to duplicate reality in the first year of the run. But by the time the program hits the fifth year and the tenth year (1975), the definitional awkwardness of the equations disappears, and the simulation begins to look like reality. Second, hundreds of programming decisions can be tested against historical reality if the model begins with a ten-year retrospective forecast. The retrospective forecast does not necessarily tie the future pattern of development to the past. It simply requires sufficient program flexibility to permit alternative futures built on a single past. Certain distortions are introduced into some variables (e.g. petroleum production) in some projections by starting the projection runs in 1965. But the loss of a perfect match between the projection run and historical reality is more than compensated for by the gain in structural validity for the model as a whole.

As stated in the introduction to the Statistical Profile (Chapter 13), the projection model contains three basic sectors—energy production, energy consumption, and net energy export potential. The energy production sector is driven by alternative resource assumptions. The energy consumption sector is driven by economic growth. The energy export potential (or import requirement) was derived as a residual sector from the difference between the energy consumption requirement and energy availability in any given year. The remaining parts of this chapter deal in turn with each sector of the model.

The Energy Production Sector

The energy production sector is the most complex part of the model in terms of the number of variables (Figure 23.1). The production sector was disaggregated by production stage (reserves, primary energy production, and secondary energy production) and by fuel (coal, natural gas, petroleum, electric power, and an unidentified future energy industry). Each stage in the production sector was governed by its own set of interlocking program equations, and each fuel industry was modeled on the basis of growth assumptions that fit the industry in question. Waste, inefficiencies, and non-energy use of hydrocarbons were subtracted from net energy production in each fuel sector to give a summary statistic for aggregate energy availability, broken down by fuel into energy available for consumption or export in the form of coal, natural gas, petroleum products, electric power, or some future energy commodity.

Future production curves are exceedingly difficult to project for the four primary energy fuels, even in situations where there is an abundance of data available and where the energy industries in question are following a fairly smooth growth pattern. Furthermore, different projection methods must be used, depending on the growth characteristics of the energy industry in question. A production growth model that might be appropriate for hydropower generation, for example, would be completely different from that required for the petroleum or natural gas industries. Hydropower production is capital-intensive, but based on a renewable resource. Petroleum and natural gas production are capital-intensive, and based on nonrenewable resources. Biogas generation is labor-intensive, and based on renewable resources. Each type of energy industry would, therefore, have a distinct growth curve determined by a different set of parametric conditions. The model must reflect this complexity or fail to capture reality to any significant degree.

Petroleum and Natural Gas Projections

My models of the Chinese energy production system focused on alternative growth curves for the petroleum and natural gas industries based on variable assumptions regarding oil and gas resources. The subsectoral model for the coal industry generated three raw-coal production curves,

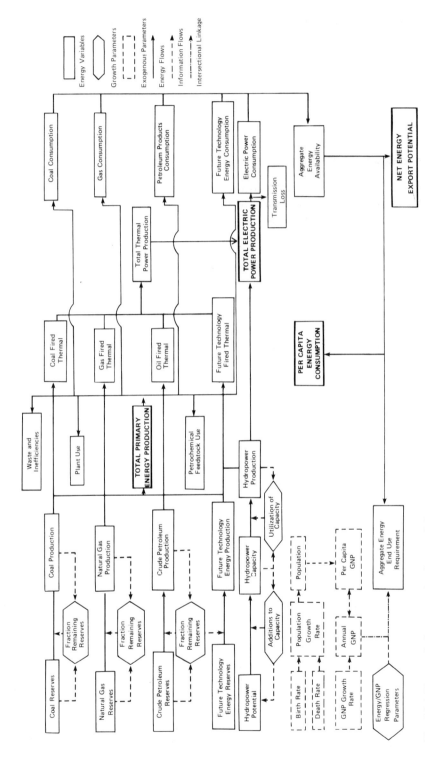

Fig. 23.1 Energy balance projection model.

reflecting the range of investment and development options open to Peking. Once developed, the subsectoral model for the electric power industry was held constant. The most accurate method of predicting oil and gas production growth rates is on the basis of projected capital investment in the short term, and on the basis of projected reserves discovery rates in the long term. Lacking data on the rate of Chinese investment in the petroleum and natural gas industries, it was necessary to rely exclusively on a long-range model based on total resource estimates and projected reserves discovery rates.

The general theoretical relationship between the total size of recoverable oil and gas resources and production growth rates is expressed in Figure 23.2. The relationship begins with the assumption that the total initial size of fossil-fuel resources in place underground is constant on the time scale of human civilization. Part of this total ("in place") resource is recoverable, the exact proportion varying with geological conditions, the development of extraction technology, and the long-range economics of extraction. The area under the curve in Figure 23.2 represents this "economically recoverable" resource for a hypothetical country and a given fossil fuel. In practice, of course, the concept of an "economically recoverable" resource is highly elastic and variable over time as new extraction technologies are introduced and as the price of the resource changes. But, in theory at least, we can visualize the economically recoverable resource as the total amount that will have been produced when extraction of the resource ceases.

As the annual production of a resource (petroleum) increases over the years, the remaining economically recoverable resource slowly dwindles.[1] At time A, when the bulk of resources remains and economic conditions are generally favorable to maximum expansion of the producing industry, production growth rates are high, reaching 15–20 percent per year in some cases, including the petroleum and natural gas industries of the People's Republic of China. As the petroleum industry continues to expand, however, the fraction of resources remaining in the ground slowly declines, carrying first the discovery rate and then the annual production growth rate downward from peak levels. At time B, which occurs when less than 50 percent of economically recoverable resources has been produced (about 35 percent in practice), the annual production growth rate declines to zero, and production peaks or levels out. As the zero growth point is reached, there are powerful economic inducements to extend production at current levels. The price rises precipitously. Government and industry may attempt to accelerate exploration. Efforts will be made to expand the rate of recovery through "secondary" and "tertiary" recovery techniques such as water or gas injection or fire flooding.

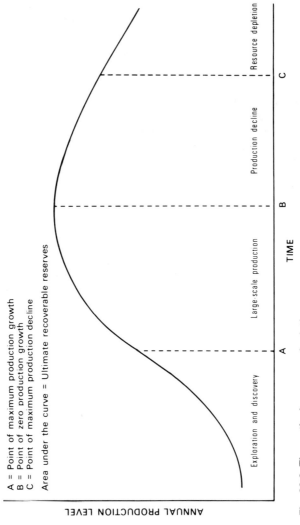

A = Point of maximum production growth
B = Point of zero production growth
C = Point of maximum production decline

Area under the curve = Ultimate recoverable reserves

Fig. 23.2 Theoretical resource depletion curve.

It must be stressed that in the late 1970's we knew very little about the "downhill" side of the resource depletion curve for crude petroleum and natural gas. Some authors assumed that the depletion side of the curve would mirror the rising production side.[2] Others believed that peak production could be extended for some time by enhanced recovery techniques or by exploiting fields that were previously considered subeconomic. One government analyst suggested that peak production would be followed by rapid decline and then recovery to a production plateau that would extend for a considerable period into the future.[3] My own view was that oil and gas depletion would occur according to a variety of general scenarios in different countries, depending on an enormous array of independent factors, including the resource geology, economic structure, and international market position of the country in question. For the Chinese case, I modeled two types of depletion curve for petroleum and natural gas—a production curve that peaks at 65 percent of remaining resources and then declines, and a production curve that reaches a plateau between 65 and 50 percent of remaining resources and then begins to decline. I attributed the plateau phase of the second curve to enhanced recovery techniques. But in applying these two curves, I discovered that a choice of one or the other makes very little difference to the projected energy balance for China within the 20-year time frame of the projections.

In general terms, once we know or assume to some order of approximation the total size of economically recoverable resources (the area under the curve) and the shape of the curve to the left of point A, we should be able to project the curve at least as far as the peak point of annual production (point B). The larger the resources, the longer production rates will continue to grow and the higher will be the peak production level. Conversely, the smaller the ultimate recoverable resource, the lower the peak production level and the earlier that rapid production decline will set in. There is, therefore, a statistical relationship between the fraction of remaining resources (the area to the right of the point reached along the curve each year divided by the total area under the curve) and the production growth rate.[4]

Three historical examples of fossil-fuel depletion curves were examined to establish an empirical relationship between the fraction of remaining reserves and production growth rates. The three cases were the Venezuelan petroleum industry, the American petroleum industry, and the American natural gas industry (Figure 23.3).[5] These three fossil-fuel industries are among the few in the world that have reached the zero production increase point, and have (we think) begun the long decline in

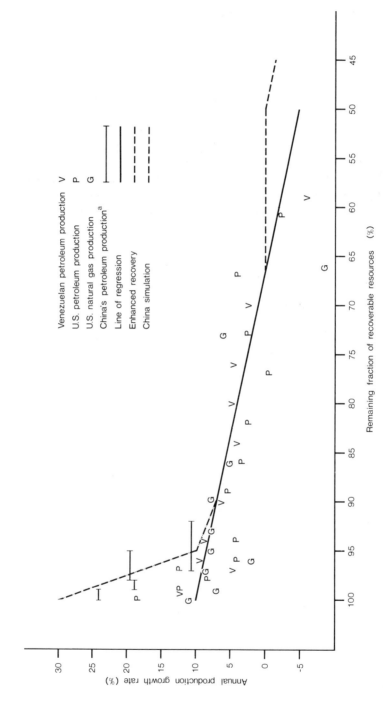

Fig. 23.3 Three historical cases of resource depletion.

production that will be characteristic of the petroleum industries of many other countries within this century.

The derivation of Figure 23.3 is itself open to interpretation and will be disputed by some analysts. Annual production growth rates for each industry were tabulated over five-year periods and plotted against the fraction of remaining reserves halfway through each five-year period. The assumed size of ultimate recoverable resources for the three cases was obviously an important factor in determining the statistical parameters of the relationship. Ultimate recoverable resources were assumed to include past production, current reserves, and estimated future discoveries. The second and third components are open to a wide range of interpretations. I set Venezuelan recoverable crude petroleum resources (excluding tar sands) at 10 billion metric tons (75 billion barrels), American recoverable crude oil resources at 35 bmt (250 bbbl), and American recoverable natural gas resources at 40 trillion cubic meters (1.4×10^{15} cubic feet).[6] (Two of the projections for the Chinese case were designed with resource assumptions similar to the Venezuelan and American cases. See Tables 24.6 and 24.7.)

Having established five-year average production growth rates and resource depletion levels, I assumed a linear relationship between the two variables and determined the parameters for that relationship, using an ordinary least-squares regression.[7] In fact, the relationship between the fraction of remaining reserves and production growth rates is not linear but an S-shaped curve.[8] However, the middle section of the "S" is close enough to linear to permit a linear interpolation between 90 percent and 50 percent of remaining reserves. Production growth rates in the Chinese case were high, between 100 and 90 percent of remaining reserves, and averaging 20–30 percent per year in the petroleum and natural gas industries. But there is recent evidence that China's crude oil production growth rates are declining toward the line of regression established in the Venezuelan and American industries. The high early growth rates in the Chinese oil and gas industries were induced by heavy government investment that came as a crisis response to the break in relations with the Soviet Union in 1960. But by the mid-1970's, rapid production growth was becoming more difficult, as the largest structures were tapped and new fields became more difficult to locate. On the basis of what one would expect from historical precedents, this does not mean that the Chinese petroleum industry is experiencing unusual difficulties, but simply that it has reached a lower growth stage in the expected development pattern imposed by a naturally falling fraction of remaining reserves. Peking would not enjoy the comparison to petroleum and natural gas industries in the market economy countries, but the basic reserves-production relationship should hold, regardless of the social structure of the producing country.

Projection of the growth pattern for the natural gas industry was accomplished in much the same manner, except that the initial growth rates were set lower than for the petroleum industry (15 percent per year). The slower initial growth rate of the natural gas industry is attributable to lower capital investment than in the petroleum industry, and to the lack of a pipeline distribution network. (Crude oil was initially shipped by rail in China.)

Now this crude method of projection will surely generate vigorous criticism from both economists and resource geologists. The economists will argue that real petroleum industry growth curves are influenced by a host of extrinsic factors, such as the industrial growth rate, the rate of capital accumulation, capital investment in the petroleum industry, and the comparative market price of petroleum. Some resource economists, in fact, would argue that the situation is quite the reverse—that economic factors determine the rate of exploration and consequently the rates of discovery and production.[9] Petroleum geologists would argue, on the other hand, that knowledge of remaining reserves is always incomplete and that the model is therefore based on false assumptions. After all, our estimates of the world's ultimate recoverable oil resources in 1945 were different by orders of magnitude from present estimates, and future estimates will surely grow to reflect new discoveries. Knowledge of China's petroleum resource base is obviously imperfect, especially from the distant vantage point of the foreign observer.

These theoretical objections were confirmed by observations of growth curves generated by the stage-three model of the petroleum industry, which was based on the M.I.T. (Meadows et al., *The Limits to Growth*) reserves-production equations. I noticed in the computer runs used for the thesis version of this study that the petroleum production curve tends to "stack up" as the assumed petroleum resource is increased. That is, under the assumptions of the original Meadows resource model, increasing the assumed resource base raises the fraction of recoverable reserves at any particular time and thus increases the projected production growth rate. This tends to raise the production curve without extending it significantly through time. Increasing the resources therefore does little to extend the life of the resource. This violates our intuitive notion of growth in the petroleum industry. Additional resources should push the time of production decline and resource depletion significantly further into the future. At root, this problem reflects the inability of the original Meadows model to capture the uncertainties and delaying effect of new reserves discoveries.

In order to meet these objections, I redesigned the model for the petroleum and natural gas industries to allow for a variable rate of reserves discoveries through time. This was accomplished by dividing the total assumed pool of resources for each industry into discovered reserves and undiscovered resources. Discovered reserves and undiscovered resources were then each set at alternative assumed levels, generating various production projections. Undiscovered resources were assumed to flow via discovery into the pool of discovered reserves. Determining the rate of discovery at any particular moment proved difficult. One could simply assume constant discovery rates through time, but this introduces an artificial linearity into the model. Ideally, one could tie the discovery rate to a dynamic model of industrial growth for the economy as a whole, incorporating both demand and capital investment into some measure of exploration activity. The available data simply do not permit such a complex and dynamic model for the Chinese case. My solution was to tie the discovery rate itself to the stage of development in the petroleum industry. The discovery rate is low in the initial phases of the petroleum industry, as it begins to mobilize the necessary exploration infrastructure and to map uncharted basins. The rate of discovery should then rise as capital flows into lucrative exploration activities and the large fields begin to be discovered. But as the giant and supergiant fields are discovered, exploration begins to focus on smaller, deeper, and more remote fields, holding the discovery rate to a relatively constant level over many years. By the time roughly half of the ultimate recoverable reserves are produced, the rate of discovery begins to decline as the pool of undiscovered resources shrinks. The decline in rate of discovery can be staved off by technological innovation or by increased capital investment. This would create a plateau in production, but ultimately the cost of new discoveries rises still further, and the rate of discovery will eventually decline.

I attempted to model this complicated series of events with a simple table function, tying the rate of new discoveries to the fraction of remaining reserves. The rate of discovery begins at zero, with 100 percent of recoverable resources still in the ground. It is then allowed to rise to 4 percent of those resources each year at 50 percent of remaining reserves, and declines once again to zero when 100 percent has been produced. The effect of this added stage in the structure of the model is to greatly extend the production curve through time as larger quantities of undiscovered resources are added in new assumed projections. DYNAMO permits modeling of multiple resource assumptions in a single computer run, greatly simplifying the programming task. For example, in the baseline projection, I modeled petroleum resources at 5 billion metric tons of discovered reserves and 3.5 billion metric tons of undiscovered resources, for a total of 8.5 bmt of recoverable resources. Then, for the low-, median-, and high-growth projections, I held discovered reserves constant, while varying the size of the undiscovered resources. The addition of resource discoveries through time greatly enhances the validity of the model, perhaps at the cost of greater complexity and an increased number of assumed initial values.

Coal Projections

The coal industry was modeled along the lines of the original M.I.T. resource depletion model, eliminating the rate of discovery as an insignificant factor in determining coal production growth rates. Coal resources in China are already known to be in excess of 1 trillion metric tons, enough to last 2,000 years at present rates of production, assuming that all of the coal could be recovered. Resources, therefore, cannot be considered a significant constraint on the growth of the coal industry. The real constraints are capital investment, the transportation infrastructure (railroads), and the size of the Chinese market for lump coal. Furthermore, the coal industry had already reached maturity in the year (1965) when the projection runs were initiated, with an annual production rate of about 240 million metric tons. The initial growth rate was set at 8 percent per year and allowed to decay slowly as the most readily accessible coal reserves are depleted. The coal production growth rate is really more contingent on Peking's energy development and export policy and on consumption limits than on reserves. But the model was unable to capture such subtleties at this stage. I projected continued growth in the coal industry, albeit at ever slower rates, through the turn of the century, when annual production of coal could be in the general vicinity of 1 billion tons per year.

Aside from the conventional fossil fuels (coal, petroleum, and natural gas), two other energy production industries were included in the model—electric power and an unspecified "future energy production" industry. The thermal and hydropower industries were separated and hydropower treated as a primary energy input with its own renewable resource potential. Thermal power production was treated as a closed loop, siphoning off available energy from coal, natural gas, petroleum, and "future production," but reinjecting available energy in the form of electric power.

Hydropower Projections

Development of hydropower production behaves differently than development of the fossil-fuel industries. Hydro is a limited but nondepletable energy resource. It can be developed at higher and higher proportions of the available potential, but there is no depletion curve analogous to petroleum or natural gas. Annual production levels for hydropower depend on the development of capacity rather than on the fraction of developed potential. The development of hydro capacity under conditions of great hydraulic potential is relatively resource-insensitive in the initial stages of the industry and relatively sensitive to capital and labor costs, social and economic dislocation factors, geographic locational factors, and development policy. This is particularly true for China, with its large hydropower potential, which does not impose practical limits on the expansion of generating capacity within the time scale of these projections. Like the coal industry, Chinese hydropower capacity will grow during the next 20 years under a set of constraints largely unrelated to ultimate hydraulic potential. In some distant future, perhaps the constraints will be reversed, as additions to capacity begin to press on available potential and further capital inputs begin to have diminishing returns.

For these reasons, the expansion of hydropower capacity was tied to growth of the electric power equipment industry. Hydro-generating equipment was assumed to have been produced and imported at an annual rate of about 600 megawatts per year in 1965, and allowed to grow thereafter at 5 percent per year. Thus, additions to installed capacity grow along a simple exponential curve. Installed capacity itself was derived from initial levels and annual additions to capacity. Production was in turn derived from installed capacity, assuming a utilization ratio of 3,000 kilowatt-hours per kilowatt. These assumptions are fairly rigid and linear compared to the dynamic characteristics of the fossil-fuel projections. But even considerable error in the projections of hydropower capacity and production would not greatly alter the primary energy balance projections through the turn of the century (Chapter 24).

Thermal Power Production

Thermal power production relies on energy inputs from the primary energy industries in a certain mix. This fuel mix for thermal power generation was difficult to simulate in the Chinese case, since we lack firm historical data. Total thermal power production was projected along a simple exponential growth curve at a rate of 10 percent per year, reaching two-thirds of current U.S. thermal power output levels by the year 2000. This is a reasonable growth assumption, since China's industrial product might be expected to grow at about 10 percent per year, based on past experience.[10] Industry will absorb the bulk of new electric power generated by additions to thermal capacity. Thermal power output should therefore grow at roughly the same pace as industrial output.

Within this overall growth plan for thermal electric power production, the contribution of each primary energy source to power generation was tied to the growth pattern for the primary energy industry itself. Thus, for example, electric power generation was assumed to consume about 10 percent of petroleum production, 10 percent of natural gas production, and 10 percent of energy production from future technologies. Thermal power production from coal was considered a residual category, making up the difference between thermal production from petroleum, natural gas, and future technologies and total projected thermal power output.

As with the projections of hydropower production, the assumptions underlying the thermal power subsector were somewhat arbitrary and linear. But the effect of different assumptions on the total energy balance is not critical within the framework of this study. If thermal power production grew at less than 10 percent per year, it would release only a negligible additional amount of petroleum or coal for export. Shifting the fuel mix within the thermal power industry would have little or no effect on the production-consumption balance or on export potential. So, to a large extent, the precise configuration of the thermal power subsector is academic in the context of China's international energy policies, but instructive in the context of China's domestic energy development pattern.

Projection of Production from Future Energy Technologies

An undefined future energy production subsector was included in order to account for possible development of one or more new energy technologies, specifically nuclear power. Future energy resources were arbitrarily set at 10 billion metric tons coal equivalent and production was started at one million metric tons coal equivalent in 1965. The growth rate for future energy production is one of the most interesting dynamic features of the projection model. Production increases from future energy technologies were tied to the remaining fraction of petroleum reserves. Thus, as the petroleum industry begins to reach resource limits on further expansion, development of future energy technologies becomes an attractive option. This feature introduces a great deal of flexibility into the projections. If China's offshore petroleum resources prove to be large and readily accessible, future energy technologies will be introduced only slowly, because of high initial capital costs. On the other hand, if offshore resources prove limited or costly to extract, capital and equipment expansion will flow toward the available new production technologies—nuclear, solar, geothermal, biomass, and possibly coal liquefaction or gasification. The program device tying future energy production technology to the fraction of remaining petroleum reserves was a table function. Increases in energy output from future technologies were allowed to expand from an initial growth rate of 10 percent per year to 25 percent as petroleum reserves declined toward the 50 percent depletion level. This is an arbitrary modeling device, but it does allow for the input of new energy production technologies over the next several decades.

This completes our review of the projection methodology for the production sector of the energy balance model used to forecast China's energy development through the year 2000. The program for each production industry was written and tested separately, and then incorporated into the dynamic and interactive equations of the energy production sector. Whenever a choice had to be made between overstepping the limits on our empirical knowledge of China's energy system and increasing the dynamic characteristics of the model, dynamic features were sacrificed. The projections therefore retain certain linearities and are inherently conservative.

The Energy Consumption Sector

The energy literature has long recognized a highly correlated relationship between energy consumption and measures of economic growth, such as the Gross National Product (GNP). Energy consumption and GNP, expressed in aggregate statistics or on a per capita basis, correlate in the 0.9 range across countries for a single year or for most single countries through time.[11] Authors who have done earlier projective analysis of China's future energy balance have modeled the relationship between energy consumption and GNP on the basis of fixed energy/GNP elasticities.[12] Growth rate elasticities, however, are subject to a wide range of error in the Chinese case, because of the volatility of China's historical energy consumption and GNP growth rates. An energy/GNP growth rate elasticity of much under 1.0 or much over 2.0 has very little theoretical meaning. However, China's energy/GNP elasticities range from negative values to large positive values, distorting average elasticities beyond statistical repair. This renders any fixed assumption regarding the energy/GNP elasticity arbitrary and meaningless. The future energy balance is highly sensitive to variation in the assumed elasticities. Clearly some other statistical approach was called for.

The basic projection method on the consumption side of the model used in this study was to stand the energy/GNP relationship on its head, treating energy consumption as a dependent variable and GNP as an independent variable in a series of linear regression equations for different historical periods in the development of the Chinese energy balance.

Thus, each unit of additional GNP was assumed to require some additional increment of energy consumption—called the "energy end-use requirement." The statistical method of ordinary least squares was used to establish correlation parameters, linear coefficients, and constants (Table 23.1). Several linear equations were derived for the period 1949–78, as well as for several subperiods, in the form:

$$\text{energy consumption} = \text{coefficient} \times \text{GNP} + \text{constant}$$

The coefficients and constants in the projection equations were varied according to the general range of historical parameters derived from China's energy development during different historical periods. Low-, median-, and high-growth projections were than constructed on the basis of these alternative estimates of the linear parameters relating energy end-use requirements to growth in the GNP.

The advantage of using a linear regression analysis is that the relationship between energy consumption and GNP appears far more regular and less variable than indicated by China's historical energy/GNP elasticity patterns. It is interesting to note the coefficients for 1961–70 and 1971–78, which were substantially lower and higher, respectively, than the general pattern. The 1960's were a decade of massive disruption in all of the energy industries. During this period, commercial energy commodities were in short supply, causing substitution by noncommercial fuels in the rural areas and tight rationing measures in the urban-industrial sector. By contrast, the 1970's were a decade of recovery and expansion in all energy industries, led by rapid growth in the oil and gas industries. The effect has been to introduce new commercial energy supplies at a rate higher than general expansion in the economy. This means that each additional increment of GNP has been bought at a higher energy "cost" than was the case before 1970. During a period of energy commodity abundance, commercial fuels are substituted for noncommercial fuels in the countryside, and industry is permitted to increase its use of energy-intensive processes. Rapid industrialization is not an energy-efficient experience for most countries. China is no exception to this rule. The energy/GNP coefficients for all periods since 1949 are high relative to international averages.

The coefficients used in the projections were generally more optimistic (efficient) than the historical experience, in order to allow for the introduction of energy use conservation. Initial coefficients were set to the values indicated in Table 23.1 for the different projections, and then allowed to decay to reflect long-range improvements in energy use efficiency. It is my impression, from a number of different perspectives, that the 1970's will turn out to have been the least energy-efficient de-

TABLE 23.1
Energy Consumption and Gross National Product

Historical period	Coefficient	Constant	R-squared	Per capita GNP growth rate (percent)
1949–1978	1.55	−78.0	0.95	4.6%
1949–1960	1.74	−90.1	0.79	6.6
1961–1970	0.91	12.8	0.78	3.2
1971–1978	2.44	−332.5	0.92	3.5
1961–1978	1.62	−97.2	0.93	3.3

Projections	Coefficients[a] 1975	2000			
Low growth	1.50	1.00	35.0	—	3.0%
Base line	1.50	1.00	23.0	—	3.5
Median growth	1.50	1.15	−5.0	—	4.0
High growth	1.50	1.15	9.0	—	5.0

Note: Ordinary least-squares regression of aggregate energy end-use and GNP using the Harvard *Time Series Processor*, version 3.4.

[a]Under the low and baseline projections, the coefficient was allowed to decay slightly faster than in the median and high projections, reflecting greater attention to energy conservation under conditions of resource constraint on production. Projected constants were set on the basis of an assumed production-consumption cross-over (zero net energy export potential) in 1972.

cade in China's drive for industrialization, at least in terms of the growth of GNP.

Having established an empirically defined range of linear relationships between energy end-use requirements and Gross National Product, some means was necessary to adequately project growth in the GNP itself. The simplest method would have been to project GNP at fixed growth rates along alternative exponential curves. This would, however, exclude the likely impact of population dynamics on future energy consumption requirements. The PRC is at the present time in the midst of its demographic transition from a condition of high death rates and high birth rates to a condition of low death rates and low birth rates. There is some lag between the drop in death rates due to improved nutrition and health care and a subsequent drop in birth rates caused by family planning and birth control. During this critical period, rates of natural increase rise to very high levels and the population expands rapidly. China experienced high rates of natural increase during the 1950's and 1960's under conditions of relative political stability and internal peace.[13] The government in Peking consequently adopted a policy favoring lower birth rates through family planning and the dissemination of birth control information and birth control devices. In the late 1970's, as China's population crossed the one billion mark, these measures were beginning to have a visible effect. The degree of effectiveness of the family planning program in China will have an impact on the rate of growth of per capita income, and, ultimately, on the growth of energy end-use requirements. In order to capture this variation, I projected GNP on the basis of alternative assumed per capita GNP growth rates and population projections in the following steps: (1) based on historical experience, per capita GNP was projected at 3–5 percent per year; (2) population levels were projected under low, median, and high birth and death rates, and an "expected" plan was selected that conforms to the work of experts on China's population dynamics;[14] (3) GNP was derived as the product of population times per capita GNP for each year under each per capita GNP projection; (4) the aggregate energy consumption requirement was projected on the basis of GNP, using alternative assumed energy/GNP coefficients; and (5) per capita energy consumption was derived from the aggregate energy consumption requirement divided by the projected population for each year.

This completes the review of the methodology of projections used on the consumption side of the basic model. It demonstrates how the low-, median-, and high-growth projections for energy end-use requirements were constructed on the basis of regression analysis, alternative energy/ GNP coefficients, and various projected rates of growth in the economy. This analysis should successfully tie the projection of future energy consumption patterns to historical trends. It avoids the difficulties of growth-rate elasticities, which are volatile and meaningless in the Chinese case. It must be emphasized that some method of projecting energy end-use requirements was needed in order to avoid the impression that energy production increases in the petroleum and natural gas industries will automatically be followed by rising oil exports. The next section deals directly with the problem of projecting China's energy export potential.

The Energy Export Sector

Projecting China's future energy commodity exports must be ranked as one of the world's most hazardous intellectual occupations. Future exports will be determined by the growth of all four primary energy industries, by the size and recoverability of offshore oil resources, by the transportation infrastructure, by the pattern of capital investment, by the world market price of crude petroleum, by the growth dynamics of the Chinese population, and by increases in China's average standard of living, to name but a few of the more important factors. All of the variables in this list are highly volatile in the Chinese case, and none would be easy to predict alone. The only relief from this bewildering complexity is what I call the "law of self-canceling marginal probabilities." It is theoretically possible that the universe will align itself in such a manner as to maximize (or minimize) China's energy commodity exports. Offshore oil resources could prove enormous and economically accessible. Inland natural gas reserves could be much larger than foreign estimates suggest. The market price of crude oil could double. China's population and economic growth could be simultaneously minimized. And the energy sector could perform at high levels of internal and external efficiency. All these events could take place simultaneously, making the PRC another Saudi Arabia. But, the probability of each such outcome is small and equal to the probability of its opposite. This makes it highly likely that breakthroughs in one factor will be canceled by catastrophes in another factor, bringing the net gain for oil exports to zero. The probability of the whole sequence of events landing on one side of the energy balance equation is the product of the marginal probabilities of all the events in the chain. If we were, therefore, to select a general scenario upon which to base our expectations and policy judgments, it would best be selected from among the many hundreds of possible futures that inhabit the space at the center of the range, well away from the zones of marginal probability. Predicting the exact outcome within the center range is impossible, given the number of variables. The best that can be expected is to provide samples of likely scenarios and compare them for common elements.

Given the sensitivity of actual energy commodity exports to an enormous array of variables endogenous and exogenous to the energy sector, I felt it necessary to simplify the future, perhaps at the cost of greater generality in the conclusions. This was done by the conceptual separation of the amount of energy that China *will* export in any given future year from the amount that China *could* export in that year. In other words, I eliminated all of the exogenous political and economic variables bearing on the year-to-year formulation of Peking's oil and coal export policy and concentrated exclusively on the energy balance itself, in particular the balance of production capacity and consumption requirements. It was simply assumed that Peking must meet its domestic energy consumption requirements first, before exporting energy commodities to other countries. Market economists will not like this assumption. They will insist that the world oil market generates a "shadow price" for Chinese oil inside as well as outside of the domestic economy and that future export decisions will be based on the comparative advantage of exports versus domestic consumption at that market price. I concede that there might be some merit to this argument for certain oil-exporting countries. Perhaps Iran, Venezuela, Nigeria, and Indonesia fall into the category of countries that have at one time or other sacrificed some portion of domestic commercial energy consumption to the international market value of oil exports. But none of these countries has a population of one billion persons whose energy consumption needs must be met as modernization proceeds. Nor have the governments of these countries placed resource sovereignty, domestic development, or self-reliance at the center of their policies. I believe that, in the Chinese case, domestic energy consumption requirements will be placed first in the list of priorities for use of available energy supplies, leaving exports as a residual. In this sense, Chinese energy development will be similar to that in the Soviet Union or the United States.

Casting the argument in a slightly different mold, the projections make it clear that high oil exports could be achieved only by holding the rise in per capita income in China to less than 3 percent. Considering that this figure is an average that includes urban and rural incomes, as well as growth in the GNP not related to personal consumption, a per capita GNP growth rate of less than 3 percent per year would mean little or no visible increase in personal living standards for the mass of Chinese people over the next two decades. I believe that this outcome would be unacceptable in a country where heavy labor and social mobilization are rationalized in terms of the goals and values of modernization, industrialization, and economic growth. A sustained period with no visible increase in personal standards of living would seriously erode the existing political legitimacy of the Chinese government. A rising per capita GNP of more than 3 percent per year will produce some visible improvement in personal living standards, but will require enormous energy inputs. The electric water pump, the threshing mill, the walking tractor, the truck for heavy transport, and the single 20-watt light bulb in the rural home are visible signs of higher per capita access to commercial energy. Multiplied across the Chinese population and across all of the activities of Chinese agriculture and industry, the increasing use of commercial energy fuels will place a staggering demand on Chinese energy industries. This steadily growing energy consumption requirement will sharply curtail the availability of energy commodities for export, regardless of the price of oil in the international market.

For these substantive reasons, as well as in the name of simplicity in the final model, energy export potential was treated as a residual sector, the difference between rising production capacity and rising consumption requirements. Note that the term "export potential" has been used throughout the study, rather than "exports." This is a notational recognition of the fact that the projected energy commodity export curve generated by each energy balance projection under alternative growth assumptions represents a maximum curve. The Chinese government could decide for a variety of market or policy reasons to export energy commodities at less than the maximum possible level in any given year. There are some indications that Peking would like to export more oil in the 1978–82 period than the Japanese market will bear. The precise level of energy commodity exports will be the result of a complex set of policy decisions by the Chinese government. All we know is that exports will fall within a ceiling value defined by the energy export potential curve under a given set of reserves and economic growth assumptions. Real energy commodity exports could be less than energy export potential, but they will not exceed the difference between domestic production capacity and consumption requirements.

One final note should be added to this discussion of the energy export sector of the model. All of the projected values for energy export potential were given in million metric tons of *oil* equivalent. This does not imply that the exports will all be in the form of crude petroleum. Some energy commodity exports will be in the form of refined petroleum products, coal, coke, and perhaps liquefied natural gas. Crude petroleum will probably remain the predominant commodity in trade, but the history of China's energy commodity trade, as well as current trade agreements, indicates that other energy commodities will be exported as well. Once again, providing projections of the energy commodity export potential in a common energy unit greatly simplifies the projection task, at the cost of greater generality in the results. Oil equivalents were chosen as the export potential unit for the sake of convenience in comparisons with other oil-exporting countries.

In sum, I repeat the argument that simple export projections based on the growth curve of the petroleum industry alone are completely inadequate and give a grossly exaggerated picture of China's future oil export potential. At minimum, some account must be made of the growth of production capacity in other energy industries and of the steady growth of domestic energy consumption. An accurate picture of energy commodity export potential can only be derived from an overview of the entire energy balance, not from the growth curve for a single fuel. The next chapter provides my version of such an overview.

Chapter 24

Alternative Energy Balance Projections

Chapter 23 provided an overview of the framework of assumptions that supports the projection program for simulation of China's future energy balance. This chapter will set out, in highly condensed form, the statistical results of the projections. We will begin with an in-depth, sector-by-sector analysis of a single projection. I have called this the "baseline projection." It shows what would happen to the Chinese energy balance over the next two decades if it continued to follow development patterns established over the last three decades. The analysis of the baseline projection follows the format of the historical energy profile (Chapter 14–21). That is, it begins with statistics on resource depletion for the primary energy fuels and moves through primary energy production, energy production growth rates, the electric power production loop, consumption requirements for commercial fuels, and energy export potential. This method of detailed statistical presentation is useful to illustrate both the structure of the model and its power in describing one possible growth pattern for the Chinese energy balance. The baseline projection results should allow the energy analyst to look "inside" the model and to compare it with similar models. Presentation of a wide range of variables for a single projection should also enable the China specialist to compare my energy balance projections with those of other authors, with their own intuitive notions of the direction of China's energy development, and with growth projections for other sectors of the Chinese economy.

Examination of one projection in depth, however, should not convey the impression that it is a "preferred scenario." A wide range of alternative assumptions has been built into the projections, generating a wide range of results. The chapter continues, therefore, with presentation of statistics describing low-, median-, and high-growth projections. I believe that these three define the boundaries of likely outcomes for the Chinese energy balance over the next 20 years. This gives us a broad but finite range of alternative energy futures, within which the precise outcome will be determined by a complex mix of resource, growth, and policy parameters. The low- and high-growth projections were generated from what I consider extreme sets of assumptions, given what we know of the geology of China's energy resources and the history of Chinese economic development. Owing to space limitations, I could present only a select group of variables to describe the low-, median-, and high-growth energy balances. The other variables are readily available, using the projection model, for those analysts who seek detailed growth information on any subsector of the energy balance, or on the projection outcome of any given set of assumptions.

I have not included a "sensitivity analysis" of the responsiveness of energy export potential to various growth parameters in this chapter. Generally speaking, I found energy export potential to be most sensitive to even minor variations in the per capita GNP growth rate. This is not a surprising finding, in view of the size of the Chinese population. Oil and gas resources ranked second as a determinant of energy export potential. If per capita GNP growth is held to a low and constant rate, then export potential proves to be highly sensitive to oil and gas resources. However, large increases in assumed oil and gas resources are counterbalanced by small increases in per capita GNP growth rates. For example, if oil and gas resources are assumed to be on the order of magnitude of original U.S. resources (a large guess for China), and the per capita GNP growth rate is allowed to rise to just 5 percent per year, the additional energy production is swallowed by additional consumption, and export potential looks much like the baseline projection. This indicates that energy export potential is even more sensitive to per capita GNP growth than to oil and gas resources. The energy/GNP coefficient also turns out to be an important determinant of energy export potential, but less important than either per capita GNP growth rates or oil and gas resource discoveries. Since I assumed improving energy-use efficiencies over time in all projections, the marginal impact of various starting efficiencies on the overall energy balance is not great. Energy exports would be highly sensitive to variable growth rates in the coal industry, but I believe the range of likely variation in future coal production will be narrow because of saturation of the domestic market for coal and continuing limits on the international market for Chinese coal. As for the electric power industry, I find that wide variations in growth rates of electric power production have little impact on energy export potential. It should be recalled in this connection that hydropower still contributes only 1 percent of China's primary energy production. Energy export potential will be sensitive to the growing use of future energy production technologies in China. However, the rate of introduction of new energy technologies (and accompanying capital requirements) will be contingent on the discovery rate for oil and gas resources. The net impact on export potential of lower oil and gas discoveries and higher growth in future energy industries (e.g. nuclear and geothermal) is negligible. I also found that energy export potential is not very sensitive to the introduction of enhanced recovery techniques on China's oilfields. At best, enhanced recovery will extend peak production rather than increasing it. If oil and gas resources turn out to be limited, as assumed in the low and baseline projections, then enhanced recovery will help China avoid becoming a heavy-energy importer in the late 1990's. But enhanced recovery will not improve the energy export picture within the time horizon of these projections, regardless of the size of oil and gas resources.

The beauty of the projection model is that it can be used to test the sensitivity of the Chinese energy balance to a very wide array of growth assumptions. It enables us to answer the major "what if" questions as new information is introduced. If foreign oil and gas resource estimates double next year, that finding can easily be plugged into the generation of an appropriate projection. The model is sufficiently interactive to permit its use in the question mode without introducing more than minor program changes. There are certain questions the model will not answer. It won't tell us, for example, how much capital Peking will invest in the coal industry between 1985 and 1990 or how many offshore drilling rigs China will buy in 1981. But the computer model will provide us with a statistical framework within which to begin analyzing the Chinese energy industries at a more detailed level, using documentary evidence, interviews, the public media, and so on. A new energy balance projection for the PRC is only as far away as a telephone connection and a quick computer run.

Baseline Projection

The baseline projection was constructed using the best available current information about energy resources and growth rates. It shows what would happen to the Chinese energy balance if present trends continued without much alteration through the turn of the century. The baseline projection was used to test the projection model against historical energy statistics for the period from 1965 through 1978 in a retrospective forecast. The retrospective forecast did not match reality completely, since most of the projected variables grew along smooth curves, eliminating the volatility of the Chinese energy sector experienced over the past decade and more. The dip in energy production caused by the Cultural Revolution, for example, does not appear in the results of the retrospective forecast, although the effect of that dip on longer-range growth rates was reflected in the model. Once the retrospective forecast had been successfully constructed using the assumptions of the baseline projection, it was simply allowed to run through the year 2000, playing out the implications of current trends. However, the baseline projection does not represent a prediction, since it rests on a conservative set of assumptions.

In the energy production sector, the key variable assumptions are crude petroleum and natural gas reserves and resources. Economically recoverable oil and gas resources were set at levels just below the estimates of Meyerhoff and Willums, which I consider the best foreign estimates available at the current time.[1] Crude petroleum resources were set at 8.5 billion metric tons (62 billion barrels). This figure was broken into 5.0 billion metric tons of discovered oil and 3.5 billion tons of additional discoveries over the period of the projection. If Meyerhoff and Willums are correct, China will eventually recover more than 5 billion tons of crude oil from onland fields and an additional 4 billion tons from offshore fields. These estimates are conservative, both within the overall range of foreign estimates of China's oil resource base, and also within the framework of the Meyerhoff-Willums probability analysis. Natural gas resources were set at 7.5 trillion cubic meters (economically recoverable), of which 5.0 tcm was designated as already discovered and an additional 2.5 tcm was assumed to be discovered within the next 20 years. Here again, the estimates were under Meyerhoff-Willums, who place ultimate natural gas recovery at 5.7 tcm onland and 2.9 tcm offshore. China's natural gas resources could be much higher, depending on the size of gas resources in inland basins, particularly the Tsaidam Basin, which is currently locked in by the lack of gas pipelines.

On the consumption side, the baseline projection was also structured around a fairly conservative set of assumptions. Per capita income (per capita GNP) was assumed to grow at an average rate of just 3.5 percent per year, well below the 4.6 percent annual growth rate that China has achieved since 1949. Per capita GNP growth rates declined to around 3–3.5 percent per year during the 1960's and 1970's. Thus the 3.5 percent growth rate represents a conservative estimate of the current trend. The energy/GNP coefficient for the baseline projection was set at an initial value of 1.5 and then allowed to decay slowly to reflect gradual improvement in the energy use efficiency of the Chinese economy, reaching about 1.0 in the year 2000. This is a conservative estimate in view of the coefficient of 1.55 derived for the 1949–78 period by regression analysis (Table 23.1). One would expect some improvement in energy use efficiency over historical coefficients as energy development proceeds.

The baseline projection did not include the likely effects of enhanced recovery on oil and gas production, and consequently on China's future energy export potential. I did run the program for the baseline projection both with and without the enhanced-recovery assumption and found that it makes only marginal difference to export potential within the time horizon of these projections. Enhanced oil and gas recovery would extend the period of peak oil and gas production through 2000 under the resource assumptions of the baseline projection. But the impact of this extension would be negligible in terms of the total energy balance. If the conditions of the baseline projection held through two more decades, China would become a net energy importer in the early 1990's. The main impact of using tertiary recovery methods on China's aging oilfields would be to reduce the necessary volume of oil imports after crossover had been reached in the energy commodity trade balance. Enhanced recovery would save the PRC about 20 million tons of oil imports in the year 2000, under the assumptions of the baseline projection. That would be about 2 percent of China's total energy consumption requirement in that year.

The base-line projection was also based on a number of other structural and substantive assumptions about the Chinese energy balance. But these assumptions are common to nearly all of the runs and were therefore described in Chapter 23.

Baseline Projection: Primary Energy Resources

Despite recent optimism about China's growing discoveries of crude oil and natural gas, particularly in the fields of the northeast and offshore areas, the overall outlook for primary energy resources is not encouraging. (See Table 24.1.) Coal resources and hydropower resources will not be a serious constraint on the growth of these energy industries through the turn of the century. Indeed, China is among the world's best-endowed countries in both bituminous coal and hydraulic potential. The coal and hydropower industries, however, will be seriously restricted by nonresource factors such as capital costs, market saturation, transmission distances, and substitution inelasticities. The coal industry could grow rapidly over the next two decades only if China were to move toward the extensive use of coal gasification and liquefaction technologies, processes that are still expensive to build and operate and that, consequently, do not compete well with oil and gas. Hydropower development suffers capital constraints, transmission inefficiencies, and problems caused by the displacement of rural populations and the inundation of useful agricultural land. Under the growth assumptions of the baseline projection, installed hydropower capacity will reach 60 GWe by the year 2000, or about 12 percent of theoretical hydraulic potential. Even this figure represents a quadrupling of installed capacity in just 20 years, a fairly liberal growth assumption.

I believe, therefore, that the size of China's oil and gas resources will be critical in determining the pace of energy development through 2000. If ultimate recovery of oil and gas from Chinese fields is only 8.5 billion tons and 7.5 trillion cubic meters, as implied by the Meyerhoff-Willums analysis and the assumptions of the baseline projection, crude petroleum resources will be 45 percent depleted and natural gas resources will be 35 percent depleted by the year 2000. That represents a serious depletion rate, based on the historical experience of the American oil and gas industries and the Venezuelan oil industry (Chapter 23). If historical experience is any guide, peak production occurs at about 35 percent depletion of ultimate economically recoverable resources. In other words, under the assumptions of the baseline projection, oil and gas production in China will peak within this century, and at fairly low output levels (Table 24.2).

As depressing as this projection might be to Peking's energy planners, it is not surprising. If the Meyerhoff-Willums estimates are accepted, China's oil and gas resources would be about 20–25 percent of the original recoverable oil and gas resources of the United States, or 40–45 percent of Venezuelan oil resources. One should not expect the Chinese to construct a first-rank oil industry on such a limited resource base. The truly disturbing feature of the baseline projection is that more than one-third of the recoverable oil and gas resources in the Meyerhoff-Willums estimate lie in the offshore basins. This implies that even with extensive investment in offshore oil development, and large-scale discoveries in the near-shore areas of the Pohai Gulf and the South China Sea, China will face a serious resource constraint on oil and gas production within the foreseeable future. The major oilfields of the northeast (Taching, Takang, and Shengli) will simply not be able by themselves to sustain a large oil and gas industry, unless the reserves in these fields are much larger than estimated by foreign geologists. Hope for China's oil and gas industries must therefore lie with large discoveries in the still untapped inland basins, and the development of the oil resources of the Taiwan-Sinzi Folded Zone, an offshore area that lies under deep and sharply contested waters (Chapter 7).

China's energy reserves picture would be very tight indeed, if the resource assumptions of the baseline projection proved to be the ultimate destiny of the petroleum and natural gas industries. This indicates that China cannot afford to ignore the issue of resource conservation. Oilfields must be developed with techniques that permit maximum recovery, even at the cost of slower production rates. Under baseline conditions, Peking's energy planners would soon be aware that oil exports are being sold at the expense of the future energy balance. We should then expect

TABLE 24.1
Baseline Projection: Primary Energy Resources

Year	Coal[a] (bmt)	Crude petroleum (bmt)[b]			
		Discovered reserves	Undiscovered resources	Annual discoveries	Remaining fraction
1965	100	5,000	3,500		100%
1966	99	4,990	3,500		99
1967	99	4,977	3,499	1	99
1968	99	4,962	3,498	2	99
1969	98	4,942	3,496	3	98
1970	98	4,918	3,492	4	98
1971	98	4,888	3,488	6	97
1972	97	4,852	3,482	8	97
1973	97	4,809	3,473	10	96
1974	97	4,759	3,463	13	95
1975	96	4,703	3,450	16	94
1976	96	4,642	3,433	19	92
1977	95	4,578	3,414	23	91
1978	95	4,509	3,390	26	90
1979	94	4,437	3,364	30	88
1980	93	4,361	3,334	34	87
1981	93	4,282	3,299	37	85
1982	92	4,200	3,262	41	84
1983	91	4,115	3,220	45	82
1984	91	4,027	3,174	49	80
1985	90	3,937	3,125	53	78
1986	89	3,845	3,072	56	76
1987	89	3,751	3,015	60	75
1988	88	3,656	2,955	63	73
1989	87	3,560	2,891	66	71
1990	86	3,464	2,825	69	69
1991	85	3,369	2,755	71	67
1992	85	3,275	2,683	74	65
1993	84	3,183	2,609	75	63
1994	83	3,093	2,533	77	61
1995	82	3,006	2,456	78	60
1996	81	2,923	2,378	79	58
1997	80	2,843	2,299	79	56
1998	79	2,768	2,219	79	55
1999	78	2,697	2,140	78	53
2000	77	2,631	2,061	78	52

[a]Measured coal reserves.　　[b]Excluding shale oil.

TABLE 24.1 *(continued)*
Baseline Projection: Primary Energy Resources

	Natural gas (tcm)				Hydraulic potential[c] (GW)	Future resources[d] (bmtce)
	Discovered reserves	Undiscovered resources	Annual discoveries	Remaining fraction		
1965	5,000	2,500		100%	500	10.0
1966	4,991	2,500		99	499	9.9
1967	4,980	2,499		99	498	9.9
1968	4,969	2,498	1	99	498	9.9
1969	4,955	2,497	1	99	497	9.9
1970	4,940	2,495	2	98	496	9.9
1971	4,922	2,493	3	98	495	9.9
1972	4,902	2,490	3	98	495	9.9
1973	4,879	2,486	4	97	494	9.9
1974	4,853	2,481	5	97	493	9.9
1975	4,824	2,475	6	96	492	9.9
1976	4,791	2,468	8	95	491	9.9
1977	4,754	2,460	9	95	490	9.9
1978	4,714	2,451	11	94	489	9.9
1979	4,670	2,439	12	93	488	9.9
1980	4,623	2,426	14	92	486	9.9
1981	4,572	2,412	16	91	485	9.9
1982	4,517	2,395	18	90	484	9.9
1983	4,459	2,377	20	89	482	9.9
1984	4,397	2,356	22	87	481	9.9
1985	4,332	2,334	24	86	479	9.9
1986	4,263	2,309	27	85	478	9.9
1987	4,191	2,281	29	83	476	9.9
1988	4,116	2,252	31	82	474	9.8
1989	4,038	2,220	34	80	472	9.8
1990	3,957	2,186	36	79	470	9.8
1991	3,873	2,149	38	77	468	9.8
1992	3,787	2,111	40	75	466	9.8
1993	3,700	2,070	43	74	464	9.7
1994	3,610	2,027	45	72	461	9.7
1995	3,520	1,982	46	70	459	9.7
1996	3,430	1,935	48	68	456	9.6
1997	3,340	1,886	50	66	453	9.5
1998	3,250	1,836	51	65	450	9.4
1999	3,162	1,785	52	63	447	9.3
2000	3,075	1,732	53	61	444	9.2

[c]Undeveloped theoretical hydraulic potential.   [d]Future energy technology resources.

to see a conservative oil export strategy in the 1980's, emphasizing coal trade rather than further development of the international market for Chinese oil. Within China, industry would be encouraged to minimize the use of oil and gas and maximize the use of coal and hydroelectric power. Offshore oil development would loom ever larger as a priority for capital investment, depending, of course, on the size and economics of recovery of offshore discoveries. Peking would probably seek accommodation on the various political issues that impede exploration for oil in contested areas of the continental shelf. Japan in particular would be sought as a partner in development of offshore oil and gas. Under limited resource conditions, however, the Japan connection will pose a dilemma for Peking. China will not want to sell much of the oil discovered in the continental shelf, the main incentive for Japanese participation in joint ventures. Finally, in the event of serious resource constraints on the oil and gas industries, Peking will invest heavily in alternative energy production technologies, particularly nuclear power, geothermal, biomass, and perhaps solar. Even maximum growth rates in these industries will increase their share of the energy production burden to only marginal levels by 2000. The baseline resource projection could even result in serious constraints on overall economic development, and in a dampening of growth in per capita income levels.

The baseline projection demonstrates that China's current energy resource situation is not encouraging. The PRC will have to work hard over the next two decades to discover and develop new oilfields. I believe that this view is shared by China's political leaders and energy planners, despite their bullish comments to foreign visitors. It is no accident that ten of the 120 large-scale projects envisioned for the Ten-Year Development Plan are new oil and gas fields.[2] Nor is it any accident that Peking has recently developed a more open attitude about the use of foreign oil technology, joint ventures in offshore oil exploration, and energy cooperation with Japan. All of these pieces fit the same jigsaw puzzle of perceptions and policy choices. Peking is still hedging its bets on the oil and gas industries and looking for ways to expand the resource base to a level that will support high levels of oil and gas production over sustained periods. If there is some genuine optimism in Chinese energy-planning circles, it is based on the historical pattern, which implies that more exploration yields steadily mounting discoveries. The history of the American petroleum industry carries essentially the same message. There have been several points, the war years for example, when the U.S. oil and gas reserve appeared to be tapering off, only to grow again with new exploration activity and new discoveries. Our uncertainty about the Chinese resource situation is sufficient to warrant caution about any single set of conclusions. The median- and high-growth projections presented below provide a picture of what will happen if history repeats itself and large new oil and gas discoveries are made in the PRC. It should be kept in mind, however, that there is no law of society or nature that guarantees the Chinese a large and expanding oil and gas resource base.

A brief note should be added regarding the figures in Table 24.1 on future technology energy resources. Energy resources for future technology production were set at an arbitrary initial value of 10 billion metric tons coal equivalent and were then depleted by current production from all forms of future technology. This manner of dealing with primary energy resources and production from future technologies is arbitrary in several ways. In the first place, some future energy technologies, such as biomass and solar, are not depletable, although there may be an outer limit on production capacity, as there is with hydropower. Second, there is no way of telling how large China's actual uranium or geothermal resources are, at least at this stage in our knowledge of China's geology. There is no reason to place future technology energy resources at 10 billion tons coal equivalent, rather than 1 billion tons or 100 billion tons. We simply do not know. Future technology energy resources were therefore treated in the model as a dead-end variable, with no feedback to the energy balance. The growth rate for future technology energy production was tied to the depletion of petroleum resources, not to the depletion of the theoretical and unmeasurable future resources for energy production from unknown technologies. The faster petroleum resources are depleted in the model, the faster production from future technologies grows. The future technology resource depletion figures were simply a heuristic device to remind us that some future energy production technologies (e.g. nuclear) also depend on depletable resources, and that China's long-range energy resources are not limited to coal, oil, gas, and hydro.

Baseline Projection: Primary Energy Production

Primary energy production statistics derived from the baseline projection further illustrate the seriousness of China's oil and gas resource position, if ultimate recovery of crude oil is less than 10 billion metric tons and ultimate recovery of natural gas is less than 8 trillion cubic meters. Several different projections were tried around the range of the Meyerhoff-Willums resource estimates, and all produced roughly the same primary energy production curves.

Under the assumptions of the baseline projections (and others as well), coal production will continue to increase through the turn of the century, but at declining annual growth rates. The growth rate for coal

TABLE 24.2
Baseline Projection: Primary Energy Production

Year	Coal[a]		Crude petroleum		Natural gas	
	Mmt	Increase	Mmt	Increase	Bcm	Increase
1970	347	7.2%	34	23.5%	20	16.1%
1971	372	6.9	42	21.1	23	15.5
1972	398	6.7	51	18.2	26	14.9
1973	425	6.5	60	14.8	30	14.1
1974	452	6.2	69	10.8	35	13.3
1975	480	6.0	77	9.4	39	12.4
1976	509	5.7	84	8.7	44	11.3
1977	538	5.4	91	7.9	49	10.1
1978	567	5.0	98	7.1	54	9.6
1979	595	4.7	105	6.6	60	9.0
1980	624	4.3	112	6.2	65	8.5
1981	651	4.0	119	5.7	71	7.9
1982	676	3.6	126	5.2	76	7.2
1983	701	3.2	133	4.7	82	6.8
1984	723	2.8	139	4.2	87	6.4
1985	743	2.3	145	3.6	93	6.0
1986	760	2.0	150	3.1	99	5.6
1987	775	2.0	155	2.5	104	5.2
1988	790	1.9	159	1.9	110	4.7
1989	805	1.9	162	1.4	115	4.2
1990	821	1.8	164	0.8	120	3.7
1991	836	1.8	165	0.2	124	3.2
1992	851	1.7	166	−0.3	128	2.7
1993	865	1.7	165	−0.9	132	2.2
1994	880	1.7	164	−1.4	135	1.7
1995	895	1.6	161	−2.0	137	1.1
1996	909	1.6	158	−2.5	138	0.6
1997	924	1.5	154	−2.9	139	0.0
1998	938	1.5	150	−3.4	139	−0.5
1999	952	1.4	145	−3.8	139	−1.0
2000	966	1.4	139	−4.2	137	−1.5

[a] Raw coal production, discounted at 0.75 mtce/mt.

TABLE 24.2 *(continued)*
Baseline Projection: Primary Energy Production

	Hydropower		Future technology		
Year	Capacity GW	Output bkwh	Mmtce	Increase	Total mmtce
1970	5	19	1	10.5%	341
1971	6	22	1	10.7	377
1972	7	24	1	10.9	414
1973	8	27	2	11.1	454
1974	9	30	2	11.4	494
1975	10	33	2	11.8	533
1976	11	36	3	12.1	573
1977	12	39	3	12.5	613
1978	13	42	3	12.9	653
1979	14	46	4	13.4	693
1980	15	50	4	13.8	732
1981	16	54	5	14.3	771
1982	18	58	6	14.8	810
1983	19	62	7	15.3	846
1984	21	67	8	15.8	881
1985	22	72	9	16.4	914
1986	24	77	11	16.9	945
1987	25	83	13	17.5	973
1988	27	88	15	18.1	1,000
1989	29	94	18	18.6	1,026
1990	31	100	21	19.2	1,052
1991	33	107	26	19.8	1,076
1992	35	114	31	20.3	1,099
1993	38	121	37	20.9	1,121
1994	40	129	45	21.4	1,143
1995	43	137	55	21.9	1,164
1996	45	145	67	22.5	1,186
1997	48	154	82	22.9	1,208
1998	51	164	101	23.4	1,232
1999	54	173	125	23.8	1,259
2000	58	184	155	24.2	1,291

production was started at 8 percent per year and allowed to decay to about 1.5 percent per year by the end of the century. Under this growth assumption, coal production will reach 750 million metric tons of raw coal in 1985 and about 1 billion tons by the year 2000. In 1975, the United States produced 575 million metric tons of standard coal, and the Soviet Union produced about 510 million tons. Even at a discount rate of 0.75 metric tons of standard coal per metric ton of Chinese raw coal, the

PRC may exceed current U.S. coal production levels by the year 2000. Meanwhile, the United States will probably have substantially increased its own coal production to provide feedstock for gasification and lique-faction processes, and will still equal or outrank China in coal output. China, the United States, and the USSR will continue to stand at the apex of the world coal industry for the next several decades.

Unlike coal, Chinese crude petroleum production levels will be highly sensitive to resource constraints. Under the limiting assumptions of the baseline projection, Chinese crude oil output will peak at about 165 million metric tons per year (3 million barrels per day) in the early 1990's. This is certainly far from the figure of 400 million tons per year (8 million barrels per day) often cited by foreign analysts as China's oil produc-tion target for 1990.[3] Crude oil production growth rates were started at 30 percent per year at 1965 and allowed to decay to about 6 percent per year in 1980, 4 percent in 1985, and 1 percent in 1990. This growth curve is not arbitrary. As elaborated in Chapter 23, it is based on the the-ory of resource depletion curves and the history of petroleum resource depletion in two other countries. Furthermore, it conforms closely to the actual pattern in the Chinese case. China's crude oil production growth rate was 7.7 percent from 1976 to 1977.[4] The model predicts 7.9 per-cent. Furthermore, even if it is argued that crude oil production will grow faster than projected by the model, if oil and gas resources are lim-ited to the Meyerhoff-Willums estimates, crude oil production will peak even sooner under higher growth-rate assumptions, and will not exceed 200 million tons per year in any case. As the median- and high-growth projections demonstrate, China's crude petroleum resources would have to be more than double the Meyerhoff-Willums estimates in order to reach production levels of 300 million tons per year by 1995, and qua-druple the Meyerhoff-Willums figures to reach production of 400 mil-lion tons per year by 1995 (Tables 24.6 and 24.7). The conclusion is obvi-ous. Either China's crude petroleum resources are much larger than es-timated by foreign geologists, or the PRC will have to be satisfied with much less than 400 million tons of oil in 1990. This illustrates once again the hazards of projecting crude oil production growth curves with abso-lutely no reference to the size of the petroleum resource base.

The baseline projection of the natural gas production curve looks much like the petroleum curve, except that natural gas started at a lower initial growth rate, and therefore lags somewhat behind development of the petroleum industry. Assuming about 7.5 trillion cubic meters of ulti-mate natural gas recovery, natural gas production will reach about 90 billion cubic meters per year in 1985, and will peak at about 140 billion cubic meters in the late 1990's. The natural gas production growth rate will drop to 9 percent in 1980, 6 percent in 1985, 4 percent in 1990, 1 percent in 1995, and zero by 2000. At peak production, the Chinese natural gas industry would be only about one-quarter the size of the U.S. natural gas industry in 1975. Again, this is not a surprising finding, since the baseline projection assumed that China has only about 20 percent of the ultimate recoverable natural gas resources that the United States had when production began.

The projection model tied hydropower production growth rates to the expansion of the Chinese hydropower equipment industry, rather than to the hydraulic resource base, for reasons explained in Chapter 23. The baseline projection assumed that in 1965 China was producing about 600 MW of new generating equipment for hydropower stations each year, and that the equipment industry then expanded at a growth rate of 5 percent per year for the entire period of the projections. This set of assumptions results in a gently declining rate of additions to hydropower capacity and hydropower output. The computer program could not conveniently provide annual growth rate figures for the hydropower industry, but hand tabulation shows a growth rate of 9.7 percent in the 1970's, about 7 percent in the 1980's, and 6 percent in the 1990's. This growth curve would result in development of about 20–25 GWe of hydropower capacity by 1985 and 60 GWe by the year 2000. Assuming a conservative utilization ratio of 3,000 kilowatt-hours per kilowatt, China will produce about 70 billion kilowatt-hours of hydroelectric power in 1985 and 180 billion kwh in 2000. That would rank China's hydropower industry of the year 2000 third in the world of 1975, behind the United States (300 bkwh) and Canada (200 bkwh). The difference is that China will have developed only 10–15 percent of theoretical hydraulic potential, and will be able to continue expanding hydropower capacity in the twenty-first century. I also experimented with a 10 percent expansion of the hydropower equipment industry, which results in high growth rates in installed capacity (unrealistic in view of the capital costs), and hydropower output of 400 billion kwh at the end of the century. This frantic pace of hydropower expansion would increase total energy production by only 25 million metric tons coal equivalent, or by 2 percent of projected total energy production in the year 2000. It is clear that the hydropower industry will not save China's energy balance in case oil and gas resources are sharply limited. This will be the case, regardless of the proportion of hydropower output that is generated in small-scale hydropower stations. Improvement of hydropower utilization ratios would also have only marginal impact on the total energy balance.

The results of projection of future technology energy production in the baseline projection are among the most interesting findings of the energy balance model. As explained in Chapter 23, I tied the growth rate for all forms of future technology energy production (FTEP) to the petroleum resource-depletion curve. As the fraction of remaining petroleum reserves declines, the growth rate for FTEP accelerates from 10 percent per year to peak growth rates of 25 percent per year. Beginning at an assumed level of one million metric tons coal equivalent in 1965, FTEP increases along its dynamic growth curve to more than 10 mmtce in 1985 and about 150 mmtce by the year 2000, or some 12 percent of total primary energy production in that year. Most of the assumed growth in FTEP from 1965 to 1978 was in the form of biogas generation, with some geothermal power production, some tidal power production, and some solar power production in small units. The retrospective forecast of FTEP is probably an exaggeration, and energy analysts may complain that the entire curve is too high. However, under conditions of sharply limited oil and gas resources, the motivation would be high for the PRC to seek additional primary energy production sources. Under these conditions, for example, the nuclear power industry will be expanded at the maximum possible rate. In the electric power subsector, I assumed that only 10 percent of FTEP will be in the form of electric power generation, primarily nuclear and secondarily geothermal. But under conditions of oil and gas resource constraints, a much higher proportion of FTEP development could be in the electric power industry. China certainly has the domestic market for rapid expansion of electric power generation. The design and construction lead times for most future energy technologies are more than a decade. However, in the past, when faced with critical energy shortages, Peking has shown a propensity for forced capital feeding of critical energy industries. Here, again, I believe that China's energy planners share this perception of possible oil and gas resource constraints and the necessity of rapid development of other primary energy production technologies. I believe this is the reason that Peking has experimented with exotic energy production technologies ranging from tidal power to controlled thermonuclear fusion (Chapter 14). The Chinese government wants to hedge its bets on the fossil-fuel industries and place a little money on the dark horses. Nuclear power is obviously the leading dark horse. As spelled out at some length in Chapter 12, I believe that the PRC will try to construct its first nuclear power station by 1985 and will keep open the option of rapid nuclear development, in case offshore oil proves incommensurate with China's burgeoning energy requirements. Nuclear power, of course, would do nothing to boost energy export potential, except in the unlikely event that Peking invests heavily in both the oil industry and the nuclear power industry simultaneously.

The statistics for total primary energy production in Table 24.2 were tabulated as the sum of production in the coal, oil, gas, hydropower, and future technology industries, weighted by energy-equivalent value and expressed in million metric tons coal equivalent. According to the baseline projection, total primary energy production will reach 900 mmtce in the mid-1980's and 1.3 billion metric tons coal equivalent (bmtce) by the end of the century. This implies a growth rate of 8 percent in the 1970's, 4 percent in the 1980's, and just 2 percent in the 1990's. (The actual growth rate for 1970–78 was 9 percent and declining.) If the assumptions of the baseline projection hold true, then Peking will face a serious decline in primary energy production growth rates in the 1990's. Once again, this reflects the conservative resource assumptions of this projection. Under these conditions, China would have little choice but to join the rest of the world in the rush on world energy commodity markets. As shown in Table 24.4, the PRC would become a net energy importer by the mid-1990's, a situation only partly relieved by enhanced oil and gas recovery. It should be kept in mind that the baseline projection allowed a generous rate of growth for new energy production technologies. The implication is that the incentive for new oil and gas discoveries in the PRC is high and will remain high for the next two decades.

On a comparative basis, the baseline projection would give China about 60 percent of the 1975 total primary energy production of the United States by the end of the century, or about 80 percent of current Soviet primary energy production. Under these conditions, the PRC would retain but improve its third-place ranking in terms of the aggregate size of the energy system.

Baseline Projection: Electric Power

Electric power production statistics are disaggregated in Table 24.3. The growth assumption for the hydropower industry was explained in the preceding section. Thermal electric power production was assumed to grow at a flat rate of 10 percent per year, paralleling the assumed growth of the total industrial product (Chapter 23). Projection of the breakdown of thermal power production by fuel (coal, petroleum, gas, and future energy technology) really amounts to sophisticated guesswork rather than empirical analysis, since we do not know the historical pattern, let alone the future. Disaggregation of the thermal power industry was accomplished by assuming that 10 percent each of oil, gas, and future technology energy production is used to generate electric power. I then simply assumed that coal-fired thermal power generation will provide the difference between the sum of oil, gas, and future-technology thermal and total thermal electric power generation. This as-

TABLE 24.3
Baseline Projection: Electric Power

Year	Thermal power production (bkwh)				
	Coal	Petroleum	Natural gas	Future	Total
1970	33	10	6	0.4	51
1971	35	12	7	0.4	56
1972	37	15	8	0.4	62
1973	40	18	10	0.5	69
1974	43	20	11	0.6	76
1975	47	23	13	0.6	84
1976	52	25	14	0.7	93
1977	58	27	16	0.8	102
1978	64	29	18	0.9	113
1979	72	31	19	1.0	125
1980	82	33	21	1.2	138
1981	92	35	23	1.4	153
1982	104	38	25	1.6	169
1983	118	40	27	1.8	187
1984	134	41	29	2.1	207
1985	152	43	30	2.4	229
1986	172	45	32	2.8	253
1987	195	46	34	3.3	279
1988	221	47	36	3.9	309
1989	250	48	38	4.6	341
1990	283	49	39	5.4	377
1991	319	49	41	6.5	417
1992	361	49	42	7.8	461
1993	407	49	43	9.4	509
1994	458	49	44	11.4	563
1995	514	48	45	13.8	622
1996	577	47	45	16.9	688
1997	647	46	46	20.7	760
1998	723	45	46	25.4	840
1999	808	43	45	31.4	928
2000	900	41	45	38.8	1,026

TABLE 24.3 *(continued)*
Baseline Projection: Electric Power

Year	Hydropower			Total electric power (bkwh)	
	Capacity (GW)	Additions (GW)	Output (bkwh)	Production	Consumption
1970	5	0.7	19	70	63
1971	6	0.8	22	78	70
1972	7	0.8	24	87	78
1973	8	0.8	27	96	86
1974	9	0.9	30	106	95
1975	10	0.9	33	117	105
1976	11	1.0	36	129	116
1977	12	1.0	39	142	128
1978	13	1.1	42	156	141
1979	14	1.2	46	172	155
1980	15	1.2	50	189	170
1981	16	1.3	54	207	187
1982	18	1.4	58	228	205
1983	19	1.4	62	250	225
1984	21	1.5	67	274	247
1985	22	1.6	72	301	271
1986	24	1.7	77	330	297
1987	25	1.8	83	362	326
1988	27	1.8	88	397	358
1989	29	1.9	94	436	392
1990	31	2.0	100	478	430
1991	33	2.2	107	524	472
1992	35	2.3	114	575	518
1993	38	2.4	121	631	568
1994	40	2.5	129	692	623
1995	43	2.6	137	760	684
1996	45	2.8	145	834	750
1997	48	2.9	154	915	823
1998	51	3.1	164	1,004	904
1999	54	3.2	173	1,102	992
2000	58	3.4	184	1,210	1,089

sumption conforms roughly to what I believe to have been the historical pattern in oil- and gas-fired thermal power generation (Chapter 17).

Under these assumptions, total thermal power generation will reach 230 billion kilowatt-hours in 1985, and about 1 trillion kwh in the year 2000. As points of comparison, U.S. thermal power generation was 1.5 trillion kwh in 1975, Soviet thermal power generation was 900 billion kwh, and Japan generated 365 billion kwh in the same year.[5] This indicates that with substantial capital investment and sustained rapid growth, China's thermal power industry will reach current Soviet levels by the end of the century. This projection may be too optimistic. However, I believe, for reasons cited throughout this book, that the Chinese electric power industry has lagged behind the rest of the energy balance and that serious efforts are being made in Peking to rectify the electric power shortages that have resulted. Given current shortages in industry and the major urban areas, I believe that future development of thermal power capacity will have to at least keep pace with the expansion of industry. If my generally optimistic view of the growth curve for thermal electric power is accurate, total electric power generation will reach 1.2 trillion kwh by the year 2000, of which roughly 15–20 percent will be contributed by hydropower. (The contribution of hydropower was 25 percent in the 1975–78 period.) This represents a reversal of the current trend toward a higher contribution from hydro. If the baseline projection is correct, the contribution of hydropower generation to total electric power output will peak at around 30 percent in the early 1980's and then decline slowly as the thermal power industry overtakes the decaying growth rate of hydro.

The contribution of oil- and gas-fired thermal to total electric power generation is highly sensitive to the resource assumptions of the baseline projection. Under limited oil and gas resource conditions, oil-fired thermal will reach a peak contribution of 25 percent of total electric power generation in 1980, and then decline relative to the aggregate size of the electric power industry. Enhanced oil recovery techniques would extend the peak level of oil-fired thermal, but would not prevent its relative decline. The contribution of gas-fired thermal would peak at less than 15 percent of total electric power output. The contribution of coal-fired thermal will grow to 65 percent in the mid-1980's and remain high throughout the period under consideration.

One of the key findings of the electric power projections is that under limited oil and gas resource conditions, the generation of electric power from future technologies could reach 40 billion kwh by the turn of the century. If this were predominantly generated in nuclear power stations, it would require a nuclear generating capacity of nearly 10 GWe, or the equivalent of ten large nuclear power stations. Considering that China currently has no nuclear power stations, this would represent a considerable outlay of capital for nuclear development. At more than $1,000 per kilowatt of installed nuclear power generating capacity, a nuclear industry of that size would cost $10–15 billion, a figure that begins to look significant in the framework of China's investment strategy. The PRC would probably prefer not to import all ten nuclear power stations, particularly at such a high cost in terms of foreign exchange. This implies that Peking will be paying a lot of attention to civilian nuclear engineering and may attempt to build some of the necessary equipment at home. The Chinese government may also find it necessary to come to terms with the existing framework of international control agreements, in order to obtain the necessary technology and equipment from abroad. The policy implications of this development are discussed in depth in Chapter 12.

Baseline Projection: Energy Consumption and Export Potential

The consumption sector of the baseline projection rests on a set of conservative growth assumptions. I adopted this strategy in order to avoid overstating energy consumption requirements, thereby understating energy export potential. One of the principal findings presented throughout this book is that China's energy export potential will be sharply limited by rising energy consumption requirements. It is possible to demonstrate this under very conservative assumptions in the consumption sector of the model. (See Table 24.4.) In fact, if per capita GNP and the energy consumption requirement are allowed to rise under more liberal assumptions, energy export potential disappears altogether, and the model projects a net energy import requirement. Each additional increment in the per capita GNP growth rate requires a large addition of assumed oil and gas resources in order to maintain net energy exports at greater than zero.

The baseline projection of energy consumption requirements began with constant growth of per capita GNP at 3.5 percent per year, reflecting the historical growth rates of 5 percent since 1949 and 3 percent since 1970. The population was projected at moderate rates that conform to median expert opinion of foreign demographers, with a gently declining birth rate and low death rate, reaching 1.3 billion by the end of the century.[6] (The projected rates of natural increase were 2.0 for the 1970's, 1.6 for the 1980's, and 1.0 for the 1990's.) Constant growth in per capita GNP and dynamic growth in population yield a projection for total GNP required to sustain the assumed pace of expansion in average living standards. This projection yielded a GNP of nearly 500 billion 1975 U.S. dollars in 1985, and nearly 1 trillion U.S. dollars in the year 2000. This implies a GNP growth rate of 5.4 percent during the 1970's, 5.1 percent during the 1980's, and 4.4 percent during the 1990's, well under historical growth rates of 7 percent since 1949 and 5–6 percent since 1970.

The consumption sector of the baseline projection also assumed an energy/GNP regression coefficient set to an initial value (1975) of 1.5

TABLE 24.4
Baseline Projection: Consumption and Export Potential

Year	Per capita GNP (dollars)[a]	Population (millions)	GNP (million dollars)[a]	Energy consumption requirement (mmtce)
1970	255	839	214	323
1971	264	855	226	344
1972	273	873	238	366
1973	283	890	252	391
1974	293	908	266	416
1975	303	926	280	444
1976	313	944	296	467
1977	324	963	312	492
1978	336	981	330	518
1979	348	1,000	348	545
1980	360	1,019	367	573
1981	372	1,038	387	596
1982	385	1,057	408	618
1983	399	1,076	429	642
1984	413	1,095	452	665
1985	427	1,113	476	690
1986	442	1,132	501	714
1987	458	1,149	526	739
1988	474	1,166	553	764
1989	490	1,182	580	789
1990	508	1,197	608	813
1991	525	1,211	637	838
1992	544	1,225	667	863
1993	563	1,239	698	888
1994	583	1,252	730	913
1995	603	1,264	763	938
1996	624	1,276	797	947
1997	646	1,288	832	955
1998	669	1,298	869	961
1999	692	1,309	906	966
2000	716	1,319	945	968

[a]Constant 1975 U.S. dollars

TABLE 24.4 *(continued)*
Baseline Projection: Consumption and Export Potential

Year	Energy availability						Per capita energy consumption (kgce/cap.)	Energy export potential[b] (mmtoe)
	Coal (mmt)	Petroleum (mmt)	Natural gas (bcm)	Electricity (bkwh)	Future (mmtce)	Total (mmtce)		
1970	229	26	15	63	1	298	384	16
1971	246	32	18	70	1	328	402	10
1972	263	39	20	78	1	361	420	3
1973	281	46	24	86	1	394	439	-2
1974	299	53	27	95	2	429	459	-8
1975	317	59	31	105	2	462	479	-11
1976	335	64	35	116	2	495	495	-18
1977	353	70	39	128	3	528	511	-24
1978	371	76	43	141	3	561	527	-29
1979	387	81	47	155	3	593	545	-33
1980	403	86	51	170	4	625	562	-35
1981	418	92	55	187	5	656	573	-41
1982	431	97	60	205	5	686	585	-46
1983	443	102	64	225	6	714	596	-49
1984	452	107	68	247	7	739	607	-50
1985	459	111	72	271	8	762	619	-49
1986	463	115	76	297	10	782	631	-46
1987	464	119	80	326	12	800	643	-41
1988	465	122	84	358	14	815	655	-34
1989	464	124	87	392	16	829	667	-27
1990	461	126	90	430	19	841	679	-18
1991	457	127	93	472	23	850	692	-8
1992	451	127	95	518	28	858	704	3
1993	443	127	97	568	34	863	717	16
1994	433	126	97	623	41	867	729	31
1995	420	124	98	684	49	868	742	47
1996	405	121	97	750	60	868	742	54
1997	388	118	95	823	74	866	741	60
1998	367	115	93	904	91	864	740	66
1999	343	111	90	992	113	862	737	70
2000	316	107	86	1,089	140	862	734	72

[b]Expressed as million metric tons oil equivalent net energy imports to conform to Chapters 20 and 21.

and declining to 1.0 by the turn of the century. This assumption is also well within the historical pattern, which has produced a coefficient of 1.5–1.7 since 1949. China's energy planners would have to emphasize use conservation of energy commodities in order to achieve the projected levels of use efficiency, particularly during a period of rapid industrialization and further substitution of commercial for noncommercial fuels. Here, again, the effort was to avoid overstating the factors that determine energy consumption requirements.

The projected statistics for energy availability were actually generated from the production sector of the model. Coal availability equals raw coal production, discounted (0.7 mtce/mt) for plant use and average energy content, minus the coal burned for electric power generation, which shows up in the column for available electric power. Crude petroleum production, natural gas production, and production of energy from future technologies were similarly discounted for plant use, petrochemical use, production inefficiencies, and use in the generation of electric power, yielding an approximation of availability of each of these fuels. Electric power production was discounted for plant use and transmission loss to yield an estimate of electric power availability (in output rather than capacity figures). Total energy availability was tabulated as the sum of the availability of the fuels and electric power, weighted by energy equivalent value. Per capita energy availability was then derived from total energy availability, minus exports, divided over the population. The energy availability statistics are quite useful in the model. First, the difference between the aggregate energy consumption requirement and total energy availability in any given year yields a net export potential or import requirement. This represents the interface between the production and consumption sides of the model. Second, the energy availability statistics provide a first-order approximation of the amounts of various fuels and electric power that can be either consumed at home or exported. (Some projections of China's oil exports exceed the total amount of oil available from domestic production under the assumptions of the baseline projection.) Third, the energy availability statistics give some basis for predicting future trends in the fuel and power mix, under different resource assumptions. Under the constrained resource assumptions of the baseline projection, coal will continue its gradual decline relative to the energy balance, contributing about 60 percent of total energy availability by 1985. The contribution of oil will remain steady at about 20–25 percent until the mid-1990's, and then decline. Gas will increase its contribution to the energy mix to 15 percent in 1995. The contribution of electric power will increase slowly at first (4 percent in 1985), and then more rapidly toward the end of the century, reaching 16 percent of energy availability in the year 2000. The contribution of future energy technologies to the energy mix will remain constant at about 1 percent or less until 1985, and then will begin to grow rapidly, exceeding 15 percent by the end of the century. Once again, these conclusions are highly contingent on the oil and gas resource assumptions of the various projections.

The statistics for export potential have been expressed in negative values as net energy imports, in order to maintain consistency with the notation used in Chapters 20 and 21 for historical energy commodity trade. The export potential figures were provided in million metric tons oil equivalent, for the convenience of those who think of China's energy trade primarily in terms of crude oil exports to Japan. Note once again the consistent use of the term "export potential" to describe this curve. This is a projection not of actual oil exports but of net energy export potential. Peking could choose to export more coal and save crude oil for domestic consumption. Or exports could be held substantially below the potential ceiling, in order to pour an additional energy supplement into the domestic economy and stimulate higher growth for industries that are energy-intensive. The curve tells us only what maximum exports of all energy commodities could be under various growth and resource assumptions. Market conditions and policy choices will determine the actual rate and mix of energy commodity exports within that ceiling.

The baseline projection shows energy export potential growing rapidly in the late 1970's and early 1980's, peaking at about 50 million tons of oil per year in the mid-1980's and then declining just as rapidly in the early 1990's. If actual energy end-use is substituted for projected consumption requirements, net export potential was 15 million tons in 1975, dropped to about 10 million tons in 1976, bounced back to 15 million tons in 1977, and reached some 30 million tons oil equivalent in 1978. If these figures reflect China's actual energy export surplus, Peking has been exporting at about three-quarters of its export potential since 1975. Apparently planners in Peking would like to export at an even higher percentage of net export potential, since they have pressed for larger oil exports to Japan and other countries in every year except 1976, when the export ceiling dropped and China failed to meet its commitments.

Despite its exaggeration of export potential in the late 1970's, I believe that the ceiling of 50 million tons oil equivalent is accurate for the mid-1980's, under the limited oil and gas resource assumptions of the baseline projection. Energy commodity exports at anything approaching that level would represent a big jump in China's energy trade over the next few years and would stimulate yet another wave of speculation regarding China's long-range oil export prospects. In other words, I expect Chinese oil to be a hot topic until 1985 or so. Nonetheless, this figure should be approached with some caution. It is quite clear, for example, that Peking could not choose to export at the projected level if oil alone were to be exported. The projected figures would take fully half of China's available petroleum during the period under consideration, or about 35 percent of total crude petroleum production. It is much more likely that the Chinese government will seek to expand its coal exports as rapidly as possible, holding crude oil exports to 15–25 percent of production, or 25–40 million tons in 1985. Assuming that Peking chose to export at 75 percent of the potential ceiling, I would guess that China will try to market 10–15 million tons of coal exports by 1985, as well as some liquefied natural gas. These levels square with the findings of the baseline projection and are reasonable in view of the current pattern of Chinese energy commodity trade. If two-thirds of the projected energy commodity exports went to the Japanese market and Japanese energy commodity trade continues to move in directions established during the 1970's, China will satisfy about 10–15 percent of Japan's oil import requirement and less than 15 percent of Japan's coal market in 1985.

An even more depressing outcome of the baseline projection is that the period of China's net energy exports will last only about 20 years, from 1973 until the early 1990's. We are already six years into that period and cumulative exports of petroleum are only about 50 million tons, an amount that Indonesia exports in a single year. Peak export potential would last about five years and then decline rapidly under the pressure of rising consumption requirements on peaking crude petroleum production. The baseline projection indicates that crossover to net energy imports would occur in the early 1990's, under constrained oil and gas resource assumptions. If the Chinese oil industry follows the experience of Venezuela and the United States, production decline will follow peak production at about 65 percent of recoverable resources still remaining. This would have a devastating effect on China's balance of energy commodity trade, resulting in net energy imports of about 50–100 million tons of oil equivalent per year (1–2 million barrels per day) by the end of the century.

It is not likely that China's energy planners would stand idly by as crossover to net energy imports was reached. The government, presumably still controlling its centrally planned economy, would place strict import controls on energy commodities, and attempt such remedial measures as accelerated exploration and enhanced recovery from existing fields. In order to model this outcome, I held peak oil and gas production levels constant at zero percent growth, from 65 percent of remaining resources to 50 percent. This has the effect of flattening and extending the peak of the petroleum production curve. I ran the baseline projection under this enhanced recovery assumption to observe the likely impact on export potential of maintaining crude petroleum production once peak levels are reached. The result for net energy trade was almost the same as the peak-and-decline model. Crossover would still be reached in 1992. The increase in energy import requirements would be less precipitous, resulting in a net saving of about 20 million tons of oil imports in the year 2000, or 2 percent of projected consumption requirements in that year. The point is that enhanced recovery alone will not save China from a considerable energy deficit toward the end of the century, without vast new oil and gas discoveries.

Now the discerning reader will have long since begun asking "what if" questions that the baseline projection simply does not answer. The most obvious one is, "What if China's oil and gas resources are much larger than estimated by Meyerhoff and Willums?" Petroleum geologists, after all, are known to be conservative, since the penalties of overestimation are costly. Furthermore, foreign geologists have a poor record in early estimates of China's oil resources, which were almost always too low by an order of magnitude (Table 14.2). If one allowed for another order-of-magnitude error in the Meyerhoff-Willums estimates, all of the fantasies about China's oil future would come true. Just how robust are the findings of the baseline projection, in view of the possibility of large errors in the structure of its assumptions?

In order to begin answering the "what if" questions and to provide a range of likely energy futures for the PRC, the following sections of this chapter will present three other possible projections. The low-, median-, and high-growth projections are presented in summary form, without the technical discussion or detailed statistical analysis that accompanied the baseline projection. One of the basic objectives was to examine the sensitivity of energy export potential to various sets of resource and growth assumptions. I did not change the computer program in any regard except through variation of explicit assumptions to generate the alternative growth projections. All of the structural assumptions and the program equations are exactly the same as the baseline projection. Every change has been recorded with the projection as an explicit assumption.

Low-Growth Projection

The low-growth projection represents a "disaster" run of the projection model. (See Table 24.5.) It illustrates what would happen if everything

TABLE 24.5
Low-Growth Projection

Year	GNP (million 1975 U.S. dollars)	Energy consumption requirement (mmtce)	Primary production[a] Petroleum (mmt)	Gas (bcm)	Total (mmtce)
1970	209	327	34	20	341
1971	219	347	41	23	376
1972	230	367	50	26	413
1973	242	389	58	30	451
1974	254	412	66	34	489
1975	267	436	72	39	527
1976	281	456	79	43	564
1977	295	477	85	48	602
1978	309	499	91	53	640
1979	325	523	97	57	678
1980	341	547	103	62	715
1981	358	565	109	67	751
1982	375	583	114	72	786
1983	393	602	119	76	819
1984	412	621	123	81	849
1985	432	640	126	86	878
1986	452	659	129	90	903
1987	473	679	130	95	925
1988	494	698	131	98	946
1989	516	716	130	102	966
1990	539	735	129	105	984
1991	561	754	126	107	1,002
1992	585	772	123	109	1,018
1993	609	790	119	110	1,035
1994	634	809	114	111	1,051
1995	659	826	108	111	1,069
1996	686	830	103	110	1,091
1997	713	833	97	108	1,116
1998	740	834	93	105	1,146
1999	769	834	88	102	1,183
2000	798	833	83	99	1,228

TABLE 24.5 *(continued)*
Low-Growth Projection

	Energy availability						Per capita energy consumption (kgce/cap.)	Energy export potential[b] (mmtoe)
Year	Coal (mmtce)	Petroleum (mmt)	Natural gas (bcm)	Electricity (bkwh)	Future (mmtce)	Total (mmtce)		
1970	229	26	15	63	1	298	390	20
1971	246	32	18	70	1	328	405	12
1972	263	38	20	78	1	359	420	5
1973	281	45	23	86	1	392	436	-2
1974	299	51	27	95	2	424	453	-8
1975	317	56	30	105	2	456	471	-13
1976	335	61	34	116	2	487	483	-21
1977	352	65	38	128	3	519	496	-28
1978	370	70	41	141	3	550	509	-34
1979	386	75	45	155	3	580	522	-39
1980	402	79	49	170	4	610	536	-43
1981	416	84	52	187	5	639	544	-50
1982	429	88	56	205	6	665	551	-55
1983	441	91	59	225	6	690	559	-59
1984	449	94	63	247	8	712	567	-61
1985	456	97	66	271	9	730	575	-61
1986	459	99	69	297	11	746	582	-58
1987	460	100	72	326	13	758	590	-54
1988	460	100	74	358	15	768	598	-47
1989	458	100	76	392	19	776	606	-40
1990	455	99	78	430	23	782	614	-31
1991	450	97	79	472	28	786	622	-21
1992	444	94	79	518	34	788	630	-10
1993	435	91	79	568	42	788	638	1
1994	425	87	77	623	53	788	646	14
1995	412	83	75	684	66	787	653	27
1996	397	79	72	750	83	787	650	29
1997	380	75	69	823	103	788	647	30
1998	360	71	64	904	129	792	642	28
1999	337	67	59	992	162	801	637	23
2000	311	64	53	1,089	203	814	631	12

[a] Coal production is identical under this scenario to the baseline projection, Table 24.2.
[b] Expressed as million metric tons oil equivalent net energy imports to conform to Chapters 20 and 21.

went wrong in Chinese energy development over the next two decades. Oil and gas resources were set at 5 billion metric tons and 5 trillion cubic meters, respectively, and it was assumed that there were no additional discoveries beyond this level of ultimate economically recoverable resources. This would place oil and gas resources at about two-thirds the baseline figures. Growth in per capita GNP dropped to 3.0 percent per year. The initial value of the energy/GNP elasticity was set at 1.5, decaying to 1.00 in the year 2000 as energy use efficiency improves. On the consumption side of the model, this represents roughly what would happen if China experienced another series of domestic or international disruptions on the order of the Great Leap Forward, the Sino-Soviet split, and the Cultural Revolution. A serious and protracted power struggle or a war on China's periphery (e.g. in Indochina) might produce this scale of disruption. Energy inefficiency would persist, as the PRC failed to modernize its industrial infrastructure. Low GNP growth would restrict the availability of investment capital for new energy industries, but would also save additional increments in the energy consumption requirement.

Under the assumptions of the low-growth projection, crude petroleum production will peak at about 130 million metric tons per year in the late 1980's. Natural gas production would peak at 110 billion cubic meters in the mid-1990's. Both oil and natural gas would then experience production decline by the year 2000. Coal would continue to be the backbone of the Chinese energy system, continuing to provide more than half of energy consumption through the turn of the century. Peking would be forced to rely increasingly on energy production from future energy technologies and might have to move into heavy development of coal gasification and liquefaction plants. Per capita energy consumption would rise only slowly, to about 600 kilograms coal equivalent per capita in the 1990's. This would leave China in the middle or low ranks of Third World countries in terms of per capita energy consumption standards, a depressing result after 50 years of energy development.

Under the conditions of the low-growth projection, China would continue to export energy commodities at increasing annual levels until the mid-1980's. In fact, energy export potential would peak at about 60 million tons oil equivalent, slightly higher than under the assumptions of the baseline projection. This illustrates the great sensitivity of export potential to a lower economic growth rate (assumed per capita GNP growth rate equals 3.0 percent) under conditions of resource constraint. It also indicates that 50 million tons oil equivalent is the lowest ceiling that we should expect on China's energy export potential under any projection. Because of rising energy consumption requirements, however, China would cross over to net energy imports in the early 1990's. If the low projection actually took place, I would expect Peking's energy planners to conserve crude oil resources, holding exports to perhaps 20–30 million tons of crude oil in 1985 and coal exports to 10–15 million tons in the same year.

How likely is the low-growth projection? The computer does not provide projections of political disruptions or the likelihood of a border war. There are some signs that China's energy balance is now moving on a trajectory well above the low-growth projection. Crude oil production was expected to pass the 100 million metric tons per year level (2 million barrels per day) in 1978 or 1979. The low-growth projection would not reach the 100 million ton level of oil production until 1980. Total primary energy production in 1978 reached about 675 mmtce, the level projected for 1979 by the low-growth projection. In general, I would expect much less exuberance from the Chinese press about the country's energy development prospects if the assumptions of the low-growth projection were correct and known to be so in Peking. Judging from the tone of press reports and the vigor of current plans to modernize by the end of the century, I believe that China's own energy planners are counting on at least the oil and gas resources assumed in the baseline projection, and that they hope for much larger oil and gas discoveries in the next five to ten years. The median and high projections examine what will happen if these hopes are borne out.

Median-Growth Projection

The median-growth projection represents what could happen to the Chinese energy balance under favorable development conditions. (See Table 24.6.) That is, if the Meyerhoff-Willums oil and gas resource estimates prove too conservative by a factor of two and Chinese geologists discover much more oil both onland and offshore over the next 20 years, ultimate recovery of crude petroleum could reasonably be set at 20 billion metric tons (150 billion barrels) and ultimate recovery of natural gas at 15 trillion cubic meters. Not all of this oil and gas would be discovered at once. I set the initial level of discovered reserves at 5 billion tons of crude petroleum and 5 trillion cubic meters of natural gas, and then introduced the balance of ultimate recovery gradually from undiscovered resources. This method of introducing new oil and gas discoveries flattens and extends the projected production curves (Chapter 23). The same method was used in the baseline projection, but with much lower assumed additional discoveries. The model automatically introduces new discoveries into the reserve pool at a rate proportional to the size of undiscovered resources and inversely proportional to the rate of depletion of initial reserves.

The consumption side of the median projection assumed a slightly higher growth rate in per capita GNP (4.0 percent per annum) and the same energy/GNP elasticity as the baseline projection. The higher per capita GNP growth rate reflects an expected increment in living standards introduced by greater energy availability. Even so, the increment (0.5 percent) is marginal and the GNP figure projected by the median

TABLE 24.6
Median-Growth Projection

Year	GNP (million 1975 U.S. dollars)	Energy consumption requirement (mmtce)	Primary energy production			
			Coal (mmt)	Petroleum (mmt)	Gas (bcm)	Total (mmtce)
1970	219	302	348	29	18	332
1971	232	325	374	35	21	365
1972	247	350	400	42	24	400
1973	262	377	428	50	27	439
1974	277	406	458	60	31	480
1975	294	437	488	70	36	524
1976	312	464	519	81	40	570
1977	331	492	551	91	46	618
1978	351	522	583	102	51	666
1979	372	553	616	112	58	714
1980	394	587	649	122	64	764
1981	418	618	681	133	71	814
1982	442	650	713	144	78	865
1983	468	684	745	156	86	917
1984	496	719	775	167	93	968
1985	524	755	804	178	102	1,019
1986	554	788	830	190	110	1,069
1987	585	820	855	202	119	1,118
1988	618	854	877	214	127	1,166
1989	651	887	895	226	136	1,212
1990	686	921	913	238	145	1,258
1991	722	955	931	250	154	1,304
1992	760	990	948	262	163	1,350
1993	799	1,025	966	273	172	1,396
1994	839	1,061	984	283	181	1,442
1995	881	1,097	1,001	293	190	1,487
1996	925	1,133	1,019	302	199	1,531
1997	971	1,170	1,036	310	207	1,575
1998	1,018	1,207	1,054	317	215	1,618
1999	1,068	1,244	1,071	323	222	1,661
2000	1,119	1,282	1,088	328	229	1,702

TABLE 24.6 *(continued)*
Median-Growth Projection

	Energy availability						Per capita energy consumption (kgce/cap.)	Energy export potential[a] (mmtoe)
	Coal (mmtce)	Petroleum (mmt)	Natural gas (bcm)	Electricity (bkwh)	Future (mmtce)	Total (mmtce)		
1970	229	22	14	63	1	290	360	7
1971	246	27	16	70	1	318	380	4
1972	264	32	18	78	1	348	401	1
1973	282	39	21	86	1	381	423	−2
1974	301	46	24	95	2	416	447	−7
1975	321	54	28	105	2	454	471	−11
1976	341	62	32	116	2	493	491	−19
1977	361	70	36	128	2	532	511	−27
1978	382	78	40	141	3	572	531	−34
1979	402	86	45	155	3	613	553	−40
1980	422	94	50	170	4	653	575	−45
1981	441	102	56	187	4	695	595	−52
1982	460	111	61	205	5	736	615	−58
1983	477	120	67	225	5	777	635	−63
1984	493	128	73	247	6	817	656	−66
1985	507	137	79	271	7	856	678	−68
1986	518	146	86	297	8	894	696	−72
1987	527	155	92	326	9	930	714	−74
1988	534	165	99	358	10	964	732	−74
1989	536	174	105	392	12	994	750	−73
1990	537	183	112	430	14	1,024	769	−70
1991	537	192	118	472	16	1,053	788	−66
1992	534	201	125	518	19	1,080	808	−61
1993	530	210	131	568	22	1,106	827	−55
1994	524	218	137	623	25	1,131	847	−47
1995	515	225	143	684	30	1,153	867	−37
1996	504	232	148	750	35	1,172	888	−26
1997	490	239	153	823	41	1,189	908	−12
1998	473	244	157	904	48	1,202	929	3
1999	452	249	161	992	57	1,213	950	21
2000	428	252	163	1,089	67	1,220	971	42

[a] Expressed as million metric tons oil equivalent net energy imports to conform to Chapters 20 and 21. Note also that coal production is expressed in million tons of raw coal, while coal availability is expressed in million metric tons coal equivalent. Hydropower production and production of energy from future technologies are not shown.

scenario is only 18 percent higher than that projected by the baseline scenario for the year 2000.

The effect of relaxed oil and gas resource assumptions on the energy balance is dramatic. Crude petroleum and natural gas production continues to rise, albeit at declining growth rates, through the turn of the century. Crude petroleum production reaches 200 million metric tons per year (4 million barrels per day) in 1987 and 300 million tons in the mid-1990's. Natural gas production increases to 100 billion cubic meters per year in 1985 and 200 billion cubic meters per year by the late 1990's. This outcome would make China an oil producer (not exporter) on the scale of Iran's oil industry in another two decades. Compared to the world of 1975, China would indeed be an "oil giant," ranking behind the USSR, Saudi Arabia, and the United States in crude oil production at the peak of the production curve. Total primary energy production would reach 1.7 billion metric tons coal equivalent by the end of the century, a level comparable to 1975 Soviet primary energy production. On the consumption side of the energy balance, the contribution of coal to the energy mix would decline steadily to 50 percent in 1990 and 35 percent in the year 2000. The oil industry, on the other hand, would increase its energy-equivalent contribution to about 30 percent in 2000. Natural gas would contribute 12 percent in 1985 and 18 percent in 2000. The contribution of electric power would rise, but much more slowly than in the baseline projection, reaching just 11 percent of the fuel and power mix by the end of the century. Production of energy from future technologies would be less than under the resource assumptions of the baseline projection, both absolutely and relative to the energy mix. There would simply be less incentive for costly investment in future technology energy production under the relaxed oil and gas resource assumptions of the median projection. Nuclear generating capacity would still reach about 500 MWe by 1985, but might be under the 10 GWe figure projected for the year 2000 by the baseline projection. A large proportion of crude oil production in the median projection would come from the offshore basins—possibly as much as half. This would make China one of the largest offshore oil producers in the world.[7] But it would also seriously restrict capital investment in civilian nuclear power, since nuclear power and offshore oil development are both capital-intensive and would be competing for limited capital and foreign-exchange resources.

The per capita energy consumption statistics and net energy export potential curve generated by the median-growth projection are not as optimistic as might be supposed by the rate of growth in primary energy production. Here, again, the large and still growing Chinese population is the critical factor. Even under the relaxed oil and gas resource assumptions of the median projection, average per capita commercial energy consumption will reach ony 650–700 kgce in 1985 and less than 1,000 kgce at the end of the century. After 50 years of rapid energy development, the People's Republic of China will have about one-fifth the average per capita energy consumption that Japan achieved in 1975, and less than one-tenth current American per capita energy consumption standards.

Energy export potential rises rapidly under the assumptions of the median projection, reaching peak levels of 70 million tons oil equivalent in the mid-1980's, and declining thereafter under pressure from domestic energy end-use requirements. The decline occurs even though the oil and gas industries continue to grow throughout the 1990's. Here again we witness the sensitivity of energy export potential to energy consumption requirements generated by economic growth. Crossover to net energy imports would be reached sometime in the late 1990's, followed by a rapid increase of net energy import requirements. The median projection illustrates beautifully the general pattern discovered in virtually all of the alternative energy balance projections. Total primary energy production outstrips the rise in domestic energy consumption for about 20–25 years, providing Peking with an exportable energy commodity surplus. But the inexorable rise of energy consumption eventually overtakes the growth of primary energy production, rising up underneath the production curve and eventually crossing it. The area between the production curve and the consumption curve looks like a long, flat bubble. The vertical distance across that bubble is the net energy export potential. The exact dimensions of the bubble are altered by various resource and growth assumptions, but its general shape remains the same under all of the likely projections.

If Peking chose to export at 75 percent of energy export potential under the assumptions of the median projection, petroleum exports would probably be in the neighborhood of 40 million tons from 1985 to 1990, a large increase in current energy commodity export levels. Coal trade would be about 20 million tons by 1990, assuming that China could find the markets and transport facilities for coal exports at that level. But the oil trade will drop off to 20 million tons by 1995 and will decline rapidly thereafter. Even if Peking decided to push oil exports to a higher proportion of export potential, it is doubtful that actual petroleum exports will exceed 50 million tons per year at the peak level reached under the assumptions of the median projection. That would make China an oil exporter at about the same level as Indonesia in 1975, with a ten-year lag. If two-thirds of China's crude oil exports went to Japan, that amount would satisfy about 15 percent of Japan's 1975 crude oil import requirements.

How realistic and likely is the median projection? I would be hard pressed to attach a probability to either the baseline or the median-growth projection. I believe that both lie well within what I would term the "likely" group of alternative energy balance projections. I consider the range of energy export potential projectd by the baseline and median scenarios (50–75 million metric tons oil equivalent in the peak years) to be an accurate designation of the area of central tendency in the spectrum of alternative energy balance projections. The level of crude oil production of the median projection for 1985 could still be achieved with an average annual growth rate of just 8 percent. If average growth rates are still running around 10 percent for the Chinese petroleum industry by 1981–82, that will be a strong indication that the median projection is likely. If crude petroleum production growth rates are closer to 5–6 percent by 1981–82, then we should begin to believe the baseline projection. The long-range outcome for the 1990's could easily lie anywhere between the baseline and median projections.

High-Growth Projection

The low-growth projection provides an analysis of what would happen under severe resource constraints and sharp economic setbacks to the Chinese energy balance. Despite what I consider the low probability of this actually occurring, it is instructive regarding the lower boundary of possible energy futures for the PRC. In a similar manner, I have constructed a high-growth projection that sets what I consider to be the upper boundary on the range of possible energy futures for China. (See Table 24.7.) I believe the high-growth projection to be possible, but not likely. If I were attaching (arbitrarily, of course) a set of probabilities to the various projections, I would attach a probability of 0.1–0.2 each to the low- and high-growth projections, and a probability of 0.6–0.8 to the range of estimates lying between the baseline and median projections.

On the production side of the energy balance, the high-growth projection assumes that oil and gas resources are in the range of the original ultimate recoverable resources of the United States. This would place China's ultimate recoverable crude petroleum resource at 35 billion metric tons (250 billion barrels) and the ultimate recoverable natural gas resource at 40 trillion cubic meters (1.4×10^{15} cubic feet).[8] Of this total quantity, I assigned 5 bmt of crude oil to discovered reserves in 1965, and 5 tcm of natural gas to the same category. The rest was placed in the undiscovered resource category, and "discovered" according to the assumptions of the model as it moved through time. This set of resource assumptions would basically quadruple the Meyerhoff-Willums estimates and be double the assumed resources of the median projection. It must be stressed from the outset that there is at present no geologic or documentary evidence to support this set of very high resource assumptions, at least outside of the PRC. The resource assumption of the high-growth scenario is simply a "what if" projection. It tells us something about the likely upper bounds on China's energy future.

The assumptions on the consumption side of the high-growth projection were actually rather conservative. I raised the annual growth rate for per capita GNP from 3.5 percent in the baseline projection and 4.0 in the median projection to just 5.0 percent. This is hardly a radical assumption, since per capita GNP grew at roughly 5 percent per year from 1949 to 1978. But it is an optimistic assumption. The per capita GNP growth rate did decline in China after 1960 and did not fully recover during the 1970's. In part this was the result of the scale effect and the low initial level of per capita GNP that had resulted from the Second World War and the Chinese revolution. But the PRC would be hard pressed to repeat the pace of the last 30 years over the next 20 years. I consider it fairly unlikely that China's per capita GNP will grow at much over 5 percent for the next 20 years.

The energy/GNP coefficient (elasticity) was set at an initial value of 1.5 in 1965 and allowed to decay slowly to 1.15 by the turn of the century. This is an optimistic elasticity assumption, given the history of China's energy/GNP coefficients. It implies sustained improvement in energy-use efficiencies throughout the Chinese economy. That would require everything to go smoothly in Chinese economic development over the next two decades and would probably also require a vigorous government energy conservation program. I consider the coefficient an expression of the most favorable possible outcome in use efficiencies in the Chinese energy balance.

The high-growth scenario projects a GNP of about 550 billion dollars for 1985 and 1.4 trillion for the year 2000, an achievement that would require a sustained 6 percent economic growth rate for the next two decades. Under the assumptions of the high-growth model, the energy end-use requirement would grow at an average rate of about 5 percent during the 1980's and about 4 percent during the 1990's, yielding aggregate energy consumption (end-use) of about 1.6 billion metric tons coal equivalent at the end of the century, which exceeds 1975 Soviet energy end-use by a considerable margin.

Growth in the petroleum and natural gas industries would be spectacular under the resource assumptions of the high-growth projection. Crude oil output would reach 220 million metric tons per year in 1985 and would reach more than 500 million tons per year in 2000, still grow-

TABLE 24.7
High-Growth Projection

Year	GNP (million 1975 U.S. dollars)	Energy consumption requirement (mmtce)	Primary energy production			
			Coal (mmt)	Petroleum (mmt)	Gas (bcm)	Total (mmtce)
1970	203	293	349	27	17	329
1971	217	318	375	32	20	361
1972	233	345	402	39	23	396
1973	250	374	431	47	26	434
1974	267	405	461	56	30	476
1975	286	439	493	67	34	522
1976	307	469	525	79	39	571
1977	328	501	559	92	45	624
1978	351	536	594	107	51	680
1979	376	573	630	122	58	740
1980	402	613	666	138	66	801
1981	430	650	702	153	75	864
1982	460	690	739	169	84	928
1983	492	732	776	185	95	995
1984	525	776	812	202	106	1,064
1985	561	823	848	219	119	1,134
1986	599	865	882	237	133	1,206
1987	638	909	914	256	147	1,279
1988	680	955	945	275	163	1,353
1989	724	1,001	973	294	179	1,426
1990	770	1,049	998	313	197	1,499
1991	818	1,097	1,020	333	215	1,572
1992	869	1,148	1,041	354	234	1,646
1993	923	1,199	1,061	374	254	1,722
1994	979	1,252	1,081	395	275	1,799
1995	1,038	1,307	1,101	415	296	1,877
1996	1,100	1,362	1,122	436	317	1,955
1997	1,166	1,419	1,142	455	339	2,034
1998	1,234	1,478	1,162	474	361	2,114
1999	1,306	1,538	1,182	492	384	2,194
2000	1,382	1,599	1,202	509	407	2,275

TABLE 24.7 *(continued)*
High-Growth Projection

Year	Energy availability						Per capita energy consumption (kgce/cap.)	Energy export potential[a] (mmtoe)
	Coal (mmtce)	Petroleum (mmt)	Natural gas (bcm)	Electricity (bkwh)	Future (mmtce)	Total (mmtce)		
1970	229	20	13	63	1	288	350	3
1971	246	25	15	70	1	315	372	2
1972	264	30	18	78	1	345	395	0
1973	283	36	20	86	1	377	420	-2
1974	303	43	23	95	2	413	446	-5
1975	324	51	27	105	2	452	473	-8
1976	345	61	31	116	2	493	497	-16
1977	367	71	35	128	2	538	521	-24
1978	390	82	40	141	3	586	546	-33
1979	413	94	46	155	3	635	573	-42
1980	436	106	52	170	3	687	601	-50
1981	459	118	59	187	4	739	626	-60
1982	481	129	66	205	4	792	653	-69
1983	503	142	75	225	5	846	680	-77
1984	525	155	84	247	6	902	709	-85
1985	544	168	94	271	6	959	739	-92
1986	563	182	105	297	7	1,017	764	-102
1987	579	197	117	326	8	1,074	791	-112
1988	593	211	129	358	9	1,131	818	-120
1989	605	226	142	392	11	1,187	847	-126
1990	613	241	156	430	12	1,241	876	-131
1991	617	256	170	472	14	1,295	905	-134
1992	619	272	185	518	16	1,347	936	-135
1993	619	288	201	568	18	1,400	968	-136
1994	617	304	217	623	21	1,452	1,000	-136
1995	614	319	233	684	24	1,504	1,033	-134
1996	607	335	249	750	28	1,554	1,067	-130
1997	598	350	265	823	32	1,602	1,102	-124
1998	586	365	282	904	38	1,648	1,138	-116
1999	571	379	299	992	44	1,693	1,174	-105
2000	552	392	315	1,089	51	1,734	1,212	-92

[a] Expressed as million metric tons oil equivalent net energy imports to conform to Chapters 20 and 21. Note also that coal production is expressed in million tons of raw coal, while coal availability is expressed in million metric tons coal equivalent. Hydropower production and production of energy from future technologies are not shown.

ing at 3–4 percent per year. This would give the PRC about the same peak output as the United States reached in the early 1970's (including natural gas liquids), not a surprising finding in view of the similarity of the resource assumption to recoverable U.S. crude oil resources. Soviet crude oil production also exceeded 500 million tons per year in the late 1970's.[9] But the projections would bring China to this level of oil production in a relatively short period, under conditions of accelerated capital investment in the oil industry. Natural gas production would follow roughly the same curve, reaching 120 billion cubic meters in 1985 and 400 bcm by the end of the century. The rapid development of the oil and gas industries would give China total primary energy production of 2.3 billion metric tons coal equivalent at the turn of the century, about what the United States produced in 1975. This outcome would represent spectacular success for China's energy development and would give economic development a tremendous boost.

The precise energy mix would be difficult to predict under such rapid growth conditions. Virtually anything could happen to the consumption and export mix of various energy commodities, depending on a wide range of economic conditions and policy choices. The high-growth scenario, following the general structure of the model, projects a decline in the relative contribution of coal to 57 percent in 1985 and 32 percent at the turn of the century. Petroleum, on the other hand, would increase its share of energy consumption to 26 percent in 1985 and 33 percent in the year 2000. The natural gas contribution would grow from 11 percent in 1978 (actual) to 13 percent in 1985 and 24 percent in 2000. Electric power consumption would grow more slowly, to 3 percent of the energy mix in 1985 and 8 percent in the year 2000. Future energy production technologies would contribute about 1 percent in 1985 and only 3 percent by the turn of the century, reflecting low incentives for investment in uncertain and capital-intensive production methods. The construction of nuclear power plants would go slowly as large oil and gas discoveries began to be made, reaching just 5 GWe (about five large plants) by the end of the century. I still predict that the first 500 MWe nuclear power station will be operating by 1985.

As optimistic as I have attempted to make the high-growth projection, certain implications are not favorable for China's long-range energy development prospects. Once again the model has projected a low-growth curve for per capita energy consumption, reaching 700 kilograms coal equivalent per capita by 1985 and just 1,200 kilograms coal equivalent by the end of the century. The figure at the end of the projected period is just 10 percent of 1975 U.S. per capita energy consumption and about 30 percent of Japan's 1975 per capita energy consumption. This would place the PRC in the upper end of the spectrum of Third World countries, assuming that the spectrum itself had not moved upward in the interim. This would give China the same per capita energy consumption as Portugal, the poorest of the European countries, in 1975. It is clear from this finding, and from the other projections as well, that China will have to do considerable research on methods of improving personal living standards at low per capita energy consumption standards. Extensive development of the public transport network will have to be undertaken to move China's population, an impossible task for the private automobile. Great attention should be paid to energy-efficient but comfortable housing designs. Consumer commodities will have to be made for long use and raw materials carefully recycled. This sort of innovation is now reaching the industrial market economy countries, but has even more urgency under more crowded population conditions. Finally, it is obvious from this finding, as well as from alternative population projections conducted early in my research, that investment in family-planning programs will be highly cost-effective in terms of the Chinese energy balance. The government should probably invest first in factories producing birth control devices or in the construction of family-planning clinics, and then consider an allocation for offshore drilling rigs or nuclear power stations. The effect of a more optimistic population growth curve on per capita energy consumption and even energy export potential would be well worth the marginal cost of such programs.

The energy export potential curve generated by the high-growth projection is more optimistic than under the oil and gas resource assumptions of the median and baseline projections, but still retains the same growth characteristics as the curves generated by the other projections. That is, energy availability exceeds energy end-use requirements for a defined period, but then consumption requirements begin to overtake availability. This produces the same bubble-shaped projection for energy export potential. If all of the miracles assumed in the high-growth projection were to come true between 1978 and 1985, energy export potential would reach 100 million tons oil equivalent per year by the mid-1980's and would peak at even higher levels by the end of the decade. This represents something like what the optimists have been telling us would happen under current resource estimates. But even the optimists have neglected to point out that the oil export bubble would bring declining energy commodity export potential in the 1990's, under the most favorable resource and growth assumptions. The peak energy export years would last for less than a decade. During that period (roughly 1985–92), the PRC would be exporting oil and other energy commodities at about the same peak levels that Venezuela reached in the late

1960's and early 1970's, assuming that Peking chose to export at or near the upper limit. Assuming that Peking exported at 75 percent of export potential, and exported both crude oil and coal in 1985, the high-growth projection would yield about 50–70 million tons per year of crude oil exports and 30–40 million tons of coal exports in the late 1980's. If two-thirds of this quantity went to Japan, China would still be satisfying less than a quarter of the Japanese energy import market. Energy commodity exports would then decline slowly toward the end of the century, although China would still have a favorable balance of energy trade in the year 2000. Once again this illustrates the powerful constraining effect of relentlessly rising energy consumption requirements.

It could be argued, of course, that a projection could be constructed that is more favorable to oil exports than those that have been presented here. It is clearly the case that if oil and gas resources turn out to be on the order of original U.S. resources and if the Chinese government consciously restricts the growth of average per capita GNP (which includes constraints on industrial growth) to 3.0 or 3.5 percent per year, China would then become a major energy commodity exporter. However, I consider the political consequences of economic growth constraints under conditions of energy plenty to be an unlikely and difficult choice for any Chinese government. Rapid growth in the energy system feeds back into the rest of the economy, stimulating higher increments of growth in per capita energy consumption. The high-growth projection would greatly benefit the development of the domestic economy, but would not necessarily lead to substantially higher energy commodity exports. In addition, of course, a rapid pace of expansion in the Chinese energy system would increase the number of planning options available to the Chinese government. One of these options would be to shave the rate of expansion of the domestic economy to release more energy for export and foreign-exchange purposes. Another option would be to encourage end-use efficiency in the domestic energy system, lowering the energy/GNP coefficient and conserving energy for the future or for export. All of the tools of economic planning will be sharper and easier to use under conditions of energy plenty than under conditions of sharp energy resource constraint. But nature, rather than human planners, will determine the level of resource constraints on the oil and gas industries.

Summary of the Alternative Energy Balance Projections

This brings to a close the theoretical, technical, and statistical presentation of the findings of the alternative energy balance projections. Once again, let me recall what was said earlier about the subjectivity of computerized projection models. The model was built in a way that reflected my own perceptions of the dimensions of the Chinese energy balance, and the relationship of that balance to China's economic space. Just as a building always represents the interface between the perceptions of the architect and the ambience of the setting, so a model always represents the interface between the modeler and reality. There is no easy escape from this dilemma, which is typical of all social, political, and economic analysis, in which the observer lives at the same level of complexity as the observed. The future is still less charted than the past.

Nonetheless, I wish to argue the validity of this exercise. The findings of the computer projections were remarkably robust under a variety of initial assumptions. The findings regarding China's energy export potential demonstrate converging results under a wide range of resource and growth projections. If anything, I have been too liberal in my assessment of the prospects for Chinese oil and coal exports. It is easy to generate projections, using exactly the same model, that result in no energy export surplus for the entire period of the 1980's and 1990's. Try, for example, setting the per capita GNP growth rate at 5 percent per year and constraining oil and gas resource discoveries to the Meyerhoff-Willums estimates. The result is a net energy import requirement for the entire period under consideration.

As for China's energy development prospects, it would be unfair to suggest that I have demonstrated that the PRC will not be an "oil giant" within this century. Indeed, "oil giant" is an appropriate term for the outcome of certain projections. But what I have discovered is that even under the most favorable of development circumstances, the Chinese energy giant will be bound hand and foot by the size of the Chinese population, and will be required to labor tirelessly toward the objective of modernization and industrialization of Chinese society and the Chinese economy. The task is and will remain stupendous. The task of raising a fifth of the world's population to modern levels will leave very little energy for export. It is true that these projections demonstrate that China will not be an energy export giant in the world market, at least within this century. As stated at the outset of the book, the giant has a dual energy personality, strong and still growing but hungry.

Reference Matter

Notes

The following abbreviations are used in the Notes:

AAPGB	American Association of Petroleum Geologists Bulletin
ARB	Asia Research Bulletin
AWSJ	Asian Wall Street Journal
CB	Current Background
CCOP	Committee for Co-ordination of Joint Prospecting for Mineral Resources in Asian Offshore Areas: Technical Bulletin
CNA	China News Analysis
CP	China Pictorial
CQ	China Quarterly
CR	China Reconstructs
CTEN	China Trade and Economic Newsletter
CTR	China Trade Report
ER	Economic Reporter
FBIS	Foreign Broadcast Information Service, Daily Report
FEER	Far Eastern Economic Review
HHS	Hsin Hua She (New China News Agency)
HQ	Hong Qi (Red Flag)
IPE	International Petroleum Encyclopedia
JMJP	Jen Min Jih Pao (People's Daily)
JPRS	Joint Publications Research Service, Translations on Communist China
MY	Minerals Yearbook: International Area Reports
NCNA	New China News Agency
NFCRRS	News From Chinese Regional Radio Stations
NYT	New York Times
OGJ	Oil and Gas Journal
PNSEA	Petroleum News: Southeast Asia
PR	Peking Review
SCMP	Survey of the China Mainland Press
SER	Survey of Energy Resources
USCBR	U.S.–China Business Review (China Business Review)
WES	World Energy Supplies

Chapter 2

1. Chang Chien, "Behind the So-Called Energy Crisis," *HQ* 270 (Feb. 1974): 83–86, trans. in *PR* 17, no. 11 (Mar. 15, 1974): 5–7.

2. Chin Hua, "Human Cognizance and Utilization of Energy Sources Is Never-Ending," *PR* 19, no. 4 (Jan. 23, 1976): 49–51.

3. T'ien Chih-ch'un, "The New and Old China as Seen from the Angle of Petroleum," *Chung Kuo Hsin Wen,* Sept. 2, 1965, pp. 12–13, in *JPRS* 32454 (Oct. 19, 1965): 11–14.

4. Chin Hua, "Utilization of Energy Sources," p. 49.

5. *Ibid.,* p. 50.

6. M. A. Adelman, "Is the Oil Shortage Real? Oil Companies as OPEC Tax-Collectors," *Foreign Policy,* Winter 1972–73, pp. 69–107.

7. Chin Hua, "Utilization of Energy Sources," p. 51.

8. Chou En-lai, "Report to the Tenth National Congress of the Communist Party of China," speech of Aug. 24, 1973, *HQ* 265 (Sept. 1973): 12; in *PR* 16, no. 35–36 (Sept. 7, 1973): 17–25.

9. Chang Chien, "Behind the So-Called Energy Crisis."

10. Chin Pei-chiang, "Energy Crisis and Scramble for Energy Resources," *PR* 16, no. 39 (Sept. 28, 1973): 12–14.

11. Ching Jan, "Trouble Ahead for the Japanese Economy," *PR* 17, no. 4 (Jan. 25, 1974): 15–17.

12. "Growing Energy Crisis," *PR* 16, no. 14 (Apr. 6, 1973): 18.

13. Chinese sources believe that profits are higher for oil corporations than for other multinationals. "American Monopoly Capitalists Use the Energy Crisis to Greatly Raise Profits," *JMJP,* Feb. 10, 1974, p. 6.

14. Mei Chu, "Energy Crisis in the United States," *FBIS,* Feb. 27, 1978, p. A-3.

15. "Scramble for Hegemony," *PR* 16, no. 39 (Sept. 28, 1973): 16–17.

16. Paul R. Ehrlich and Anne H. Ehrlich, *Population, Resources, Environment: Issues in Human Ecology* (San Francisco, 1970), pp. 53–58; Ralph E. Lapp, "The Logarithmic Century—Charting Future Shock," Annual Managers Conference, Minneapolis, Aug. 20–22, 1973.

17. Richard P. Runyan and Lawrence Rocks, "The Energy Crisis," in Robert H. Connery and Robert S. Gilmour, eds., *The National Energy Problem* (Lexington, Mass., 1974) p. 4.

18. David C. White, "The Energy-Environment-Economic Triangle," *Technology Review* 76, no. 2 (Dec. 1973): 19.

19. Sherman H. Clark, "The Changing World of World Energy," presented to Professional Journalism Fellowships, Stanford University, Nov. 22, 1972; Joshua Goldstein, "The World Energy Situation—Some Implications," manuscript, Dept. of Political Science, Stanford University, Aug. 1973; J. P. Charpentier, "World Energy Consumption," Research Memorandum, International Institute for Applied Systems Analysis, Laxenburg, Austria, Dec. 1973; Chauncey Starr, "Realities of the Energy Crisis," in Lon C. Ruedisili and Morris W. Firebaugh, eds., *Perspectives on Energy* (New York, 1975) pp. 8–16.

20. A. J. Surrey and A. J. Bromley, "Energy Resources," *Futures,* Feb. 1973, pp. 90–107; Ernst R. Berndt and David O. Wood, "An Economic Interpretation of the Energy-GNP Ratio," in Makrakis, pp. 21–30.

21. J. D. Adams, R. L. Foley, and R. L. Nielsen, "Energy Conservation in Perspective of International Energy Requirements," in Makrakis, pp. 516–30.

22. "Increase Urged in Fuel Sources," *NYT*, Dec. 12, 1972, p. 69; William D. Smith, "Energy Crisis: Shortages Amid Plenty," *NYT*, Apr. 17, 1973, p. 1; H. A. Merklein, "The Energy Crisis: Some Causes and Effects," *World Oil* 178, nos. 2, 4 (Feb., Mar , 1974).

23. John P. Lewis, "Oil, Other Scarcities, and the Poor Countries," *World Politics* 27, no. 1 (Oct. 1974): 72.

24. Runyan and Rocks, "The Energy Crisis," pp. 1–2.

25. James P. Grant, "Energy Shock and the Development Prospect," in Senate Committee on Interior and Insular Affairs, *Implications of Recent Organization of Petroleum Exporting Countries (OPEC) Oil Price Increases* (Washington, D.C., 1974), p. 73.

26. Senator Clifford Hansen, in Paul W. McCracken et al., *The Energy Crisis* (Washington, D.C., 1974), p. 3; Ford Foundation Energy Policy Project, *A Time to Choose: America's Energy Future* (Cambridge, Mass., 1974), p. 9.

27. Adelman, "Is the Oil Shortage Real?" p. 72.

28. Marc J. Roberts, "Is There an Energy Crisis?," manuscript in the Stanford University Energy Information Center (9.4/R646; probably 1974), pp. 18–19.

29. Adelman, "Is the Oil Crisis Real?"; Gilbert Burck, "The Greatest Monopoly in History," *Fortune*, Apr. 1973, pp. 153–54; Fred C. Allvine and James M. Patterson, *Highway Robbery: An Analysis of the Gasoline Crisis* (Bloomington, Ind., 1974); Kevin P. Phillips and Patrick H. Codell, "Public Doubts the Gravity of the Energy Crisis," *Seattle Post-Intelligencer,* June 23, 1975.

30. "The National Energy Outlook," *Shell Oil,* Mar. 1973; Foster Associates, *Energy Prices: 1960–1973* (Cambridge, Mass., 1974); Michael C. Jensen, "Petrodollar Outlook," *NYT,* Feb. 13, 1975, p. 1; Juan de Onis, "OPEC to Restudy Prices If Dollar Sags," *NYT,* Mar. 8, 1975; Ezra Solomon, *The Anxious Economy* (Stanford, Calif., Stanford Alumni Association, 1975); J. William Fulbright, comments in McCracken et al., *The Energy Crisis,* p. 81; Walter J. Levy, "Implications of Exploding World Oil Costs," in Senate Committee, *Implications of OPEC Oil Price Increases,* pp. 21–43; articles by Ekstein, Bernstein, and Morgan Guarantee Trust Co., *ibid.*

31. Senate Committee on Interior and Insular Affairs, *International Energy Program: A Plan for Sharing Energy Imports in Time of Emergency and Cooperating with Other Energy Programs* (Washington, D.C., 1975).

32. "OPEC Production Controls Urged to Cut Crude Surplus," *OGJ* 73, no. 13 (Mar. 31, 1975): 48.

33. William D. Smith, "Sagging Oil Prices Give Consumers Some Benefit," *NYT,* Feb. 18, 1975, p. 1.

34. Terry Robards, "Ship Industry in a Crisis as Oil-Tanker Use Falls," *NYT,* Mar. 8, 1975.

35. "Floor Price in Oil Asked for Europe," *NYT,* Feb. 14, 1975.

36. Genevieve C. Dean, "Science, Technology, and Development: China as a 'Case Study,' " *CQ* 51 (July–Sept. 1972): 520.

37. "Chairman Hua Kuo-feng's Speech at the National Conference on Learning from Taching in Industry," *PR* 20, no. 21 (May 20, 1977): 13.

Chapter 3

1. Chou En-lai, "Report to the Tenth National Congress of the Communist Party of China," Aug. 24, 1973, in *PR* 16, nos. 35–36 (Sept. 7, 1973): 17–25.

2. "Hegemony Cannot Decide World History," *HQ* 226 (Oct. 1973): 17–22, trans. in *PR* 16, no. 48 (Nov. 30, 1973): 4–6.

3. Chou En-lai, "Report to the Tenth Party Congress," p. 24.

4. Michael B. Yahuda, "Chinese Foreign Policy after 1963: The Maoist Phases," *CQ* 36 (Oct.–Dec. 1968): 93–113.

5. Huang Chan-p'ing, " 'Underdeveloped Economics' Is the New Colonialist Theory," *HQ*, Oct. 8, 1963, pp. 67–73; "Awakening and Growth of the Third World," *PR* 17, no. 3 (Jan. 18, 1974): 11; "Resolutely Support the Just Demands of the Third World," *JMJP*, Apr. 9, 1974, p. 1; "Speech of Teng Hsiao-p'ing, Head of the Delegation of the People's Republic of China at the Special Session of the UN General Assembly," *JMJP*, Apr. 11, 1974, p. 1; "The Superpowers Exploit Third World Mineral Resources," *JMJP*, Apr. 13, 1974, p. 6; "Important Victories of the Third World in United Struggle Against Hegemonism," *JMJP*, May 5, 1975, p. 1.

6. *WES* 18 (1975), Table 1.

7. "The Awakening Strength of the Third World in the Struggle for Unity," *JMJP*, Jan. 23, 1974, p. 6; "Third World Countries Urge Changes in Unequal International Economic Relations at UN General Assembly Special Session," *JMJP*, Apr. 17, 1974, p. 6; "Chairman Teng Hsiao-p'ing's Speech"; "Representatives of Third World Countries Speak in UNCTAD Meeting," *JMJP*, Aug. 26, 1974, p. 6; "The Success of the Just Struggle of the Oil Producing Countries is Undeniable," *JMJP*, Dec. 28, 1974, p. 6; Genevieve C. Dean, "Science, Technology, and Development: China as a 'Case Study,' " *CQ* 51 (July–Sept. 1972): 520.

8. T'ien Chih-ch'un, "The New and Old China as Seen from the Angle of Petroleum," *Chung Kuo Hsin Wen*, Sept. 2, 1965, pp. 12–13, in *JPRS* 32454 (Oct. 19, 1965): 11–14.

9. *Ibid.*

10. Ikonnikov, pp. 96–99; Wu and Ling, p. 41.

11. "Consolidating Achievements in Gasoline Savings," *Ta Kung Pao*, Dec. 1, 1960, p. 3; "Transportation Workers in Szechuan Province Economize Fuel and Increase Transportation Volume," *Kung Jen Jih Pao*, Dec. 21, 1960, p. 2.

12. "Large Hydropower Station Completed in Colombia," *HHS* 9333 (Aug. 4, 1974): 11.

13. "Resolution on Permanent Sovereignty over Natural Resources," *PR* 16, no. 19 (May 11, 1973): 19; "Great Victories in the United Third World Struggle Against Hegemonism," *JMJP*, May 5, 1974, p. 1; "Third World Unites to Preserve Sovereignty and Protect National Resources," *JMJP*, May 6, 1974, p. 6.

14. Chou Hua-min, "China's Principled Stand on Relations of International

Economy and Trade," speech to third UNCTAD plenary session, *PR* 15, no. 17 (Apr. 18, 1972): 11–14.

15. Huang Ming-ta, "The Reliable Way for the Developing Countries to Develop Their National Economy," speech to 30th session of U.N. Economic Commission for Asia and the Far East, Colombo, Sri Lanka, March 29, 1974, in *ER* 2 (Apr.–June 1974): 14.

16. The term for "self-reliance" (*tzu-li*) compares closely to that for "self-strengthening" (*tzu-chiang*). For the historical reference, see John K. Fairbank, Edwin O. Reischauer, and Albert M. Craig, *East Asia: The Modern Transformation* (Boston, 1965), p. 315.

17. Fu Yi-fu, Deputy Director of the Shanghai Petrochemical Complex, quoted in "Technology Import and Self-Reliance," *PR* 21, no. 49 (Dec. 8, 1978), p. 14. Note that this reference postdates China's initial discussions of joint off-shore development with foreign oil companies.

18. For example, A. A. Meyerhoff's report of Iranian petroleum exports to China from 1960 to 1966, esp. Table 3, p. 1569.

19. Tanzer, pp. 379–80.

20. *WES* 15–18 (1972–75), Table 2.

21. Juan de Onis, "Mastery over World Oil Supply Shifts to Producing Countries," *NYT,* Apr. 16, 1973, p. 1; Juan de Onis, "Politics and Instability of Prices Tearing World Oil Prices Apart," *NYT,* Aug. 24, 1973, p. 1.

22. Taching Oilfield Workers Critics Organization, "The Success of the Just Struggle of the Oil Producing Countries is Undeniable," *JMJP,* Dec. 28, 1974, p. 6.

23. "Fight to Defend Petroleum Rights," *PR* 15, no. 11 (Mar. 17, 1972): 19; "Agreement with Western Oil Consortium to Terminate," *PR* 16, no. 7 (Feb. 16, 1973): 20; "Iranian People's New Achievement," *PR* 16, no. 33 (Aug. 17, 1973):17; "Iran Marks First Anniversary of Oil Day," *HHS* 9332 (Aug. 3, 1974): 44–45.

24. "A New Coal Field Discovered in Northeast Iran," *JMJP,* Aug. 14, 1974, p. 6.

25. "Kuwait National Assembly Delegation," *PR* 15, no. 29 (July 21, 1972), p. 4; "Safeguarding Oil Rights," *PR* 17, no. 14 (Apr. 5, 1974): 28–29.

26. "Foreign Minister Chi Peng-fei Meets Arab Diplomatic Envoys to China," *PR* 15, no. 12 (Mar. 24, 1972): 3.

27. "Kuwait Refuses to Lift the Oil Boycott," *JMJP,* Jan. 24, 1974, p. 6; "An Historical Undertaking in the Struggle Against Imperialism and Hegemonism," *JMJP,* Dec. 26, 1974, p. 6.

28. "Social-Imperialist Expansion in the Middle East: The True Face of a False Friend," *PR* 16, no. 37 (Sept. 14, 1973): 17; "False Friend with a Tongue of Honey and a Dagger Heart," *JMJP,* May 5, 1974, p. 6.

29. "Soviet Price—Far Too Low," *PR* 16, no. 28 (July 13, 1973): 21; "How the Soviet Revisionists Exploit the Third World," *JMJP,* Apr. 13, 1974, p. 6.

30. Frank J. Gardner, "Chinese Tattle on the Soviets," *OGJ* 71, no. 32 (Aug. 6, 1973): 37.

31. "Some Eastern European Countries Take Measures to Reduce Oil Imports from the Soviet Union," *JMJP,* Sept. 14, 1975, p. 6.

32. "Soviet Revisionism Is One of the Biggest Plunderers of Third World Raw Materials," *ER* 2 (Apr.–June 1974): 10.

33. Gardner, "Chinese Oil Flow Up," pp. 35–39; *USCBR* 4, no. 5 (Sept.–Oct. 1977): 54.

34. François Charbonnier, "Sahara Oil," *FEER* 43, no. 4 (Jan. 23, 1964): 145; François Charbonnier, "Helping Ben Bella," *FEER* 43, no. 12 (Mar. 20, 1964): 601.

35. "President Boumedienne Arrives in Peking," *PR* 17, no. 9 (Mar. 1, 1974): 5.

36. "Asian, African, and Latin American Countries Protect National Resources," *JMJP,* May 25, 1974, p. 6; "New Natural Gas Fields Discovered in Tunisia," *HHS,* June 2, 1975, p. 11.

37. "Somalia Increases Electric Power Output," *HHS,* June 2, 1975, p. 8.

38. *USCBR* 2, no. 5 (Sept.–Oct. 1975): 59.

39. *USCBR* 2, no. 4 (July–Aug. 1975): 56.

40. *USCBR* 3, no. 4 (July–Aug. 1976): 57.

41. "PRC–Aided Powerplant Turned Over to Ethiopia," *FBIS,* Feb. 21, 1978, p. A-15.

42. "Venezuelan National Assembly Passes a Law Decreeing that the President Has the Power to Raise the Price of Oil Exports to the U.S. at Any Time," *JMJP,* Jan. 8, 1971, p. 6; "Developing Venezuela's Petroleum Output," *PR* 16, no. 10 (Mar. 9, 1973): 16; "Venezuela Raises the Posted Price of Oil to Protect National Sovereignty," *JMJP,* Jan. 5, 1974, p. 6; "Venezuela to Send Observers to Foreign Oil Companies," *HHS* 9347 (Aug. 18, 1974): 24.

43. "China Establishes Diplomatic Relations with Venezuela," *PR* 17, no. 27 (July 5, 1974), p. 5.

44. "Trinidad and Tobago Oil Mission Leaves Peking for Shanghai," *HHS,* June 9, 1975; "China Establishes Diplomatic Relations with Trinidad and Tobago," *PR* 17, no. 26 (July 28, 1974): 3.

45. "Ecuador: Restricting Foreign Oil Monopoly," *PR* 16, no. 2 (Jan. 12, 1973): 20; "Seventh Rise in Petroleum Reference Price," *PR* 16, no. 48 (Nov. 30, 1973): 23; "Ecuador Raises Taxes of Foreign Oil Companies," *JMJP,* Nov. 16, 1974, p. 6.

46. "Several Latin American Countries Actively Develop Oil Production," *JMJP,* Aug. 15, 1974, p. 6.

47. *USCBR* 3, no. 6 (Nov.–Dec. 1976): 63.

48. *USCBR* 1, no. 3 (May–June 1974): 56.

49. *USCBR* 2, no. 1 (Jan.–Feb. 1975): 57.

50. "China, Brazil Sign Trade Agreement in Peking," *HHS,* Jan. 7, 1978, trans. in *FBIS,* Jan. 10, 1978, p. A-12.

51. "Brazil Deaf to U.S. Resentment Over Nuclear Pact with FRG," *HHS,* Feb. 2, 1978, trans. in *FBIS,* Feb. 2, 1978, p. A-15.

52. "Opening the Pipeline," *FEER* 92, no. 20 (May 14, 1976): 5.

53. "Aid from New Delhi," *FEER* 93, no. 35 (Aug. 27, 1976): 5.

54. Salamat Ali, "Close Military Collaboration," *FEER* 98, no. 40 (Oct. 7, 1977): 88.

55. *USCBR* 3, no. 2 (Mar.–Apr. 1976): 59; *USCBR* 4, no. 5 (Sept.–Oct. 1977): 59.

56. Salamat Ali, "Close Military Collaboration," p. 88.

57. *PNSEA* 9, no. 1 (Apr. 1978): 3; *USCBR* 5, no. 2 (Mar.–Apr. 1978): 61.

Chapter 4

1. *WES* 20 (1971–75): Table 2.

2. John Gittings, "The Origins of China's Foreign Policy," in David Horowitz, ed., *Containment and Revolution* (Boston, 1967), p. 206.

3. Allen S. Whiting, "Sinkiang and Sino-Soviet Relations," *CQ* 3 (July–Sept. 1960): 32–41.

4. *IPE,* 1975, p. 196.

5. Hirotada Eto, "Energy Resources of the People's Republic of China," *Japan Science and Technology* 13, no. 1 (1972): 33–48, in *JPRS* 55470 (Mar. 17, 1972): 2–10.

6. Joseph Lelyveld, "China Is Increasing Oil Export Deals," *NYT,* Jan. 5, 1974, p. 35.

7. Brian Heenan, "China's Petroleum Industry: Part I," *FEER* 49, no. 13 (Sept. 23, 1965): 565–67.

8. Colina MacDougall, "Vague Claims," *FEER* 52, no. 6 (May 12, 1966): 302; "Karamai Oilfield Production," *Ta Kung Pao,* Apr. 27, 1966, p. 1, in *JPRS* 37566 (Sept. 13, 1966): 39–43.

9. "China's Petroleum Industry," *Ching Chi Tao Pao,* Sept. 9, 1969, p. 15, in *JPRS* 49146 (Oct. 28, 1969): 31–32; "Petroleum Industry," *PR* 15, no. 47 (Nov. 24, 1972): 17–18.

10. "Simultaneous Progress in Economy of Fuel Consumption and High Productivity of Transportation," *Ta Kung Pao,* Nov. 2, 1960, p. 3, in *JPRS* 6866 (Mar. 8, 1961): 102–4; "Reform Gasoline-Saving Techniques, Develop the Potential Strength, and Use Less Gasoline to Transport More Goods," *Ta Kung Pao,* Oct. 28, 1960, p. 3, in *JPRS* 6866 (Mar. 8, 1961): 64–69.

11. "In Chengtu the public buses use natural gas as a fuel, each vehicle carrying a balloon of it on top, as was done in Peking with manufactured gas at the time of the fuel shortage in the early sixties. Szechuan is rich in natural gas, so it might as well be used." Rewi Alley, "Among the Tibetans and Chiang," *Eastern Horizon* 12, no. 5 (1973): 41.

12. Chin Chi, "China Follows Her Own Path in Developing Industry—Taching, a Striking Example," *CP,* Sept. 1975, pp. 6–15.

13. "Lanchow Oil Refinery Converted into a Large-Scale Chinese Style Refining Base," *JMJP,* Apr. 25, 1960, p. 2, in *JPRS* 35261 (Apr. 29, 1966): 23–31; "Karamai Oilfield Production," *Ta Kung Pao,* Apr. 27, 1966, p. 1, in *JPRS* 37566 (Sept. 13, 1966): 39–43.

14. Genevieve C. Dean, "Energy in the People's Republic of China," *Energy Policy* 2, no. 1 (Mar. 1974): 36.

15. Colina MacDougall, "More with the West," *FEER* 41, no. 13 (Sept. 26, 1963): 801–4; Alexandra Close, "Ups and Downs," *FEER* 46, no. 1 (Oct. 1, 1964): 5–6; Daniel and Lois Dougan Tretiak, "Moscow's Trade with Asia," *FEER* 51, no. 5 (Feb. 3, 1966): 204–8.

16. Wu and Ling, pp. 223–32; Smil, "Exploiting China's Hydro Potential," p. 21.

17. Colina MacDougall, "The Power Question," *FEER* 40, no. 1 (Apr. 4, 1963): 6–7.

18. Lin Hung, "China's Growing Power Industry," *ER* 4 (Oct.–Dec. 1974): 36.

19. "China to Have Atomic Reactor This Year," *HHS,* May 23, 1957, in *SCMP* 1539 (May 28, 1957): 1.

20. Peter D. Weintraub, "China's Minerals and Metals," *USCBR* 1, no. 6 (Nov.–Dec. 1974): 44.

21. *USCBR* 3, no. 4 (July–Aug. 1976): 57; Peter Weintraub, "China's Moscow Connection," *FEER* 93, no. 27 (July 2, 1976): 71.

22. The chronology of the Sino-Soviet border confrontation presented here was taken from Thomas W. Robinson, "The Sino-Soviet Border Dispute: Background, Development, and the March 1969 Clashes," *American Political Science Review* 66, no. 4 (Dec. 1972): 1175–1202.

23. *Ibid.,* pp. 183–87.

24. Edith Lenart, "Peking's Interest in Europe," *FEER* 78, no. 49 (Dec. 2, 1972): 27–28.

25. "Sabre-Rattling Soviets," *FEER* 89, no. 29 (July 18, 1975): 6.

26. Russell Spurr, "The Kremlin's Reliance on Blitzkrieg," *FEER* 90, no. 44 (Oct. 31, 1975): 33–34.

27. "China and Soviet Meeting on Border Rivers," Reuters, Aug. 12, 1977, in *NYT,* Aug. 13, 1977, p. 5.

28. Koji Nakamura, "Icy Melting Point," *FEER* 71, no. 12 (Mar. 20, 1971): 27–28.

29. Bruce Nussbaum, "Key to Asia's Future," *FEER* 77, no. 28 (July 8, 1972): 40–41.

30. Koji Nakamura, "The Tanaka Letter," *FEER* 79, no. 11 (Mar. 19, 1973): 22.

31. "From China, A Warning," *FEER* 80, no. 18 (May 7, 1973): 5.

32. Koji Nakamura, "Treading the Siberian Tightrope," *FEER* 80, no. 19 (May 14, 1973): 6–8.

33. Koji Nakamura, "Chinese Wedge," *FEER* 80, no. 21 (May 28, 1973): 14.

34. Koji Nakamura, "A Losing Game," *FEER* 82, no. 42 (Oct. 22, 1973): 18–19; "Tokyo's Troubles," *FEER* 82, no. 42 (Oct. 22, 1973): 61.

35. Koji Nakamura, "Partners in Siberian Energy," *FEER* 83, no. 8 (Feb. 25, 1974): 56–57.

36. William Shawcross, "A Draft from the Open Door," *FEER* 84, no. 13 (Apr. 1, 1974): 30–32.

37. "Oil Pact on the Rails," *FEER* 84, no. 16 (Apr. 22, 1974): 38.

38. Koji Nakamura, "Toward a Siberian Commitment," *FEER* 84, no. 18 (May 6, 1974): 61–64.

39. Koji Nakamura, "Japan Balances on a Siberian Tightrope," *FEER* 86, no. 45 (Nov. 15, 1974): 41.

40. Alan Sanders, "Tapping Siberia's Riches," *FEER* 87, no. 5 (Jan. 31, 1975): 58–61.

41. James Laurie, "American Finance Drying Up," *FEER* 87, no. 5 (Jan. 31, 1975): 63.

42. Koji Nakamura, "A Rethink in Japan," *FEER* 87, no. 5 (Jan. 31, 1975): 62–63.

43. Dev Murarka, "Growth Pace Curbed," *FEER* 87, no. 5 (Jan. 31, 1975): 62.

44. Alan Sanders, "Tackling Siberia's New Railway," *FEER* 88, no. 17 (Apr. 25, 1975): 47–48.

45. Miles Hanley, "Outlet for Siberia's Riches," *FEER* 92, no. 21 (May 21, 1976): 51.

46. "The 'BAM' Secret," *PR* 20, no. 30 (July 22, 1977): 23–24.

47. The validity of these rumors is subject to some doubt, since no nuclear power plants appear in the current five-year development plan for Siberia. See Tracy Dahlby, "Japan Waits for Soviet Proposals," *FEER* 94, no. 44 (Oct. 29, 1976): 43–44.

48. Foreign Minister Gromyko visited Japan January 9, 1976, for the express purpose of preventing the signing of a draft Sino-Japanese peace treaty that included an antihegemony clause. Koji Nakamura, "Caught in a Peace Triangle," *FEER* 91, no. 6 (Feb. 6, 1976): 22–23.

49. James Laurie, "Siberia: Thaw in the Freeze," *FEER* 86, no. 49 (Dec. 13, 1974): 67.

50. Bruce Nussbaum, "Dusting Off Siberian Gas Plans," *FEER* 92, no. 21 (May 21, 1976): 50–52.

51. Koji Nakamura, "The Tanaka Letter," *FEER* 79, no. 11 (Mar. 19, 1973): 22.

52. John E. Moore, ed., *Jane's Fighting Ships: 1976–77* (London), p. 127.

53. Koji Nakamura, "Chinese Wedge," *FEER* 80, no. 21 (May 28, 1973): 14.

54. "Sabre-Rattling Soviets," *FEER* 89, no. 29 (July 18, 1975): 6.

55. Nayan Chanda, "Sino-Soviet Rivalry: Islands of Friction," *FEER* 90, no. 50 (Dec. 12, 1975): 28–29.

56. "China 'South Sea' Claims," *FEER* 93, no. 34 (Aug. 20, 1976): 5; "The Enemy Below," *FEER* 93, no. 36 (Sept. 3, 1976): 5.

57. Dean, "Energy in the People's Republic of China," p. 36.

58. *Ibid.*, p. 43.

59. *Ibid.*, p. 46.

60. "Biggest Afro-Asian Partner," *FEER* 24, no. 4 (Oct. 26, 1961): 229; Lois Dougan Tretiak, "On Bended Knee," *FEER* 53, no. 13 (Sept. 29, 1967): 626.

61. Harald Munthe-Kaas, "Chou's Journey," *FEER* 52, no. 12 (June 23, 1966): 585.

62. "China and Oil—What to Expect," p. 2.

63. Wang, "The Mineral Industry of Mainland China," *MY*, 1965, p. 1107.

64. *CTEN* 237 (July 1975).

65. "Chinese Oil Discussed," *Internationale Wirtschaft*, Jan. 4, 1972, p. 1.

66. Ling, p. 32.

67. "Some Eastern European Countries Take Measures to Reduce Oil Imports from the Soviet Union," *JMJP*, Sept. 14, 1975, p. 6.

68. Leo Goodstadt, "Chinese Bottlenecks," *FEER* 78, no. 41 (Oct. 7, 1972): 39–41.

69. National Council for U.S.–China Trade, *China's Petroleum Industry*, p. 75.

70. Paul Strauss, "Ports Get High Priority," *FEER* 91, no. 7 (Feb. 13, 1976): 74–75.

71. *USCBR* 3, no. 3 (May–June 1976): 58.

72. Peter Weintraub, "China: Sounding a Warning," *FEER* 94, no. 42 (Oct. 15, 1976): 56.

73. *USCBR* 4, no. 1 (Jan.–Feb. 1977): 53.

74. *USCBR* 5, no. 2 (Mar.–Apr. 1978): 57.

75. "Chairman Hua's Fruitful Visit to Rumania," *PR* 21, no. 34 (Aug. 25, 1978): 6–15.

76. "On China's Cessation of Aid to Albania," Note from the Chinese Ministry of Foreign Affairs, July 7, 1978, *PR* 21, no. 29 (July 21, 1978): 20–23.

Chapter 5

1. *USCBR* 3, no. 2 (Mar.–Apr. 1976): 51.

2. "Grasp the Key Link in Running the Country Well and Promote a New Leap Forward in the National Economy," *JMJP* (Apr. 19, 1977), trans. in PR 20, no. 18 (Apr. 29, 1977): 21–25.

3. "Plant and Plant Technology Sales to China," *USCBR* 3, no. 4 (July–Aug. 1976): 41.

4. National Council for U.S.–China Trade, *China's Petroleum Industry*, p. 22.

5. Irwin Millard Heine, "China's Merchant Marine," *USCBR* 3, no. 2 (Mar.–Apr. 1976): 7–18.

6. "China and Oil—What to Expect," p. 1.

7. "U.S. Quietly Begins Talks with Chinese on Financial Claims," *NYT*, May 2, 1977, p. 1.

8. Harold C. Hinton, *Communist China in World Politics* (New York, 1966), p. 265.

9. For a chronology of U.S. involvement in Indochina, see Committee of Concerned Asian Scholars, *The Indochina Story* (New York, 1970), pp. 318–39.

10. "Melting the Ice," *FEER* 72, no. 19 (May 8, 1971): 74.

11. "Quarterly Chronicle and Documentation: The Nixon Visit," *CQ* 50 (Apr.–June 1972): 390–402.

12. "Quarterly Chronicle and Documentation," *CQ* 54 (Apr.–June 1973): 420–22.

13. "U.S. Quietly Begins Talks with Chinese on Financial Claims," *NYT,* May 2, 1977, p. 1.

14. For example, Peter D. Weintraub, "Peking's Oil Strategy," *NYT,* Jan. 5, 1975; Henri Hymans, "Peking Takes a Coy Line on Oil," *FEER* 91, no. 8 (Feb. 20, 1976): 39.

15. Donald K. White, "Bay Plant to Refine China's Oil," *San Francisco Chronicle,* Nov. 22, 1978, p. 1; William K. Stevens, "U.S. to Get Low-Sulfur Chinese Oil," *NYT,* Nov. 22, 1978, p. D-1.

16. "Exploring China," *FEER* 85, no. 37 (Sept. 20, 1974): 44; *USCBR* 3, no. 6 (Nov.–Dec. 1976): 51.

17. *USCBR* 2, no. 5 (Sept.–Oct. 1975): 47; "China, Despite Death of Mao, Opens Plants Built by U.S. on Time," *NYT,* Oct. 26, 1976, p. 51.

18. "CDC Gets the Green Light: Export Controls," *USCBR* 3, no. 6 (Nov.–Dec. 1976): 51.

19. "U.S. Agrees to Sell China a Computer with Defense Uses," *NYT,* Oct. 29, 1976, p. 1.

20. Michael Morrow, "Oil: Catalyst for the Region," *FEER* 86, no. 51 (Dec. 27, 1974): 26–28.

21. "Atomic Aid for China," *FEER* 86, no. 39 (Oct. 4, 1974): 5.

22. "Peking Stays Aloof on Power Policy," *FEER* 86, no. 46 (Nov. 22, 1974): 56.

23. "Quarterly Chronicle and Documentation," *CQ* 45 (Jan.–Mar. 1971): 209. Author's emphasis.

24. Information on Sino-Canadian energy delegations was drawn from National Council for U.S.–China Trade, *China's Petroleum Industry,* pp. 74–86.

25. Hans Heymann, "Acquisition and Diffusion of Technology in China," U.S. Joint Economic Committee, *China: A Reassessment,* p. 725.

26. Wageman et al., pp. 1611–43.

27. Harrison, "China: The Next Oil Giant," pp. 12–13.

28. *USCBR* 3, no. 3 (May–June 1976), p. 51.

29. The Houston conference was sponsored by the National Council for U.S.–China Trade (Washington, D.C.) and was attended by representatives of American universities, petroleum equipment industries, and the government. For a report on the Houston conference, see National Council for U.S.–China Trade, *China's Petroleum Industry.* Other workshops on the subject included the Stanford Workshop on Chinese Energy Policy (June 2–3, 1976), sponsored by the Social Science Research Council and the U.S.–China Relations Program of Stanford University. A sequential workshop was held at Wingspread (Racine, Wisconsin) in July 1977, sponsored by the Johnson Foundation. For a report of the Stanford workshop, see Fingar and Bachman. The Wingspread meeting was reported in Douglas P. Murray and Thomas Fingar, "Memorandum of Discus-

sion on China's Energy: Domestic Development and International Implications," mimeo. report, U.S.–China Relations Program, Stanford University, July 18–19, 1977.

30. *PNSEA* 9, no. 1 (Apr. 1978), p. 2.

31. Chung Chih-ping, "World Advances Amidst Turbulence," *PR* 17, no. 1 (Jan. 4, 1974): 20.

32. "World in Great Disorder: Excellent Situation," *PR* 17, no. 3 (Jan. 18, 1974): 7–11.

33. "False Friend with a Honey Tongue and Dagger Heart," *JMJP*, May 5, 1974, p. 6.

34. "Peking Expected to Stress Europe," *NYT*, Sept. 11, 1973, p. 15.

35. "Worker's Movement Gathering Momentum in Western Europe," *PR* 17, no. 9 (Mar. 1, 1974): 22.

36. Malcolm Subhan, "Peking: Pushing for a Pact in Europe," *FEER* 91, no. 7 (Feb. 13, 1976): 103.

37. *USCBR* 4, no. 3 (May–June 1977): 57; "EEC and Asia," *FEER* 100, no. 16 (Apr. 21, 1978): 35–70.

38. National Committee for U.S.–China Trade, *China's Petroleum Industry*, p. 84.

39. *USCBR* 3, no. 3 (May–June 1976): 58.

40. Colina MacDougall, "Red and Less Experts," *FEER* 61, no. 28 (July 11, 1968): 101–2.

41. Edith Lenart, "China Buys in Paris," *FEER* 82, no. 45 (Nov. 12, 1973): 49–50; Yuan, "China's Chemicals," pp. 37–52.

42. Harald Munthe-Kaas, "Peking's Search for Technology," *FEER* 90, no. 45 (Nov. 7, 1975): 32–33.

43. *USCBR* 5, no. 3 (May–June 1978): 61.

44. Peter Weintraub and Melinda Liu, "China Buys Its Way Towards a Vision of Self-Reliance," *FEER* 101, no. 27 (July 7, 1978): 34–35; Anthony Rowley, "Peking Intrigues the World," *FEER* 102, no. 43 (Oct. 27, 1978): 39–43.

45. "China's Boom Is Europe's Boom," *NYT*, Nov. 25, 1978, p. 29.

46. *CTR* 16, no. 10 (Oct. 1978): 8.

47. "Moscow Warns Against Jet Sales," *Honolulu Advertiser*, Nov. 24, 1978, p. 1; Richard Burt, "U.S. Neutral on West Europe's Arms Sales to Peking," *NYT*, Nov. 8, 1978, p. A-3.

48. Andreas Freund, "French Get Trade Pact with China," *NYT*, Dec. 5, 1978, p. D-1.

49. "Quarterly Chronicle and Documentation," *CQ* 53 (Jan.–Mar. 1973): 200. Author's emphasis.

50. *Ibid.;* "Quarterly Chronicle and Documentation," *CQ* 57 (Jan.–Mar. 1974): 213.

51. *USCBR* 1, no. 6 (Nov.–Dec. 1974): 63; "Peking Oil Strategy," *NYT*, Jan. 5, 1975.

52. *USCBR* 2, no. 4 (July–Aug. 1975): 54.

53. *USCBR* 4, no. 2 (Mar.–Apr., 1977): 54.

54. *USCBR* 3, no. 4 (July–Aug. 1976): 56; *USCBR* 3, no. 6 (Nov.–Dec. 1976): 63.

Chapter 6

1. *WES* 20 (1971–75), Tables 2, 6, and 10.
2. Harrison, *China, Oil, and Asia,* pp. 147–57.
3. Lee, *Japan Faces China,* has been used as an authoritative reference on the history of Sino-Japanese political and commercial relations since World War II; the quotation is from p. 1. Other book-length references on Sino-Japanese relations include Jansen, *Japan and China,* and Kato, *The Japan-China Phenomenon.*
4. Hsiao, "Prospects," p. 735.   5. Lee, p. 23.
6. *Ibid.,* p. 25.   7. *Ibid.,* p. 32.
8. *Ibid.*   9. *Ibid.,* p. 136.
10. *Ibid.,* p. 160.   11. *Ibid.,* p. 145.
12. Hsiao, "Prospects," p. 738.
13. Jansen, p. 499.
14. Hsiao, "The Sino-Japanese Rapprochement," pp. 104–5.
15. Lee, p. 106.
16. I had the good fortune to be in Peking at the time the Nixon visit was announced. See Committee of Concerned Asian Scholars, *China!,* chap. 11.
17. Kato, p. 60.
18. Hsiao, "The Sino-Japanese Rapprochement," p. 106.
19. *Ibid.,* pp. 108–10.
20. *Ibid.,* p. 114.
21. Daniel Wit and Alfred B. Clubock, "The United States and Japanese Atomic Power Development," *World Politics* 8, no. 4 (July 1956): 515–33.
22. Bernard Gwertzman, "U.S. and Japan Agree on Formula for Nuclear Plant," *NYT,* June 15, 1977, p. A-11.
23. Hsiao, "Prospects," p. 728.
24. *Ibid.,* pp. 721–27.
25. *Ibid.,* pp. 727–34.
26. Susumu Awanohara, "Trade Progress, Yes; But Peace Treaty, No," *FEER* 98, no. 40 (Oct. 7, 1977): 80.
27. *USCBR* 4, no. 6 (Nov.–Dec. 1977): 52; *USCBR* 5, no. 1 (Jan.–Feb. 1978): 57.
28. For the text of the agreement, see *USCBR* 5, no. 2 (Mar.–Apr. 1978): 46–47.
29. "Japan Hoping to Widen Trade with China," *NYT,* Nov. 24, 1978, p. D-1.
30. Lee, p. 136.
31. Dick Wilson, "Trade Across the China Sea," *FEER* 45, no. 10 (Sept. 3, 1964): 429–31.
32. *CTEN* 231 and 234 (Jan. and Apr. 1975).
33. *USCBR* 1, no. 4 (July–Aug. 1974): 22; *USCBR* 1, no. 6 (Nov.–Dec. 1974): 42, 63.

34. *USCBR* 2, no. 2 (Mar.–Apr. 1975): 55.

35. *USCBR* 2, no. 5 (Sept.–Oct. 1975): 57.

36. *USCBR* 3, no. 1 (Jan.–Feb. 1976): 53; *USCBR* 3, no. 2 (Mar.–Apr. 1976): 58; *USCBR* 3, no. 3 (May–June 1976): 58.

37. Colina MacDougall, "Finding the Gusher," *FEER* 43, no. 13 (Mar. 26, 1964): 658; Colina MacDougall, "Production Records," *FEER* 53, no. 1 (Sept. 29, 1966): 621–24.

38. Lee, p. 175. The four conditions, announced April 28, 1970, prohibited Chinese trade with Japanese companies that (1) were selling military equipment to South Korea or Taiwan; (2) had large investments in South Korea or Taiwan; (3) were supplying U.S. military forces in Indochina; or (4) were subsidiaries of U.S. companies or engaged in joint enterprises with U.S. companies.

39. John G. Roberts, "Tanaka's Auspicious Omens," *FEER* 77, no. 39 (Sept. 23, 1972): 29–31; Leo Goodstadt, "Chinese Bottlenecks," *FEER* 78, no. 41 (Oct. 7, 1972): 39–41; Koji Nakamura, "China: Political Deal," *FEER* 79, no. 4 (Jan. 29, 1973): 33.

40. "Quarterly Chronicle and Documentation," *CQ* 54 (Apr.–June 1973): 416.

41. The International Oil Trading Company was established with an initial capital of 100 million yen and included Nippon Steel, Tokyo Electric Power Company, the Japan Industrial Bank, Idemitsu Kosan, Maruzen, Daikyo, and Kyodo. It was headed by Yosomatsu Matsubara, former president of Hitachi Shipbuilding. See Koji Nakamura, "Sino-Japanese Trade," *FEER* 79, no. 4 (Jan. 29, 1973): 44; Barry Wain, "The Realities of Self-Reliance," *FEER* 82, no. 39 (Oct. 1, 1973): 23–24.

42. Lee, p. 125.

43. Hudson, "Japanese Attitudes."

44. "Tokyo's Tangled Options," *FEER* 81, no. 29 (July 23, 1973): 32–33.

45. Nicholas Ludlow, "U.S. Companies and China's Oil Development," *NYT,* Mar. 3, 1974, sec. 3, p. 2.

46. Koji Nakamura, "Tripartite Pressure," *FEER* 86, no. 39 (Oct. 4, 1974): 41–42.

47. "Chinese Oil Tanker's First Voyage to Japan," *PR* 16, no. 39 (Sept. 28, 1973): 21.

48. J. O. Ronall, "China as an Oil Exporting Nation," *NYT,* Jan. 5, 1975, sec. 3, p. 3.

49. *CTEN* 232 (Feb. 1975); Williams, 239.

50. *USCBR* 1, no. 6 (Nov.–Dec. 1974): 63..

51. Price data were taken from various issues of *USCBR* and from National Council for U.S.–China Trade, *China's Petroleum Industry.*

52. *USCBR* 2, no. 1 (Jan.–Feb. 1975): 56.

53. "All Peking's Fault," *FEER* 92, no. 14 (Apr. 2, 1976): 43.

54. *USCBR* 2 no. 4 (July–Aug. 1975): 54.

55. Susumu Awanohara, "Snags Facing China's Oil Exports," *FEER* 90, no. 48 (Nov. 28, 1975): 42, 47.

56. *USCBR* 2, no. 5 (Sept.–Oct. 1975): 48; *USCBR* 2, no. 6 (Nov.–Dec. 1975): 62.

57. *USCBR* 3, no. 1 (Jan.–Feb. 1976): 53.

58. Henri Hymans, "Tokyo's Bid to Curb Chinese Oil Flow," *FEER* 91, no. 4 (Jan. 23, 1976): 41–42.

59. A Nippon Steel delegation led by Yoshiro Inayama went to China on January 13, 1976, to discuss the barter of 2–3 million tons of rolled steel for Chinese crude oil in 1976. See *USCBR* 3, no. 2 (Mar.–Apr. 1976): 59.

60. This debate was subsequently revealed by the winning faction in its 1977 campaign against the "Gang of Four." See "Foreign Trade: Why the 'Gang of Four' Created Confusion," *PR* 20, no. 9 (Feb. 25, 1977): 16–18.

61. Wrightman, pp. 31–35.

62. Susumu Awanohara, "Japan Wary of Peking Power Play," *FEER* 92, no. 17 (Apr. 23, 1976): 128–30.

63. Peter Weintraub, "China: Ideology, Then Oil," *FEER* 92, no. 25 (June 18, 1976): 36–38; *USCBR* 3, no. 3 (May–June 1976): 57; Susumu Awanohara, "Japan-China Business Suffers," *FEER* 93, no. 33 (Aug. 13, 1976): 43.

64. "Foreign Trade: Why the 'Gang of Four' Created Confusion," *PR* 20, no. 9 (Feb. 25, 1977): 16–18; *USCBR* 4, no. 1 (Jan.–Feb. 1977): 6–7; "Actively Strengthen Construction and Management," *JMJP*, Mar. 19, 1977, p. 4.

65. For the 1970–75 crude petroleum production rates, see Table 16.5. For the 1976 growth rate, see "Petroleum and Coal-Mining Industries Achievements," *PR* 20, no. 3 (Jan. 14, 1977): 7.

66. The crude oil production growth rate for January–June 1977 was 10.6 percent. See "All-Round Growth of Industrial Production," *PR* 20, no. 29 (July 15, 1977): 3.

67. Ross H. Munro, "Production of China's Oilfield at Taching May Have Peaked," *NYT*, Dec. 27, 1976, p. D-2.

68. Susumu Awanohara, "Peking's Pledges to Tokyo," *FEER* 92, no. 22 (May 28, 1976): 112.

69. Weintraub, "China: Ideology, Then Oil."

70. For example, in 1973, Overseas Petroleum Corporation, a Japanese consortium, purchased part of British Petroleum's holdings in Abu Dhabi, providing for an assured annual crude oil supply of 21 million kiloliters for 30 years. See "Japanese Oil Deal," *FEER* 79, no. 1 (Jan. 8, 1973): 30.

71. *WES* 20 (1971–75): 67.

72. *USCBR* 3, no. 4 (July–Aug. 1976): 55.

73. "China Sets New Date for 5th 5-Year Plan," *NYT*, Oct. 28, 1976, p. 9.

74. "Waiting for China's Oil Orders," *FEER* 94, no. 47 (Nov. 19, 1976): 5.

75. Drew Middleton, "China Is Reported Seeking to Conclude a Long-Term Oil Export Agreement with the Japanese Government," *NYT*, Feb. 13, 1977, p. 12.

76. Teng Hsiao-ping was appointed Vice-Chairman of the Party, Vice-Chairman of the Military Affairs Committee, Chief of Staff, and Vice-Premier, all positions just one rung below Party Chairman Hua Kuo-feng. There was

some speculation that Teng might eventually be appointed Premier, a move that would put him on a nearly equal rank with Hua. See David Bonavia, "Dismantling Parts of Maoism—But Not Mao," *FEER* 98, no. 40 (Oct. 7, 1977): 39–41.

77. Brendon Jones, "U.S. Study Sees Trade Increase with Pragmatic Post-Mao China," *NYT,* Aug. 11, 1977, p. 39.

78. *USCBR* 4, no. 2 (Mar.–Apr. 1977): 57.

79. Susumu Awanohara, "Trade Progress, Yes; But Peace Treaty, No," *FEER* 98, no. 40 (Oct. 7, 1977): 80.

80. "China and Japan Sign Peace and Friendship Treaty," *PR* 21, no. 33 (Aug. 18, 1978): 8.

81. Ashton, p. 306.

82. Colina MacDougall, "East European Trade," *FEER* 39, no. 11 (Mar. 14, 1963): 542.

83. Harrison, *China, Oil and Asia,* p. 63.

84. National Council on U.S.–China Trade, *China's Petroleum Industry,* p. 76.

85. Leo Goodstadt, "Politics and Prices in Canton," *FEER* 82, no. 41 (Oct. 15, 1973): 41–43.

86. *USCBR* 2, no. 4 (July–Aug. 1975): 38, 54.

87. Henri Hymans, "Japan Eyes Peking's Liquid Gas," *FEER* 91, no. 8 (Feb. 20, 1976): 37–39; *USCBR* 3, no. 1 (Jan.–Feb. 1976): 52. Also reported in many other sources.

88. Dr. Norman Pruvost (Lawrence Livermore Laboratories) comments to the Workshop on China's Energy Policy, Stanford University, June 2, 1976. See Fingar and Bachman, p. 21.

89. "Chinhuangtao-Peking Oil Pipeline Completed," *PR* 18, no. 29 (July 18, 1975): 6.

90. "Taching Oil Pipeline Reaches Peking," *CR* 24, no. 10 (Oct. 1975): 15–16.

91. Paul Strauss, "Peking: The Drive for Expansion," *FEER* 91, no. 4 (Jan. 23, 1976): 42.

92. U.S. CIA, *China: Oil Production Prospects,* p. 25.

93. Strauss, "Peking: The Drive for Expansion."

94. Hymans, "Tokyo's Bid to Curb Chinese Oil Flow."

95. "A Modern Deepwater Oil Port," *JMJP,* June 7, 1976, p. 1; "Dairen Constructs a New Harbor," *JMJP,* July 22, 1976, p. 1.

96. George Lauriat, "Chinese Chartering," *FEER* 98, no. 40 (Oct. 7, 1977): 69–71.

97. Completion of the 50,000-dwt tanker "Hsihu" at the Dairen shipyard was reported in early 1977. See George Lauriat, "Containers at Whampoa?" *FEER* 95, no. 6 (Feb. 11, 1977): 45–46.

98. Lauriat, "Chinese Chartering."

99. *USCBR* 3, no. 1 (Jan.–Feb. 1976): 54.

100. Christopher Lewis, "The Independence Seekers," *FEER* 87, no. 9 (Feb. 28, 1975): 25–30; Paul Strauss, "Ports Get High Priority," *FEER* 91, no. 7 (Feb. 13, 1976): 74–75; National Council for U.S.–China Trade, *China's Petroleum Industry,* p. 107; *USCBR* 3, no. 6 (Nov.–Dec. 1976): 55.

101. *USCBR* 3, no. 5 (Sept.–Oct. 1976): 55; *USCBR* 3, no. 6 (Nov.–Dec. 1976): 55.

102. *USCBR* 1, no. 6 (Nov.–Dec. 1974): 62; *USCBR* 3, no. 2 (Mar.–Apr. 1976): 58–59; *USCBR* 3, no. 4 (July–Aug. 1976): 56; Peter Weintraub, "China: Sounding a Warning," *FEER* 94, no. 42 (Oct. 15, 1976): 56.

103. Shipping costs to Japan were estimated by one source in the $0.70–0.80 per barrel range, about the same as from the Middle East. See Wrightman, "Japan and China's Oil," p. 34; Peter Weintraub, "Limits on China's Oil Exports," *FEER* 95, no. 3 (Jan. 21, 1977): 100–103.

104. CIA, *China: Oil Production Prospects,* p. 11.

105. *USCBR* 3, no. 3 (May–June 1976): 57.

106. "The Oil Bonanza Turns Sour," *FEER* 86, no. 47 (Nov. 29, 1974): 5; David A. Andelman, "Thais Reject Chinese Oil as Too Waxy to Refine," *NYT,* Sept. 19, 1975, p. 3.

107. Peter Weintraub, "Slowing Down or Dying?," *FEER* 93, no. 40 (Oct. 1, 1976): 55–56; Weintraub, "Limits on China's Oil Exports."

108. George Lauriat, "Awaiting the Rush of Chinese Crude, If Any," *FEER* 98, no. 40 (Oct. 7, 1977): 67–69.

109. CIA, *China: Oil Production Prospects,* p. 11.

110. *USCBR* 4, no. 3 (May–June 1977): 53.

111. Alistair Wrightman, "How Japan Finances Trade with China," *USCBR* 2, no. 2 (Mar.–Apr. 1975): 32; Susumu Awanohara, "Airing Japan-China Trade Problems," *FEER* 88, no. 14 (Apr. 4, 1975): 39.

112. *USCBR* 2, no. 6 (Nov.–Dec. 1975): 62.

113. Susumu Awanohara, "China Finds an Ardent New Suitor in Japan," *FEER* 102, no. 44 (Nov. 3, 1978): 38–44.

114. Ronall, "China as an Oil Exporting Nation."

115. Weintraub, "Slowing Down or Dying?"

116. *USCBR* 3, no. 4 (July–Aug. 1976): 55; *USCBR* 3, no. 6 (Nov.–Dec. 1976): 61.

117. "China—Capitalist in Hong Kong," *NYT,* Feb. 11, 1977, p. D-1.

Chapter 7

1. This general description of the Chinese continental shelf was derived from a series of geological survey reports published annually in the *CCOP Technical Bulletin* (1968–76), by the Committee for Coordination of Joint Prospecting for Mineral Resources in Asian Offshore Areas, an international scientific research agency sponsored by the United Nations Economic Commission for Asia and the Far East (ECAFE). Note that ECAFE was renamed the Economic and Social Council for Asia and the Pacific (ESCAP) in 1975. The text in this chapter will refer to ECAFE, since that was the name of the organization during the period when the CCOP surveys were conducted. Area and volumetric estimates for the continental shelf were from Willums, "China's Offshore Petroleum," p. 12.

2. Emery et al., p. 11.

3. *Ibid.,* p. 11.

4. *Ibid.*, pp. 11–12.

5. *Ibid.*, p. 41.

6. For a recent, exciting, and historically accurate account of the shadow-play among these governments, the oil companies, and the United States and Chinese governments in the wake of the CCOP survey, see Harrison, *China, Oil, and Asia.* This book was the result of more than 300 interviews with public and private officials in Asia, the United States, and Europe, conducted under the auspices of the Carnegie Endowment for International Peace. An earlier version of the Harrison findings appeared in *Foreign Policy* 20 (Fall 1975): 3–27, and aroused a wave of speculation in the United States regarding China's offshore oil potential.

7. Harrison, *China, Oil, and Asia,* Figs. 5–8.

8. See M. L. Parke et al., and Emery and Ben-Avraham.

9. Emery and Ben-Avraham, p. 120.

10. Harrison, *China, Oil, and Asia,* Fig. 10.

11. Ishiwada and Ogawa, "Petroleum Geology."

12. Emery and Niino, "Stratigraphy."

13. Mainguy, p. 106; Dalton, "Developments in 1967," p. 1585.

14. Dalton, "Developments in 1968," pp. 1801–3; Humphrey, "Developments in 1969," pp. 1561–62; Humphrey, "Developments in 1970," pp. 1647–49.

15. "Business Briefs," *FEER* 73, no. 31 (July 31, 1971): 58; Park, "Oil Under Troubled Waters," p. 233.

16. Ishiwada and Ogawa, p. 24; Scheidecker, "Developments in 1976."

17. The legal details of this agreement will be discussed below. See "Offshore Oil Agreement with Japan," *ARB* 3, no. 9 (Feb. 28, 1974): 2471; "Agreement Between South Korea and Japan on Continental Shelf Oil Exploration," *ARB* 3, no. 10 (Mar. 31, 1974): 2544; "At Last Japan Ratifies the Joint Oil Development Pact," *ARB* 7, no. 2 (July 31, 1977): 347.

18. Dalton, "Developments in 1967," p. 1578.

19. The first companies granted concessions were (from south to north) Conoco, Amoco, Gulf, Oceanic, and Clinton. A Texfel concession was signed in June 1972. Kilroy, Superior, and Comoro signed in 1973. Humphrey, "Developments in 1970," pp. 1635–41; Kennett, p. 2095; Bowman, p. 2134.

20. Harrison provides a detailed account of the incident in *China, Oil and Asia,* pp. 1–9.

21. "Taiwan—Offshore Drilling Programme," *ARB* 3, no. 7 (Dec. 1973): 2311.

22. Kennett, p. 2095.

23. Bowman, Table 2, p. 2152.

24. Caldwell, p. 1984.

25. Fukien Front radio broadcast November 1, 1974, reported in *ARB* 4, no. 7 (Dec. 31, 1974): 33.

26. Central News Agency dispatch, date unknown, as reported in *ARB* 4, no. 9 (Feb. 28, 1975): 53.

27. Scheidecker, "Developments in 1975," p. 1916. Scheidecker did not report the rumored second Conoco gas discovery, nor was it listed in Table 2, which provides an annual *AAPGB* summary of East Asian well locations and specifications. Table 2 also missed three wells north of Taiwan indicated in a map (Fig. 10) accompanying the same article.

28. "Discovery of Gas Well off Kaohsiung," *ARB* 5, no. 7 (Dec. 31, 1975): 157.

29. "Two U.S. Companies Pull Out of Oil Search," *ARB* 6, no. 4 (Sept. 30, 1976): 248; Scheidecker, "Developments in 1976," p. 1841.

30. "First Offshore Drilling Vessel Built," *ARB* 4, no. 10 (Mar. 31, 1975): 63.

31. Harrison, *China, Oil, and Asia,* p. 118.

32. HUNTEC, Ltd., "Offshore Geophysical Survey."

33. Borsum et al., "Aeromagnetic Survey."

34. The initial concessionaires were Gulf (Apr. 15, 1969), Shell (Jan. 28, 1970), Texaco-Chevron (Feb. 27, 1970), and Wendell-Phillips (Sept. 24, 1970). Kennett, p. 2091.

35. Bowman, p. 2130.

36. Caldwell, p. 1980.

37. Scheidecker, "Developments in 1975," p. 1912.

38. "Statement by Foreign Ministry Spokesman," *PR* 16, no. 12 (Mar. 23, 1973): 4.

39. Harrison, *China, Oil, and Asia,* p. 130.

40. *Ibid.,* p. 132. According to Harrison, Gulf denied these rumors. For other petroleum industry reports that the Gulf wells were dry, see Bowman, p. 2130.

41. Kennett, p. 2091.

42. "Japanese Delay in Ratification of Agreement on Joint Development of Continental Shelf," *ARB* 3, no. 11 (Apr. 30, 1974): 2617.

43. "South Korea—Offshore Oil Exploration," *ARB* 6, no. 9 (Feb. 28, 1977): 299; Scheidecker, "Developments in Far East in 1976," p. 1837. One onland oil strike was reported near Pohang in 1975. See Susumu Awanohara, "Tokyo: Anxiety over Oil Pact," *FEER* 91, no. 5 (Jan. 30, 1976): 43–44.

44. John Burgess, "North Korea Seeks Help in Offshore Oil Search," *Washington Post,* Dec. 12, 1977, p. A-10.

45. Philippines, Bureau of Mines, "Oil Exploration," and Humphrey, "Developments in 1970," pp. 1654–55.

46. Tanner and Kennett, p. 1830.

47. *Ibid.,* Table 9, p. 1844.

48. Kennett, p. 2094.

49. Bowman, p. 2133.

50. "Japan's Interest in Philippines Offshore Oil," *ARB* 3, no. 8 (Jan. 31, 1974): 2387; "Philippines–Joint Oil Prospecting," *ARB* 4, no. 3 (Aug. 31, 1974): 2936.

51. *USCBR* 3, no. 4 (July–Aug. 1976): 56.

52. Caldwell, p. 1982.

53. Scheidecker, "Developments in 1975," pp. 1914–15; "Integrated Area for Oil Exploration," *ARB* 5, no. 4 (Sept. 30, 1975): 122.

54. "Philippines: First Oil Discovery," *ARB* 5, no. 11 (Apr. 30, 1976): 192–93; "Oil Flow in South Nido I Well," *ARB* 7, no. 3 (Aug. 31, 1977): 356.

55. Leo Gonzaga, "A Shot in the Arm for Philippines Oil Search," *FEER* 93, no. 34 (Aug. 20, 1976): 34–35.

56. The discovery, announced Feb. 21, 1978, tested at 9,540 bbl/day. See "Oil Production Ahead for the Philippines?", *ARB* 7, no. 6 (Nov. 30, 1977): 380; Pete Ucko, "Oil Found in the Philippines," *Honolulu Advertiser,* Feb. 22, 1978, p. B-1.

57. Humphrey, "Developments in 1970," p. 1635. For the sake of simplicity the country will be referred to here as "Cambodia," despite two changes in its official designation during the period under consideration.

58. W. E. Kennett, "Petroleum Developments in 1972," p. 2091.

59. Caldwell, p. 1980.

60. Tanner and Kennett, p. 1831.

61. Kennett, p. 2095.

62. Bowman, p. 2135.

63. Caldwell, p. 1985; "South Vietnam—Oil Exploration," *ARB* 3, no. 10 (Mar. 31, 1974): 2552.

64. "First Offshore Oil/Gas Trace," *ARB* 4, no. 4 (Sept. 30, 1974): 6.

65. "Discovery of Oil and Gas Off the Coast," *ARB* 4, no. 11 (Apr. 30, 1975): 74; Scheidecker, "Developments in 1975," p. 1916.

66. "Saigon's Statement on Oil Exploration Dispute with Khmer," *ARB* 4, no. 5 (Oct. 31, 1974): 14.

67. Harrison, *China, Oil, and Asia,* Fig. 3.

68. Bowman, p. 2132.

69. "Exploration of Tonkin Oil with Japan and Italy," *ARB* 3, no. 6 (Oct. 1973): 2226; "JPDC to Study North Vietnam's Offshore Oil," *ARB* 3, no. 8 (Jan. 31, 1974): 2387.

70. "U.S. Oil Firms Withdraw," *ARB* 4, no. 12 (May 31, 1975): 83.

71. "Petroleum Agreement with Iraq," *ARB* 5, no. 3 (Aug. 31, 1975): 114.

72. Scheidecker, "Developments in 1975," p. 1917; "Government to Allow Entry of Foreign Oil Companies and Other Investors," *ARB* 6, no. 10 (Mar. 31, 1977): 307.

73. "South Vietnam to Revive Oil Exploration," *ARB* 5, no. 5 (Oct. 31, 1975): 135.

74. "Government May Invite Oil Companies," *ARB* 5, no. 12 (May 31, 1976): 206; Nayan Chanda, "Hanoi Anxious to Begin Search," *FEER* 92, no. 22 (May 28, 1976): 113–14; "Oil Firms in Secret Talks with Hanoi," *ARB* 6, no. 2 (July 31, 1976): 226.

75. "Foreign Participation in Oil Industry," *ARB* 6, no. 7 (Dec. 31, 1976): 277.

76. Harrison indicates (personal communication) that Norway was to have rendered the assistance through the United Nations Development Program and that Vietnam is still reluctant to permit this type of foreign assistance in the pe-

troleum industry. See also "Norway to Drill for Oil Off Coast," *ARB* 6, no. 5 (Oct. 31, 1976): 258; *PNSEA* 7, no. 10 (Jan. 1977): 46.

77. The new concessionaires may recover discovery costs and buy up to 42 percent of production at 7–10 percent below market. See "Vietnam—New Oil Strike South of Hanoi," *ARB* 7, no. 4 (Sept. 30, 1977): 364; "Vietnam Signs Contracts, Finds Onshore Oil," *World Oil* 185, no. 6 (Nov. 1977): 29.

78. A "graben" is a single- or double-faulted block structure, many kilometers wide and deep (like a giant bathtub), that captures sediment of a sufficient depth to cause hydrocarbon migration into trap structures around its fringe.

79. Ho Ping-ti quoted Chinese sources to the effect that reserves were on the scale of the Middle East in "China Is the Country with the Richest Oil Resources," *Ch'i Shih Nien Tai* (Hong Kong, Feb. 1975), pp. 6–14, in *JPRS* 64685 (May 2, 1975): 1–21. Horton R. Connell reported an early U.S. oil industry estimate of 50 billion metric tons in "China's Petroleum Industry," p. 2160. Park and Cohen cited a total resource estimate of 70 billion tons in "China's Oil Weapon," p. 31. Early Japanese projections of Chinese oil production in 1980 of over 200 million tons per year were based on exaggerated offshore resource speculation.

80. Maurice Terman, "Geological Constraints on Chinese Petroleum Development," comments to the Workshop on China's Energy Policy, Stanford University, June 2, 1976, reported by Fingar and Bachman, pp. 28–34. Willums and Terman discussed their alternative methods of estimation at this workshop.

81. Yen Tun-shih, Director of the Institute of Petroleum and Chemical Engineering, Ministry of Petroleum and Chemical Industries, PRC, "The Meso-Cenozoic Tectonic Framework of Eastern China," seminar given to the Menlo Park branch of the U.S. Geological Survey, October 22, 1975. A similar lecture was reported in Walter Sullivan, "Scientists Say Continental Collisions Formed Asia," *NYT,* Oct. 9, 1975, p. 1.

82. For a general description of the Uinta Basin structure, see *IPE,* 1976, pp. 262–64.

83. Terman, "Geological Constraints," in Fingar and Bachman, p. 32. Harrison reports that Professor Necmettin Mungan, a Canadian petroleum engineer who has visited Taching, disputes Terman's analogy with the Uinta Basin on the grounds that the stratigraphic traps in China's northeast oilfields are larger than those in the Uinta Basin. See Harrison, *China, Oil, and Asia,* p. 37.

84. Willums, "China's Offshore Oil," chap. 2.

85. Meyerhoff and Willums, pp. 103–212.

86. *Ibid.,* p. 202.

87. Also reported in Willums, "China's Offshore Petroleum," esp. p. 12.

88. In 1974, U.S. proved recoverable resources were rated at 5.6 billion metric tons and ultimate recoverable resources at three to four times this figure. Proved recoverable natural gas resources were rated at 7.5 billion cubic meters, with ultimate recoverable resources several times higher. Middle East proved recoverable crude petroleum resources were rated at 41.4 billion metric tons and ultimate recoverable resources were at least twice proved resources. World Energy Conference, *Survey of Energy Resources, 1974,* pp. 102–13.

89. "Tiaoyu and Other Islands Have Been China's Territory Since Ancient Times," *PR* 15, no. 1 (Jan. 7, 1972): 13–14; Shih Ti-tsu, "South China Sea Islands, Chinese Territory Since Ancient Times," *PR* 18, no. 50 (Dec. 12, 1975): 10–15.

90. Kim Woodard, "Chinese International Behavior Under Stress: A Content Analysis of Chinese Diplomatic Notes During the Sino-Indian Border Crisis," M.A. thesis, Graduate School of International Studies, University of Denver, June 15, 1967.

91. Park, "Oil Under Troubled Waters."

92. Harrison indicates that the Japanese government has never made its median-line claim on the continental shelf explicit (personal communication). However, Choon-ho Park points out that the midline principle for international sea zone demarcation was incorporated into two laws passed by the Diet on May 2, 1977. The laws were the Territorial Sea Law (Law Number 30) and the Provisional Law Governing Japanese Fisheries Zones (Law Number 31). See *Jurist Magazine* (Tokyo) 647 (Sept. 1, 1977): 78–79. In any case, the pattern of preliminary Japanese exploration concession areas in the East China Sea would confirm the reliance of the Japanese government on the midline criterion.

93. Li, "China and Offshore Oil."

94. *Ibid.,* p. 147.

95. *Ibid.,* p. 148.

96. "Business Briefs," *FEER* 73, no. 31 (July 31, 1971): 58.

97. Harrison, *China, Oil and Asia,* p. 172.

98. "Far Eastern Roundup," *FEER* 76, no. 17 (Apr. 22, 1974): 4.

99. "News Roundup," *FEER* 78, no. 49 (Dec. 2, 1972): 5.

100. "There's a Catch," *FEER* 80, no. 18 (May 7, 1973): 5.

101. Koji Nakamura, "Political Concessions on a Fisheries Pact," *FEER* 89, no. 36 (Sept. 5, 1975): 22.

102. U.S. Department of State, translation of "Fisheries Agreement." Professor Choon-ho Park notes that the map accompanying this translation contains a serious error at the southern end of the "trawl-free zone."

103. I am indebted for the thrust of this argument to a discussion with Professor Choon-ho Park, who also kindly provided the documentation. For the quote see Douglas M. Johnston and Edgar Gold, "The Economic Zone in the Law of the Sea: Survey, Analysis and Appraisal of Current Trends," Law of the Sea Institute Occasional Paper 17 (University of Rhode Island, June 1973): 28. The Law of the Sea Institute has recently moved to the University of Hawaii.

104. United Nations Third Conference on the Law of the Sea, "Informal Negotiating Text," Sixth Session, May 23 to July 15, 1977. Available in English as UN Doc. A/Conf.62/WP.10/Corr.3 (July 27, 1977). Quotation from Art. 76, p. 52.

105. *Ibid.,* Art. 83, p. 55.

106. "Struggle for a New Code," report on the 5th Session of the U.N. Law of the Sea Conference, *PR* 19, no. 32–33 (Aug. 9, 1976): 27.

107. Emery and Niino, esp. p. 25.

108. Some sources suggest that the South Korean position is based consistently on natural prolongation. However, a comparison of Maps 7.1 and 7.2 shows that Seoul has granted concessions reaching to the midline in the Yellow Sea, in an area where the midline lies to the southwest (Chinese side) of the line of greatest depth on the shelf. South Korea has also accepted a midline settlement with Japan north of the Joint Development Zone. See note 110 below, and Sam Kim-O, "Hands Across the Sea-Bed," *FEER* 83, no. 7 (Feb. 18, 1974): 39–40.

109. Susumu Awanohara, "Miki Faces Seabed Wrangle," *FEER* 88, no. 16 (Apr. 18, 1975): 37–38; Susumu Awanohara, "Tokyo: Anxiety Over Oil Pact," *FEER* 91, no. 5 (Jan. 30, 1976): 43–44.

110. For a text of the two agreements and a map showing the boundaries, see U.S. Dept. of State, "Continental Shelf Boundary."

111. "Statement by Spokesman of Foreign Ministry," Feb. 4, 1974, in *PR* 17, no. 6 (Feb. 8, 1974): 3; "Reiterating China's Stand on Japan–South Korea Agreement for Joint Development of the Continental Shelf," *PR* 20, no. 23 (June 3, 1977): 7; " 'Japan–South Korea Continental Shelf Agreement' Opposed," *PR* 20, no. 23 (June 3, 1977): 28–29.

112. I am indebted to Selig S. Harrison for this point. Compare "Statement of China's Foreign Ministry," June 13, 1977, in *JMJP*, June 14, 1977, p. 1, and "Violation of Our Country's Sovereignty Over the Continental Shelf Is Impermissible," *JMJP*, June 14, 1977, p. 6. Both documents are translated together in *PR* 20, no. 25 (June 17, 1977): 16–17.

113. *Ibid.*, "China's Sovereignty Over Continental Shelf Is Inviolable," *PR* 20, no. 25 (June 17, 1977): 16–17.

114. Susumu Awanohara, "Oil Pact Delay Upsets Seoul," *FEER* 96, no. 19 (May 13, 1977): 25; Susumu Awanohara, "Fukuda Sets His Sights on Peking," *FEER* 96, no. 23 (June 10, 1977): 13.

115. Chen Huang, "The Legal Tussle for Asia's Seas," *FEER* 84, no. 20 (May 20, 1974): 45; "Oil in Troubled Waters," *FEER* 87, no. 8 (Feb. 21, 1975): 5.

116. "North Korea Sets 'Military' Line Off Coast, Barring Foreign Craft," *NYT*, Aug. 2, 1977, p. 2.

117. The Spratleys are 1,100 miles south of Taiwan. In early 1974 Taiwan was reported to have four naval ships in the area, in addition to its garrison. South Vietnam and the Philippines also maintained small forces on some of the islands. Hanoi has replaced the Saigon military forces in the area with its own units. The Philippine government has recently strengthened its air and naval power in the area and has built an airstrip on one of the islands. See "China's Dispute Over Neighboring Islands Shifts from the Paracels to the Spratleys," *ARB* 3, no. 9 (Feb. 28, 1974): 2443; Rodney Tasker, "Stake-Out in the Spratleys," *FEER* 99, no. 8 (Feb. 24, 1978): 11–12.

118. William Glenn, "Scramble for Flyspecks," *FEER* 69, no. 36 (Sept. 5, 1970): 42.

119. Li, pp. 149–50.

120. Bowman, p. 2152.

121. Scheidecker, "Developments in 1975," Fig. 10 and pp. 1924–25.

122. Harrison, *China, Oil, and Asia,* pp. 173–81.

123. "Statement of the Ministry of Foreign Affairs of the People's Republic of China," *PR* 15, no. 1 (Jan. 7, 1972): 12; "Sato Government Tries to Annex China's Tiaoyu and Other Islands," *PR* 15, no. 14 (Apr. 7, 1972): 18.

124. Hudson, p. 706.

125. See note 117 above.

126. "China's Silence over South Vietnam's Claim to Spratley Islands," *ARB* 3, no. 6 (Nov. 1973): 2209–10.

127. Chen Huang, "A Matter of Legality," *FEER* 83, no. 8 (Feb. 25, 1974): 25–28.

128. Bernard Wideman, "Marcos Listens to the Peking Tune," *FEER* 93, no. 31 (July 30, 1976): 28–29.

129. Bernard Wideman, "Manila Probes a Sensitive Spot," *FEER* 92, no. 22 (May 28, 1976): 115; Leo Gonzaga, "A Shot in the Arm for Philippines Oil Search," *FEER* 93, no. 34 (Aug. 20, 1976): 34–35.

130. "China's Silence over South Vietnam's Claim to Spratley Islands," *ARB* 3, no. 6 (Nov. 1973): 2209–10.

131. "China and South Vietnam in Violent Conflict over Paracels," *ARB* 3, no. 8 (Jan. 31, 1974): 2366–67.

132. Michael Morrow, "Today Hsisha, Tomorrow . . .?," *FEER* 83, no. 4 (Jan. 28, 1974): 32; "Statement by Spokesman of Chinese Ministry of Foreign Affairs," Jan. 11, 1974, in *PR* 17 no. 3 (Jan. 18, 1974): 3; "Statement of the Chinese Ministry of Foreign Affairs," (Jan. 20, 1974) in *PR* 17, no. 4 (Jan. 25, 1974): 3–4.

133. "China's Dispute Shifts to Spratleys," p. 2443.

134. *Ibid.,* p. 2443.

135. "Chiang Ching Helped Foster an Evil Plot in 'Hsi Sha Battle,'" *JMJP,* Mar. 17, 1977, p. 3.

136. Chen Huang, "The Legal Tussle for Asia's Seas," p. 45; "Oil in Troubled Waters," *FEER* 87, no. 8 (Feb. 21, 1975): 5.

137. "Baring the Truth," *FEER* 88, no. 15 (Apr. 11, 1975): 5.

138. Fox Butterfield, "China Reasserts Claim to Islands," *NYT,* Nov. 27, 1975, p. 10; Shih Ti-tsu, "South China Sea Islands, Chinese Territory Since Ancient Times," *PR* 18, no. 50 (Dec. 12, 1975): 10–15.

139. "Vietnam's Sea Rights Extended to 200 Miles," *NYT,* May 22, 1977, p. 5.

140. *USCBR* 4, no. 5 (Sept.–Oct. 1977): 39.

141. "Soviet Bombers Spotted by Japan over East China Sea," *ARB* 2, no. 4 (Sept. 1972): 1166.

142. Koji Nakamura, "Chinese Wedge," *FEER* 80, no. 21 (May 28, 1973): 14.

143. "The Enemy Below," *FEER* 93, no. 36 (Sept. 3, 1976): 5.

144. "Southeast Asian Countries Strengthen Struggle to Protect Oil Sovereignty," *JMJP,* Sept. 10, 1975, p. 6.

145. See note 124 and "Quarterly Chronicle and Documentation," *CQ* 54 (Apr.–June 1973): 416.

146. Bowman, p. 2127.

147. "International Joint Oil Exploration in Asian Waters," *ARB* 3, no. 11 (Apr. 30, 1974): 2617.

148. "Japan–South Korea Continental Shelf Agreement Opposed," *PR* 20, no. 23 (June 3, 1977): 28–29.

Chapter 8

1. Petroleum Publishing Co., "Search for Oil Will Focus Offshore," pp. 282–85.

2. Michel Grenon, "Global Energy Resources," *Annual Review of Energy* 2 (1977): 81.

3. Council on Environmental Quality, *OCS Oil and Gas: An Environmental Assessment,* vol. 1 (Washington, D.C., 1974), p. 19.

4. Don E. Kash et al., *Energy Under the Oceans: A Technology Assessment of Outer Continental Shelf Oil and Gas Operations* (Norman, Okla., 1973), p. 315.

5. These figures refer to market economy countries only. My estimate is based on figures from "Worldwide Report," *OGJ* 75, no. 53 (Dec. 26, 1977): 97–190.

6. Robert E. King, "World-wide Activity Slows Due to Economics, Politics," *World Oil* 183, no. 1 (July 1976): 41–47.

7. Council on Environmental Quality, *OCS Oil and Gas,* p. 20.

8. CIA, *China: Oil Production Prospects,* Fig. 15, pp. 16–17.

9. "Newly Built Taching Oilfield," *PR* 17, no. 21 (May 24, 1974): 15–17.

10. *Ibid.,* p. 15.

11. "Takang, Studying Taching, Has Five Years of Great Development," *JMJP,* Jan. 6, 1976, p. 2.

12. CIA, *China: Oil Production Prospects,* Fig. 7, p. 9; National Council for U.S.–China Trade, *China's Petroleum Industry,* p. 32.

13. CIA, *China: Oil Production Prospects,* p. 16.

14. *Ibid.*

15. Meyerhoff and Willums, p. 189.

16. *Ibid.*

17. "Jenchiu—a New High-Yielding Oilfield," *PR* 21, no. 41 (Oct. 13, 1978): 3–4. For comparative per-well productivity in Indonesian offshore fields, see Scheidecker, "Developments in 1975," Table 1, pp. 1917–21.

18. Meyerhoff and Willums, p. 189.

19. "A Visit to Taching Oilfield," *CR* 13, no. 10 (Oct. 1974): 8–14; "Visitors' Reports on Taching and Shengli Oil Fields," *China News Summary* 571 (June 18, 1975).

20. *USCBR* 1, no. 1 (Jan.–Feb. 1974): 29–30.

21. Harrison, *China, Oil, and Asia,* pp. 74–82.

22. *Ibid.,* pp. 77–78; Meyerhoff and Willums, p. 205.

23. Chin Yun-shan, "Relief and Bottom Sediment."

24. "South China Sea Investigated," *PR* 21, no. 5 (Feb. 3, 1978): 30.

25. Harrison, *China, Oil, and Asia,* p. 75; "Completion of Exploratory Survey of Gulf of Chihli," *ARB* 3, no. 11 (Apr. 30, 1974): 2619.

26. "Airborne Magnetic Survey of Coastal Waters," *PR* 21, no. 31 (Aug. 4, 1978): 28.

27. "South China Sea Investigated," *PR* 21, no. 5 (Feb. 3, 1978): 30.

28. "China's First Ocean Scientific Research," *PR* 19, nos. 32–33 (Aug. 9, 1976): 4, "PRC Completes Oceanographic Research Project," *FBIS*, July 20, 1977, p. E-17.

29. "China's First Floating Drilling Vessel for Sea Exploration," *CP*, April 1975, p. 5.

30. Williams, p. 238.

31. *USCBR* 4, no. 5 (Sept.–Oct. 1977): 39; *CTR* 16, no. 6 (June 1978): 3; *CTR* 16, no. 7 (July 1978): 9; *PNSEA* 9, no. 3 (June 1978), supplement; *PNSEA* 9, no. 5 (Aug. 1978): 11.

32. For example, Peking contracted to purchase the "Hakuryu II" from Mitsubishi for $22.6 million in December 1973. The contract was later abrogated and delivery refused in a disagreement over the final purchase price. See Harrison, *China, Oil, and Asia*, p. 68.

33. "How China Built Her First Off-Shore Rig," *Hsinhua News Bulletin*, June 4, 1975, p. 1.

34. "China's First Floating Drilling Vessel for Sea Exploration," *CP*, April 1975, p. 5.

35. *USCBR* 3, no. 4 (July–Aug. 1976): 44.

36. *USCBR* 4, no. 5 (Sept.–Oct. 1977): 38–39.

37. *USCBR* 4, no. 5 (Sept.–Oct. 1977): 39.

38. *USCBR* 4, no. 6 (Nov.–Dec. 1977): 43: *USCBR* 5, no. 1 (Jan.–Feb. 1978): 36.

39. *PNSEA* 9, no. 3 (June 1978), supplement; *Ocean Industry* 13, no. 6 (June 1978): 112; *USCBR* 5, no. 3 (May–June 1978): 42–43.

40. *CTR* 16, no. 6 (June 1978): 10.

41. *PNSEA* 9, no. 4 (July 1978): 11.

42. *PNSEA* 9, no. 4 (July 1978), supplement. In addition to the rigs listed in Table 8.1, Harrison's interviews identified another rig, the "Pailung," a drill-ship purchased from Ishikawa-Harima in 1969 for $11 million. The existence of this transaction, however, is still subject to some doubt. The "Pailung" never surfaced in the foreign press before Harrison discovered it through his interviews in the mid-1970's. This contrasts sharply with the foreign interest generated by Chinese purchase of the "Fuji" in 1972. Furthermore, the Chinese name "Pailung" means "White Dragon," which is the same as the Japanese name "Hakuryu." Harrison himself reports that China declined delivery of the Hakuryu II from Mitsubishi, after contracting for its purchase in December 1973. In any case, it is highly doubtful that the present Chinese regime would name anything "White Dragon." Finally, some sources have identified the "Pailung" as a semisubmersible, which would again indicate confusion with the Hakuryu II. Compare Harrison, *China, Oil, and Asia*, pp. 62 and 68; see also *PNSEA* 8, no. 8 (Nov. 1977): 33.

43. Willums projects offshore production of about 46 million tons by 1980 and the discovery of more than 2 billion metric tons of crude oil in 114 offshore

fields by 1985 under a "moderate" set of assumptions. This projection is unrealistically high in view of the present pace of the offshore exploration program. See comments by Willums in Fingar and Bachman, p. 34; Willums, "China's Offshore Petroleum," p. 13.

44. *USCBR* 4, no. 2 (Mar.–Apr. 1977): 54.

45. Harrison reports (*China, Oil, and Asia,* p. 76) that two additional seismic survey ships were imported from Japan (Sumitomo).

46. *USCBR* 4, no. 5 (Sept.–Oct. 1977): 39.

47. *CTR* 16, no. 6 (June 1978): 8.

48. This account of North Sea development relies on Robert E. King, "North Sea Joins Ranks of World's Major Oil Regions," *World Oil* 185, no. 7 (Dec. 1977): 35–46.

49. *Financial Times,* Sept. 7, 1977, p. 6.

50. "Petroleum Delegation Departs U.S. for Japan," *FBIS,* Feb. 1, 1978, p. A-1; James Cook, "Oil for the Lamps of Tokyo?" *Forbes,* Feb. 6, 1978, pp. 37–38; "Potential Giant: Peking Experts Visit U.S.," *Time,* Feb. 6, 1978, p. 57; *USCBR* 5, no. 2 (Mar.–Apr. 1978): 12–13.

51. U.S. Senator Henry M. Jackson, who chairs the Senate Energy and Natural Resources Committee, visited energy units in the PRC in February 1978; see "Jackson Says China Wants U.S. Oil Skill," *NYT,* Feb. 23, 1978, p. D-1.

52. "Ministry Holds 3-Day Discussion of World Oil Techniques," *FBIS,* Feb. 28, 1978, p. E-18.

53. Jason Mugar, "Why China Is Moving Offshore," *PNSEA* 9, no. 1 (Apr. 1978): 608.

54. "National Finance and Trade Conference," *PR* 21, no. 30 (July 28, 1978): 3.

55. "Vice-Chairman Li Hsien-nien on Finance and Trade," speech to the National Finance and Trade Conference, June 20, 1978, excerpts, *PR* 21, no. 30 (July 28, 1978): 15–17.

56. *PNSEA* 9, no. 3 (June, 1978): 4.

57. Henry Scott-Stokes, "China Strengthens Its Ties with Japan," *NYT,* July 23, 1978, p. 9.

58. *USCBR* 5, no. 3 (May–June 1978): 41.

59. The Teng estimate was first quoted in September 1977; see Melinda Liu, "Sobering Thought in the Oil Rush," *FEER* 102, no. 44 (Nov. 3, 1978): 45; *USCBR* 4, no. 6 (Nov.–Dec. 1977): 58.

60. *CTR* 16, no. 7 (July 1978): 9.

61. *PNSEA* 9, no. 5 (Aug. 1978): 4.

62. *PNSEA* 9, no. 5 (Aug. 1978), supplement.

63. "China and Japan Sign Peace and Friendship Treaty," *PR* 21, no. 33 (Aug. 18, 1978): 6; "China-Japan Treaty of Peace and Friendship Goes into Effect," *PR* 21, no. 43 (Oct. 27, 1978): 3.

64. *CTR* 16, no. 10 (Oct. 1978): 7.

65. Melinda Liu, "China's Export Initiative," *FEER* 101, no. 31 (Aug. 4, 1978): 47–48.

66. Susumu Awanohara, "Japan's Moscow-Peking Equation," *FEER* 101, no. 33 (Aug. 18, 1978): 45–46.

67. "Partners for Prosperity," *FEER* 102, no. 41 (Oct. 13, 1978): 5.

68. "China's New Export Strategy," *CTR* 16, no. 9 (Sept. 1978): 2.

69. Susumu Awanohara, "Japan Gives an Extra Push to Its Trade with China," *FEER* 101, no. 38 (Sept. 22, 1978): 96–97.

70. Susumu Awanohara, "China Finds an Ardent New Suitor in Japan," *FEER* 102, no. 44 (Nov. 3, 1978): 38–42.

71. Anthony Rowley, "Peking Intrigues the World," *FEER* 102, no. 43 (Oct. 27, 1978): 39–43.

72. Susumu Awanohara, "Peking's Yen for the U.S. Dollar," *FEER* 102, no. 41 (Oct. 13, 1978): 44–45.

73. Kathleen Teltsch, "Peking, in a Shift, Is Seeking U.N. Aid," *NYT,* Nov. 16, 1978, p. A-5.

74. Denis Peiris, "Change of Time but Not Tempo," *FEER* 102, no. 45 (Nov. 10, 1978): 38–40.

75. Nayan Chanda, "A Bear Hug from Moscow," *FEER* 102, no. 46 (Nov. 17, 1978): 8–10.

76. David Bonavia, "The Marxist and the Monarchy," *FEER* 102, no. 46 (Nov. 17, 1978): 10–12.

77. Tim Williams, "Vietnam Wants American Oil Firms," *PNSEA* 9, no. 5 (Aug. 8, 1978): 8–9.

78. Roderick O'Brien, "Vietnam's Offshore Claims," *PNSEA* 9, no. 4 (July 1978): 19–20.

79. Ian Brodie, "China–U.S. Relations Are in Tattered Shape," *FEER* 98, no. 40 (Oct. 7, 1977): 60–61.

80. Burt Solomon, "China Shifts Its Energy Gears," *Energy Daily* 6, no. 206 (Oct. 25, 1978): 1.

81. *PR* 21, no. 44 (Nov. 3, 1978): 6.

82. Burt Solomon, "U.S., China Set Tentative Agenda in Energy," *Energy Daily* 6, no. 215 (Nov. 7, 1978): 1–3.

83. "U.S. Offers to Aid China in Energy Development," *NYT,* Nov. 7, 1978, p. 69.

84. Susumu Awanohara, "An Ill Wind from the Senkakus," *FEER* 100, no. 17 (Apr. 28, 1978): 10–12.

85. "Another Victory for the Principle of Self-Reliance: Domestically Produced 300,000 KW Water Cooled Generator Commissioned," *JMJP,* June 16, 1976, p. 1, trans. in *PR* 19, nos. 32–33 (Aug. 9, 1976): 22.

86. "Why China Imports Technology and Equipment," *PR* 21, no. 41 (Oct. 13, 1978): 11–13.

87. *Ibid.,* p. 11.

88. *Ibid.,* p. 13.

89. "Machine-Building in High Gear," *PR* 21, no. 40 (Oct. 6, 1978): 19.

90. *USCBR* 1, no. 1 (Jan.–Feb. 1974): 22; Park and Cohen, p. 39.

91. Joanna Lee, "Whampoa Works on Stream," *PNSEA* 9, no. 5 (Aug. 1978): 16–17.

92. "Monopoly Moves," *FEER* 81, no. 37 (Sept. 17, 1973): 47; "Mao's Men in Manila," *FEER* 82, 48 (Dec. 3, 1978): 34.

93. Bernardino Ronquillo, "Manila's Growing Ties," *FEER* 77, no. 33 (Aug. 12, 1972): 34–35.

94. Leo Goodstadt, "Grim Struggle in Canton," *FEER* 80, no. 19 (May 14, 1973): 38–39.

95. Jidbhand Kambhu, "Chatichai in China: Starting Slowly," *FEER* 83, no. 2 (Jan. 14, 1974): 13.

96. "A Conspicuous Silence," *FEER* 83, no. 9 (Mar. 4, 1974): 5.

97. Bernardino Ronquillo, "The Last Touches to Peking Accord," *FEER* 85, no. 33 (Aug. 23, 1974): 26–28.

98. Bernardino Ronquillo and Bernard Wideman, "Coming to Terms with Peking," *FEER* 86, no. 39 (Oct. 4, 1974): 13–14.

99. "The Oil Bonanza Turns Sour," *FEER* 86, no. 47 (Nov. 29, 1974): 5.

100. *ARB* 4, no. 6 (Nov. 30, 1974): 22.

101. Chou En-lai, "Report on the Work of the Government," Speech to the Fourth National People's Congress, January 13, 1975, *PR* 18, no. 4 (Jan. 24, 1975): 25.

102. "Southeast Asian Countries Strengthen Struggle to Protect Oil Sovereignty," *JMJP*, Sept. 10, 1975, p. 6.

103. David A. Andelman, "Thais Reject Chinese Oil as Too Waxy to Refine," *NYT*, Sept. 19, 1975, p. 3.

104. Susumu Awanohara, "China's Deficit Here to Stay," *FEER* 88, no. 25 (June 20, 1975): 36–37.

105. Kedar Man Singh, "Nepal: Threatened by an Oil Blockade," *FEER* 86, no. 49 (Dec. 13, 1974): 71; Michael Morrow, "Oil: Catalyst for the Region," *FEER* 86, no. 51 (Dec. 27, 1974): 26–28; *ARB* 4, no. 12 (May 31, 1975): 81; Ho Kwan Ping, "Singapore Aims to Bridge the China Gap," *FEER* 90, no. 49 (Dec. 5, 1975): 37–38.

106. Kuo Chi, "Foreign Trade: Why the 'Gang of Four' Created Confusion," *PR* 20, no. 9 (Feb. 25, 1977): 16–17.

107. Arnold Zeitlin, "China Halts Oil Exports—Proved No Bargain in Manila," *Washington Post*, May 23, 1976, p. M-6; Bernard Wideman, "Marcos Listens to the Peking Tune," *FEER* 93, no. 31 (July 30, 1976): 28–29.

108. *USCBR* 3, no. 5 (Sept.–Oct. 1976): 57.

109. Peter Weintraub, "Slowing Down or Dying?" *FEER* 93, no. 40 (Oct. 1, 1976): 55–56.

110. For example, a large Chinese team attended the Southeast Asian Conference on Offshore Oil in Singapore during February at the lowest point in monthly oil trade with Japan. *USCBR* 3, no. 2 (Mar.–Apr. 1976): 52.

111. *ARB* 5, no. 8 (Jan. 31, 1976): 164; Lauriat, "China's Emerging Tanker Fleet."

112. *USCBR* 3, no. 5 (Sept.–Oct. 1976): 54.

113. "China—Capitalist in Hong Kong," *NYT,* Feb. 11, 1977, p. D-1; *USCBR* 4, no. 4 (July–Aug. 1977): 32.

114. *USCBR* 4, no. 5 (Sept.–Oct. 1977): 55.

115. *USCBR* 4, no. 6 (Nov.–Dec. 1977): 56.

116. *ARB* 7, no. 6 (Nov. 30, 1977): 383.

117. "China: A Good Word for ASEAN," *Asia Week* 3, no. 38 (Sept. 23, 1977): 12; Salamat Ali, "Close Military Collaboration," *FEER* 98, no. 40 (Oct. 7, 1977): 88.

118. Hua Kuo-feng, "Unite and Strive to Build a Modern, Powerful Socialist Country!," Report to the Fifth National People's Congress, Feb. 26, 1978, *PR* 21, no. 10 (Mar. 10, 1978): 7–40.

119. David Bonavia, "Old Faces in the New Team," *FEER* 99, no. 11 (Mar. 17, 1978): 20–22.

120. Fang Yi, "Outline Plan for the Development of Science and Technology, Relevant Policies and Measures," *PR* 21, no. 14 (Apr. 7, 1978): 6–14; David Bonavia, "Better Read than Red," *FEER* 100, no. 14 (Apr. 7, 1978): 28–29.

121. "Agreement on Oil Supply to Philippines Reached," *FBIS,* Feb. 1, 1978, p. A-6; *USCBR* 5, no. 2 (Mar.–Apr. 1978): 54; *PNSEA* 9, no. 6 (Sept. 1978): 5.

122. *CTR* 16, no. 1 (Jan. 1978): 4–5; *CTR* 16, no. 5 (May 1978): 10; *USCBR* 5, no. 3 (May–June 1978): 71.

123. *PNSEA* 9, no. 1 (Apr. 1978), supplement: "An Optimistic Kriangsak," *FEER* 100, no. 16 (Apr. 21, 1978): 31; *USCBR* 5, no. 3 (May–June, 1978): 71.

124. *CTR* 16, no. 6 (June 1978): 11.

125. "Teng Begins Southeast Asian Tour to Counter Rising Soviet Influence," *NYT,* Nov. 6, 1978, p. 1.

126. "Malaysia Warns China Against Interference," *NYT,* Nov. 11, 1978, p. 1.

127. Henry Kamm, "Singapore Enjoying Incongruous Visits," *NYT,* Nov. 7, 1978, p. 11.

128. Susumu Awanohara, "China Finds an Ardent New Suitor in Japan," *FEER* 102, no. 44 (Nov. 3, 1978): 40–42; "All Peking's Fault," *FEER* 92, no. 14 (Apr. 2, 1976): 43.

129. *PNSEA* 9, no. 3 (June 1978), supplement.

130. *CTR* 16, no. 7 (July 1978): 10.

131. *Ibid.,* p. 10; Melinda Liu, "China Learns from Hong Kong," *FEER* 101, no. 33 (Aug. 18, 1978): 49–51; *CTR* 16, no. 9 (Sept. 1978): 3–11.

132. Shim Jae Hoon, "Pyongyang Tries a New Ball Game," *FEER* 100, no. 17 (Apr. 28, 1978): 12.

133. "The Kremlin Helps Create 'Two Koreas,' " *PR* 21, no. 38 (Sept. 22, 1978): 23.

134. Susumu Awanohara, "Pyongyang Ponders the New Alliance," *FEER* 102, no. 43 (Oct. 27, 1978): 13–15.

135. "The Soviet Connection," *FEER* 100, no. 24 (June 16, 1978): 7.

136. "Partners for Prosperity," *FEER* 102, no. 41 (Oct. 13, 1978): 5; *USCBR* 5, no. 3 (May–June 1978): 71.

137. Liu Mei-yun, "Taiwan Looks to Import Coal," *PNSEA* 9, no. 3 (June 1978): 13; William Kazer, "Taiwan's Gas Hopes Evaporate," *FEER* 100, no. 25 (June 23, 1978): 100.

138. Sheilah Ocampo, "A Quiet Soviet Guest," *FEER* 102, no. 44 (Nov. 3, 1978): 16.

139. "Moscow Changes Its Attitude Toward ASEAN," *PR* 21, no. 31 (Aug. 4, 1978): 16–17.

140. Park and Cohen, p. 39.

141. Ling, p. 79; "Quarterly Chronicle and Documentation," *CQ* 52 (Oct.–Dec. 1972): 790.

142. "Oil Based Industrial Complex Developed in South China," *Wen Hui Pao,* Oct. 30, 1971, p. 3, trans. in *JPRS* 54934 (Jan. 14, 1972): 17–20.

143. *ARB* 5, no. 3 (Aug. 31, 1975): 113; National Council for U.S.–China Trade, *China's Petroleum Industry,* p. 50. I have based the estimates in Chapter 20 on the figures provided by the National Council.

144. USCBR 2, no. 6 (Nov.–Dec. 1975): 64.

145. "China-Korea Friendship Oil Pipeline," *PR* 19, no. 5 (Jan. 30, 1976): 24.

146. *Ibid.*

147. "Trade Talks in Peking." *FEER* 89, no. 35 (Aug. 29, 1975): 5.

148. "Time Will Tell the True from the False," *PR* 21, no. 30 (July 28, 1978): 26–29.

149. Lynn Yamashita, "A Return for Their Money," *FEER* 93, no. 31 (July 30, 1976): 45–46; "Vietnam's Ningping Electric Power Plant Victoriously Constructed," *JMJP,* Aug. 13, 1976, p. 5.

150. *USCBR* 3, no. 3 (May–June 1976): 59.

151. *USCBR* 4, no. 2 (Mar.–Apr. 1977): 56–57.

152. John Burgess, "North Korea Seeks Help in Offshore Oil Search," *Washington Post,* Dec. 12, 1977, p. A-10.

153. David Bonavia, "Chairman Hua's Korea Nuances," *FEER* 100, no. 20 (May 19, 1978): 13–14; *PNSEA* 9, no. 4 (July 1978): 5.

154. *USCBR* 4, no. 6 (Nov.–Dec. 1977): 60.

155. "Protest Against Viet Nam's Encroachments upon Chinese Territory," *PR* 21, no. 39 (Sept. 29, 1978): 23.

156. Henry Kamm, "Laos Backs Vietnam in Dispute Despite Chinese Troops in North," *NYT,* July 23, 1978, p. 3.

157. *PNSEA* 9, no. 3 (June 1978): 4.

158. "Sino-Vietnamese Pact Spurs Cambodian Pact," *NYT,* Nov. 6, 1978, p. 31.

159. "Soviet Revisionists Plunder Mineral Resources," *PR* 17, no. 27 (July 5, 1974): 29; "Robbing Mongolia's Minerals," *PR* 18, no. 29 (July 18, 1975): 28.

160. Quoted in John Parke Wright, "Hong Kong: Oil Center for South China," *PNSEA* 9, no. 5 (Aug. 1978): 10–12.

Chapter 9

1. " 'Economic Integration' Impairs State Sovereignty," report of an article in the Romanian party paper *Era Socialista,* in *PR* 17, no. 27 (July 5, 1974): 27–

29; "Documents of the 5th Non-Aligned Summit Conference: Economic Declaration," *PR* 19, no. 36 (Sept. 3, 1976): 11–12.

2. Li Chiang, Minister of Foreign Trade, People's Republic of China, "New Developments in China's Foreign Trade," *China's Foreign Trade* 1 (1974), trans. in *CR* 23, no. 7 (July 1974): 14–15.

3. "China Supports Demands for U.N. Charter Revision," speech by Pi Chi-lung to November 25, 1975, session of the Sixth Committee of the U.N. General Assembly, in *PR* 18, no. 50 (Dec. 12, 1975): 9.

4. Mikdashi, *The Community of Oil Exporting Countries;* "The OPEC Process," *Daedalus* 104, no. 4 (Fall 1975): 203–15.

5. Mikdashi, pp. 147–49.

6. Mira Wilkins, "The Oil Companies in Perspective," *Daedalus* 104, no. 4 (Fall 1975): 159–78.

7. "OPEC's 21st Conference Decides to Adopt Measures to Raise the Posted Price of Oil," *JMJP,* Jan. 3, 1971, p. 5.

8. "Joint Struggle Wins New Victory," *PR* 15, no. 4 (Jan. 28, 1972): 20; "Oil Exporting Countries: New Victory," *PR* 15, no. 14 (Apr. 7, 1972): 19.

9. "Prices Up 11.9 Percent," *PR* 16, no. 25 (June 22, 1973): 19; "OPEC Extraordinary Conference," *PR* 16, no. 39 (Sept. 28, 1973): 21.

10. *PR* 16, no. 48 (Nov. 30, 1973): 10–11; "Treating Countries Differently," *PR* 17, no. 1 (Jan. 4, 1974): 26.

11. Romano Prodi and Alberto Clo, "The Oil Crisis: Europe," *Daedalus* 104, no. 4 (Fall 1975): 91–112; Yoshi Tsurumi, "The Oil Crisis: Japan," in *ibid.,* pp. 113–27.

12. "Great Victories in the Struggle of the Oil Exporting Countries," *JMJP,* Dec. 26, 1974, p. 6, and numerous other articles.

13. Ulf Lantzke, "The OECD and Its International Energy Agency," *Daedalus* 104, no. 4 (Fall 1975): 217–27.

14. "Western Oil Consumers' Conference," *PR* 17, no. 8 (Feb. 22, 1974): 21; "Relationship Towards Arab Countries Changes," *PR* 17, no. 29 (July 19, 1974): 21–22; "An Historical Undertaking in the Struggle Against Imperialism and Hegemonism," *JMJP,* Dec. 26, 1974, p. 6; "Call for 'Dialogue' with the Developing Countries," *PR* 18, no. 25 (June 20, 1975): 21.

15. "Resolute Oil Struggle Attacks Hegemonism," *JMJP,* Sept. 6, 1975, p. 6.

16. "Latin American Heads of State Accuse the American Trade Law of Interference with the Developing Countries," *JMJP,* Jan. 7, 1975, p. 6.

17. "Resolute Oil Struggle Attacks Hegemonism."

18. "OPEC Decides to Raise Oil Prices," *JMJP,* Sept. 29, 1975, p. 4.

19. "Decision to Raise Oil Price," *PR* 20, no. 1 (Jan. 1, 1977): 48.

20. John P. Lewis, "Oil, Other Scarcities, and the Poor Countries," *World Politics* 27, no. 1 (Oct. 1974): 63–86.

21. *WES* 21 (1978), Table 2. On the other hand, the Third World as a region exports 65 percent of its primary energy production (Table 10.6).

22. "Chiao Kuan-hua's Speech at the 29th Session of the UN General Assembly," *CB,* Apr. 22, 1975, pp. 9–12.

23. "OPEC Establishes an Aid Fund for the Third World," *JMJP*, Apr. 11, 1974, p. 6.

24. *CTEN* 236 (June 1975): 3.

25. "OPEC Decides to Raise Oil Prices," *JMJP*, Sept. 29, 1975, p. 4.

26. "How Imperialism Plunders the Developing Countries," *PR* 15, no. 17 (Apr. 28, 1972): 16; "Chinese Representative Exposes Big-Power Hegemonism," *PR* 16, no. 29 (July 20, 1973): 8–10.

27. "Resource Exporting Countries Unite to Protect Sovereignty," *JMJP*, Aug. 16, 1974, p. 6; "Third World Countries Unite in Struggle to Defend Raw Materials Resources," *ER* 2 (Apr.–June 1974): 10.

28. Scott R. Pearson, "Prospects for Multination Commodity Cartels," colloquium, Food Research Institute, Stanford University, Oct. 17, 1975.

29. Weintraub, "China's Minerals and Metals," pp. 39–48.

30. *USCBR* 2, no. 5 (Sept.–Oct. 1975): 58.

31. *USCBR* 3, no. 3 (May–June 1976): 60.

32. "Oil Struggle Developing in Depth," *PR* 19, no. 4 (Jan. 23, 1976): 51.

33. Dick Wilson, "China and the European Community," *CQ* 56 (Oct.–Dec. 1973): 647–66.

34. "Fruitless Trade Negotiations," *PR* 15, no. 3 (Jan. 21, 1972): 21; "Common Market to Be Enlarged," *PR* 15, no. 5 (Feb. 4, 1972): 22–23; "The Nine-Nation Summit Conference," *PR* 15, no. 43 (Oct. 27, 1972): 17–23; "Common Market to Establish 'Free Trade Area' with Mediterranean Countries," *PR* 15, no. 47 (Nov. 24, 1972): 21; "Association with Developing Countries," *PR* 16, no. 32 (Aug. 10, 1973): 20; "Superpower Rivalry in Middle East Expedites West European Unity," *PR* 16, no. 49 (Dec. 7, 1973): 13–14.

35. *CTEN* 232 (Feb. 1975): 2.

36. "China and E.E.C. Establish Official Relations," *PR* 18, no. 20 (May 16, 1975): 5; "Establishment of Relations with China Hailed," *PR* 18, no. 26 (June 27, 1975): 18.

37. "C.M.E.A.—Soviet Revisionism's Instrument for Neo-Colonialism," *ER* 3 (July–Sept. 1974): 44; see also *PR* 17, no. 27 (July 5, 1974): 24–26.

38. "CMEA Ridden with Difficulties," *PR* 20, no. 6 (Feb. 4, 1977): 22–23.

39. Liang Hsiao, "Economic Cause of Soviet Revisionism's World Hegemony Bid," *HQ* 10 (1975), in *PR* 18, no. 45 (Nov. 7, 1975): 18–21.

40. "Third World Role in International Affairs," *PR* 16, no. 1 (Jan. 5, 1973): 18–20; "Struggle for National Economic Development," *PR* 16, no. 7 (Feb. 16, 1973): 6–7, 12.

41. *Ibid.*

42. "Opposing Trans-National Companies," *PR* 16, no. 8 (Feb. 23, 1973): 20.

43. "Resolution to Reform Inter-American System," *PR* 16, no. 17 (Apr. 27, 1973): 20.

44. "Community and Common Market Established," *PR* 16, no. 32 (Aug. 10, 1973): 21; "Setting up Latin American Economic System," *PR* 18, no. 33 (Aug. 15, 1973): 28; "Third Lima Declaration," *PR* 16, no. 33 (Aug. 17, 1973): 19; "Latin American Organization of Energy," *PR* 16, no. 46 (Nov. 16, 1973): 23.

45. "Defense of Oil Resources," *PR* 16, no. 52 (Dec. 28, 1973): 17; "Latin American Countries Strengthen Cooperation and Develop National Economies," *JMJP*, Jan. 31, 1974, p. 6.

46. "The First Arab-African Cooperation Meeting Opens in Cairo," *JMJP*, Jan. 24, 1974, p. 6.

47. Named the U.N. Economic Commission for Asia and the Far East (UNECAFE) before 1975. "Oppose Big Powers Seeking Hegemony: China at UNECAFE," report of speech by An Chih-yuan to Apr. 12, 1973, 29th plenary session, *PR* 16, no. 16 (Apr. 20, 1973): 13–15; "Support the Struggle of the Developing Countries in Asia and the Far East Against Imperialism and Hegemonism," report of speech by Huang Ming-ta to Mar. 29, 1974, session, *PR* 17, no. 14 (Apr. 5, 1974): 22–24.

48. "Year of Decline for U.S. Imperialism," *PR* 15, no. 3 (Jan. 21, 1972): 16–17; "Unite to Win Still Greater Victories," New Year's editorial, *PR* 15, no. 1 (Jan. 7, 1972): 8–11.

49. "Huang Hua Sends Note to U.N. Secretary-General Urging U.N. and All Its Related Organizations to Immediately Cease All Contact with Chiang Kai-shek Clique," *PR* 15, no. 3 (Jan. 21, 1972): 15.

50. "Refuting Y. A. Malik," *PR* 15, no. 3 (Jan. 21, 1972): 5–6; "Unite to Defend Economic Resources and Oppose Superpower Exploitation," *JMJP*, Apr. 13, 1974, p. 6.

51. "The Group of 77," *JMJP*, June 4, 1974, p. 5.

52. "China Supports Demands for U.N. Charter Revision," *PR* 18, no. 50 (Dec. 12, 1975): 9; "Who Are For and Who Are Against?: U.N. Security Council Holds Meetings in Africa," *PR* 15, no. 4 (Jan. 28, 1972): 12–13.

53. "Third U.N.C.T.A.D. Opens in Santiago," *PR* 15, no. 16 (Apr. 21, 1972): 13–15; "China's Principled Stand on Relations of International Economy and Trade," report of speech by Chou Hua-min at third UNCTAD plenary session, *PR* 15, no. 17 (Apr. 28, 1972): 11–14; "Resolution on International Trade," *PR* 15, no. 22 (June 2, 1972): 17–18.

54. "Resolution on Permanent Sovereignty over Natural Resources," *PR* 16, no. 19 (May 11, 1973): 19–20.

55. "Discussion on Drafting 'Charter of Economic Rights and Duties of States,'" *PR* 16, no. 33 (Aug. 17, 1973): 12–14.

56. "Premier Chou Greets 4th Conference of Heads of State and Government of Non-Aligned Countries," *PR* 16, no. 37 (Sept. 14, 1973): 6; "GATT in Session," *PR* 16, no. 39 (Sept. 28, 1973): 21; "Chairman of Chinese Delegation Chiao Kuan-hua's Speech," *PR* 16, no. 40 (Oct. 5, 1973): 10–17.

57. "Speech by Teng Hsiao-p'ing, Chief Delegate of the PRC at the UN General Assembly Sixth Special Session," *JMJP*, Apr. 11, 1974, p. 1, in *PR* 17, no. 16 (Apr. 19, 1974): 6–11.

58. "Chinese Delegation Holds Receptions," *JMJP*, Apr. 4, 1974, p. 1.

59. "Third World Countries Advocate Changing Unequal Economic Relations at the Sixth Special Session," *JMJP*, Apr. 17, 1974, p. 6.

60. "Great Victory of the Third World Struggle Against Hegemonism," *JMJP,* May 5, 1974, p. 1, in *PR* 17, no. 19 (May 10, 1974): 11–13.

61. "Huang Hua's Speech at the U.N. Special Session," *CB,* Sept. 17, 1974, p. 54.

62. "Representatives of Third World Countries Demand Implementation of the Declaration and Programme of the Sixth Special Session," *JMJP,* Aug. 26, 1974, p. 6; "The Chinese Government Will Continue to Carry Out Resolutely Chaiman Mao's Revolutionary Line and Policies in Foreign Affairs," speech by Chiao Kuan-hua at UNGA Session of Oct. 5, 1976, in *PR* 19, no. 42 (Oct. 15, 1976): 12–15.

63. "Speech by Chiao Kuan-hua," at the 30th Session of the UN General Assembly, Sept. 26, 1975, *PR* 18, no. 40 (Oct. 3, 1975): 10–17.

64. "13th Session of UN Trade and Development Board," *PR* 16, no. 38 (Sept. 21, 1973): 23.

65. "UN Industrial Development Commission Meetings Open," *JMJP,* May 5, 1974, p. 6.

66. *CTEN* 233 (Mar. 1975): 4.

67. "UN Conference on Law of the Sea Recommended," *PR* 16, no. 44 (Nov. 2, 1973): 13.

68. "Conference on the Law of the Sea," *PR* 17, no. 26 (June 28, 1974): 15–16; "U.N. Conference on the Law of the Sea," *PR* 17, no. 27 (July 5, 1974): 9–11; "Chinese Delegation Leader Chai Shu-fan's Speech," *PR* 17, no. 26 (July 12, 1974): 11–14.

69. "An Chih-yuan Refutes Japanese Representative's Absurd Statement about Tiaoyu Island," *PR* 15, no. 11 (Mar. 17, 1972): 10–11.

70. "Chinese Delegation Leader Chai Shu-fan's Speech."

71. "UN Sea-Bed Committee: The Struggle in Defense of Maritime Rights," *PR* 16, no. 13 (Mar. 30, 1973): 9–11, 12.

72. Li, pp. 143–62.

73. "Sharply Attack U.S.-Soviet Hegemonist's Exploitation and Monopolization of International Sub-Sea Resources," *JMJP,* Sept. 5, 1976, p. 6.

74. "Debate on the Question of Straits for International Navigation," *PR* 17, no. 31 (Aug. 2, 1974): 9–10.

75. "Chinese Delegation Leader Chai Shu-fan's Speech."

76. "China's Stand on the Question of the Human Environment," *PR* 15, no. 24 (June 16, 1972): 5–8, 13.

77. "Chinese Delegation Makes Statement on 'Declaration on Human Environment,' " *PR* 15, no. 25 (June 23, 1972): 8–9.

78. "International Marine Pollution Conference," *PR* 16, no. 46 (Nov. 16, 1973): 22.

79. Mira Wilkins, "The Oil Companies in Perspective," *Daedalus* 104, no. 4 (Fall 1975): 159–78; Robert B. Stobaugh, "The Oil Companies in the Crisis," in *ibid.,* pp. 179–202.

80. Fei Chou, "Moscow's Transnational Corporations Go by the Name 'Joint-Stock Companies,' " *PR* 19, no. 22 (May 28, 1976): 23–24.

Chapter 10

1. See Table 14.1. All statistics for China presented in this chapter were derived from the analysis in the Statistical Profile. Reserve and resource data are from World Energy Conference, *Survey of Energy Resources, 1974; IPE,* 1978, p. 270; Ford Foundation, *Nuclear Power,* p. 81. Production and consumption data were obtained from United Nations, Department of International Economic and Social Affairs, *World Energy Supplies.* Growth-rate and distribution tabulations are the responsibility of the author.

2. *IPE,* 1978, p. 270.

3. I am unaware of any previous public estimate of China's uranium reserves. This figure refers to recoverable U_3O_8 at $30 per kilogram at 1975 prices.

4. Production of U_3O_8 for 1975. Ford Foundation, *Nuclear Power,* p. 81.

5. OECD, *Uranium: Resources, Production, and Demand.*

6. CIA, *China: Energy Balance Projections,* p. 33.

7. Chauncey Starr, "Energy and Societal Development," paper presented to the Institute for Energy Studies seminar series, Stanford University, April 7, 1975, Fig. 7.

8. George Lauriat, "Costly Alternatives for Asia's Gas," *FEER* 101, no. 35 (Sept. 1, 1978): 85–89.

Chapter 11

1. A project is afoot that may provide in-depth research on each energy industry and on energy consumption patterns. It was initiated by a workshop at Stanford University in June 1976 and continued with another workshop at Wingspread, Racine, Wisconsin, in July 1977. Sponsors have included the Social Science Research Council, the Johnson Foundation, and Stanford's U.S.–China Relations Program.

2. CIA, *China: Oil Production Prospects,* p. 11.

3. Russell Spurr, "The Kremlin's Reliance on Blitzkrieg," *FEER* 90, no. 44 (Oct. 31, 1975): 33–34.

4. "Soviet Secrets Take Flight," *FEER* 95, no. 10 (Mar. 11, 1977): 5.

5. Soviet technicians conducted gravimetric and magnetic surveys on the Sungliao Plain in 1956 and seismic surveys in 1957. The first Chinese press report of exploration was in 1959: "Several Thousand Geologists Explore the Sungliao Plain in Search of Crude Oil," *JMJP,* May 6, 1959, p. 5. This article said that exploration began in 1956.

6. In July 1960, 1,390 Soviet technical and support personnel left the Sungliao basin as part of the general departure of Soviet technical personnel from China. Akio Akagi and Morihito Sato, "Taching Oilfield and China's Industrial Technology," *Shizen,* May 1974, pp. 62–73, in *JPRS* 64466 (Apr. 2, 1975): 16–37.

7. Wilfred Burchett, "Chinese Tap Taching Potential," *FEER* 83, no. 2 (Jan. 14, 1974): 45–46; Akagi and Sato, p. 28.

8. "Twelve Glorious Years," *HHS,* Jan. 2–7, 1973, in Ling, pp. 228–41.

9. Editorial in *JMJP,* Jan. 2, 1966, in Ling, pp. 151–53.

10. "Twelve Glorious Years," Jan. 4, 1973, in Ling.

11. Akagi and Sato, "Taching and Industrial Technology," p. 25.

12. "Taching Oilfield Achieves High Standards," *HHS*, Sept. 29, 1969, in *JPRS* 49030 (Oct. 10, 1969): 33–35.

13. Colina MacDougall, "Filling the Gap," *FEER* 44, no. 3 (Apr. 16, 1964): 159–61.

14. Kucho Kudo, "Petroleum Industry Booms at Taching," *Gijutsu Janaru*, Feb. 28, 1969, p. 8, in *JPRS* 47855 (Apr. 18, 1969): 14–21.

15. "Forum of Workers Learning from Taching," *NFCRRS* 144 (Feb. 10, 1966): 28.

16. Steve Charles, "China's Leap Forward," *FEER* 68, no. 17 (Apr. 23, 1970): 46.

17. R. H. Leary, "Mystery Matters," *FEER* 57, no. 8 (Aug. 24, 1967): 390.

18. Party Committee of the Taching General Petrochemical Plant, "Release Latent Forces and Increase Production," *HQ* 254 (Oct. 1972): 48–51, in Ling, pp. 214–26.

19. Kudo, "Petroleum Industry Booms at Taching."

20. Chou En-lai was reported to have criticized the Taching workers sharply for leaving the oilfield. Wang, "The Mineral Industry of Mainland China," *MY*, 1967, vol. IV, p. 201; Colina MacDougall, "The Economic Cost," *FEER* 57, no. 4 (July 27, 1967): 195–99; Colina MacDougall, "Mounting Costs," *FEER* 57, no. 9 (Aug. 31, 1967): 401–2; Colina MacDougall, "Counting the Cost," *FEER* 57, no. 13 (Sept. 28, 1967): 619–21; Colina MacDougall, "Refined Bottleneck," *FEER* 64, no. 19 (May 8, 1969): 349.

21. MacDougall, "Refined Bottleneck."

22. *Ibid.*

23. "Taching Oilfield Achieves High Standards."

24. *Ibid.*

25. Hung Yu, "China's Taching Oilfield Expanded at Top Speed," *ER* 4 (Oct.–Dec. 1974): 30. Taching now includes at least five subfields. See Li Ch'eng-jui, "Talk on Small Industry" (June 13, 1975), to the Rural Small Scale Industries Delegation to the PRC (June 13–July 8, 1975), National Academy of Sciences, Washington D.C., p. 9.

26. "Release Latent Forces and Increase Production."

27. "How China's First Long Pipeline Was Built," *ER* 1 (Jan.–Mar. 1975): 32.

28. "A Modern Deepwater Oil Port—Dairen's New Port Completed Ahead of Schedule," *JMJP*, June 7, 1976, p. 1; "Dairen Constructs a New Harbor with High Speed, High Quality, and an Advanced Technological Standard," *JMJP*, July 22, 1976, p. 1.

29. "Taching Oil Pipeline Reaches Peking," *CR* 24, no. 10 (Oct. 1975): 15–16.

30. Paul Strauss, "Peking: The Drive for Expansion," *FEER* 91, no. 4 (Jan. 23, 1976): 42.

31. Leo Goodstadt, "China: Earthquake Rocks a Key Province," *FEER* 87, no. 9 (Feb. 28, 1975): 35.

32. Peter Weintraub, "Shake-Up for China's Economy," *FEER* 93, no. 33 (Aug. 13, 1976): 44–45.

33. "Peking General Petrochemical Works Takes Class Struggle as Principle, Deeply Criticizing Teng, Achieving New Victories in Anti-Quake Struggle," *JMJP*, Aug. 16, 1976, p. 2.

34. "Dwindling Resources," *FEER* 93, no. 36 (Sept. 3, 1976): 5.

35. By the time of Mao's death, Taching's standing had been eroded to the point that a report on mourning activities at the oilfield was buried among messages from other units. See "Mao Tse-tung's Thought Will Forever Guide the Proletarian Struggle of the Taching Workers," *JMJP*, Sept. 15, 1976, p. 5.

36. "Appointment of Hua as Party's Chairman Confirmed by Peking," *NYT*, Oct. 13, 1976, p. 1; "Mao's Widow, 3 Shanghai Radicals Reported Held for Plotting Coup," *NYT*, Oct. 12, 1977, p. 1.

37. Jen Ping, "A Brilliant Historic Document," *PR* 19, no. 47 (Nov. 19, 1976): 12–14; "Taching Oil Workers Denounce 'Gang of Four,' " *PR* 19, no. 47 (Nov. 19, 1976): 17–18.

38. "Chairman Hua Receives Representatives to Three Learn-from-Taching Conferences," *PR* 19, no. 52 (Dec. 24, 1976): 6; "Party Central Committee Calls for Upsurge in Learning from Taching," *PR* 20, no. 6 (Feb. 4, 1977): 3–4; "Big Campaign Develops Quickly in Capital to Study Taching," *JMJP*, Mar. 11, 1977, p. 1; "Taching Begins 'Three Great Discussions,' and Everyone Condemns the 'Gang of Four,' " *JMJP*, Mar. 26, 1977, p. 1; "National Conference on Learning from Taching in Industry Opens," *PR* 20, no. 18 (Apr. 29, 1977): 3–5; Peter Weintraub, "Taching's Theme Is Growth," *FEER* 96, no. 18 (May 6, 1977): 51–52; "Chairman Hua Inspects Taching," *PR* 20, no. 19 (May 6, 1977): 29.

39. "Chairman Hua Kuo-feng's Speech at the National Conference on Learning from Taching in Industry," *PR* 20, no. 21 (May 20, 1977): 7–14; "Vice-Chairman Yeh Chien-ying's Speech at the National Conference on Learning from Taching in Industry," *PR* 20, no. 21 (May 20, 1977): 15–19; Yu Chiu-li, "Mobilize the Whole Party and the Nation's Working Class and Strive to Build Taching-Type Enterprises Throughout the Country," *PR* 20, no. 22 (May 27, 1977): 5–23.

40. Ross H. Munro, "Production of China's Oilfield at Taching May Have Peaked," *NYT*, Dec. 27, 1976, p. D-2.

41. *USCBR* 3, no. 4 (July–Aug. 1976): 51.

42. CIA, *China: Oil Production Prospects*, p. 9.

43. Akagi and Sato, "Taching Oilfield and Technology," p. 17.

44. *Ibid.*, p. 31.

45. *Ibid.*, p. 29.

46. Hirotada Eto, "Energy Resources of the People's Republic of China," *Japan Science and Technology* 13, no. 1 (1972): 33–48, trans. in *JPRS* 55470 (Mar. 17, 1972): 2.

47. Akagi and Sato, "Taching Oilfield and Technology."

48. "Chinese Oil Discussed," *Internationale Wirtschaft*, Jan. 4, 1972, p. 1; CIA, *China: Oil Production Prospects*, p. 11.

49. Kudo, "Petroleum Industry Booms at Taching"; Colina MacDougall, "Taching Spirit," *FEER* 51, no. 8 (Feb. 24, 1966): 380–81.

50. Meyerhoff, p. 1569; Meyerhoff and Willums, p. 109.

51. For example, Kambara puts Taching "proved plus probable reserves" at 0.4 billion metric tons. See Tatsu Kambara, "The Petroleum Industry in China," *CQ* 60 (Dec. 1974): 711.

52. Ling, p. 56.

53. Colina MacDougall, "A Propaganda Leap," *FEER* 63, no. 12 (Mar. 20, 1969): 529; Colina MacDougall, "Refined Bottleneck"; Steve Charles, "China's Leap Forward."

54. The estimates of Taching's refinery capacity were from the following sources: 1966, Kudo; 1970, Wang, "Mineral Industry," *MY*, 1970, p. 225; 1973, Burchett, "Chinese Tap Taching Potential"; 1976, CIA, *China: Oil Production Prospects,* p. 11.

55. *USCBR* 3, no. 6 (Nov.–Dec. 1976): 43.

56. The three estimates for the number of wells were from the following sources: 1965, Kudo; 1968, Wang, "Mineral Industry," *MY,* 1968, p. 199; 1969, *Internationale Wirtschaft,* 1972; 1976, Meyerhoff and Willums, p. 176.

57. For example, see Ling, p. 130; National Council for U.S.–China Trade, *China's Petroleum Industry,* p. 29; Williams, p. 258.

58. CIA, *China: Oil Production Prospects,* p. 9.

59. For one journalist's despair over conditions at Taching, see Ross H. Munro, "Taching Oilfield, a Place of Endless Grey Desolation," *Globe and Mail,* Toronto, Apr. 6, 1977, p. 10.

60. Estimates regarding the number of oilfield workers at Taching have varied from 40,000 to "several hundreds of thousands." There were probably about 100,000 workers in the early construction phase from 1960 to 1963. The number may then have dropped to less than 50,000. The usual figure given in the mid-1970's was 60,000 oilfield workers and 500,000 people living in the Taching area. See Wang, "Mineral Industry," *MY,* 1967, p. 193; "Visitors' Reports on Takang and Shengli Oil Fields," *China News Summary* 571 (June 18, 1975); Akagi and Sato, "Taching Oilfield and Technology"; Russ H. Munro, "Production of China's Oilfield at Taching May Have Peaked," *NYT,* Dec. 27, 1976, p. D-2; Chiang Shan-hao, "Combining Urban and Rural Life," *PR* 20, no. 22 (May 27, 1977): 24–27, 29.

61. Burchett, "Chinese Tap Taching Potential."

62. "1205 Team Drills Over 127,000 Meters," *PR* 15, no. 4 (Jan. 28, 1972): 8–9.

63. Ch'ing Sheng, "Taching—A New Type of Petroleum Field in China," *Chung Kuo Hsin Wen,* Apr. 7, 1966, pp. 9–10, in *JPRS* 35747, May 25, 1966, pp. 13–17, esp. p. 16.

64. *USCBR* 4, no. 3 (May–June 1977): 45.

65. Ch'ing Sheng, "Taching—A New Type of Petroleum Field." Most of the detail on living conditions at Taching comes from this article. See also Chiang Shan-hao, "Taching Impressions," a four-part series in *PR* 20, nos. 19–22 (May 6–27, 1977).

66. *Ibid.*

67. *Ibid.*

68. *Ibid.*

69. The Taching Oilfield Party Committee was said to have "strengthened its leadership over the enterprise" in 1971. "It timely analyzed and studied the situation throughout the oilfield and in each subordinate unit, improved management, sent cadres to help grassroots units and brought the enthusiasm of the workers and cadres into fuller play." "Taching Oilfield Fulfills 1971 State Plan," *HHS,* Jan. 2, 1972, in Ling, pp. 198–99.

70. Eto, p. 6.

71. *Ibid.,* p. 6.

72. Munro, "Taching Oilfield, a Place of Endless Grey Desolation."

73. Eto, p. 6.

74. "Oil Production Technology," *HHS,* Jan. 2, 1966, in Ling, p. 149.

75. *Ibid.,* p. 150.

76. "Twelve Glorious Years," Jan. 3, 1973.

77. Min Yu, "Taching Oilfield Developed under the Direction of the Thought of Mao Tse-tung," *HQ* 13 (Dec. 6, 1965): 23–28, in *JPRS* 33699 (Jan. 11, 1966): 36–54.

78. *Ibid.*

79. *Ibid.*

80. *Ibid.*

81. "Oil Production Technology."

82. "Twelve Glorious Years," Jan. 6, 1973.

83. *Ibid.*

84. Ling, p. 12.

85. Dr. Necmattin Mungan, in comments to the Workshop on China's Energy Policy, Stanford University, June 2, 1976.

86. *Ibid.*

87. Chang Chun, "How China Developed Her Oil Industry," *CR* 23, no. 10 (Oct. 1974): 2–7.

88. Ling, pp. 129–31.

89. "Release Latent Forces and Increase Production," p. 48.

90. *Ibid.,* p. 50.

91. "Taching Oilfield," *HHS,* Jan. 1, 1966, in Ling, p. 148.

92. "Twelve Glorious Years," Jan. 5, 1973, p. 3.

93. "Production High Tide in Petroleum Stirred by Technical Innovations," *Kung Jen Jih Pao,* Dec. 8, 1965, p. 1, in *JPRS* 33622 (Jan. 10, 1966): 6–8.

94. *Ibid.,* p. 7.

95. *Ibid.,* p. 6.

96. *Ibid.*

97. " 'Iron Worker' Struggles On at Taching," *JMJP,* Nov. 16, 1974, p. 1; Chiang Chan-hao, "Far More Than Oil," *PR* 20, no. 19 (May 6, 1977): 40–45.

98. "Victory of the Self-Reliance Guideline: Our Oil Industry Surpasses the 1973 Plan," *JMJP,* Nov. 24, 1974, p. 1.

Chapter 12

1. Park and Cohen, pp. 118–19; Smil, *China's Energy,* p. 205; CIA, *China: Energy Balance Projections,* p. 29.

2. *ARB* 4, no. 8 (Jan. 31, 1975): 41.

3. Park and Cohen, p. 40.

4. Willums, "China's Offshore Petroleum," p. 13; C. Y. Cheng, U.S. Dept. of Commerce, quoted in Harrison, *China, Oil, and Asia,* p. 24.

5. "Drilling Speeds Up This Year," *PR* 21, no. 40 (Oct. 6, 1978): 20.

6. Harrison, *China, Oil, and Asia,* p. 12; *USCBR* 4, no. 4 (July–Aug. 1977): 13.

7. CIA, *China: Oil Production Prospects,* p. 22.

8. Park and Cohen, pp. 116–17.

9. CIA, *China: Energy Balance Projections,* pp. 11–15.

10. Smil, *China's Energy,* pp. 204–10.

11. "China May Become Major Oil Producer," *NYT,* May 29, 1975, p. 51.

12. Susumu Awanohara, "Japan Gives an Extra Push to Its Trade with China," *FEER* 101, no. 38 (Sept. 22, 1978): 96–97.

13. *Ibid.,* p. 97.

14. CIA, *China: Oil Production Prospects,* p. 7.

15. Meyerhoff and Willums, p. 103.

16. Meyerhoff gave a round estimate in barrels (70 billion bbl). A. A. Meyerhoff, "Petroleum Geology—People's Republic of China," Circum-Pacific Energy and Mineral Resources Conference, Honolulu, Aug. 1, 1978.

17. Harrison attaches a "better than fifty-fifty chance" to this outcome; *China, Oil, and Asia,* pp. 19–20.

18. Susumu Awanohara, "Energy Policy Priority or a Major Bottleneck," *FEER* 98, no. 50 (Dec. 16, 1977): 48–49.

19. "Chairman Hua Kuo-feng's Speech at the National Finance and Trade Conference on Learning from Taching and Tachai," July 7, 1978, *PR* 21, no. 30 (July 28, 1978): 7.

20. Burt Solomon, "U.S., China Set Tentative Agenda in Energy," *Energy Daily* 6, no. 215 (Nov. 7, 1978): 2.

21. *CTR* 16, no. 2 (Feb. 1978): 3.

22. "China Dresses Its Coal for Market," *PNSEA* 9, no. 3 (June 1978): 12–13.

23. "U.S. and Japan in Energy Pact," *NYT,* Nov. 20, 1978, p. D-10.

24. *CTR* 16, no. 4 (Apr. 1978): 1.

25. Susumu Awanohara, "Japan Gives an Extra Push to Its Trade with China," *FEER* 101, no. 38 (Sept. 22, 1978): 97.

26. Susumu Awanohara, "China Finds an Ardent New Suitor in Japan," *FEER* 102, no. 44 (Nov. 3, 1978): 39–40.

27. *Ibid.,* pp. 40–41.

28. William K. Stevens, "U.S. to Get Low-Sulfur Chinese Oil," *NYT,* Nov. 22, 1978, p. D-1.

29. *CTR* 16, no. 10 (Oct. 1978): 8.

30. *PNSEA* 9, no. 6 (Sept. 1978), supplement.

31. Fang Yi, "National Outline Plan for the Development of Science and Technology, Relevant Policies and Measures," Speech to the National Science Conference, Mar. 18, 1978, *PR* 21, no. 14 (Apr. 7, 1978): 6–14, 17.

32. Eduardo Lachica, "China Purchases Nuclear Plants from France,"*AWSJ,* Dec. 6, 1978, p. 3.

33. Solomon, "U.S., China Set Tentative Agenda in Energy," p. 3.

34. "Talk with the American Correspondent Anna Louise Strong," Aug. 1946, *Selected Works of Mao Tse-tung,* vol. 4 (Peking, 1961), p. 100.

35. Mao Tse-tung, "On the Ten Great Relationships," Apr. 25, 1956, *PR* 20, no. 1 (Jan. 1, 1977): 12–13. Jason C. Hu argues that the Chinese showed interest in acquiring atomic weapons as early as 1951 and points out that the establishment of the Sino-Soviet Scientific and Technical Cooperation Commission in October 1954 led to a "scientific and technical assistance" agreement in April 1955 that mentioned the development of "atomic energy for peaceful purposes." The decision to develop atomic weapons may therefore have been earlier than 1955, and the Soviet pledge to supply research reactors and nuclear materials may have antedated the October 1977 agreement. Personal communication from Jason C. Hu, Balliol College, Oxford, Feb. 14, 1979.

36. Halperin, *China and the Bomb,* p. 74.

37. J. R. Nix, "Report on Foreign Travel to China," Theoretical Division, Los Alamos Scientific Laboratory, University of California, Los Alamos, New Mexico, June 1, 1977, mimeo.

38. "China Extracting Uranium from Own Ores," *SCMP* 1539 (May 28, 1957): 1; Bodhan O. Szuprowicz, "China's Trade with Nonmarket Nations," *USCBR* 5, no. 3 (May–June 1978): 29.

39. *Ibid.,* p. 29.

40. Halperin, *China and the Bomb,* pp. 79–80. The original source is a remarkable document that illustrates Chinese acrimony over Soviet arms control negotiations with the United States. The Chinese press printed the full text of the Soviets' note and their response. See "Statement by the Spokesman of the Chinese Government: A Comment on the Soviet Government's Statement of August 3," Aug. 15, 1963, *PR* 6, no. 33 (Aug. 16, 1963): 7–19.

41. Halperin and Perkins, p. 99; "Premier Chou En-lai on World Situation and China's Foreign Policy," *HHS,* Feb. 10, 1978, trans. in *SCMP* 1712 (Feb. 13, 1978): 1.

42. Halperin, *China and the Bomb,* p. 80.

43. *Ibid.,* p. 75.

44. Szuprowicz, "China's Trade," p. 29.

45. *Ibid.,* p. 29.

46. Pollack, pp. 39–40.

47. *Ibid.,* p. 40.

48. Halperin and Perkins, p. 102.

49. *Ibid.,* p. 123. China's original non-first-use pledge was contained in the announcement of its first atomic test. Chou En-lai subsequently cabled all heads

of government, asserting the defensive nature of the Chinese weapon and repeating the non-first-use pledge. See "China Successfully Explodes Its First Atom Bomb," Chinese Government Statement, Oct. 16, 1964, *PR* 7, no. 42 (Oct. 16, 1964): ii–iii; "Premier Chou Cables Government Heads of the World," Oct. 16, 1964, *PR* 7, no. 43 (Oct. 23, 1964): 6.

50. Charles H. Murphy, "China's Place in Nuclear Stakes," *FEER* 67, no. 16 (Apr. 16, 1970): 18.

51. Pollack, p. 53.

52. Chang Wen-yu, "Modernizing the Motherland," *PR* 21, no. 40 (Oct. 6, 1978): 26–27.

53. Nix, "Foreign Travel," pp. 2–4, 6–7, 11.

54. "Device for Thermonuclear Experiments," *CR* 14, no. 7 (July 1975): 22–23.

55. Chinese research on radioactive isotopes dates to the 1950's. See Hu Tsu-hua, "Protection Against Radioactive Materials," *Kohsueh Hsinwen* 34 (1959): 11. For more recent experiments, see "Radioactive Isotopes Utilized," *PR* 16, no. 51 (Dec. 21, 1973): 23; "Various Uses of Radioactive Isotopes," *CP* 351 (Sept. 1977): 30–33.

56. "Exchange of Physicists," *China Exchange Newsletter* 4, no. 5 (Aug. 1977): 4.

57. "Atomic Aid for China," *FEER* 86, no. 39 (Oct. 4, 1974): 5.

58. "Peking Stays Aloof on Power Policy," *FEER* 86, no. 46 (Nov. 22, 1974): 56.

59. *USCBR* 3, no. 1 (Jan.–Feb. 1976): 56.

60. *USCBR* 3, no. 5 (Sept.–Oct. 1976): 58.

61. "Nuclear Link?" *FEER* 94, no. 46 (Nov. 12, 1976): 5; *USCBR* 4, no. 1 (Jan.–Feb. 1977): 55.

62. "Exchange of Nuclear Physicists," *China Exchange Newsletter* 4, no. 5 (Aug. 1977): 4.

63. *USCBR* 4, no. 4 (July–Aug. 1977): 34.

64. *USCBR* 4, no. 5 (Sept.–Oct. 1977): 58.

65. *Ibid.*, p. 58; *USCBR* 4, no. 6 (Nov.–Dec. 1977): 57.

66. Personal communication from Dr. Mark Goldstein, Environment and Policy Institute, East–West Center, Honolulu.

67. Report in the *Hongkong Standard,* Dec. 27, 1973, cited in "Proposed China-Hongkong Nuclear Power Reactor," *ARB* 3, no. 8 (Jan. 31, 1974): 2391.

68. Huang Sheng-nien, "On Atomic Energy," *Kohsueh Shihyen* 12 (Dec. 1974): 13–15, trans. in *JPRS* 65241 (July 16, 1975): 14–22.

69. *CTR* 16, no. 9 (Sept. 1978): 11.

70. *USCBR* 4, no. 5 (Sept.–Oct. 1977): 50; Weintraub, p. 53.

71. "China Successfully Conducts a New Hydrogen Bomb Test," *PR* 19, no. 48 (Nov. 26, 1976): 10; "Peking Announces Test of 22nd Device," *NYT,* Sept. 18, 1977, p. 5.

72. Pollack, p. 53; International Institute for Strategic Studies, *The Military Balance.*

73. For example, "The Soviet Union and U.S. Sign the So-Called Treaty on Peaceful Underground Nuclear Explosions," *JMJP*, May 31, 1976, p. 6; "What Does the Failure of the Moscow Talks Signify?" *PR* 20, no. 16 (Apr. 15, 1977): 20–21.

74. Huang Hua, "Soviet-U.S. Rivalry for Hegemony Is Irreversible," speech at the meeting of the U.N. General Assembly First Committee, Nov. 8, 1976, *PR* 19, no. 47 (Nov. 19, 1976): 28–29.

75. Clough et al., p. 63.

76. "New Tsars' Deeds Don't Match Words," *PR* 20, no. 6 (Feb. 4, 1977): 27; "Renewed Demand for Soviet Signing of Additional Protocol II," *PR* 20, no. 19 (May 6, 1977): 47.

77. "4-Point National Salvation Proposal," *PR* 20, no. 6 (Feb. 4, 1977): 29.

78. "Brezhnev Snubbed," *PR* 20, no. 5 (Jan. 28, 1977): 30.

79. Hua Kuo-feng, "Unite and Strive to Build a Modern, Powerful Socialist Country!" Report to the Fifth National People's Congress, Feb. 26, 1978, *PR* 21, no. 10 (Mar. 10, 1978): 27.

80. Fang Yi, "Outline Plan for the Development of Science and Technology, Relevant Policies and Measures," speech to the National Science Conference, Mar. 18, 1978, *PR* 21, no. 14 (Apr. 7, 1978): 6–14, 17.

81. "Project for High-Energy Accelerator," *PR* 22, no. 23 (June 9, 1978): 3–4.

82. Solomon, "U.S., China Set Tentative Agenda," p. 3.

83. "More Magazines and Newspapers," *PR* 21, no. 31 (Aug. 4, 1978): 26; "Atomic Energy for Farm Use," *PR* 21, no. 31 (Aug. 4, 1978): 26.

84. *USCBR* 5, no. 2 (Mar.–Apr. 1978): 45.

85. "Electric Power Delegation Departs West Germany for France," *FBIS*, Feb. 2, 1978, p. A-7; "Atomic Power Study Team Ends Visit to France," *FBIS*, Mar. 9, 1978, p. A-17.

86. "PRC Nuclear Experts Begin Cooperation Talks in Rome," *FBIS*, Mar. 15, 1978, p. A-22; *PNSEA* 9, no. 1 (Apr. 1978): 5.

87. *PNSEA* 9, no. 5 (Aug. 1978): 6.

88. *USCBR* 5, no. 3 (May–June 1978): 61; "China May Use French Technology to Build Nuclear Power Plant," *Hsingtao Jihpao*, May 7, 1978, p. 8.

89. *PNSEA* 9, no. 3 (June 1978): 7; *CTR* 16, no. 8 (Aug. 1978): 10.

90. *USCBR* 5, no. 3 (May–June 1978): 41.

91. *PNSEA* 9, no. 3 (June 1978): 7.

92. Richard Burt, "White House Endorses French Sale of a Nuclear Power Plant to China," *NYT*, Nov. 25, 1978, p. 1.

93. Eduardo Lachica, "China Purchases Nuclear Plants from France," *AWSJ*, Dec. 6, 1978, p. 3.

94. Andreas Freund, "French Get Trade Pact with China," *NYT*, Dec. 5, 1978, p. D-1.

95. Frank Ching, "China Signs 10-Year Pact with Sweden Calling for a Sharp Increase in Trade," *AWSJ*, Dec. 8, 1978, p. 3.

96. "British Power Group Meets China Officials," *AWSJ*, Dec. 9, 1978, p. 5.

97. Colina MacDougall, "Chinese Mission to Discuss Australian Uranium Purchases," *Financial Times*, Feb. 8, 1978, p. 3; *USCBR* 5, no. 2 (Mar.–Apr. 1978): 57.

98. "Tokyo Weekly Hints Sino-Japanese Uranium Trade Pact in Offing," *Nuclear Fuel*, Oct. 39, 1978, p. 2.

99. Wang, *The People's Republic of China*, p. 27.

100. *Ibid.*

101. Weintraub, p. 53.

102. U.S. Department of Energy, *Uranium Industry*, p. 83.

103. OECD, *Uranium*, p. 23.

104. Power Reactor and Nuclear Fuel Development Corp., *Development of Power Reactors and Nuclear Fuels: Japan* (Tokyo, 1978), p. 25.

105. Szuprowicz, "Electronics in China," p. 33.

106. Hsin Ping, "Utilization of Nuclear Energy and the Struggle Against Hegemony," *PR* 21, no. 15 (Apr. 14, 1978): 12.

107. Salamat Ali, "Pakistan's Atomic Dilemma," *FEER* 101, no. 36 (Sept. 8, 1978): 18–19.

108. David Fishlock, "Peking Offers Pakistan Nuclear Technology," *Financial Times*, Aug. 15, 1978; *PNSEA* 9, no. 6 (Sept. 1978): 6.

109. "Brazil Deaf to U.S. Resentment over Nuclear Pact with FRG," *FBIS*, Feb. 2, 1978, p. A-15.

110. *CTR* 16, no. 7 (July 1978): 8.

111. Unidentified news clipping and personal communication from Jason C. Hu, Balliol College, Oxford, Aug. 15, 1978.

112. Liu Mei-yun, "Taiwan: Big Chips on the Atomic Square," *PNSEA* 9, no. 6 (Sept. 1978): 17.

113. Michael Richardson, "Hanoi's Nuclear Hand-Me-Down," *FEER* 100, no. 21 (May 26, 1978): 8.

114. Nayan Chanda, "Vietnam Prepares for the Worst," *FEER* 100, no. 23 (June 9, 1978): 10.

115. Huang Hua, "Superpower Disarmament Fraud Exposed," speech to the UNGA Special Session on Disarmament, May 29, 1978, *PR* 21, no. 22 (June 2, 1978): 5–13.

116. "The Struggle Goes On," *PR* 21, no. 28 (July 14, 1978): 29.

Chapter 13

1. PRC, State Statistical Bureau, *Ten Great Years*.

2. Wu and Ling, *Economic Development and Energy Resources*.

3. Darmstadter et al.; U.N. Dept. of Economic and Social Affairs, *World Energy Supplies;* World Energy Conference, *Survey of Energy Resources*.

4. Eckstein, *Growth and Trade*.

5. Edgar Snow, "Talks with Chou En-lai: The Open Door," *New Republic* 164, no. 4 (Mar. 27, 1971): 20.

6. The SITC publications used for this work were four studies of the U.N. Dept. of Economic and Social Affairs: *Standard International Trade Classification,*

1961–; *Trade Commodity Statistics,* 1952–; *World Trade Annual,* 1963–; and *Supplement to the World Trade Annual,* 1963–. Also used were U.N. Economic Commission for Africa, *African Trade Statistics,* 1962–; and U.N. Economic Commission for Asia and the Far East, *Foreign Trade Statistics of Asia and the Far East,* 1962–.

7. Harvard Institute of Economic Research, *Time Series Processor,* Version 2.7.

8. Pugh, *DYNAMO II User's Manual.*

9. Dennis L. Meadows et al., *Dynamics of Growth in a Finite World;* Donnella H. Meadows et al., *The Limits to Growth.*

10. Harrison, "China: The Next Oil Giant," pp. 3–27; Cohen, pp. 28–49.

11. U.N. Dept. of Economic and Social Affairs, *World Energy Supplies,* no. 20 (1977): xx.

12. Wu and Ling, p. 108.

13. Elliot, pp. 10, 130.

14. CIA, *China: Energy Balance Projections,* Appendix A; Williams, Table 3, note 1; Smil, *China's Energy,* p. 139; CIA, *China: The Coal Industry,* p. 13, Table 5, note 1.

15. *WES* 20 (1977): xiv; U.S. CIA, *China: Oil Production Prospects,* pp. 11, 13.

16. Darmstadter et al., p. 3.

Chapter 14

1. These four categories are consistent with, but not identical to, the categories used in *Survey of Energy Resources,* 1974, which have been based on more than two decades of energy reserves data compilation experience. The general reserves categories employed by *SER* are proved recoverable, probable recoverable, ultimate recoverable, and total resources.

2. *SER,* 1974, p. 52.

3. Ikonnikov, p. 155. See also CIA, *China: The Coal Industry,* pp. 2–3. The CIA figures confirm the general figure of 1.5 trillion tons of total coal reserves, although the CIA rates only 50 percent of this recoverable. The breakdown of coal reserves by region and type also vary slightly between the CIA and Ikonnikov analyses. But both were ultimately drawn from Soviet data.

4. *Ibid.,* p. 101.

5. K. P. Wang in comments to the Workshop on China's Energy Policy, Stanford University, June 2, 1976.

6. Wang, *PRC: New Industrial Power,* p. 11.

7. Ikonnikov, p. 98.

8. *Ibid.,* pp. 105–54.

9. "Rich Deposits of Bituminous Shale," *PR* 21, no. 51 (Dec. 22, 1978): 39.

10. The view that China's oilfield development pattern was determined by distance and transportation factors is common. See, for example, Kambara, p. 713; Smil, *China's Energy: Achievements, Problems, and Prospects,* pp. 35–38. For a detailed analysis by oilfield, including aerial maps, see CIA, *China: Oil Production Prospects.*

11. *IPE,* 1975, p. 196.

12. Professor Necmattin Mungan, a Canadian petroleum engineer who has visited Taching, indicates that the early water-injection system used at Taching was a "line drive" system, which maximizes the rate of oil extraction (the crude oil production growth rate) at the cost of a lower ultimate recovery rate. Newly developed formations have the "nine spot" water injection system, which maximizes the ultimate recovery rate at the cost of a somewhat lower extraction rate. Comments at the Workshop on China's Energy Policy, Stanford University, June 3, 1976.

13. "K'o-la-mai Increases Crude Oil Production," *JMJP,* Dec. 16, 1960, p. 3, in *JPRS* 8172 (Apr. 27, 1961): 36–38; "Oil Production in the Karamai Region," *Ta Kung Pao,* Mar. 9, 1961, p. 3, in *JPRS* 8550 (July 12, 1961): 25–27; "A Glimpse of Karamai–the Oil City," *Chung Kuo Hsin Wen,* Mar. 16, 1963, pp. 11–12, in *JPRS* 19691 (June 14, 1963): 45–47; "Karamai Oilfield Production," *Ta Kung Pao,* Apr. 27, 1966, pp. 1–2, in *JPRS* 37566: 39–43; "Karamai Oilfield's Revolution in Production Grows Daily," *JMJP,* Dec. 23, 1974, p. 1.

14. "A Visit to Takang Oilfield," *China Reconstructs* 13, no. 10 (Oct. 1974): 8–14; "Visitors' Reports on Takang and Shengli Oil Fields," *China News Summary* 571 (June 18, 1975); "Newly Built Takang Oilfield," *PR* 17, no. 21 (May 24, 1974): 15–17.

15. Takang's 1975 crude oil production growth rate was 16 percent. "Takang, Studying Taching, Has Five Years of Great Development," *JMJP,* Jan. 6, 1976, p. 2.

16. Shengli's 1975 crude oil production growth rate was 34 percent. "Shengli Strides Forward with Great Force," *JMJP,* Jan. 6, 1976, p. 2.

17. Dr. Maurice Terman in comments to the Workshop on China's Energy Policy, Stanford University, June 2, 1976.

18. *Ibid.*

19. *IPE,* 1975, p. 196; Ling, p. 56.

20. Williams, p. 253; Kambara, p. 710; *IPE,* 1975.

21. "Tsaidam—A Rising Industrial Base," *PR* 14, no. 48 (Nov. 26, 1971): 9–11; "Mainland China's Oil Growth-Rate Dips Sharply in 1972," *OGJ* 71, no. 9 (Feb. 26, 1973): 28–29.

22. "Yumen Oilfield Holds Fast to Production," *JMJP,* Dec. 18, 1960, p. 2; "Yumen Oilfields Take Winter Precautions," *Ta Kung Pao,* Sept. 5, 1962, p. 1, in *JPRS* 15766 (Oct. 18, 1962): 24–25; "Yumen Petroleum Output Up," *JMJP,* Aug. 2, 1969, p. 4, in *JPRS* 48741 (Sept. 3, 1969): 18.

23. For a history of the Szechwan oilfields, see Weller, pp. 1430–49.

24. "Jenchiu—A New High-Yielding Oilfield," *PR* 21, no. 41 (Oct. 13, 1978): 3–4.

25. "Gas for Industrial and Home Use," *PR* 17, no. 27 (July 5, 1974): 31; Meyerhoff and Willums, "Petroleum Geology."

26. Compare Meyerhoff, p. 1574, and Meyerhoff and Willums, p. 103.

27. "Szechwan Expands Natural Gas Output," *NCNA,* Jan. 15, 1975, in *FBIS,* Jan. 16, 1975, pp. J1–J2. See also "Tapping Natural Gas in Szechuan," *PR* 16, no. 47 (Nov. 23, 1973): 23; "Szechwan Province Speeds Up Development of Gas Fields," *ER* 1 (Jan.–Mar. 1975): 34.

28. Dr. Norman Pruvost, Workshop on China's Energy Policy, Stanford University, June 2, 1976.

29. For example, "Search for Gas," *FEER* 28, no. 1 (Jan. 7, 1960): 19; "Shanghai Develops Water, Gas, and Transportation Services," Radio Shanghai, Sept. 29, 1972, in *JPRS* 57476 (Nov. 10, 1972): 31–32.

30. Ling, p. 25.

31. Meyerhoff, p. 1579.

32. Interview with K. Yamamoto, Bridgestone Liquified Gas Co., Feb. 27, 1975, quoted by Norman Pruvost in comments to the Workshop on China's Energy Policy, Stanford University, June 2, 1976.

33. K. P. Wang in comments to Workshop on China's Energy Policy, Stanford University, June 2, 1976.

34. World Energy.Conference, *Survey of Energy Resources*, 1974, p. 173.

35. *WES* 21 (1978): 168.

36. Smil, "Exploiting China's Hydro Potential," esp. p. 19.

37. *SER*, 1974, p. 187.

38. Smil, "Exploiting China's Hydro Potential," p. 20. For a detailed analysis of the constraints operating on China's hydropower development, see Smil, *China's Energy*, chap. 3.

39. "Power Industry in 1971," *PR* 15, no. 2 (Jan. 14, 1972): 23; "Water Conservancy and Power Industry," *PR* 15, no. 50 (Dec. 15, 1972): 15–16; "Large Numbers of Hydropower Stations," *PR* 16, no. 47 (Nov. 23, 1973): 22; "China's Power Industry Surpasses 1973 Plan," *ER* 1 (Jan.–Mar. 1974): 7; Tang Chung-nan, of the Ministry of Power and Water Conservancy, in comments to the Rural Small Scale Industries Delegation to the PRC, June 14, 1975.

40. "Building Power Plants in Shansi," *PR* 15, no. 40 (Oct. 6, 1972): 31; "Szechuan's Small Hydroelectric Stations," *PR* 15, no. 46 (Nov. 17, 1972): 22; "For More Electricity," *PR* 16, no. 12 (Mar. 23, 1973): 4; "A Commune Along the Red Flag Canal," *CR* 13, no. 8 (Aug. 1974): 14–19, 38; "Chingchung County Speeds Up Construction of Small Hydropower Stations," *JMJP*, May 22, 1974, p. 4; "The Rural Masses of Sinkiang Speed Construction of Small Hydropower Stations," *JMJP*, May 25, 1974, p. 3; "Every Drop of Water Utilized," *CR* 14, no. 12 (Dec. 1975): 24–27.

41. "Power Industry Makes Big Headway," *PR* 17, no. 8 (Jan. 22, 1974): 23; "Kwangtung's Fengtsuen County Hydropower Station Completed," *JMJP*, May 19, 1974, p. 4; "China's Biggest Hydro-Power Station," *Pr* 18, no. 7 (Feb. 14, 1975): 11–12, 21; "China's Biggest Hydro-Electric Power Station Goes into Operation," *ER* 1 (Jan.–Mar. 1975): 36; "Construction of the Liuchiahsia Hydropower Station Completed" and "Success in Renovating Sanmen Gorge Project," *CP*, Apr. 1975, pp. 6–7; visit to the Yellow River Exhibit Hall, Chengchow, Honan, by the Rural Small Scale Industries Delegation to the PRC, June 28, 1975; "Anhwei's Ch'entsuen Hydropower Station on the Ch'ingyi River Victoriously Constructed," *JMJP*, Aug. 23, 1975, p. 1; "Large Hydropower Station in Anhwei Province," *PR* 18, no. 40 (Oct. 3, 1975): 30.

42. For an exhaustive list of power plants in China with a greater than 30 MW capacity, see Clarke, "China's Electric Power Industry," *USCBR,* pp. 30–31.

43. Hsieh, p. 20.

44. *Ibid.*

45. "China Extracting Uranium from Own Ores," *NCNA,* May 23, 1957, in *SCMP* 1539 (May 28, 1957): 1; *MY,* 1964, p. 1166.

46. Weintraub, p. 53.

47. *MY,* 1969, p. 207; Szuprowicz, "China's Trade with Nonmarket Nations," p. 29.

48. *MY,* 1965, p. 1107.

49. Hsieh, pp. 3–6.

50. "China to Have Atomic Reactor This Year," *NCNA,* May 23, 1957, in *SCMP* 1539 (May 28, 1957): 1; Carin, p. 48; Hsieh, pp. 20–21.

51. CIA, *China: Energy Balance Projections,* p. 4, note 2.

52. Alexander Tseng, "China's Scientific and Technological Development," lecture at Stanford University, Feb. 24, 1973.

53. Huang, "On Atomic Energy." Text of the translation corrected by the author for grammatical and spelling errors. First quote from p. 14.

54. *Ibid.,* p. 18.

55. Professors Shen Yuen-ron and Tien Chang-lin (University of California, Berkeley), in comments during a lecture on "Physics and Engineering in the PRC," Center for East Asian Studies, Stanford University, Nov. 1, 1974.

56. "Protection Against Radioactive Materials," *Ko Hsueh Hsin Wen* 34 (1959): 11.

57. Hsieh, p. 48.

58. Quoted in *ibid.,* pp. 58–59.

59. "Radioactive Isotopes Utilized," *PR* 16, no. 51 (Dec. 21, 1973): 23.

60. Hua Kuo-feng, "Unite and Strive to Build a Modern, Powerful Socialist Country!," Report on the Work of the Government delivered at the First Session of the Fifth National People's Congress on Feb. 26, 1978, *PR* 21, no. 10 (Mar. 10, 1978): 7–40.

61. Fang Yi, "Outline National Plan for the Development of Science and Technology, Relevant Policies and Measures," speech to the National Science Conference, Mar. 18, 1978, *PR* 21, no. 14 (Apr. 7, 1978): 6–14, 17.

62. Eduardo Lachica, "China Purchases Nuclear Plants from France," *AWSJ,* Dec. 6, 1978, p. 3.

63. "Project for High Energy Accelerator," *PR* 22, no. 23 (June 9, 1978): 3–4.

64. "Solar-Energy Boiler on Tibetan Plateau," *PR* 15, no. 37 (Sept. 15, 1972): 23; "Solar Energy Used in Lhasa," *PR* 19, no. 8 (Feb. 20, 1976): 23.

65. "Solar Energy Stoves," *PR* 17, no. 40 (Oct. 4, 1974): 38.

66. "Peking Using Solar Energy on an Experimental Basis," *Boston Globe,* Aug. 31, 1975, AFP Hong Kong.

67. "60 Research Projects Completed by Tientsin U.," summary of translations from *Ta Kung Pao,* Dec. 18–24, 1975. Translation source unknown.

68. Geothermal Power Generation Experimental Group, Kwangtung Province, "An Experimental Geothermal Power Station," *Ko Hsueh Shih Yen* 6 (1971): 36–37, in *JPRS* 60673 (Dec. 3, 1973): 1–7.

69. Ko Tze-yuan, "Tibet's Abundant Geothermal Resources," *Ta Kung Pao,* Apr. 8, 1976.

70. Notes of the Rural Small Scale Industries Delegation to the PRC, July 8, 1975; Shen, p. 1.

71. Dr. Vaclav Smil in comments to the Workshop on China's Energy Policy, Stanford University, June 2, 1976. Smil also estimated the energy input from human labor and animal labor in China, although such estimates are far more precarious than for firewood and crop residues. Smil's estimates were based on inferences from the number of rural families, the total amount of agricultural production and resulting crop wastes, and so on.

72. "Cooking with Garbage," *Friendship Journal,* Jan. 1976, p. 7.

73. *Ibid.*

74. Smil, "Energy Solution in China," p. 28.

75. "Shanghai Marsh Gas Use," Radio Shanghai, Dec. 30, 1971, in *JPRS* 55269 (Feb. 24, 1972): 21; "Marsh Gas Used in Rural China," *PR* 16, no. 2 (Jan. 12, 1973): 22, "Szechwan Marsh Gas," Radio Peking, Jan. 3, 1974, in *JPRS* 61103 (Jan. 30, 1974): 25.

76. "Device for Thermonuclear Experiments," *CR* 14, no. 7 (July 1975): 22–23.

77. "Laser Research and Application," *PR* 16, no. 52 (Dec. 28, 1973): 19.

Chapter 15

1. G. E. Pearson, "China's Mineral Wealth a Key to Industrial Power," *FEER* 28, no. 16 (Apr. 21, 1960): 839–41; G. E. Pearson, "Minerals in China," *FEER* 36, no. 10 (June 7, 1962): 513–15; Colina MacDougall, "Black Diamonds," *FEER* 41, no. 4 (July 25, 1963): 212.

2. Andrew Nathan, "China's Lagging Coal Mines," *FEER* 42, no. 7 (Nov. 14, 1963): 354–56; Colina MacDougall, "China's Industrial Upsurge," *FEER* 49, no. 10 (Sept. 2, 1965): 421–23.

3. CIA, *China: The Coal Industry.*

4. "Raise the Level of Mechanization for Rapid Development of the Coal Industry," *HQ,* Jan. 5, 1978, pp. 30–33, trans. in *FBIS,* Feb. 1, 1978, p. E-7.

5. "Annual Targets Met Ahead of Schedule," *PR* 21, no. 50 (Dec. 15, 1978): 5.

6. "1978 Grain and Coal Output," *PR* 22, no. 2 (Jan. 12, 1979): 7–8.

7. "January Coal Production Increases 24 Percent," *FBIS,* Jan. 31, 1978, p. E-26; "First Quarter Production Plans Overfulfilled," *PR* 21, no. 14 (Apr. 7, 1978): 4–5; "Upswing in Industrial Production," *PR* 21, no. 17 (Apr. 28, 1978): 3; Jen Min, "Learn-from-Taching Movement Surges On," *PR* 21, no. 28 (July 14, 1978): 13–17.

8. CIA, National Foreign Assessment Center, *Handbook of Economic Statistics, 1978,* p. 91.

9. "Machine-Building in High Gear," *PR* 21, no. 40 (Oct. 6, 1978): 19.

10. Liao Chien, "Development of China's Coal Mining Industry," *Jinmin Chukoku (People's China)* 10 (1964): 86–88, trans. in *JPRS* 28048 (Dec. 30, 1964): 14–17; Shelton, *MY,* 1974, p. 262. Shelton lists another seven major combines in excess of 10 mmt/year capacity, five in the 5–10 mmt/year range, and another 50 in the 1–5 mmt/year range. A number of new mines in the medium range have been added since 1974, and in late 1978 and early 1979 Peking contracted with foreign firms for the construction of several additional underground and open-cast mines in the large 20–30 mmt/year range. The new mines will not be in service until the mid-1980's.

11. Based on estimates from *MY* and Table 17.1.

12. Dean, "Energy in the PRC," p. 37.

13. *Ibid.,* p. 36.

14. G. E. Pearson, "China's Coal Washery," *FEER* 23, no. 5 (Feb. 4, 1960): 152.

15. "Quarterly Chronicle and Documentation," *CQ* 5 (Jan.–Mar. 1961): 162.

16. Solomon, pp. 1–3.

17. Important book-length studies of China's petroleum industry include Cheng, *China's Petroleum Industry,* and Ling, *The Petroleum Industry.* Shorter studies include Hardy, "Chinese Oil"; Kambara, "The Petroleum Industry in China"; Koide, "China's Crude Oil Production"; National Council for U.S.–China Trade, *China's Petroleum Industry;* and Williams, "The Chinese Petroleum Industry."

18. CIA, *China: Oil Production Prospects.*

19. Jen Min, "Learn-from-Taching Movement Surges On," *PR* 21, no. 28 (July 14, 1978): 15.

20. "Drilling Speed Up This Year," *PR* 21, no. 40 (Oct. 6, 1978): 20.

21. Ross H. Munro, "Production of China's Oilfield at Taching May Have Peaked," *NYT,* Dec. 27, 1976, p. D-2. Production at Taching may be leveling out as of the late 1970's, but new oilfields in other parts of the country continue to add production capacity at 8–10 mmt per year.

22. Author's estimate, based on earlier estimates in Kambara, p. 710; *MY,* 1971, p. 234; and Cheng, p. 32.

23. Kambara, p. 702; Meyerhoff, pp. 1579–80; Williams, p. 252.

24. Meyerhoff, "Chinese Oil Discussed," p. 1578; National Council for U.S.–China Trade, *China's Petroleum Industry,* p. 43; Cheng, p. 101. The National Council based its report of the fictitious pipeline on Cheng, and Cheng based his report on the Taiwan source.

25. The date of construction of the Tiehling–Dairen pipeline has not been clearly established. See Meyerhoff, "Chinese Oil Discussed," p. 1578.

26. "How China's First Pipeline Was Built," *ER,* Jan.–Mar. 1975, p. 32; "Taching Oil Pipeline Reaches Peking," *CR* 24, no. 10 (Oct. 1975): 15–16.

27. Ling, p. 79.

28. CIA, *China: Oil Production Prospects,* p. 25.

29. *Ibid.*

30. Ling, p. 77.

31. Williams, p. 347; Smil, "Energy in China," p. 60, note 16.

32. George Lauriat, "Containers at Whampoa?" *FEER* 95, no. 6 (Feb. 11, 1977): 45–46.

33. George Lauriat, "China's Emerging Tanker Fleet," *PNSEA* 7, no. 7 (Oct. 1976): 11–14; U.S. CIA, National Foreign Assessment Center, *Handbook of Economic Statistics, 1978,* p. 163.

34. National Council for U.S.–China Trade, China's Petroleum Industry, pp. 47–48; CIA, *China: Oil Production Prospects,* p. 26; "A Modern Deepwater Oil Port—Dairen's New Port Completed Ahead of Schedule," *JMJP,* June 7, 1976, p. 1.

35. CIA, *China: Oil Production Prospects,* p. 26.

36. Smil, *China's Energy.*

37. For example, Stephanie Green, "Shengli Journal," *USCBR* 5, no. 1 (Jan.–Feb. 1978): 31–35.

38. Kambara, p. 712.

39. CIA, *China: Oil Production Prospects,* p. 26.

40. Kochu Kudo, "Petroleum Industry Booms at Ta-ch'ing," *Gijutsu Janaru,* Feb. 28, 1969, p. 8, in *JPRS* 47855 (Apr. 18, 1969): 14–21.

41. George Lauriat, "Awaiting the Rush of Chinese Crude, If Any," *FEER* 98, no. 40 (Oct. 7, 1977): 67–69.

42. "Kao-chou Petroleum Plant Produces Diesel Oil," *JMJP,* Dec. 16, 1960, p. 3, in *JPRS* 8172 (Apr. 27, 1961): 39–41.

43. "Lanchow Oil Refinery Converted into a Large-Scale Chinese Style Refining Base," *JMJP,* Apr. 25, 1960, p. 2, in *JPRS* 35261 (Apr. 29, 1966): 23–31.

44. Kambara, p. 712.

45. Alva Lewis Erisman, "China: Agriculture in the 1970's," U.S. Joint Economic Committee of Congress, *China: A Reassessment,* Table 2, p. 333.

46. Development Center Research Division, Organization for Economic Cooperation and Development, *Supply and Demand Prospects for Fertilizers in Developing Countries* (Paris, 1968), pp. 174–91. The production of nitrogen in Brazil also required 0.36 billion kwh/mmt electric power input.

47. "Peking's New Petrochemical Complex," *PR* 14, no. 5 (Apr. 14, 1972): 4; Shih Hua-chien, "Construction Design of the Peking Main Petrochemical Plant Discussed," *Chien Chu Hsueh Pao* 1 (1973): 14–19, in *JPRS* 64523: 1–21.

48. "The Petroleum Chemical Industry Is a Good Example for the Diversified Utilization of Resources," *JMJP,* Mar 1, 1966, p. 5, in *JPRS* 34755 (Mar. 28, 1966): 7–10; "Petroleum Refining and the Petrochemical Industry," in Taching Oilfield Writing Group, *Petroleum Refining and Petrochemicals,* chaps. 3 and 5, in *JPRS* 65034 (June 18, 1975): 4–30.

49. Chi Wen-hu, "The Shanghai Petroleum Machine Parts Factory Improves Quality of Products," *Kung Jen Jih Pao,* Feb. 5, 1961, p. 1, in *JPRS* 8345 (May 25, 1961): 65; Hu Kuang, "Development of Chinese Petroleum Machinery Industry," *Chung Kuo Hsin Wen,* Sept. 28, 1965, p. 17, in *JPRS* 33122 (Dec. 1, 1965): 40–42.

50. Prior to 1954, China's only petroleum machinery industry was the ma-

chine shop of the Shanghai Refinery. "Medium and Small-Scale Plants Producing Petroleum Machinery in Quantity," *Chieh Fang Jih Pao,* Oct. 11, 1964, p. 1; *JPRS* 28642 (Feb. 4, 1965): 18–20.

51. Hu Kuang, "Development of China's Petroleum Industry."

52. *MY,* 1965, p. 1120.

53. Heymann, p. 719. See also Chapter 22.

54. Smil, "Energy in China," p. 61.

55. Szuprowicz, "China's Trade with Nonmarket Nations," p. 27.

56. Lynn Yamashita, "A Return for Their Money," *FEER* 93, no. 31 (July 30, 1976): 45–46.

57. "Szechuan Expands Natural Gas Output," *FBIS,* Jan. 16, 1975, p. J-1; "Szechuan Province Speeds Up Development of Gas Fields," *ER,* Jan.–Mar. 1975, p. 34. The same quote is in both sources.

58. U.N. Dept. of Economic and Social Affairs, *Statistical Yearbook,* 1951, p. 139; *MY* 2 (1953): 334.

59. U.S. Dept. of the Interior, Bureau of Mines, "World Natural Gas, 1975," Table 1.

60. "Tapping Natural Gas in Szechuan," *PR* 16, no. 47 (Nov. 23, 1973): 23.

61. "Shanghai Water, Gas, and Transportation Services," Radio Shanghai, Sept. 29, 1972, in *JPRS* 57476 (Nov. 10, 1972): 31–32.

62. "Gas for Industrial and Home Use," *PR* 17, no. 27 (July 5, 1974): 31.

63. Smil, "Energy in China," p. 64 note 33.

64. Dr. Norman Pruvost, quoting interview with K. Yamamoto, Bridgestone Liquified Gas Co. (Feb. 27, 1975), in comments to Workshop on China's Energy Policy, June 2, 1976.

65. *USCBR* 3, no. 1 (Jan.–Feb. 1976): 53.

66. "Gas for Industrial and Home Use," *PR* 17, no. 276 (July 5, 1974): 31.

67. Wu Cheng-chun, "The Development of the Gas Industry," *JMJP,* Nov. 14, 1964, p. 5, in *JPRS* 27876 (Dec. 16, 1964): 22–25.

68. For a rare recent article see Clarke, "China's Electric Power Industry," *USCBR.* A valuable synopsis of the hydropower industry may be found in Smil, *China's Energy,* chap 3.

69. Chi Ti, "Industrial Modernization," *PR* 21, no. 26 (June 30, 1978): 7–9.

70. Ashton, p. 307, Table 5, note 2.

71. Smil, "Exploiting China's Hydro Potential," p. 25, Smil, "Energy in China," pp. 62–63; Smil, *China's Energy,* p. 90; CIA, *China: Energy Balance Projections,* p. 29.

72. "300,000 KW Water Turbine Generating Set," *PR* 17, no. 40 (Oct. 4, 1974): 37; "Domestically Produced 300,000 KW Water-Cooled Generator Commissioned," *JMJP,* June 16, 1976, p. 1.

73. "Every Drop of Water Utilized," *CR* 14, no. 12 (Dec. 1975): 24–27.

74. "Hydroelectric Power," *Chung Kuo Hsin Wen,* Oct. 22, 1975, p. 4, in *JPRS* 66987 (Mar. 18, 1976): 34.

75. For example, see "Chingchong County Rapidly Develops Hydropower," *JMJP,* May 22, 1974, p. 4.

76. *WES* 20 (1977), Table 20.

77. Wu and Ling, Appendix A.

78. Ashton, p. 310; Dean, "Energy in the PRC," p. 46.

79. Ashton, p. 309.

80. Clarke, "China's Electric Power Industry," *Chinese Economy Post-Mao*, p. 416.

81. Clarke, "China's Electric Power Industry," *USCBR*, pp. 28–29.

82. Dean, "Energy in the PRC," p. 50.

83. "PRC Expressed Interest in Energy Project with FRG," *Handelsblatt* (Düsseldorf), Sept. 8, 1975, p. 4, in *JPRS* 65903 (Oct. 10, 1973): 1.

84. Author's observation based on trade returns from partner countries.

85. "Power Output Rises, but Less Coal Used," *HHS* (Mukden), May 10, 1949, in *NCNA Daily News Release* 10 (May 11, 1949): 3.

86. Ashton, p. 310.

87. "National Symposium in Coal and Electricity," Radio Chengtu, Oct. 26, 1965, in *NFCRRS* 130 (Oct. 28, 1965): 45.

88. Smil, "Energy in China," p. 68.

89. Wu and Ling, p. 107.

90. The "heat rate" refers to the amount of coal required per kilowatt-hour of electric power produced. Data on heat rates are extremely rare in the Chinese literature. One plant that reported its average heat rate in 1965 was producing at a coal requirement of 0.457 kgce/kwh, which is under the projected series, but probably refers to a model unit. "Power Station Saves Coal," Radio Chengtu, July 10, 1965, in *NFCRRS* 115 (July 15, 1965): 40.

91. "Water Conservancy and Power Industry," *PR* 15, no. 50 (Dec. 15, 1972): 15–16; "Power Industry Makes Big Headway," *PR* 17, no. 8 (Feb. 22, 1974): 23.

92. "Two New Hydropower Stations," *PR* 20, no. 43 (Oct. 21, 1977): 31–32.

93. Chi Ti, "Industrial Modernization," *PR* 21, no. 26 (June 30, 1978): 7–9.

94. Dean, "Energy in the PRC," p. 44.

95. John W. Lewis, in comments to Workshop on China's Energy Policy, Stanford University, June 2, 1976.

96. Smil, "Exploiting China's Hydro Potential," p. 26.

97. "China Completes Its First 330 Kv. Extra-High Tension Line," *ER* 1 (Jan.–Mar. 1975): 37.

98. Reichers, pp. 86–111.

99. Szuprowicz, p. 33.

100. "New Electronic Computer," *PR* 16, no. 41 (Oct. 12, 1973): 22.

101. Szuprowicz, p. 22.

102. "More Radios and Television Sets," *PR* 16, no. 41 (Oct. 12, 1973): 22–23.

103. Reichers, pp. 87–89.

104. Szuprowicz, p. 39.

Chapter 16

1. Smil, *China's Energy*, pp. 67–73.

2. *Ibid.*, p. 72.

Chapter 17

1. U.S. Dept. of the Interior, Bureau of Mines, *Minerals Yearbook;* Usack and Egan, Table 2, p. 271. Usack and Egan in turn based their crude steel production figures on CIA data. See CIA, National Foreign Assessment Center, Handbook of Economic Statistics, 1978, p. 102. Peking recently announced figures for steel production for 1949 (0.158 mmt), 1958 (8 mmt), 1960 (18.7 mmt), 1977 (23.71 mmt), and 1978 (31.7 mmt). These figures generally confirm the CIA estimates of crude steel output and inferentially confirm Usack and Egan's series for China's coke requirement. See "Steel Output Tops 30 Million Tons," *PR* 21, no. 51 (Dec. 22, 1978): 20–22.

2. Smil argues on the basis of Usack and Egan's estimates that China's coking industry requires one-fourth the national raw coal consumption, which would have placed the coal requirement for coke at 125 million tons of raw coal in 1977. See Smil, "China's Energetics," p. 356. I do not accept this argument. Usack and Egan argue that the Chinese coking industry is very wasteful, requiring as much as 5 tons of raw coal for production of a single ton of metallurgical coke. However, this argument is undocumented except for reference to figures supplied for 1958 (the height of the Great Leap Forward) by Wu and Ling in their 1963 book. In estimating the coal requirement for coke production in China, I use the average U.N. conversion figure of 1.54 metric tons of standard coal per metric ton of coke. This tabulates to about 2 metric tons of Chinese raw coal required to produce one metric ton of metallurgical coke.

3. Clarke, "China's Electric Power Industry," *USCBR,* p. 28.

4. "Szechuan Expands Natural Gas Output," *NCNA,* Jan. 15, 1975, in *FBIS,* Jan. 16, 1975, p. J-1.

5. Kuo Chi, "Foreign Trade: Why the 'Gang of Four' Created Confusion," *PR* 20, no. 9 (Feb. 25, 1977): 17.

6. My estimates of China's thermal efficiency factors are supported by Clarke, "China's Electric Power Industry," *USCBR,* p. 28.

7. *WES* 20 (1977), Table 20.

8. Clarke, "China's Electric Power Industry," *USCBR,* p. 26.

9. *Ibid.,* p. 34; Smil, *China's Energy,* p. 72.

10. Clarke, "China's Electric Power Industry," *USCBR,* p. 34.

11. *WES* 20 (1977), Table 19.

12. Smil, *China's Energy,* p. 39.

13. *Ibid.*

14. Wu and Ling, pp. 69, 98; Smil, *China's Energy,* p. 150; CIA, *China: Oil Production Prospects,* Table D-1, note 1, p. 26.

15. Alva Lewis Erisman, "China: Agriculture in the 1970's," U.S. Joint Economic Committee of Congress, *China: A Reassessment,* pp. 334–35.

16. "Actively Strengthen Construction and Management," *JMJP,* Mar. 19, 1977, p. 4; Jen Min, "Learn-from-Taching Movement Surges On," *PR* 21, no. 28 (July 14, 1978): 14.

17. Jen Min, "Learn-from-Taching Movement Surges On," p. 14.

Chapter 18

1. "Bunkers" are fuel oil sales to international shipping and transport. No bunkers data are available for China. See *WES* 18 (1975), pp. viii–ix.

2. *WES* 20 (1977), Table 2.

3. Rawski, "China and Japan"; Wu and Ling, pp. 69, 90, 98; CIA, *China: Energy Balance Projections,* p. 33.

4. CIA, *China: Energy Balance Projections,* p. 33.

5. Field, "Civilian Industrial Production," p. 150.

6. *WES* 20 (1977), pp. 28–29.

7. *WES* 20 (1977), Tables 2 and 21.

Chapter 19

1. GNP estimates from 1949 through 1975 are from CIA, *PRC: Handbook of Economic Indicators.* GNP estimates for 1976 to 1978 were the author's, based on an assumed growth rate of 3 percent in 1976 and 5 percent in 1977 and 1978. All GNP figures are in 1975 U.S. dollars.

2. Banister, "Fertility and Mortality." See also Judith Banister, *China's Pattern of Population Growth* (Stanford, Calif., forthcoming).

3. *WES* 20 (1977), Table 2.

4. All energy commodity price information refers to 1975 and was taken from the notes of the Rural Small Scale Industries Delegation to the People's Republic of China, which visited the PRC from June 13 to July 8, 1975. Professor Thomas G. Rawski compiled the energy commodity price statistics gathered by the delegation at different enterprises during the course of the visit.

Chapter 20

1. Williams, p. 262; Ling, Table 6, p. 32; Meyerhoff, p. 1569.

2. CIA, *China: Oil Production Prospects,* p. 26.

3. *USCBR* 2, no. 1 (Jan.–Feb. 1975): 56, *USCBR* 2, no. 5 (Sept.–Oct. 1975): 57.

4. *China Trade Report* 16, no. 4 (Apr. 1978): 1–2.

5. Phijit Chong, "China-Japan Coal Talks," *CTR* 16, no. 2 (Feb. 1978): 4.

6. Williams, p. 262; National Council for U.S.–China Trade, *China's Petroleum Industry,* p. 50; *USCBR* 5, no. 5 (Sept.–Oct. 1978): 38.

7. The data are available as follows: (Philippines) *CTR* 16, no. 5 (May 1978): 10; (Iran) Irfan Parviz, "Iran Selling Goods Worth $30 Million to China," *Tehran Journal* 24, no. 6979 (Sept. 1, 1977): 2; (Brazil) *USCBR* 5, no. 5 (Sept.–Oct. 1978): 38.

8. Park and Cohen, p. 43; Smil, "Energy in China," p. 73; Williams, p. 239.

9. Peter Weintraub, "Limits on China's Oil Exports," *FEER* 95, no. 3 (Jan. 21, 1977): 100–103.

10. Cohen and Park, p. 126; *CTR* 16, no. 1 (Jan. 1978): 4–5; *PNSEA* 9, no. 5 (Aug. 1978), supplement.

11. *CTR* 16, no. 4 (Apr. 1978): 1–2.

12. China's highly visible Vice-Premier, Teng Hsiao-p'ing, recently placed

China's total oil resources at 400 billion barrels (55 bmt), a figure that would put China on a par with the Middle East. Exaggerations of this sort are intended for the ears of potential oil importers. *CTR* 16, no. 4 (Apr. 1978): 6.

13. *USCBR* 2, no. 2 (Mar.–Apr. 1975): 55.

14. *USCBR* 3, no. 1 (Jan.–Feb. 1976): 53.

15. Henri Hymans, "Japan Eyes Peking's Liquid Gas," *FEER* 91, no. 8 (Feb. 20, 1976): 37–38.

16. Cranfield, p. 24; *CIA, China: Oil Production Prospects,* pp. 5, 11, 13.

17. *CTR* 16, no. 6 (June 1978): 11.

Chapter 22

1. Heymann, pp. 716–29; National Council for U.S.–China Trade, *China's Petroleum Industry,* pp. 98–115.

2. Lauriat, "China's Emerging Tanker Fleet."

3. The contract stipulation was relaxed for tankers.

4. Hua Kuo-feng, "Unite and Strive to Build a Modern, Powerful Socialist Country," report to the First Session of the Fifth National People's Congress, Feb. 26, 1978, *PR* 21, no. 10 (Mar. 10, 1978): 19–26.

5. CIA, *China: The Coal Industry,* p. 3.

6. Ikonnikov, pp. 105–14.

Chapter 23

1. Various publications by M. King Hubbert, including "Energy Resources," in John Yannacone, ed., *Energy Crisis: Danger and Opportunity* (St. Paul, Minn., 1974), pp. 43–150; "Energy Resources of the Earth," in *Energy and Power,* special issue of *Scientific American,* Sept. 1971, republished under the same title (San Francisco, 1971), pp. 30–40; *U.S. Energy Resources. A Review as of 1972* (U.S. Senate, Committee on Interior and Insular Affairs, Washington, D.C., 1974).

2. Hubbert, *U.S. Energy Resources,* Fig. 18, p. 55.

3. T. M. Garland, M. Carrales, and J. S. Conway, "Assessment of U.S. Petroleum Supply with Varying Drilling Efforts," U.S. Dept. of the Interior, Bureau of Mines Information Circular 8634 (Washington, D.C., 1974); Richard P. Sheldon, "Petroleum Exploration Frontiers," paper presented to the American Association of Petroleum Geologists, Pacific Section Meetings, Bakersfield, Calif., Apr. 21, 1977, esp. Fig. 4.

4. This general methodology was used in the Club of Rome studies (Donnella H. Meadows et al., *The Limits to Growth*) conducted at the Massachusetts Institute of Technology. There is a good analogy between information constraints at the global level and information constraints facing the foreign analyst examining the Chinese energy production system. The equations used in the natural resources sector of the M.I.T. model were highly suggestive for the Chinese case. See Dennis L. Meadows et al., pp. 371–408, esp. p. 405.

5. Data on the Venezuelan petroleum industry were taken from Franklin Tugwell, *The Politics of Oil in Venezuela* (Stanford, Calif., 1975), pp. 132, 182–83.

6. Data on Venezuelan petroleum resources were taken from Tugwell,

ibid., and from Richard Nehring, *Giant Oil Fields and World Oil Resources,* prepared for the CIA (Santa Monica, Calif., June 1978), esp. p. 32. The Nehring estimates exclude future discoveries, which I estimated at 25 bbbl. See Chapter 24, note 8, for sources on U.S. oil and gas reserves and for a breakdown of reserve and resource estimates for Venezuela and the United States.

7. The equation describing the line of regression is: growth rate equals 0.3 times the fraction of the remaining reserves minus 20. R-squared ran around 0.6, depending on the data subset.

8. Hubbert, *U.S. Energy Resources,* Fig. 27, p. 77.

9. M.A. Adelman, "Is the Oil Shortage Real? Oil Companies as OPEC Tax-Collectors," *Foreign Policy,* Winter, 1972–73, pp. 69–107; M. A. Adelman, *The World Petroleum Market* (Baltimore, 1972).

10. China's rate of industrial growth averaged 13 percent per year from 1949 to 1974, 22 percent during the 1950's, just 5 percent during the 1960's, and 8–10 percent in the early 1970's. Field, "Civilian Industrial Production," p. 150.

11. Documented in numerous studies. See Darmstadter et al., p. 32, for one of the best-known formulations. The fixed nature of the energy/GNP relationship has recently been challenged by some authors on the basis of deviant cases. See Lee Schipper and Allan J. Lichtenberg, "Efficient Energy Use and Well-Being: The Swedish Example," *Science* 194, no. 4269 (Dec. 3, 1976): 1001–16.

12. Energy/GNP elasticity is defined as the ratio of energy consumption growth rates to GNP growth rates, averaged over time. For application of this method to projection of China's energy balance, see Kambara, p. 716; Smil, "Energy in China," p. 80; CIA, *China: Energy Balance Projections,* p. 13.

13. Judith Banister, "Fertility and Mortality," pp. 515–16.

14. *Ibid.,* pp. 520–21; John Aird, "Population Estimates and Projections, 1953–2000: China—Model 2," Foreign Demographic Division, Bureau of Economic Analysis, U.S. Dept. of Commerce, April 1976 projections.

Chapter 24

1. Meyerhoff and Willums, p. 103.

2. Chi Ti, "Industrial Modernization," *PR* 21, no. 26 (June 30, 1978): 7.

3. See, for example, Japanese sources cited by Harrison in *China, Oil, and Asia,* p. 12, note 6.

4. National Council for U.S.–China Trade, as quoted in Chapter 15, note 20, and indicated in Table 14.2.

5. *WES* 20 (1977), Table 20.

6. Banister, pp. 515–16, 520–21; John Aird, "Population Estimates and Projections, 1953–2000: China–Model 2," Foreign Demographic Division, Bureau of Economic Analysis, U.S. Dept. of Commerce, April 1976 projections.

7. In 1975, Saudi Arabia was the world's largest offshore oil producer at 120 million tons, followed by Venezuela at 110 million tons and the United States at 70 million tons. Under the median projection I would expect China to reach 50 million tons of offshore production in the late 1980's. *WES* 20 (1977), Table 6.

8. The exact estimates for U.S. oil and gas resources were: (1) crude oil—past production (1975) 106 billion barrels, current reserves 61 bbbl, projected discoveries 82 bbbl; (2) natural gas—past production 481 trillion cubic feet, current reserves 439 tcf, projected discoveries 450 tcf. Betty M. Miller et al., "Geological Estimates of Undiscovered Recoverable Oil and Gas Resources in the United States," Geological Survey Circular 725, U.S. Dept. of the Interior, Geological Survey (Washington, D.C., 1975).

9. *WES* 20 (1977), Table 6.

Bibliography

Introductory Note

This bibliography is intended as a research tool for those pursuing depth analysis of China's energy policies and energy development. It includes English-language materials, statistical sources, and government documents that might be of use in that research. It includes occasional general references on international energy problems but only those general books and articles that are cited repeatedly in the text. It excludes the hundreds of individual articles from the Chinese press and other mass media used as documentation throughout the book. The reader will note occasional entries in the bibliography, marked with an asterisk (*), that were obtained too late for inclusion in the text or footnotes, but which may be of value for further research on the subject. The author would appreciate notification of any works of note on China's energy policy or energy development that have escaped his attention. Entries are in simple alphabetical order by author, or by title when no author is given.

Albers, John B. *Summary Petroleum and Selected Mineral Statistics for 120 Countries, Including Offshore Areas,* U.S. Geological Survey, Professional Paper no. 817. Washington, D.C., 1973.

Ashbrook, Arthur G. "China: Economic Overview, 1975," *China: A Reassessment of the Economy.* U.S. Joint Economic Committee of Congress, Washington, D.C., July 10, 1975, pp. 20–51.

Ashton, John. "Development of Electric Energy Resources in Communist China," *An Economic Profile of Mainland China,* vol. 1. U.S. Joint Economic Committee of Congress, Washington, D.C., 1967, pp. 297–316.

Audridge, Larry. "Mainland China Striving to Boost Crude Exports," *Oil and Gas Journal* 73, no. 1 (Jan. 6, 1975): 26–28.

Banister, Judith. "Current Fertility and Mortality in the People's Republic of China." Ph.D. dissertation, Food Research Institute, Stanford University, August 1977.

*Bartke, Wolfgang. *Oil in the People's Republic of China: Industry, Structure, Production, Exports.* Hamburg, West Germany, 1977.

Bosum, W., E. G. Kind, and J. H. Koo. "Aeromagnetic Survey of Offshore Areas Adjoining the Korean Peninsula," *CCOP Technical Bulletin* 4 (June 1971): 1–23.

Bosum, W., et al. "Aeromagnetic Survey of Offshore Taiwan," *CCOP Technical Bulletin* 3 (May 1970): 1–34.

Bowman, J. D. "Petroleum Developments in Far East in 1973," *American Association of Petroleum Geologists Bulletin* 58, no. 10 (Oct. 1974): 2124–56.

Brazil, Ministerio da Fazenda, Secretaria da Receita Federal, Centro de Informações, Econômico-Fiscais. *Comércio Exterior do Brasil* (annual).

Caldwell, R. D. "Petroleum Developments in Far East in 1974," *American Association of Petroleum Geologists Bulletin* 59, no. 10 (Oct. 1975): 1977–2010.

Carin, Robert. *Power Industry in Communist China.* Union Research Institute publication, Hong Kong, 1969.

Ceylon (Sri Lanka), H.M. Customs Bureau. *Ceylon Customs Returns.* Colombo (annual).

Chan, Leslie W. *The Taching Oilfield: A Maoist Model for Economic Development.* Canberra, Australia, 1974.

Chang Kuo-sin. "Situation Report on China's Oil Production," *Chinese Viewpoint Newsletter* 3, nos. 4–6 (Feb. 3–23, 1974).

Cheng Chu-yuan. *China's Petroleum Industry: Output Growth and Export Potential.* New York, 1976.

Chin Yun-shan. "Initial Study of the Relief and Bottom Sediment of the Continental Shelf of the East China Sea," *Haiyang yu Huchao* 5, no. 1 (Feb. 1963): 71–85, trans. in *JPRS* 50252 (Apr. 7, 1970): 12–36.

"China and Oil—What to Expect," *China Briefing Backgrounder,* Nov. 22, 1974, pp. 1–3.

CIA, *see under* United States.

Clarke, William W. "China's Electric Power Industry," *China Business Review* 4, no. 5 (Sept.–Oct. 1977): 23–37.

———. "China's Electric Power Industry," *Chinese Economy Post-Mao.* U.S. Joint Economic Committee of Congress, Washington, D.C., Nov. 9, 1978, pp. 403–35.

———. "China's Steel: The Key Link," *U.S.–China Business Review* 2, no. 4 (July–Aug. 1975): 27–40.

Clough, Ralph N., et al. *The United States, China, and Arms Control.* Washington, D.C., 1975.

Cohen, Jerome Alan, and Choon-ho Park. "China's Oil Policy," in Shao-chuan Leng, ed., *Post-Mao China and U.S.–China Trade* (Charlottesville, Va., 1977).

Colombia, Departmento Administrivo Nacional de Estadistica. *Anuário de Comércio Exterior* (annual). Bogotá.

Committee of Concerned Asian Scholars. *China! Inside the People's Republic.* New York, 1972.

Connell, Horton R. "China's Petroleum Industry—An Enigma," *American Association of Petroleum Geologists Bulletin* 58, no. 10 (Oct. 1974): 2157–72.

Cranfield, John. "Mainland China Gearing Up to Boost Oil Exports," *Oil and Gas Journal* 73, no. 32 (Aug. 11, 1975): 21–24.

Daily, James W. "Hydropower: A Mirror of Self-Reliance," *Mechanical Engineering* 97, no. 5 (May 1975): 32–33.

Dalton, Howard W. "Petroleum Developments in Far East in 1967," *American Association of Petroleum Geologists Bulletin* 52, no. 8 (Aug. 1968): 1574–91.

———. "Petroleum Developments in Far East in 1968," *American Association of Petroleum Geologists Bulletin* 53, no. 8 (Aug. 1969): 1789–1807.

Darmstadter, Joel, Perry D. Teitelbaum, and Jaroslav G. Polach. *Energy in the World Economy: A Statistical Review of Trends in Output, Trade, and Consumption Since 1925.* Baltimore, 1971.

Dean, Genevieve C. "Energy in the People's Republic of China," *Energy Policy* 2, no. 1 (Mar. 1974): 33–54.

———. "Science, Technology, and Development: China as a 'Case Study,'" *China Quarterly* 51 (July–Sept. 1972): 520–34.

Donnithorne, Audrey. "China's Cellular Economy: Some Trends Since the Cultural Revolution," *China Quarterly* 52 (Oct.–Dec. 1972): 605–19.

———. *China's Economic System.* London, 1967.

Eckstein, Alexander. *Communist China's Economic Growth and Foreign Trade.* New York, 1966.

Ecuador, Ministerio de Finanzes, Oficina Nacional de Presupuesto, Departamento de Estadísticas Fiscales. *Anuário de Comércio Exterior* (annual).

Elliot, Iain F. *The Soviet Energy Balance: Natural Gas, Other Fossil Fuels, and Alternate Power Sources.* New York, 1974.

Emery, K. O., and Zvi Ben-Avraham. "Structure and Stratigraphy of the China Basin," *CCOP Technical Bulletin* 6 (July 1972): 117–40.

Emery, K. O., and Hiroshi Niino. "Stratigraphy and Petroleum Prospects of Korea Strait and the East China Sea," *CCOP Technical Bulletin* 1 (June 1968): 13–27.

Emery, K. O., et al. "Geological Structure and Some Water Characteristics of the East China Sea and the Yellow Sea," *CCOP Technical Bulletin* 2 (1969): 3–43.

Energy-Economics Institute of Japan (Nihon Energi Keizai Kenkyujo). *The Present Situation of the Oil Industry in China* (Chugoku Sekiyu Sanyo no Genjo). Naigai Jijo, Kaisetsu no. 43, Tokyo, May 31, 1976. In Japanese.

*Esposito, Bruce. *The Chinese Petroleum Industry: Myth and Reality.* U.S. Department of State, Foreign Area Research Paper 28177. Washington, D.C., 1977.

Eto, Hiratada. "Energy Resources of the People's Republic of China," *Japan Science and Technology* 13, no. 1 (1972): 33–48, trans. in *JPRS* 55470 (Mar. 17, 1972): 2–10.

Field, Robert Michael. "Chinese Communist Industrial Production," *An Economic Profile of Communist China.* U.S. Joint Economic Committee of Congress, vol. 1, Washington, D.C., 1967, pp. 269–93.

———. "Civilian Industrial Production in the People's Republic of China, 1949–74," *China: A Reassessment of the Economy.* U.S. Joint Economic Committee of Congress, Washington, D.C., July 10, 1975, pp. 146–74.

Fingar, Thomas, and David Bachman. "China's Energy Policies and Resource Development," report of a workshop conducted by the Stanford U.S.–China Relations Program, Stanford, Calif., June 1976.

Ford Foundation, Nuclear Energy Policy Study Group. *Nuclear Power: Issues and Choices.* Cambridge, Mass., 1977.

Gardner, Frank J. "Chinese Oil Flow Up, but Much Larger Gains Needed," *Oil and Gas Journal* 69, no. 13 (Dec. 13, 1971): 35–39.

*Green, Stephanie R. "Taching/Pohai Journal," *China Business Review* 5, no. 6 (Nov.–Dec. 1978): 10–20.

Halperin, Morton H. *China and the Bomb.* New York, 1965.

———. "The Perspective from China and Japan," in Mason Willrich and John B. Rhinelander, eds., *SALT: The Moscow Agreements and Beyond* (New York, 1974), pp. 209–22.

Halperin, Morton H., and Dwight H. Perkins. *Communist China and Arms Control.* New York, 1965.

*Hardy, Randall W. *China's Oil Future: A Case of Modest Expectations.* Boulder, Colo., July 1978.

———. "Chinese Oil: Development Prospects and Potential Impact," mimeographed paper from the Center for Strategic and International Studies, Georgetown University, Nov. 1976.

Harrison, Selig S. *China, Oil, and Asia: Conflict Ahead?* New York, 1977.

———. "China: The Next Oil Giant," *Foreign Policy* 20 (Fall 1975): 3–49.

Harvard Institute of Economic Research. *TSP: Time Series Processor.* Technical Paper no. 12. Cambridge, Mass., July 1975.

Heymann, Hans. "Acquisition and Diffusion of Technology in China," *China: A Reassessment of the Economy.* U.S. Joint Economic Committee of Congress, Washington, D.C., July 10, 1975, pp. 678–729.

Hong Kong, Census and Statistics Department. *Hong Kong Trade Statistics* (monthly and annual). Hong Kong.

Hsiao, Gene T. "Prospects for a New Sino-Japanese Relationship," *China Quarterly* 60 (Oct.–Dec. 1974): 720–49.

———. "The Sino-Japanese Rapprochement: A Relationship of Ambivalence," *China Quarterly* 57 (Jan.–Mar. 1974): 101–23.

Hsieh, Alice Langley. *Communist China's Strategy in the Nuclear Era.* Englewood Cliffs, N.J., 1962.

Huang Shen-nien. "On Atomic Energy," *K'o Hsueh Shih Yen* 12 (Dec. 1974): 13–15, trans. in *JPRS* 65241 (July 16, 1975): 14–22.

Hudson, Geoffrey. "Japanese Attitudes and Policies Towards China in 1973," *China Quarterly* 56 (Oct.–Dec. 1973): 700–707.

Humphrey, Wilson. "Petroleum Developments in Far East in 1969," *American Association of Petroleum Geologists Bulletin* 54, no. 8 (Aug. 1970): 1551–66.

———. "Petroleum Developments in Far East in 1970," *American Association of Petroleum Geologists Bulletin* 55, no. 9 (Sept. 1971): 1634–56.

HUNTEC, Ltd. (Toronto, Canada). "Report on the Offshore Geophysical Survey in the Pohang Area, Republic of Korea," *CCOP Technical Bulletin* 1 (June 1968): 1–12.

Ikonnikov, A. B. *Mineral Resources of China.* Geological Society of America, Microform Publication no. 2. Boulder, Colo., 1975.

India, Department of Commercial Intelligence and Statistics. *Monthly Statistics of the Foreign Trade of India* (annual). Calcutta, India.

International Institute for Strategic Studies. *The Military Balance* (annual). London.

Iraq, Ministry of Planning, Central Statistical Organization, Department of General Trade Statistics. *Annual Foreign Trade Statistics.* Baghdad, Iraq.

Ishiwada, Yasufumi, and Katsuro Ogawa. "Petroleum Geology of Offshore Areas Around the Japanese Islands," *CCOP Technical Bulletin* 10 (Dec. 1976): 23–34.

Jansen, Marius B. *Japan and China: From War to Peace, 1894–1972.* Chicago, 1975.

Japan, Ministry of Finance. *Japan Exports and Imports* (monthly and annual). Tokyo.

Kambara, Tatsu. "The Petroleum Industry in China," *China Quarterly* 60 (Dec. 1974): 699–719.

Katili, John A. *Mineral Resources Assessment in East-Asian Offshore Areas; a Unique Cooperation Between Advanced and Developing Countries, Government Agencies, and Universities.* Indonesia, Ministry of Mines and Energy, Jakarta, n.d.

Kato, Shuichi. *The Japan-China Phenomenon: Conflict or Compatibility?* Trans. by David Chibbett. New York, 1975.

Kennett, W. E. "Petroleum Developments in Far East in 1972," *American Association of Petroleum Geologists Bulletin* 57, no. 10 (Oct. 1973): 2085–2108.

Klingman, Charles L. "The Mineral Industry of the People's Republic of China," *Minerals Yearbook: International Area Reports*. U.S. Department of the Interior, Bureau of Mines, Washington, D.C., 1971 and 1972.

Koide, Yoshio. "China's Crude Oil Production," *Pacific Community* 5, no. 3 (Apr. 1974): 463–70.

Kudo, Kochu. "Petroleum Industry Booms at Taching," *Gijutsu Janaru*, Feb. 28, 1969, p. 8, trans. in *JPRS* 47855 (Apr. 18, 1969): 14–21.

Kuwait, Planning Board, Central Office of Statistics. *Yearly Bulletin of Foreign Trade Statistics*.

Lauriat, George. "China's Emerging Tanker Fleet," *Petroleum News: Southeast Asia* 7, no. 7 (Oct. 1976): 11–14.

Lee Chae-jin. *Japan Faces China: Political and Economic Relations in the Post-War Era*. Baltimore, 1976.

Li, Victor H. "China and Offshore Oil: The Tiao-yu Tai Dispute," *Stanford Journal of International Studies* 10 (Spring 1975): 143–63. Also in Bryant Garth, ed., *China's Changing Role in the World Economy* (New York, 1975), pp. 143–63.

Ling, H.C. *The Petroleum Industry of the People's Republic of China*. Stanford, Calif., 1975.

Ludlow, Nicholas. "China's Oil," *U.S.–China Business Review* 1, no. 1 (Jan.–Feb. 1974): 21–28.

Mainguy, M. "Regional Geology and Petroleum Prospects of the Marine Shelves of Eastern Asia," *CCOP Technical Bulletin* 3 (May 1970): 91–107.

Makrakis, Michael S. *Energy: Demand, Conservation, and Institutional Problems*. Cambridge, Mass., 1974.

Malaysia, Department of Statistics. *Peninsular Malaysia Annual Statistics of External Trade*. Kuala Lumpur.

*McGarry, Michael G., and Jill Stainforth, eds. *Compost, Fertilizer, and Biogas from Human and Farm Wastes in the People's Republic of China*. Translation of Chinese documents published by the International Development Research Centre, Ottawa, 1978.

Meadows, Dennis L., et al. *Dynamics of Growth in a Finite World*. Cambridge, Mass., 1974.

Meadows, Donnella H., Dennis L. Meadows, Jorgen Randers, and William W. Behrens. *The Limits to Growth: A Report for the Club of Rome's Project on the Predicament of Mankind*. New York, 1972.

Meng, Chao-yi. "Geological Concepts Relating to the Petroleum Prospects of Taiwan Strait," *CCOP Technical Bulletin* 1 (June 1968): 143–53.

Mexico, Secretaría de Industria y Comercio, Dirección General de Estadístico. *Anuario Estadístico del Comercio Exterior de los Estados Unidos Mexicanos* (annual).

Meyerhoff, A. A. "Developments in Mainland China, 1949–1968," *American Association of Petroleum Geologists Bulletin* 54, no. 8 (Aug. 1970): 1567–80.

Meyerhoff, A. A., and J.-O. Willums. "Petroleum Geology and Industry of the People's Republic of China," *CCOP Technical Bulletin* 10 (Dec. 1976): 103–215.

Mikdashi, Zuhayr. *The Community of Oil Exporting Countries: A Study in Governmental Cooperation.* London, 1972.

National Coal Association. *World Coal Trade* (annual). Washington, D.C.

National Council for U.S.–China Trade. *China's Petroleum Industry.* Special Report 16. Washington, D.C., June 1976.

National Petroleum Council. *Impact of Oil Exports from the Soviet Bloc.* Washington, D.C., 1962.

"The Oil Crisis in Perspective," *Daedalus,* special issue, 104, no. 4 (Fall 1975).

Organization for Economic Cooperation and Development. *Uranium: Resources, Production, and Demand.* Joint Report by the OECD Nuclear Energy Agency and the International Atomic Energy Agency. Paris, 1977.

*Otsuka Masanobu. "China's Energy Economy and Foreign Trade," *Monthly Report of Chinese Economic Research.* Japan External Trade Organization, Tokyo, 1975.

Pakistan, Ministry of Finance, Planning, and Development, Statistical Division. *Foreign Trade Statistics of Pakistan* (quarterly and annual). Karachi.

Park Choon-ho. "Oil Under Troubled Waters: The Northeast Sea-Bed Controversy," *Harvard International Law Journal* 14, no. 2 (Spring 1973): 212–60.

———. "The South China Sea Dispute: Who Owns the Islands and the Natural Resources?" *Ocean Development and International Law Journal* 5, no. 1 (1978): 27–59. Also in *Harvard Law School Studies in East Asian Law,* China no. 26. Cambridge, Mass., 1978.

Park Choon-ho and Jerome Alan Cohen. "The Politics of China's Oil Weapon," *Foreign Policy* 20 (Fall 1975): 28–49.

Parke, M. L., K. O. Emery, Raymond Szymankiewicz, and L.M. Reynolds. "Structural Framework of the Continental Margin in the South China Sea," *CCOP Technical Bulletin* 4 (June 1971): 103–41.

People's Republic of China, State Statistical Bureau. *Ten Great Years.* Peking, 1960.

Petroleum Publishing Company. *International Petroleum Encyclopedia* (annual). Tulsa, Okla.

Philippines, Bureau of Mines, Mineral Fuels Division. "A Review of Oil Exploration and Stratigraphy of Sedimentary Basins in the Philippines," *CCOP Technical Bulletin* 10 (Dec. 1976): 55–102.

Poland, Statystyka Polski Glowny Urzad Statystyczny. *Rocznick Statystyczny Handlu Zagranicznego* (annual). Warsaw.

Pollack, Jonathan D. "China as a Nuclear Power," in William H. Overholt, ed., *Asia's Nuclear Future* (Boulder, Colo., 1977), pp. 35–65.

Pugh, Alexander L. *DYNAMO II User's Manual*, 4th ed. Cambridge, Mass., 1973.

Rawski, Thomas G. "China and Japan in the World Energy Economy," in Edward W. Erickson and Leonard Waverman, eds., *The Energy Question: An International Failure of Policy*, vol. 1 (Toronto, 1974), pp. 101–19.

———. "Recent Trends in the Chinese Economy," *China Quarterly* 53 (Jan.–Mar. 1973): 1–33.

Reichers, Philip D. "The Electronics Industry in China," *People's Republic of China: An Economic Assessment.* U.S. Joint Economic Committee of Congress, Washington, D.C., 1972, pp. 86–111.

Richman, Barry M. *Industrial Society in Communist China.* New York, 1969.

Romania, Ministerul Comertului Exterior. *Comertul Exterior al Republicii Socialiste Romania: Culegere de Date Statistice* (annual).

Scheidecker, William R. "Petroleum Developments in Far East in 1975," *American Association of Petroleum Geologists Bulletin* 60, no. 10 (Oct. 1976): 1908–46.

———. "Petroleum Developments in Far East in 1976," *American Association of Petroleum Geologists Bulletin* 61, no. 10 (Oct. 1977): 1832–79.

Scott, R. W. "Oil and Gas in China," *World Oil* 187, nos. 6–7 (Nov.–Dec. 1978).

Shelton, John E. "The Mineral Industry of the People's Republic of China," *Minerals Yearbook: International Area Reports.* U.S. Department of the Interior, Bureau of Mines, Washington, D.C., 1973 and 1974.

Shen, Richard T. "Transcription of Notes from the Water Resources Delegation to the People's Republic of China, August 19–September 19, 1974," San Jose, Calif., mimeo.

Singapore, Department of Statistics. *Singapore External Trade Statistics* (annual).

Smil, Vaclav. "China Opts for Small Scale Energy Techniques," *Energy International* 13, no. 2 (Feb. 1976): 17–18.

———. "China's Energetics: A System Analysis," *Chinese Economy Post-*

Mao. U.S. Joint Economic Committee of Congress, Washington, D.C., Nov. 9, 1978, pp. 323–69.

———. *China's Energy: Achievements, Problems, and Prospects.* New York, 1976.

———. "China's Energy Performance," *Current History* 73, no. 429 (Sept. 1977): 63–67.

———. "Energy in China: Achievements and Prospects," *China Quarterly* 65 (March 1976): 54–81.

———. "Energy in the PRC," *Current Scene* 13, no. 2 (Feb. 1975): 1–16.

———. "Energy Solution in China," *Environment* 19, no. 7 (Oct. 1977): 27–31.

———. "Exploiting China's Hydro Potential," *International Water Power and Dam Construction* 28, no. 3 (Mar. 1976): 19–26.

Smil, Vaclav, and Kim Woodard. "Perspectives on Energy in the People's Republic of China," *Annual Review of Energy* 2 (1977): 307–42.

Solomon, Burt. "China to Double Coal Production by 1987, Quadruple It by 2000," *Energy Daily* 6, no. 235 (Dec. 8, 1978): 1–3.

Szuprowicz, Bohdan O. "China's Trade with Nonmarket Countries," *China Business Review* 5, no. 3 (May–June 1978): 15–32.

———. "Electronics in China," *U.S.–China Business Review* 3, no. 3 (May–June 1976): 21–43.

*Szuprowicz, Bohdan O., and Maria R. Szuprowicz. *Doing Business with the People's Republic of China: Industries and Markets.* New York, 1978.

Tanner, J. J., and W. E. Kennett. "Petroleum Developments in Far East in 1971," *American Association of Petroleum Geologists Bulletin* 56, no. 9 (Sept. 1972): 1823–45.

Tanzer, Michael. *The Political Economy of International Oil and the Underdeveloped Countries.* Boston, 1969.

Thailand, Department of Customs. *Foreign Trade Statistics of Thailand* (monthly and annual). Bangkok.

Tregear, Thomas R. *An Economic Geography of China.* New York, 1970.

Union of Soviet Socialist Republics. *Vneshniaia Torgovlia SSSR* (annual). Moscow.

United Nations, Department of Economic and Social Affairs, Statistical Office. *Commodity Trade Statistics* (also *Trade Commodity Statistics*). Statistical Papers, Series D (annual). New York.

———. *Standard International Trade Classification,* Statistical Papers, Series M (occasional). New York.

———. *Statistical Yearbook.* New York.

———. *Supplement to the World Trade Annual* (annual). New York.

———. *World Energy Supplies,* Statistical Papers, Series J (annual). New York.

————. *World Trade Annual.* New York.

United Nations, Economic Commission for Africa. *African Trade Statistics.* Statistical Bulletins, Series B, Trade by Commodities (annual). New York.

United Nations, Economic Commission for Asia and the Far East. *Foreign Trade Statistics of Asia and the Far East* (annual 1962–69). Bangkok.

————. *Statistical Yearbook for Asia and the Far East.* Bangkok.

United Nations Development Program, Office of Technical Support for Regional Offshore Prospecting in East Asia. "The Offshore Hydrocarbon Potential of East Asia: A Decade of Investigations," *CCOP Technical Bulletin* 11 (Oct. 1977): 1–68.

United States, Central Intelligence Agency. *China: Energy Balance Projections.* Washington, D.C., Nov. 1975.

————. *China: The Coal Industry.* Washington, D.C., Nov. 1976.

————. *China: Oil Production Prospects.* Washington, D.C., June 1977.

————. *People's Republic of China: Handbook of Economic Indicators.* Washington, D.C., Aug. 1976.

————. *People's Republic of China: International Trade Handbook.* Washington, D.C., Oct. 1976.

United States, Central Intelligence Agency, National Foreign Assessment Center. *Handbook of Economic Statistics, 1978.* Washington, D.C., Oct. 1978.

United States, Department of Commerce, Bureau of the Census, Foreign Trade Division. *U.S. Exports,* Schedule B, Commodity by Country; and *U.S. General Imports,* Schedule A, Commodity by Country (monthly and annual.) Washington, D.C.

United States, Department of Energy. *Statistical Data of the Uranium Industry.* Grand Junction, Colo., Jan. 1, 1978.

United States, Department of the Interior, Bureau of Mines. *Mineral Facts and Problems,* Bulletin no. 650. Washington, D.C., 1970.

————. *Minerals Yearbook: International Area Reports.* (Annual.) Washington, D.C., 1963–75.

————. "World Natural Gas, 1975," *Mineral Industry Surveys.* Washington, D.C., May 27, 1977.

United States, Department of State, Bureau of Intelligence and Research, Office of the Geographer. "Continental Shelf Boundary and Joint Development Zone: Japan–Republic of Korea," *Limits in the Seas* 75 (Sept. 2, 1977).

————. "Fisheries Agreement: China-Japan," *Limits in the Seas* 70 (April 6, 1976).

United States, Department of State, Office of Media Services, Bureau of

Public Affairs. *Background Notes: People's Republic of China.* Washington, D.C., May 1972.

United States, Federal Power Commission, Bureau of Power. *World Power Data* (annual, 1962–69). Washington, D.C.

United States, Joint Economic Committee of Congress. *China: A Reassessment of the Economy.* Washington, D.C., July 10, 1975.

———. *Chinese Economy Post-Mao,* vol. 1. Washington, D.C., Nov. 9, 1978.

———. *An Economic Profile of Mainland China,* vol. 1. Washington, D.C., 1967.

———. *People's Republic of China: An Economic Assessment.* Washington, D.C., 1972.

United States, National Academy of Sciences, Committee for Scholarly Communication with the People's Republic of China. *Rural Small-Scale Industries Delegation to the People's Republic of China, June 13–July 5, 1975.* A trip report. Washington, D.C., 1975.

Usack, Alfred H., and James D. Egan. "China's Iron and Steel Industry," *China: A Reassessment of the Economy.* U.S. Joint Economic Committee of Congress, Washington, D.C., July 10, 1975, pp. 264–88.

Wageman, John M., Thomas W. C. Hilde, and K. O. Emery. "Structural Framework of East China Sea and Yellow Sea," *American Association of Petroleum Geologists Bulletin* 54, no. 9 (Sept. 1970): 1611–43.

Wang, K. P. "China's Mineral Economy," *Chinese Economy Post-Mao.* U.S. Joint Economic Committee of Congress, Washington, D.C., Nov. 9, 1978, pp. 370–402.

———. "The Mineral Industry of Mainland China," *Minerals Yearbook: International Area Reports.* U.S. Department of the Interior, Bureau of Mines (1963–70). Washington, D.C.

———. "The Mineral Resource Base of Communist China," *An Economic Profile of Mainland China.* U.S. Joint Economic Committee of Congress, Washington, D.C., 1967, pp. 167–80.

———. *The People's Republic of China: A New Industrial Power with a Strong Mineral Base.* U.S. Department of the Interior, Bureau of Mines, Office of International Data and Analysis. Washington, D.C., 1975.

Weintraub, Peter D. "China's Minerals and Metals," *U.S.–China Business Review* 1, no. 6 (Nov.–Dec. 1974): 39–53.

Weller, J. Marvin. "Petroleum Possibilities of the Red Basin of Szechuan Province," *Bulletin of the American Association of Petroleum Geologists* 28, no. 10 (Oct. 1944): 1430–39.

Williams, Bobby A. "The Chinese Petroleum Industry: Growth and Prospects," *China: A Reassessment of the Economy.* U.S. Joint Economic Committee of Congress. Washington, D.C., July 10, 1975, pp. 225–64.

Willums, Jan-Olaf. "China: Major Oil Exporter of the '80s?" *Ocean Industry* 9, no. 4 (Apr. 1974): 180–84.

———. "China's Offshore Oil: Application of a Framework for Evaluating Oil and Gas Potentials Under Uncertainty." Ph.D. dissertation, Department of Ocean Engineering, Massachusetts Institute of Technology, Sept. 1975.

———. "China's Offshore Petroleum," *China Business Review* 4, no. 4 (July–Aug. 1977): 6–14.

Woodard, Kim. "The International Energy Policies of the People's Republic of China." Ph.D. dissertation, Department of Political Science, Stanford University, Aug. 1976.

———. "People's China and the World Energy Crisis: The Chinese Attitude Toward Global Resource Distribution," *Stanford Journal of International Studies* 10 (Spring 1975): 114–42. Also in Bryant Garth, ed., *China's Changing Role in the World Economy* (New York, 1975), pp. 114–42.

World Energy Conference. *Survey of Energy Resources.* New York, 1962, 1968, and 1974.

World Power Conference. *Statistical Yearbook of the World Power Conference.* London, 1936–54.

Wrightman, Alistair. "Japan and China's Oil—Proceeding with Caution," *U.S.–China Business Review* 3, no. 2 (Mar.–Apr. 1976): 31–37.

Wu, Yuan-li, and H. C. Ling. *Economic Development and the Use of Energy Resources in Communist China.* New York, 1963.

Yuan, Sy. "China's Chemicals," *U.S.–China Business Review* 2, no. 6 (Nov.–Dec. 1975): 37–52.

———. "An Inside Look at China's HPI," *Hydrocarbon Processing* 53, no. 4 (Apr. 1974): 105–6.

Yugoslavia, Federal Institute for Statistics. *Statistics of Foreign Trade of the Socialist Federal Republic of Yugoslavia* (annual). Belgrade.

Index